THE ORIENTAL INSTITUTE OF THE UNIVERSITY OF CHICAGO

STUDIES IN ANCIENT ORIENTAL CIVILIZATION • NO. 44

NIPPUR NEIGHBORHOODS

ELIZABETH C. STONE

THE ORIENTAL INSTITUTE OF THE UNIVERSITY OF CHICAGO

STUDIES IN ANCIENT ORIENTAL CIVILIZATION • *NO. 44*

CHICAGO • ILLINOIS

Library of Congress Catalog Card Number: 86-63702
ISBN: 0-918986-50-8
ISSN: 0081-7554
The Oriental Institute, Chicago

Published 1987. Printed in the United States of America

To

L. S.

TABLE OF CONTENTS

LIST OF TABLES

LIST OF ILLUSTRATIONS

Figures

Plates

(at end of volume)

PREFACE

In the course of preparing a dissertation entitled "The Social and Economic Organization of Old Babylonian Nippur," I read the texts which are included in this volume and examined, if briefly, the published and unpublished records of the second and third seasons of the University of Chicago's excavations at Nippur. At the time I was struck both by the richness and variety of the available information and by the narrow approach of the publication. Once my dissertation was behind me, I thought to attempt a more detailed reanalysis of this evidence. My plan at the outset was to use the information available from the archaeological contexts of the tablets to flesh out some of the ideas that had come out of my dissertation. Almost immediately I discovered serious discrepancies between the publication and the field records; at this point my task was expanded to include an attempt to resolve these differences.

As the solution to the purely archaeological problems led to the unraveling of the sequence of occupation in the two residential areas, it became increasingly clear that these data, together with the tablets, contained clues to the very nature of the organization of the ancient Mesopotamian city—clues to the nature and organization of Mesopotamian neighborhoods. But the results of this study form no more than a web of inference, falling far short of the levels of proof that are required of modern archaeologists. This shortcoming is inherent in the nature of the data. The excavations upon which this study was based were conducted three and a half decades ago, at a time when the standards of modern archaeology had still to be articulated, while the very nature of textual evidence precludes rigorous hypothesis testing. At this point we must be content to search for a fit between the two available sources of information, archaeological and textual, and hope that any conclusions drawn may serve as the basis of hypotheses which can be tested in the course of future excavations.

Because of both the long time involved in this study and its interdisciplinary nature, many people have helped or influenced me. McGuire Gibson first suggested that I work on the Old Babylonian period at Nippur; he provided me with the opportunity to excavate at Nippur—an experience which has made me much more sympathetic with its earlier excavators than I might otherwise have been—and has always been willing to share his perceptions of the site with me. Thanks to him and to the Ford Foundation which provided me with a Travelling Fellowship, I visited Iraq in 1975, collated, studied, and photographed the Iraq Museum tablets which are in this volume, and spent a season digging at Nippur. My stay in Baghdad was greatly eased by the generosity of Dr. Isa Salman, Director-General of Antiquities, and Dr. Fawzi Rashid, Director of the Iraq Museum, who allowed me free access to the Nippur materials, by the museum staff, who provided me with a never-ending stream of tablets to examine, and by Dr. Abdul-hadi al-Fuadi, who made it possible for me to travel to provincial museums to examine their collections. Nicholas Postgate not only made life very comfortable by inviting me to stay in his house while I was in Baghdad, but also helped me to translate the more difficult passages which I encountered.

Åke Sjøberg, Curator of the Babylonian Collection of the University Museum, has submitted with seeming goodwill to my scouring the collection for unpublished and partially published contracts from Nippur and has given me all the necessary resources to photograph and publish what I found. Meanwhile, the Director of the University Museum, Robert H. Dyson, Jr., very kindly allowed me to rummage in the storerooms in search of unpublished complete vessels, and to examine and draw them. Every trip to Philadelphia was both profitable and enjoyable.

It was the Oriental Institute, though, which bore the brunt of my endeavors. The various directors of the Institute—J. A. Brinkman, Robert McC. Adams, and Janet Johnson—the Curator of the Museum, John Carswell, and the Museum Registrar, Anita Ghaemi, allowed me to copy the field plans and notes, to study and photograph the tablets, and to draw unpublished pots. Most long-suffering though were those associated with the tablet collection. Over the years Robert Whiting, Irving Finkel, Maureen Gallery, Martha Roth, and Matthew Stolper have put up with my ignorance and given me the benefit of their knowledge of Sumerian and Akkadian language and prosopography.

The many trips to Chicago and Philadelphia to copy and collate texts and notes, and the subsequent research, were funded in part by two grants from the State University of New York. My initial trip in 1978 to Xerox all the field notes was paid for by a S. U. N. Y. Stony Brook Faculty Grant-in-Aid, while a S. U. N. Y. University Award made it possible for me to hire Angelo Fegan to print my photographs and Matthew Knopf to work on the object typologies.

My greatest intellectual debts are to Miguel Civil and to Robert McC. Adams. The first taught me what little Sumerian I know and gave me the benefit of his deep understanding of Mesopotamian society, while the second, by demanding clarity of thought and a firm sense of problem, has given my work what rigor it possesses. To both I owe a debt I can never hope to repay.

Finally I must thank those who helped me with the present manuscript. Mari Walker typed one version or another of the manuscript, while Jeanne Stone helped with the proof-reading. In addition, all or part of a draft version of the book was commented on by Robert McC. Adams, Norman Yoffee, Lawrence Stone, Jeanne Stone, and Paul Zimansky. The last named especially identified areas of fuzzy thinking and ensured that my ideas were not too lost in the vagaries of my style. Finally, Lisa Jacobson, under the supervision of Walter Farber and Miguel Civil, tried to turn my very amateur Assyriology into something more generally acceptable. I have benefited greatly from the comments of all who read the manuscript, although of course all errors of fact or interpretation are entirely my responsibility.

Last, but by no means least, I must thank the excavators of TA and TB, Carl Haines and Donald McCown. I was fortunate enough to spend a day with the former shortly before his untimely death. I learned a great deal about those early seasons from that conversation; had he lived or had I known at that time what questions to ask, I would have gained much more. Without their detailed notes and plans this study would have been impossible. If I appear to be critical of their work in places it is only because these records have provided posterity with the wherewithal to challenge their interpretations. Many other excavation reports remain unchallenged because the basic data either no longer exist or never did.

ABBREVIATIONS

ARN	M. Çığ, H. Kızılyay, and F. R. Kraus. *Altbabylonische Rechtsurkunden aus Nippur.* Istanbul: Milli Egitim Basimevi, 1952.
BE 6/2	Arno Poebel. *Babylonian Legal and Business Documents from the Time of the First Dynasty of Babylon Chiefly from Nippur.* University of Pennsylvania University Museum, The Babylonian Expedition of Pennsylvania, Series A, Cuneiform Texts, vol. 6, part 2. Philadelphia, 1909.
CAD	*The Chicago Assyrian Dictionary.* 14 vols. to date. Chicago/Glückstadt: J. J. Augustin, 1956-.
Cornell	Elizabeth C. Stone and David I. Owen. *Adoption in Old Babylonian Nippur and the Archive of Mannum-mešu-liṣṣur.* Winona Lake: Eisenbrauns, in press.
Hussey	Mary I. Hussey. "The Conveyance of Land Dated in the Reign of Ellil-bani," *Journal of the American Oriental Society* 36 (1916): 34-36.
N	Unpublished tablet in the University Museum.
Ni	Tablets mentioned in Fritz R. Kraus, "Nippur und Isin nach Altbabylonischen Rechtsurkunden," *Journal of Cuneiform Studies* 3 (1951): 1-228.
OECT 8	G. R. Hunter. *The Sayce and Weld Collection in the Ashmolean Museum: Sumerian Contracts from Nippur.* Oxford Editions of Cuneiform Texts, vol. 8. Oxford, 1930.
OIMA 1	Elizabeth C. Stone and Paul E. Zimansky. *Old Babylonian Contracts from Nippur I.* University of Chicago Oriental Institute Microfiche Archives, vol. 1. Chicago, 1976.
OIP	Oriental Institute Publications. Chicago, 1924-.
PBS 8/1	Edward Chiera. *Legal and Administrative Documents from Nippur, Chiefly from the Dynasties of Isin and Larsa.* University of Pennsylvania University Museum, Publications of the Babylonian Section, vol. 8, no. 1. Philadelphia, 1914.
PBS 8/2	Edward Chiera. *Old Babylonian Contracts.* University of Pennsylvania University Museum, Publications of the Babylonian Section, vol. 8, no. 2. Philadelphia, 1922.
PBS 13	Leon Legrain. *Historical Fragments.* University of Pennsylvania University Museum, Publications of the Babylonian Section, vol. 13. Philadelphia, 1922.
TIM 4	J. J. A. van Dijk. *Cuneiform Texts: Old Babylonian and Juridical Texts.* Texts in the Iraq Museum, vol. 4. Wiesbaden, 1967.
Toledo	Steven Langdon. "Miscellenea Assyriaca II," *Babyloniaca* 7 (1914): 67-80 (Text 14).
YOS 14	Stephen D. Simmons. *Early Old Babylonian Documents.* Yale Oriental Series: Babylonian Texts, vol. 14. New Haven, 1978.

Chapter 1

Introduction

The publication in 1967 of D. McCown and R. C. Haines, *Nippur I: Temple of Enlil, Scribal Quarter, and Soundings* (hereafter OIP 78) provided the first long stratified sequence of ceramics and other objects from southern Mesopotamia, and as such is still the standard to this day. In the absence of any comparable sequence other than that excavated in the 1930s in the Diyala region,[1] OIP 78 has served as the basis against which finds from other sites in the area could be dated. But even as the utility of this work was lauded, the lack of detailed discussion of the methodology employed in the excavation of the architectural levels[2] and in assigning absolute dates to such levels led to a mild degree of doubt as to the validity of the results.

A brief examination of some of the cases in which this sequence has been applied highlights some of the difficulties encountered. Hansen, in his discussion of the Nippur sequence,[3] notes that "The pottery types covering the period from the Third Dynasty of Ur to the end of the First Dynasty of Babylon . . . present a continually evolving series." The inability to differentiate between these levels led Adams in his survey first to group Ur III and Isin-Larsa sites separately from Old Babylonian,[4] and later to make a break between early Isin-Larsa and Late Larsa times.[5] This uncertainty in assigning politically meaningful dates to ceramic types has resulted in a situation whereby "the most useful distinction . . . would be precisely that which is most uncertain, intended to illuminate with settlement pattern data the political and institutional changes accompanying the rise of the kingdom of Larsa."[6] Until recently it was assumed that this uncertainty was due to the nature of the

[1] Pinhas Delougaz, *Pottery from the Diyala Region,* OIP 63 (Chicago: University of Chicago Press, 1952). As is to be expected from an excavation conducted in the 1930s, one cannot be 100% certain of the stratigraphic assessment of the Diyala materials. Furthermore, the Diyala region is far from the Mesopotamian heartland, and, relevant for our purposes, Isin-Larsa and Old Babylonian materials were not particularly well represented.

[2] Richard Ellis in his review of Donald E. McCown and Richard C. Haines, *Nippur I: Temple of Enlil, Scribal Quarter, and Soundings,* OIP 78 (Chicago: University of Chicago Press, 1967), in the *Journal of Near Eastern Studies* 31 (1972): 205, states:

> For instance, p. 58 of the present book describes the discovery of a floor within the doorless foundation of a room; since it is hard to see how a floor could be used in an inaccessible room, it is concluded that the floor belonged to an earlier period and that the foundations of a later house cut into it. This is very probably true, and it is impossible for someone who was not there to say what could or could not have been seen. . . .

An examination of the field notes suggests that the excavators themselves very probably were in no position to know what was to be seen. The notes show that they did not divide up the labor of supervising the work; rather all notes on the Enlil temple, TA, TB, and the soundings were made by Haines, while McCown merely noted on occasion that a particular locus had been dug down to a certain level by a certain date. This suggests that in many instances the only people in a position to know exactly what was unfolding were the local workmen, who took no notes.

[3] Donald Hansen, "Relative Chronology of Mesopotamia, Part II," in *Chronologies in Old World Archaeology,* ed. Robert W. Ehrich (Chicago: University of Chicago Press, 1965), p. 210.

[4] Robert McC. Adams and Hans J. Nissen, *The Uruk Countryside* (Chicago: University of Chicago Press, 1972), p. 37.

[5] Robert McC. Adams, *Heartland of Cities* (Chicago: University of Chicago Press, 1981), p. 171.

[6] Adams and Nissen, *Uruk Countryside,* p. 37.

data, and therefore irremediable, but the current excavator of Nippur, McGuire Gibson, reports that by now they have been able to refine the sequence.

These chronological considerations were not, however, the reasons that prompted this work. As an archaeologist I regretted my inability to determine the artifactual inventories of each house, as an anthropologist I was disturbed by the lack of discussion of the functional organization and development of the domestic areas, and as an Assyriologist I deplored the relegation of the tablets to the role of mere conveyers of chronological data.

In addition to its chronological significance, the publication of OIP 78 provided the first opportunity for a study of the organization and development of ancient Mesopotamian neighborhoods. Two separate areas of domestic architecture had been excavated, TA and TB, both of which had levels dating to the Isin-Larsa and Old Babylonian periods. Furthermore, unlike the similar excavations at Ur (which would not be fully published until ten years later),[7] the Nippur data provide an evolving sequence of such structures. Finally, in addition to the published materials, details of the stratigraphy of the two areas and of the findspots of the associated pots, tablets, and other objects were preserved in the original field notes, to which J. A. Brinkman, then director of the Oriental Institute, very kindly allowed me access.

Current understanding of Mesopotamian residential areas comes almost entirely from textual sources and as such is meager in the extreme. The boldest attempt to describe the organization of ancient Mesopotamian cities was made by Oppenheim:

> The city contained the palace of the ruler, the temples of the city's gods, private dwellings arranged along the small, narrow, often crooked or dead-end streets, and a few wider streets mostly near the gates. It was divided into several quarters, each of which seems to have had its own gate through the walls surrounding the entire complex.[8]
>
> The Mesopotamian city had no obvious ethnic or tribal affiliations; it forms a primary social organization as a community of families of apparently equal status.[9]
>
> The inhabitants of the city's neighborhoods or wards (*bābtum*) regulated their local affairs from sanitation to security, under an official called *ḫazannum* who was installed, apparently by the king, for irregular but considerable lengths of time.[10]

Although one might question some of the assumptions implicit in this description of the organization of the Mesopotamian city, it compares well with the standard definition of the spatial organization of the preindustrial city provided by Sjøberg:

> Typically, all or most of the city is girdled by a wall. Inside, various sections of the city are sealed off from one another by walls, leaving little cells, or subcommunities, as worlds unto themselves.[11]

Many basic questions as to the nature and functioning of the Mesopotamian version of this organization remain unanswered. What was the basic residential unit? How large were these units? What was the basis for their composition? What was the relationship between large institutions and such residential areas? How were the different units separated from one another? What common features were to be seen in all such units? Were residential units grouped into large quarters? If any of these questions are to be answered through a reanalysis of the Nippur data, a model of urban organization must first be established against which

[7] Sir Leonard Woolley and Sir Max Mallowan, *Ur Excavations, vol. 7: The Old Babylonian Period* (London: British Museum Publications, Ltd., 1976).

[8] A. Leo Oppenheim, "Mesopotamia—Land of Many Cities," in *Middle Eastern Cities,* ed. Ira Lapidus (Berkeley and Los Angeles: University of California Press, 1969), p. 6.

[9] Ibid., pp. 7–8.

[10] Ibid., p. 9.

[11] Gideon Sjøberg, *The Preindustrial City* (New York: Free Press, 1960), p. 91.

these data can be compared. Although all preindustrial cities exhibit some form of neighborhood differentiation, this differentiation is most strongly developed in medieval Islamic cities. Furthermore, since continuity in general social organization between ancient Mesopotamian and later Middle Eastern cultures seems clear,[12] there is no *a priori* reason to reject the supposition that the urban patterning typical of Middle Eastern cities in more recent times might have had parallels with the earliest cities in the area, those of ancient Mesopotamia. Detailed information on the organization of residential quarters is available for Fez,[13] Damascus,[14] Aleppo,[15] Cairo,[16] Baghdad,[17] Herat, Isfahan, and Bam.[18] Scholars discussing urban centers as disparate as Herat and Damascus agree that

> in most pre-industrial Muslim cities, the population is segregated into residential quarters which are social as well as geographical entities. . . . In these quarters people are bound together by ties of religion, occupation, family or common origin.[19]

> Small groups of people who believed themselves bound together by the most fundamental ties—family, clientage, common village origin, ethnic or sectarian religious identity, perhaps in some case fortified by common occupation—lived in these neighborhoods.[20]

These ties did not, however, follow class lines; each neighborhood[21] contained individuals belonging to all classes, although some may have had a higher percentage of notable families residing in them than others.[22] Furthermore, not only did the wealth and status of individual quarters change over time,[23] but,

> whereas the nomenclature of the earliest *ḥārāt* [neighborhoods] showed a preoccupation with ethnic and tribal affiliations, the names of the later *ḥārāt* sometimes revealed the dominant occupational or commercial functions of the area.[24]

It appears that in newly created cities[25] and in cities in the process of expansion, newly urbanized villagers attempted to re-create village life within the city. As the cities matured, however, urban institutions and ties of clientage became the dominant unifying features. The groups that occupied these neighborhoods were quite small, usually numbering between 500 and 1,000 persons, although larger groups were also known.[26] Typically, each quarter had

[12] Robert McC. Adams, "Strategies of Maximization, Stability and Resilience in Mesopotamian Society, Settlement and Agriculture," *Proceedings of the American Philosophical Society* 122 (1978): 329–35.

[13] Roger Le Tourneau, *Fez in the Age of the Marinides* (Norman: University of Oklahoma Press, 1961).

[14] Jean Sauvaget, "Esquisse d'une histoire de la ville de Damas," *Révue des études islamiques* 8 (1934): 425–80.

[15] Jean Sauvaget, *Alep,* Bibliothèque archéologique et historique, vol. 36 (Paris: Paul Geuthner, 1941).

[16] Janet Abu-Lughod, *Cairo, 1001 Years of the City Victorious* (Princeton: Princeton University Press, 1971).

[17] Guy Le Strange, *Baghdad during the Abbasid Caliphate* (Oxford: Oxford University Press, 1900); Jacob Lassner, *The Topography of Baghdad in the Early Middle Ages* (Detroit: Wayne State University Press, 1970).

[18] Heinz Grube, *Iranian Cities* (New York: New York University Press, 1979).

[19] Paul English, "The Traditional City of Herat, Afghanistan," in *From Medina to Metropolis,* ed. L. Carl Brown (Princeton: Darwin Press, 1973), p. 82.

[20] Ira Lapidus, "Muslim Cities and Islamic Societies," in *Middle Eastern Cities,* ed. Ira Lapidus (Berkeley and Los Angeles: University of California Press, 1969), p. 49.

[21] The terms *neighborhood* and *quarter* are often used synonymously by medieval Islamic scholars. However, in some cases the term *quarter* is used to refer to larger divisions within the city, such as the Christian Quarter, which might be made up of a number of *ḥārāt,* or neighborhoods. In this work the word *neighborhood* will be used to refer to the minimal social and residential unit, the Arabic *ḥāra,* while the word *quarter* will be reserved for larger units.

[22] André Raymonde, "Essai de géographie des quartiers de résidence aristocratique au Caire au XVIIIième siècle," *Journal of the Economic and Social History of the Orient* 6 (1963): 59–103.

[23] Ibid.

[24] Abu-Lughod, *Cairo,* p. 24.

[25] Edmond Pauty, "Villes spontanées et villes créées en Islam," *Faculté des lettres de l'Université d'Alger: Annales de l'Institut d'études orientales* 9 (1951): 52–75.

[26] Ira Lapidus, *Muslim Cities in the Later Middle Ages* (Cambridge: Cambridge University Press, 1984), p. 85.

its own mosque, bath, and local market. Usually these institutions were located along a main street from which narrow culs-de-sac provided access to the residences. The houses of different quarters often backed onto each other, but in other instances they were separated by major arteries. In times of political stress, or when friction between residents of different quarters was at its height, the quarters would sometimes be walled. Access to each quarter under normal circumstances was limited to a single street; gates could be built at either end, which could then be closed at night or when fighting broke out in the city.[27] Each neighborhood was governed by a leader chosen by the government from among the leading families of the neighborhood. Although his principal duty was to collect taxes (and to mediate with the government when these demands could not be met), he also was responsible for the maintenance of law and order in his neighborhood and for enforcing sanitary rules.[28] Thus Islamic neighborhoods were cities in miniature, each tied together by ethnic identity, religion, clientage, or occupation, with internal circulation patterns, the most basic institutions, and their own administration. The question which remains to be answered is to what extent this model fits the ancient Mesopotamian city in general, and Isin-Larsa and Old Babylonian Nippur in particular.

Before turning to the archaeological data from Nippur, a look at information derived from ancient Mesopotamian textual sources is in order. An examination of references to the word *bābtum,* usually translated "city ward," in Isin-Larsa and Old Babylonian contexts in the *CAD*[29] shows that the *bābtum* served as the locus of the administration of justice in cases where an individual, in spite of being warned, continued a practice which constituted a hazard to his neighbors, where someone bore false witness against a member of his ward, and where a woman wished to divorce her husband.[30] If one assumes that Mesopotamian *bābtum*s were bound, at least in part, by kinship, and that endogamy was practiced, then each of these cases would have been more of concern to groups like the small, closely knit residential units known from medieval Islamic cities than to the city as a whole. Furthermore, the very word *bābtum* is the feminine form of *bābu* ("gate"), suggesting either, following Oppenheim,[31] that each city gate led into its own *bābtum,* or that access to these residential units could be controlled by gates that existed within the city.

Further evidence on the composition of *bābtum*s is available from texts from both Nippur and other Mesopotamian cities in the Old Babylonian period. First, Gelb published a list of Amorites from Isin-Larsa Eshnunna.[32] This list divides the Amorites into kinship groups, each one of which is called a *bābtum.* Yoffee contests Gelb's interpretation of these *bābtum*s as tribal segments with no spatial implications and suggests that the term was used to refer to residential units which in this instance were based on kinship.[33] He goes on to publish a text from Kish which suggests that at least some residential kin groups occupied Kish in the Old Babylonian period.

A number of scholars have studied the Isin-Larsa and Old Babylonian "family archives" from various cities in Mesopotamia. The general picture presented,[34] although often vague,

[27] Gustav E. von Grunebaum, *Islam: Essays on the Nature and Growth of a Cultural Tradition* (London: Routledge and Paul, Ltd., 1961), pp. 147-48.

[28] Lapidus, *Muslim Cities,* pp. 92-93.

[29] *CAD,* vol. B, pp. 9-14.

[30] BE 6/2 58, a text from Old Babylonian Nippur, records a case, heard in front of the assembled members of her *bābtum,* of a woman requesting a divorce on the grounds of abandonment.

[31] Oppenheim, "Mesopotamia—Land of Many Cities," p. 6.

[32] Ignace J. Gelb, "An Old Babylonian List of Amorites," *Journal of the American Oriental Society* 88 (1968): 39-46.

[33] V. Donbaz and Norman Yoffee, *Old Babylonian Texts from Kish Conserved in the Istanbul Archaeological Museums* (Malibu: Undena Publications, in press).

[34] Charles F. Jean, *Larsa d'après les textes cunéiformes* (Paris: Librairie Orientalist Paul Geuthner, 1931); Fritz R. Kraus, "Nippur und Isin nach altbabylonischen Rechtsurkunden," *Journal of Cuneiform Studies* 3 (1951): 1-228.

suggests that kinship played a not inconsiderable role in the organization of urban society.[35] In some cases, especially Dilbat and Kutalla, more detailed information has been available, and partial reconstructions of the "quartiers d'habitation" have been attempted,[36] although the available data are inadequate to clarify the relationship uniting their residents. One study of the Dilbat texts[37] indicates that while kinship played an important role in determining economic behavior initially, behavior dictated by extra-kin ties to urban institutions increased as time went on. It credits this transformation to the direct intervention of Ḫammurabi of Babylon. Other factors, such as a shift from a kinship orientation of the neighborhood to one more aligned to urban institutions, similar to that described by Abu Lughod for Cairo (see above), are not considered.

Whereas Dilbat and Kutalla merely provide hints as to the physical organization of the cities, the texts from Sippar are more detailed. The Isin-Larsa and Old Babylonian texts with which Harris[38] was concerned were all almost certainly excavated in the *gagûm,* usually translated "cloister," the walled residential area occupied by the Sippar *nadītums*. This area was overseen by an individual called a *ḫazannum,* whose main responsibility was to keep the peace and maintain sanitation—the same tasks assigned to those in charge of the *ḥārāt* in medieval Islamic cities. The Sippar *gagûm* was clearly a specialized residential area, one reserved for a particularly secluded group, but elsewhere the term *ḫazannum* is used to refer to the individual responsible for maintaining order in other residential areas.

Ḫazannum is translated "chief magistrate of a town, of a quarter of a large city, a village or large estate—mayor, burgomaster, headman" by the *CAD*.[39] Unfortunately for our purposes, this term occurs but rarely in Old Babylonian texts, mostly in witness lists, because, perhaps, of the general paucity of administrative documents from this period. In general the *ḫazannum* is an administrator of a built-up area, in charge of keeping the peace, ensuring the legality of transactions, and maintaining sanitation. Oppenheim[40] describes him as selected by the king, a circumstance that parallels that of the leaders of medieval Islamic *ḥārāt*. In both cases it seems important to take the evidence for royal appointment with a grain of salt; it is most likely that such royal selection represented no more than the ratification of the already-existing leaders of the residential units.

The preceding examination of references to the terms *gagûm, bābtum,* and *ḫazannum* suggests the presence in ancient Mesopotamian cities of residential units enjoying a measure of administrative independence. What is not clear, however, is the size of the units involved. Were *bābtums* equivalent to the large quarters of medieval cities, such as those occupied by religious minorities and themselves made up of a number of *ḥārāt* (neighborhoods), or were they in fact equivalent to the neighborhoods themselves? At present the only evidence that can be brought to bear is inferential, and therefore highly suspect. The infrequency with which these terms are used may suggest that most of their concerns were with groups small enough that complex record-keeping was not necessary.

At this point it is appropriate to turn to the evidence from the city of Nippur itself. A cursory look at the texts provides only ambiguous evidence relevant to the topic at hand. First, neighbors, even when they are not brothers who have received shares of the same

[35] Fritz R. Kraus, *Vom mesopotamischen Menschen der altbabylonischen Zeit und seiner Welt,* Mededelingen der Kroninklijke Nederlandse Akademie van Wetenschappen, Afd. Letterkunde. Nieuwe Recks-Deel 36-No. 6 (Amsterdam: North-Holland Publishing Co., 1973), pp. 46–49.

[36] Dominique Charpin, *Archives familiales et propriété privée en Babylonie ancienne* (Geneva: Librairie Droz, 1980), especially pp. 169–71; Tom B. Jones, *Paths to the Ancient Past* (New York: Free Press, 1967), pp. 148–64.

[37] Michael J. Desroches, *Aspects of the Structure of Dilbat during the Old Babylonian Period* (Ann Arbor: University Microfilms, 1978), pp. 477–82.

[38] Rivkah Harris, *Ancient Sippar* (Istanbul: Nederlands Historisch-archaeologisch Instituut, 1975).

[39] *CAD,* vol. 6, Ḫ, p. 163.

[40] Oppenheim, "Mesopotamia—Land of Many Cities," p. 9.

pieces of property, quite often witness each other's documents, purchase property from each other, and even marry their children to each other. Some of these patterns might be seen merely as the product of their residential proximity, but since property exchange and especially marriage seem to have been governed by kin affiliation, one might conclude from these data that neighbors were often kinsmen, albeit not close enough for this relationship to be obvious from their patronymics. Another scrap of evidence is that streets were very often named after individuals living on them. Although it is possible that this naming pattern simply indicated ownership of the right-of-way, it may also have identified the family which dominated that section of the town. Not all areas appear in this guise; some, perhaps whole neighborhoods, perhaps much smaller areas, seem to have been largely given over to craftsmen of various kinds. In BE 6/2 10, the house which was awarded to the plaintiff abutted the houses of bakers and carpenters.

Without archaeological data, the textual evidence cannot give a true picture of the organization of residential life in Mesopotamian cities. But an examination of the plans of Isin-Larsa and Old Babylonian domestic areas at Ur[41] and Tell Harmal[42] and the earlier house plans from the Diyala,[43] Abu Salabikh[44] and Tell Taya[45] may be more revealing. The domestic areas from Tell Asmar and Khafajah in the Diyala most resemble patterns expected from areas organized into neighborhoods. Khafajah has a walled area housing those associated with the Temple Oval[46] while at Tell Asmar major roads may separate one area of domestic housing from another.[47] At Ur, contemporary with the TA and TB areas at Nippur, two distinct areas of domestic architecture have been excavated. Although clear neighborhood boundaries cannot be identified within the excavated areas, the pattern of culs-de-sac and narrow alleyways[48] is similar to the street pattern characteristic of Islamic cities. Tell Harmal, on the other hand, shows no such pattern; there the houses are organized into regular, rectangular blocks.[49] However, the small size of the site may well have obviated the need for divisions into quarters; if the site were occupied by a single unified group, then the outer wall would have served to exclude outsiders.[50] Finally, residential patterns can be determined from surface mapping carried out at both Abu Salabikh and Tell Taya. Although the survey data from Tell Taya is not always easy to interpret, the domestic structures seem to be grouped around small streets or squares.[51] The surface clearance of the West Mound at Abu Salabikh, on the other hand, has exposed at least three, apparently residential areas, bounded by curvilinear walls. The excavator, J. N. Postgate, has suggested that these enclosures represent separate quarters, each occupied by an extended household.[52] At Abu Salabikh, the compounds must have had populations much lower than those suggested for the Islamic neighborhoods. However, the area covered by each compound is much the same as that occupied by a

[41] Woolley and Mallowan, *Ur Excavations, vol. 7,* pls. 122, 124, and 128.

[42] Taha Baqir, *Tell Harmal* (Baghdad: Directorate-General of Antiquities, 1959).

[43] Pinhas Delougaz et al., *Private Houses and Graves in the Diyala Region,* OIP 88 (Chicago: University of Chicago Press, 1967).

[44] J. N. Postgate, *Abu Salabikh Excavations, vol. 1: The West Mound Surface Clearance* (London: British School of Archaeology in Iraq, 1983).

[45] Julian E. Reade, "Tell Taya (1972–73): Summary Report," *Iraq* 35 (1973): 155–87.

[46] Delougaz, *Private Houses,* pl. 14.

[47] Ibid., pl. 26.

[48] Woolley and Mallowan, *Ur Excavations,* vol. 7, pls. 122, 124.

[49] Baqir, *Tell Harmal,* fig. 1.

[50] The entire site of Tell Harmal covers an area of no more than 1.8 hectares. Following Adams (*Heartland,* p. 69) we may apply the population estimate figure of 125 persons per hectare. This gives an estimated population for Tell Harmal of around 225 persons, a number small enough to suggest that this was indeed no more than a single group.

[51] Reade, "Tell Taya," pls. LIX and LX.

[52] J. N. Postgate, "Excavations at Abu Salabikh, 1978–1979," *Iraq* 42 (1980), pp. 98–102; idem., "Abu-Salabikh" in *Fifty Years of Mesopotamian Discovery,* ed. John Curtis (London: British School of Archaeology in Iraq, 1982), p. 59.

typical Islamic city quarter. Thus it is possible that such compounds may represent kernals from which an entire neighborhood might emerge in the course of urban expansion. The archaeological evidence as currently available, therefore, is mixed, neither confirming nor denying the existence of neighborhood organization in ancient Mesopotamian cities.

The evidence presented above, although far from compelling, allows the formulation of the hypothesis that the main residential units in Mesopotamian cities were small face-to-face communities or neighborhoods, probably with populations of around 500 to 1,000 persons. It is suggested that these were united by ties of kinship, clientage or occupation, and that they probably had a minimal level of internal administration. It seems likely that these units were grouped together into large quarters, areas perhaps now represented by the numerous mounds which together make up most Mesopotamian tells. It is the investigation of these small neighborhoods which will be the focus of this work.

No understanding of the nature and organization of Mesopotamian neighborhoods is possible until a comprehensive study has been made of the associated textual, archaeological, and architectural data from one or more neighborhoods. It is this linkage of textual information to that derived from artifacts and architectural plans of house and street patterns which is the fundamental methodology of this study.

The reanalysis of the Isin-Larsa and Old Babylonian levels in areas TA and TB at Nippur is designed to elicit information on the nature of ancient Mesopotamian neighborhoods through an investigation of the relationships which bound residents of contiguous houses together. Since the origin, development, and change of neighborhoods is also at issue, it will first be necessary to investigate the chronology of the two areas under consideration. This exercise should also prove helpful to those in the future who may wish to use the Nippur sequence purely for comparative chronological purposes.

The sources used in this reanalysis fall into three categories: the publication (OIP 78), the field notes and plans, and the artifacts, especially the tablets, which were found in the course of the excavations. OIP 78 is quite detailed in its discussion of stylistic changes noted in the pottery and objects found in TA and TB, but the chronological significance of the remains, architectural and artifactual, is relegated to a mere four pages. Although many details of the houses themselves are to be found in the section on the structural remains, there is little discussion of the stratigraphy and modification of the two areas, an exercise which is essential for an examination of the artifactual inventory.

Before the reanalysis could begin, some amendments to the way in which the data were presented in OIP 78 were needed. First, since only in the case of a few selected houses[53] were all of the finds from a single room or locus listed together, such a locus-by-locus list of objects had to be prepared. This information is included in this volume as Appendix II. However, before this information could be collected, a much more significant difficulty had to be overcome. The stratigraphy as published differs significantly from that observed in the field fifteen years earlier, especially for the TA area. No locus-by-locus list of artifacts could be prepared until the two numbering systems could be married. Furthermore, in working through these data, it became clear to me that these *ex post facto* adjustments to the stratigraphic record introduced confusion into an otherwise fairly logical system.

As a result of the nature of the publication—the brevity of the architectural descriptions, the incompleteness of the artifact catalog, and the confusion of level designations—it has been necessary to rely very heavily on the original field notes and plans. First in importance were the "plot records," which included notes on stratigraphic and architectural details of each locus, often accompanied by a plan. The notes on the Isin-Larsa and Old Babylonian levels of TB, excavated during the second season, are generally quite complete, their plans

[53] OIP 78, pp. 115–16.

often including both architectural details and the findspots of the more significant artifacts. But the notes on the contemporary levels of TA, excavated in the third season, tend to be very brief and are only rarely accompanied by plans. The notes taken at the end of the third season are almost nonexistent.

These plot records were supplemented by the plane-table sheet plans of the architecture of the different levels (see pls. 1–9). In some respects they were similar to those published in OIP 78, in that they usually grouped several floor levels together on a single plan. This practice was most evident in the third-season TA plans. However, they do record information not included in the publication—namely, the elevations of the tops and bottoms of many of the walls and of most of the floors. Furthermore, the field plans reflect the stratigraphy as it had been seen on excavation, not as it was later reassessed. These plans and plot records, together with the comments by Haines in OIP 78 on the architecture, make up the available data base for the analysis of the succession of structures in TA and TB.

Like the plot records and plans, the books recording the objects found in the course of the excavations were also more comprehensive for the TB material than for the artifacts excavated in TA. For both seasons, there is preserved a locus-by-locus list of all finds (excluding potsherds), object and tablet catalogs, and sheets made out describing some, but not all, of the pots and burials encountered. In the second season only, separate books were kept recording the pottery and those other artifacts which were discarded.

The most useful of these registers were the locus-by-locus catalogs. For each locus there is a list of all objects found (usually excepting the tablets) together with the date of discovery, a P-number, indicating that the object was a pot, an N-number, meaning that this was an object important enough to be registered in the object catalog, or a D-number, indicating that the object was merely noted and discarded. Some items were listed, such as metal fragments, which never received a number before they were thrown away. Most objects were accompanied by a crude sketch, which, in the case of the objects to be discarded, was often the only record of what the artifact looked like. In the catalog kept for the second-season material from TB, the pots were accompanied by the type number which had been assigned to that particular shape. Unfortunately, this information was not recorded in the third-season TA catalog. Other information which appeared more sporadically were the negative numbers of those items which had been photographed and the N-numbers of those pots and discards which were elevated to object status at the end of the season.

Separate object and tablet catalogs were kept during both the second and third seasons. The tablet catalogs record the N-T number given to each tablet, the findspot, and a brief summary of the content of each tablet found, together with the museum numbers of those tablets that ended up in Chicago or Philadelphia. The summaries of the contents seem in general to be quite accurate, and heavy reliance was placed on this source in the course of this work. The object catalog was similar, in that it recorded the N-number, the date the object was found, the findspot, and a description of the object. The most important aspect, though, was the detailed sketch of each object that it included.

During the second season, special catalogs were kept for the pots and for the discards. Since neither recorded information that was not already available in the locus-by-locus catalog, they were not very useful. However, since the pot type numbers were recorded in the pot catalog, had such a record been kept for the third season (where type numbers were omitted from the locus-by-locus catalog), the difficulties encountered in attempting to type the third-season pottery would have been avoided.

Finally, for some of the pottery from both TA and TB, pot sheets were filled out which describe the ware and treatment of each vessel, as well as the number, findspot, and ceramic type. In some instances, a measured drawing was attached. Also useful were the burial sheets, which recorded all pertinent information about each burial, but since this information is largely reproduced on pages 120–44 of OIP 78, they did not add much to our knowledge. Also available, but useful only in explaining the many problems which beset the expedition, were the letters and diaries which were written during the excavations.

The only available records of the analytical work conducted by the excavators were the type cards for the pottery. Each card provided a list of all those vessels which fell into a particular type, together with their findspots. Unfortunately, some of these type cards were missing, while others omitted the pots that were found in TA.

In general, the records kept of the results of the second and third seasons at Nippur, while in most cases detailed enough to permit an attempt to answer some of the questions on neighborhood composition posed above, leave much to be desired. On the one hand it is easy to criticize the excavators. By the 1950s attention should have been paid to potsherds as well as to complete vessels, stratigraphic (as opposed to architectural) associations should have been noted, etc. However, much of the blame for the condition of the notes must be placed on the inadequate staffing of the excavation. Not only was a staff of only about five supervising the work of a huge crew excavating in numerous different, and disparate, locations on the extensive mound at Nippur, but nearly all field notes were taken by the architect, Haines. In these circumstances it is more remarkable that the records are as good as they are. These excavations were further complicated by an uncertainty as to the directorship of the excavation, an uncertainty which undermined the efficiency of the project. Finally, the retirement of McCown from the field before the publication of OIP 78 resulted in a book which was more the salvaging of an abandoned project than a unified volume. In these circumstances, much though I might bewail the inadequacy of the records in the pages of this work, the very fact that this book could be written at all is testimony to the amount of information retrieved from a project beset with problems.

The first step in my analysis of these data was to organize them on a locus-by-locus basis. All information on the architecture, stratigraphy, features, objects, discards, pottery, and tablets for every level in every locus was collected and summarized in one place. Once this was accomplished, the next step was to establish the relationship between the level designations given in the field and those published in OIP 78.[54] This was accomplished primarily through an examination of the pottery and objects which had level designations provided for them in both OIP 78 and the field notes. Also useful were the typed version of the TA field notes and the third-season tablet catalog, in both of which the field designations had been crossed out and the published designation substituted. Fortunately, both the published and the eliminated designations remained legible. Once this list of equivalences had been established, it became possible to make the concordance seen in the first three columns of Appendix I. Since, for reasons detailed in chapter 3, it appeared that the stratigraphy observed in the field was likely to be a better representation of reality than that in OIP 78, the final step was to adjust the designations where the field notes indicated that this was appropriate.[55] Finally, each locus was examined to determine the extent to which disturbance from above might have made findspot information suspect. The results of this exercise can be seen in the last column of Appendix I and in the plans, plates 10–35.

With the completion of the analysis of the architecture and stratigraphy, the next task was to examine the artifacts. Since in OIP 78 the emphasis had been on stylistic analysis, it seemed better to concentrate here on functional criteria. To this end, the various classes of artifact were organized into typologies. In the case of the pots, an attempt was made to

[54] I have been told by McGuire Gibson that a level/locus chart had been prepared by Haines, but at the time when I was working on this project no such chart could be found.

[55] See chap. 3 for a more detailed discussion. In many instances the field notes indicate the equivalence of differently named floor levels in adjacent loci. These adjustments had to be included in any revision of the stratigraphy.

duplicate the typology published in OIP 78. This procedure was not as simple as it might have been for a number of reasons. First, the type numbers given to the vessels in the field were not the same as those used in OIP 78. To a large extent equivalences could be drawn by comparing published vessels with their type designations in the field notes, but in some instances there was no one-to-one correlation, especially in the case of subtypes. Second, as noted above, the record for the third-season pots, those from TA, was less complete than that for the second season. Since the TA pottery differed somewhat from that from TB (see chap. 5), this resulted in some types being less well correlated. Thus in Appendix II, some vessels have been given only tentative numbers, while others that should probably have been typed remain untyped.

The typologies of the other objects presented less of a problem. They were divided into two categories: figurines and plaques, and "tools." The former was divided into a series of types based on the kind of figure or scene that was depicted, while the latter, which included everything from jewelry to weapons to seals, was divided into functional categories. These types were used in chapter 5 to discern functional differences between various kinds of loci and between TA and TB, and are described in Appendix III.

One last category of artifact, probably the most important, was considered: the tablets. In most instances the tablets themselves were not examined, and only the descriptions of their contents as listed in the tablet catalogs taken into consideration.[56] By far the largest group of tablets were the school, literary, mathematical, and lexical texts, which, while they provide a wealth of information on the Sumerian language and literature, tell no more about the society that wrote them than that scribal education was being conducted. Other classes of texts, such as accounts, letters, and administrative texts, while they tell something about the types of activities practiced by those whose actions they recorded, fail to identify these people through the use of patronymics. Thus these types of texts cannot be used to tell an individual's kinship position or his network of associates. It is only the contracts, with their use of the patronymic and their listing of witnesses and of the owners of neighboring property, that can do that, and these, therefore, are the texts which were examined in detail and which are published in Appendices IV and V and in plates 36–94.

The tablets are the most informative of all the artifacts found at Nippur, but before we go on to an examination of what they and the other archaeological data can tell us about the social and economic makeup of the residents of TA and TB, a word is in order on their findspots. The separation normally found between the documentary and other data from Mesopotamian archaeological sites is often justified by the assumption that tablets are usually found in garbage dumps, not in their original contexts. Such an assumption obviates the need to distinguish between those tablets which were discarded in antiquity and those which were found in the place where they were used. Tablets are frequently found in pots within houses or lying against the walls of the houses, suggesting that they had been stored by their owners in pots on the ground or in baskets or on shelves attached to the walls, as at Ebla.[57] Such archives would have been deposited archaeologically at times when the building was destroyed or rebuilt under circumstances in which the tablets were no longer of any value. Furthermore, if the breaking of a tablet was an indication that the transaction recorded in it was null and void, then the finding of tablet fragments in domestic contexts may indicate no more than that not all of the broken tablet was cleared away before it was trodden into the floor. Other tablets were discarded, as can be determined by their discovery together with remains of other trash. However, even in this instance, it makes more sense to postulate that this trash derived from those living in the vicinity than that it reflects the

[56] If those tablets which were examined, the contracts, are a fair test, they indicate that the tablet catalog was quite accurate in its assessment.

[57] Paolo Matthiae, *Ebla, An Empire Rediscovered* (New York: Doubleday, 1981), p. 151.

activities of those living on the other side of town. Thus, if our interest is in the makeup of urban neighborhoods, it is reasonable to suppose that tablets found in a particular place reflect the activities of those who had lived in that neighborhood.

This work, therefore, will be devoted to an examination of the texts, pottery, objects, architecture, and stratigraphy of TA and TB to see how these can shed light on the organization of residential neighborhoods in Isin-Larsa and Old Babylonian Nippur. The following chapter gives a short socioeconomic history of the city. Its aim is to pinpoint those events which are likely to have affected the lives of all residents of Nippur. This is followed by two chapters, the first of which contains a house-by-house discussion of the finds from TA, while the second repeats this procedure for TB. Chapter 5 discusses each class of artifact to determine variations in time and space and provides a chronology for the levels in TA and TB. Finally, chapter 6 returns to the basic theme of neighborhood composition and discusses how the data from TA and TB contribute to an understanding of this issue.

Chapter 2

Nippur in the Isin-Larsa and Old Babylonian Periods

The discussion of an aspect of ancient Mesopotamia, in this instance domestic areas of the city of Nippur, remains largely meaningless unless it is viewed in the context both of the cultural and physical environment of Mesopotamia as a whole and of the sociopolitical history of the specific time and place in question. To set the scene, this chapter will begin with a discussion of the cultural ecology of southern Iraq, indicating the limits imposed on the society by the environment which it is exploiting. This is followed by an overview of the current state of knowledge of the social, political, and economic history of Nippur in the period under discussion. It is against this background that the detailed investigation of the residential areas of Nippur in the early second millennium will take place.

The period under consideration, ca. 1970–1720 B.C.,[1] was a critical period in Mesopotamian history. It witnessed the last sputterings of Sumerian influence and the shift in dominance from south to north. Furthermore, the close of this period was marked by a dark age, apparently accompanied by, or perhaps even partially caused by, an inability to maintain the old pattern of exploitation of the alluvium. One cannot but expect these factors to have affected the local population at Nippur, especially in the realm of social and economic life.

CULTURAL ECOLOGY

In Mesopotamia, as in perhaps no other center of early civilization, the external environment and its potentiality for human exploitation served to limit the types of social and political groups living there. Devoid of resources other than the alluvium and the water that flowed through it, in an area of minimal rainfall, the irrigation economy of ancient Mesopotamia was fragile and susceptible to misuse.[2] Mesopotamia is essentially a flat desert traversed by two rivers, the Tigris and the Euphrates. Although enough rain falls in the winter months to provide pasturage, it is not sufficient for dry farming. Since the bed of the principal source of irrigation in antiquity, the Euphrates River, lies above plain level, confined by high levees, flow irrigation can be practiced with little difficulty. However, at times of flood the water courses become unstable, frequently changing their beds, and the excess water drains into the interriverine basins to form somewhat saline marshes characterized by large stands of tall reeds. In addition, the high evaporation rate and saline groundwater often result in salinization of the soil if overirrigation or insufficient fallowing is practiced.

In its natural state, southern Mesopotamia is made up of two separate ecological niches, desert and marsh. The former, found in areas where water from the Tigris and Euphrates

[1] All dates B.C. are based on the Middle Chronology as presented by J. A. Brinkman in A. Leo Oppenheim, *Ancient Mesopotamia: Portrait of a Dead Civilization*, 2d ed. (Chicago: University of Chicago Press, 1977), pp. 336–37.

[2] Thorkild Jacobsen, *Salinity and Irrigation Agriculture in Antiquity* (Malibu: Undena Publications, 1982), especially pp. 52–56.

rivers does not reach, supports some scattered deep-rooted plants such as camel thorn (*Alhagi maurorum*) and *Artemisia* on a year-round basis and a more varied flora in the spring. The marshes, in contrast, consist of large, slow-moving or stagnant areas of relatively shallow water, the result of the overflowing of the rivers into the basins which lie between them. These marshes support large stands of reeds and have plentiful fish and waterfowl. Exploitation by man of the desert for grazing and the marshes for fish, fowl, and reeds has been characteristic of the Mesopotamian landscape for at least six millennia, but these natural habitats served only as refuge areas, with the bulk of the population occupying the artificial environment of the irrigated zone. Canal irrigation allowed the cultivation of dates and vegetables near the watercourses and cereal cultivation in the more distant fields. In addition, these settled farmers received wool, milk, and meat from desert herders, and fish, fowl, reeds, and perhaps pork from the marsh dwellers, giving grain, the "staff of life," in exchange. Yet in spite of this reciprocal pattern of economic interdependence, the irrigated areas could grow only at the expense of the deserts and marshes; the larger the area cultivated, the smaller the area left as desert, and the more water used for irrigation, the less available for marsh formation. Furthermore, the Mesopotamian environment is both restrictive in the types of agricultural exploitation possible and extremely sensitive to abuse.[3] Although the richness of the alluvium allowed ancient Mesopotamia to become the "breadbasket of the East," the uncertainties of the water supply, together with salinization as the penalty for overcultivation or overirrigation, meant that there was a high potential for economic collapse under conditions of mismanagement. This environmental instability limited the number of viable socioeconomic systems to those with the built-in risk-sharing attributes of tribal, feudal,[4] or state redistributive structures.[5]

Such redistributive systems ensure that long-range needs are not neglected for short-term goals. Under tribal management, the corporate group collectively owns and works the land. Agricultural products are distributed primarily according to need, although status may also be somewhat reflected.[6] When an individual or large institution controls a large tract of land, the produce is redistributed to workers either in the form of wages or as a share of the crop. In this instance, although the landowner receives a share of the produce, the laborer or sharecropper is still assured of an income. In both cases, it is in the interest of those in control to prevent short-term gains (by overcultivation) from resulting in long-term loss (by salinization)

[3] Robert McC. Adams, "Factors Influencing the Rise of Civilization in the Alluvium: Illustrated by Mesopotamia," in *City Invincible—A Symposium on Urbanism and Cultural Development,* ed. Carl H. Kraeling and Robert McC. Adams (Chicago: University of Chicago Press, 1960), pp. 24–46; idem, *Land behind Baghdad* (Chicago: University of Chicago Press, 1965); idem, "Patterns of Urbanism in Early Southern Mesopotamia," in *Man, Settlement and Urbanism,* ed. Peter J. Ucko, Ruth Tringham, and G. W. Dimbleby (London: Duckworth and Co., 1972), pp. 735–50; idem, "Historic Patterns of Mesopotamian Irrigation Agriculture," in *Irrigation's Impact on Society,* ed. Theodore Downing and McGuire Gibson, Anthropological Papers of the University of Arizona 25 (Tucson: University of Arizona Press, 1974), pp. 1–6; idem, "Strategies of Maximization, Stability and Resilience in Mesopotamian Society, Settlement and Agriculture," *Proceedings of the American Philosophical Society* 122 (1978): 329–35; idem, *Heartland of Cities* (Chicago: University of Chicago Press, 1981); Robert McC. Adams and Hans J. Nissen, *The Uruk Countryside* (Chicago: University of Chicago Press, 1972); P. Buringh, "Living Conditions in the Lower Mesopotamian Plain in Ancient Times," *Sumer* 13 (1957): 30–57; Robert A. Fernea, *Shaykh and Effendi: Changing Patterns of Authority among the El-Shabana of Southern Iraq* (Cambridge: Harvard University Press, 1970); McGuire Gibson, "Violation of Fallow and Engineered Disaster in Mesopotamian Civilization," in *Irrigation's Impact,* ed. Downing and Gibson, pp. 7–19; Jacobsen, *Salinity and Irrigation;* Thorkild Jacobsen and Robert McC. Adams, "Salt and Silt in Ancient Mesopotamian Agriculture," *Science* 128 (1958): 1251–58; A. P. G. Poyck, *Farm Studies in Iraq,* Mededelingen van de Landbouwhogeschool, vol. 62, no. 1 (Wageningen: H. Veeman & Zonen N. V., 1952).

[4] I am using the term *feudal* here in its broader, Marxist, sense, referring to all landlord-peasant relationships, not to the narrower meaning used to describe the situation in medieval Europe and Japan.

[5] Fernea, *Shaykh and Effendi;* Poyck, *Farm Studies;* Elizabeth C. Stone, "Economic Crisis and Social Upheaval in Nippur in the Old Babylonian Period," in *Mountains and Lowlands: Essays in the Archaeology of Greater Mesopotamia,* ed. Louis D. Levine and T. Cuyler Young, Jr. (Malibu: Undena Publications, 1977), pp. 267–89.

[6] Fernea, *Shaykh and Effendi,* p. 91.

and to ensure that the produce is equitably divided. In each instance the individual is protected by his association with a larger institution.

In ancient Mesopotamia, as in modern Iraq, small farm owners have existed who have benefitted but little from the protection afforded by membership in such a large economic institution. Poyck[7] demonstrates that small farm owners in Iraq are poorer than sharecroppers, and his data show that their poverty is the result of the overcultivation which they have to practice when their family size exceeds the carrying capacity of their plot. These farm owners could not survive on their meager harvests were it not for the wages that they receive during their annual migrations to Baghdad to work in the construction industry. In this case, only the possibilities for wage labor make possible the continuance of such small-scale economic units.

Mesopotamia has always been a pluralistic society. Not only have there been herders, marsh dwellers, and agriculturalists; urbanites and villagers; bureaucrats and laborers; but tribal and feudal-state-controlled economies as described above must always have coexisted. Although at different times one mode of organization may have dominated over the other, no matter whether corporate or individual control was the norm, other forms of organization, such as small-farm ownership, must always have been of minor significance.

Like economic organization, social organization can also be understood in terms of alternative and complementary roles, as reflected in the title of Robert Fernea's *Shaykh and Effendi,* a study of a modern Iraqi town. The sheikh is the leader of a social group whose membership is based upon kinship ties, while the effendi owes his position to his institutional link with the state government. This distinction between lineage members and bureaucrats dates back to the dawn of history. The first scribes were employees of the nascent Mesopotamian state, and from the fourth millennium B.C. onward they were employed to keep track of the activities of the temple and palace personnel. Those so recorded were defined by their occupational and institutional ties. In rare texts like the Maništušu obelisk,[8] on the other hand, we catch glimpses of the more rural groups whose organization was based on kinship. Although these distinctions can be made, we must not lose sight of the fact that the bureaucrats too must have had kinsmen; but surviving documents make it appear that their kinship positions were less important in defining their roles in society than their positions in the bureaucracy.

These alternate modes of social organization are closely related to those of economic organization. The locus of corporate land ownership is generally a lineage or tribe, a social unit based on kinship. Conversely, those whose livelihood is controlled by the state, whether they receive wages or are sharecroppers, have their landlord as a common bond. However, this correlation is not automatic. Today, tribal groups may be sharecroppers,[9] or an unrelated group may form an agricultural commune. There is evidence of kin groups having a virtual monopoly of positions of importance in small institutions in ancient Mesopotamia.[10] For this reason, it seems best to keep the potential modes of economic organization conceptually separate from those of social organization.

NIPPUR SOCIAL INSTITUTIONS

Before discussing the changes in social and economic organization in the Isin-Larsa and Old Babylonian periods, it is appropriate to describe the nature of the major social institutions

[7] Poyck, *Farm Studies,* p. 74.

[8] Igor M. Diakonoff, "The Rise of the Despotic State in Mesopotamia," in *Ancient Mesopotamia,* ed. Igor M. Diakonoff (Moscow: "Nauka" Publishing House, 1969), p. 183; idem, "On the Structure of Old Babylonian Society," in *Beiträge zur sozialen Struktur des alten Vorderasien,* ed. Horst Klengel (Berlin: Akademie Verlag, 1971), pp. 15–31.

[9] Fernea, *Shaykh and Effendi,* p. 12.

[10] Richard Zettler, personal communication.

which can be documented for this period. Our understanding of the structure and organization of Mesopotamian society in the Old Babylonian period is better than for most other periods of Mesopotamian history,[11] but yet not adequate when approaching data concerned with a specific city—in this case Nippur. A cursory examination of the available textual record from different Old Babylonian cities leads to the conclusion that major differences existed between the types, significance, and an economic impact of social institutions in the various cities.[12] As a consequence, the bulk of this section is based solely on texts found at Nippur, primarily the approximately five hundred private contracts, some of which are published in this volume for the first time.[13]

These texts contain sufficient evidence for it to be possible to identify clearly both people and property in most cases. Almost every personal name is accompanied by a patronymic, a profession, or both. This not only pinpoints an individual when involved in different transactions, but frequently allows the reconstruction of genealogies.[14] In addition to providing information on the kinship position of the transacting parties, the texts provide the names of the owners of neighboring plots. In some cases it is possible to reconstruct maps of the real estate involved; more often, however, we can tell only who lived in the same neighborhood, or shared interests in the irrigation and cultivation of particular fields or orchards. The texts also provide some insight into the associates of the transactors. Each text includes a list of the names of the witnesses who were chosen as advocates for the two parties in the contracts.

[11] Kraus, *Vom mesopotamischen Menschen.*

[12] Compare, for example, the picture presented by Michael J. Desroches's study of texts from Dilbat in northern Mesopotamia (*Aspects of the Structure of Dilbat during the Old Babylonian Period* [Ann Arbor: University Microfilms, 1978]) with that presented by Dominique Charpin, who examined texts from the southern cities of Kutalla and Ur (*Archives familiales et propriété privée en Babylonie ancienne* [Geneva: Librairie Droz, 1980]).

[13] The texts used in this study can be found in BE 6/2, PBS 8/1, PBS 8/2, PBS 13, *ARN,* OIMA 1, OECT 8, YOS 14, TIM 4, Hussey, Toledo, and Cornell, and Elizabeth C. Stone and David I. Owen, *Adoption at Nippur in the Old Babylonian Period and the Archive of Mannum-mešu-liṣṣur.* (Forthcoming). Additional texts are published in M. Çığ and H. Kızılyay, "Fünf Tontafeln mit neuen Daten aus der altbabylonischen Period," *Belletin* 26 (1962): 20–44.

[14] Genealogical reconstructions were primarily based on profoundly subjective judgments; the nature of the material made this a necessity, thus few hard and fast rules could be applied. The two rules that *were* strictly followed were, first, that at least two different connections had to be established between individuals before they were accepted as belonging to the same genealogy, and second, that the assignment of members to a genealogy had to make chronological sense.

The basic building block used in the reconstruction of the genealogies was the father-son link. The difficulty came in determining, for instance, whether or not the Ududu who is a son in one case and a father in another represents a single individual. Once it was established that it was chronologically possible for the two roles, those of father and son, to have been played by the same individual, the search for verification could be initiated.

First, it had to be established whether the name itself was common. If it was, then the link had to be treated with some suspicion. If, however, that name only occurred in those two roles, then it was considered more probable that it referred to the same person.

The second step was to investigate property relationships. Since property was passed from father to son, the property transactions of the individual (in his two roles) were expected to treat the same pieces of residential property, fields, or orchards in the same named tract, or the same temple office. However, even if they dealt with different pieces of property, this would not prove that they did not reflect the transactions of one person, since individual estates were often made up of many plots of land and many temple offices, any one of which could have been recorded in the text.

The third step was to look at the other people involved in the transaction. The nature of the inheritance system was such that neighboring plots were likely to be owned by relatives. Thus, if the two roles were found in texts where the owners of neighboring plots were either the same or related to each other (brothers, sons, etc.), then this was taken to suggest that the two roles were probably united in one individual. Similarly, since witnesses were usually either kinsmen, neighbors, or associates, when the same people occurred as witnesses on texts in which our individual appears in both his roles, or when witnesses of one text were related to those of another text, then again there were grounds for belief that the roles concern the same person. Finally, since transactions were frequently between brothers or other kinsmen, once the genealogy had been roughed out, the veracity of the genealogy was strengthened if members of the same genealogy were found to do business with each other, witness each other's texts, and own contiguous property.

Genealogical links, then, were considered to be "established" when two positive pieces of evidence were available, namely, when two property links or two personal links were identifiable, or where one of each could be found.

These witnesses, therefore, can be understood as representing some of the associates of the transacting parties. In a sufficient number of cases, the same name or (better still) group of names occurs on several documents, providing information not only on the genealogical relationships between individuals, but also on how these kinship ties were reflected in residential patterns and in business associations.

This data base has allowed the identification of three social institutions[15] which were important at Nippur between around 1920 and 1720 B.C. These were patrilineal lineages, the temple office association,[16] and the *nadītums*. Following a description of the ideal form of each institution will be a discussion of how they changed over time. The purpose is to show how they interacted with each other and with the other social groups which were in Nippur, and how all were affected by the more important political events of the time.

The evidence suggests that one of the basic elements in Nippur society was the lineage, a modification of an ideal of a corporate group based on patrilineal kinship ties. Those that can be identified were usually quite shallow, only about four generations deep, although the lineage that controlled TA (see chap. 3) was somewhat deeper. Lineage members generally owned similar and often contiguous property, a result of partitive inheritance, and they usually witnessed each other's documents, indicating a degree of communal interest. The evidence suggests that alienation restrictions on land prevented fields and orchards, perhaps also houses, from being sold outside the lineage.[17] Marriage practices may also have served to keep wealth within the family; although we have very little evidence, there are some suggestions[18] that patrilateral endogamy, as practiced in the Middle East today, may also have been the rule in ancient Nippur.[19] Slim evidence also exists which suggests that some judicial actions, especially those which concern familial or marital problems, may have been settled within kin-based neighborhoods.[20]

These lineages seem similar to the ideal Middle Eastern tribes described in modern ethnographies[21] where land is owned and worked in common, patrilateral endogamy is

[15] I use the term *institution* to refer to these social units because the behavior patterns of the individuals who made up their memberships suggest that, at least at one level, these represented corporate groups. However, the textual record does not refer to named corporate groups. The difficulty when using written sources is to know whether such omissions mean that such units did not exist, or simply that they had no significance for the types of transactions so recorded. In this case one may hypothesize that although these "institutions" were social units of some real significance, they did not enjoy the legal status which would have led to their inclusion as reference points in the economic and legal texts, which are all that record the social and economic behavior of the ancient inhabitants of Nippur.

[16] Temple offices were offices associated with particular temples which could be owned for a certain number of days out of the year. These offices were heritable, and by 1800 B.C. were alienable as well. A few offices had associated prebend fields, but the best estimate of the value of these offices is that they entitled the owner to a share of the sacrifice. See Stone, "Economic Crisis;" and Marcel Sigrist, "Ninurta à Nippur" (Ph.D. diss., Yale University, 1976), pp. 309–44, who demonstrates that many of the temple offices which are known from the Old Babylonian contracts were important early in Isin-Larsa times. Finally, temple office ownership apparently carried with it a certain amount of status; the offices were used as titles, and their owners were often called upon to witness such official documents as court cases. However, it is far from clear whether the Old Babylonian officeholders owed any obligations to the temple.

[17] Elizabeth C. Stone, "The Social Role of the *Nadītu* Women in Old Babylonian Nippur," *Journal of the Economic and Social History of the Orient* 24 (1982): 50–70.

[18] Elizabeth C. Stone and David I. Owen, *Adoption in Old Babylonian Nippur and the Archive of Mannum-mešu-liṣṣur* (forthcoming), where a girl marries her adoptive father's brother's son.

[19] Samuel Greengus ("Old Babylonian Marriage Ceremonies and Rites," *Journal of Cuneiform Studies* 20 [1966]: 55–72; and "The Old Babylonian Marriage Contract," *Journal of the American Oriental Society* 89 [1969]: 505–32) suggests that this practice may have been common in other Old Babylonian cities.

[20] Constance Cronin ("Kinship in the Code of Hammurabi," paper read at the Annual Meetings of the American Anthropological Association, Toronto, November 27–30, 1972) has suggested that the *bābtum*, translated "city ward" by the *CAD*, vol. B, pp. 9–14, might be better understood as the physical manifestation of a lineage. In BE 6/2 58, a court record which concerned the maltreatment of a woman by her husband, the locus of the trial was the *bābtum*, perhaps indicating that such offenses were subject to familial judicial authority.

[21] See, for an example, Fernea, *Shaykh and Effendi*, p. 78.

practiced, and judicial and military affairs are conducted by the tribe as a corporate group. These tribes have charismatic leaders whose positions *tend* to be passed within the same branch of the family, although this cannot be guaranteed. It is this type of organization that Adams suggests as the "resilient" element in Mesopotamian society, that element which retained sufficient flexibility to cope with political or economic disaster.[22]

All modern ethnographies describe how this ideal tribal system has been modified through contact with state governments;[23] the same modification was experienced by the Nippur lineages. By the Isin-Larsa period, any military functions that they might have had were gone, judicial functions were weak or nonexistent, and land was in individual rather than corporate hands. Thus, if the lineages originally resembled the ideal type, their functions had been largely curtailed by the beginning of the period under consideration and, as we shall see, were to undergo further weakening throughout the Isin-Larsa and Old Babylonian periods.

An aggravating factor in the progressive weakening of the lineages was the rise of other, more urban based, associations whose membership was drawn from disparate lineages. One such association was that based on the ownership of temple offices. In the Ur III period, these offices were apparently part of the temple bureaucracies which were prevalent at that time. By the Isin-Larsa period, however, it appears that they had become a kind of private property which could have been passed on to the heirs of the owner. When temple offices became alienable shortly before 1800 B.C., they carried none of the alienation restrictions which applied to the more traditional kinds of property, i.e., fields and houses.[24] The special characteristics of temple offices as a form of property seem to have led to the establishment of a large loosely organized socioeconomic group consisting entirely of temple officeholders.

It is difficult to know how the bonds between such officeholders were formed; perhaps common rites in the temples whose offices they controlled led to a degree of solidarity, or perhaps their frequent activities as witnesses to court cases brought them together. Whatever the cause, it resulted in the development of a loosely knit organization in which an officeholder could draw on any other member of the group to witness his transactions or to purchase his property. This practice contrasted with normal real estate transactions, which, at least before 1750 B.C., had to be between kinsmen and witnessed by kinsmen. Since most or all members of the temple office group were also members of their natal lineages, often important members, the economic ease of transactions in temple offices must have led to a conflict between their two memberships. In the end, the economic advantages of the habits of the more freewheeling temple group apparently outweighed the tradition associated with the lineages, for when economic conditions and political control weakened, the temple office association apparently became the dominant group in the society, and even fields were being exchanged between unrelated officeholders. In the later years of Samsuiluna, although the names of an officeholder's kinsmen are usually known, all of his economic dealings were with other members of the temple group, and not with members of his family.

While the temple office association can be seen as the antithesis to the lineage, a third institution, that of the *nadītum*s, was both an intrinsic part of the lineage system, while at the same time, like that of the temple officeholders, it forged interlineage ties. *Nadītum*s were unmarried women who were drawn from the major branches of some lineages and provided with land for their support. The evidence suggests that a close *nadītum* relative was necessary for acceptance into the institution, so that only some lineages had *nadītum*s. It seems likely

[22] Adams, "Maximization and Resilience."

[23] Hanna Batatu (*The Old Social Classes and the Revolutionary Movements of Iraq* [Princeton: Princeton University Press, 1978], pp. 63-152) has an extremely good discussion of the manipulation of tribal groups by the Ottoman, British, and Iraqi governments.

[24] Of the various classes of property exchanged, only temple offices are almost never exchanged between known kinsmen, in contrast to the majority of real estate transactions.

that this practice served both to provide for women who were outside the marriage market, perhaps because of their high status, and to consolidate property holdings which would otherwise be divided on inheritance. Although these women often lived in a particular area set aside for them, they maintained very close economic ties with their brothers. The property which they had received was at least partly controlled by these brothers, yet the *nadītum* was always recorded as the sole owner at times of property transfer. However, most of the economic transactions of the *nadītums* were with fellow *nadītums*, women who were drawn from other lineages. Thus, as with the temple office owners, the *nadītum* institution brought members of different lineages together, but in this case interlineage contact did not result in a divorce of the members from their natal lineage.[25]

The next question is how the lineages, the temple office group, and the *nadītum* institution interacted and changed over time. Although many residents of TB and especially TA were members of these institutions, it is the dynamics of their interactions with each other, with other groups at Nippur, and with outside political forces which one might expect to find reflected in the archaeological record.

SOCIOECONOMIC HISTORY

In seeking the roots of the social institutions which were of importance in the Isin-Larsa and Old Babylonian periods, it is first necessary to describe briefly what is known of Nippur in the Ur III period. Ur III documentation from Nippur, like that from other cities, is mostly in the form of the receipts and accounts produced by the bureaucracy. While this material rarely reveals much about socioeconomic organization, certain features of Ur III Nippur are worth noting: First, some high political and religious offices, including the nu-èš and the ugula-é, which occur in Old Babylonian contracts, were heritable in Ur III times and were dominated by a single family.[26] Second, although Ur III real estate purchase documents are extremely rare, those which have been preserved generally can be ascribed to Nippur.[27]

This evidence from Ur III Nippur shows that in spite of the great differences between the Ur III and Old Babylonian textual record, the societies had significant similarities. First, in the Ur III period, kinship ties were extremely important, even for the highest office holders. Indeed, some of the highest religious and secular positions were passed from father to son. However, there is no evidence here that extended kinship groups, like the Isin-Larsa lineages, played a significant role in the city's affairs. Second, in the Ur III period, although temple offices were not divisible, at least some were heritable. However, in Ur III the position ugula-é, for example, was held uniquely by the man who was in charge of the running of that temple. By Old Babylonian times, when up to one hundred men may have shared a single office, the ownership of an office can have had little to do with the bureaucratic activities implied by the title. Third, although real estate sale was all but unknown elsewhere in Ur III times, a few transactions are known from Nippur, indicating that some private property must have existed at that time. Finally, since the word used for *nadītums* at Nippur was simply the Sumerian lukur, meaning priestess,[28] the *nadītum* institution may already have been in existence in Ur III times. Perhaps the *nadītums* had been established as a way of providing for girls whose high status made it difficult for them to find suitable husbands.[29]

[25] For a more detailed discussion of the Nippur *nadītums*, the reader is referred to Stone, "Social Role."
[26] William W. Hallo, "The House of Ur-Meme," *Journal of Near Eastern Studies* 31 (1972): 87–95.
[27] Piotr Steinkeller, "Sale Documents of the Ur III Period" (Ph.D. diss., University of Chicago, 1977).
[28] *CAD*, vol. N, pp. 63–64.
[29] Stone, "Social Role," p. 65.

Thus, in Ur III Nippur, it seems that kin-based groups and perhaps also *nadītums* were important elements in the society, while those controlling heritable temple offices were at the pinnacles of power. What remains unclear is how those elements of Nippur society which controlled real estate and cultivated it outside the state agricultural system[30] were tied into the urban power structure. As long as this remains a mystery, no full understanding of the socioeconomic changes associated with the shift in power from Ur to Isin is possible.

Išbi-Erra, the first king of Isin, gained control of Nippur in the sixth year of Ibbi-Sîn (2022 B.C.), when the latter appointed him (at his request) as the defender of Nippur and Isin. Within six years, Išbi-Erra had attained independence, and within twenty years he had wrested control of Sumer from Ur with a little help from the Martu, the Elamites, and the Suam.[31] Of the many cities in Mesopotamia, Nippur was probably the least affected by these events. The ending of the bala offerings after 2026 B.C.[32] must have led to some belt-tightening, but since Nippur was controlled by Isin, which was rich in grain, it cannot have experienced the famine that plagued the south in 2021 B.C.[33] However, the departure of the royally appointed governor, Dada,[34] and the imprisonment of the sanga, Ni-dugani,[35] must have had a quite profound effect on the urban bureaucracy. Nevertheless, administrative texts from TA (see Appendix III) and elsewhere at Nippur[36] indicate that although the external controls were absent, most of the internal aspects of the Ur III administrative activities were continued in Isin-Larsa times.

Evidence about the early years of Isin's domination over Nippur is virtually nonexistent, but it is clear that at some time in the mid-twentieth century B.C., much of Sumer and especially Nippur were devastated by war. An inscription of Išme-Dagan[37] and the "Lamentation over the Destruction of Nippur"[38] name Išme-Dagan as the king responsible for reestablishing the cult of Enlil and Ninlil at Nippur and for restoring peace to the area. This warfare must have had a profound effect on the inhabitants of Nippur, and it may be significant that it is after that time, around 1920 B.C., that the first Old Babylonian style contracts were written at Nippur. The earliest contracts from Ur also date to about this time,[39] but at other cities they do not appear until later.[40]

These contracts indicate that patrilineal lineages were residing in Nippur by 1920 B.C. Their members individually owned real estate, including temple offices, which could be divided up on inheritance[41] and sold, except for the temple offices, to other members of the same kin group. It is possible to interpret these first contracts as evidence of rural-based, property-owning lineages moving into the city. The point of departure for this discussion, all admittedly hypothetical, is that the disaster recorded in the Lamentation for Nippur really happened and that at Nippur it was this event that served as the turning point in the city's

30 Diakonoff, "Rise of the Despotic State."

31 Thorkild Jacobsen, "The Reign of Ibbi-Suen," *Journal of Cuneiform Studies* 7 (1953): 41–44.

32 William W. Hallo, "A Sumerian Amphictyony," ibid. 14 (1960): 96.

33 Jacobsen, "Reign of Ibbi-Suen," pp. 41–42.

34 Hallo, "House of Ur-meme," p. 95.

35 Jeremy A. Black, "A History of Nippur, from the Earliest Times to the End of the Kassite Period" (B.Phil. thesis, Oxford University, 1975), pp. 41–44.

36 Sigrist, "Ninurta à Nippur," pp. 85–86.

37 Black, "History of Nippur," p. 45.

38 Dietz Otto Edzard, *Die "Zweite Zwischenzeit" Babyloniens* (Wiesbaden: Otto Harrassowitz, 1957), pp. 86–90.

39 Hugo H. Figulla and William J. Martin, *Ur Excavations: Texts V: Letters and Documents of the Old Babylonian Period* (Philadelphia: University of Pennsylvania Press, 1953).

40 Ronald F. G. Sweet, "On Prices, Moneys and Money Uses in the Old Babylonian Period" (Ph.D. diss., University of Chicago, 1958).

41 Division of temple offices is documented, albeit in a roundabout way, from as early as 1890 B.C., close in time to the earliest contract known from Nippur. *ARN* 57, which is contemporary with *ARN* 58, can be related through personal names to *ARN* 4 + PBS 8/1 2, which is dated to the reign of Būr-Sîn, around 1890 B.C. *ARN* clearly concerns the division of temple offices, in this case nar-ships.

social and economic history, rather than the end of the Ur III period itself.[42] The "enemy" that caused the destruction mourned in the Lamentation for Nippur is not named,[43] and it seems possible that they were none other than members of semi-independent rural tribal groups. Išme-Dagan's restoration of the cult of Nippur seems to have been associated with reversing the trend towards the "scattering of the people."[44]

It seems possible that this event provided the circumstances for the introduction of some new groups into the city and for a restructuring of the bureaucracy. It seems likely that the urban sector might have been prepared to share some of their wealth and power with the rural population in exchange for a more peaceful relationship. What I suggest is that a deal was struck whereby some of the rural tribal leaders moved into the cities, together with some of their followers, and received in exchange some of the wealth which accompanied the holding of temple offices. Those remaining in the countryside would have found themselves locally leaderless but retaining ties of kinship, perhaps reinforced by marriage, with the new urban elements.

A number of issues must be discussed before it is possible to accept the hypothesis discussed above as the best explanation of the available evidence. The first question is whether the people whose records first appear in the form of contracts more closely resemble urban or rural groups. In this early period they appear highly cohesive, with bonds of kinship apparently dictating social behavior. Drawing parallels with more recent history, this pattern would appear more characteristic of rural than long-term urban populations. In the texts property appears to be individually recorded, but there are retained elements of communal ownership, a behavior pattern generally felt to be more characteristic of rural groups. Among the property which they control are temple offices which can be inherited. The early texts record the control of whole or half offices, suggesting either that these offices had been in the family for only a short period of time or that they were neither heritable nor divisible before the time of the first contracts. My hypothesis would suggest that the offices became heritable and divisible at the time that they were given to these families. The large amount of agricultural land controlled by these groups again appears to be more consistent with these groups having a rural background than with their having an urban, Ur III past. Finally, one text refers to some property having been the gift of the king of Isin, supporting the idea that these people were being provided with sources of wealth.

The hypothesis advanced here of a rural origin for the kin groups whose activities are recorded in the Isin-Larsa and Old Babylonian contracts provides an avenue for explaining how Ur III property-control patterns could have been so transformed in the subsequent period. Two aspects are involved here: the divorce of temple offices from the services previously expected of their holders and their becoming both heritable and divisible, and second, the introduction of the ownership of agricultural land on the part of urbanites. In the Ur III and early Isin-Larsa period temple offices were, literally, offices held in temples. The individual named the overseer of the temple (ugula-é) was responsible for the workings of the temple concerned, in exchange for which he received certain emoluments. In late Isin-Larsa and Old Babylonian times, one individual could "own" complete offices of more than one kind and attached to more than one temple,[45] or as little as one and a half days' worth of one office (or 0.004 of a total office). It is inconceivable that at this time these offices required of their

[42] Although many such lamentations are apparently merely literary compositions and not true historical records, in this case Išme-Dagan's own inscriptions tend to support the suggestion that this text records a real event.

[43] Although "at *TCL* 15.15 ii 13 he is identified as 'ti-da-nu-um, the desert nomad'" (Black, "History of Nippur," p. 46), this might well be one way of describing a rural tribal population that had run amok.

[44] Black, "History of Nippur," p. 45.

[45] As indicated above, an individual could inherit at least some offices in the Ur III period and, in some cases, is seen as holding the titles of more than one office (Hallo, "House of Ur-Meme"), but the Ur III period does not witness the multiplicity of offices seen in the later Isin-Larsa and Old Babylonian periods. It seems possible that the seeds for

holders the services which had been expected during Ur III hegemony. No texts have been preserved indicating which of the many owners was responsible for performing the temple duties on which dates, and the performance of all the duties attached to multiple offices would have been impossible. Therefore, one cannot escape the conclusion that the temple offices mentioned in the later texts, although called by the same names and presumably derived from those of the earlier period, had been transformed from titles associated with services into property pure and simple.

The scenario which I am suggesting argues that private ownership of agricultural land was introduced by the rural groups who moved into the city. The temple offices, on the other hand, would have been transformed in order to provide incentives for the ingress of these potential troublemakers. While tribal sheikhs were capable of receiving the benefits of office holding, they would not have had the experience needed for the running of a temple. The alternative explanation, that the kin groups whose activities are recorded on the contracts were old urbanites who had reorganized themselves, cannot explain from where they could have obtained the agricultural land which they suddenly appear to control, nor why the temple offices should have been transformed.

In summary, it is suggested that following the attack on Nippur described in the Lamentation, Išme-Dagan and his successors initiated a program designed to pacify the countryside. Like the British during the mandate period,[46] they brought the tribal leaders into the cities where they could be controlled, but unlike the British, this action took place during a period of relative political weakness, so they were forced also to take in some of their followers. Moreover, to tempt them in, the urbanites had to give up some of their wealth and power, which emerges in the texts in the form of transformed temple offices. Išme-Dagan, meanwhile, protected the urban character of Nippur by exempting the population from military service and taxes and rebuilding the major shrines.[47]

The political climate within which these land-based lineages settled into urban life was one of constant warfare. Between 1870 and 1793 B.C., as seen in year dates, Nippur changed hands between Isin and Larsa every few years (see table 1). These outside events form the backdrop to a more localized political struggle which developed as the lineage leaders attempted to carve out a significant role for themselves within the affairs of the city. One may postulate that the leaders, who had already received so much as a result of the shift into the city, would have spent the early years of the nineteenth century B.C. consolidating their power and wealth. This process, though, could only be accomplished at the expense of lineage unity. Without corporate land ownership lineage power must now have been based on the amount of property owned personally by the leaders, not collectively by the lineage, therefore property acquisition by the leaders would be the first step in consolidating power. However, since houses, fields, and orchards, the only alienable property at that time, held traditional alienation restrictions that prevented their sale outside the lineage, the main branches could only acquire property at the expense of the minor branches. Moreover, this acquisition of property by the main branch had to be an ongoing process. Since inheritance was essentially partitive, the estate which formed the basis for the power of one generation would be divided when the next generation took over.[48] Property relationships would also have affected lineage power. Since inherited property now formed the basis of leadership, when a new leader came

the transformation documented for the Isin-Larsa period were sown in Ur III as some of those whose power was based on office holding tried to pass that power on to their sons.

[46] Batatu, *Old Social Classes.*

[47] Black, "History of Nippur," p. 47.

[48] There is no record of concubines being taken as second wives in Nippur in the Isin-Larsa and Old Babylonian periods, but if they were, one would expect the rich leaderships to have been the ones to have them. The consequence of this would have been more sons among whom the property had to be divided.

TABLE 1. ISIN-LARSA DATES AT NIPPUR

Isin	Date	Larsa
Ur-Ninurta	1923–1896	
Būr-Sîn	1895–1874	
	1873(?)–1872	Sumu-el
Lipit-Enlil	1871(?)	
	1870	Sumu-el
Lipit-Enlil	1869(?)	
	1868–1867	Sumu-el
Irra-imittī	1866–1861	
Enlil-bāni	1860–1844(?)	
	1843	Sîn-iddinam
	1842–1841	Sîn-erībam
Enlil-bāni	1840(?)–1838(?)	
	1837	Sîn-iqīšam
Zambija	1836–1834	
Īter-pīša	1833–1831	
Ur-dukuga	1830–1828	
	1827–1823	Warad-Sîn
	1822–1815	Rīm-Sîn
Damiq-ilišu	1814–1811	
	1811–1810	Rīm-Sîn
Damiq-ilišu	1809–1803	
	1802–1797	Rīm-Sîn
Damiq-ilišu(?)	1796–1794	
	1793–1763	Rīm-Sîn

to be chosen, the choice would have been based more on his inheritance expectations than on his personal qualifications. Any attempt to transfer leadership from one branch to another would have had to have been accompanied by a major land sale, which made such a transfer unlikely. Finally, the conversion of liquid capital into land which all this would have entailed was not without risks of its own. Mesopotamian agricultural production was always unreliable, with individually owned small field plots the most vulnerable to the effects of political or environmental instability. Those most vulnerable would have been the members of the minor branches of the lineages, those whose small land holdings may have led them to overcultivate even in good years, bringing with it the risk of salinization. Nevertheless, a series of bad harvests, whether caused by poor water management or marauding armies, could have left even the leaders with property that they could not sell and debts that they could not pay.

The lineages were not, of course, unaware of many of these difficulties, and they devised means for mitigating their effects. All lineages for which we have adequate records adopted specific strategies for avoiding excessive partition of property, although each lineage apparently developed its own *modus operandi*. First, since the eldest son always received an extra 10% "preference portion," this could be modified to avoid some of the disadvantage of partitive inheritance. This was accomplished by leaving the temple offices intact to the eldest son and compensating the younger sons with increased shares of other types of property, sometimes even with silver. This practice was presumably not forbidden by traditional rules of inheritance because temple offices were not traditional property, while at the same time the links of the offices with the temples, important urban institutions, must have given their holders access to an important source of both political and economic power. A second strategy was to omit some sons from property inheritance altogether. The evidence suggests that these were often older sons, so it may be that they preferred to take their patrimony early in the form of moveable wealth rather than wait until their father died. These sons were sometimes able to use this wealth to rebuild propertied estates through the purchase of real estate from their brothers or cousins. The net result was that estates tended to be either quite large or very small, with very few of intermediate size.

A third strategy for consolidating property was available only to those lineages that already had women in the *nadītum* institution. Here property could be kept together by being given to *nadītum* daughters before the sons inherited. Thus a block of land could be manipulated by the leaders yet not liable to subdivision at death. A second advantage was that through *nadītum*s, control of property could be transferred from one lineage to another. Thus a rich lineage leadership could acquire property from someone other than its minor branches, while a poor one could find the liquid assets needed to pay its debts. *Nadītum* membership rose sharply in this mid Isin-Larsa period as its potential for avoiding some of the pitfalls of partitive inheritance became clear.[49]

Without evidence as to how the *nadītum* institution came into existence, it is impossible to tell why some families were able to participate in it when others could not. Most of those families that had *nadītum* members may have been long-term Nippur residents, whereas those with no *nadītum*s may have been more recent immigrants. These immigrant families could gain membership in the *nadītum* institution only through adoption. Unfortunately, although several texts from Nippur which might concern adoption and *nadītum*s have been published, all are in too fragmentary a condition for full understanding to be possible.[50]

The evidence is much more detailed on other uses of adoption as means of solving economic difficulties. Some debt-ridden families, although rich in property, were unable to convert their real estate holdings into liquid capital through sale. Since temple offices could not be alienated before 1800 B.C. and since only close kinsmen could purchase land from each other, legitimate buyers were often hard to find.[51] Marriage with an heiress must have been the most attractive solution, but when heiresses were unobtainable,[52] the adoption of a rich but propertyless man became an option. This individual would use his capital to pay off his adoptive father's debts and in exchange would inherit the property.[53] The adoptee would also be in a position to wield political power, but whether as a lineage member or only as an individual is not clear. Since lineages were based on land ownership and kinship, such an adoption must have been an admission of failure on the part of the lineage in question since the giving of lineage land to an outsider was normally unthinkable. It is perhaps a measure of the economic weakness of the lineages, though, that there is no evidence to suggest that adoption was ever used by one lineage to gain control over the resources of another; those with sufficient wealth to be valuable as adoptees were always outsiders.

This weakness of the lineages was largely due to their inability to deal effectively with the problems that arose as a consequence of the conflict between the demands of the urban economy and traditional values, the most serious of which resulted in a continuing economic split between the leadership and the minor branches. This split must be seen as the root cause of the breakup of the lineages during the Old Babylonian period. However, the inability of many of the leaders themselves to maintain important positions in Nippur may be due in part

[49] See also, Stone, "Social Role," pp. 67–68.

[50] Stone and Owen, *Adoption in Nippur* (forthcoming).

[51] This situation has parallels where debt-ridden owners of entailed property had to devise complex strategies for relieving the situation; see David Kannadine, "Aristocratic Indebtedness in the Nineteenth Century: The Case Reopened," *Economic History Review* 30 (1977): 624–50.

[52] Marriage to an heiress was complicated by a preference for endogamous marriages.

[53] For examples of this practice, see Stone and Owen, *Adoption in Nippur* (forthcoming).

to the inflexibility of a system which equated access to power with inherited wealth. The flexibility of the traditional organization whereby personal qualifications played an important role in the transfer of leadership ensured strong leaders. Only one example of the transfer of power from one branch of a lineage to another has been preserved, and that was the subject of litigation for the following seventy years.

In the Ninlil-zimu family (see chap. 3), leadership generally went to the eldest son of the previous leader, although in some instances elder sons who received their patrimony early in exchange for economic independence may have been passed over. Leadership was accompanied by the control of one of the most prestigious temple offices at Nippur, the $gudu_4$-ship of Ninlil. Although detailed evidence is lacking on this point, a time seems to have come when the successor, perhaps an only son, was extremely incompetent, perhaps even half-witted. At all events, leadership was transferred to another branch of the family, accompanied by the temple office; a field plot is all that was given in exchange.

This event had several consequences. First, the sons of the ousted leader, realizing what they had lost as a result of their father's incompetence, appealed to the monarchy for redress, identifying themselves as sons of their paternal grandfather. This meant both that outside powers were being introduced into lineage affairs, and that the weakness of the lineage system as it then was stood revealed for all to see. The second consequence of this shift of power was that some of the stresses on lineage unity that had been building up came to a head. From that time forth, the leadership became increasingly separated from the minor branches, and more importantly, this separation could be exploited by outside forces. The third consequence was that, perhaps for the first time at Nippur, a temple office had been given for exchange. Once temple office alienation was permitted, the growth of the most potent challenge to lineage power, the temple office group, became possible.

The various strategies adopted by the lineages during the unstable political climate of the mid Isin-Larsa period were not sufficient to stem the tide of lineage dissolution, but before the old sources of power could fall, new nuclei had to be developed. It was these nuclei which slowly came into being during the last years of the Isin-Larsa era. The conquest of Isin by Rīm-Sîn in 1792 B.C. led to a thirty year period of peace at Nippur, the first since Isin and Larsa had begun vying for control of Mesopotamia. Yet the ending of political unrest could not bring with it an end to the inequalities and imbalances in the social system which had grown up during the previous century. Already existing trends continued, but a new factor was added. Temple offices could now be freely alienated, but unlike the traditional house and field property whose potential buyers were restricted to kinsmen, temple offices carried no such restrictions. Thus temple office exchange could take place between members of different lineages.

One must assume that owners of offices in the same temples, whether members of the same family or not, must have had a certain amount of contact. In addition to whatever activities may have been associated with the temple itself, they shared such civic duties as the witnessing of court cases. When temple offices became alienable, the contacts that already existed between office owners and the absence of traditional alienation restrictions attached to this new property allowed the owners to exchange offices not only with other members of their lineages but with other unrelated officeholders as well. For the first time lineages without *nadītums* found a way to exchange property for liquid capital outside the lineage. Henceforward, significant interlineage economic transactions, through the medium of officeholders, became possible.

At this time the lineage leaders still controlled considerable amounts of real property, but the amassing of these estates had been accomplished at the expense of minor branches, whose holdings were by now no more than marginal. This disparity in sizes of holdings is seen in the size of inherited estates dating to the first half of the eighteenth century B.C.;

property owners were polarized into the rich and the poor.[54] Since the leaderships had milked dry the rest of the lineages, they must have been eager to find other groups with whom they could make transactions. The leaders, by that time, had more in common with other leaders than they did with lesser members of their own lineages, so the lineage as a viable social institution was doomed.

Although the conditions described above were present at Nippur when Rīm-Sîn gained control of the south in 1793 B.C., it was not until Hammurabi's conquest some thirty years later that the consequent economic changes were felt. For the last two decades of Rīm-Sîn's control, virtually no private economic texts have been preserved.[55] This absence may simply reflect the inadequacies of our sample, or it may reflect some kind of ban on private transactions for that period.

The situation was changed dramatically by the conquest by Hammurabi of Babylon, which took place in 1763 B.C. Not only was there a brief interruption in the peace, but evidence of private economic activity resumed, some of it actively managed by the new monarch. Most important from our point of view is what seems to have been his attitude towards the lineages. Hammurabi apparently was suspicious of any potential source of power in Nippur and therefore encouraged the minor branches to bring complaints against the leaders, as seen in the court case described above. This practice exacerbated the friction between the leaders and their followers, and may have hastened the lineages' demise.

The increase in economic activity that coincides with the conquest by Hammurabi reveals how the changes which took place in the previous three decades had affected Nippur society. First, it becomes clear that the *nadītum* institution was much less important than it had been before.[56] Presumably, their loss of power was due to the new, less cumbersome, channels for interlineage economic interaction that had opened up in the meantime. Second, there is a significant increase in the number of loan and rental texts preserved from this period.[57] The exact significance of these texts is unclear, but they may suggest that lineage cohesion had become so weak that members of the minor branches could no longer rely on their leaders for help in the form of loans or leases when they experienced economic stress. Hammurabi appears to have made available credit and rental land in order to help those members of minor branches who were in trouble. However, although temporary relief was at hand, the need for this relief was the result of lineage weakness, and its provision led to further weakening of the traditional social structure.

The accession of Samsuiluna made little difference, except that where Hammurabi was an active king, trying to stave off trouble as soon as it appeared, Samsuiluna left things to take care of themselves. For the first eight years of his reign, loans and rental continued to be common, as were other signs of distress, such as the adoption of wealthy outsiders by debt-ridden landowners.

In Samsuiluna's ninth year the political stability established by his father was shattered when all of southern Babylonia, including Nippur, fell into the hands of Rīm-Sîn II of Larsa. Within a year, Samsuiluna had successfully regained control, but the evidence suggests that this strife led, whether through intent or carelessness, to a fatal destruction of the supply of irrigation water to the southern area. All of the southern cities were abandoned, while cities in central Babylonia, like Nippur and Isin, suffered considerably.[58] The economic crisis of

[54] See Stone, "Economic Crisis," p. 284.

[55] Ibid., fig. 5, p. 278.

[56] Stone, "Social Role," p. 69.

[57] Stone, "Economic Crisis," p. 285. The exact significance of the discovery of unbroken loan documents is not clear. It may be either a measure of the number of loans which were extended or a measure of the number of loans which remained outstanding.

[58] Ibid., p. 270.

1739 B.C. probably was the death blow to the lineages. The poor members sold their land to whomsoever would buy it and left town. Only those who had enough property, especially in temple offices,[59] stayed and bought the property of those who had left, paying only a fraction of its previous value.[60] Many of those who bought this property were the wealthy outsiders who had entered the property-owning group through adoption.[61] Much of the property that they had bought consisted of temple offices, acquired from those who owned too little for it to benefit them. However, they also bought house and field property, and in such cases the traditional alienation restrictions seem to have been abandoned. Sometimes the sale was written up as a redemption document as though the previous sale ensured the present unrestricted alienation, but probably whatever legal authority that had been responsible for maintaining the alienation restrictions was no longer a force to be reckoned with.

This economic crisis spelled the end of lineage power and allowed the temple office association to take its place. Even those members of the old lineages who remained at Nippur seem to have maintained virtually no contact with the other members of their families, but called instead on their fellow officeholders to act as their witnesses. Meanwhile the most successful of these officeholders were men like Mannum-mêšu-liṣṣur[62] and Atta,[63] who had been born outside the property-owning group.

From 1739 B.C. until around 1730 B.C. Nippur remained half abandoned. Slowly Samsuiluna tried to reestablish an adequate water supply,[64] and by 1730 B.C. Nippur was enough on the road to recovery for the judges to return and try to redress the many wrongs which had been perpetrated during the intervening decade. From 1730 to 1720 B.C., life returned to normal at Nippur. Complaints were heard, commodities were lent, land was brought, sold, rented, and bequeathed. Although these inheritance contracts show that some had amassed great wealth during the crisis, the old order was gone and it was the temple office association that seems to have dominated the property owners.

It is possible that the wealthy landowners of this time had dreams of founding new lineages, but if so those dreams were stillborn. In Samsuiluna's twenty-eighth year, Nippur fell into the hands of Iluma-ilu, the king of the Sealands. The Sealands, presumably, were the marshes which resulted from the overflowing of the Euphrates from its western bed.[65] These marshes would have been the only part of southern Mesopotamia capable of supporting permanent habitation, and that must have been distinctly non-urban in character. It is symbolic of the weakness of the Old Babylonian state in the latter years of Samsuiluna that such a group was able to conquer Nippur and the rest of central Babylonia. This conquest proved fatal for Nippur. The irrigation system may have been patched together earlier, but

[59] Since temple office ownership presumably gave rights to a share of total temple income, even if this income was sharply curtailed by the prevailing economic conditions, some income would remain. In the case of field ownership, if it was no longer receiving irrigation water, then it became virtually worthless.

[60] Ibid., p. 280.

[61] Stone and Owen, *Adoption in Nippur* (forthcoming).

[62] Ibid.

[63] Albrecht Goetze, "The Archive of Ātta from Nippur," *Journal of Cuneiform Studies* 18 (1964): 102–13. See also chap. 4.

[64] H. V. Hilprecht (*Exploring the Bible Lands during the Nineteenth Century* [Philadelphia: A. J. Holman and Co., 1903], p. 481) describes an inscription of Samsuiluna in which he states: "Samsuiluna . . . dug 'the Euphrates of Nippur' and erected the dam of 'the Euphrates of Nippur' along it." If this inscription is to be dated to this post-crisis period, it may represent Samsuiluna's attempt to ensure the continuance of Nippur as a city.

[65] It appears that the bulk of the Euphrates' flow was to the west, near its present course, and not through the middle of Babylonia as before. An examination of the Old Babylonian and earlier irrigation canals shown in Adams, *Heartland*, figs. 29–31 and 33, indicates that Nippur was watered at that time by canals that had a roughly north-south flow. In the Kassite period (ibid., fig. 34) when Nippur was reoccupied, the canals trend from the northwest, suggesting that new canals had been dug to provide irrigation water for Nippur. These led from the new bed of the Euphrates, southeast to Nippur. The entire direction of the flow of irrigation system had been changed.

this second conquest led to its complete failure. One year later, Nippur was abandoned, not to enjoy full urban renaissance until late in the Kassite period.

For the period under consideration, the end of Ur III to the abandonment in 1720 B.C., archaeological evidence for domestic life at Nippur is preserved in the two separate excavation areas of TA and TB. It will be the task of the rest of this volume to examine these archaeological data and their associated texts to determine how the social and political events outlined above were reflected in the everyday life of Nippur's population. More significantly, an examination of the character and composition of neighborhoods will be attempted, with emphasis on how such organization allowed the inhabitants to survive the social and political turbulence of the time.

Chapter 3

TA

INTRODUCTION

TA, an area of 20×40 meters is located in the center of a small eminence at Nippur known as Tablet Hill. Work there began in 1948 and continued until 1952, but it was only during the 1951–1952 season that the Isin-Larsa and Old Babylonian levels were excavated. Finds were recorded by level and locus (the horizontal area excavated as a unit, usually a single room). The levels were generally considered to have extended over the entire area of TA and were not locus specific, and each level was further subdivided into two or three floors. As published in OIP 78, levels X to XIV seem to have been Isin-Larsa and Old Babylonian in date.

Different systems of field recording permitted either more or less reworking on the part of the excavator after the fieldwork was completed. The system employed in these excavations at Nippur, where level designations were felt to be area-wide in significance, was one which assumed little or no later reassessment. Moreover, the somewhat hit-or-miss nature of the elevations taken on the architectural remains and the lack of any drawn profiles[1] provide few data upon which any such reassessment could be undertaken. In spite of this, the Old Babylonian levels were completely reorganized back in Chicago, and in a way which on closer observation seems unwarranted. In the field, levels VIII to XIII were the levels yielding Isin-Larsa and Old Babylonian materials, not levels X to XIV as in OIP 78. Correlations between the published level designations and those recorded in the field do not now exist,[2] but they can be reconstructed by comparing the levels assigned to objects in OIP 78 with those in the field catalog.[3]

The approximate correlations between the two sets of level designations are as shown in table 2, although level X floor 4 and level X floor 4 foundation designations in OIP 78 are equivalent to a wide variety of field designations. The variability in these designations is reflected in the recorded elevations of the floors in these levels. Table 3 shows that the elevations of levels X-4 and X-4 foundation had higher standard deviations than those of other levels. Although clearly it is unwise to expect contemporary occupation to take place at the same elevation in all areas, especially when houses are built on a mound, one expects the range of variation to be reasonably consistent from one level to another.[4]

[1] The profile drawings illustrated in OIP 78 (pl. 78 for those of TA) are merely reconstructions based on elevations, not drawn profiles.

[2] Although the sheets recording these correlations exist, they could not be found at the time that I was working through the field notes.

[3] In addition, both a later transcript of the locus-by-locus field notes and the tablet catalog had the field level designations crossed out and replaced by those used in the publication. Since both sets of designations were legible, this greatly eased the task of correlating the two sets of level and floor numbers assigned to each locus.

[4] Only the elevations of field level VIII floor 3 show high variability. Indeed, the elevations for this level seem generally disturbing since in addition to the high standard deviation, the mean elevation is *lower* than that of the preceding level IX. However, the explanation of this phenomenon is quite simple. It will be shown later that only part of TA was occupied in level IX; the rest was abandoned for a time. The elevations that were taken for level VIII floor 3 fall into two moieties. On the one hand, there are three elevations, all over 92 m, which were taken from the area

TABLE 2. Rough Correlations between the Level Designations as Assigned in the Field and Those Used in OIP 78

Field Level	Published Level
VIII-1	X-1
VIII-2	X-2
VIII-3	X-3
IX-1	X-4
IX-2	X-4 foundation
X-1	XI-1
X-2	XI-2
X-3	XI-3
XI-1	XII-1
XI-2	XII-2
XI-3	XII-3
XII-1	XIII-1
XII-2	XIII-2
XII-3	XIII-3
XIII	XIV
XIV	XV

These high standard deviations of elevations of levels as published in OIP 78 can be compared with those of the elevations taken in the field.[5] This comparison, as shown in table 3, makes clear that the standard deviations of the elevations of field level IX are considerably less than those of level X floor 4 and level X floor 4 foundation as published in OIP 78.

These discrepancies between the two systems of designations and the high standard deviations associated with that used in OIP 78 make it possible to question whether the publication might not reflect a reorganization of levels that was in excess of what was necessary. This suspicion is strengthened when looking at the brief section on chronology in OIP 78. McCown writes:

> Perhaps the most remarkable fact concerning the dated, stratified tablets is how "unstratified" they are. . . . At best, cuneiform tablets can provide only a reasonable approximation of the date of the level in which they are found.[6]

His explanation for this phenomenon is that it is due both to a habit of keeping some tablets over long periods of time and to the intrusion and disturbance that are the result of the digging of drains and foundations. The first problem can be eliminated by taking each dated

---

that had had level IX occupation; on the other hand, there are another three elevations, all below 91.50 m, which come from the area without level IX occupation. The partial abandonment of TA during level IX led to an uneven rise in ground level and consequent variability in elevation. This variability continued throughout level VIII, hence the higher standard deviations seen in this level when compared with level X. Furthermore, although all loci had level VIII floors, only a few had an extra floor requiring the use of the floor 3 designation. Thus the larger sample sizes for level VIII floors 2 and 1 reduced this variability.

[5] The field designations used in this comparison are not in all instances exactly as they were assigned in the field. In the course of the excavations, inconsistencies were observed and were recorded in the notes. A typical example of such observations, in this instance for locus 190, reads "[level] x [floor] 1 equals [level] IX of [locus] 188 against the top of [level] X wall. [Level] X [floor] 2 equals [level] X [floor] 1 of [locus] 188." The adjustments which have been made by me to the stratigraphy simply followed these instructions.

[6] OIP 78, p. 74.

TABLE 3. Elevations of Upper Levels as Assigned in OIP 78 and in the Adjusted Field Stratigraphy

Level	*N*	Mean	Range	*s*
		OIP 78		
X-1	25	92.42	92.95–91.95	0.277
X-2	29	92.01	92.68–91.47	0.301
X-3	10	91.86	92.16–91.16	0.281
X-4	19	91.42	91.90–90.36	0.445
X-4 fdn.	9	91.31	91.53–90.48	0.417
XI-1	12	90.88	91.18–90.58	0.173
XI-2	9	90.56	90.93–90.20	0.275
XI-3	1	90.33	. . .	. . .
		Adjusted Field Stratigraphy[a]		
VIII-1	25	92.46	92.86–91.97	0.279
VIII-2	36	92.04	92.68–91.47	0.275
VIII-3	6	91.70	92.16–91.27	0.386
IX-1	10	91.83	92.92–91.70	0.077
IX-2	7	91.40	91.61–91.16	0.133
X-1	17	90.88	91.18–90.91	0.162
X-2	16	90.52	90.91–90.20	0.205
X-3	3	90.21	. . .	. . .

[a] The adjusted field stratigraphy is that assigned in the field with the addition of those changes recommended in the field notes.

table as no more than a *terminus post quem*. All objects likely to be intrusive should have been noted in the field, but in cases where such information is absent, the stratigraphic context of all objects deriving from loci which were disturbed should be treated with suspicion.

With these cautions in mind, a look at the dated tablets listed on pages 75 and 76 of OIP 78 suggests that there may indeed be some problems with the published stratigraphy. From level X-4 to level X-1 of the publication come tablets from good contexts dating to the last three years of Nippur's Old Babylonian occupation. When the level designations as assigned in the field are used, this situation is somewhat ameliorated since the level spread is then reduced to levels VIII-3 to VIII-1. In most instances (see pl. 78 of OIP 78) floors 1 to 3 in this level all represent accumulation within the same construction period; level X-4, which is generally equivalent to level IX as designated in the field, is associated with an earlier building phase. Given the excavation techniques, floor distinctions within levels probably do not mean very much, but the more major level distinctions which were based on new construction and carefully noted by Haines must be taken seriously. Thus a lack of time difference between floors within field-designated level VIII is not disturbing the way it is when encompassing the published level X, which included more than one phase of construction.

These results, although sketchy, led to the suggestion that any new work on the TA materials might be easier to conduct were the field designations, including those modifications suggested in the field notes, used as a basis of the analysis. Given the nature of the records and the amount of time that has elapsed since the excavations, it is difficult to prove decisively that one system approximates reality more closely than another. However, since the time of the publication, work with the textual sources has suggested, as outlined in the previous chapter, that Nippur in the Isin-Larsa and Old Babylonian periods might have experienced a more turbulent history than had been thought heretofore. The next step in this introduction to the archaeological remains from TA is to determine whether these stratigraphical problems might be resolvable when the impact of historical events on domestic life is taken into account.

In the previous chapter three events which one might expect to be reflected in the archaeological record were noted: the destruction of Nippur during the reign of Išme-Dagan, the economic crisis of 1739 B.C. that led to a partial abandonment of the city, and the final abandonment in 1720.[7] If we address ourselves to the last two events, one might expect the crisis and abandonment levels to be characterized by concentrations of artifacts, especially pots and tablets which were either too fragile for transportation or irrelevant to those living outside Nippur.

A comparison of numbers of tablets, whole vessels, and small finds from loci in TA is presented in table 4. Two distinct periods of artifact concentration can be noted in the field stratigraphy, whereas the published stratigraphy merely indicates that the upper levels of TA yielded more artifacts than the lower. The two periods of artifact concentration, occurring in levels X and VIII of the field stratigraphy,[8] correlate well with the historically known crisis of 1739 B.C. and the abandonment of 1720 B.C., especially when the dated tablets found in them are taken into consideration. Since tablets serve as *termini post quem,* only the latest date in any tablet group[9] has been noted in table 5. Using the field stratigraphy, the latest date for level VIII was 1721 B.C., the year before the final abandonment of the city, while that for level X was 1739 B.C., the year of the commencement of the economic crisis. Using the published stratigraphy, however, the pattern is inconsistent: the compression of dates from levels X-4 to X-1 noted above is seen, and furthermore, level X-4 foundation would date to 1739 B.C., surely an inappropriate time for new construction to be taking place. Finally, level XI, roughly equivalent to level X in the field stratigraphy, had only one dated tablet, from 1797 B.C.

These data show that the changes in the stratigraphy effected by the excavators after their return from the field placed all tablets dating to the reign of Samsuiluna in an expanded level X. In such circumstances, each assigned level could be seen as lasting for approximately the same amount of time, perhaps the sixty years which is the average life span of a mud-brick house. In fact, the dated tablets and artifact inventories showed that little time elapsed between levels X and VIII as excavated in the field. In adjusting their stratigraphy so that each assigned level represented approximately an equal span of time, the excavators obscured the evidence for the instability and change that characterized the later years of the reign of Samsuiluna.

The remaining historical event, the suggested attack and "destruction" of Nippur around 1950 B.C., must now be considered. Although one should not assume that the city was razed to the ground—and indeed there is no evidence for such total destruction—this attack was serious enough to occasion the composition of a lament, and the restoration of peace was significant enough for Išme-Dagan to commission an inscription commemorating that event.

[7] Different types of events are more or less likely to be reflected in the archaeological record. Changes in government, for example, since their effects on the general population is subtle, can rarely, if ever, be identified archaeologically, whereas social and economic changes which radically affected the entire population are more likely to leave their mark. It is regrettable that the designation of artifacts and phases in Mesopotamian archaeology uses a nomenclature which is based on the very type of change, change in political power, that has the least impact on material culture.

[8] The subdivisions of major levels, called floors, are, as noted above, probably of little significance. In the field, level distinctions were made when periods of new construction were noted; floor distinctions represent no more than layers of ash or other debris, some of which represents the decay of abandoned buildings.

[9] A tablet group is defined as those texts found in the same locus and with the same floor and level designation. One overall level may therefore have several tablet groups.

TABLE 4. LEVELS WITH CONCENTRATIONS OF ARTIFACTS
(more than ten artifacts per locus per level)

Locus	OIP 78 Levels	Adjusted Field Levels
184	X-1	VIII-1
173	X-1 to X-3	VIII-2
178	X-3	VIII-2
187	X-4	VIII-3
188	X-4	VIII-3
174	X-4 to X-4 fdn.	X-1 to X-2
191	X-4 to XI-2	X-1 to X-2
205	X-4 to XI-2	X-1 to X-3
188	XI-1	X-2
184	XI-1 to XI-2	X-2 to X-3
189	XI-2	X-2

NOTES: Disturbed loci, whether the result of burials or other sources of disturbance, have been omitted from this table. By adjusted field levels I refer to the designations assigned in the field with the addition of those changes recommended in the field notes.

OIP 78 shows a large number of burials set into the remains of level XIII. Since these burials were cut into the walls of level XIII and underlie some of the walls of level XII, one must assume that they were dug during the period of time that elapsed between the destruction of level XIII and the subsequent building of XII. In addition, the considerable degree of continuity in plan observable between levels XII and XIII suggests that but a short time elapsed between the two. At first glance, then, these burials would seem to be exactly what one might expect to find as evidence of the attack on Nippur that was recorded in the lament, evidence of the burial of the dead and the rebuilding of the city. However, table 5 shows that dated tablets from apparently reliable contexts place the level XIII/XII transition some 50 to 100 years after Išme-Dagan's reign. This chronological evidence would make such an association between the burials and the attack untenable were it not that a closer examination both of the reconstructed section shown in plate 78 of OIP 78 and of the elevations suggests the presence of a hiatus in settlement that was not taken into account when level designations were assigned in the field.

The domestic structures published as level XII seem not all to have been occupied at the same time. Whereas House K, the small structure to its west, and perhaps locus 217[10] had continuous occupation from levels XII to XI in OIP 78, there was a hiatus in settlement in the rest of the area. This meant that House K, occupied by members of one of Nippur's most important lineages, was fronted by a large open space.[11] Furthermore, a break in settlement,

[10] The stratigraphic assessment of locus 217 is somewhat of a problem. The notes for locus 205 indicate that this was the only level X (field designation; equivalent to level XI of OIP 78) locus in the southern portion of the excavation area which had the remains of earlier construction immediately beneath it. This evidence of continuity is similar to that which I will argue for House K. Beneath this construction was found what has been described as fill, and in that fill was found a tablet (Text 3) dating to about the same time as the texts from the earliest floor levels of House K. Beneath that is the architecture of locus 217, which seems to tie in well with the remains from the rest of the earliest levels of TA.

[11] In field level XI-3 (published level XII-3), the entrance chamber in House K would have opened onto an open space a little higher than the floor level. At the door to the street the ground would have sloped up in a 1:8.5 incline, a very shallow slope. At the higher floors this slope would have been even less.

TABLE 5. The Latest Dated Tablet of Each Group Found in TA

OIP 78		Adjusted Field Stratigraphy[a]	
Level	Date	Level	Date
X-1	1721, 1732, 1733, 1743, 2047	VIII-1	1721, 1732, 1733, 1743
X-2	1732, 1744	VIII-2	1737, 1744, 2047
X-3	1739, 1762	VIII-3	1723, 1739, 1742, 1755, 1762
X-4	1723, 1741, 1742, 1755, 1755	IX-1	1755
X-4 fdn.	1739		
XI-1	1793	X-1	1741, 1793
		X-2	1739
XII-1	1860–1837	XI-1	1860–1837
XII-3	ca. 1840	XI-3	ca. 1840
XIII-1	1843	XII-1	1843
XV	2028–2004	XIV	2028–2004

[a] The adjusted field stratigraphy is that assigned in the field with the addition of those changes recommended in the field notes.

like that caused by the creation of this open area, would explain the radical change in plan between the architecture of level XII (OIP 78 designation) and that from level XI and above.

The evidence for this hiatus comes primarily from the elevations. First, in level XI in OIP 78, Houses K and Q appear to be on a slight rise, suggesting that this area may have had more construction than the rest of TA. Second, whereas the elevations of Houses K and Q evidence the kind of occupational continuity that is seen in the upper levels of TA,[12] this is not the case for the area to the south. There, with the exception of locus 205, between 0.5 and 1 m of nonarchitectural levels separate the level XII (as published) remains from the level XI architecture that lay above. Moreover, the area separating House K from most of the rest of TA was not excavated down to this level, so there never was any stratigraphic evidence to tie the two blocks of architecture together. If these data are taken to suggest that the north-eastern portion of TA was a little later than the southern in level XII of OIP 78, then the two tablets which appeared to mark the level XIII/XII boundary can be shown to derive from contexts which are probably somewhat later than the rest of the area. In these circumstances, the burials dug into level XIII would fit chronologically with the attack on Nippur recorded in the Lamentation for Nippur.

Earlier in this chapter, the stratigraphic designations as assigned in the field appeared to be more accurate than those included in the publication; here it seems that even the field designations for some levels are suspect. For this publication, I propose a scheme which, while staying as close to the stratigraphy as published in OIP 78 as possible, also indicates the areas where major revisions are needed. I propose to divide both level X and level XII into two, calling them levels XA, XB, XIIA, and XIIB. In this way the distinction between levels VIII and IX as assigned in the field is maintained in the differences between levels XA and XB. Similarly, the level XII architecture of house K and its neighbor is assigned to level XIIA, while that of the rest of the excavation area, seemingly earlier in date, is assigned to level XIIB. What is not clear, and cannot be clear, is whether the lower levels of XIIA were contemporary with the upper levels of XIIB, or if one followed the other. A rough indication of the relationship between the schemes used in the field, in OIP 78, and in this volume is presented in table 6; a detailed locus-by-locus comparison can be found in Appendix I.

[12] In TA, the normal pattern is to find that the elevation of the base of one level was *lower* than the elevation of the top of the walls of the previous level. This pattern, perhaps the result of the cutting in of foundations into the remains of earlier walls, clearly indicates continuity of occupation.

TABLE 6. ROUGH COMPARISONS BETWEEN LEVELS AS ASSIGNED IN THE FIELD, IN OIP 78, AND IN THIS VOLUME

Adjusted Field Stratigraphy[a]	OIP 78	This Volume	Latest Dated Tablets
VIII-1 to VIII-3	X-1 to X-3	XA-1 to XA-3	1721, 1723, 1732, 1733, 1737, 1739, 1742, 1743, 1744, 1755, 1762, 2047
IX-1 to IX-2	X-4 to X-4 fdn.	XB-1 to XB-2	1755
X-1 to X-3	XI-1 to XI-3	XI-1 to XI-3	1739, 1741, 1793
		XIIA-1 to XIIA-3	ca. 1840
XI-1 to XI-3	XII-1 to XII-3		
		XIIB-1 to XIIB-3	1843, 1860–1837
XII-1 to XII-2	XIII-1 to XIII-2	XIII-1 to XIII-2	...
XIII	XIV	XIV	...
XIV	XV	XV	2028–2004

[a] The adjusted field stratigraphy is that assigned in the field with the addition of those changes recommended in the field notes.

Under the scheme proposed here, the lower four levels, levels XIV to XIIA, represent most or all of the two centuries of Isin-Larsa domination, while the upper three, levels XI to XA, represent the mere four decades that the Babylonian dynasty controlled Nippur. The "destruction" of Nippur during the reign of Išme-Dagan came between levels XIII and XIIB, and level XI can be associated with the economic crisis. Level XB was found only in the north and east parts of the excavation area and represents those houses that continued to be occupied during the decade of Nippur's partial abandonment. Level XA represents the rebuilding that followed the easing of the crisis and the total abandonment of the city around 1720 B.C.

The establishment of the stratigraphic scheme provides a framework within which the archaeological data, in the form of texts, artifacts, and architecture, can be ordered. It is on this framework that the detailed discussion of the evidence for daily life in Isin-Larsa and Old Babylonian Nippur will be founded.

TA GENERAL

The plans (pls. 10–24) of the TA excavation area make its purely domestic nature quite clear. A street running approximately from northeast to southwest was bordered by houses, usually quite small, whose irregular plans (excepting House K) suggest that they were constructed without the benefit of an architect. Their walls rarely met at right angles, and although a few ideal patterns of room arrangement can be detected,[13] in practice these were usually significantly modified by the available space. House K, however, is different. Its walls meet at right angles, and its plan is remarkably similar to the typical plan of contemporary domestic structures at Ur.[14] The siting of this house is also unique in that, unlike buildings in TA, House K had no party walls.

[13] Elizabeth C. Stone, "Texts, Architecture and Ethnographic Analogy: Patterns of Residence in Old Babylonian Nippur," *Iraq* 43 (1981): 24.

[14] Sir Leonard Woolley and Sir Max Mallowan, *Ur Excavations, vol. 7: The Old Babylonian Period* (London: British Museum Publications, Ltd., 1976), pl. 22, for example.

Three houses have staircases (Houses J, K, and G), but there is no compelling reason to take these as evidence of a second story; with flat-roofed houses, access to the roof is always desirable. The widths of the walls of these houses are the same (60 cm) as those of other structures; probably not thick enough to support a second story.[15] These staircases were generally added after the initial construction and were not kept up in subsequent rebuildings. The textual evidence tends to support the contention that single-story construction was the norm at Nippur. The many Nippur contracts that concern house plots, from TA and elsewhere, never mention the existence of a second floor, a feature which surely would have affected house value, whereas the texts from Sippar[16] often mention the sale or rental of rooms on an upper story. Furthermore, the Old Babylonian structures recently excavated at Tell ed-Der are characterized by thick walls (ca. 1 m) and staircases, perhaps indicating the presence of second stories in the Sippar region.[17]

An examination of the identifiable property boundaries over time essentially suggests continuity, although minor, probably accidental, changes can be seen. Continuity seems to have been maintained by using old wall stubs as foundations. Although this practice usually resulted in a general similarity in the location of houses, this was not the case with streets. Narrow alleyways were widened by the destruction of series of rooms, wide roads were encroached on by new construction, and, in one instance, a narrow street was closed by the addition of a doorway.

The naming of streets at Nippur may shed some light on this phenomenon. In spite of one instance of a "Wall Street," most roadways were identified by the use of personal names. It is possible that these streets were in fact owned, or at least controlled, by the families whose head is so named. The "owner" of the street would thus have every right to encroach on it if he wished to do so. One can envisage Nippur, then, as having major arteries, like Wall Street, which were inviolable, with a network of small alleyways in between which, if not privately controlled, could be modified by the people who lived on them. Since much of TA in level XIIA was an open area fronting House K, it seems likely that the entire area was controlled by the Ninlil-zimu family that lived there.

The domestic nature of TA is generally confirmed by an examination of the tablets that were found in the houses (see table 7). The texts fall into two main categories, private documents (contracts, letters, accounts) on the one hand and educational materials (literary, lexical, school, and mathematical texts) on the other. Notably absent are administrative documents and accounts pertaining to the functioning of public institutions. the large number of school and literary texts suggests, perhaps, a high degree of literacy since they were found in almost every house (see table 8), while the extremely large number of such texts found in House F suggests that it might have been the location of a small scribal school. Most of the literary and school texts were found in level XI, the level associated with the disruption of settlement of 1739 B.C. It seems possible that some of the first to flee from the worsening economic conditions may have been the scribes; indeed, this crisis seems to have spelled the end, at least for several centuries, of Nippur's position as Mesopotamia's cultural center.[18]

[15] Carol Kramer ("An Archaeological View of a Contemporary Kurdish Village: Domestic Architecture, Household Size and Wealth," in *Ethnoarchaeology,* ed. Carol Kramer [New York: Columbia University Press, 1979], p. 148) indicates that today, second stories are built only when the wall is approximately 1 m in thickness. Walls 60 cm thick are used only in one-story construction.

[16] Rivkah Harris, *Ancient Sippar* (Istanbul: Nederlands Historisch-archaeologisch Instituut, 1975), pp. 22, 30–31.

[17] Leon de Meyer, *Tell ed-Der II* (Leuven: Editions Peeters, 1978), plans 2–6.

[18] Jacob J. Finklestein (*Late Old Babylonian Documents and Letters,* Yale Oriental Series, vol. 13 [New Haven: Yale University Press, 1972], pp. 11–13) notes that the later Old Babylonian texts at Kish include references to the maintenance of cults originating in Uruk and personal names generally associated with Uruk. These data are evidence of the movement of at least some elements of the population of southern Mesopotamia to the more northerly cities as a result of the economic difficulties that beset the south during the reign of Samsuiluna.

TABLE 7. Tablet Distribution by Level in TA

Text Type	Level						
	XA	XB	XI	XIIA	XIIB	XIII	Total
Private contract	27	2	28	0	3	0	60
Private letter	1	1	7	0	0	1	10
Private account	10	2	5	4	0	1	20
Temple account	0	0	0	0	0	0	0
Administrative	0	0	0	0	0	0	0
Literary, lexical, mathematical, school	41	23	1427	2	1	2	1496
Miscellaneous	2	1	2	0	0	0	5
Total	81	29	1469	6	4	4	1591

TABLE 8. Distribution of Lexical, Literary, School, and Mathematical Texts by House

House	Number of Texts
E	1
F	1407
G	28
H	13
I	4
J	4
K	22
L	0
M	1
M	1
O	1
P	3
Q	0

Table 9 shows that approximately 60% of the scribes who figure as witnesses on contracts disappear from our records at this time; while an additional 25% apparently left the city but returned when the crisis was over. Although the writing of contracts did not cease during the crisis period, the number of scribes available to do the work was much smaller than in any other period.

The textual and archaeological evidence, then, indicate that TA was a residential area, occupied by small property owners, one of whom may also have run a scribal school. The history of occupation in TA was far from stable. Following the "description" during the reign of Išme-Dagan in the twentieth century B.C., the area was rebuilt, but in level XIIA much of it was given over to open space, symbolizing, it seems, the importance of the residents of House K. During level XI the area was built up again, until the economic crisis of 1739 B.C. led to a partial abandonment and a marked drop in scribal activity. Finally, after a brief recovery, the entire city was abandoned in 1720 B.C.

TABLE 9. SCRIBAL ACTIVITY

Scribes who wrote tablets before, during, and after the crisis	2
Scribes who wrote tablets before the crisis	8[a]
Scribes who wrote tablets before and after but not during the crisis	4[b]

[a] The scribes apparently stopped work in 1739 B.C. in two cases, in 1738 in three cases, and in 1737 in three cases.

[b] The gaps in the records of these scribes were as follows: 1738–1722, 1738–1724, 1736–1722, 1736–1727.

What follows is a house-by-house analysis of the occupational history of TA over a period of nearly three centuries. The discussion begins with levels XIII and XIIB, the early Isin-Larsa houses, which follow a plan different from that which characterizes the Old Babylonian period. There will ensue a discussion of these later levels, levels XIIA to XA. Throughout, the adjusted stratigraphy outlined above will be followed (see also Appendix I).

THE LOWER LEVELS

The organization of TA changed with level XIIA, so the discussion of the lower levels, XIII to XIIB, will be treated separately here. By the time the excavators reached these strata, they were pressed for time by the impending Iraqi summer, which spelled the end of the third season, and were hampered by the considerable depth of the archaeological remains. They were therefore compelled both to step up the pace of excavation and to restrict the area. The northeastern portion of TA, the area in which the very important House K was found in later levels, remained unexcavated, and the scanty notes and confusing circulation plans recorded for the rest of the area testify to the speed with which they were working. Nevertheless, despite these shortcomings, some features of these earlier houses in TA can be noted which differ significantly from those of the later levels.

HOUSE J

House J, located in the northwestern portion of TA, is the one structure that shows some continuity from level XIII through level XA, although, like most of the rest of TA, it was replaced in level XIIA by the large open space that fronted House K. The continuity in plan of House J from before to after this period of nonoccupation is hard to explain. Since nearly 1 m of fill separated the tops of level XIIB walls from the level XI floors, one cannot assume that the level XIIB wall stubs remained visible; perhaps in excavating foundation trenches for the level XI construction, they came across the old walls and decided to follow them to provide a better footing. The field notes do indicate the presence of level XI foundations but provide no further details.[19]

In level XIII, the earliest excavated level of House J, it was entered through the partially paved courtyard, locus 209,[20] which in turn gave on to two small rooms, loci 232 and 233, and

[19] The field sheets provide only the elevations of the lower floors of level XI and of the top of the level XII walls. No information is available on the depth of the level XI foundations beneath the first floor.

[20] I assume that the area to the northeast was a street at this time, but since it was later closed off, and since at this level it was not excavated, it is impossible to be sure.

presumably to a western series of rooms, now in the baulk. This pattern of entrance through a courtyard, seen also in Houses L and M (see below), was common at this time, but in later levels access to houses tended to be by way of an entrance chamber.

The finds from levels XIII and XIIB of House J tell us little about its inhabitants. The literary tablets, cylinder seal, and seal impression found in level XIII suggest some degree of literacy and prosperity, while the bone awls found in locus 233 in level XIIB may indicate that the residents were artisans of some kind. The burial of a child, accompanied by a string of beads and two pots, in level XIII-1(?) of locus 233 may simply be one of the many burials that were found sunk into the level XIII remains, but it is also possible that it is the result of the death of a child of the level XIIB residents.[21]

House J, then, the only building on the west side of the street, was a small, simple structure, entered by way of the courtyard. In plan and features it was much like other houses in TA dating to the same time. Like much of the rest of TA it was abandoned in level XIIA, and the area that it had occupied became part of the large open space in front of House K.

House L

House L was a small structure that was occupied in levels XIII and XIIB. Like many other level XIII houses, it was apparently entered through the courtyard, locus 227, and when in level XIIB the entrance shifted to locus 225, it seems likely that the location of the courtyard also changed. Only three loci can be definitely associated with the house, although locus 236 may also have been part of this structure. In level XIII, locus 228 is said to have had two doorways, one connecting it with the rest of House L and one connecting it with House M; in level XIIB it had no doors preserved. Since the door connecting locus 228 with House M is not shown on the field plan, although it is mentioned in the notes, I suggest that that door may only have existed in level XIII floor 2, and that level XIII floor 1, the room had been transferred from House M to House L.[22] In these circumstances, one might expect locus 228 to have remained part of House L in level XIIB. In that case it might have been a storage room with a high sill. Locus 236 may have served a similar function since again no doors have been found to connect it with either House L or M.

The only finds from House L came from locus 226 in level XII, probably a storage room. No tablets were found here, only some plaques and figurines, as well as a weight and a chisel. In general, the finds do not help to determine the occupation of the residents of this house.

House M

Access to House M was by way of a large court or open area, locus 220,[23] which in level XIII was used as an area of bread baking as indicated by the presence of a bread oven and some sunken pots. In level XIIB several rooms were built into this court—loci 221, 222, and

[21] In OIP 78, p. 144, this burial is said to have been found in level XII, which is equivalent to our level XIIB, and the burial sheet which was filled out for 3B 75 records it as being found in field level XI (level XIIB here) and shows two pots but makes no mention of any associated beads. However, in the list of finds from TA 233, 3N 470, a string of beads, is recorded as being found within the skeleton of a field level XII (level XIII here) burial. Finally, 3B 75 is shown on the field plan of level XII, not on that of level XI. My conclusion, then, is that 3B 75 was a burial with two pots and a string of beads, and that it was found in level XIII, but the evidence is certainly contradictory.

[22] These doors have been shown on the plans (pls. 10 and 11). I must confess, however, that the evidence on this point is extremely unreliable.

[23] This open space was somewhat disturbed, so it is possible that it was originally smaller than it appears now. Here the brevity of the field notes makes understanding difficult.

223—but since no doors have been found, their functions remain unclear. Similar rooms were also found in level XIII, loci 239, 240, and 241, but again their lack of doors and finds make interpretation impossible.

From the court, access to House M proper was gained through a wide corridor, locus 219, which led in level XIII into the central courtyard of the house, locus 229/231. From there one had to go through a small anteroom, locus 237, to get to the main living room, locus 230. This plan was considerably modified in level XIIB. At that time the corridor joining the house with the open area, locus 220, was much narrower, and the house itself much larger. Again, however, the corridor led directly into a court, which was separated from the main living room by an anteroom. As noted above, it seems likely that in level XIII floor 2, locus 228 was also part of House M, but by floor 1 it appears to have formed part of House L.

The finds from this house were not noteworthy, mostly plaques and figurines, although a statue fragment found in level XIII locus 231 might possibly indicate a secondary religious function for the room. Pottery was rare and tablets were absent[24] in this house, but seals were found in both levels.

House M was the only area excavated down to levels XIV and XV, though only in locus 230. Finds from level XV included an Ur III text which has led to the assignment of this level as Ur III in date. No recorded finds came from level XIV, but the excavators believed it to be early Isin-Larsa in date.

House R

To the southeast of House M was the small complex of rooms that is called here House R. In level XIIB all that was excavated was a large court, locus 218. Locus 216 apparently belonged to a separate structure. In level XIII, however, the plan is a little clearer. From the court, locus 218, access was gained to two small rooms, loci 243 and 246, and perhaps also to the larger room locus 217,[25] although no door was discovered in excavation. The jewelry, plaques, and pottery found in this house testify to its domestic functions, but in general too little was excavated to permit any firm conclusions.

The Burials

A number of burials were found dug from level XIIB into level XIII (see OIP 78, p. 144). The evidence is not clear, however, as to when exactly they were set in, but it seems likely that they were excavated at the end of level XIII and before the construction of level XIIB since in two cases they clearly cut level XIII walls, and in two other instances they are partly under the walls of level XII.[26] We have related this group of burials with the attack on Nippur

[24] A marriage contract (Text 1) is said to have been found in level XIIB-1 "under the north wall." Since no notes were taken, it is impossible to tell whether this tablet was found under the level XIIB-1 wall (in which case it would belong in level XIIB-2) or below the level XI wall. The text itself is not included in the list of dated tablets on pp. 75–76 of OIP 78, and in the field notes an original change from a field designation of level XI-1 to a published designation of XII-1 was revised with a final designation of level XI foundations. The late date of the tablet (1792 B.C.) indicates that this late change might be the most likely, so the tablet has been assigned to locus 180 level XI foundations.

[25] As noted above, the assignment of 217 is fraught with difficulties. It appears that its successor, locus 205, was built before the level XI occupation. Beneath that was fill, within which a tablet, Text 3, was found, and beneath that was the level XIII locus. It appears from this that in level XIIB, locus 217 was not in existence. It seems probable that at that time it was included within the courtyard, locus 218.

[26] It should not be surprising that these burials do not significantly underlie the level XII walls. If, as is suggested, the setting in of the burials and the building of the level XII houses took place at about the same time, the

made during Išme-Dagan's reign and recorded in the "Lamentation over the Destruction of Nippur." The evidence from TA does not support the idea of a total disaster; the houses do not show signs of burning and look as though they were rebuilt immediately. In addition, the burials, though not particularly rich, were quite orderly and usually contained a pot or two and an occasional string of beads.

These burials contrast with those found in the later levels of TA in that they contained a cross section of the population—adults, adolescents, and children—whereas in later levels only groups of infants were found; both the early and the late burials, though, were set into the remains of domestic structures. Because of both the nature of the burials and corroborative textual evidence, I suggest that these Isin-Larsa deaths were the result of war, while the later, Old Babylonian, infant deaths were the result of famine or epidemic disease. Since intramural burial does not seem to have been practiced normally in Isin-Larsa and Old Babylonian Nippur, I assume that only those burials resulting from unusual circumstances would be found in TA.

Conclusions

In conclusion, the lower levels of TA consisted of a number of small, domestic structures, all entered by way of the courtyard. Although small finds were not particularly rare, these levels have not yielded the wealth of textual evidence that was to characterize the later houses. Between levels XIII and XIIB a number of burials were dug into the remains of earlier houses, but there is no reason to postulate a substantial hiatus in settlement. In level XIIA all of the area excavated in XIIB, except perhaps locus 217, was turned into a large open space.

THE UPPER LEVELS

House K

House K was a large, well-built structure whose organization of rooms can be compared to contemporary houses from Ur.[27] With its formal plan, lack of party walls, and baked-brick foundations (or damp course), House K stands apart from the haphazard arrangement of rooms and courts generally seen in TA. In its siting and construction, House K appears as the dominant structure in TA, an impression that is supported by the luxury items and tablets which it contains. Two texts found in level XI indicate that this house was occupied by members of the Ninlil-zimu lineage, probably one of the most important of the families that dominated Nippur in the mid-to-late Isin-Larsa period.

The incomplete excavation of House K and the presence nearby of trenches of the University of Pennsylvania's original excavations make it entirely possible that the other tablets concerning the activities of the Ninlil-zimu family, now in museums in Philadelphia and Istanbul, originated in the nether regions of House K. In any event, there are now twenty-seven tablets which describe the activities of six generations of the descendants of Ninlil-zimu and cover almost all of the two centuries in which Isin-Larsa and Old Babylonian

builders would have generally avoided placing their walls over newly dug graves because of the likelihood of subsidence. It is not likely that these burials were set in during the occupation of level XIIB, since there seems to be no reason to have gone to the trouble of undercutting the walls of the house for two of the burials.

[27] Woolley and Mallowan, *Ur Excavations, vol. 7,* especially pl. 22.

contracts were written at Nippur (see table 10). At times, the exact genealogical relationships between lineage members is somewhat difficult to determine, but the best approximation of the family tree as we know it is as shown in figure 1.

The actions of members of the Ninlil-zimu lineage determined the occupational history of TA. From when they are first seen as residents of House K, this family dominated the neighborhood. Consequently, a lengthy excursis on what is known of their history is essential if an understanding of some of the forces that shaped neighborhood development at Nippur is to be achieved.

Of the texts describing the activities of the Ninlil-zimu family, nine, including the two from House K, have no date preserved. Nevertheless, it is possible to arrange all in rough chronological order (see table 10). The earliest text appears to be *ARN* 20 + OIMA 1 52. Although damaged, it may be interpreted as the inheritance document of Abba-kalla, Im-ši-ŠI, KA-Damu, and Lu-dingirra, the sons of Ninlil-zimu, and to date to approximately 1800 B.C.[28] The amount of property represented in this text is much greater than that of any other text from Nippur, especially when one considers that probably only about a half or even a third of the text is preserved. Clearly, at this early time, the Ninlil-zimu family was one of the great property-owning families of Nippur, and certainly the wealthiest family in TA. The family owned a full year of the most prestigious temple office in the city, a gudu$_4$-ship of Ninlil, as well as three other more minor offices. The preserved portion of the first column of this tablet suggests that the brothers came to some agreement over the disposition of these offices, and from *ARN* 23 + PBS 8/2 169 it appears that the eldest son, Abba-kalla, received most, if not all, of these offices intact. In addition, much of this family's strength apparently lay in the very large area of unbuilt urban property (kislaḫ) that they owned. The text describes over 1,000 square meters of such property, and 150 years later, text PBS 8/2 129 shows that this Ninlil-zimu's great-great-grandsons still controlled a similar amount. Furthermore, one of the tablets found in House K, Text 4, also concerns a sizeable kislaḫ plot. Here, the same four brothers as appeared in *ARN* 20 + OIMA 1 52 are recorded as the recipients of the kislaḫ,

[28] There are some difficulties with this interpretation, all of which stem from the fragmentary nature of the text. First, none of the suggested heirs is specifically described as an heir in the text as preserved. The preserved portion of the text probably only represents about one-third of the whole, so it is likely that the clauses naming the heirs were on the portion of the tablet which is now missing. The four suggested heirs do occur on the tablet in ways which are usually associated with heirs, and two, probably three, of the names are preserved on seal impressions, a virtual guarantee of heirship. However, a phrase occurs in the second column of the tablet which has been interpreted by the publishers of this text as indicating that a Bigamatum was one of the heirs. I would prefer to interpret this phrase, which reads ha-la-ba bi-ga-ma/ku-tum, as simply a descriptive phrase referring to the piece of house property listed on the preceding line. In the first place, house plots are usually described as using the name of the owner of the neighboring plot. In this instance this descriptor is replaced by the phrase in question, which I assume refers to the man who had inherited the property in the past. Secondly, a list of property to be inherited usually lists similar property together, beginning with the various classes of real estate and ending with moveable property. In this text, this ha-la-ba phrase falls in the midst of a listing of house property. Finally, in 70% of inheritance texts from Nippur, the ha-la-ba phrase is either preceded or followed by a horizontal line; in this case, the line is absent, although a similar line is found in column I marking off the description of the eldest son's preference portion, indicating that such lines were used in this text. The preceding argument disposes, I hope, of Bigamatum as a possible heir.

A second problem is that of the date of the tablet. Both the actual date and the witness list are broken away. An examination of the names in the text and on the seals almost suggests an early Samsuiluna date (some 130 years later than the date suggested here) since an Im-ši-ŠI (E-4) and a KA-Damu (E-5), both sons of Ninlil-zimu (D-3), occur in PBS 8/2 129, which dates to 1745 B.C. I suggest that this is a case of two sets of related individuals having been given the same names, a pattern known from elsewhere in Mesopotamia. The reasons for this are as follows: First, PBS 8/2 129, together with OIMA 1 48, suggests that Im-ši-ŠI and KA-Damu were the sole heirs of Ninlil-zimu, whereas *ARN* 20 + OIMA 1 52 lists four heirs. Second, fig. 2 shows that much of the property given to the eldest son in *ARN* 20 + OIMA 1 52 shows up in his own inheritance document, *ARN* 23 + PBS 8/2 169, dated to 1867 B.C. This evidence suggests that *ARN* 20 + OIMA 1 52 should be dated to around 1880 B.C. Thus the later Ninlil-zimu, Im-ši-ŠI, and KA-Damu group simply represents the reusing of names of dead forebears.

TABLE 10. THE NINLIL-ZIMU TEXTS

Date	Text	Contents
n.d.	*Arn* 20 + OIMA 1 52	Abba-kalla, Im-ši-ŠI, KA-Damu, and Lu-dingirra inherit from Ninlil-zimu
n.d.	Text 4	Abba-kalla, Im-ši-ŠI, KA-Damu, and Lu-dingirra divide a plot of kislaḫ
1867	*ARN* 23 + PBS 8/2 169	Enlil-maš-zu, Damu-azu, and Lu-Ninurta inherit from Abba-kalla
1860–1873	YOS 14 321	Enlil-maš-zu and Damu-azu divide property
n.d.	Text 5	Enlil-maš-zu pays his employees
1810	PBS 8/1 12	Ududu and Ninurta-rīm-ilī inherit from Lu-Ninurta
1816–1794	PBS 8/1 18	Ninlil-zimu sells field and orchard to Nanna-mansum
n.d.	*ARN* 22	Ninlil-zimu sells field to Nanna-mansum
(n.d.	see OIMA 1 48	Ninlil-zimu sells field to Zijatum)
1793	Text 1	Ipquatum, Abum-waqar, and Uqâ-ilam witness
n.d.	*ARN* 142	Iddin-Damu, Damiq-ilišu, and others inherit from Ninurta-zimu
1789	*ARN* 31	Ipquatum and Abum-waqar witness
n.d.	PBS 8/1 92	Uqâ-ilam and Sin-nāši witness
1762	PBS 8/1 82	Nanna-zimu witnesses
1760	BE 6/2 10	Mār-erṣetim and Mutum-ilum bring suit against Iškur-girra and Ipqatum
1758	BE 6/2 11	Aḫī-šagiš and Iddinjatum witness
1756	BE 6/2 14	Sîn-išmeanni brings suit against Mār-erṣetim
1755	*ARN* 70	Enlil-dingir and Iddin-Ninurta exchange fields
1751	OIMA 1 12	Ekur-andul exchanges kislaḫ with Iddin-Ninurta
1745	OIMA 1 13	The heirs of Ninlil-zimu, Enlil-zamen, Dingir-luti, and Ninurta-mansum divide a kislaḫ plot that had once belonged to Im-ši-ŠI
1745	PBS 8/2 129	KA-Damu and Im-ši-ŠI agree to the division of their shares
n.d.	*ARN* 176	Enlil-dingir redeems a field from Nanna-adaḫ
1739	BE 6/2 30	Mār-erṣetim, Mutum-ilum, and Ipqatum ask for a new trial
1739	OIMA 1 19	Damu-iddinam buys a temple office from Ubajjatum
1738	OIMA 1 22	Damu-iddinam buys a field from Ina-Ekur-rabi
1738	OIMA 1 23	Damu-iddinam buys a field from Uta-u-lumeša
n.d.	OIMA 1 48	Damu-iddinam redeems a field from Ninnutum and Nūr-Šamaš
1737	BE 6/2 43	Igi-šag and Sîn-išmeanni inherit from Enlil-dingir

and although the text was neither sworn, witnessed, nor dated, it seems likely that it was an addendum to the original inheritance document.[29]

In addition to kislaḫ, *ARN* 20 + OIMA 1 52 also describes large areas of field, orchard, and house property. Some of the fields and orchards are said to have been along the *ḫiritum*, or moat, which flowed along the northeast wall of the city of Nippur;[30] this property must have been within easy walking distance of the city making it prime real estate. Finally, the

[29] Groups of heirs do not normally appear on a single text except in situations which related to inheritance.
[30] Samuel N. Kramer, *The Sumerians* (Chicago: University of Chicago Press, 1963), following p. 64.

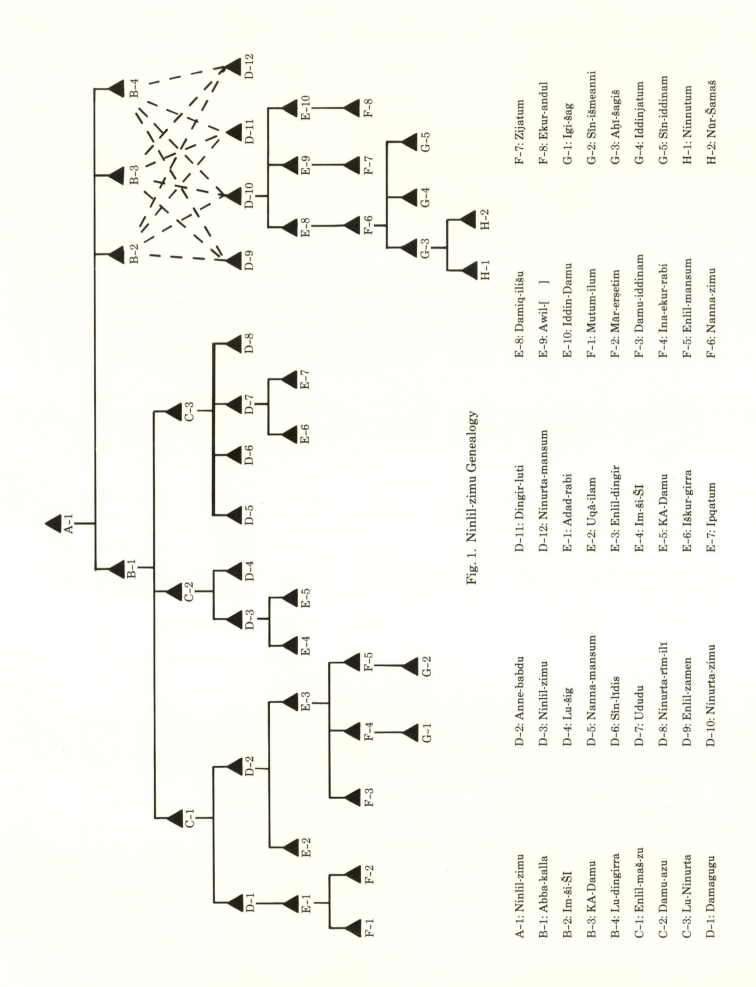

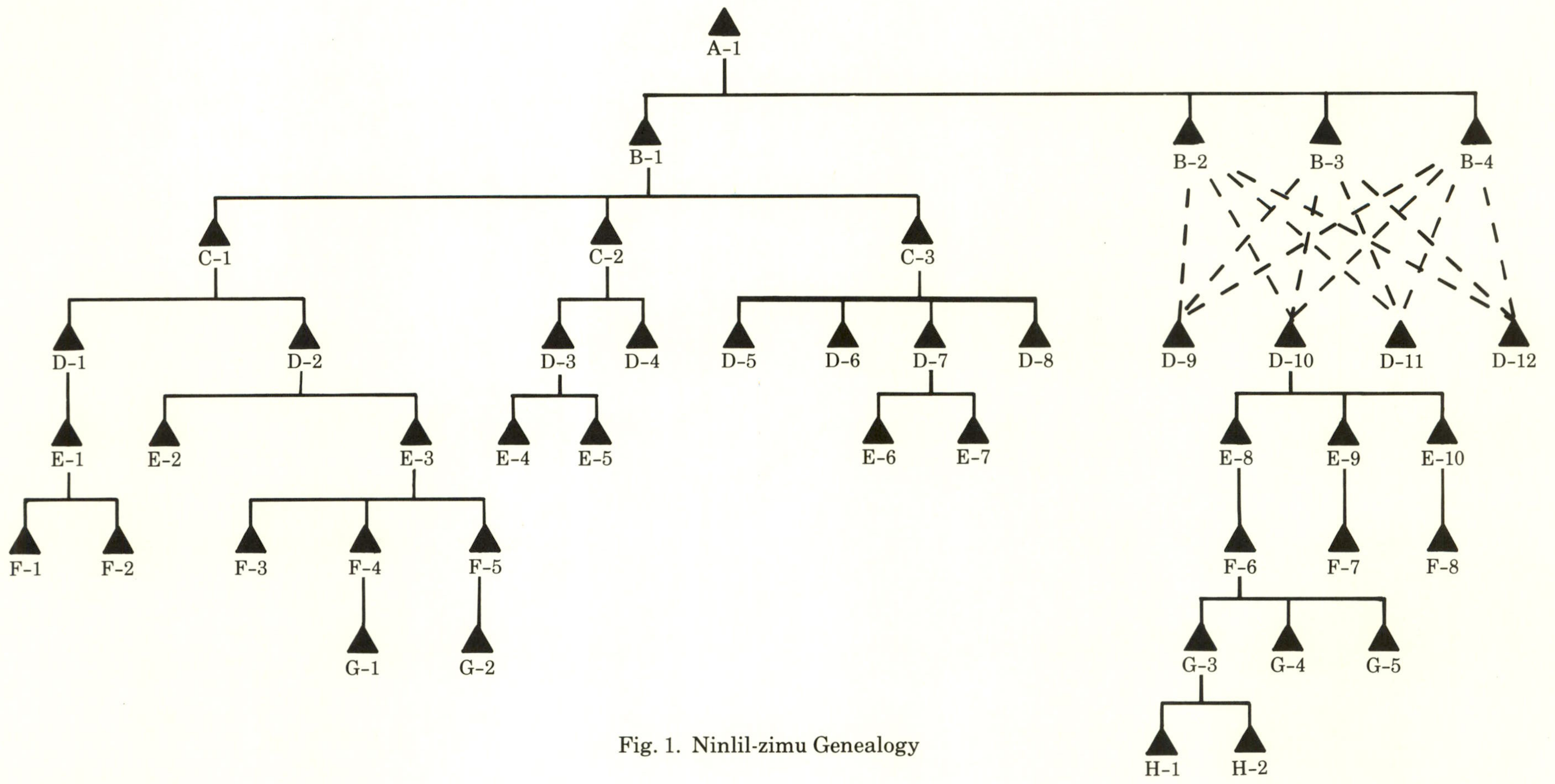

Fig. 1. Ninlil-zimu Genealogy

A-1: Ninlil-zimu
B-1: Abba-kalla
B-2: Im-ši-ŠI
B-3: KA-Damu
B-4: Lu-dingirra
C-1: Enlil-maš-zu
C-2: Damu-azu
C-3: Lu-Ninurta
D-1: Damagugu
D-2: Anne-babdu
D-3: Ninlil-zimu
D-4: Lu-šig
D-5: Nanna-mansum
D-6: Sîn-līdis
D-7: Ududu
D-8: Ninurta-rīm-ilī
D-9: Enlil-zamen
D-10: Ninurta-zimu
D-11: Dingir-luti
D-12: Ninurta-mansum
E-1: Adad-rabi
E-2: Uqâ-ilam
E-3: Enlil-dingir
E-4: Im-ši-ŠI
E-5: KA-Damu
E-6: Iškur-girra
E-7: Ipqatum
E-8: Damiq-ilišu
E-9: Awil-[ ]
E-10: Iddin-Damu
F-1: Mutum-ilum
F-2: Mār-erṣetim
F-3: Damu-iddinam
F-4: Ina-ekur-rabi
F-5: Enlil-mansum
F-6: Nanna-zimu
F-7: Zijatum
F-8: Ekur-andul
G-1: Igi-šag
G-2: Sîn-išmeanni
G-3: Aḫī-šagiš
G-4: Iddinjatum
G-5: Sîn-iddinam
H-1: Ninnutum
H-2: Nūr-Šamaš

family also owned at least three houses, one of which must have been house K. There are references to the é-libir-ra, or old house, and to the é-murub$_4$, or middle house, as well as to ordinary house property.

In summary, *ARN* 20 + OIMA 1 52, probably the earliest inheritance text known from Nippur, describes the division of a very considerable estate between the four sons of Ninlil-zimu. Although all other property was apparently divided, the temple offices went intact to the eldest son, Abba-kalla. The addendum, Text 4, not only confirms the association of the four brothers, but also places at least some of this family in House K of TA.

The tradition of leaving all temple offices to the eldest son was continued in the next generation. *ARN* 23 + PBS 8/2 169 (1867 B.C.) is the inheritance document of Abba-kalla (B-1), the eldest son of Ninlil-zimu (A-1). In this text he gives all of the temple offices that he had received from his father to his eldest son, Enlil-maš-zu (C-1), and divides his other property between all three sons, giving the two younger sons, Damu-azu (C-2) and Lu-Ninurta (C-3), extra property as equalization in lieu of offices. Although the total estate described in this text is not quite as great as that of *ARN* 20 + OIMA 1 52, it is still quite considerable, and much of the property is identical with that in the earlier document (see fig. 2).

As was the case with the earlier generation, the work of dividing the property on inheritance could not be concluded by the writing of a single document. YOS 14 text 321 describes a further division of field and orchard property between the two elder sons, Enlil-maš-zu and Damu-azu. At first glance, given that at least some of this property is said to have been part of the third brother's, Lu-Ninurta, inheritance, it seems possible that this text was written as a consequence of the untimely death of Lu-Ninurta. However, since other texts make clear that Lu-Ninurta lived to raise four sons, such an explanation seems unlikely. More probably, this text represents merely a redisposition of Abba-kalla's estate.

Although YOS 14 321 is damaged and difficult to understand in places, column II lines 9–12 may provide a clue both to the position of the Ninlil-zimu family and to the reasons behind the writing of this text. At least some of the property under consideration was a gift from the king, Enlil-bani, to the family, a gift made after the original estate had been divided amongst the heirs. The writing of this text must have been prompted by this unanticipated increase in the size of the family estate. The significance placed on this transaction is further emphasized by the presence of the two surviving paternal uncles as witnesses.

YOS 14 321 makes clear the importance of this third generation of the Ninlil-zimu family both in the city of Nippur and in southern Mesopotamia in general. This significance is underlined by an additional text which was found in the remains of House K. Text 5 records the employees of Enlil-maš-zu (C-1), the eldest brother, and the wages that he paid them. Although unfortunately the record of the property that Enlil-maš-zu left to his sons has not been preserved, Text 5 and YOS 14 321 show him to have been a man of sufficient substance both to have received gifts of property from the king and to have provided employment to others.

The only inheritance text from this third generation to be preserved is that of the youngest son, Lu-Ninurta (C-3). He had four sons, but only two of them were named as heirs[31] in this document, and the usual preference portion for the eldest son is missing. Ududu (D-7)

[31] Ududu is said to be dumu-šeš-gal, the son of the eldest brother, but in all other texts he is referred to as a son of Lu-Ninurta and a brother of Lu-Ninurta's other sons. The seal of this text shows traces which would be compatible with Ududu, son of Lu-Ninurta. However, if he were really a grandson, then one might suggest that Damagugu (D-1) was the eldest son of Lu-Ninurta. But if this were the case, it becomes difficult to explain how Lu-Ninurta came to have the temple office that had been inherited by Enlil-maš-zu. Also, in PBS 8/1 18 Ududu (D-7) and Adad-rabi (E-1) occur on two consecutive lines without a reference to the fact of their being brothers, which makes it unlikely that this was in fact the case. My conclusion is that the use of the term dumu-šeš-gal was either a scribal error, or it was used because the real eldest son, perhaps Nanna-mansum (D-5), was not included in the inheritance; but the data are open to other interpretations.

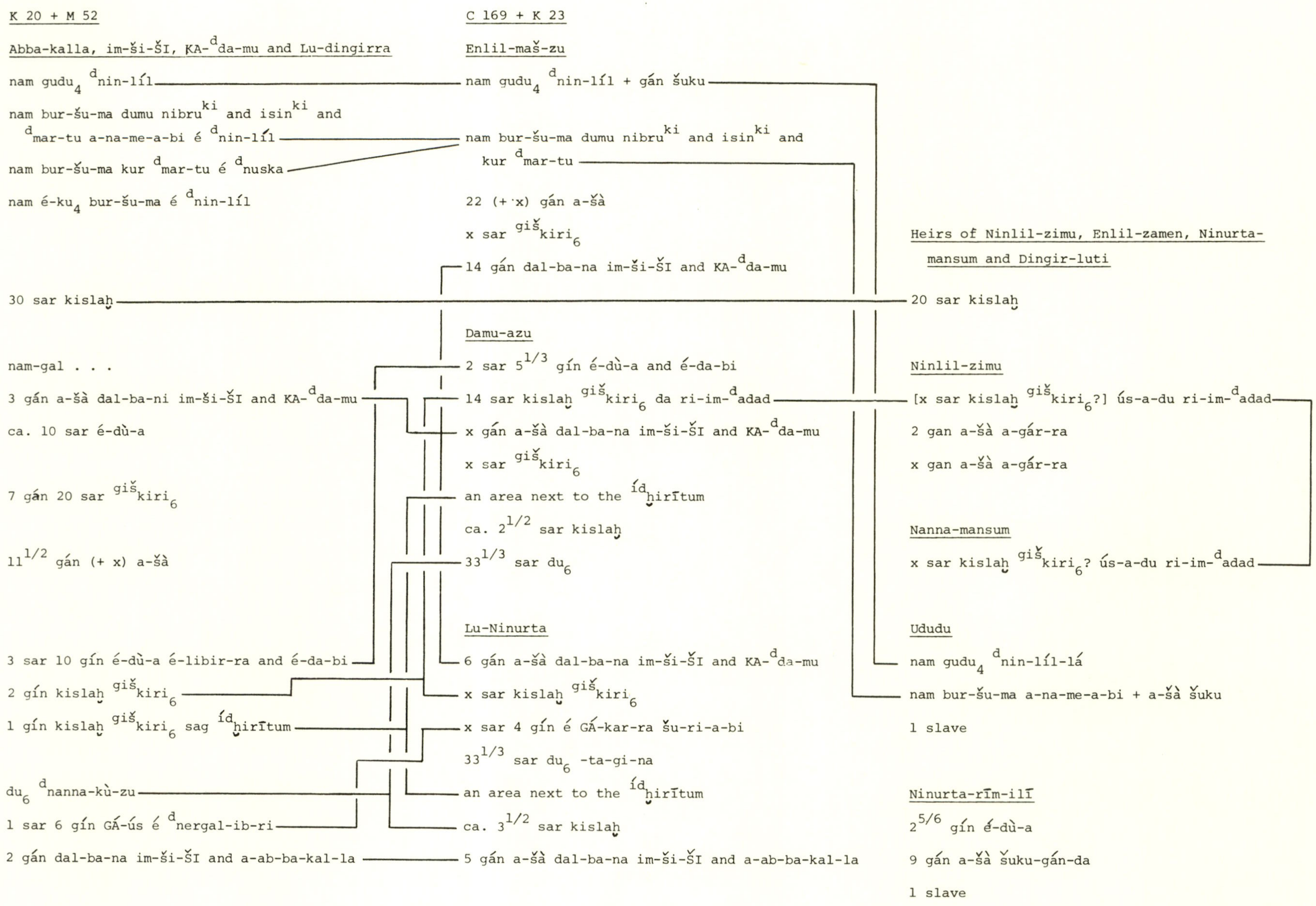

Fig. 2. Ninlil-zimu Family Property

received a gudu₄-ship of Ninlil, another temple office,[32] some furniture, and a slave; while the younger brother received sizeable house and field property, a slave, and some silver. The total amount of real estate involved and the presence of slaves show that this family was still quite wealthy.

The activities of the original Ninlil-zimu's grandchildren remain unknown, but texts concerning some of his great-grandchildren are preserved. PBS 8/1 18 and *ARN* 22 both record the sale of property by a second Ninlil-zimu (D-3), the son of Damu-azu, to his first cousin Nanna-mansum (D-5), the son of Lu-Ninurta. These two texts show this family to have been very close-knit. The sale of field and orchard property in PBS 8/1 18 names Ninlil-zimu's father's older brother, Enlil-maš-zu (C-1), as the owner of the neighboring field and his own brother Lu-šig (D-4) as the owner of the adjacent orchard. In *ARN* 22, Nanna-mansum's brother Sîn-līdiš (D-6) was the neighbor in the field sale. Included as witnesses on at least one of these texts were the family members, Anne-babdu (D-2), Ududu (D-7), Lu-šig (D-4), and Adad-rabi (E-1). These texts show that Nanna-mansum, in spite of being excluded from his father's inheritance document, had the means to acquire property and apparently did so from the hands of his cousin, Ninlil-zimu.

Although chronologically the next texts are those concerning the sons of Adad-rabi (E-1), in the Enlil-maš-zu branch of the family, it seems best to continue to discuss the activities of the descendants of Damu-azu. In OIMA 1 13 (1745 B.C.), a large piece of unbuilt house property (kislaḫ) was divided among several of the "descendants" of the older Im-ši-ŠI (B-2). The recipients were the heirs of the younger Ninlil-zimu (D-3), whom we have already met, and also the heirs of Enlil-zamen (D-9), Dingir-luti (D-11), and Ninurta-mansum (D-12), none of whom can be placed with any confidence in the genealogy. Although it seems likely that all were the descendants of the earlier Ninlil-zimu (A-1), it is not clear on what basis this later Ninlil-zimu (D-3) was chosen as a recipient of this property, rather than any of the other grandsons of Abba-kalla. The property to be divided may have been a square or part of a city block. It was an area of some 700 square meters, bordered on three sides by streets. One of the streets was the Wall Street noted above, which may signify that the property was at the edge of town, next to the city wall.

One month later, a new text was written, PBS 8/2 129, in which the two sons of Ninlil-zimu (D-3) agreed to the division of this property. During the intervening month several things seem to have happened. In the first place, instead of receiving one-quarter of the total, 5 sar, as they had been allocated in OIMA 1 13, they had apparently been allotted the extra preference portion usually granted the eldest son and had received a total of 6⅔ sar of the kislaḫ.[33] Secondly, it appears that Im-ši-ŠI (E-4) purchased the remainder of the property from the three other heirs, while his brother, KA-Damu (E-5) bought virtually all of the rest of the city block. Together, they owned an area of well over 1,000 square meters. This text indicates that as late as 1745 B.C., a time when many of the lineages were in a state of decline, the Ninlil-zimu family still controlled sizeable tracts of land within Nippur.

The elder branch of the family, on the other hand, seems to have done less well. The sons of Enlil-maš-zu are known only as witnesses, but the record of his more distant descendants is more informative. Enlil-maš-zu's great-grandsons Mār-erṣetim (F-2) and Mutum-ilum (F-1) first occur in a court dispute (BE 6/2 10) with their cousins Iškur-girra (E-6) and Ipqatum (E-7), the sons of Ududu. Apparently, at some time in the past, probably over fifty years before this text was written, Adad-rabi (E-1) had received a field from Ududu in exchange for

[32] It is not clear how Lu-Ninurta came by this property, since in the previous text (*ARN* 23 + PBS 8/2 169) these temple offices were given to the eldest son, Enlil-maš-zu. It is possible, however, that Ududu had already made the exchange with his cousin Adad-rabi (E-1) (or that his father had made it for him) that was to be under dispute in the later texts BE 6/2 10 and BE 6/2 30.

[33] PBS 8/2 154 may be a portion of the case of this later inheritance text, but it could equally well be the case to a second copy of OIMA 1 13.

his $gudu_4$-ship of Ninlil.[34] Although the text does not mention the grounds for complaint, it seems likely that the temple office, which in this family always had been left to the eldest son intact and had not been divided on inheritance, conferred a leadership role on its owner. This hypothesis is strengthened by the fact that it was temple offices—nontraditional, urban-based property—which were treated in this way. When Ududu received Adad-rabi's temple office, then, the main source of power in the lineage moved from the eldest branch to a younger one. The evidence suggests that Adad-rabi was a man whose personal abilities were not up to the demands of the position into which he was placed at birth. Even his sons, when they fought to regain the rights that they had lost, preferred to be called the sons of Damagugu, who was their grandfather, the last member of this branch of the family to have kept the property and power intact.

By this time, during the reign of Hammurabi, over a century after the earliest text, it appears that the basic principles behind lineage organization had been sufficiently modified that Adad-rabi's sons could feel that the property and leadership that had been squandered by their father should have been theirs by right. The rest of the lineage may have been satisfied with a shift in leadership from one branch to another, but Adad-rabi's sons were not, and asked Hammurabi for redress. The king acceded to their request, probably more to undermine current sources of political power at Nippur than because he believed in the justice of their cause. The council of Nippur, however, did not rule in their favor, although they attempted to satisfy them by the award of a piece of house property, apparently in a commercial district,[35] owned by the sons of Ududu.

The sons of Adad-rabi were not satisfied with a decision that did not restore their lost power and that gave them property that may have been outside the normal residential quarter of that lineage. Five years later they had quarrelled so badly with their neighbors that the matter had to be taken to court, and on the very eve of the economic crisis they again appealed to the king, now Samsuiluna, to give them a new trial.

Although the intervention of the courts did not succeed in reversing intralineage decisions on the distribution of property and power, these court cases demonstrate the weakness of the system as it had evolved. Not only were the lineages liable to interference by the crown in what had previously been considered internal affairs, but the conflict between the inheritance of property and power and the nature of the lineage as a corporate group is made clear by the discontent of the sons of Adad-rabi.

Not all of this branch of the family were discontent, though; while the descendants of Enlil-maš-zu's eldest son fared poorly, those of his younger son, Anne-babdu, did better. Texts recording the purchases of both Anne-babdu's son Enlil-dingir (E-3) and his grandson Damu-iddinam (F-3) have been preserved. The latter apparently did not wait for his father's death to receive his patrimony in the form of real estate; it must be assumed that he received moveable commodities at the time of his majority. It is in the latest text to be associated with this genealogy that we find evidence of Damu-iddinam's disinheritance. BE 6/2 43, dated to 1737 B.C., is the inheritance text of his father, Enlil-dingir. Instead of being recorded as one of the heirs, Damu-iddinam is simply listed as one of the witnesses, his presence, one must assume, indicating that he was satisfied with his omission from the body of the text. Damu-iddinam was wise to have taken his inheritance early. His father, Enlil-dingir, apparently lived a long time, so long that his two other sons predeceased him. His heirs in BE 6/2 43 were his grandsons, Damu-iddinam's nephews.[36]

[34] This exchange on the part of Ududu must have been of property that he was to inherit later, not property that he already owned. This practice is not unknown at Nippur; see Elizabeth C. Stone and David I. Owen, *Adoption in Old Babylonian Nippur and the Archive of Mannum-mešu-liṣṣur* (forthcoming).

[35] The owners of neighboring plots are described as bakers and carpenters.

[36] These relationships were not clearly described in the text. From OIMA 1 22, we know that Ina-ekur-rabi was the son of Enlil-dingir and the brother of Damu-iddinam. His son, Igi-šag, is then recorded in BE 6/2 43 as an heir. Enlil-mansum is described as the šeš-ad-da of Ina-ekur-rabi's son, Igi-šag. Although the primary meaning of

Damu-iddinam seems to have used his early inheritance to take advantage of the falling prices associated with the economic crisis of 1739 B.C. and buy property. Among other things, he purchased temple offices and thus became a member of the temple office association whose power in Nippur's economy was becoming increasingly conspicuous. Most of his business transactions were with and were witnessed by members of this association, not with other members of his family, but in OIMA 1 48 he bought property which had previously been sold by Ninlil-zimu (D-3) to a more junior branch of the family.

Although this junior branch can be traced for five generations, it occupies an uncertain position in the Ninlil-zimu genealogy. Ninurta-zimu (D-10) was probably a son of either Im-ši-ŠI, KA-Damu, or Lu-dingirra, the three younger sons of the founder of the family, since he acts as a witness to Lu-Ninurta's inheritance document, PBS 8/1 12. Ninurta-zimu's membership in the Ninlil-zimu family is strongly suggested by the terms of his own inheritance document. In *ARN* 142, he follows the family practice of maintaining common property and of leaving temple offices undivided to the eldest son—a practice not followed by members of other Nippur lineages. The other members of this branch are known largely from their witnessing activities. Apart from witnessing texts of other Ninlil-zimu family members, they occur on texts written by their neighbors, the Imgur-Sîn family.[37] Finally, in OIMA 1 48, Damu-iddinam redeemed some property from his distant cousins Ninnutum (H-1) and Nūr-Šamaš (H-2).

Despite difficulties in linking this branch of the family to the rest of the genealogy, the pattern of naming reinforces the internal evidence of the texts in indicating a relationship. Echoes of Ninlil-zimu are to be found in the names Ninurta-zimu and Nanna-zimu. As might be expected, the texts do not suggest that this group was as rich and powerful as the more senior branches, but even this segment of the Ninlil-zimu family was far from impoverished.

Altogether, the twenty-seven texts which describe the activities of the Ninlil-zimu family show it as one of the wealthiest and most important families in Nippur. The property it controlled in mid Isin-Larsa times was immense, and even at the time of the economic crisis of 1739 B.C., when the Nippur lineages were in eclipse, at least one member of the family, Damu-iddinam, was in a position to purchase the property that others were selling in panic. This is not to say that the family did not have its difficulties; the legal squabbling over the transfer of leadership from one branch to another and the invocation of outside powers to force changes in the internal organization of the lineage are hardly indicative of harmony. Nevertheless, these outside forces, namely agents of the crown, although they may have wished to weaken the lineage, were largely unsuccessful, and the family continued rich and powerful.

The success of this lineage over so long a time period probably lay in the strategies used for property consolidation. Not only were some sons excluded from property inheritance, but some real estate remained under joint ownership and all temple offices were passed to the eldest son. Since the holders of these temple offices were people of importance in the city of Nippur as a whole, not just in the family, it would be through these officeholders that the lineage would have been able to exercise influence in a broader sphere. A tradition of wielding power through office ownership allowed members of this family to assume positions of

šeš-ad-da is "father's brother," which would make Enlil-mansum and Ina-ekur-rabi brothers, as shown in fig. 1, it may also refer to any agnatic kinsman of an ascendant generation. If this usage were the one employed here, then the two could have been more distantly related than shown in fig. 1. However, since inheritance texts usually divide property between sons and their descendants, the term šeš-ad-da should probably be taken literally, in which case the reconstruction shown in fig. 1 represents reality.

[37] The Imgur-Sîn family is best known for its connections with the family of Ur-Pabilsag (see Stone and Owen, *Adoption in Nippur*, forthcoming), with which it formed ties by marriage. However, the closeness of its ties with this branch of the Ninlil-zimu family are made clear by BE 6/2 11, a text belonging to the Imgur-Sîn family, which is witnessed by Aḫī-šagiš (G-3) and Iddinjatum (G-4), and by PBS 8/1 82, in which Nanna-zimu (F-6) witnesses a text of the Ur-Pabilsag family.

importance in the temple office association even as the power of lineage membership went into eclipse. Thus the strategies adopted by the Ninlil-zimu family were not only successful in maintaining wealth and power at the time when lineages were significant political forces within the city, but were also adaptable enough to allow its members to continue in positions of importance long after the lineage as a unit had lost significance.

These texts, rich as they are, are not the only source of information on the importance of the Ninlil-zimu family; their home, House K, offers further testimony about their fortunes and influence on their neighbors.

The first evidence for House K is in level XIIA, when it stood apart from any other building and had a large open space in front of it. It is not known whether House K had earlier manifestations in level XIIB or below, but since this first excavated level of House K coincides with a radical reorganization of TA and contains texts referring to the founding members of the Ninlil-zimu family, it is probably that level XIIA represents the time when the family first established itself in TA.[38]

The plan of House K in level XIIA is closely paralleled by those of many houses found by Woolley at Ur.[39] Compare, for example, House K with the famous number 3 Gay Street from Ur[40] (see fig. 3): Both House K locus 197 and Gay Street room 1[41] are entrance chambers; both are at the left of the house and open only into the courtyard. To the right of the entrance chamber is the staircase, respectively locus 198 and room 3. The stairs differ slightly—at Nippur it is entirely of brick and is contained in locus 198, continuing up over a brick arch, whereas at Ur only the first flight was in room 3, with the second flight, made of wood, continuing over room 4, a "bathroom." The house at Nippur has no room that would be equivalent to room 4—indeed, no evidence has been preserved to indicate what, if any, were the sanitary arrangements of the inhabitants of TA.

Next to the stairway of House K, and beside the bathroom of the Ur house, was the kitchen, loci 199 and 200, and room 5 respectively. In both cases the kitchen occupies a corner of the house, although the doors are in different walls. In House K only two other rooms have been preserved, loci 235 and 196, both of which were probably used as living rooms; at number 3 Gay Street three such rooms, rooms 6, 7, and 9, were found, while room 8 may have been a storeroom.

The similarities between these two houses from Ur and Nippur are striking. In both structures there is an obvious division between service rooms, on the same side of the courtyard as the entrance chamber, and living rooms, which lay to the back of the house. In addition, the distribution of the service rooms was identical. This identity of pattern suggests that a mental template of the "ideal" house may have existed in southern Mesopotamia at this time. However, the fact that only a few houses conformed to this template suggests either that this house plan was designed to accommodate an "ideal" family, which may not actually have been particularly common, or that only houses built by architects on unconfined lots could follow the plan exactly. It is possible that the structural division of a house into service and living areas, a division not common at Nippur, is related to the ownership of household slaves. *ARN* 20 + OIMA 1 52 is one of the very few contracts from Nippur that includes mention of household slaves. Slaves, although still rare at Ur, occur more often in documents from that city than in those from Nippur, as do houses following this plan. It is possible,

[38] The notes indicate that in one very limited deep sounding, the excavators found a considerable depth of mud brick beneath the baked-brick foundations (or damp course) of the wall. This mud brick may be the remains of an earlier version of House K, or alternatively, the builders may have followed the line of earlier construction. This mud brick may also indicate that the builders of House K in level XIIA included a substantial mud-brick foundation.

[39] Woolley and Mallowan, *Ur Excavations, vol. 7.*

[40] Ibid., pp. 96–97, pl. 22.

[41] For the rest of this discussion, I will refer to rooms in House K as loci, and rooms in the Gay Street house as rooms, thus obviating the need specifically to identify to which structure I am referring.

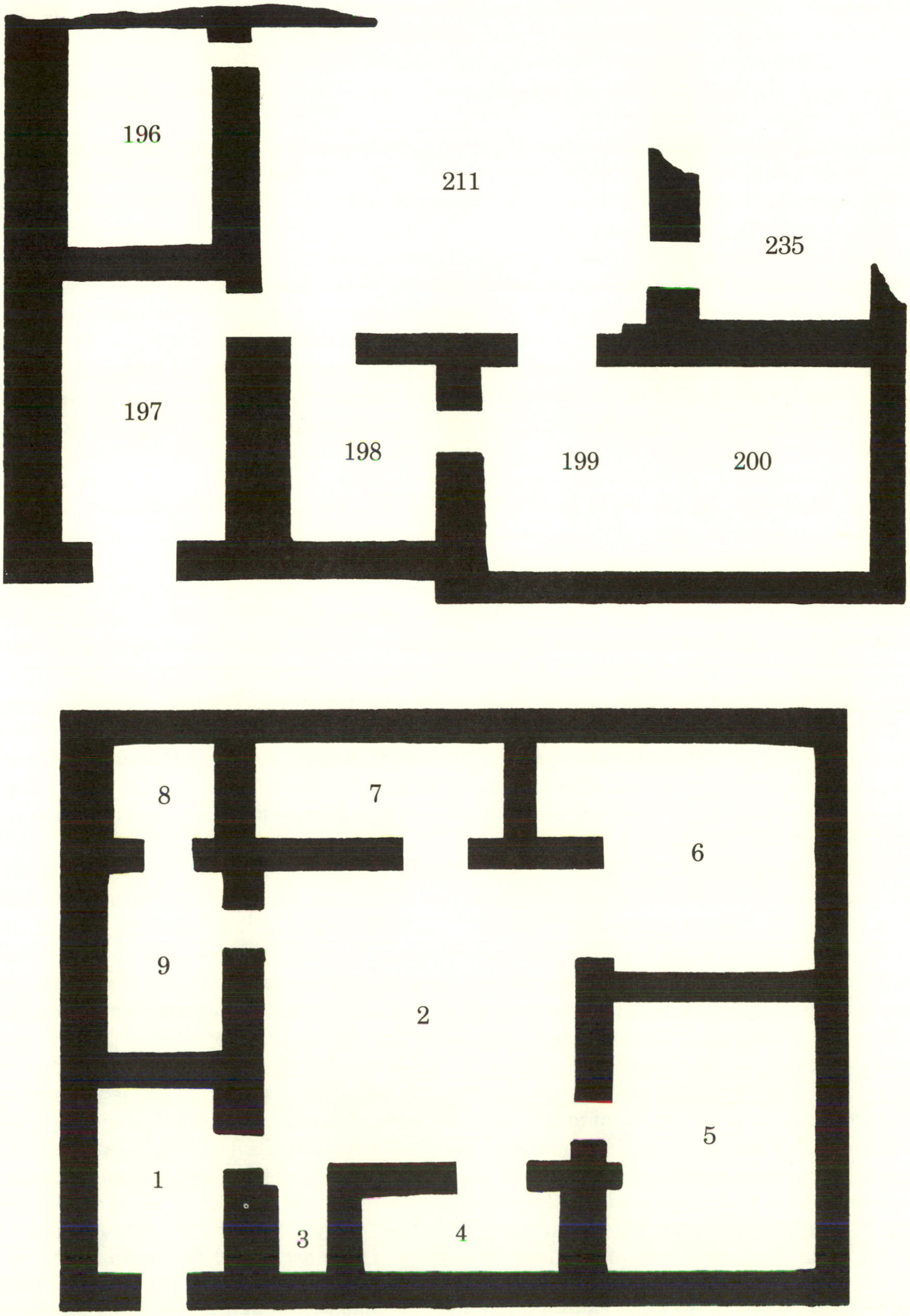

Fig. 3. TA House K and Number 3 Gay Street at Ur

then, that the division of service from living areas was a feature of house construction for owners of household slaves, of which the Ninlil-zimu family was one.

The objects found in level XIIA of House K also reflect this division. Apart from one literary fragment found in the kitchen, locus 199, and a small fragment of an animal figurine found in the entrance chamber, locus 197, all finds from this level came from the two "living rooms," loci 196 and 235 (both of which were only partially excavated), and from the courtyard, locus 211. Generally they were not particularly noteworthy—mostly figurines, plaques, pottery, etc.—but a fragment of shell inlay in locus 196 and two cylinder seal impressions from the courtyard may reflect the family's wealth. The best attestation of their wealth, however, remains the two tablets, Texts 4 and 5, found in locus 196. Considering how little of the living area was excavated (most of locus 196, a corner of locus 235, none of the back rooms), however, this evidence is abundant enough.

Thus in level XIIA, House K was a large, well-planned structure occupied almost certainly by the senior branch of the Ninlil-zimu family. It may be surmised that the large open space outside its front door was under its control. In subsequent levels much of the empty space in TA was filled in, and the plan of House K became less easy to understand.

The plan of House K in levels XI and XB seems to indicate one section cordoned off from the bulk of the building. Changes in the circulation pattern permitted no access between loci 196 and 197 and the rest of House K—in fact no entrance to the latter is to be found in the excavated area.

Three explanations for these architectural modifications are possible. First, House K may have had a suite of two rooms, loci 196 and 197, serving as entrance chambers, with locus 196 leading into the main portion of the house via unexcavated rooms at the back of the house. This suggestion may be strengthened by the presence of a second entrance, this time from the alleyway, locus 168, again in the loci 196/197 pair, in level XB. It must be admitted that such a pattern was unusual, but the importance of this family may have necessitated a more complex entrance area. The second alternative is that loci 196 and 197 were rooms which were set aside for the conduct of business, with the main entrance to the domestic part of the house located either in the unexcavated areas to the northeast or in the southeastern part of the house, an area that was disturbed by a later, possibly Kassite, pit. Separate business and residential areas are evidenced elsewhere in TA and in TB. Finally, loci 196 and 197 may have formed a separate structure. This seems improbable, however, because the two loci differ considerably in shape and organization from other small houses known from this area (see Houses G and H below) and from TB.

Assuming that one of the first two explanations of this architectural configuration is correct, the finds from these loci may be examined to help in determining the truth. Unfortunately, although finds in the main portion of House K were common in levels XI and XB, only a few literary and school tablets were found in loci 196 and 197. Few conclusions can be drawn from these data; they are certainly not plentiful enough to serve as evidence for the presence of a scribal school and clearly do not indicate any specialized business activity. The exact function of this pair of rooms must remain unknown, and the texts may simply have been dumped in these rooms at the time of the level XA rebuilding.

This level XA rebuilding apparently changed House K from a residential structure into an open working area consisting of one large courtyard, with loci 166 and 177 separated from one another by a brick sill and from the street by a wall. To the north and west of this courtyard were some small rooms (loci 159, 169, 165), whose relationship to the courtyard remains unclear. Unfortunately, locus 159, the room that was most obviously attached to the courtyard, was largely destroyed by a later pit. In the courtyard itself the area to the west, locus 166, is said to have contained many potsherds. The most complete pieces, and those with decoration, were recorded, but it is not clear whether these vessels, all of which were broken, represent anything more than a paving of the floor with potsherds, a practice that is not unknown in ancient Mesopotamia. The area to the east, locus 177, was also paved, but in this case the more usual form of paving, baked bricks, was employed. This latter locus also contained a large (but unspecified) number of milling stones. Otherwise the finds from the area were meager, and none were in context or in sufficient numbers to be deemed significant. One is left with the impression that in level XA, House K formed a large, open work area used, among other things, for the grinding of grain.

In conclusion, in the Isin-Larsa period House K served as a residence for one of the most important property-owning lineages of Nippur, the Ninlil-zimu family. In the early part of the Old Babylonian period the house continued to be occupied, probably by later generations of the same family, but with a changed circulation pattern. By the end of the Old Babylonian occupation of Nippur, House K had ceased to be a residential unit; instead the area that it had once occupied had been transformed into a large, open work area.

House Q

Although only two rooms of House Q were excavated, enough is preserved to make it clear that this building was the only one other than House K to be occupied during level XIIA. The remains of one room, called locus 194 in the lower levels and locus 162 in level XA, are preserved from level XIIB until Nippur was abandoned in 1720 B.C., but the only information preserved on the room to the northeast comes from levels XB-1 (locus 208) and XA-2 (locus 172). Almost no architectural details are preserved from this latter room, but in level XA-2 a fragment of an inheritance document was found, naming one Imgur-Ninurta as the heir to some fields (Text 6). The fragmentary nature of the text, though, and its somewhat dubious archaeological context do not allow us to assume that it refers to the owner of House Q.[42]

The available information on the room through which the house was entered is much more complete, although not always easy to interpret. For almost all of its history, this room (locus 194/162) was wider than any other roofed area in TA or TB. It was a full 3 m wide, whereas elsewhere most rooms did not exceed 2.15 m, probably the distance that can be comfortably spanned by beams of split palm logs.[43] Even at Ur, with the exception of the enigmatic "chapels," rooms were rarely wider than 2.75 m. The most logical conclusion is that this locus served as an open courtyard for much or all of its history.

It has been noted above that in the lower levels of TA most houses were entered through the courtyard. Thus House Q was not exceptional in level XIIB in having a large courtyard which opened directly onto the street and which was used, from time to time, for bread making. It retained the older pattern even in level XI, when separate entrance chambers were common. A fireplace built in level XB-1 may indicate some special function for this court, while the small walls, or pilasters, that divided the locus in level XA-3 may have allowed it to be partially roofed, but it is to the evidence from level XA-2 that we must turn for an understanding of the peculiarities in plan of House Q.

[42] Although an Imgur-Ninurta was the father of the residents of House H, Text 6 is in such a fragmentary condition and the name is sufficiently common that one cannot suggest that the two Imgur-Ninurtas represent the same person.

[43] In spite of an exhaustive search, I have been unable to discover any source which discusses how wide a room can be spanned by split palm logs. The texts indicate that doors at least were frequently made of this material, and the small width of most rooms suggests that poplar wood was not generally used for construction. In TA only loci 201 and 205 were wider than 2.15 m, around 2.8 m. These rooms were clearly the most important rooms of fairly sizeable houses, and therefore, the extra cost of obtaining hardwood for roof beams might have been acceptable. An entrance chamber would hardly justify such treatment. See Hans Nissen, "Survey of an Abandoned Modern Village in Southern Iraq," *Sumer* 24 (1968): 107–14.

In level XA-2, the last true occupation level in the house, the locus was again undivided. Here, the excavators note that the area had a thick layer of vegetable material, probably straw, on the floor. The presence of straw, in addition to the door sockets and high baked-brick sills[44] associated with this house, suggests that the area may have been used to house animals. It is perhaps here that one can find the explanation for the differing modes of entrance that have been seen in TA houses.

Entrance by way of a separate chamber is basically incompatible with the keeping of domestic animals in the courtyard in view of the inconvenience of having livestock traversing a room used for receiving outsiders. Textual evidence of the keeping of domestic animals by private urban property owners in Nippur exists only in the Isin-Larsa period.[45] After political stability was established with the conquest of Isin by Rīm-Sîn, animal husbandry by urban residents appears to have become less common, and domestic architecture was consequently modified. The residents of House Q were exceptional in maintaining an entrance via the courtyard until Nippur was abandoned in 1720 B.C., exceptional also, perhaps, in continuing to keep animals in the city.

With the rest of House Q remaining unexcavated, an understanding of the entire plan is denied to us, and any further modifications that might have been associated with animal husbandry remain unknown. In general, House Q must be seen as a house entered through a courtyard that was used for keeping animals and bread baking. It is not clear what relationship existed between the residents of Houses K and Q, except that these were the only two buildings occupied in TA in level XIIA, and both were occupied throughout the economic crisis.

House J

House J is the only structure in TA, other than Houses K and Q, to evidence rough continuity of plan from level XIIB to level XI, but unlike Houses K and Q, House J was abandoned during level XIIA. House J, when it was rebuilt in level XI, was one of the first houses to encroach on the space that had been left open in front of House K. As they prepared the ground for construction, the builders must have encountered the old wall stubs and decided to use them for foundations.

In spite of the similarity in plan between the level XIIB structure (see above p. 38) and that built in level XI floor 2, the circulation pattern was quite different. Whereas the level XIIB house, like most other houses of that period, was entered through the courtyard, the level XI entrance chambers had gained popularity and House J was entered through locus 160. Furthermore, the other small room, locus 163, was now entered directly from the courtyard. The plan of House J in level XI-2 continued until Nippur was abandoned, the only changes being the construction of a staircase in locus 163 in level XI-1, the appending of a bakery (see House P below) in level XA-2, and the inclusion of the newly enclosed locus 164 in level XA-1.

Locus 164 seems to have been an alleyway in levels XI and XB, although the constriction of its opening may indicate that access was restricted. In level XA floor 1, however, the locus was closed off by a wall and turned into a room of House J. Since there is some textual evidence to suggest that streets may have been individually or family owned, if changes in

[44] In general, the notes for the second-season excavations in TB refer frequently to baked-brick foundations, sills, features, etc., while those from the third-season excavations in TA refer to such features but rarely. But since there are occasional references to the use of baked brick in TA, such as this one, it is assumed here that this distinction in the frequency of reference to baked brick reflects real differences between the two areas, and not simply differences in note taking.

[45] Unfortunately, of the five contracts from Nippur that mention animals, only two can be securely dated, and a third can be dated approximately. All three dates seem to fall during the reign of Rīm-Sîn, either just before or just after his conquest of Isin. The five texts are *ARN* 33, *ARN* 50, OIMA 1 66, TIM 4 1, and TIM 4 20.

the plans of House J and of the structure to the west obviated the need for this alleyway, there would have been nothing to stop its owners from converting the extra space into a room.

The finds from House J shed no additional light on these architectural changes. Only mundane household goods, mostly pottery, were found, and there is no evidence of either literary or economic pursuits. Nevertheless, not only were the residents of House J some of the first to build in the open space fronting House K, but their economic base was such that they were largely unaffected by the 1739 B.C. crisis. Like all other Nippurites, though, they abandoned their home in 1720 B.C.

House P

Although not built until level XI floor 1, House P is discussed here because of its close relationship to House J, especially in the later levels. Only a small portion of the building lies within the excavation area; that portion which does indicate that it was always a quite modest structure. As constructed, House P had two doors to the street, one in locus 170 and one in locus 158. Because so little of it has been excavated, it is hard to tell whether these two doors indicate the presence of two separate buildings, but the small size of locus 158 makes it more likely that a single establishment with two doors was involved. Similar houses have been found in TB, and there each door provided access to either the private or the public sector of the building. If House P falls into this category, then locus 158 would represent that part of the house set aside for business purposes, and locus 170 the entrance chamber of the domestic sector.

Unfortunately, House P has yielded few artifacts, perhaps because of its small exposure, but the barrel weight found in level XI of locus 158 may testify to the conduct of commercial activities in that area. Furthermore, if the unnumbered space to the northwest of locus 158 was a room and not a courtyard, then its door socket might represent the further separation of locus 158 from the rest of the house.

Whatever the business of the residents of House P, it permitted them to remain at Nippur for the duration of the 1739 B.C. crisis, when other residents of TA left the area. The plan of House P remained unchanged throughout level XB, but in level XA, after the crisis had eased, it underwent some significant changes.

The evidence from locus 158 suggests that in level XA this building belonged to a baker (*muḫaldim*), an occupation known from several witness lists. A series of bread ovens in locus 158, accompanied by a large amount of ash, and a furnace in locus 170, testify to this activity. Elsewhere, bread ovens were either found in courtyards (as in locus 188 of House G and probably locus 162 of House Q) or in kitchens, which were usually rooms tucked away into the far corner of the house (as in locus 191 of House F, locus 163 of House J, and locus 200 of House K). In House P, evidence of baking is not only located in a room which opens into the street, but each oven shows evidence of continuous rebuilding, perhaps indicating that more than one such oven was in use at one time. Associated with these ovens were a series of shallow dishes, of pottery type 21 in level XA floor 2 and perhaps type 7 in floor 1 (see chap. 5). They are described variously as small dishes or saucers in the field notes, but no measured drawings are preserved. If this room were used as a bakery, perhaps these small saucers were similar to those used for the oil and water needed for bread making in the Middle East today: "The dough is taken from the mixing pan and moulded into fist-sized balls on a flour-sprinkled board. A small dish of oil or water is placed nearby to put on her hands so that the dough will not stick."[46]

[46] Louise E. Sweet, *Tell Toqaan: A Syrian Village,* Anthropological Papers of the Museum of Anthropology, University of Michigan, no. 14 (Ann Arbor: University of Michigan Press, 1960), p. 133.

It is unfortunate that so little of House P has been excavated. In level XA floor 2, a door between loci 163 and 158 suggests that it was a shop attached to the neighboring House J. However, the notes also indicate a possible blocking of both the door to the street and the door to House J in level XA floor 1. If the blocking of the door to the street went all the way to the lintel, it seems less likely that this room served commercial purposes, but if it were only a partial blocking, then it may have been used as a shop counter. Such fixed barriers between the populace and the baker are features commonly seen in the Middle East today.

The bakery that was housed in level XA House P was certainly more modest than one of a similar date uncovered on the West Mound in the course of most recent excavations;[47] House P was probably a small bakery designed to serve the needs of the immediate locality, rather than a large state-run institution like that on the West Mound. It may not be coincidental that most of the other houses in TA had no bread ovens in level XA, although they were quite common items of domestic furniture in the earlier levels.

In summary, in spite of its small exposure, House P has slight evidence of commercial activity from its founding in level XI, culminating in its use as a local bakery in level XA. It is possible that it was these commercial activities that allowed the residents of House P to survive the 1739 B.C. economic troubles and remain at Nippur.

House F

House F was a sizeable structure with a living room at the back of the house, several small subsidiary rooms on one side of the small courtyard, and an entrance chamber in the front. It was probably the first sizeable building to occupy the eastern portion of the open area that fronted House K, and it served as a scribal school throughout level XI. After a hiatus in level XB, coinciding with the economic crisis, the house was rebuilt in level XA, probably by a new group of people.

Level XI House F produced by far the largest number of school, lexical, literary, mathematical, etc., tablets of any house in TA. The total of over thirteen hundred tablets and fragments found here suggests that this structure housed a scribal school. There exist copious descriptions of such schools,[48] but without an adequate description of their physical properties most scholars have considered them to have been large formal institutions.[49] However, recently Sumerologists[50] have described scribal training as taking place in more modest surroundings. House F would represent such a school.

The tablets were found primarily in the large back room, locus 205, some built into a bench and a box, and others along the walls. Perhaps these latter were originally on shelves or in bags attached to the walls. Only a few school texts found their way into the two rooms at the side of the courtyard, loci 184 and 189, but many tablets, tablet fragments, and (if I interpret the field notes aright) much unformed tablet clay was found in locus 191, perhaps indicating this as an area where old tablets were turned into new tablet clay.[51] Locus 191 appears to have served also as a kitchen, or at least as a locus for bread baking, since two

[47] Judith A. Franke, "Area WB," in *Nippur 12,* ed. McGuire Gibson, Oriental Institute Communications, no. 23 (Chicago: Oriental Institute, 1978), pp. 54–65.

[48] See Samuel Noah Kramer, "Schooldays: A Sumerian Composition Relating to the Education of the Scribe," *Journal of the American Oriental Society* 69 (1949): 199–215.

[49] See, even, OIP 78, p. 148.

[50] Miguel Civil, *Materials for the Sumerian Lexicon,* vol. 14 (Rome: Pontificum Institutum Biblicum, 1979), pp. 7–8.

[51] The relevant passage in the notes reads "X-3 [our XI-3] is base of red tablet clay fill. Not a good laid floor but with *tanour* [bread oven] in corner." Civil (ibid., p. 7) states that old tablets were quite rapidly melted down so that their clay could be reused by the fledgling scribes.

bread ovens were found there, accompanied by a shallow dish similar to those associated with bread baking in House P (see above) and elsewhere. The entrance chamber, locus 203, was only partially excavated, while the courtyard (locus 192) remains somewhat of a puzzle. This courtyard, small though it was, had benches built on two sides and is said to have had a box which contained a large vessel filled with small pots. No record other than the field notes remains of these vessels, but it is possible that since this locus was unnumbered at the commencement of its excavation, its finds were recorded as coming from other loci in the house, or remained unrecorded.

The nature of this school may be reconstructed as follows: The entrance chamber, locus 203, gave access to the courtyard, locus 192, an area that was probably used for instruction in good weather. Benches against the walls provided the teacher and pupils with places to sit, while the baked-brick box held a large jar of water for use in keeping the tablet clay the correct consistency. Perhaps the small pots found in the jar were used by the students to dip the water that they needed. Most tablets, however, were kept in the large schoolroom at the back of the house. Here again there is the necessary furniture, a bench and a box, but in this case they were made of the most readily available raw material, old tablets. The walls of this room had bags or shelves on them to hold the tablets, and, if the finds from this room are anything to go on, were decorated with plaques whose themes tended to be religious in nature. Rooms 184 and 189 may have been the private domain of the teacher, but even his kitchen, locus 191, was much used by the school. In addition to normal culinary activities, this kitchen was the place where old tablets were soaked and turned into new tablet clay.

So much of House F seems to have been devoted to scribal teaching that it seems unlikely that it could have served much of a domestic purpose. However, the bread ovens and pottery imply that it also served as a residence of the schoolmaster, with rooms 184 and 189, small though they were, kept private. It seems unlikely, however, that such a resident scribe could have had a family. Even if the schoolroom, locus 205, were used as a living room at night, there would have been nowhere for the wife and children to have had privacy during the day. Thus, if we assume a resident schoolmaster, he was probably unmarried.

The crisis of 1739 B.C. apparently ended these scribal activities. Scribal training was probably an indulgence which could not be maintained in times of economic adversity. When the House F scribe and his colleagues in other parts of the city left Nippur, they left behind the evidence of their teaching activities, evidence without which both our knowledge and our awareness of Sumerian literature would have been considerably reduced.

Shortly thereafter, House F was rebuilt and reoccupied, apparently by a new group of people. Apart from a few fragments of school tablets, presumably left over from the previous occupation, the finds from level XA House F were entirely domestic in nature. The house apparently belonged to Ubar-Baʾu, since we have a text dating to 1769 B.C. (Text 11) in which he and two others were allocated some temple office property. His ownership of these offices before the crisis may have enabled him to remain at Nippur throughout and have placed him in a position to acquire House F.

Text 12 concerns the activities of the two sons of Ubar-Baʾu, Ninurta-rīm-ilī and Ištar-kīma-ilija, and is dated to 1721 B.C., a few months before the abandonment of Nippur. The two brothers exchange house plots. Since these plots were not next door to each other, it did not seem likely that both could have been located in the TA excavation area. However, the tablet was found in House F, and it seemed reasonable to suppose that one of the house plots recorded in Text 12 might actually have been House F. The areas of the various loci of House F are given in table 11,[52] and if locus 192 is assumed to have been a courtyard, then the total floor space of House F is 60 gín, or 1 sar, exactly the size of the house plot given by

[52] See Stone, "Texts, Architecture and Ethnographic Analogy," p. 20, for the methodology used.

TABLE 11. THE AREAS OF THE LOCI IN HOUSE F

Locus	Area (m^2)	Area (gín)
205	15.90	27.04
184	4.32	7.35
189	3.36	5.71
191	6.72	11.43
203	5.28	8.98
Total	35.58	60.51

Ištar-kīma-ilija to Ninurta-rīm-ilī. In addition, the neighboring house is described as belonging to Utaulu-ḫeti. Only one man of that name is known from Nippur, and he was a scribe who practiced from 1761 B.C. until 1739 B.C., and then resumed work in 1731 B.C. Of the seventeen surviving texts which this man wrote, 29% were part of the Atta archive found in TB and 18% concerned the activities of the Ninlil-zimu family. He also wrote one of the texts found in House N, Text 31. He apparently lived in the area east of House F, or perhaps even in House G. Indeed, it is even possible that it was he who ran the scribal school before the crisis, returning to Nippur later to continue his secondary activity of contract writing.[53]

Of the other texts found in level XA of House F, only one may be related to the Ubar-Baʾu family. Text 13, dated to 1743 B.C., describes the purchase of an orchard plot. Unfortunately, the name of the purchaser was broken away, but that man may well have been Ubar-Baʾu or one of his sons.[54] The remaining texts from XA-1, though, do not concern these residents of House F. One, Text 14, describes a house rental, but the principals are not identified by patronymics, and the property is undescribed. Another, Text 15, an adoption dated to 1734 B.C., has no names in common with any other contract from Nippur; while Text 16's early date (1885–1874 B.C.) may indicate that it was derived from the earlier school, where it could have served as a model. Only Text 17 indicates a connection with other residents of TA, and that is very tenuous. The seller of a house plot in this 1784 B.C. text could be the brother of the Rīm-Adad who occurs in texts found in House I. In *ARN* 36 an otherwise unidentified Nannatum disinherits Rīm-Adad, the son of Šagiš-kīnum. This last name is not at all common at Nippur and is recorded as the patronymic of Ur-dukuga, the seller in Text 17. More common is the name Nannatum, but it is just conceivable that the Nannatum who disinherited Rīm-Adad in *ARN* 36 was the same person as the resident of House N of that name, especially since a second resident of House N, Amurru-šemi, was also involved in a disinheritance case. Such a connection is possible, not probable, but without it Text 17 joins Text 15 as an unexplained tablet.

The tablets from level XA House F, then, cannot be described as consistent in pattern. Some, like Text 12, seem fairly convincing as the records of the last owners of House F. With others, it seems that the connection is tenuous at best. Since the tablets were found in two groups, Texts 11–14 and Texts 15–17, it is possible that the former group was left behind by the House F residents, while the latter group reflects the chaos associated with the final abandonment of Nippur. Here, as with the two different sets of texts found in level XA House I (see below), it may be argued that these contracts found in the upper levels of TA may have

[53] One cannot know whether the teaching scribes also worked as contract and other document writers.

[54] The purchaser is the one who would have retained the tablet that recorded the transaction.

been part of the abandonment debris and thus cannot be related to the structure in which they were found. Only in situations where the texts seem to represent an archive, or where they can be directly related to the building in which they were found, is there good reason to believe that these level XA-1 texts were found where they were left by their owners.

Apart from the tablets, all of which were found in locus 184, the level XA house had few finds. A badly worn seal was found in locus 184, and a bronze pin and a miniature pot were found in locus 182. Room 184/189 was decorated with plaques, but unlike the more heroic motifs that adorned the earlier schoolroom, these motifs show that this latter resident's taste ran to the pornographic.

Some changes in plan occurred; in level XA-2, locus 184 had access only through loci 189 or 182, while in level XA-1 it was merged with locus 189 and had a door to the courtyard, locus 192. The significance of this change, however, remains unclear. In general, level XA House F was simply an unassuming domestic structure, quite different in function from the scribal school that preceded it.

House N

House N is a partially excavated structure located north of House F and was probably founded at about the same time, or perhaps a little later. Together Houses F and N closed off the east side of the open area. House N has a coherent plan only in level XI, although it also shows evidence of occupation in level XA. Like House F it was abandoned in XB as a result of the troubles of 1739 B.C., and before its reoccupation in level XA, two of its rooms were used for burials. The house consisted of a courtyard (locus 174), a secondary room which opened onto the courtyard (locus 210, which in level XA is called locus 175), and a probable storage room (locus 202, called locus 183 in level XA) with access only through locus 210 and containing a storage alcove (locus 214). As excavated, the house has no entrance chamber; a street or alleyway must therefore have existed east of the excavated area to provide access.

Although the abandonment of House N during the economic crisis has yielded a rich assortment of objects and tablets in the level XI courtyard, the use of the rest of this structure as a burial ground during level XB effectively destroyed any evidence from the inside of the house. Seven or more infant burials were found cut into level XI loci 214 and 202. These burials, which must have been dug from the bottom of what would have been level XB, suggest the possibility that the crisis of 1739 B.C. was accompanied by an outbreak of epidemic disease or famine that resulted in high infant mortality. The infants buried in House N probably came from families living in those parts of TA that were still occupied during the crisis.

As a result of these burials, only the finds from the courtyard, locus 174, can be considered evidence for the level XI occupation of House N. Fortunately, these finds were very rich and included sizeable archives of tablets from both floors of level XI.[55] The tablets found on the two floors differ from each other in both style and content. Nevertheless, the principals in the two sets of tablets are related, and both archives show how these individuals (one must assume the residents of House N) maintained ties with other residents of TA, including those of House K (see fig. 4 and tables 12 and 13).

The majority of the texts found in the upper level, level XI-1, of locus 174 were loan or rental texts which concerned Mār-erṣetim and Nannatum. In contrast, those from the lower

[55] These floors were originally labeled X-1 (our XI-1) and IX-1 (our XB-1), but the field notes indicate that the floor described as X-1 (our XI-1) was in fact equivalent to X-2 (our XI-2) elsewhere. This evidence suggests that the floor we are calling XI-2 was a true living surface; whereas level XI-1 represents the junk that was left at the time of the 1739 B.C. abandonment.

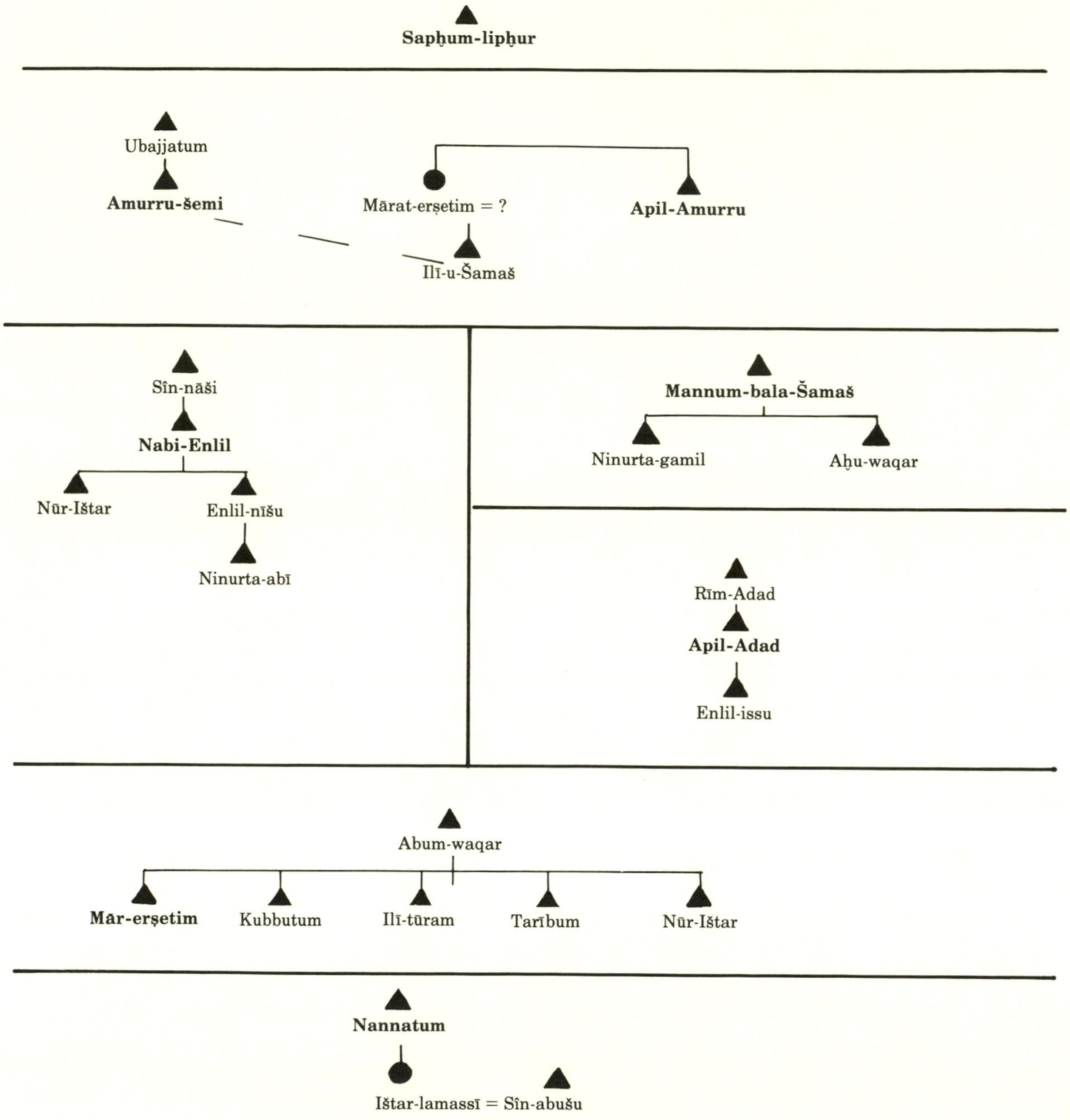

Fig. 4. House N Residents

TABLE 12. The House N Texts

Text	Date	Saphum-liphur	Amurru-šemi	Apil-Amurru	Mār-erṣetim	Nabi-Enlil	Apil-Adad	Nannatum	Mannum-bala-Šamaš	Others	Findspot
Text 18	1786	†									174 XI-2
Text 19	n.d.	†	†								174 XI-2
Text 20	1764	†	†								174 XI-2
Text 21	1764	†	†								174 XI-2
Text 22	1750		†								174 XI-2
Text 23	1745		†								174 XI-2
Text 24	n.d.		†								174 XI-2
Text 25	1743		†	†					†		174 XI-2
Text 26	1743		†	†							174 XI-2
ARN 81	1744			†	†					Imguʾa family	. . .
TIM 4 28	1751				†					Imguʾa family	. . .
Text 27	1750				†						174 XI-1
Text 28	1749				†						174 XI-1
ARN 125	1741				†						. . .
BE 6/2 30	1739				†					Ninlil-zimu family	. . .
PBS 8/2 150	1739				†						. . .
Text 55	n.d.				†	†					179 XA-1
Text 29	1741				†		†				174 XI-1
Text 30	1749–1721					†					174 XI-2
Text 31	1740					†					174 XI-2
Text 54	1743					†	†				179 XA-1
Text 49	1743						†				185 XA-1
Text 50	1742						†				185 XA-1
PBS 8/1 28	1785								†		. . .
Text 32	1740							†			174 XI-1
Text 33	n.d.							†			174 XI-1
Text 34	1739							†			174 XI-2
BE 6/2 42	1737							†			. . .
Text 35	1923–1896										174 XI-2
Text 36	1873–1869										174 XI-2
Text 37	1833–1831										174 XI-2
Text 38	1745										174 XI-2
Text 39	n.d.										174 XI-2
Text 40	n.d.										174 XI-1
Text 41	n.d.									destroyed	174 X-2

TABLE 13. ACTIVITIES OF HOUSE N RESIDENTS

Saphum-liphur	Sale, purchase, and exchange of é ki-šub-ba
Amurru-šemi	Purchase and exchange of é ki-šub-ba, collection of grain for payment, disinheritance
Apil-Amurru	Sale of é ki-šub-ba, receives grain loan
Mār-erṣetim	Lends grain, borrows silver, gives offices, exchanges property, witnesses court case
Nabi-Enlil	Exchanges property, adopts a son, is testator, rents a field, buys é ki-šub-ba
Apil-Adad	Rents property, sells é ki-šub-ba, rents out field and house
Mannum-bala-Šamaš	Sells é ki-šub-ba, gives grain for purchase
Nannatum	Borrows wool, lends grain, betroths daughter, receives offices

level, XI-2, were more often concerned with the permanent exchange of real property. More interesting, however, are the apparently foreign traditions which were reflected in many, but not all, of the level XI-2 texts. Characteristically, these tablets[56] are more angular in shape than most Nippur contracts, with a flatter obverse. They also show use of a different stylus, in that the signs are impressed less deeply and the script is more cursive. The majority of the texts concern the sale or exchange of ruined house property, but in all instances they employ the phrase é ki-šub-ba instead of é KI.KAL or é libir-ra, the terms usually used in Nippur texts. Not only are many of the personal names Akkadian names not otherwise known from Nippur, or indeed from southern Babylonia, but they rarely include the patronymic. The phraseology is also different. The verbal phrase used in most sale texts from Nippur is in-ši-in-ša$_{10}$, but all of these texts omit the second in, rendering the phrase in-ši-ša$_{10}$, as is normal in texts from Ur[57] and sometimes from Isin.[58] The exchange documents (Texts 20 and 21) also use a different formulary, much of the text being written in Akkadian. The oath at the end of the text is more abbreviated than is usual at Nippur, while the text of this type that was found in House I (Text 58) is even more unusual in that the oath, instead of being to an unnamed king, is to the gods Nanna and Utu and to the king Samsuiluna. Finally, unlike the Nippur property transfers where clay bur-gul seals of the sellers were employed, these texts were either sealed with a stone cylinder seal belonging to one of the witnesses or not sealed at all. In sum, this group of tablets differs in prosopography, style, and content from all other Nippur texts, so much so that we may be justified in referring to it as a "foreign" archive and in concluding that the early residents of House N originated from some other part of Mesopotamia, bringing with them their tradition of naming and contract writing.

These unusual texts from level XI-2 were concerned with the sale and exchange of é ki-šub-ba or ruined house property, by Saphum-liphur and Amurru-šemi. It is not clear whether or not this property was in Nippur, although Text 25 strongly suggests that the principals were at least part-time residents of the city. In this text, Amurru-šemi was collecting

[56] The tablets in question are Texts 18–21 and 26. PBS 8/1 28 and Text 58 also share foreign traits, while Texts 24 and 26 concern some of the same people. Text 34 is an unusual text that shares some of the characteristics of the other texts in the "foreign" group. The other texts found in this group, Texts 24, 30–31, 35–39, and 41 appear to be normal Nippur contracts.

[57] Hugo H. Figulla and William J. Martin, *Ur Excavations: Texts V: Letters and Documents of the Old Babylonian Period* (Philadelphia: University of Pennsylvania Press, 1953), texts 131–83.

[58] Charles Jean, "Nouveaux contrats de Larsa," *Revue d'Assyriologie* 26 (1929): texts 1, 2, 4, and 5.

varying amounts of grain from eight people in order to arrive at the sum needed to purchase a house plot (perhaps the same plot as that recorded in Text 26) from Apil-Amurru. Since one of these providers of grain was a *nadītum* of Ninurta, a class of person known only from Nippur, it seems that Nippur residents were concerned in this transaction.

In spite of this reference to a typical Nippur resident, Text 25 remains unique. Not only is it the only text to describe the sources of revenue for a house purchase, but many of the listed donors replace the patronymic with other, often bizarre, forms of identification. One is identified by his mother's name, one by that of his son, one by his father's brother, while a fourth is described simply as a resident of Apil-Amurru's house. In the last case it is possible that his gift of grain was designed to ensure his continued residence in that structure, even after a change in ownership. With the others no such simple explanation is possible unless this text represented collective debt repayment. If so, those described in the normal way may have been repaying debts contracted by themselves, while those with unusual forms of identification, debts contracted by their sons or mothers.[59]

The inheritance document of Nabi-Enlil (Text 31), a more typical Nippur text found in this level, may help to explain the place of origin of this group of outsiders. Part of the estate is a total of 1 sar of house property located in the town of Iaḫalpilum, known from the Old Babylonian itineraries[60] and to be located somewhat to the south of Assur, on the Tigris. Such a northern origin for these foreigners would help to explain their Akkadian names and the frequent use of Akkadian in the texts. However, the formulary used in the sale texts is most similar to that used at Isin[61] and Ur,[62] while the inclusion of the gods Nanna and Utu and of the current king's name in the oath (Text 58) is typical of contracts from southern Mesopotamia.[63] Although these contradictory features make identification of the place of origin of these foreigners difficult (unless one postulates a generalized expatriate population), the interest of Nabi-Enlil and his family in distant Iaḫalpilum cannot but be of significance.

In sum, the group of texts found in level XI-2 of locus 174 appears to have belonged to a group of foreigners living at Nippur. The infrequent use of patronymics inhibits the determination of relationships that might have existed between those whose texts were found in House N, a difficulty not helped by the eclectic nature of the texts themselves. Within this archive are texts which are wholly "foreign" in style, those which are typically Nippurite, and those which seem to be somewhere in between. One must conclude that this mixture resulted from an interaction between imported and local traditions. While the é ki-šub-ba transactions may have concerned property outside Nippur and therefore have retained a foreign style, the local style of the others must reflect an interest on the part of their principals in aspects of the economy of Nippur. The evidence suggests that over time this group became increasingly acculturated.[64]

The texts from the upper level of locus 174, level XI-1, are in some senses quite different from those from the earlier levels, although of the two later residents of House N, one, Nannatum, had one of his texts included in the XI-2 archive, while the other, Mār-erṣetim,

[59] It is therefore possible that Amurru-šemi was a moneylender. Although no extant texts indicate that he had lent grain or silver, Text 23 shows him to have been a borrower of grain. It could be significant that the other lenders of grain and silver documented from Nippur are also recorded as borrowers. Such individuals, then, should be understood as dealers in these commodities, not simply as usurers.

[60] William W. Hallo, "The Road to Emar," *Journal of Cuneiform Studies* 18 (1964): 69–70.

[61] Jean, "Nouveaux contrats."

[62] Figulla and Martin, *Ur Excavations: Texts V*, text 131, for example.

[63] See, for example, Charles Jean, *Contrats de Larsa*, Textes cunéiformes du Louvre, vol. 10 (Paris: Paul Geuthner, 1926), pl. IX.

[64] In those texts in which patronymics were used, and in which either the father's or the son's name was otherwise unattested from Nippur, there are twelve cases of an unknown father's name and only one of an unknown son's name. This might indicate that foreign fathers were giving their sons typical Nippur names.

had had dealings with one of the principals of that earlier group of texts. The evidence suggests that Mār-erṣetim was a dealer in commodities, possibly as an agent of the temple, who also owned some property, including perhaps House N, at Nippur. Mār-erṣetim is recorded as borrowing silver without interest from the god Šamaš and lending grain both with and without interest to other individuals. Four hematite weights found at this level may represent the tools of his trade. In addition to his receiving an interest-free loan from the god Šamaš, two other texts suggest that Mār-erṣetim's activities were not purely personal. In a unique text, *ARN* 125, he redistributes temple offices, while in BE 6/2 30, he joins other officials in witnessing a request for justice by two of the descendants of Ninlil-zimu, members of the family that occupied House K, the dominant building in TA. This makes possible the suggestion that his commercial activities were conducted less as an individual than as an agent of the temple.

The other man whose texts were found in level XI-1 of locus 174 also dealt in commodities and land. In texts 32 and 33 Nannatum, a holder of a nu-èš office, is recorded as the lessee of a field and the borrower of grain; he is also the one person whose affairs were recorded in texts from both floors of this locus. Text 34, found in level XI-2, is yet another unique text which, if interpreted aright, records the betrothal of Nannatum's daughter to Sîn-abušu. The purpose of this written betrothal becomes clear on an examination of BE 6/2 42, where Nannatum receives his son-in-law's gala offices and his inheritance until his son-in-law's death. This betrothal must have been recorded on clay in order to establish the basis for the extraordinary transaction recorded in BE 6/2 42.

In addition to this clear evidence of continuity between the residents of House N in both floors of level XI, the tablets from level XI-1 show that Mār-erṣetim and Nannatum, the residents of House N at the time of the 1739 B.C. crisis, also maintained ties with their neighbors in House I (see below). Patterns of shared witnesses indicate a connection between the residents of House N and Ipqu-Enlil, a middleman involved in House I transactions. This link, due perhaps in part to both Ipqu-Enlil and Nannatum holding nu-èš offices, may help to explain the discovery of a text of the House N type in one of the rooms of House I. More importantly, however, taken together with the fact that Mār-erṣetim witnessed a text of the Ninlil-zimu family living in House K, these texts demonstrate the degree to which the residents of TA shared economic concerns.

One may conclude that House N was occupied by an immigrant group, who became intimately involved in the economic affairs of Nippur, and especially of TA. They were some of the first to build in the open area fronting House K; together with House F, House N closed off the east side. They were probably primarily involved in the lending of silver and barley, but also dealt in real property. The earliest residents of House N, those whose texts show most obvious foreign influence, seem to have been quite isolated, but by 1739 B.C. the household had become acculturated and was thoroughly involved in the affairs of the city. Their tie, albeit tenuous, with the inhabitants of House K may indicate that they first came to Nippur as a result of the Ninlil-zimu family's patronage; while that with a resident of House I may be related to their ownership of similar offices. In spite of these ties, House N was abandoned at the time of the crisis and was used for infant burial. It was later rebuilt, but its residents have left no evidence of their concerns.

House I

House I, together with Houses H and G, was first built somewhat later than Houses F and N. With the construction of these buildings, TA ceased to be characterized by open space; Houses G, H, and I reduced what had once been a sizeable plaza to a T-intersection.

The tablets found in House I have done more for our understanding of the organization of domestic space than any other texts. Elsewhere[65] I have explored in detail the implications of the architecture of House I and its associated artifacts; here I will confine myself to summarizing those findings where they are relevant to understanding the architectural and occupational history of the building and its relationship to other buildings in TA.

The stratigraphy of House I, coupled with the documentary evidence, illustrates the pitfalls inherent in the assignment of levels to a whole excavation instead of on a locus-by-locus basis. The stratigraphic evidence from Houses F and N shows clearly that this area was abandoned in level IX, and the documentary evidence found in House I indicates that the structure was in existence by 1742 B.C., which should coincide with level XI, and that it was neglected between 1738 and 1734 B.C., equivalent to level XB. The excavators though, in keeping with their overall view of the area, recorded the existence of living floors in what is called here level XB-1 and all three floors of XA. In the absence of any field notes discussing the remains which they had called level IX (equals level XB in this publication), it seems appropriate to reassess the level designations, changing a scheme which has the building occupied only after 1739 B.C. to one where it is occupied from 1750 and 1720 B.C., with a period of semiabandonment in the middle. This latter scheme required some alterations to the level designations as assigned in the field (see Appendix I).

House I and its observable architectural modifications can be correlated with information contained in six of the contracts which were found within it.[66] Details of the transactional history of House I are contained in plates 25 and 26 and in table 14. Having accepted the idea that the texts in question (Texts 42–47) refer to House I (see tables 14 and 15), it is possible to reconstruct events as follows: In 1742 B.C., at the death of Ilum-nāši, House I was divided amongst his four sons, Enlil-mansum, Ṭāb-balāṭum, Ur-dukuga, and Enlil-galzu. The first and third sons apparently had little use for this property, since shortly after this Ṭāb-balāṭum was in possession of Enlil-mansum's share, and Enlil-galzu had that of Ur-dukuga. In 1738 B.C., during the economic crisis, Ṭāb-balāṭum sold his double share to an outsider, Ipqu-Enlil, leaving Enlil-galzu as the only original heir still holding a section of House I. Although Enlil-galzu and Ipqu-Enlil maintained their ownership of the building for the next four years, the worst of the crisis period, the archaeological evidence, such as it is, suggests that the building was not occupied. However, around 1734 B.C. it was renovated, probably at the same time as House H was built (see below), and Ipqu-Enlil sold one room of his share to Enlil-nīšu and Etel-pî-Ištar, the new neighbors living in House H. However, Enlil-galzu, the remaining original heir, owned the property that separated House H from that part of House I owned by Ipqu-Enlil. In order to sell the rest of his part of the house, Ipqu-Enlil effected an exchange of plots with Enlil-galzu and immediately afterwards sold all of his property to the owners of House H. The final transaction, dating to 1732 B.C., records a dissolution of the partnership of the brothers Enlil-nīšu and Etel-pî-Ištar which left one in possession of House H and the other with their holdings in House I.[67]

The tablets upon which the previous reconstruction was based were found in two different rooms. Texts 46–47 were found in locus 185, while Texts 42–45 came from locus 178. The field notes, however, suggest that these texts were all originally part of a single cache, but that they had spilled through the door between loci 178 and 185. Both loci, as is to be expected, were part of the house that was finally acquired by the owners of House H.

Several other texts, mostly contracts, were also found in locus 185. The field rental, Text 51, was apparently another text belonging to Etel-pî-Ištar, the final owner of this part of

[65] Stone, "Texts, Architecture and Ethnographic Analogy."
[66] Ibid.
[67] For more details see ibid.

TABLE 14. The House I Transactions

Date	Text	Enlil-mansum	Ṭāb-balāṭum	Ur-dukuga	Enlil-galzu	Ipqu-Enlil	Enlil-nīšu	Etel-pî-Ištar	Price (shekels per gín)
1742/4/20	Text 42	157 + 173 (31 gín)	178 + 185 (19 gín)	179a + 179b + 155 (19 gín)	152 (19 gín)				inheritance
		157 + 173 (31 gín) - - - →		179a + 179b + 155 (19 gín) - - →					
1738/5/18	Text 43		157 + 173 + 178 + 185 (50 gín) ——→						0.120
1734/ - /2	Text 44					173 (20 gín) ——→			?
1733/3/ -	Text 45				179a + 179b → (10 gín) ←	157 (10 gín)			Ipqu-Enlil pays extra 0.050
1733/3/ -	Text 46					179a + 179b (10 gín) ——→			0.117
						178 + 185 (20 gín) - - - →			. . .
1732/5/25	Text 47						←½ (173 + 178 + 185 + 179a + 179b) (25 gín)		0.107

Note: Broken lines indicate transactions inferred from, but not directly evidenced by, the textual record.

House I, as may have been Text 52, which is now completely illegible. The other texts found in this room, as well as those found in locus 179, cannot be so easily associated with House I. Indeed, these texts, three from locus 185 (Texts 48–50)[68] and three from locus 179 Texts 53–55), are closely related to texts found in the neighboring House N (see above). These tablets mostly concern the activities of Apil-Adad (and his father Rīm-Adad) and Nabi-Enlil, both of whom are principals in texts found in House N. This relationship is seen most clearly in the texts from locus 179: Text 55 concerns Mār-erṣetim, a resident of House N, while Text 54 is written in a style known only from that building. Since the witnessing patterns of the tablets which describe the sale of House I suggest that the middleman in these transactions, Ipqu-Enlil, may have had some economic ties with the residents of House N, it is possible that the unrelated House I texts may have been deposited originally during Ipqu-Enlil's ownership of the structure.

However, even if these spurious tablets were deposited first by Ipqu-Enlil, this does not explain their discovery in the latest occupation level of the building, a level that should date to 1720 B.C., more than ten years after he had sold his interest in that structure. Explanations for this do not come easily; perhaps these tablets simply testify to the chaotic conditions which must have accompanied the final abandonment of the city, conditions which may have been accompanied by some looting. But it is also possible that the chronological disconformity may be more the result of some confusion in the recording of the levels in House I.

House H

Although House H is the structure which can be associated with Etel-pî-Ištar and Enlil-nīšu, the final purchasers of much of House I, no tablets which concern their activities were found there. This is probably because the tablets which recorded the House I transactions remained the property of the brother that retained ownership of that house, Etel-pî-Ištar, rather than of the brother who stayed in House H, Enlil-nīšu. Instead, the texts found in House H apparently concern those who lived in this part of TA before 1739 B.C. These texts are said to come from the lowest floor of level XA, which should be dated to around 1734 B.C., the date of the rebuilding of the house by Etel-pî-Ištar and Enlil-nīšu. It is possible, however, that they really belonged to the level XI occupation but were mistakenly thought to have come from the upper level.[69]

Very little is known about House H in the earliest levels because when it was rebuilt around 1734 B.C., its deep foundations destroyed all traces of the previous building.[70] Although it may have been larger before, in level XA House H was a very modest structure consisting of only three rooms and a courtyard. Nevertheless, it was built with some care. Both the

[68] Texts 48 and 50 were found on the day before Texts 46 and 47, suggesting that the latter were near the door of locus 178, where the other House I texts were, and Texts 48 and 50 were in some other part of the room.

[69] It is clear from the field notes that the levels as excavated were based more on rough perceptions of architectural continuity than on the identification of true living floors. In these circumstances, confusion is easily possible between materials that belonged to one floor and those from the preceding or succeeding level. In this instance the picture is further complicated by the deep foundations of the level XA reconstruction, which largely destroyed all previous building. In most instances the confusion experienced makes little difference in our understanding of the occupational history of Nippur, but in cases like this one, where we are postulating a hiatus in occupation and a change of ownership, small stratigraphic differences can take on a greater significance. If the finds from level XA-3 House H had failed to show both internal consistency and a pattern congruent with their originating from a level XI House H, I would have dismissed them as from dubious context, but I find the pattern to be too consistent for that. Consequently, I will treat these level XA-3 finds as evidence for level XI occupation, and leave open the question of how they came to be found in level XA-3.

[70] The neighboring House G has shallower level XA foundations. Consequently, a few traces of what may have been a level XI House G/H remain.

TABLE 15. THE AREAS OF THE LOCI IN HOUSE I

Locus	Area (m^2)	Area (gín)
157	7.55	12.84
173	10.64	18.09
178	7.02	11.94
185	5.85	9.95
179a	2.55	4.34
179b	4.00	6.80
155	6.04	10.27
152a	8.80	14.96
Total	52.45	89.19
155 + 152a + 157	22.39	38.07
173 + 178 + 185 + 179a + 179b	30.06	51.12
Area of house I recorded in text 42	. . .	88.00

courtyard (locus 187) and the entrance chamber (locus 176) were paved, while the doors in the house featured baked-brick sills, jambs, and door sockets. Although these features were not unknown in other TA houses, only in House H were they so well preserved.

Although the artifactual inventory was neither plentiful nor noteworthy, clay tablets were found in each of the rooms and in the courtyard of House H, most of which (12 texts) were school fragments. Most of these tablets were found in level XA-3 and may have originated in earlier levels (see above), including the three contracts which were found in loci 180, 187, 176. The tablet found in the courtyard (locus 187) is the most enigmatic. This text, Text 57, is a silver loan which unfortunately omits all patronymics. The loan took place in 1755 B.C., and the name of the lender, Lipit-Ištar, is a quite common name at Nippur. If he could be identified with the Lipit-Ištar, son of Imgur-Ninurta, known as a buyer and seller of field property in TIM 4 texts 24 and 25, then it is possible that he was the elder brother of Etel-pî-Ištar and Enlil-nīšu, the final owners of House H. But this remains mere speculation in view of the facts that the TIM 4 tablets rarely show connections with the TA texts, that money-lenders are not usually property owners, and that without patronymics clear identification is impossible.

More interesting and informative are Text 58 (1762 B.C.) from locus 180 and Text 59 (1739 B.C.) from locus 176. These two tablets were clearly left over from the previous inhabitants of this structure, the family of Sîn-magir.[71] Little is left of Text 58, but the seal impression indicates that the principals in this text were Sîn-magir's wife and daughter. In Text 59 Sîn-magir's son Imgur-Sîn rents a field at the time of the economic crisis.

Although these texts alone tell us little of the relationship between this family and other occupants of TA, the witnesses in Text 58 and the principals in Text 59 link them to other texts describing the activities of the same family. In a text dating to 1755 B.C., *ARN* 70, another son of Sîn-magir, Iddin-Ninurta, a nu-èš like many other residents of TA, exchanged field plots with Enlil-dingir, a member of the Ninlil-zimu family associated with House K. In a text written four years later, OIMA 1 12, this same individual exchanges kislaḫ with Ekur-

[71] It is the discovery of two tablets concerned with the activities of the same family but found at opposite ends of the same house that suggests that these tablets were found in context.

TABLE 16. THE AREAS OF THE LOCI IN HOUSE G

Locus	Area (m^2)	Area (gín)
181	9.24	15.72
190	7.26	12.34
Total	16.50	28.06

andul, a member of one of the junior branches of that family. These texts indicate that these early residents of House H, like those of House N, had clear ties with the dominant Ninlil-zimu lineage.

Further interconnections between residents of the TA area can also be discovered through an examination of the witnesses and neighbors recorded in *ARN* 70 and OIMA 1 12. In addition to Bēl-šunu, who witnessed both texts and text 58 (found in House H), *ARN* 70 records Ibbi-Enlil as a witness. This same individual witnessed Text 34, a text belonging to Nannatum, the nu-èš who occupied House N. Finally, demonstrating that Sîn-magir's family were indeed the pre-crisis owners of House H, OIMA 1 12 records Ilum-nāši as the neighbor of Iddin-Ninurta; Ilum-nāši was the original owner of House I, the house adjoining House H.[72]

It is not easy to summarize the occupational history of House H, but the evidence suggests the following account: House H, probably a large structure that included the area later occupied by House G, was first built by Sîn-magir in the early years of Hammurabi. At Sîn-magir's death the area later occupied by House G went to Iddin-Ninurta, while House H itself when to another son, Imgur-Sîn. Iddin-Ninurta allowed his share to fall into disrepair and exchanged it for a larger plot elsewhere with Ekur-andul.[73] As with Text 42 from House I, the areas of roofed floor space in House G approximate the half sar of kislaḫ recorded in OIMA 1 12 (see table 16). House H, meanwhile, probably remained in the hands of his brother Imgur-Sîn until the events of 1739 B.C. drove him from Nippur. Five years later, Enlil-nīšu and Etel-pî-Ištar rebuilt the structure, in the process destroying much of the evidence of the earlier building.

Throughout, the texts associated with House H suggest a close relationship between Sîn-magir's family and other residents of TA, especially with the Ninlil-zimu family, who occupied the large House K. The ties between the residents of Houses H, I, N, and K suggest that before the 1739 B.C. crisis interrupted both settlement and economic networks, the residents of TA maintained close economic ties, some of which may reflect ties of kinship which cannot yet be reconstructed completely.

HOUSE G

In the discussion of House H, it has been suggested that House G was founded late in level XI and that it originally formed part of a single structure with House H. It seems likely

[72] Since the name Ilum-nāši is very rare at Nippur, occurring in only one other context, it seems unlikely that we are dealing here with two individuals of the same name.

[73] OIMA 1 12 indicates that the plot Iddin-Ninurta received was located next door to one that he already owned. This suggests that he owned two plots, one of which was House G. This text therefore records the disposing of House G in order to attain a larger plot elsewhere. His ownership of this second plot may indicate why Iddin-Ninurta allowed House G to fall into disrepair.

that the House G section of the building was left in disrepair for longer than the House H part. Indeed, OIMA 1 12 implies that by 1751 B.C. House G was no longer maintained as a place of residence. Although the level XA foundations have destroyed much of the level XI remains, it appears that reconstruction of House G did not take place until after the rebuilding of House H in 1734 B.C. Although architectural details are well preserved for level XA House G, artifacts are not. Consequently, information is lacking which might tell us whether the structure was still occupied by the branch of the Ninlil-zimu family that had bought it in 1751 B.C.

House G consisted of a living room in the rear (locus 181), a courtyard (locus 188), and a small entrance chamber (locus 190). The house probably was occupied only in level XA floors 2 and 3, with floor 1 simply representing the decay of the structure. Level XA-3 was the earliest level in the rebuilding, but yielded few finds other than a few school tablets, which occurred in all rooms. As in House H, some of these tablets may belong to level XI, and some perhaps originated in the neighboring House F, which served as a scribal school at that time (see above). However, one account tablet said to be from this level was dated to Samsuiluna 27 (1723 B.C.), shortly before the final abandonment of the city. The remains from level XA-3 should therefore be considered to represent occupational debris in the house, with level XA-2 as the abandonment level. The general paucity of objects and features associated with level XA-3 may be considered the result of continuous occupation, while the good preservation of features and the larger artifactual inventory of level XA-2 must be due to the abrupt abandonment of the house at that time.

In level XA-3, the entrance chamber (locus 190) had a bench running around the three sides away from the doors, while in the courtyard (locus 188) a stairway to the roof was built which arched up and over the bread oven. This staircase continued in use through level XA-2 when, presumably at the time of the abandonment of the house, three infant burials were placed beneath its overhang, cutting into the earlier bread oven. It has been suggested earlier that the infant burials in House N might indicate that epidemic disease or famine accompanied the economic crisis of 1739 B.C.; perhaps these burials in House G indicate that the abandonment of the city in 1720 B.C. might also have been associated with high infant mortality. Both of these upheavals are also reflected in scattered domestic items left behind in House G. Pottery, a whetstone, weights, and the like remain from the later level, while, in spite of the paucity of undisturbed remains from level XI, pottery, school tablets, and no less than four spindle whorls (or model chariot wheels) were found. Unfortunately, since none of the tablets found in the structure refer to its inhabitants, no further conclusions are possible.

House E

House E was the last house to be constructed in TA. Unlike the other houses in the area, it had to conform to the available space, molding itself against the irregular north walls of Houses N and I and sprawling lengthwise in order to accommodate a street between it and House K. House E appears to have been continuously occupied from about the time of the accession of Samsuiluna, or a little after (around 1750–1740 B.C.), until shortly before the final abandonment of Nippur in 1720 B.C., a period of less than thirty years. Unlike most of the other houses in the eastern part of TA, House E shows no evidence of hasty abandonment. It was one of the few houses to be occupied during the crisis of 1739 B.C., and when its inhabitants left the house for good, they did so in an orderly manner several years before whatever cataclysm depopulated Nippur in 1720 B.C. Since the final level of House E predates the final abandonment of the city, it is impossible to tell whether the objects associated with this upper level were left by its occupants or whether they represent the trash thrown away by the residents of neighboring houses. In any event the number of such objects is small.

Throughout most of its history, House E exhibited a fairly standard plan, albeit elongated. A small entrance chamber led into a courtyard, which in turn gave on to a living room on the far side and to a small subsidiary room next to the entrance chamber. This plan was maintained except for a short time in level XB, when the entrance shifted and was by way of the courtyard. Above, I mentioned the possibility that direct entrance via the courtyard might have been associated with urban animal husbandry. It is possible that this was the case here; certainly the keeping of animals during a period of uncertainty would have served to broaden the economic base of the family concerned. However, it must be stressed that in this instance, since at that time the neighboring House I was probably unoccupied, the position of the entrance may have been changed to allow the residents to avoid the depressing sight of decaying mud brick.

The finds from House E, as indicated earlier, were meager. A few figurines and plaques were found, mostly in the courtyard (locus 153), and a hematite cylinder seal, well-made and largely unworn (OIP 78, pl. 112:14), was found in level XB of this same court. The seal identifies its owner as Maṣija, the daughter of Sîn-erībam. Since House E shows evidence of continuous occupation, it may be assumed that this seal was deposited, presumably by accident, during a period of normal occupation, indicating perhaps that Maṣija was one of House E's residents. Since personalized cylinder seals such as this one are rare at Nippur both as excavated artifacts and as seal impressions on tablets, this seal probably belonged to a person of some importance. The name Maṣija is not otherwise attested at Nippur, while her father's name, Sîn-erībam, is too common to allow identification. Since she is a woman, it is possible that Maṣija was a *nadītum,* although if such were the case, one would normally expect the seal to so identify her. Nevertheless, despite these difficulties, if this seal implies that House E was occupied by a woman of sufficient importance to have had her own seal, this may explain why House E continued to be occupied throughout the economic crisis. Furthermore, if Maṣija were a *nadītum,* and therefore unmarried, the modest size of House E might be related to the small size of her household, and should not be taken as an indication of poverty.

Of the two tablets found in House E, one was a small school tablet and one a contract, Text 60. Both were found towards the top of level XA, in contexts such that they might have been thrown into the house with some trash. Text 60 is a contract in which a Sîn-imguranni and an Apil-Adad agree on the responsibility for cultivating two fields. Sîn-imguranni has no patronymic and therefore cannot be related to any other individual of that name, but it is just possible that this Apil-Adad was the same as the father of Enlil-issu and Nabi-Enlil who had dealings with Mār-erṣetim, a resident of House N. Such an identification, however, is purely speculative and, if this text were deposited after Maṣija had left the house, does not relate to the occupation of that building.

Conclusions

The textual, architectural, and artifactual evidence from TA indicates that this area, perhaps from the beginning, was occupied by small property owners. These inhabitants of TA seem generally to have built their houses without the aid of architects, often using the old wall stubs for foundations. In spite of the continuity in property lines that resulted from this practice and from traditional patterns of ownership, both major events in Nippur's history and small-scale changes effected through sale of exchange modified the character of TA over time.

Although a deep sounding uncovered fragments of earlier architecture, the earliest levels to show a coherent plan date to the early Isin-Larsa period. These early houses differ from those which succeeded them in that the door to the street provided access directly to the courtyard. The large amount of organic material found in House Q supports the view that courtyards without entrance chambers might have been used for keeping animals. Certainly the few contracts which mention animals are generally early in date. Animals may have been kept by Nippur residents during the Isin-Larsa period because warfare and unrest outside the walls occasionally made grazing a dangerous occupation and meat delivery impossible.

The literary composition entitled the "Lamentation over the Destruction of Nippur" indicates that at one time, during the reign of Išme-Dagan, active warfare penetrated the city itself. Testimony of this may be found in the burials dug into the level XIII houses. Intramural burial was unusual in Nippur in the Isin-Larsa and Old Babylonian periods and seems to occur only in time of crisis. The evidence suggests that much of the city was damaged and many people killed, but that those who survived buried their dead and rebuilt their houses along much the same lines as before.

I have suggested earlier that this attack on Nippur might not represent an incursion by a foreign city, but rather raiding by the rural population. I have further suggested that this problem of rural-urban friction might have been solved by the co-opting of the leaders of these rural, tribal groups by the royal powers. This is perhaps evidenced in Level XIIA TA, where the entire area was razed and given over to the Ninlil-zimu family, one of the most important lineages whose activities are reflected in the Isin-Larsa and Old Babylonian texts. If my reconstruction is correct, this family had been one of the foci of rural unrest. To stem future rebellion, the king moved them to the city, provided them with a large area of urban real estate, and co-opted the leaders with gifts of real estate and temple offices. In TA, this is characterized by an obliteration of earlier occupation and the founding of House K, the only architect-built structure, and the largest one, known from TA in the early second millennium B.C. The rest of TA remained open space.

In terminal Isin-Larsa and early Old Babylonian times, represented by level XI of TA, this open space began slowly to fill in. The earliest houses to be built seem to have been those serving special functions that might have been of use to the Ninlil-zimu family. At least some of the area to the west of the street, for example, contained shops. House P had a large enough number of bread ovens to serve as a bakery. No evidence ties the residents of this western area of TA directly to the lineage whose leadership occupied House K, but none excludes such a relationship. They may have been lineage members whose land holdings were so small that their activities did not need to be recorded in writing.

At about the same time, in the southeast, House F was built to serve as a scribal school. Although a single scribe may have lived in this building, all rooms show evidence of his teaching activities. The scribal school was abandoned in 1739 B.C., and although scattered school texts were found in the upper levels, there is no evidence for scribal schools from post-crisis Nippur.

At about the same time as the construction of House F, House N was founded, apparently by a group of outsiders who had taken up residence at Nippur during the reign of Rīm-Sîn. Their early texts suggest a somewhat isolated community, but by 1739 B.C. this group had become assimilated and developed clear ties with the members of the Ninlil-zimu lineage and other residents of TA. Although some of these ties may have been formed through marriage or adoption, it seems most likely that commercial transactions were the basis of most of these links.

While Houses P, F, and N were probably built by patrons of the Ninlil-zimu family, in the case of those which were founded later (Houses G, H, I, and E), the situation is less clear. These houses were purely domestic structures, occupied by individuals who cannot be shown to be members or patrons of the Ninlil-zimu family. It may not be coincidental that the founding of these houses is relatively late, after the time when Hammurabi began his campaign to undermine the influence of the Nippur lineages. Nevertheless, the influence of

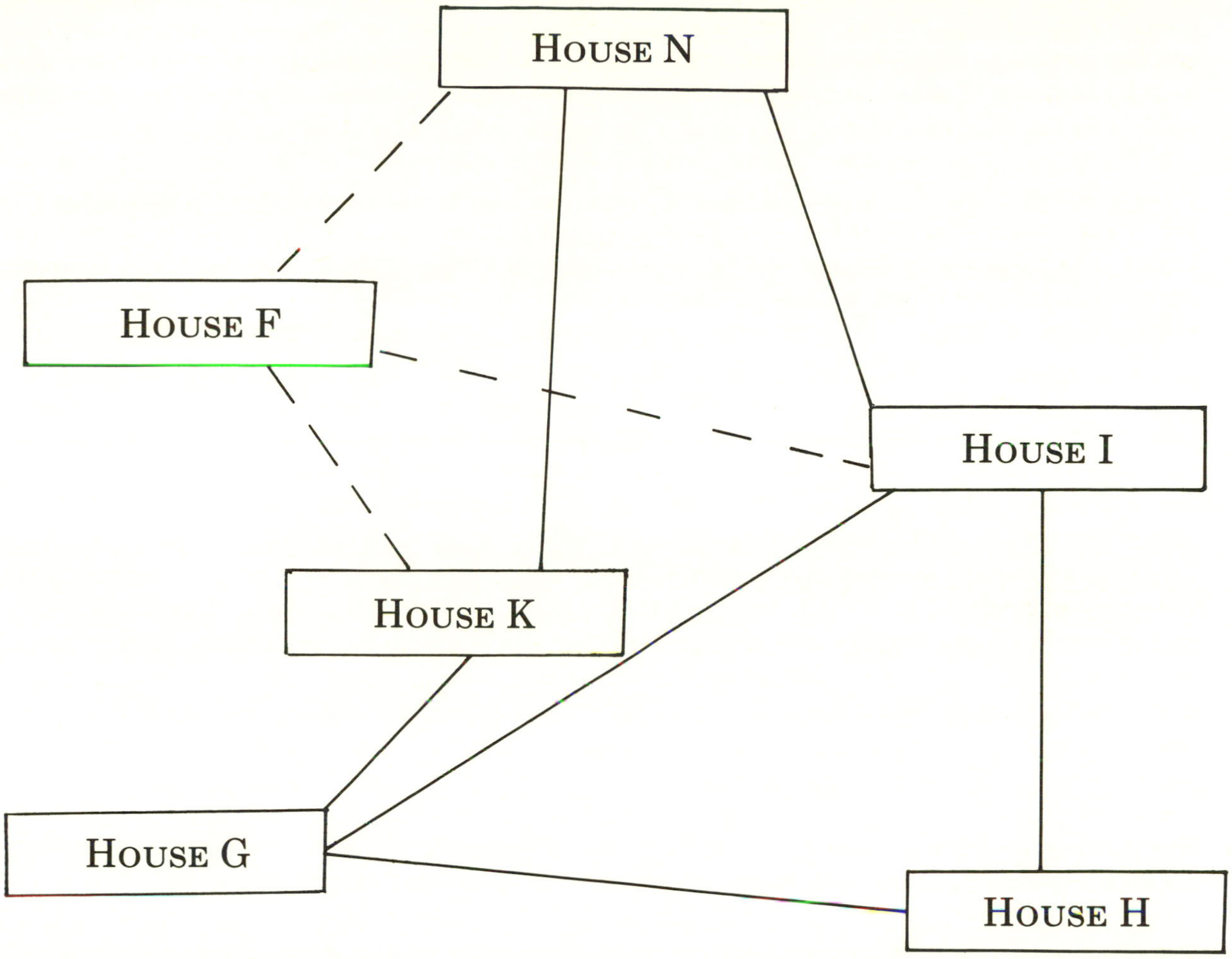

Fig. 5. Interconnections between TA Residents

the residents of House K is clear. As demonstrated by figure 5, the residents of TA maintained close economic ties. Indeed, when the owner of House G was looking for a buyer for his property, it was a distant member of the Ninlil-zimu family who was the purchaser.

An examination of level XI TA reveals a pattern which is significantly different from that seen in the early levels. First, entrance to the houses is no longer by way of a courtyard but is through a small entrance chamber. At the same time, the antechamber attached to the levels XIII and XIIB living rooms is no longer present. Presumably the entrance chamber now served the same function of isolating the family from strangers as the antechamber had done before. Secondly, unlike the early houses, which closely resembled each other in size, organization, and associated finds, the level XI houses show significant differences. While House K was a large, well-built structure with a separate kitchen and a brick stairway to the roof, many of the other houses in TA were much smaller. House G, for example, probably owned by a minor branch of the family, consisted of only an entrance chamber, a courtyard, and a living room, clearly quite a modest structure. Furthermore, the finds from the larger, better-appointed houses generally included more luxury items than did those from the smaller houses. Here it seems that the wealth differences seen in the textual record were mirrored in the differences in size, quality, and appointments of the houses in TA.

The economic crisis of 1739 B.C. was marked by falling real estate prices, hasty sales, and the partial abandonment of TA. Those who were rich enough, like the residents of House K, or who served essential functions, like the baker in House P, remained in the city, while many of the others, including the scribe who ran the school in House F, disappeared. With this second crisis came another set of burials, but this time they were multiple infant burials with few grave goods.

When economic conditions improved some six years later, TA was fully reoccupied. The new occupants were very different from their predecessors. Most striking in the level XA data is the change in the role of House K. Its occupants no longer dominate the area, and the character of the building itself suggests that it had ceased to serve as a residence. Indeed, although all houses were now occupied, and although evidence on the activities of their residents is plentiful, the ties that bound TA together in the earlier levels no longer existed. It is possible that similar ties would have been established with time, but Nippur's days were numbered. In 1720 B.C. it was abandoned. The residents left many objects, especially pottery and tablets, in their houses, and again buried their infant dead. If this abandonment was triggered by a crisis similar to that which occurred two decades earlier, this time its effects were permanent; Nippur served only as a burial ground for nomadic groups for several centuries and was not reoccupied until late in the Kassite period.

In general, TA was an area occupied by private property owners. Most of the changes in social and economic organization seen in texts from the city of Nippur as a whole are reflected in the archaeology of TA. The only significant event not so reflected is the rise and fall of the *nadītum*s, but this is not unexpected since the Ninlil-zimu family, who dominated the area, did not participate in that institution. The archaeological data from TA have supplemented the information available from the texts. The advent of the lineages as urban territorial units and the increasing polarization of wealth that followed were reflected on the ground. The same data illustrate how the crisis of 1739 B.C. affected different population groups and how it transformed the social fabric. In sum, as it details the organization of a small residential area, TA serves as a microcosm for the study of changes which affected all of Isin-Larsa and Old Babylonian Nippur.

Chapter 4

TB

TB, lying some 30 to 40 m to the east of TA, was located at the base of an area which had been excavated in the nineteenth century by the University of Pennsylvania. These earlier excavations had removed much of the later overburden, making possible the uncovery of early levels which could not be reached in TA. Much of the upper Old Babylonian levels in TB had already been removed, but this allowed the excavators to reach Ur III and earlier levels over a fairly wide area. Whereas in TA it was the later Old Babylonian levels that had the best exposure, in TB the earlier Isin-Larsa levels provide most of the data with which we are concerned.

THE STRATIGRAPHY

The stratigraphy of TB, unlike that of TA, needs little reorganization. The publication (OIP 78) followed the stratigraphy that, with the exception of a few alterations, had already been proposed in the field. Furthermore, the staffing problems that resulted in loose supervision and scanty note-taking in the third season (when the Old Babylonian levels in TA were uncovered) were not a major factor in the second season. Consequently, the stratigraphic assessment presented here differs little from that in OIP 78. The changes suggested here are quite minor: First, as was the case in TA, the labeling of foundations has been altered. Where in the publication foundations were given the designations of the levels into which they were cut, here they bear those of the occupation levels with which they should be associated—that is, the levels from which they were dug. Second, in some instances, locus designations have been consolidated; where a number of locus numbers were used to define a large open space or a street, without the existence of any clear boundaries between loci, it seemed more useful to use only a single focus designation (see Appendix I).

There remains one area where the stratigraphic changes proposed here are more substantial. One structure, House F, had levels which were called IV-high in the field notes. In OIP 78 these levels, along with the lower levels that the field notes describe as IV-1, were all called IV-1. Since there existed architectural continuity between levels designated III-1 and IV-high in the field notes, since these IV-high levels were considerably higher in elevation than the other IV-1 levels, since the field notes contain no reference to the existence of any III-2 levels in the affected loci, and since the tablets and ceramics from these levels seem largely contemporary with those found in level III and later than those from the rest of level IV, the designation of these levels has been changed from IV-high to III-2 in this volume (see Appendix I).

In spite of the lack of serious stratigraphic problems encountered in considering the TB material, and in spite of the greater detail of the TB notes, many of the same difficulties arose when approaching the TB material as had been encountered in the case of TA. First, in almost all instances architectural details (such as wall bonding) which would allow a better understanding of the constructional history of the area are still lacking. Second, the greater detail of the TB notes makes it clear that level designations, especially of objects, should be taken only as rough estimates. Much of the time the notes state, "we seem to be between levels." The result of this rough-and-ready approach to stratigraphy is a considerable variability in floor elevations; it is common to find that elevations for two connecting rooms may differ by as much as 40 cm. Such discrepancies can be explained by assuming that the excavators, having dug through the actual floor, recorded the elevation of the point at which they stopped work. My own experience at Nippur had made me aware of the difficulty encountered in identifying floors at that site, presumably the result of the use in antiquity of reed mats as substitutes for prepared and plastered floors. The TB notes confirm what was suspected for TA, that floor level designations represent only rough indications of true findspots. To conclude on a more optimistic note, though, the TB notes contain much information in the form of drawings and detailed descriptions that was not only not available for TA but also never included in OIP 78.

TB GENERAL

Probably the most interesting result of this study is the discovery that TA and TB do not represent similar domestic areas. TA, with its unplanned architecture and many private documents, seems to have been an area occupied by small property owners, but TB, with planned architecture and many administrative documents, was apparently the residential quarter for landless employees of the state. Indeed, as is shown in table 17, no contracts which indicate the ownership of property (inheritance and sale texts) were found in TB levels III to I.[1] Those contracts which did come to light were all rentals, loans, or adoptions, contracts which do not necessarily imply property ownership on the part of the holder of the text. Whereas in TA no administrative documents or temple accounts were found, they were quite plentiful in TB. If those accounts whose public nature is not specifically stated in the tablet catalog are included, administrative and account texts make up some 25% of the tablets from the Isin-Larsa and Old Babylonian levels of TB.

An overview of both the TB architecture (see pls. 27–34, and OIP 78, pls. 58–64) and the associated texts (see table 17) suggests that the character of TB changed over time. In the Ur III period it was an area of public buildings serving public functions.[2] In the Isin-Larsa period, these public functions continued, but, with time, the structures which housed these activities took on an increasingly domestic appearance. By the Old Babylonian period, TB was occupied by bureaucrats who transacted their business in domestic structures presumably provided by their employers. By the end of this period, some of the bureaucrats had apparently been able to break into the property-owning group, as witnessed by the Atta archive.

The following detailed discussion of the TB evidence takes into account not only these changes in the organization of the TB neighborhood, but also the ways in which the differences in the populations of TA and TB were reflected in differences in the archaeological record. Two observations may be made with reference to TB as a whole. First, the TB structures are of more regular and permanent construction than those of TA. The walls meet at close to right angles, baked-brick is frequently used in foundations (damp courses), sills, and jambs,

[1] The Atta archive, which was found in level E, is an exception (see Albrecht Goetze, "The Archive of Ātta from Nippur," *Journal of Cuneiform Studies* 18 [1964]; and below).

[2] Although this volume is not immediately concerned with the Ur III period, in TB there exists continuity between the Ur III levels and the Isin-Larsa material which is the subject of this work, and therefore, it seems appropriate to take the Ur III information into consideration in our discussion of change in this urban setting.

TABLE 17. TB TEXTS

Type of Text	Level D	E	I	II	III
Contract indicating property ownership	0	24	0	0	0
Contract not indicating property ownership	2	1	5	3	0
Letter	1	0	2	1	2
Account	0	6	20	9	1
Temple account	0	1	4	2	44
Administrative	0	2	2	1	0
School (literary, lexical, etc.)	12	32	43	103	12
Miscellaneous	0	4	0	5	0
Ur III	0	2	4	2	4

and the houses bear a close resemblance to house plans which have been found scratched into clay tablets.[3] These features suggest that the TB houses were built by professional—or at least experienced—architects.

The second observation that can be made is that the effects of the economic crisis of 1739 B.C. were more subtle in TB than in TA. Although the excavation of much of the relevant levels of TB took place in the 1890s, the scraps that do survive do not show the sharp break in settlement and in scribal activities noted for TA. Instead, the TB evidence suggests a continuity of settlement and merely a slow decrease in scribal activities. Such a pattern is to be expected in an area where the occupants had close ties to the large, more stable, state institutions. In TA where these ties were less direct, the effects of economic uncertainty were felt more strongly.

In the following pages a house-by-house discussion of the remains from TB will be presented. Since in this area no clear succession of construction can be ascertained, the discussion will begin in the southwest and move clockwise around the area. Level III remains, however, will be discussed separately at the beginning since the basic pattern of settlement in TB was not established until level II.

LEVEL III

With the exception of House V, the basic plan of Isin-Larsa and Old Babylonian TB was not established until level II. Level III seems to represent a period of transition between the Ur III public architecture and the more private buildings which characterized the Old Babylonian period. Much of level III, though, was badly disturbed by the foundations of later structures, and even Area C, underlying the later House C, may have been affected by this later phase of construction. Only in the south are there undisturbed remains; House F in level III floor 2 and House E in floor 1 were both found in a relatively good state of preservation.

Level III is the earliest level that can be considered Isin-Larsa in date, with the ceramics and texts from level IV suggesting a terminal Ur III occupation. The many changes in plan and organization of TB seen in levels V through II suggest that the transition from Ur III to Isin-Larsa resulted in numerous shifts in the organization of this, apparently administrative,

[3] See OIP 78, pl. 52.

area. Though the simple passage of time could account for the accumulation observed between levels V and II, the artifactual and textual data indicate that this accumulation derived from a shorter period of repeated and abrupt upheaval.

House F

House F is the earliest Isin-Larsa structure uncovered in TB. At the time that it was built, the rest of the area that was undisturbed by later foundations seems to have been either open space or ruins. House F cannot be described as strictly residential in function since this building, replete with courtyards, had no features indicative of domestic activities preserved.

The building was entered through an elaborate doorway leading into a large courtyard, locus 216, with baked-brick foundations and a baked-brick pavement. Locus 216 was rich in finds, including beads, seals, seal impressions, and ceramics. In spite of some evidence of disturbance, it seems likely that the majority of the objects were found *in situ*.

Locus 216 gave access to a large room, locus 203, which contained, in addition to a number of beads, two stone drill heads. These finds may help to explain the beads and other jewelry that dominate the contents of this house. Although the presence of one drill head could have been the result of chance, two such items are more likely to reflect past activities. These drill heads, together with the beads, suggest that House F may have been a lapidary workshop during the time of its occupation.

Two doors lead from locus 203 into a second courtyard, locus 70. This court is unremarkable, although it continues the pattern of rich finds, especially jewelry, that has been seen elsewhere in this house. To the north of locus 70 lies a small room, locus 201, whose northern extent is not now known. This seems to have been a storeroom, yet it was constructed with baked-brick foundations. To the west, across the courtyard from locus 203, a second double doorway led into locus 206.

Locus 206 had the richest finds of any room in this building. A cache of pottery, jewelry, and tablets was found in the northern part of the room. Although the exact disposition of these objects is not entirely clear, it seems that a number of shallow bowls may have contained shell beads, gold rings, and tablets. The texts make clear the administrative function of the area. Two tablets are Ur III in date, but the remaining ten seem to be dated to the early Isin-Larsa period, especially to the reign of Išme-Dagan. Those definitely of Isin-Larsa date are temple accounts, while the others are receipts and accounts of food and beer—the latter, at least, for cult purposes. In the center of this room, against the west wall, was a reed-covered platform, again associated with pottery and jewelry, while in the south was a drain and a reed basket. The importance of this room is obvious, even if its exact function is not.

Beyond locus 206 lay a third court, locus 217, whose western limit remains unexcavated. As elsewhere in the building, its finds included a number of shell rings, although spindle whorls and a weight may testify to some other, nonlapidary activity.

The nature and quantity of the artifacts found in this building may be explained by the burials which were dug into its remains. Together these imply not only that this area was abandoned rapidly, but also that the cause of the abandonment had resulted in loss of life. In the discussion of the TA remains, it was suggested that the attack on Nippur which is recorded in the "Lamentation over the Destruction of Nippur" might be reflected in the series of burials which separated TA levels XIII and XIIB. It seems probable that the destruction of House F and the associated burials (see below) were the result of the same event; indeed, the latest dated tablets from House F were written during the reign of Išme-Dagan, the king associated with this event. In TA this disruption of settlement was followed by a rebuilding of the area with little change in architectural configuration. This was not the case for TB. The change in plan and organization that is observable between level III floor 2 House F and floor 1 House E suggests that by the time that peace was restored, the organization of administrative activities had been altered.

House E

House E is a well-planned, well-constructed, but short-lived structure, built partly over the remains of House F. It was founded in level III floor 1, but by level II the area it occupied had been abandoned. Unlike the earlier House F, this building is more noteworthy for its architectural features than for its objects, so its function remains largely unknown. But for the first time in TB, House E contains elements that indicate purely domestic functions.

The house was entered through an odd-shaped chamber, locus 163, which connected the court, locus 70, to a large open area, locus 153. Four rooms led off this court, loci 101, 162, 156, and 175. Locus 162, in spite of its relatively large size, may have served as a storeroom, as evidenced by its lack of architectural elaboration and a number of shallow bowls which were found in one corner. Loci 101 and 156, on the other hand, had baked-brick sills or jambs and well-plastered walls. Although these architectural details suggest that these may have been living rooms rather than storerooms, the few bowls and vases that were found in them provide no additional clues.

The last room that led from the courtyard, locus 175, is of more interest. It appears to have been the antechamber to a small, self-contained group of rooms, consisting of a bathroom, locus 174, which had baked-brick paving on the floor and a broken jar for a drain; a storeroom, locus 171; and a probable living room, locus 500. Since this room lay entirely outside the limits of excavation, its size and disposition remain unknown. However, the remains of the walls and doors suggest that it was quite substantial. It is possible that the antechamber, locus 175, may have been unroofed since the storeroom (locus 171) had a baked-brick sill, a feature usually found in doorways leading from a room to an unroofed area, but since locus 171 also had baked-brick in its foundations, perhaps this sill is of less significance. Whether or not it was roofed, locus 175 seems to have served as a secondary entrance chamber, for a large jar[4] from this locus is similar to other round-based water jars known from other entrance chambers (see chap. 5).

It is possible that the peculiarities of the House E plan represented a transition between the public buildings found below and the domestic units typical of the later levels. Although TB was apparently used for administrative purposes at all times, during the Ur III period as well as the earliest Isin-Larsa time (level III floor 2), these activities took place in buildings which were entirely public in nature and function, whereas in the late Isin-Larsa and Old Babylonian periods, administrative activities took place in domestic structures. If House E were such a transitional structure, perhaps the rooms in the front of the house, loci 163, 101, 162, and 156, served public functions, while the apartment at the back served as the private residence of the administrator. If so, then its plan may represent the beginnings of the secularization of administrative activities which took place during the Isin-Larsa period.

[4] Registered objects from locus 175 include 2N 1066, a footed burial jar, type 18. This cannot be the same as the "typical round-bottomed pot—badly broken" which the notes say was found near the door to locus 171. This latter was probably a type 19 water jar (so it appears in the sketch) but was not registered because of its fragmentary condition. 2N 1066 is said merely to be from level III and probably came from lower down. Perhaps yet another burial was sunk into level III-2, of which only this vessel remains.

House W

House W was a small domestic structure occupied only in level III floor 1, although its baked-brick foundations penetrated down to floor 2. Access was by way of a small entrance chamber, locus 168, which in turn gave onto the court, locus 169, and to a larger room, locus 172. The latter may have been a bathroom since it contained a fragment of baked-brick paving with a drain in it, but it seems to be larger than most bathrooms, though not completely excavated. The court, locus 169, had a reed screen against the southeast wall and a small sunken area in the south corner, but was otherwise unremarkable, as were the finds; a cylinder seal, seal impressions, figurines, beads, and some pottery were all that came from House W. In general, House W seems to have been a small domestic structure; apart from the cylinder seal and seal impressions, there is no evidence to suggest any nondomestic activities.

To the north of House W lies a large open area, locus 167, which is the immediate predecessor of locus 502, to be discussed below. At this level no traces of features or architecture exist within this area. A wall separates locus 167 from the street, locus 166, and along this wall were found a number of shallow dishes—their function is obscure, but they are not unlike the bowls found against the walls of the courtyard of the house in WB.[5] In addition to these bowls, this area was rich in finds of all kinds, including figurines, stone bowls, and beads. These finds, unfortunately, are no help in determining the function of this area, if indeed it was any more than a place for trash disposal.

House X

House X consisted of two rooms, loci 182 and 184, and a courtyard, locus 177. No door was found connecting these rooms either to the street or to the courtyard, presumably a result of the poor state of preservation of the remains. Like House W, House X was unremarkable: the small locus 184 had what appeared to be a baked-brick drain in the south corner, possibly indicating the presence of a bathroom; the second room had no features. The finds from both rooms were limited to some ceramics, the odd figurine and copper fragment. Little more can be said about the court, locus 177, except that in the northwest sector (the only portion preserved), a number of figurine fragments were found. Like House W, House X seems to have been a small domestic structure of no particular interest. The functions of the large courtyards, locus 167 north of House W and locus 177 south of House X, are more of a problem; their presence in these levels, together with the large open space in Area C (see below), suggests that in level III open space was in greater demand than in either earlier or later levels.

Area C

Area C was a large open area, broken here and there by fragments of walls, occupying the entire northwestern portion of TB in level III. All evidence suggests that at least the northern portion was used as a dump, although in level III floor 1 the area in front of the door to House E cannot have been overly cluttered with refuse. The scraps of architecture east of locus 153 (loci 178, 186, and 173) could have represented structures associated with the court, but if so the few finds associated with them provide no clue as to what their functions might have been.

[5] Judith A. Franke, "Area WB," in *Nippur 12,* ed. McGuire Gibson, Oriental Institute Communications, no. 23 (Chicago: Oriental Institute, 1978), fig. 41.

In locus 187, in the north of TB, the excavators note irregular lenses of ash, again suggesting trash disposal. This area, called Area Q in later levels, continued to be used as a garbage dump in level II. The excavators were less specific about the deposits in locus 153, but the concentration of finds from this area, the lack of any mention of good floors, and the cache of tablets found in the north corner, all suggest that it too, at least in part, was simply an accumulation of refuse. The tablets from this cache date to about the same time as those found in House F (see above) and are very similar in content, although many concern sheep as well as bread and cereals. The tablets from locus 153 were apparently discarded in level III floor 1, but their similarities to those from House F suggest that they may have originated in that building. It is possible that they were excavated in antiquity when graves were being dug or when House E was under construction, and then thrown away in locus 153. This possibility of secondary deposition militates against associating these texts with the activities of any of the level III floor 1 residents of TB. However, one may assume that discarded trash was not moved further from its point of origin than necessary, and this, plus the similarities to texts from good contexts, suggests that they do refer to the activities of TB residents in general.

In conclusion, Area C was a large open area with only scrappy remains of architecture. At least part of Area C was occupied by a midden. In level III TB, enclosed open space must have been valued since loci 216, 220, 221, 191, 153, 167, 177, and 187 were all large, unroofed areas. For TA it was suggested that some of the architectural peculiarities noted in the earlier levels might have been due to the keeping of livestock in private dwellings during the unsettled political climate of the Isin-Larsa period. A similar argument can be made for TB, not that the large enclosures were used for keeping privately owned livestock, but rather that they were used for holding the animals needed for the temple sacrifice. Clearly, the evidence in support of such a suggestion is thin, but the Isin-Larsa administrative texts found in TB discuss the distribution of sheep and cattle as well as of bread, and there must surely have been a place to put the animals prior to slaughter.

The Burials

The significance of burials in both TA and TB is difficult to assess since it is always much easier to determine the level into which a burial was dug than that from which it came. Nevertheless, it is clear that quite a large number of graves were dug from level III TB into level IV.[6] This may not be surprising since much of TB was open at that time, and indeed many of the burials were found beneath these open spaces. However, enough burials were found dug into the walls of House F and beneath the walls of House E to make it clear that they are not just an example of the phenomenon of using any available space as a cemetery.

The evidence, such as it is, indicates that the burials were dug from immediately above level III floor 2, i.e., at the time of the transition from level III floor 2 to floor 1. The only structures clearly extant at this time, Houses E and F, differ considerably in plan one from the other, and the richness of the finds from House F may be taken as an indicator of rapid abandonment. As in TA, which also has a series of burials which date to the same time, these burials may be testimony to the attack on Nippur which occurred during the reign of Išme-Dagan and which is described in the "Lamentation over the Destruction of Nippur."[7] However, whereas the TA burials were very simple, those in TB were much richer. Considerable

[6] OIP 78 provides a complete description of the burials, and they are included in Appendix II of this volume. The burials in question are 1B 276, 282, 287, 288, 289, 290–291, 292, 295–297, 299, 300, 301, 302, 305, and 3B 13a–b.

[7] Deitz Otto Edzard, *Die "Zweite Zwischenzeit" Babyloniens* (Wiesbaden: Otto Harrassowitz, 1957), pp. 86–90.

amounts of pottery were often associated with the remains, as well as jewelry and occasional items in bronze. This implies that the administrators who lived in TB in the early Isin-Larsa period commanded considerable wealth even after an episode of looting and destruction, and were still able to provide the dead with grave offerings.

Conclusions

In summary, TB in the early Isin-Larsa period was mostly open space, used for trash disposal and perhaps also for holding animals destined for temple sacrifices. In the lower floor, only House F was preserved, a structure which had served, apparently, as both a lapidary workshop and an administrative center. This building—together with TA and perhaps all of Nippur—was destroyed in an attack, after which the dead were buried and the area was rebuilt. It is in this later level, level III floor 1, that are found the first examples of purely domestic buildings in the area, Houses W and X, and House V to be discussed below. The area once occupied by House F was also rebuilt, but its successor, House E, although it seems to have been used for public functions in the front, included a private apartment in the rear.

Level III seems to represent the transition from the Ur III practice of having administrative activities located in large public buildings to the Old Babylonian habit of locating administrative activities in private dwellings. It thus set the stage for the construction in level II, presumably by a state institution, of a series of domestic buildings which would serve both as dwellings and as the loci of administrative activity for the later residents of TB.

LEVELS II THROUGH D

Level II of TB sees the founding of Houses A, B, C, D, S, and T, the major buildings in the area. The construction of these houses set the basic architectural pattern of TB, which was to remain largely unchanged until Nippur was abandoned around 1720 B.C. Although in the subsequent discussion little in the way of architectural change will be noted, this does not necessarily mean that TB was immune to social change over this period. Such changes can be seen in the details of the internal features of the buildings and in artifacts, not in the broad pattern.

As in the previous chapter, the discussion will use as its basic unit the house—an architectural unit sharing a common circulation pattern—or an area, an open space characterized by little in the way of architecture.

House A

House A is a partially excavated structure located at the western edge of the excavations. Along with House B (see below), it was first built in level II-2, its foundations cutting into and destroying any previous structures. Since only small rooms surrounding a medium-sized courtyard have been exposed, the living rooms probably remain in the unexcavated portion of the house. In level II-2, the earliest occupied level of the building, two large, round-based jars, presumably for liquid storage, were found sunk into the floor of the courtyard by the west wall. Near them was an account tablet which recorded oil used for libations. These indications that the building served administrative and storage functions are supported by the level II finds from the small rooms, loci 50, 60, and 61. A receipt found in locus 60 and an administrative text from locus 50 both reflect administrative activity, while the various vessels found in the latter room, perhaps including the three storage jars said to be from the foundations,[8] further indicate that the function of at least the excavated portion of the building was storage.

If House A served administrative functions in level II, it is not clear whether these activities continued into level I. Finds from this period were scanty, but two probable field rentals found in the courtyard[9] might be interpreted as indicating that House A residents were conducting business for themselves in level I, whereas they had worked for a state institution in level II. However, since ample documentation exists for apparently private rental documents in this period actually serving public ends,[10] perhaps not too much weight should be placed on these rentals.

Possibly related to House A are loci 147, 151, and 152. Loci 147 and 151 are found only in levels D and E, levels in which the rest of House A had been disturbed by the nineteenth-century excavations. Locus 152, on the other hand, is completely or partially preserved in levels I and II. All three are small rooms that lay to the west of the courtyard of House A, but in no case is their connection with House A at all clear. Locus 152 may not in fact have been a room at all, but instead may have been built as a burial chamber. In level II it is preserved as a mud-brick box which contained eight infant burials. Since this structure, although damaged, also existed in level I, it seems likely that this locus and its burials were set in place towards the end of level I, perhaps at the time of the 1739 B.C. economic crisis. These infant burials may thus be related to the similar and contemporary infant burials found in TA House N. Above, grouped infant burials in TA have been taken as possible indicators of epidemic disease or famine associated with both the crisis of 1739 B.C. and the final upheaval that led to the abandonment of Nippur in 1720 B.C. The discovery of similar burials in TB not only strengthens this argument, but shows that while the crisis had less effect on the residents of TB than on those of TA, food shortages and ill health were perhaps common to both areas.

House R

House R consists of a series of loci which show little in the way of intelligible plans. The entire area was badly disturbed in levels D and E by modern excavations, and in the south even in level I. Locus 22, which appears to have been an open area extending to the south, was so badly disturbed that its original form cannot even be approximated. However, in level I floor 1, in the northeast corner, part of the floor was preserved and contained two *tanour*s

[8] If these jars had originally been buried with their mouths at floor level, their remains could have been found in the foundation levels.

[9] Although neither Text 63 nor Text 64 are complete enough for one to be able to tell the exact nature of their contents, except that they concern field plots, the evidence strongly suggests that Text 63 and probably Text 64 were field rentals. In the case of Text 63, the tablet is unsealed and concerns a large plot of land. Nippur field sale texts generally concern small plots and are sealed, whereas rental texts are frequently unsealed and on average describe larger plots. The logical conclusion is therefore that Text 63 was a rental text. Text 64 presents more of a problem. The size of the plots described in the text, a total of 6 *ikû*, is more characteristic of rentals than of sales, but the tablet is sealed, perhaps with a bur-gul seal, usually a mark of permanent exchange of property. On the other hand, no other text, sale or rental, has a seal impression above the first line of the text, so conclusions based on normal usage are difficult. The remains of the seal impression suggest the use of a single seal referring to a single individual, yet multiple owners of the fields in question are recorded. If this seal belongs to one of the witnesses, then the text is probably a rental of some kind, but if it belongs to one of the owners of the plot, Mār-erṣetim or Šagubum, then the text is probably a sale. Since my understanding of the TB area supposes that real property ownership was not a characteristic feature, and since this is the only text which could disprove this theory, I prefer to interpret it as one concerned with temporary, not permanent, exchange of property. Clearly, however, this position is far from proven.

[10] See, for example, Rivkah Harris, "The Archive of the Sin Temple in Khafajah (Tutub)," *Journal of Cuneiform Studies* 9 (1955): 37–39.

(bread ovens) and many of the small shallow dishes which appear to have been associated with bread making. The presence of more than one *tanour* and the large amount of associated pottery may imply bread-baking activities of a commercial nature, similar to those documented from area WB at Nippur.[11] However, with only one corner of the locus free from disturbance and no readily understandable associated architecture, the exact nature of this activity must remain unclear.

Since no doors have been found in locus 1 except in level I floor 1, it seems likely that this represents foundations in the lower levels. Locus 2, on the other hand, appears to have been a courtyard. In level I floor 1 a door is preserved which links loci 1 and 2, but that is all that was preserved of locus 2 at that time. In the lower levels, although somewhat better preserved, locus 2 cannot be associated with any known structure. The only architectural features which follow any expected pattern are loci 28, 29, and 101 in level II floor 2, a courtyard flanked by two rooms, but the lack of access to the complex, combined with an absence of finds and few notes, inhibits the drawing of conclusions.

House B

House B is a substantial, well-planned building, notable for the large size of most of its rooms. The earlier excavations of Peters and Hilprecht cut away much of the structure, but it was well preserved and apparently undisturbed in level II. The presence of some baked-brick foundations and brickbats in level II suggests that the baked-brick pavings and features preserved in level I may originally have existed also in level II, but that the bricks were robbed at the time of the level I rebuilding.

The most noteworthy feature of House B in the large number of school texts that were found, especially in level II[12] These texts came primarily from three rooms, loci 10, 45, and 12. However, since those texts attributed to locus 45 were found in the doorway to locus 10, they may in fact have originated in locus 10. The presence of these texts implies that in level II House B, at least one of the functions of the courtyard[13] was the education of fledgling

[11] Franke, "Area WB," pp. 54-65.

[12] Several difficulties are encountered in determining the exact level designations of the tablets from House B. Although the majority of the school texts from this house are said to come from level II floor 1, a designation of level II floor 2 might be better. In locus 10, the area from which all of the texts probably originated, the tablets are designated as from II-1, although in the notes they are described as occurring some 15 cm below floor 1, or only a few centimeters above the II-2 floor. More disturbing is the note that from above the level I floor 1 platform in locus 10 "several tablets were found." Unfortunately only one tablet is recorded from this level, and this is an Ur III text said to come from the bottom of a later well.

In locus 12 school tablets are again said to come from level II floor 1, but they are not mentioned in the notes. And in locus 45 school tablets are recorded as coming from II-1, but in the notes appended to a sketch of the locus they are said to have been found between II-1 and II-2, while in the notes themselves they are described as coming from above level II floor 1 and below level I.

Because of this conflicting testimony, I have preferred to retain the level II floor 1 designation for these texts. As noted at the beginning of this chapter, confusion in level designation is characteristic of the TB data; the tablets from House B merely provide a good example of this confusion.

[13] In OIP 78 (p. 56) it is suggested that locus 10 was a large central room rather than a courtyard. This suggestion is similar to that made for the Diyala (Pinhas Delougaz et al., *Private Houses and Graves in the Diyala Region,* OIP 88 [Chicago: University of Chicago Press, 1967], pp. 146-48), where all houses were interpreted as having large central rooms surrounded by ranges of smaller rooms. There are four difficulties with this interpretation. The width of these loci (locus 10 is well over 3 m wide) raises the question of how they were roofed. Without evidence for central roof supports, one must assume substantial beams. Trees capable of spanning such a distance were not common in the southern Mesopotamian plain. A second difficulty is that if these were rooms, even if they themselves had clerestories, the ranges of rooms around them would have been deprived of access to light and air. Yet these outer rooms often have features which suggest that they were actively lived in. Third, as noted in chap. 3, studies of modern villages suggest that walls such as those found in TB that are less than 1 m in width do not have the

scribes. This evidence of educational activity, though, is not sufficient to allow House B to be dubbed a scribal school, as was the case with TA House F. Scribal activity in House B was limited to only two rooms of the house, and the evidence for it was much less pronounced. The building lacked the benches and water containers which were related to scribal teaching in the TA example. Consequently, while it is likely that some scribal training took place in House B, the building was never wholly given over to this activity.

Finds and features from other loci are less noteworthy. The presence of an unfinished bead and a blank cylinder seal in locus 17 *might* suggest, but hardly represents conclusive evidence, of lapidary activity. The elaborate paving in level I floor 2 of locus 59 points to its use as a bathroom, as do the remains of baked bricks from level II and its baked-brick foundations. Bathrooms were rare at Nippur in the Old Babylonian period—in marked contrast to their ubiquity at Ur in the same period. The presence of a bathroom in House B, together with the excellent construction of the house as a whole, indicates that this was an important structure, but the finds from this house do not indicate any particular degree of wealth.

Area Q

The poor preservation of Area Q and its location close to the limits of excavation prevent full understanding, while the many architectural modifications noted by the excavators indicate that its function must have changed over time. In level II floor 2, there was a large open area, locus 120, with a couple of rooms, loci 108 and 121, to the west, although the relationship between these three loci remains unclear. In both the open area, and in one of the rooms, locus 121, numerous school tablets and seal impressions were found.[14] Locus 108, while it yielded no such tablets, gave access both to locus 121 with its many tablets and to House B, which was also characterized by scribal activity.

Several questions are raised by these finds. First, the relationship between House B and Area Q must be established. House B appears a self-contained unit with its entrance through locus 45, but instead of leading to a street, this entrance chamber gives onto a court with clear access only from the range of rooms to the north.[15] The evidence of scribal activity in the structures to the north and to the south of this court suggest that these two complexes may have been related.

The second question refers to the open area, locus 120. Since it has no clear access except from the street, locus 42, and since its contents include much ash but little in the way of true floors, one may conclude that this was a cul-de-sac primarily used for garbage disposal—hence the concentration of objects found there.[16] The presence of school tablets and seal impressions similar to those found on the floors of House B and in locus 121 suggests that the residents of these two structures used locus 120 as their trash heap.

A similar situation prevailed in level I, although from level II floor 1 onwards the northern extent of the open area was limited by the remains of a wall. In OIP 78 the

strength to support a second story. Finally, the standard house plan in the Middle East today is based on a central courtyard. It seems improbable that in antiquity this pattern was any different.

[14] Some of the seals preserved belong to the gudu$_4$ Abba-kalla, the eldest son of Ninlil-zimu and the owner of TA's House K.

[15] It is possible, of course, that an additional doorway existed which was missed by the excavators.

[16] One would expect a garbage dump to have been primarily made up of broken potsherds, yet virtually no pottery was registered from this locus. However, since only complete vessels were recorded, and since it is usually broken vessels which are thrown away, this lack of pottery from locus 120 is more likely the result of the selection process in registration than a true measure of what was found.

excavators attempted to reconstruct the level I floor 2 architecture to the west of the open area, but too little remains to make this effort fully convincing. By level I floor 1, however, the whole area appears to have formed a street, providing direct access from the entrance chamber of House B, locus 45. In level E this street was narrowed, and the structure to the north, known largely from the records of the nineteenth-century excavations, was given an extra range of rooms. Yet in spite of its reduced size this locus still served as a northwest-southeast artery, and in spite of its transition from a garbage dump to a street, Area Q remained at all times an area serving public functions.

House C

House C is a large, sprawling, double-courtyard house that existed only in level II; in level I it was subdivided into Houses C-1 and C-2. The large size of the structure and some of its special features indicate that it may have been used for more than just residential purposes—but the few tablets and artifacts found there give no clue as to what that activity might have been.

The house was entered, like most houses of this time, through an entrance chamber, locus 122. This room gave access to the first courtyard, locus 159, and possibly to a corridor-like room, locus 157, as well. The presence of a bench in locus 122 may indicate that it was used as a waiting room at the entrance of the house proper.

The special function of locus 109 may have been the reason that access to this house was more tightly controlled than usual. A small table was built against the south wall and possibly a bench (the notes are unclear on this point) against the west wall of level II floor 1. A headless stone statue (OIP 78, pl. 146:2) was found above the bench, while other finds from this room include a figurine and a plaque. Furthermore, instead of being entered from the courtyard as is the case for most rooms, access was provided through the small corridor or anteroom, locus 157, designed in such a way that the view of the interior of locus 109 was restricted until the visitor was at the door.[17] This limitation of access, the internal features, and associated artifacts all suggest that this room served as a small private chapel, similar to those known from Ur.[18] Significant differences exist, however, between this room and the "chapels" from Ur. While at Ur chapels were generally very large and located at the back of the house, this room is of average size and is near the entrance chamber. Moreover, the Ur chapels often had tombs beneath the floor, whereas in House C, the only Old Babylonian house at Nippur to contain brick tombs, these tombs were found some distance from room 109, beneath the rear courtyard, locus 30. Thus, if locus 109 served some religious purpose, its functions must have been somewhat different from those of the chapels at Ur. Its proximity to the entrance chamber and the presence of an otherwise inexplicable vestibule suggest that if this room was indeed a chapel, it served the public, not just the private family.

[17] The final field plan and the published plan both show doors between loci 122 and 157, and between loci 109 and 132. However, it must be noted that the more detailed plans of the loci attached to the field notes indicate no such doors. If there were no door between loci 122 and 157, then the corridor, locus 157, would have served more effectively as an anteroom.

The plan of the locus attached to the notes also shows no door between loci 109 and 132. Instead, the level II floor 2 west wall of locus 109 is seen as serving as a bench in level II floor 1, with an extra wall, to the west of this bench, as the somewhat destroyed wall of the room in level II-1. This interpretation of the brickwork in this room accords better with my interpretation of the special function of this room. I suspect that the reason behind the confusion here is that in drawing the complete plan of TB for all of level II, the details of the architectural changes which took place between the two floors were missed.

[18] Sir Leonard Woolley and Sir Max Mallowan, *Ur Excavations, vol. 7: The Old Babylonian Period* (London: British Museum Publications, Ltd., 1976), pp. 29–30.

The only other noteworthy feature in the front half of the house is in locus 159, where a *tanour* and fireplace are indications of a kitchen. Cooking activities also took place in locus 14, towards the back of the house, where another *tanour* was found, associated with the usual shallow bowls. In OIP 78 a point is made of the lack of access between loci 14 and 104, resulting in a division of the house into two sections. Such a situation makes sense since it provides a front courtyard, locus 159, for public activities and a back courtyard for the private family. In addition, locus 104, the most remote room attached to the front, or public, courtyard has two semicircular niches in the east wall, again pointing to some special function. Regrettably, the central portion of the house is too badly disturbed to permit understanding of how passage between the two sections of the house was affected. The break in the wall between loci 123 and 132 may be simply the result of the nineteenth-century excavations, although it is also possible that this was the location of the door that joined the two parts; alternatively, access may have been through locus 158.

Three brick-lined tombs were sunk beneath the rear courtyard, locus 30, probably from level II–1 into floor 2 and below. Unfortunately, the burials originally associated with the tombs were disturbed so that the wealth of their grave goods is now not known. However, the very fact that they were disturbed and their placement in brick tombs indicate that they may have been quite rich. Like the private chapel, locus 109, brick tombs sunk beneath the floor have parallels at Ur. Although these Nippur tombs are not located beneath the chapel as was common at Ur, their correlation in a single structure may be significant.

House C-1

In level I the large House C of level II was divided to make two separate structures, called Houses C-1 and C-2. Unfortunately, the remains of both houses, and especially C-1, were disturbed by the nineteenth-century excavations at Nippur. In view of this disruption, the few artifacts recorded from these levels could well have originated elsewhere.

In level I floor 2, House C-1 was entered through locus 89, a large room or small court with a well-built oven in the south corner (see OIP 78, pl. 68). The rear of the house was largely destroyed, although parts of two possible living rooms, loci 32 and 18, were preserved. In the notes, the courtyard, locus 30, is said to have had *tanour*s against the east end of the south wall, but we are not told how many there were, nor is there any plan in which they are illustrated. These scrappy notes, combined with the poor preservation of the structure, make interpretation difficult.

In OIP 78, the excavators suggest that this house may have served as a bakery, with the front room, locus 89, as the shop, complete with oven. The argument that the front of the structure was used for nondomestic purposes is compelling, but it is less certain that breadmaking was the activity involved. The oven found in this locus is not of the *tanour* variety normally associated with breadmaking, and the entire configuration differs markedly from the small bakery in TA and from the structure associated with the large-scale baking area in WB.[19] Nevertheless, there is little doubt that this house was entered through a room, or more probably a court, which was used primarily for some commercial purpose.

Such activity *may* have been continued in level I floor 1, but here the house was even less well preserved. The available evidence shows that the entrance had been moved to the north, and instead of an entrance chamber, the house was entered through a large enclosed court—a feature most unusual for this time period. One room, locus 43, seems to have been associated with this court and may have served some industrial or commercial purpose. The rear,

[19] Franke, "Area WB," pp. 54–65.

presumably domestic, portion of the house was almost completely destroyed by the earlier excavations.

House C-2

House C-2 was also badly disturbed. In level I-2 its plan is by and large coherent; entered through the entrance chamber, locus 103, a court probably gave access to the fairly well-preserved range of rooms to the southeast. There was little of note from these loci; finds were few and the only features of interest were a *tanour* in locus 102, suggesting a kitchen, and some mud-brick paving or the remains of a bench in locus 44. The rear two rooms, loci 14 and 19, must have been used as storerooms since access to light, especially in room 19, must have been virtually nonexistent.

In level I floor 1 there was a change; the house apparently lost the rooms to the southeast and became a single, long, narrow structure. Entrance was now effected through a very small room, with locus 58 beside it possibly serving as a bathroom. In location, this bathroom is very similar to that in House B, locus 59. The rest of the house consisted of a small court and a living room with, presumably, the same two storerooms in the back, loci 14 and 19. If these two rooms were indeed used as storerooms, this house devoted much more space to storage than was usual.

In OIP 78, the excavators assigned loci 25, 24, and 13 to House C-2. Clearly, with all of the northwestern part of these rooms destroyed, there is no absolute basis for determining whether these rooms were linked to House C-2. However, since there is incontrovertible evidence that these three loci formed the separate structure here called House T in level I floor 2 and below, it seems best to assume that in level I floor 1 they were also part of House T.

House T

In level I floor 1 House T was a small, poorly preserved structure, sandwiched between Houses C and D. At no time did it have more than three rooms, with the central one, locus 24/107, probably serving as a courtyard. This building is noteworthy in that at no time did the front room, locus 25/112, have any apparent doors. The excavators asumed that there must have been blocked doorways, but the consistency of its doorless state suggests another explanation. In level I floor 2, the lack of a good floor might indicate that we are dealing with foundations, but this is not the case in level II. Here, the walls were rebuilt between the two floor levels and were preserved 10–20 cm high at each floor. It seems possible that this room was used for a purpose that required high doorsills, sills of such a height that they could not be distinguished in the walls as preserved. The small size of the structure and its plan is not inconsistent with the idea that locus 25/112 served as a shop, but other features that might have confirmed such a hypothesis are lacking. No storage jars were noted from locus 13/106, no account texts were found, and though one sealed bulla came from locus 106, its association with two school tablets weakens it as evidence of economic activities. In short, except for the peculiarities of the architecture and its small size, no evidence was preserved to support the suggestion that House T served as a shop, or indeed to support any other interpretation.

House D

House D is a large, well-planned structure first built in level II and occupied until the end of level D. The upper levels—D, E, and to a lesser extent level I floor 1—were badly disturbed by the nineteenth-century excavations. Although House D displays the typical plan of a courtyard surrounded by rooms, it is peculiar in that the courtyard was very large and the rooms quite small. Only one room, locus 136/53, is 2.5 m in width; all the others are less than 2 m, and sometimes much less. Despite the narrowness of the rooms, the house was well constructed, with many baked-brick doorsills and sockets, and some baked brick used in walls and pavings.

House D was best preserved in level II, where the entire building was undisturbed. It was entered through locus 113, which in turn gave access to the other rooms via the paved court, locus 137. On the northwest, southwest, and northeast sides of the court were long, narrow rooms whose functions remain unclear since they had few finds, but which might have served as storage magazines. In OIP 78 (p. 57), the excavators posit that the narrowest of these rooms, locus 139, may have contained a staircase to the roof, although the notes make no reference to any mud-brick construction. Locus 139 is of an unusual shape to have had a stair; both the two preserved stairways in TA and those at Ur were located in small square rooms. However, at Tell ed-Der, one house had a staircase in a room very similar in size, shape, and organization to locus 139. If a stair was really located in this locus, it must have been supported by an arch, otherwise the second door to the room would not have led anywhere. But if such an arch had existed, its architectural details would have been described in detail by Haines. Conclusions are difficult to draw, but it seems that more evidence is needed before such a stairway can be demonstrated.

Only loci 136 and 142 show signs of occupation, and these are the only rooms of comfortable dimensions. In locus 136 the floor had much ash, and in the west corner of the room a jar and a pot were found *in situ* on floor 1 of level II. Since in level I this room was used as a kitchen, it is possible that the heavy concentration of ash on the floor indicates a similar function in level II. Locus 142, on the other hand, may have served as a place of business. Associated with level II floor 1 were weights, several blades, and a number of cylindrical jars (type 27). Although it is impossible to reconstruct exactly what took place here, the evidence points to something being cut, weighed, and placed in jars.

The only other noteworthy feature of the level II house is locus 82. In level II floor 1 this small room was separated from locus 110 by a wall, yet no doorway was found. The small size of the room is compatible with a storage function, and high doorsills that have not been preserved may be taken for granted. Regrettably since no elevations were taken on the walls and floors, the height of such sills is unknown.

The finds from level I House D are more informative but less reliable since most of the central portion of the house was destroyed by trenches dug during the course of the nineteenth-century excavations. Access to the house was still through the entrance chamber to the north, now called locus 48, which likewise gave onto the courtyard, although in floor 2 there was a second door to locus 67. The courtyard was again flanked to the southwest and northeast by long narrow rooms, and the west and south corners contained small storage rooms. As in level II the two rooms to the southeast had the most evidence of domestic activity. Locus 53 certainly served as a kitchen; in level I floor 2 it had a cooking stove, and throughout level I there was much ash and some utilitarian pottery. Activities of perhaps a more commercial nature are associated with locus 77. On floor 2, three overturned bowls were found in one corner, along with a pestle or polisher, while on floor 1 lay several business documents, accompanied by more pottery and a cylinder seal. Regrettably, since the southwest portion of this room was disturbed by the earlier excavations, one cannot tell how many of these objects were found *in situ*. The finds from this locus thus hint at enterprises of a commercial nature, but fail to provide firm proof.

More intriguing is the presence of school tablets throughout this building at level I floor 1. A cache of over twenty was found on the small piece of undisturbed floor in locus 63, while most other loci in the house produced one or two. It is possible that the unusually large courtyard in House D may have been used, at least in level I, as a locus of scribal activity—some special function is necessary to explain its excessive size. Although circumstances suggest the existence of a locus of scribal training in level I-1 House D, it cannot be demonstrated conclusively because the nineteenth-century excavators removed so much of the contents of the courtyard.

It is possible, though, that these school tablets represent no more than dumped debris since, although very badly disturbed by the early excavators, the fragments of levels E and D House D indicate at least a change in circulation pattern, if not a complete reorganization of space. Most of the center of the structure is gone. Locus 53, the kitchen that had been tucked away in the back corner of the house in previous levels, had by then been transformed into an entrance chamber. Without better preservation though, the significance of this change remains unclear.

House S

Since only part of House S lay within the excavation area, it is impossible to obtain full understanding of the size and circulation pattern of the structure. However, if the central locus, variously numbered 68, 84, and 141, was a courtyard, as suggested by the baked-brick paving found in level D, then the house was probably quite small, with rooms on only two, or perhaps three, sides of the court.

In level II three rooms are preserved, locus 143 near the street, locus 141 (probably the courtyard),[20] and locus 144 at the back. None of these rooms was completely excavated, and the only known doorway was that between loci 141 and 143. Locus 143 was heavily burned in level II floor 2, perhaps indicating its use as a kitchen; but no stove or oven was found in the excavated remains. Locus 144, disturbed by a later burial, had a drain set into the floor in level II floor 2[21] but so little of this locus survives that its exact nature and function defies interpretation.

The remains of House S in levels I and above are even more fragmentary, since much of its southeastern part was disturbed by the early excavators. In level I floor 2, the doors which joined the three loci were all preserved, strengthening the idea that this house was a small, narrow structure with a central courtyard. Locus 95 had a door to the street, locus 42, and must therefore have served as the entrance chamber. It had a second door that gave on to locus 84, probably a court.[22] From there, access was gained to the back of the house, locus 96. In level I floor 1, the walls were less well preserved and the door between locus 95 and the street was not found. Although locus 96 was almost completely destroyed at this level, it contained a *tanour,* suggesting that it was used as a kitchen, as its predecessor, locus 143, had been in level II.

The fragmentary remains of level E offer a pattern similar to that of level I floor 1, but in level D the area previously designated as locus 95 was divided into two rooms, with the

[20] The identification of locus 141 as a courtyard is strengthened by the discovery of baked-brick paving. Although this is shown on the published plan as occurring in level III, the notes indicate that it was found 50 cm above the level III-high floor. Unfortunately, the elevation readings which would have indicated whether such a position was best associated with level II or with level III were not taken. However, the notes also indicate that the walls of this locus stopped 20 cm above the level III-high floor; therefore, this paving must have been 30 cm above the base of these walls. Unless these lower walls had more than 30 cm of foundations dug into the remains of the previous level, this paving must be assigned to level II and directly associated with House S.

[21] As in locus 141, this feature is shown in the published plan as part of the foundations in level III, yet the notes and their associated plan make it clear that on excavation the top of this drain was found in level II.

[22] 73% of the entrance chambers in TA and TB had doors only to the courtyard. Of the remaining 27%, most gave access to the court and also to another room, as in House D.

southeastern room and the court, locus 68, having baked-brick paving. Although no door to the street was noted, the area was so close to the limit of excavation that it is possible that the small paved room in the southeast was the entrance chamber.[23] Level D was rich in finds, but the disturbance was so widespread that the context of these finds is insecure.

In short, House S was a small, long-lived structure to the south of House D. As excavated, it could have been as small as House T, but it seems more likely that it had an extra set of rooms to the south which were outside the excavation area. The rear room, locus 96, contained evidence which suggests its use as a kitchen, so since other organizational aspects of this house indicate it as a domestic rather than a commercial structure, it must have had a living and perhaps a storage room in the unexcavated area to the south.

House O

Across the street from House S lay House O, the source of the Atta archive.[24] House O, together with House N, was founded in level I floor 1, its foundations cutting into floor 2 and destroying the remains of the previous structure, House U (see below). Only three rooms of this building lay within the excavation area, one of which, the courtyard (locus 76), was badly disturbed in the upper levels D and E by a tunnel cut by Peters in the nineteenth century. Although the three rooms which lie within Area TB are sufficient to form a small structure in their own right, having living, storage, and courtyard areas, the absence of a door to the street and the apparent importance of its owner suggest that the original house was of the large, square type, similar to Houses B and D, rather than the long, narrow type represented by Houses T and perhaps S.

The finds from House O indicate that domestic functions were predominant. The use of locus 174 for storage is indicated not only by its position in the house, but also by the pottery found in level I floor 1: vases, a potstand, a large storage jar, and small dishes which may have served as lids. It may be assumed that this function persisted in levels D and E, where the absence of an identifiable doorway again suggests a raised threshold. In the living room, locus 75, little was found except in level E-2, where the Atta archive was encountered heaped up in the south corner of the room and covered by an inverted storage jar. Nearby lay a cylinder seal and two weights, items which might have been associated with the business transacted by Atta, the owner of the house. Some pottery and a milling stone were also found, testifying to more domestic activities.

The artifactual inventory indicates that House O served as both the home and the workplace of Atta, a successful entrepreneur to judge from his texts. Although the architectural remains of House O are scanty, traces of black paint and colored plaster found on the walls of locus 75, together with its stone door socket and baked-brick foundations, indicate that in its construction and decoration, House O reflected the importance of its resident. Had undisturbed levels in the rest of the house been excavated, more examples of the special character of this building would doubtless have been forthcoming.

Although the architecture and associated artifacts tell something about Atta, the primary source for his activities is the Atta archive. These texts were published by Goetze in 1964,[25] but deserve a reconsideration at this time for several reasons. First, Goetze's article merely describes the contents of the tablets; he did not attempt to place Atta's activities within the context either of Nippur society as a whole or of TB in particular. Secondly, Goetze's lack of

[23] Courts and entrance chambers are more frequently paved than all other rooms except bathrooms.
[24] Goetze, "Archive of Ātta."
[25] Ibid.

TABLE 18. THE ATTA TEXTS

Date	Text	Contents	Price (shekels per day)
ca. 1780–1760	68	Damiq-ilišu sells Ḫabannatum's offices to X (the name of the purchaser is now broken away)	?
1747/6	69	Atta and Imgur-Ninurta buy offices from Ipqatum	0.62
1747/11	70	Atta and Imgutum (Imgur-Ninurta) buy offices from Ubar-Šamaš	0.76
1740/8	71	Atta buys offices from Nuska-nīšu	0.7–0.53
1740/10	72	Šamaš-muballiṭ buys offices from Igmil-Sîn	0.33
1739/3	73	Adad-tajjār buys offices from Sîn-imguranni and Tarībatum	0.12
1739/4	74	Atta buys offices from Ilīma-lulim and Abikkua	0.34
1739/10	75	Atta buys offices from Ilī-iddinam	0.2
1739/11	76	Atta(?) buys offices from Abija and X	?
1738/ -	77	Atta buys something	?
1738/5	78	Atta buys offices from Lipit-Ištar	0.56
1738/6	79	Atta buys offices from Alutaḫi and Damiq-ilišu	0.06–0.08
1738/8	80	Atta buys offices from Enlil-NI-[ ]	?
1736/11	81	Atta buys offices from Tarībatum	0.13
1736/ -	82	?	?
1727/ -	83	Sîn-magir buys Ḫunābatum and Annum-pî-Ištar's offices from Annum-pî-Ištar and KA-Ninurta	0.06
1726/3	84	Atta buys offices from Sîn-magir	0.07
n.d.	85	Atta buys offices from Sîn-[ ]	?
n.d.	86	Damu-iddinam and [ ]-i-bi-[ ] exchanges offices with Enlil-nīšu and Alijatum	?
n.d.	87	X buys offices from Lipit-Ištar	0.56(?)
n.d.	88	Atta buys offices from Damu-iddinam	?
n.d.	89	Atta buys offices from Apil-Šamaš	0.21
n.d.	90	Atta buys offices from Nabi-Šamaš and Annum-pî-Šamaš	0.22
n.d.	91	Atta buys offices from Iddin-Ištar	0.3–0.23

familiarity with Nippur prosopography, combined with the generally poor condition of the tablets, led to some errors of identification (see Appendix VI for a list of corrections to Goetze's original publication). Since these errors are more serious because no photographs and few copies were published, it seems appropriate to prepare new copies of the entire archive.[26]

The Atta archive consists of 24 tablets (see table 18), all damaged to a greater or lesser extent, concerning the buying and selling of temple offices. Of these, seventeen are purchase documents in which Atta is at least one of the buyers,[27] and five are purchase documents in which the buyer was someone other than Atta.[28] The remaining two tablets are too badly

[26] See Texts 68-91 (pls. 74-92). An examination of Goetze's copies shows that some of the tablets now contain less information than they did when he read them. Given the very crumbly condition of the entire corpus, one must assume that some tablets have continued to deteriorate since they were excavated and baked. This situation pertains to all tablets published in this volume, but in most instances it is possible to collate now-missing passages by means of the casts which were made at the time of discovery. Regrettably, no casts or molds currently exist of those tablets whose originals are now in Chicago, and among these are some of the most problematic of the texts from the Atta archive.

[27] The texts in question are Texts 69–71, 74–81, 84–85, and 88–91.

damaged to allow the identification of the buyer; one may not even be a sale text.[29] It is probable that the purchase documents in which Atta is not mentioned represent records of earlier transactions which were handed to Atta at the time of his purchase of the property concerned.[30]

Atta was first mentioned in 1747 B.C. when he began to buy temple office property in partnership with his brother Imgur-Ninurta (sometimes shortened to Imgutum). Two further brothers, Ipqu-Damu and Ipqu-erṣetim, appear as witnesses. There followed a gap of seven years, by which time his partnership with his brother had been dissolved. Acting alone, from 1740 until 1736 B.C., Atta vigorously pursued a policy of buying up temple offices, with his brothers Ipqu-Damu an Enlil-nada occasionally acting as witnesses. After 1736 B.C. his activities seem to have been curtailed, but Text 84, dated to 1726 B.C., shows that he was still at the old game.

Atta's purchases concentrated on offices in the Utu/Šamaš temple, but offices in the Kisal Ekurra, the Nuska temple, the temple of Inanna-anaka, and the temple of Lugal-aba and Abkumaḫ are also mentioned (see table 19). The texts give the impression that Atta was trying to consolidate his hold over particular offices. There are only two mentions of real estate: a prebend field that accompanied the offices in Text 71, and 8½ sar of orchard property in Text 82 (and two offices in the Ninlil temple and the Kisal Ekurra). Unfortunately, this last text is too badly damaged for it to be possible to tell what it was about. The offices and the orchard are said to be part (or all?) of the inheritance of Imgur-Ninurta, but without a patronymic it is impossible to tell whether this property went to Atta's brother or to another man of that name. The seal on the tablet is no help since it lists the names of two brothers, Damu-eribam and Ninurta-muballiṭ, who are otherwise unknown. Understanding of this text is further complicated in that neither the traces that follow Imgur-Ninurta's name nor the oath are consistent with the text being a sale document. Indeed, the oath appears to have something missing since the critical phrase (mu lugal in-pà) follows immediately after a second mention of the orchard property, without a verb to indicate what the participants were swearing to. Altogether, this text raises more questions than it answers, and permits a variety of interpretations.

First, the text may simply concern the sale or transfer of an inheritance. If the recipient of this inheritance was not Atta but merely someone from whom Atta bought temple offices,[31] then it need not imply that Atta ever owned any real estate at all. If, on the other hand, Atta was the recipient of the property listed in Text 82, then he owned not only temple offices but also a small orchard plot. Finally, if the Imgur-Ninurta who was the heir to the property was Atta's brother of that name, then it is possible to suggest that Atta also received property through inheritance from his father, unless Imgur-Ninurta was the adopted son of a property

[28] These are Texts 72–73, 83, 87, and the exchange text 86.

[29] In Text 68 the name of the purchaser is completely illegible. Text 82 may be concerned with inheritance rather than with sale.

[30] Sîn-magir, the buyer in Text 83, was almost certainly the seller in Text 84; not only are the names the same, although part of the patronymic in Text 83 is broken off, but the two texts share a number of witnesses. One of the participants in the exchange Text 86 was the seller in Text 88. Unfortunately, the dates of the latter two texts are broken, as are most of the witnesses.

[31] In this case one must assume that this text was given to Atta when he purchased the temple offices that were included. The absence of Atta's purchase document for these offices is not a cause for concern since it would be a mistake to assume that all of Atta's texts have been preserved. The poor condition of this archive is the result of the late nineteenth-century excavators coming very close to discovering it, therefore leaving the texts close to the damaging effects of wind and weather for the next half-century until their discovery in the 1950s. Most of the tablets which have been preserved are fairly complete; it seems likely that less complete examples would have been weathered out of existence. Indeed, in the tablet catalog, 2N-T 765 and 781 are described as mere lumps of clay—other such fragments may not even have been saved.

TABLE 19. ATTA'S TEMPLE OFFICE PURCHASES

Text	Date	Office	Temple	Days	Price (shekels)
69	1747/6	ì-du$_8$	Kisal é-kur-ra	7½	5⅔
70	1747/11	gudu$_4$	é^{d}Utu	10	30½
		ugula-é		10	
		ì-du$_8$		10	
		bur-šu-ma		10	
71	1740/8	gudu$_4$	é^{d}Nuska and field	5	10½
		^{lu}ŠIM		5	
		and ?		. . .	
74	1739/4	gudu$_4$	é^{d}Utu	5	8½
		^{lu}ŠIM		5	
		ugula-é		5	
		ì-du$_8$		5	
		bur-šu-ma		5	
75	1739/10	gudu$_4$	é^{d}Utu	5	6
		ugula-é		5	
		^{lu}ŠIM		5	
		ì-du$_8$		5	
		kisal-luḫ		5	
		bur-šu-ma		5	
76	1739/11	?	?	5(?)	4⅓
78	1738/5	gudu$_4$	é^{d}Inanna-a-na-ka	15	25
		^{lu}ŠIM		15	
		bur-šu-ma		15	
79	1738/6	gudu$_4$	é^{d}Lugal-a-ba and Ab-kù-maḫ	22½	5⅓
		ugula-é		22½	
		ì-du$_8$		22½	
		kisal-luḫ(?)		22½	

owner. These three interpretations all have very different implications for understanding Atta's place in Nippur society.

For added perspective it is useful to compare the Atta archive to the group of texts which it most closely resembles, the Mannum-mêšu-liṣṣur archive.[32] On the surface, at least, their similarity is striking. Both archives provide evidence for the multiple purchase of temple offices during the reign of Samsuiluna, and neither conforms to the pattern of transacting and witnessing within a single family that is usual at Nippur (see table 20). Moreover, the

[32] Many of the texts of this archive are published in OECT 8. Additional texts may be found in Elizabeth C. Stone and David I. Owen, *Adoption in Old Babylonian Nippur and the Archive of Mannum-mešu-liṣṣur* (forthcoming). BE 6/2 38 and 64 and TIM 4 54 also belong to this archive.

TABLE 19. Continued

Text	Date	Office	Temple	Days	Price (shekels)
80	1738/3	?	é^{d}Utu	?	5
81	1736/11	gudu$_4$ ugula-é ^{lu}ŠIM ì-du$_8$ kisal-luḫ bur-šu-ma	é^{d}Utu	10 10 10 10 10 10	7½
84	1726/3	gudu$_4$ ugula-é í-du$_8$ bur-šu-ma(?)	é^{d}Lugal-a-ba and Ab-kù-maḫ	22½ 22½ 22½	6⅓
85	1749–1721/12	gudu$_4$ and ?	è^{d}Utu	30 . . .	?
88	n.d.	ì-du$_8$ and ?	è^{d}Utu	36(?) . . .	28(?)
89	n.d./6	gudu$_4$ ^{lu}ŠIM ugula-é ì-du$_8$ kisal-luḫ	é^{d}Utu	10 10 10 10 10	10⅓
90	n.d.	gudu$_4$ ^{lu}ŠIM kisal-luḫ bur-šu-ma (ugula é) (ì-du$_8$)	é^{d}Utu	5 5 5 5 5 5	6⅔
91	n.d.	gudu$_4$ ugula-é and ?	é^{d}Utu	5 5 . . .	4½

archives share two seal-cutters and five other witnesses, indicating at least a degree of contact.[33]

I have discussed elsewhere[34] how the Mannum-mêšu-liṣṣur archive may be viewed as a record of the activities of a wealthy but propertyless man able to enter the property-owning

[33] The two bur-guls are Awilija and Idišum. The others are Adad-tājjar son of Ḫummurum, Lu-Enlilla the agrig son of Eluti, Ninurta-rāʾim-Zērim son of Nanna-mansum, Ninurta-mansum son of Tarībum, and Ilī-iddinam son of Ibbi-Enlil.

[34] Stone and Owen, *Adoption in Nippur*.

TABLE 20. ATTA'S WITNESSES

Name	Text 68	69	70	71	72	73	74	75	76	77	78	79	80	81	82	83	84	85	86	87	88	89	90	91
Atta so. Narām-Sîn		A	A	A			A	A	A	A	A	A	A	A			A	A			A	A	A	A
Imgur-Ninurta so. Narām-Sîn		A	A																					
Ipqu-Damu so. Narām-Sîn														W			W	W			W			
Ipqu-erṣetim so. Narām-Sîn		W	W																					
Enlil-nādā so. Narām-Sîn								W																
Nuska-nīšu so. Adda-dugga				W			W			W							W							
Nuratum, gudu$_4$, so. Lu-Ninurta											W	W								W				
Lipit-Ištar so. Dingir-mansum											A									A				
Sîn-magir so. Enlil-nāṣir																A	A							
Tarībatum so. Elâ														A								W		
Enlil-mudammiq so. Rīm-Ištar																W	W							
Ninurta-gamil so. Urdukuga																W	W							
Appâ, gudu$_4$ Inanna, so. Ibbi-Sîn							W				W													
Elletum, gudu$_4$ Ninurta, so. Lu-Ninurta							W			W							W	W						
Enlil-mansum, gudu$_4$ Ninurta, so. Lu-Ninurta							W	W																
Awilija bur-gul				W	W		W				W	W				W			W		W	W		
Enlil-muballiṭ dub-sar										W	W	W		W					W	W	W			
Utaulu-heti dub-sar				W	W		W	W								W								
Idišum bur-gul		W				W							W	W										
Appatum bur-gul								W										W						

NOTE: A = actor W = witness.

class through adoption, who took advantage of his newly won status to amass a considerable amount of property—mostly in the form of temple offices—during the economic crisis of Samsuiluna 11. The question here is the extent to which the Mannum-mêšu-liṣṣur and Atta archives represent similar situations.

Discovering Atta's antecedents is no easy matter. The name of his father, Narām-Sîn, is not common at Nippur. It occurs frequently in the Atta archive and occasionally elsewhere as the father of Atta, Imgur-Ninurta, and their three witnessing brothers. The same name is also recorded for the father of Bēltani, a *nadītum* of Ninurta, and of Damiq-ilišu, both of whom were moneylenders. The dates of all references to Narām-Sîn are compatible with a single man being the father of all seven individuals. Confirmation of this hypothesis may be found in BE 6/2 22, in which Damiq-ilišu lends silver and grain. This text gives the borrower as the brother of Atta's most frequent witness, Nuska-nīšu, while two of the witnesses are also known from the Atta archive. The first witness listed was Enlil-nādā, son of Narām-Sîn and one of the brothers who witnessed Atta's texts. The third witness was a Ḫabil-kīnum, with no recorded patronymic. Ḫabil-kīnum is not a common name at Nippur, but an individual so named is recorded as a witness to a text in the Atta archive. These data permit the suggestion that the moneylender Damiq-ilišu may have been another of Atta's brothers.

The *nadītum* Bēltani is more of a problem to identify. None of the participants and witnesses in this text (BE 6/2 13) can be connected with the Atta archive,[35] and it is dated to the reign of Hammurabi, while the texts known to be connected with Atta all date to the reign of Samsuiluna.[36] If this Bēltani was the sister of Atta, then one must assume either that Bēltani, like most *nadītums*,[37] came from an old established, propertied family, or that she was one of those who became a *nadītum* through adoption.[38] If the latter was the case, what probably enabled her to join the *nadītums* of Nippur was her father's wealth—wealth which is surely reflected in her activity as a moneylender.

These data hardly paint a full picture of Atta's antecedents but imply that he came from a family that was wealthy but probably without real property. The discovery of his texts in TB, an area apparently occupied by landless administrators, his brother's (and perhaps his sister's) activities as a moneylender, and the similarity of his archive with that of Mannum-mêšu-liṣṣur, all suggest that Atta was a first-generation property owner.

Thus House O was occupied during the reign of Samsuiluna by Atta, who, perhaps with some help from his brother, was able to become a property owner.[39] Between 1747 and 1726 B.C. he purchased a number of temple offices. He concentrated his activities in the years 1739

[35] The scribe of this text, Utaulu-ḫeti, is also known from the Atta archive, but since scribes and seal-cutters regularly witness contracts written by many disparate groups, such a link cannot be considered significant.

[36] Although the difference in actual dates is only a matter of a few years, the difference between the reigns of Hammurabi and Samsuiluna may be significant. While the evidence from Nippur does not support the contention that Hammurabi had outlawed land sales (as suggested by Michael J. Desroches, *Aspects of the Structure of Dilbat during the Old Babylonian Period* [Ann Arbor: University Microfilms, 1978], pp. 197–202), the increase in property transfers that followed Hammurabi's death may have been in part a result of the change in kingship, and the political and economic events which marked Samsuiluna's reign must also have influenced the economic climate. It is possible to suggest, therefore, that entrepreneurs may have had more freedom of action during the reign of Samsuiluna than in his father's lifetime.

[37] See Elizabeth C. Stone, "The Social Role of the *Nadītu* Women in Old Babylonian Nippur," *Journal of the Economic and Social History of the Orient* 24 (1982): 50–70.

[38] This is not a pattern that is well attested at Nippur, although it was a common practice among *nadītums* at Sippar as noted by Rivkah Harris, *Ancient Sippar* (Istanbul: Nederlands Historisch-archaeologisch Instituut, 1975), p. 309. At Nippur, all adoption documents that concern *nadītums* are too badly damaged for one to tell exactly who was adopting whom, let alone what the nature of the adoptive relationship was to be (see Stone and Owen, *Adoption in Nippur*). However, by drawing parallels with Sippar and understanding adoption practices at Nippur, it seems quite possible that this was one means of *nadītum* recruitment at Nippur.

[39] Perhaps Text 82 indicates that his brother Imgur-Ninurta was adopted into a property-owning family, and that Atta, by going into partnership with his brother in the early years, was able to take advantage of this connection to gain a foothold in the property-owning group.

and 1738 B.C. taking advantage of the panic selling and lowered prices associated with the economic crisis. House O was apparently primarily a place of residence, although the tablets, weights, and cylinder seal that were found in locus 75 suggest that Atta also used his house as his place of business.

House N

House N is a small, poorly preserved structure located to the north of House O. An entrance chamber gave access to the courtyard, locus 66, but from there the pattern of organization becomes less clear. In OIP 78, plates 62 and 63, a small bathroom is reconstructed next to this entrance chamber, but since most of locus 66 and the rooms to its southwest were almost entirely destroyed by a nineteenth-century tunnel, there is no certainty that this room ever existed. It is clear that the court provided access to the living room, locus 56, which in turn gave on to a small storage room, locus 65—a pattern which is almost exactly mirrored in the neighboring House O. Houses N and O were constructed at the same time in level I floor 1, and it is possible that their similarity in plan may indicate that a single design was followed in both cases.[40]

No clues survive concerning the occupants of House N, and indeed many aspects of its construction history remain obscure. It was badly disturbed in levels D and E, somewhat disturbed in level I floor 1, and level I floor 2 was the only level which the excavators felt was largely intact. Even there neither wall plaster nor good floors were found, probably because this was a foundation level. Thus the various objects found in this building cannot necessarily be associated with its occupation. Furthermore, such information as is available on levels D and E indicate that the courtyard, locus 66, was used for trash disposal, and thus that the house was no longer occupied at that time.

House U

Beneath Houses N and O in level II was the large structure which is called House U in this volume. All that remains of this building are the foundations. Not a single doorway was found between any of the rooms, and all walls were unplastered. The excavators note two building phases, which they designated level II floors 1 and 2. However, given the nature of the structure, the upper material should probably be considered to be the foundations from level I, and the lower material the foundations from level II.

These data suggest that some previous structure, perhaps existing in level II floor 2, was razed to permit the construction of House U in level II floor 1. The deep foundations of House U destroyed nearly all traces of this earlier building, but some features such as the basin in locus 131 and the ovens in loci 145 and 149 remained. The foundation walls of House U in level II probably went down to the floor level of the previous structure but did not cut it. Thus although good floors with walls that go down to them were found, the two were probably not contemporary. In level I floor 2, House U was apparently rebuilt on approximately the same plan. Again, during construction the walls of the previous level were destroyed, leaving only the foundations. Thus the surface that has been called level II floor 1 by the excavators (here called level I foundations) was probably the depth to which the foundations were excavated at the time of the rebuilding.

[40] If this were the case, then House O could not have had the extra range of rooms to the south, outside the excavation area, that was postulated above.

Houses N and O (see above) were built towards the end of level I, and their deep foundations again disturbed all previous construction beyond recognition. The lowest levels of House N were foundations, and this was almost certainly the case for similar levels in House O.[41] Thus, House U simply represents the foundations of successive rebuildings whose superstructures were destroyed by later construction. In these circumstances none of the finds from this area can be associated with any particular house or set of activities.

The walls of Houses N and O approximate the same lines as the foundations of House U below. The most likely explanation of this continuity is that House U represents the foundations of earlier examples of Houses N and O. In this scenario, the level II House N would have had its courtyard in locus 131, with loci 129, 133, 138, and 127 as the rooms of the house, and the rest of House U would have been the earlier House O.[42] If this were the case, then Houses N and O must have been twin domestic units that were rebuilt at level II and at floors 1 and 2 of level I. In every instance the two houses were built together.

Area P

Area P takes in all of the remains on the east side of the street between Houses N and U to the south and House V to the north. Most of this area was disturbed, below by ancient pits and foundations, above by the late nineteenth-century excavations. As a consequence the finds cannot be associated with the architecture with any confidence, and it is almost impossible to make sense of the architectural remains themselves.

At level II floor 2, all of area P appears to have been a single open space, designated here locus 502. No wall has been preserved separating it from the street, so it is possible that it was some kind of public square. Close to the center was a small platform, and a small bin had been built against the south wall. One wall fragment shows on the plan in the midst of this area. This could have been no more than part of a foundation cutting down from above, but if not, it may indicate that instead of being an open space, locus 502 was built up like the rest of TB, and the remains were so badly disturbed that the architecture was not identified by the excavators. Further evidence of disturbance was the discovery of a statuette head found in this level which joined a base found in level I floor 2, immediately above. The two parts of the statue were probably both in a single pit which was missed at the time of excavation. Although the wall fragment may be indicative of construction in this area, the presence of the pit strengthens the argument that locus 502 was an open area; pits are rarely dug in houses but are commonly found in open spaces.

Whether or not this area was open in level II-2, by floor 1 it was largely built up. Locus 118, an open area to the north, may have served a function similar to locus 502 below, but by level I it had been walled off from the street. The presence of a bread oven in one corner suggests one function for this area, but may also indicate that locus 118 served a private function and was attached to the two rooms to its south, loci 114 and 125. Locus 114 was an entrance chamber that gave access to locus 125, but the limits of the excavation area make it impossible to know how the circulation pattern was continued.

South of these messy remains were four rooms, loci 140, 117a and b, and 126, which together formed a single short-lived domestic unit in level II floor 1. The plan is quite clear.

[41] The notes do not even suggest that House O was excavated down to level I floor 2, although the I-2 field plan shows the walls continuing down. It seems best, therefore, to assume that like the neighboring House N, which was built at the same time, House O had deep foundations.

[42] The wall that separates locus 145 from locus 146 makes this reconstruction a little more difficult, since it is here that one might expect to find the courtyard of the early House O, but the disturbance by an old University of Pennsylvania tunnel and the brevity of the notes prevent further understanding of the architecture.

Locus 140 was the entrance chamber and opened into the court, with its southern portion made into a small storage area through the addition of a thin partition wall. This house differs from the normal plans in the organization of loci 117a and b. Locus 117a had its own door to the street[43] and may have been designed to separate the domestic portion of the house from loci 117a and b when outsiders came to the latter portion to conduct business.

Heavy disturbance in level I makes understanding very difficult, but it appears that at that time Area P was separated from House N by a street, locus 83. Although locus 81 may suggest the existence of a small structure to the north of this street, much of the area may have been open, again similar to the earlier locus 502. However, the fragments of brickwork which were found here and there in the area could also be the remains of houses whose walls were almost completely destroyed by later disturbance. Levels D and E, on the other hand, show ample evidence of construction in the entire area, both over the old open area to the north and over the street to the south, although the broken walls and lack of doors prevent the reconstruction of a believable plan.

Area P, then, remains poorly understood. It is possible that for much of its history all or part of it was an open area, serving some communal purpose. Despite the signs of burning from time to time, the evidence does not support the idea that it was used primarily for trash disposal as was common in other open areas (such as Area Q). It seems more likely that the scraps of architecture found in this area were the remains of temporary structures of some kind. Perhaps Area P was used as a marketplace or as a place to keep animals. Unfortunately, the notes provide little to go on.

House V

House V is the only building in TB founded in level III that continued largely unchanged throughout the Isin-Larsa and Old Babylonian periods. Yet since it was located in the northern corner of TB, no more than a small fraction of this house lay within the excavation area. In level III floor 1, the house was entered from the street through a small entrance chamber, locus 128, which was disturbed by a later pit. This room opened into locus 185, perhaps the court since it had baked-brick foundations.[44] A bread oven was located in one corner, but most of the rest of the locus was disturbed by a drain that descended through it. If locus 185 was not the court, these features might suggest that it was used as a kitchen.[45] It had a second door to locus 189, while the entrance chamber also gave onto locus 183. Two chalices were found in this house, but their significance remains obscure. Other finds were rare and decidedly utilitarian.

The house remained much the same in level II, although the small size of locus 115 (locus 185) suggests that it was the far room, locus 130, that served as the courtyard. Like locus 185 below, locus 115 had a bread oven, and the drain that had disturbed the lower level had its origin in level II floor 2. Both this room and locus 116 had pots sunk into the floor. A thick layer of ash associated with level II floor 2 hints that the house might have been destroyed by fire.

[43] Although the published plan indicates a blocked doorway between the street and locus 117a, neither the notes nor the field plan indicate such blocking. Although it is possible that the doors to the street in loci 117a and 140 were not used at the same time, it is clear from OIP 78, pp. 57-58, that the excavators assumed that such a blocking must have existed and therefore added it to the plan.

[44] Since the baked-brick foundations are in the wall that separates loci 185 and 189, either of these loci could have been the courtyard, although locus 185 is probably the better candidate since entrance chambers usually lead directly to the court. However, the small size of this locus in later levels indicates that it would have made a very inadequate courtyard.

[45] Bread ovens are generally located either in a special room, usually tucked away into a corner of the house, or in the courtyard.

In level I the general pattern is again similar, although the circulation pattern changed. Entrance was probably effected through locus 100, while the old entrance chamber, now called locus 99, served as the kitchen, as evidenced by a bread oven and a sunken pot. Finds from locus 91, probably the courtyard, include four account tablets concerned with payments of grain and flour and a grain loan, implying that the occupants were concerned with supervising the flow of cereal commodities. Like other such texts from TB, they indicate public rather than private activities.

In short, House V was a well-appointed, well-built structure that was very stable in plan and generally well preserved. Its plan in levels II and III was unusual in that, unless our interpretation of room functions is at fault, the entrance chamber lay between the street and other rooms, not between the street and the court, but so little of the house has been excavated it is difficult to tell whether there might have been a second entrance. If this were the case, then loci 128 and 183/116 may have been used only for business and have been kept separate from the domestic part of the house. By level I, however, this scheme was abandoned, and the main entrance of House V was by a door probably located in the northern part of locus 100, or via a room to the north of that. Perhaps this latter is where the domestic entrance in levels II and III had been.

CONCLUSIONS

TB was an area of Nippur occupied by landless administrators. Their large houses were built for them by architects, probably employed by a temple, and were used for both business and residence. While their ties to large institutions apparently protected the TB residents from the worst effects of the 1739 B.C. economic crisis, they were very much at the mercy of the changes in administrative practice that were associated with the transition from Ur III to Isin-Larsa control.

One of the most significant aspects of the TB sequence is the way in which it illustrates the transition between Ur III and Old Babylonian administrations. The Ur III levels of TB (OIP 78, pls. 53–54, 56–59) were characterized by large public buildings which generally lack domestic features. The late Isin-Larsa and Old Babylonian structures (this volume, pls. 27–34; OIP 78, pls. 61–64), on the other hand, are small in size and replete with evidence of residential occupation. In both cases, however, their construction suggests that professional builders had been employed, and in both cases their occupants were administrators. The buildings in TB level III show the transition from one form to the other. House F, dateable to the earliest years of the Isin-Larsa era, was very similar to the Ur III style of building, albeit on a smaller scale, while its contents also suggest purely public activities similar to those associated with Ur III buildings. The many items of shell and stone, together with some drill heads, suggest that the building housed a lapidary workshop, while the tablets indicate that its residents were concerned with the administration of comestibles for temple consumption. This reconstruction of the functions of House F is in contrast to that for House E, built immediately afterwards. House E, although probably still largely devoted to administrative functions, included a residential apartment in the rear of the building. This house shows how shortly after the fall of the Ur III state the physical separation that had existed between domestic and administrative activities had begun to break down.

This shift in organization of administration must be related to the unsettled political conditions that characterized the early years of Isin-Larsa control. Unrest is reflected in the archaeological record by the large number of burials which were found in TB level III and which can be compared to the similar phenomenon observed in TA level XIII. These burials and the subsequent rebuilding of both TA and TB are interpreted here as the physical manifestations of the event recorded in the "Lamentation over the Destruction of Nippur."

Even where this turmoil did not result in death and destruction, it must have had a profound effect on the administration of the city. Unlike the Ur III and Old Babylonian levels in TB, much of the area in level III not disturbed by later foundations seems to have been given over to open space. Some was used for trash disposal, but not all. Since the contemporary administrative texts from TB concern the distribution of animals among other things, it is likely that much of this open space was used to pen animals, and the end of neighboring Drehem as a locus for animal distribution[46] may be related to this phenomenon. Not only would the animals that were ready for temple sacrifice have been penned in the city, but when the hinterland was unstable, pasturing the animals in the countryside may have been too risky.

By level II, this need for open space had abated, and the pattern of occupation that was to characterize Old Babylonian TB was established. Houses A, B, C, D, S, and T, and perhaps also Houses N and O, were all founded in level II and continued largely unchanged until Nippur was abandoned in level D. All were well-constructed, planned houses, many quite large in size, and all were primarily domestic buildings.

Although this spate of new construction might indicate a lack of continuity between levels III and II, this is not the case. Not only did House V continue largely unchanged, locus 502 continued to be used for penning animals, and Area Q for garbage disposal, but the residents of TB continued the administrative activities of their predecessors. Now, however, these activities took place within domestic rather than public buildings, although the house in Area P, and perhaps House V, may have continued the policy of a separation of business and residential quarters that had characterized House E.

The careful planning seen in the construction of these buildings, as well as the presence of many administrative and account documents and the absence of private real estate contracts, suggests that the TB houses were built and owned by large institutions to house their employees, and not owned by their occupants. Nevertheless, the houses indicate a degree of independent action not hitherto observed. House A, although containing evidence indicating that it was used for the storage and disbursement of liquids for libation, also yielded two field rental documents. At least one function of the substantial House B seems to have been the education of fledgling scribes; perhaps House D was also used as a school. The finds in this latter building, though, also suggest the processing of goods, perhaps a more standard administrative activity. Not only are both houses B and D characterized by considerable amounts of baked-brick and generally well-appointed rooms, but both had oversized courtyards.

The largest house in TB was House C, which was originally built around two courtyards, the front one apparently for public purposes, complete with its own cooking facilities, and that in the rear reserved for the private family. Near the front door was what might have been a small chapel; if so, its plan suggests that it was for general use, not just for the family. The religious overtones of this house are continued in the rear portion of the house where several brick tombs were uncovered. In level I House C was broken up into two smaller buildings, which, where undisturbed by later excavations, show evidence of production of an industrial or commercial character.

In contrast, the smallest houses show little evidence for nondomestic activities, although House T may be better described as a shop. Houses V, S, N, O, and the house in Area P, none of which have been fully excavated, all present a largely domestic aspect, although House V and that in Area P seem to have had double entrances. House O differs little from its neighbors, but by level E-2, dating to around the time of the 1739 economic difficulties, its owner had broken with the traditions of TB and become a private property owner.

[46] Tom Jones and John Snyder, *Sumerian Economic Texts from the Third Ur Dynasty* (Westport: Greenwood Press, 1961).

In spite of the disturbance that characterized these upper levels in TB, this economic upheaval does not seem to have resulted in the partial abandonment of the area that had been noted in TA. Like TA, scribal training came to a halt, and group infant burials were found. In spite of these indicators of distress, some TB residents were able to profit from the resulting chaos. The unsettled conditions in the city seem to have resulted in a lowering of social barriers, a condition which permitted the resident of House O, Atta, to change status from administrator to property owner. Atta, perhaps the son of a moneylender, was able to use his family's wealth to purchase temple offices from the impoverished property owners who fled Nippur at the time of the crisis. With this activity the characterization of TB as an area occupied exclusively by administrators becomes inappropriate. Had Nippur's Old Babylonian occupation continued, the entire tenor of the neighborhood might have changed. However, a few years after Atta's last transaction, TB, along with the rest if Nippur—and indeed all of central Babylonia—was abandoned.

In general, the material from TB provides insight into the way in which the Ur III bureaucracy was transformed in the Isin-Larsa and Old Babylonian periods. The initial change was in the locale of administrative activities; first, residential apartments were attached to administrative buildings, and then many of these public activities simply took place in private dwellings. Nevertheless, these houses appear to have been built and owned by the institutions involved. By the time of the reign of Samsuiluna, the separation that had previously existed between administrators and property owners began to break down. The wealth of the administrators and the poverty of many property owners led to a relaxation of alienation restrictions, making possible the first ownership of real property by TB residents.

Chapter 5

Artifact Distributions

Much of OIP 78 was devoted to a description of the various classes of artifacts found in TA and TB, and there is no need to repeat those observations. However, since the architecture and artifacts were discussed by two different authors in two different chapters, the relationship between artifacts and their architectural contexts remained largely uninvestigated. To make up for this deficiency, this chapter will explore the differences between the TA and TB artifacts, the relationship between room functions and artifacts, and changes in these distributions over time. In this study, a clear distinction will be maintained between artifacts from apparently good contexts and those from loci which were disturbed. Finally, a new chronological scheme will be presented, based both on artifactual distributions and on our reassessment of the stratigraphy of TA and TB.

An attempt has been made to establish rough typologies for all artifact classes. New typologies are suggested for figurines and tools, but that laid out in OIP 78 for the pottery has been followed here. In Appendix III, these typologies are described, providing references to the published illustrations in OIP 78. In many cases, the type categories are not as precise as one might hope. Many tools and figurines were given D, or discard, numbers and were therefore not fully registered; they were only crudely sketched and described before being thrown away. This more limited registration procedure meant that for more than one-half of all plaques, figurines, jewelry, seals, and tools, the minor details which constitute aspects of style are too often irretrievably lost. The sketches and brief descriptions, though, indicate the subject matter of figurines and the functions of other objects, such that the cultural distinctions between erotic and heroic plaques, between arrowheads and clay rattles can still be discerned.

Pottery, the backbone of archaeological research, will be the first of the classes of artifact discussed. This will be followed by a review of the distribution of the tablets, which are treated as a class of artifact, albeit one with several levels of meaning. The other two artifact categories to be examined are "tools"—including blades, weights, jewelry, and seals—and plaques and figurines. The chapter will end with a reconsideration of the chronology of TA and TB in the light of this discussion of the artifacts.

POTTERY

The ceramic typology set out in OIP 78 forms the basis for our examination of the distribution of pottery types in TA and TB,[1] although it was not always easy to determine which type number had been assigned to a given pot, and pottery drawings were rare. For the ceramics from TB, there was a pot catalog which assigned field type numbers (different from those published in OIP 78) to all vessels—unfortunately, no such record existed for the

[1] As indicated in chap. 1, in general only complete or reconstructable vessels were recorded.

pottery from TA. The only TA pots with such field numbers were those for which pot sheets describing the ware had been filled out. In addition, an incomplete series of type cards was preserved which listed all vessels assigned to a particular field type. These type cards allowed the typing of most TA ceramics, but for some vessel types this information was only complete for that material which had been excavated in the first and second seasons, i.e., from the Isin-Larsa and Old Babylonian levels of TB.

Once as many vessels as possible had been provided with field type numbers, it was possible to use the published pottery to draw equivalences between the type numbers of OIP 78 and those used in the field. Sometimes no one-to-one agreement in subtypes could be found, in which case no subtype designations were given to undrawn and unpublished pottery.[2] Finally, for much of the undesignated pottery from TA, it was possible to suggest probable types based on the sketches and descriptions made in the field. Where there is any doubt,[3] it is noted by the presence of a query in Appendix II. Nevertheless, it must be stressed that at least some of the pottery from TA and perhaps also some from TB which were assigned a type of publication can no longer be so assigned with the information now available and are described here as untyped.

This effort to correlate the field data with types recorded in the publication was not entirely successful; in very few cases does the number of examples of a particular type from a particular level exactly match that given in OIP 78. Moreover, some inconsistencies can be noted in the latter document. For example, although generally only complete vessels were noted, the sherds of the painted pots (type 24) were so distinctive that they were frequently recorded, especially those from TB. The high count for this type in TB levels D and E is the result of counting sherds as though they were complete vessels. Similar sherds were noted from TA but they were excluded from the vessel counts from this area. Thus, while some discrepancies between the published frequencies and those reconstructed here are certainly due to incomplete assignment of types on my part, others are the result of the method of counting employed by the excavators.

A second difference between the analysis of pottery attempted here and that in OIP 78 is that I prefer to use only those clear representatives of a type which were found in unimpeachable contexts, while they included those from areas which had suffered disturbance. In figure 6, clear types from good contexts are distinguished from those vessels where there may be doubt over either the type designation or the context.

An examination of figure 6 shows differences between TA and TB pottery, but these may largely be attributed to differential preservation in the two areas. Whereas in TA the upper levels are well represented, in TB it was the lower levels which were well preserved. Thus while TB had many examples of early types, TA has many of the later types.

Some notes on the distribution of these types are in order. First, four shallow bowl types were identified: types 7, 8B, 21, and 22. Type 7 is hard to distinguish from type 21,[4] while type 8B is hard to distinguish from type 22, as confirmed by the more recent policy of treating each

[2] In addition to the pottery drawn in the field, the directors of the University Museum and the Oriental Institute generously allowed me to draw the unpublished pottery from the Isin-Larsa and Old Babylonian levels of TA and TB that is housed in their collections. Unfortunately, only a small fraction of the pottery excavated was taken home from the field; most was noted and discarded.

[3] In some instances, there is no question of the appropriate type designation—as in the case of painted pots (type 24). A sketch of such a pot cannot be mistaken for any other type.

[4] The work was complicated by an absence of any record of type 7 bowls from TA, although they must have existed since they are mentioned in OIP 78. The only important type card missing TA examples was that for type 7, and since type cards for 8B and 21 included examples from TA, it seemed most likely that the shallow bowls for which no type numbers could be found belonged in type 7, and they were so designated. Since the number and distribution of these type 7 bowls approximate the number and distribution of type 7 bowls described in OIP 78, this designation seems to have been appropriate.

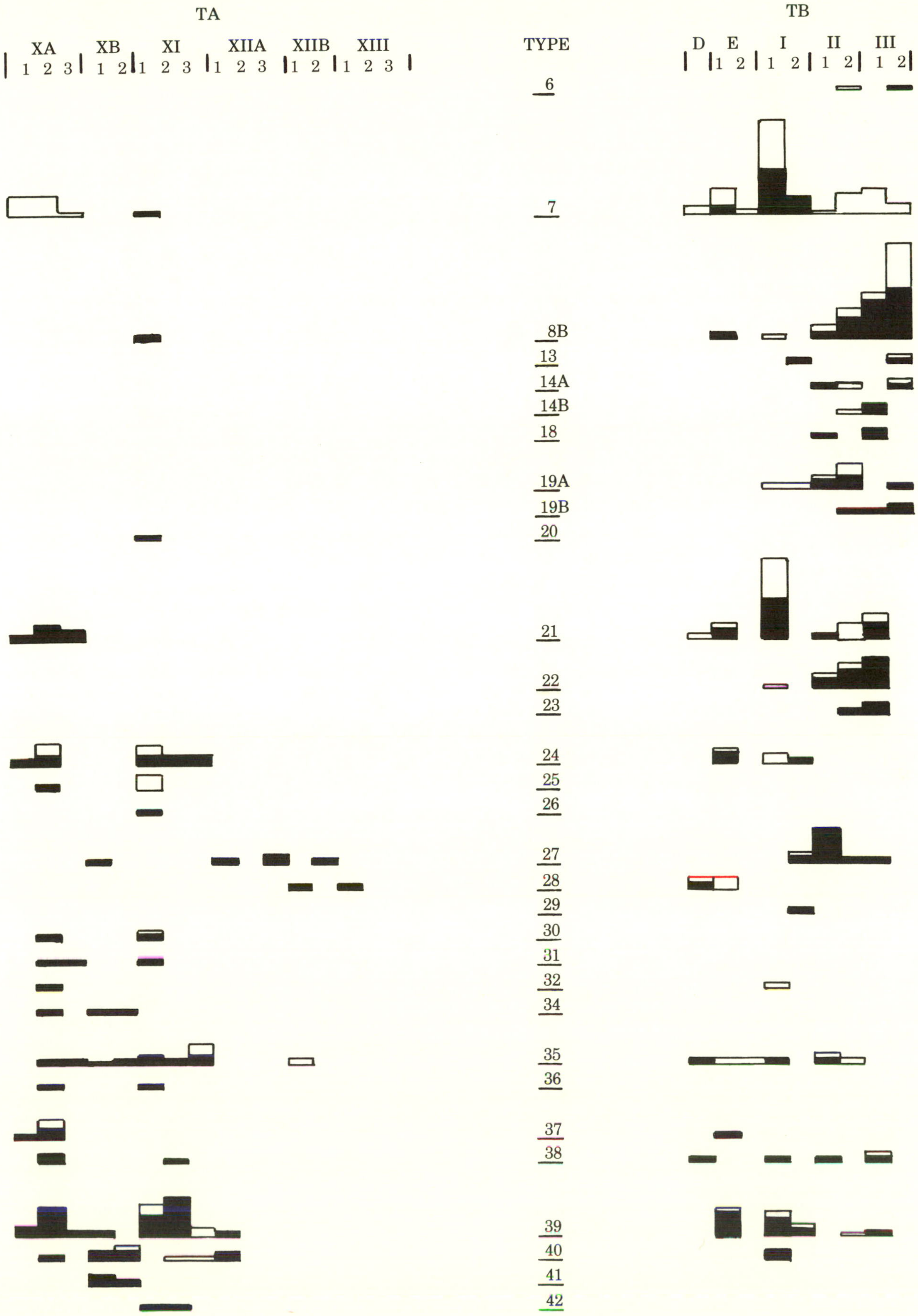

Fig. 6. Pottery from TA and TB

pair as a single type when found at Nippur.[5] Although it is clear that types 8B and 22 were generally earlier in date, and types 7 and 21 found throughout the Isin-Larsa and Old Babylonian levels, they are all probably best treated as variations on a single theme.

The painted jars (type 28) also present problems, since the TB examples are late, while the TA example is early. The latter, though, is illustrated on plate 91 of OIP 78 (item 17) and appears to be slightly unusual, suggesting that it might have been mistyped. Thus if we eliminate this vessel, then all painted jars occur in the upper levels of TB. In these circumstances, though, one must consider whether the absence of type 28 vessels from the upper levels of TA is significant. Since, as noted above, more examples of late types are expected from TA than from TB, it is possible that painted jars were used largely by bureaucrats. However, the sample is so small that it may be no more than a result of sampling error.

The more striking association between pottery types and rooms or features is that between shallow bowls and bread ovens. Twenty-seven percent of all shallow bowls (types 7, 8B, 21, and 22) were found in the four percent of the loci in TA and TB that contained bread ovens. Especially noteworthy are concentrations of such vessels in loci with multiple bread ovens. In the Middle East today, where bread is still made in the same way as at ancient Nippur, women usually provide themselves with a shallow dish of water or oil which they use to wet the dough to the correct consistency.[6]

During the most recent excavations at Nippur, a large Old Babylonian structure, House A, was excavated in area WB.[7] Texts describing the receipt of flour and the disbursement of bread, combined with archaeological evidence of numerous bread ovens, led the excavators to suggest that this structure served as a bakery. Although not directly associated with the ovens, one of the more curious features of this building was the pairs of shallow bowls found against the walls in many of the rooms. It seems possible that in this commercial bakery, the preparation of dough took place in rooms separate from those where the bread was actually baked. Furthermore, the fact that these bowls were found in pairs might indicate that two bowls were necessary, perhaps one for oil and one for water. At the very least, there is again an association between shallow bowls and bread-making activities.

Potstands, together with the round-based (types 19A and B) and pointed-based (types 40A, B, and C) jars which they were designed to hold, were found almost exclusively in entrance chambers, courts, and living rooms. As in the Middle East today, these jars were made of slightly porous clay and were used to hold drinking water. At night the jars would have been placed in the courtyard so that evaporation from the jar's surface could cool its contents, the round and pointed bases, supported by potstands, providing maximum surface area for better cooling. By day these jars would have been moved to sheltered entrance chambers and living rooms, where visitors and family members could help themselves to their contents.[8]

Other vessels frequently found in the main, or living, rooms of houses were the decorated wares. The painted pots (types 24 and 35), the painted cup (type 39A), and the stamped vase (type 27) are all typically found in main rooms, while the undecorated bottle (type 37) was found in no other kind of room. The decoration on these vessels, their generally small size, and their forms all suggest that they were primarily used for serving food and drink.

[5] Judith A. Franke, "Area WB," in *Nippur 12*, ed. McGuire Gibson, Oriental Institute Communications, no. 23 (Chicago: Oriental Institute, 1978), p. 75, fig. 59.1.

[6] See, for example, Louise E. Sweet, *Tell Toqaan: A Syrian Village,* Anthropological Papers of the Museum of Anthropology, University of Michigan, no. 14 (Ann Arbor: University of Michigan Press, 1960), p. 133.

[7] Franke, "Area WB," pp. 54–61.

[8] See Sweet, *Tell Toqaan,* p. 120. I have been unable to find detailed descriptions of this practice in ethnographies, but have observed it in operation in Iran, Iraq, and Syria.

Other associations are less clear.[9] As might be expected most pottery came from the courtyards and the subsidiary rooms, many of which were used for storage, and not from entrance and living rooms. However, there do not seem to be particular ceramic types associated with either the storerooms or the courts, although type 14B, a squat pot, was frequently found in the courtyards. Unfortunately, the function of this pot remains unclear.

TABLETS

In previous chapters the differences between the tablets from TA and those from TB have been noted. Whereas TA yielded many private contracts concerned with property transfers, TB had none (with the solitary exception of the Atta archive); on the other hand, whereas in TB many temple accounts and some administrative documents were found, TA had none. Here, these differences and their implications will be examined in more detail.

Unlike other artifact categories, where the establishment of a typology often involves somewhat arbitrary divisions of a continuum, tablets fall into clearly defined categories. A distinction may be made between private activities, public activities, and educational activities. The first category includes contracts, private accounts, and letters; the second, palace and temple accounts and administrative documents; while the third includes school, literary, lexical, and mathematical texts.

The private documents provide the most information on the activities of the Old Babylonian Nippurites, and by far the most informative of these are the contracts. Not only do these texts include information on an individual's kinship position and often on the property that he owns, but dates place him in time, and witness lists provide a measure of his wider circle of associates. Some contracts, like sales and inheritance documents, must have belonged to owners of property, while others, such as rentals and loans—and even some adoption and marriage contracts—do not imply such property ownership. This distinction is important when contracts are found in good archaeological context, since the type of contract may or may not indicate whether the resident of the house was a property owner.

Two other subcategories of private document are important: letters and accounts. Since the letters lack both patronymics and dates, and since no particular professions are indicated by their receipt, they tell us little about their owners. The accounts are also not as informative as one might wish. In the first place, few are dated and patronymics are not used, again making it difficult to identify the transactors. Secondly, it is often extremely difficult to tell a private account from a public one. In many cases a temple or palace official wrote texts in his own name when he was conducting institutional business. Such texts, to modern eyes, are indistinguishable from private accounts. In consequence many institutional accounts have been probably misidentified as private accounts. Despite these drawbacks, the private accounts and especially the letters record further examples of individual action, albeit less informative than contracts.

Only those tablets which are undoubtedly concerned with the economic affairs of large institutions, in most cases temples, are here treated as institutional accounts, while the rare administrative texts form yet another category. Together, the institutional accounts and

[9] In attempting to determine such associations, only complete vessels from loci which appear undisturbed were examined. Thus many vessels from contexts which were disturbed—even if only by the presence of the later drain or burial—were discounted. Sherds were also discounted, since almost all of them came from a single type, the painted pot (type 24). Although many of the difficulties encountered in working with the pottery would have been greatly eased had all diagnostic sherds been noted, when the sherds come from only one type, then these data are merely misleading.

TABLE 21. TABLET DISTRIBUTIONS

TA							TB				
XA	XB	XI	XIIA	XIIB	XIII	Text Type	D	E	I	II	III
11(4)	...	11	...	...	...	Property contract	...	24	...	...	...
3(6)	...	15(1)	1	1	1	Nonproperty contract	... (2)	... (1)	4(1)	4	... (1)
1	... (1)	3(1)	...	...	... (1)	Letter	... (1)	...	2(2)	... (1)	1(2)
5(7)	1(1)	15	2	...	... (1)	Account	...	2(2)	7(2)	4	1(2)
...	...	...	...	...	...	Institutional account	1	1(2)	11(7)	3(2)	12(34)
...	...	...	...	...	...	Administrative document	...	1(1)	... (2)	1	...
36(3)	5(16)	1426(4)	1	1(1)	2	School text	5(9)	21(10)	37(8)	81(8)	1(10)

NOTE: Numbers in parentheses indicate numbers of tablets from poor or disturbed archaeological contexts.

administrative documents provide clear evidence for the bureaucratic and administrative activities conducted by the residents of the domestic structures in TB.

An examination of the distribution of tablet types over time (see table 21) reveals that different classes of document were common at different times. Earliest were the institutional accounts, most of which came from level III of TB, although other, later, texts of this kind occurred occasionally in the upper levels. Most noninstitutional text types were common in the late Isin-Larsa and early Old Babylonian levels, especially those contracts which did not imply property ownership, such as school texts and private accounts. Only the contracts which concerned property transfer were most common in the upper levels.

What conclusions can be drawn from this temporal variation? In the first place, Nippur's status as Mesopotamia's center of learning at this time seems to be based on a very short period of intense activity. Only in level XI of TA and in levels II and I of TB are large numbers of school tablets found. Although some such texts come from later levels of TA and TB, they were scattered and are best interpreted as earlier tablets deposited in later levels. In the discussion of the TA materials, it was suggested that the economic difficulties which beset Nippur during the reign of Samsuiluna may have resulted in a migration of the scribes to the safer cities to the north and thus in the closing of Nippur's scribal schools. The evidence from TB tends to support such a scenario.

Secondly, the tablet distributions from TB suggest that although institutional accounting was common in the early Isin-Larsa period,[10] this rapidly ceased to be the case. As noted above, some of the private accounts and even some loans[11] may actually refer to the transaction of an institution's business by its agent. Thus, it seems that as the locus of administrative activities shifted from public to private dwellings in the late Isin-Larsa and Old Babylonian periods, so too did institutional accounting become more personalized. This is not to say that institutional activities themselves differed significantly.

Finally, while the distribution of school texts and institutional accounts reflects changes in the *modus operandi* of governmental servants and educators, the distribution of the contracts points to changes in the activities of private individuals. The large number of contracts found in the upper levels of TA and TB is the direct result of the 1739 B.C. economic crisis. Since the associated economic hardships affected individuals more than institutions, it is these private documents that reflect the destabilizing effect of economic uncertainty.

[10] Although the many graves and foundations which cut into TB level III mean that none of these institutional accounts were found in completely undisturbed loci, in many instances the part of the locus in which they were found seems to have been undisturbed. Nevertheless, some degree of doubt must always be attached to the findspots of these tablets.

[11] The evidence suggests that some moneylenders who occur frequently on loan texts were simply agents of the state institutions which undertook to provide the loans.

The significance of tablet findspots is not always clear. Most were found in courtyards and in main, or living, rooms, although some subsidiary rooms housed tablets. Tablets were frequently kept in pots, or perhaps on shelves or in baskets attached to the wall; except in trash areas, no tablets were found in the center of a locus. Unlike other artifacts, tablets were not items of daily use—rather, they were written to record an event and stored. The only exception to this practice is the school tablet, which was apparently often melted down after use. In those houses which were loci of scribal training, TB Houses B and D, and TA House F, school tablets were generally found throughout the structure.

TOOLS

"Tools" is used here as an umbrella term to cover many different classes of artifacts with different cultural implications. The major categories are jewelry, weights, seals and sealings, weapons, blades, manufacturing tools, toys, stone bowls, and tools used in the production of textiles. Clearly such a collection of widely divergent types cannot be treated as a whole. Ethnographic universals would suggest that items such as drills and chisels pertain to male manufacturing activities and spindle whorls to female domestic behavior; arrowheads and maceheads have to do with war, or at least hunting, while rattles and whistles were the playthings of children. This variety among the items here referred to as tools calls for their subdivision into meaningful categories.

To a large extent, the typology adopted here follows the list of items on pages 96–113 of OIP 78. However, because this discussion is limited to such finds as may have cultural significance, it is that cultural significance which has provided the organizational principle. Thus in OIP 78, jewelry was divided according to its ornamental function—into rings, bracelets, pendants, etc.—while here the only distinction is whether or not it is made of metal. Jewelry is deposited in an archaeological setting in one of three ways: First, and most common, jewelry may have accompanied the dead at the time of burial; second, it may have been lost; and third, the findspot may have been its place of manufacture. In the first two cases the cultural implications of the burial or loss of a ring as opposed to a pendant are minimal. If, on the other hand, the item is found in its place of manufacture, then distinctions between lapidary and metalwork become significant. It is for these reasons that lapidary and metalwork have been distinguished, while rings and bracelets have not.

For most other tool categories, the catalog in OIP 78 could be followed more closely. However, in the publication, arrowheads and maceheads were treated quite separately because they were made of different materials—whereas here, function is held more significant than manufacture, so they form a single category of weapons. Flint blades, on the other hand, are distinguished from metal blades since the differences in raw material have broad implications for manufacturing, function, and the wealth of their owners. Of the tools used in manufacturing, awls and chisels have been grouped together, as have drills and drillheads, and whetstones and polishers. In each case, the members of the pair are hard to distinguish one from the other and are normally used in related activities. Seals and seal impressions have been grouped together since the latter imply the presence of the former—in OIP 78 sealings were hardly noted. Stone bowls, needles, and spindle whorls each form clear individual categories, although the last can be confused with the wheels of clay chariots.[12] Clay rattles are the items most often classified as toys, but here clay whistles are also included in this category. Many other classes of items are listed in OIP 78, but these were either very rare or

[12] Where there exists doubt about whether an item was a spindle whorl or a chariot wheel, it has been counted in both categories.

absent in the Isin-Larsa and Old Babylonian periods. Also, the many copper/bronze fragments which were found have been omitted from consideration since they could have been part of jewelry, needles, chisels, blades, weapons, or nails. The discussion will therefore be limited to those items which occur with the most frequency and which seem to tell us the most about the activities of the TA and TB residents.

In examining the tools from TA and TB it will occasionally be useful to compare the frequency of occurrence of items found in TA with those from TB. However, since TA was generally smaller in area than TB, since the upper levels of TB were more heavily disturbed than those of TA, and since the Isin-Larsa and Old Babylonian materials have been divided into nine floors in TB and into sixteen floors in TA, any simple comparison of frequencies is rendered meaningless.

Many methods of making comparisons of object frequency between two excavated areas have been suggested, but most have unacceptable built-in assumptions, and all rely upon more detailed information than was recorded during the course of the TA and TB excavations. An attempt has been made here to arrive at a series of correction factors, one for each level, which if multiplied by the number of finds would allow comparison between different levels and different areas. The total number of finds, excluding tablets and potsherds,[13] was used in this calculation. The correction factors are designed to adjust the frequency of items found so that each level would have 100 items and each area 10 levels. These numbers were chosen because they did not depart too far from reality. To calculate the correction factors, the number of objects from each level was divided into 100. To correct for the differences in the number of excavation levels between the areas, the correction factors from TA levels were divided by 1.6 since TA had sixteen levels, while those from TB by 0.9 since TB had nine levels. These correction factors are listed in table 22. Clearly such a method is very crude, but more sophisticated techniques are inappropriate when the data-recording techniques themselves leave so much to be desired.

The first observation to be made from the table 22 results is that, in general, objects other than pottery and figurines were less common in TA than in TB (although items of domestic use, such as needles and spindle whorls, were somewhat more common in TA than in TB). Whereas in TB 40% of all items found were tools of one kind or another, only 30% of those from TA fall into this category. Most items differed little between the two areas. The only categories where the differences are striking are jewelry and weapons.

Jewelry

Turning first to jewelry, the various modes of deposition noted above are clearly visible in the archaeological record, and they contributed to the differences in distribution of these items in TA and TB. In general, jewelry was more common in TB than in TA, perhaps because those living in TB were slightly wealthier and more likely to wear jewelry than those in TA. This pattern is confirmed by an examination of the grave goods associated with the TB level III and the TA level XIII burials. The TB burials were often accompanied by jewelry in the form of beads, pendants, etc., while these items were rare in the TA burials.

[13] Potsherds have not been included for this calculation because their recording was irregular. Tablets, on the other hand, were recorded well. However, since they tend to be found in large caches—over 1,000 tablets found in one area of TA, for instance—their inclusion would have greatly distorted the results. As has been noted above, tablets were not items of daily use, as were the pottery, figurines, and tools; rather they were written to record an event and then stored, or they were used in the process of scribal training and then thrown away or stored until the need for new tablet clay led to their reuse. Both of these situations sometimes led to uneven storage of large numbers of tablets.

TABLE 22. Distribution of Tools

Level	No.	Correction Factor	Jewelry T-1, T-2		Weapons T-3		Manufacturing T-6, T-7, T-8		Sewing T-9, T-11		Seals T-12		Weights T-10		Blades T-4, T-5		Toys T-13		Stone bowls T-14	
			No.	Adjusted	No.	Adjusted	No.	Adjusted	No.	Adjusted	No.	Adjusted	No.	Adjusted	No.	Adjusted	No.	Adjusted	No.	Adjusted
TA:																				
XA-1	42	1.49	9	13.41	1	1.49	1	1.49	...	...	3	4.50	3	4.50	1	1.49	...	...	1	1.49
XA-2	66	0.95	4	3.78	2	1.89	2	1.89	1	0.95	4	3.78	8	7.56	...	...	...	...	...	...
XA-3	16	3.90	3	11.71	...	...	...	...	...	...	...	...	...	...	1	3.90	...	...	...	...
XB-1	18	3.47	...	...	...	...	1	3.47	...	...	2	6.95	...	...	...	...	...	...	...	...
XB-2	14	4.46	...	...	...	...	...	...	...	...	...	...	...	...	1	4.46	...	...	...	...
XI-1	43	1.45	1	1.45	...	...	...	...	2	2.90	1	1.45	4	5.80	...	...	1	1.45	...	...
XI-2	20	3.12	...	...	...	...	...	...	4	12.50	...	...	1	3.12	...	...	...	...	...	...
XI-3	31	2.01	2	4.02	...	...	1	2.01	1	2.01	1	2.01	1	2.01	...	...	...	...	...	...
XIIA-1	6	10.42	...	...	...	...	...	...	...	...	...	...	...	...	...	...	...	...	...	...
XIIA-2	2	31.30	...	...	...	...	...	...	...	...	...	...	...	...	...	...	...	...	...	...
XIIA-3	12	5.21	1	5.21	...	...	1	5.21	...	...	3	15.63	...	...	...	...	...	...	...	...
XIIB-1	25	2.50	3	7.50	...	...	3	7.50	1	2.50	2	5.00	3	7.50	...	...	...	...	...	...
XIIB-2	6	10.42	...	...	...	...	...	...	...	...	2	20.84	...	...	...	...	...	...	...	...
XIII-1	33	1.89	3	5.67	...	...	...	...	2	3.78	1	1.89	2	3.78	...	...	...	...	...	...
XIII-2	28	2.23	2	4.46	1	2.23	2	4.46	1	2.23	3	6.69	1	2.23	...	...	4	8.92	1	2.23
XIII-3	4	15.63	...	...	...	...	...	...	...	...	1	15.63	...	...	...	...	...	...	...	...
Total	366		28	57.21	4	5.61	11	26.03	12	26.87	23	84.37	23	36.50	3	9.85	5	10.37	2	3.72
TB:																				
D	34	3.27	4	13.08	1	3.27	4	13.08	...	...	...	...	2	6.54	1	3.27	2	6.54	...	...
E-1	46	2.42	2	4.84	...	...	...	...	1	2.42	4	9.68	...	...	1	2.42	...	...	1	2.42
E-2	13	8.55	...	...	...	...	...	...	1	8.55	2	17.10	2	17.10	...	...	...	...	1	8.55
I-1	90	1.23	7	8.61	1	1.23	2	2.46	4	4.92	7	8.61	4	4.92	2	2.46	...	...	...	...
I-2	43	2.58	4	10.32	1	2.58	1	2.58	...	...	7	18.06	2	5.16	...	...	...	...	...	...
II-1	123	0.90	8	7.02	1	0.90	1	0.90	1	0.90	42	37.80	4	3.60	7	6.30	3	2.70	1	0.90
II-2	109	1.02	17	17.34	2	2.04	8	8.16	1	1.02	22	22.44	4	4.08	3	3.06	...	...	5	5.10
III-1	127	0.87	12	10.44	4	3.48	3	2.61	...	...	7	6.09	2	1.74	1	0.87	...	...	3	2.61
III-2	142	0.78	29	22.62	2	1.56	2	1.56	5	3.90	18	14.04	3	2.34	5	3.90	...	...	5	3.90
Total	727		83	94.27	12	15.06	21	31.35	13	21.71	109	133.82	23	45.48	20	22.28	5	9.24	16	23.48

Those items of personal decoration which were found outside graves and the lapidary workshop in level III of TB show no distinct pattern of distribution in either TA or TB. Apparently the chance of losing a bead or earring in the houses with their floors of reed mats was as great as in the streets and courtyards. Thus the occasional beads and other items noted throughout TA and TB tell us little about the lives of the residents other than that those living in TB were more likely to sport bead necklaces and other jewelry.

Weapons

The distribution pattern of the weapons (T-3), mostly arrowheads and maceheads, was quite different and showed marked patterning. As can be seen in table 22, weapons are nearly three times more common in TB than they are in TA, but in both areas they are concentrated at the beginning and end of the sequence. Political unrest characterized the beginnings of the Isin-Larsa period and the last two decades of Nippur's Old Babylonian occupation. Between these two periods, during the reigns of Rīm-Sîn of Larsa and Hammurabi of Babylon, was half a century of relative peace. The weapons were concentrated in the early Isin-Larsa levels of TB III and TA XIII, and in the late levels TB D and TA XA. Although the association between weapons and particular types of loci is not clear, only four weapons were found inside rooms; all others came from open spaces, streets, courtyards, or from loci whose functions are unclear or are foundations. The exact significance of these data is not clear, but perhaps the weapons found in TA level XIII and TB level III reflect the penetration of political unrest into the streets of Nippur, as has been suggested above on the basis of burials and historical accounts of the destruction of Nippur. Perhaps this is also the explanation for the weapons found in the latest Old Babylonian levels of TA and TB. The eruption of open fighting within the confines of the city might well have precipitated the abrupt abandonment which is so well documented in the archaeological record. No further conclusions can be drawn, but the association between weapons and periods of political instability seems clear.

Manufacturing, Sewing, and Blades

Those items which can truly be described as tools can be divided into three categories. First are the manufacturing tools—the awls, chisels, drills, whetstones, and polishers (T-6, T-7, T-8)—which must have been used by smiths, carpenters, etc., in the pursuit of their trades. Second are those items used in domestic manufacture, especially in textile working—the needles and spindle whorls (T-9, T-11)—which must have been used by the women as part of their daily activities. Finally, there are the stone and bronze blades (T-4, T-5), which could have been used for both domestic and manufacturing activities. Other items here characterized as tools are the stone bowls (T-14), whose function is obscure, and toys (T-13).

An examination of the distribution of these items shows that while manufacturing tools occurred in small numbers in both TA and TB in all periods, tools associated with domestic production were a little more common in TA. This pattern fits our interpretation of the two areas in that only in TA were domestic activities predominant. The most significant differences in distribution, however, can be seen in those items whose functions are least clear: blades and stone bowls. Both of these items are considerably more common in TB than in TA, especially in the early levels, but since their social significance is obscure, this difference in patterning does not lead to any conclusions.

Weights and Seals

Interpretation of the two categories left for last, the weights (T-10) and seals and sealings (T-12), is easier since both were used in economic activities, sealing and weighing commodities.

With regard to the weights, it is important to establish the kinds of materials that they were used to weigh. Most weights were small items, of usually only a few grams, presumably designed for use with small balances. Since silver was used as a medium of exchange at this time, since the weights themselves often weigh about 1 shekel or less, and since other commodities, such as grain and flour, were measured by volume and not by weight, it seems reasonable to suggest that these weights were used primarily for weighing silver. As such, they should be considered items related to commercial, not domestic, activities.

Weights were common in both TA and TB, but their distributions were different. In TA they were generally found in groups either in courtyards or in main rooms. These groups of weights were probably used together in commercial activities; indeed in one instance they were found together with some loan texts, suggesting that they may have been used to weigh out the silver that was lent. In TB, weights were generally found singly and were not associated with any particular type of loci, although pairs of weights were found in two rooms in contexts similar to those of TA. These TB data are not easy to interpret, but perhaps here weights were used more commonly and for more varied transactions than was the case in TA.

With respect to the other items associated with commercial activities, seals and sealings, there is a striking difference between the finds from TA and those from TB. The ratio of seals to sealings in TA was 3:2. In TB it was less than 1:5. In both areas sealing activities were more common in the early periods, and courtyards and main rooms were the usual findspots.

It is not difficult to associate this discrepancy in sealing activities with the differences in occupation between these two areas that have already been noted. The seals from TA, especially those from the early levels, were probably used to seal private documents. Although bur-gul seals, perishable clay seals made for a single transaction, were more commonly used for sealing contracts, some loans and rentals, and many early Isin-Larsa contracts were sealed with stone seals. The TA seals were therefore used for sealing texts, and the relative paucity of seal impressions from TA is probably an indication that these people were not in the habit of receiving sealed consignments of goods. The opposite was true in TB. Seal impressions on bullae and on clay jar stoppers were common, especially in the lower levels, as were texts describing the receipt and disbursement of the types of goods that would have come in these sealed containers. But seal impressions, many of which seem to have come from trash heaps, were also common in TB level II. Careful examination of these impressions shows that some, but not all, were sealed by the owner of TA House K. Thus these impressions, though found in TB, represent the consignment of goods by the chief resident of TA, albeit acting in his official capacity as a $gudu_4$ of the Ninlil temple. Two explanations of the presence of these sealings can be advanced: First, the impressions came from goods which had been sealed by an inhabitant of TA but which had been opened by a resident of TB, the impressions then being discarded. Second, they had been discarded by the TA resident in the garbage dump closest to the back of his house, a dump which just happened to be located in TB (see pl. 30). Regardless of which explanation is correct, the prevalence of sealings in TB from contexts other than trash heaps and their relative absence in TA must be seen as further testimony of the administrative functions of the TB area as compared with TA.

FIGURINES

Clay figurines and plaques were found throughout TA and TB in all levels. Their variety impeded the establishment of a typology; some types were clear, such as the nude female figurines and plaques, but others, such as male figurines, had no standard form. The typology presented here (see Appendix III) is an attempt both to be comprehensive and to make distinctions of social significance. However, since in many instances, the categorizing of an item is based on only a rough sketch, or sometimes only a description, observations on stylistic changes within categories were impossible.

Before examining the distributions of the figurines, their function must first be established. In OIP 78, the excavators interpreted all plaques and figurines as being of magical or religious significance. While this must certainly be the case in many instances, some of the many animal figurines and boats could also have been toys.

A second point of difference arises over the interpretation of the purpose of the female figurines. The excavators rejected the idea that the nude female figurine might have been used in fertility magic, as documented in later texts. Their reasons for this rejection were that these figurines were more common in the Old Babylonian period than they were in the later levels contemporary with the texts which describe their use as charms. However, archaeological preservation depends on many factors, one of which is the composition of the artifact. It is possible that the infrequency of such figurines in later levels resulted from their very popularity, a popularity that could have led to their manufacture from unbaked clay instead of the baked clay of earlier periods.[14] A parallel may be drawn from the Old Babylonian evidence. In TA the most common type of seal impression was that made from the clay bur-gul seal, but no such seals have been found in the area. Several stone cylinder seals, on the other hand, have been found. This is due presumably to differing usage patterns between stone and clay seals and, more significantly, to the different rates of preservation of stone seals in comparison with unbaked clay seals. The possibility that the nude female figurines were used in the same kinds of magical practices as are documented in the later texts therefore cannot be ruled out.

Support for this hypothesis comes from an analysis of the distribution pattern of the nude female figurines and plaques. The female figurines are extremely rare in TA but common in TB, especially in the early levels, with most stratified examples found in streets, courts, and open areas. The plaques depicting nude females, on the other hand, were found in TA and TB in both living and open spaces, but were more common in the later levels of TB and in the earlier levels of TA. The model beds and erotic plaques, both of which may also be associated with fertility magic, were too rare to reveal a significant pattern of distribution.

Conclusions from such data are necessarily tentative since magical and religious beliefs are very hard to elucidate from the material record, but nevertheless a pattern may be observed similar to that which might be expected were these items used for magical purposes. The presence of female figurines in public areas of TB suggests that the practice of burying such a figurine in a place where a man's ladylove might walk over it and thus become enamored of the burier, as documented in later periods,[15] may have a history reaching back into the Old Babylonian period and earlier. In TB, especially in the early levels, much of the area was devoted to open space and streets, and even the buildings were of a public nature. It is in precisely such a public environment that seduction magic of this kind is to be expected; one's chances of success were the charm buried in a private area would have been much less.

The function of the female plaques, on the other hand, seems to have been different. These were found more often inside houses, which suggests that, like the other plaques, they were used as wall decoration. It is possible that they, and perhaps the pornographic plaques and model beds, were used in the home as fertility amulets. If this were the case, it is not surprising that they were found in both TA and TB, and in TB especially in the later levels when the domestic character of the area comes to the fore.

[14] Although the Mesopotamian archaeological record is replete with unbaked clay artifacts (most notably tablets) which have been preserved, these have generally been found in situations where they were buried under considerable amounts of debris. Where such objects have spent any time close to the surface, and thus in a position to suffer alternating periods of wet and dry, preservation is poor or nonexistent.

[15] Robert Biggs, *ŠA.ZI.GA.: Ancient Mesopotamian Potency Incantations,* Texts from Cuneiform Sources, vol. 2 (Locust Valley: J. J. Augustin, 1967), p. 70.

The distribution of the other figurines and plaques shows no such clear pattern. Those items that might have been no more than toys—animal figurines and chariots—were found throughout TA and TB. The other plaques, many of which had clear religious motifs, were also found in both areas, mostly in houses and courts, but their distribution does not clarify whether they were used as icons or simply as decoration, albeit of a religious nature.

CHRONOLOGY

One of the purposes of this artifact study was to construct a relative chronology between TA and TB, and to try to match that with known events in the history of Nippur. Although this exercise was attempted by the original excavators, it is worth repeating for three reasons: First, the changes suggested here regarding the stratigraphy for TB and especially TA imply a reevaluation of the chronology of the two areas. Second, the data from TA and TB were originally analyzed on the assumption that archaeological remains accumulated at a steady rate, an assumption that has since been shown to be untrue. Finally, in attempting to fit a chronology to the archaeological remains, the excavators did no more than attach generalized political/archaeological terms to levels. It is now possible to go further and to associate particular levels with events in Nippur's history.

The two most useful artifact classes for establishing chronologies are tablets and pottery. The dated tablets from undisturbed loci serve as *termini post quem* for the levels in which they were found, while variations in pottery style reflect the changing fashions of the time. Beyond this, varying distributions of artifacts may be associated with particular social, economic, or political events in the history of the city.

An examination of the dated tablets yields table 23, which records the latest dated tablet from each level. Tablets from apparently undisturbed contexts have been distinguished from those from areas which show evidence of later disturbance, and the number of dated tablets from each level has been recorded to help evaluate these data. This table signifies no more than that the level in which the dated table was found can be no earlier than that date. In levels where very few dated tablets were found, it is quite possible for the level to be later than the date on the tablet. In both TA and TB the last several levels—TA level XA floors 1-3 and TB D and E1-2—are all dated to the last years of Nippur's Old Babylonian occupation. It seems probable that TA level XA-3 and TB level E-2 were the last occupation levels, with those above simply representing the period of abandonment. In addition, the dated tablets from TA level XI show that level XB represented the period when Nippur was partially abandoned, between about 1739 and 1730 B.C. Area TB, on the other hand, shows no such period of abandonment—it must be assumed that bureaucrats were less affected by the crisis than were small farmers. Thus TA level XI may be roughly equated with TB level I and both described as the latest pre-crisis levels. The dated tablets indicate that these levels in TA and TB may represent the long period of peace in this part of Mesopotamia that followed the conquest of Isin by Rīm-Sîn in 1793 B.C. and continued until Samsuiluna's weakness brought on the political and economic troubles that triggered the 1739 B.C. crisis.

For the lower levels of both areas, dated tablets from good contexts are much less common. However, if, as the evidence suggests, the early Isin-Larsa temple accounts from level III floors 1 and 2 of TA can be considered contemporary with the loci in which they were found, TB level III floor 2 must be the earliest level of Isin-Larsa occupation. Since the slim evidence from TA levels XIV and XV suggests that they were Ur III in date, perhaps TA level XIII should be seen as roughly equivalent to TB level III floor 2. TB level III floor 1 and TA level XIIB would then seem to be roughly equivalent, dating perhaps between about 1940 and 1870 B.C., while TB level II and TA level XIIA can be assigned dates of between around 1870 and 1800 B.C. This chronology is shown in table 24, but it must be stressed that the dates

TABLE 23. The Latest Dated Tablets from TA and TB

Level	Tablets from Good Contexts		Tablets from Disturbed Contexts	
	Date[a]	No.[b]	Date[a]	No.[b]
TA:				
XA-1	1721	8	1732	5
XA-2	1737	3	. . .	. . .
XA-3	1723	4	. . .	. . .
XB-1	1755	1	. . .	. . .
XB-2	. . .	. . .	. . .	. . .
XI-1	1738	5	. . .	. . .
XI-2	1739	14	. . .	. . .
XI-3	. . .	. . .	1793	1
XIIA-1	. . .	. . .	. . .	. . .
XIIA-2	. . .	. . .	. . .	. . .
XIIA-3	1860[c]	. . .	1840	1
XIIB-1	. . .	. . .	1860–1837	1
XIIB-2	. . .	. . .	. . .	. . .
XIII	. . .	. . .	. . .	. . .
TB:				
D	1740	1	. . .	. . .
E-1	1743	2	. . .	. . .
E-2	1724	18	. . .	. . .
I-1	1750	4	1801	1
I-2	1809	1	1749–1721	3
II-1	1872	4	1842	1
II-2	. . .	. . .	1762	1
III-1	2037	2	1935–1923	14
III-2	. . .	. . .	1935–1923	5
IV	2028–2004	22	. . .	. . .

[a] Date of latest tablet.

[b] Number of dated tablets from level.

[c] This date is approximate, but we know that the people mentioned on the tablets were active at about this time.

assigned, especially to the early levels, are to be considered mere approximations and that the true dates of the levels may be considerably different. Furthermore, while TA and TB were excavated as though whole areas were rebuilt every so often, in actuality each area was probably continually under partial construction. Thus some temporal overlap between successive levels must be expected. Only the partial abandonment of both areas may be considered events which affected most or all of an area.

To obtain confirmation of the chronology proposed here, the archaeological remains and the distributions of artifacts must be examined. Turning first to the archaeological remains, it is apparent that both areas are characterized by a level of human burials. In previous chapters these burials, dug into level XIII of TA and level III-2 of TB, have been interpreted as the burying of the dead following the attack on Nippur that is commemorated in the "Lamentation over the Destruction of Nippur." If this is correct, then both sets of burials took place around 1940 B.C., as shown in table 24. These are not, however, the only burials encountered.[16] Group infant burials have been found in the upper levels of both TA and TB.

[16] Burials were also dug into both TA and TB after the period of abandonment that followed 1720 B.C., but these burials do not date to the period under consideration.

TABLE 24. SUGGESTED CHRONOLOGY FOR TA AND TB

TB	TA	Suggested Dates B.C.
		1720
D/E	XA	
		1730
I-1	XB	
		1740
I-2	XI	
		1800
II	XIIA	
		1870
III-1	XIIB	
		1940
III-2	XIII	
		2000

These burials were apparently dug in TA levels XA and XB and in TB level I,[17] all of which can be dated to the 1739 and 1720 B.C. crises. It has been suggested above that the instability of settlement that marked the last two decades of Nippur's Old Babylonian occupation might have been accompanied by famine, and perhaps also epidemic disease, to which these burials may bear sad testimony. If this interpretation holds up, then the assignment of dates to the upper levels shown in table 24 is supported by the archaeological evidence.

The last elements to be examined in this discussion of chronology are the artifact distributions. The most potent chronological tool here is the pottery, which in general seems to confirm the scheme laid out in table 24. If the discussion is limited only to those vessels from unassailable stratigraphic contexts (see fig. 6), the following pattern can be observed: Many of the types which are found in the upper levels of TA, where pottery is common, are rare or absent in TB, where the upper levels were badly disturbed and poorly represented. Similarly, the early types from TB are rarely found in TA, where the early levels yielded little pottery. Such a pattern tends already to confirm our suggested chronology, but a look at the distribution of types 24, 27, and 39—types which are found in both areas—serves as further verification. Type 24 is found in TA levels XI to XA and in TB from levels I to D; type 27 is found in TA levels XIIA and XIIB and TB levels III-1 to I-2; and type 39 is found in TA levels XI, XB, and XA, and in TB levels I and E. Finally, if, following the scheme in table 24, the pottery distributions from TA and TB are combined, a distribution pattern emerges which conforms to expectations of normal increase and decrease in popularity of styles (see fig. 7).[18]

Two of the other artifact categories appear to vary over time in both areas. The most significant are the concentrations of literary and school texts. These concentrations, not the scattered texts of this kind, seem to be found in loci of scribal training, places where a single scribe educated a few boys in his home. I have suggested above (p. 117) that these schools closed at the time of the economic crisis of 1739 B.C. and that the concentrations of school tablets—at least in TA—represent the abandonment of such schools. In TB two such concentrations have been found. The earliest occurs in House B level II floor 1 and the second in House D level I floor 1. Given the uncertainty of our crossdating, these two concentrations in TB would seem to be roughly contemporary with the tablets found in TA House F level XI

[17] There is also some slim evidence of a similar burial dug in TB level D.

[18] Fig. 7 conforms roughly to the evaluation of the ceramic sequence made by the current excavator of Nippur, McGuire Gibson (personal communication).

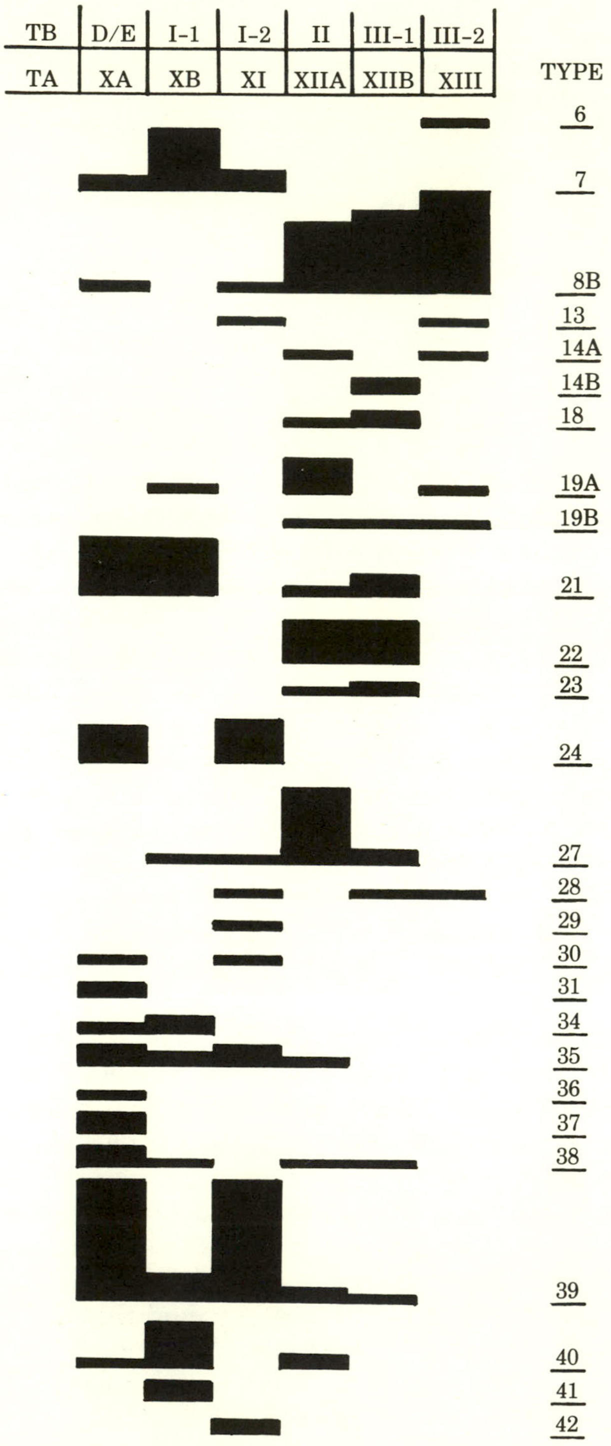

Fig. 7. Ceramic Chronology

floors 1–3. This evidence suggests that Nippur's small schools were probably already in place at the time of Rīm-Sîn's conquest of Isin in 1792 B.C. and that they prospered for about half a century until the economic crisis of 1739 B.C. left Nippur no longer capable of supporting a scribal class for which such schools were a preparation.

The second artifact type which may help confirm the chronology is the weapons. Weapons were common in TB only in levels D and III, and were found in TA only in levels XA and XIII. Following the chronology proposed here, these levels of weapon concentration will be found to date precisely to the times in Nippur's history when periods of political unrest are documented which might have made ownership of such items desirable.

The chronology outlined in table 24 allows all the available data—the stratigraphy, burials, tablets, pottery, weapons, etc.—to be associated with the known events in Nippur's history. This fit was made possible by the revised stratigraphy which has been introduced in this volume. This new stratigraphic assessment not only permits an understanding of the data from TA and TB as reflections of the history of the time, but has also tightened the chronological span for many of the ceramic types published in OIP 78 (which remains the type sequence for southern Mesopotamia) and has belied the statement that "the most remarkable fact concerning the dated, stratified tablets is how 'unstratified' they are. . . . At best, cuneiform tablets can provide only a reasonable approximation of the date of the level in which they are found."[19] On the contrary, once their depositional history is finally known and understood, the tablets from TA and TB become powerful indicators not only of the date but also of the character of the levels in which they were found.

[19] OIP 78, p. 74.

Chapter 6

Conclusions

So far this book has been concerned with the finer details of the data; the moment has now come to step back and view the evidence from TA and TB in the aggregate and attempt some generalizations which contribute to the understanding of Mesopotamian civilization as a whole. This chapter begins with a review of the evidence by comparing and contrasting the two excavation areas. Where TA and TB exhibit similarities in patterning, these features must be related to elements of basic culture shared by all Nippurites or to commonly experienced historical events. Where differences are noted, they underscore the richness and variety of Nippur society. Finally, an attempt will be made to answer the questions posed at the outset of this work about the size, composition, and significance of urban neighborhoods, the nature of the separation between them, and the relationship between large urban institutions and these residential units.

In OIP 78, TA and TB were considered to be two samples from a single population of domestic housing. This view stressed the elements of similarity between the two areas, elements which resulted from the domestic character of the two. In both TA and TB the houses were of mud brick and were probably never more than one story high. They usually shared party walls, so cooperation between neighbors was necessary. Most had an entrance chamber, at least one storeroom, a courtyard, and a living room, but there were exceptions. In some instances an entrance chamber or storeroom would be omitted, and in the larger houses that had multiple living rooms, specialized rooms such as bathrooms, kitchens, and stairways were sometimes found. Yet in spite of differences in house size and complexity, it is clear that each nuclear family received living, storage, and courtyard space, with access to the entire structure usually controlled by an entrance chamber.[1] The houses found in TA and TB not only resemble the architectural plans found occasionally on clay tablets,[2] but the same basic ideas are seen in house plans from the other Old Babylonian cities like Ur,[3] Sippar,[4] Shaduppum,[5] Isin,[6] etc.

In addition to the purely residential structures, both TA and TB have small buildings which may best be interpreted as shops. House P in TA seems to have served as a bakery, at least in its later phases, and its similarity to House T in TB suggests that the latter was also

[1] Elizabeth C. Stone, "Texts, Architecture and Ethnographic Analogy: Patterns of Residence in Old Babylonian Nippur," *Iraq* 43 (1981): 19–34.

[2] See OIP 78, pl. 52.

[3] Sir Leonard Woolley and Sir Max Mallowan, *Ur Excavations, vol. 7: The Old Babylonian Period* (London: British Museum Publications, Ltd., 1976).

[4] Leon de Meyer, *Tell ed-Der II* (Leuven: Editions Peeters, 1978).

[5] Taha Baqir, *Tell Harmal* (Baghdad: Directorate-General of Antiquities, 1959).

[6] B. Hrouda, ed., *Isin-Išān Baḥrīyāt I,* Bayerische Akademie der Wissenschaften philosophisch-historische Klasse, Abhandlungen neue Folge, vol. 79 (Munich: Verlag der Bayerischen Akademie der Wissenschaften, 1977); idem, *Isin-Išān Baḥrīyāt II,* Bayerische Akademie der Wissenschaften philosophisch-historische Klasse, Abhandlungen neue Folge, vol. 87 (Munich: Verlag der Bayerischen Akademie der Wissenschaften, 1981).

a commercial establishment of some kind. These shops were apparently scattered here and there amongst the houses, not grouped together. However, it may be that only those shops that provided staples for the residents were located amongst the houses, while others may have been grouped in as yet unexcavated commercial areas of the town. In the residential quarters at Ur,[7] the excavators identified similar shops, but there, small suqs, or local market or production areas, such as "Store Street" and "Bazaar Alley" in the AH area were also found.

The residents of both TA and TB supplemented the goods provided by these production centers by their own industry; not only do domestic bread ovens testify to bread baking on the household level, but in both areas the keeping of small numbers of domestic animals may have been common, at least in the early levels. The practice of omitting the entrance chamber and giving access to the house directly by way of the courtyard, seen especially in the early levels of TA, may be related to the urban animal husbandry evidenced in contemporary texts. With the omission of the entrance chamber, both people and animals had direct access to the courtyard, but the privacy of the family was maintained by the addition of an anteroom between the courtyard and the main living area. In the larger houses, this separation was effected by means of two courtyards, that in the rear reserved for the domestic unit, with a reception room located between the two courts. In all cases the houses were provided with both private quarters for the family and a room that could be used for entertaining outsiders, whether it was located next to the street, between the court and the living room, or between the two courts.

In addition to the use of enclosed courtyards for stabling animals, the Isin-Larsa levels of TB, and to a lesser extent TA, also were characterized by the presence of some quite sizeable, walled, open areas. Although the evidence suggests that in later times such areas were used primarily for trash disposal, during the early periods it seems likely that they were used for holding, on a short-term basis, large flocks of animals. If the courts and enclosures were used for these purposes, and if the concerns of both private and public documents are anything to go on, then animal husbandry must have been of importance to all segments of Nippur society in the early to mid Isin-Larsa period. By the Old Babylonian period, however, references to livestock in texts are rare, and the archaeology shows that in the residential areas accommodations were no longer made for their maintenance.

It seems probable that this keeping of animals in an urban setting was related to the political instability that characterized the early part of the Isin-Larsa period—instability which was also reflected in the distribution pattern of weapons and burials. In both TA and TB, the few weapons that were found, mostly maceheads and arrowheads, were concentrated in the lower levels, especially in open areas and courts. Furthermore, both TB level III and TA level XIIB were disturbed by burials of adults, adolescents, and children which were cut into the walls and rooms. Such a practice was unusual since occupied areas were not customarily used for burial. Since the sets of burials in TA and TB were contemporary, it seems likely that the warfare that characterized the Isin-Larsa period may have penetrated the city of Nippur itself, and that these burials represent the rebuilding of the city and burial of the dead that followed this event. This catastrophe was perhaps the one recorded in the "Lamentation over the Destruction of Nippur" and hinted at in other Išme-Dagan inscriptions.

The initial rebuilding of both TA and TB showed little change from the pattern established earlier, but perhaps a half century later both TA and TB experienced a complete change in plan. TB level II and TA level XIIA may represent the time when the kings of Isin secured control of the area and were able to turn their attention to the running of the city. In any event, the pattern that was then established was to persist for the remaining two centuries of early second millennium occupation. The basic character of these new configurations seems

[7] Woolley and Mallowan, *Ur Excavations,* vol. 7, pls. 122 and 124.

not to have differed from that shown in the earlier levels. TB had been a locus of administrative activity in Ur III and early Isin-Larsa periods, and so it continued, while the more purely domestic nature of TA also persisted. Nevertheless, in both areas the alterations in plan are to be related to changes in the population structure, especially in TA.

The new organization of these two areas was associated with an increase in the wealth and security of the city. The most obvious manifestation of this increase in well-being was the increased importance attached to literacy. Both TA and TB had what appear to be loci of scribal education. These were not actual schools, but the private houses of the teachers. They are characterized by a courtyard adapted for teaching, sometimes with one or more benches for teacher and students to sit on and a water container so that all could keep their tablet clay the proper consistency. These houses usually had quantities of school, literary, and lexical tablets in all rooms, although most were concentrated in the court and in the one room which may have been used as a classroom in inclement weather. It seems likely that most of TA and TB's residents had their children educated by these scribes since school tablets have been found in nearly every house. Unfortunately, Nippur was unable to maintain this level of sophistication. The schools flourished at the end of the Isin-Larsa period and during the reign of Hammurabi, but the unrest and probable ecological disruption that characterized the reign of Samsuiluna spelled the end of these schools. Nippur's post-crisis economy was too fragile to be able to support nonessential services; presumably the scribes who had been responsible for making Nippur Mesopotamia's cultural center moved to the cities in the north which were unaffected by the changes in water supply or turned their hands to other pursuits. Although scattered school texts were found in the post-crisis levels of both TA and TB, there is no evidence that they represent ongoing scribal education.

In addition to the closing of the scribal schools, there is evidence to suggest that the crisis had a more direct effect on the population. In both TA and TB, the remains of small rooms were used as a kind of burial vault and filled with jars containing the bodies of dead infants, with no other grave goods. Since these infants were deposited around 1739 B.C., they may indicate that the crisis was associated with famine and perhaps epidemic disease.

In TA—and perhaps TB—more infant burials mark the end of Old Babylonian occupation, suggesting that similar conditions may have accompanied the final abandonment of the city in 1720 B.C. It appears that the entire city, and indeed the rest of central Babylonia, was deserted from then until quite late in the Kassite period. The abandonment was apparently quite rapid, but orderly, with those items, like pottery and tablets, which were hard to transport or which had no value outside the city left in the houses. There is no evidence of looting; rather the houses seem slowly to have crumbled. In the succeeding centuries the entire area was used as a burial ground, presumably by nomadic groups who camped in the ruins of the city. It was at least three centuries later that Nippur and the rest of southern Mesopotamia were reclaimed from the desert and marshes through the building of new irrigation canals which allowed a renaissance of urban life in the area.

The similarities between TA and TB outlined above show that all Nippurites shared similar residential patterning and were affected by the same political and economic events. The similarities in house plans between TA and TB and the presence of shops among the houses indicate that different neighborhoods were similarly structured in terms of both house style and access to resources. Furthermore, the scribal schools that were found in both areas, together with the school tablets from other houses, suggest that scribal education was available to most members of this urban society. These features, together with the similarities in the artifactual inventories from TA and TB, show that any differences between the two areas did not affect basic elements in their social life.

TA residents might have shared general aspects of culture with those of TB, but their occupations were distinct. For the most part the residents of TA seem to have been small property owners, while those of TB were generally officials tied to the temple bureaucracy. In

TA many of the texts found concern the buying and selling of property, especially houses. In the case of House I especially, it was possible to demonstrate that the property described in the texts was the same as the house in which the texts were found.[8] In TB, on the other hand, the only contracts found were loans, rentals, and one adoption fragment, which do not of themselves imply real property ownership on the part of the retainers of the tablets. The texts which were common in TB were the temple accounts and administrative documents testifying to the bureaucratic pursuits of the residents of that area, types of documentation which were absent in TA. In sum, the evidence suggests that the residents of TA gained their livelihood through the management of privately held real estate and temple offices, while those of TB were landless bureaucrats.

These differences in property ownership were reflected in the architecture of the two areas. The houses in TA were very variable in size, shape, organization, and quality of construction, as one might expect where the buildings had been constructed by their owners. In contrast, in TB, where housing was apparently provided by the dominant institution, the houses were generally large, uniform in plan, and well constructed. In short, the houses in TA reflect the varying whims and competence of their owner-builders, while those in TB were constructed following formalized plans prepared by architects employed by the dominant institution, and made few concessions to the individual needs of the families which resided in them.

The size and organization of the houses in TA suggest that most housed no more than a nuclear family, although extended family residence was practiced in some instances (Houses I and K). Such a pattern is very similar to that observed in villages in the Middle East today,[9] where extended family residence is the stated ideal, even if it is only for a relatively short period during the life of a generation that such an ideal is obtainable. As is the case in the area today, TA showed the flexibility in property lines that is a feature of a residential area characterized by fissioning extended families. The architectural changes experienced by House I are a good example of this process.

The houses in TB, on the other hand, are not only much larger but exhibit little alteration in plan over time. This is what one would expect in an area of "public housing." They seem to have been built to house the ideal extended family; in the absence of private ownership the TB residents were unable to alter their living space to accommodate changes in family demography.

Not all variation in house size and complexity can be attributed to family size. In TA wealth differences must also have played a role. Unfortunately our ability to pinpoint variations in wealth is extremely limited; nevertheless, it appears that TA housed both the very rich residents of House K and the poor baker living in House P. Such wealth differences between neighbors are less apparent in TB.

Thus, although sharing aspects of general culture and history, TA and TB show marked distinction both in architecture and in the texts describing the activities of their residents. Since TA and TB are but 30 m apart, and since the evidence from the two areas suggests profound differences, it seems highly likely that they represented two distinct neighborhoods.

The differences which distinguish TA from TB are precisely those which defined neighborhoods in medieval Islamic cities.[10] Both TA and TB appear as residential districts whose occupants are united by ties of clientage and, in the case of TA, of kinship. Class distinctions, on the other hand, do not seem to have been reflected in the patterns of residence, as

[8] See also Stone, "Texts, Architecture and Ethnographic Analogy."

[9] Richard T. Antoun, *Arab Village* (Bloomington: Indiana University Press, 1972); Carol Kramer, *Village Ethnoarchaeology: Rural Iran in Archaeological Perspective,* Studies in Archaeology (New York: Academic Press, 1982); Patty-Jo Watson, *Archaeological Ethnography in Western Iran,* Viking Fund Publications in Anthropology, no. 57 (Tucson: University of Arizona Press, 1979).

[10] See, for example, Ira Lapidus, *Muslim Cities in the Later Middle Ages* (Cambridge: Cambridge University Press, 1984).

evidenced by the proximity of Houses P and K in TA, buildings which housed people of very different wealth and influence. Both areas are characterized by a street system based on a series of narrow culs-de-sac, some of which may have been closed by gates (locus 164 in TA, locus 42 in TB). It remains unclear how the neighborhoods were separated. While references to property next to "Wall Street" in texts belonging to members of the Ninlil-zimu family of TA might be taken as an indication that neighborhoods were walled, a look at the circulation patterns of TA and TB (pl. 35) suggests more that the houses of the two areas simply backed on to one another. Furthermore, the segregation of the two areas was not total. Not only were texts written by residents of the two quarters sometimes witnessed by the same individuals, especially the professionals, scribes, and seal-cutters, but seal impressions of the resident of TA's House K were found discarded in TB, albeit only about 20 m from the back of his house.

The most striking difference between TA and TB, and that which first led to the supposition that they represented distinct neighborhoods, was in the occupations of the two groups of residents. Nevertheless, occupation alone does not seem to have served to define neighborhoods. Instead, as was the case in medieval Islamic cities, the character of a neighborhood was often defined by a kernel institution. In TA the Ninlil-zimu family seems to have served as that kernel, drawing into the area kinsmen and clients, most of whom, like the Ninlil-zimu family, were concerned with the management of real estate and temple offices. In TB the kernel must have been the temple or temple storehouse whose administrators lived in the area. Here, no information on the backgrounds of the residents is preserved, but it seems likely that at least some of them may have been the descendants of those who had worked in the area in Ur III and Isin-Larsa times.

TA and TB differ not only in their core institutions but also in their histories. Setting aside TA's levels XIII and XIIB, for which so little information is available, TA may be viewed as a new neighborhood, and TB as an old one. Clearly TB level II and TA level XIIA, both of which date to mid Isin-Larsa times, around 1900–1880 B.C., involved a thorough reorganization of settlement, but while in TA an old residential area was cleared to make way for newcomers, in TB continuity in occupation suggests that the new houses were designed to provide the same population with a more attractive environment. Thus the types of activities recorded in the early texts—accounting for libations and other temple offerings, providing animals for the temple sacrifice, and administering temple lands—apparently continued to be the main occupation of TB residents in the late Isin-Larsa period. However, in keeping with the times, these activities were now conducted from residential structures, while their occupants also rented fields and loaned and borrowed silver and grain.

Some of these apparently private documents may be no more than records of public activities conducted in the name of the official responsible for such action, but this cannot be true of all such texts. Some surely represent individual action on the part of the TB residents, behavior that was unthinkable in Ur III or early Isin-Larsa times. Rental of land, dealing in silver and barley, and perhaps even the teaching of scribal arts may represent new possibilities for individual economic action that opened up in late Isin-Larsa times. It is possible that the realization of this degree of economic independence was the result of proximity to the much more autonomous neighborhood of TA. Nevertheless, even at the end of its Old Babylonian occupation, when some residents were largely concerned with private transactions, TB remained primarily a neighborhood of administrators.

The history of TA is both more complicated and more volatile. No evidence bearing on the nature of the TA residents for the early Isin-Larsa period has been preserved, but the general picture is of a somewhat impoverished area, perhaps one that was even losing population. Around 1880 B.C. the entire area was apparently razed to make way for the entry of a new group. At first, most of the excavated area was left as an open area dominated by House K, a building which was owned and occupied by the founding members of the large, powerful Ninlil-zimu lineage. Not only was this family to dominate the property owners of Nippur for the next one and a half centuries, but at the time of the founding of House K, it controlled vast amounts of real estate. In addition to the large holdings of house, field, and orchard property, the family owned an unbuilt urban area at least twice the size of TA, and no fewer than four complete temple offices.

It is not easy to understand how such wealth had been accumulated and how such a family was able to take over a section of the city, but what evidence there is suggests that this was a rural lineage which moved into the city at this time, lured at least in part by gifts of property from the king. No matter what its origins, the wealth of the Ninlil-zimu family and the location of its house placed it in a position to dominate the neighborhood. After perhaps as much as eighty years, the neighborhood of which TA is a sample became sufficiently crowded that the open area, possibly used by the Ninlil-zimu leadership for public meetings, began to fill in. Although one cannot identify all those who built their houses in TA, most of the first were clients of the dominant family. Some, like the resident of House F, provided services for the neighborhood as a whole, in this case the establishment of a small scribal school. Others, such as the residents of House N, were outsiders who moved into Nippur, apparently under the protection of the family living in House K. Over time, the assimilation of this group can be documented as sons were given typical Nippur names and became involved in the affairs of the city. The interest of the Ninlil-zimu family in these foreigners is not entirely clear, but since they seem to have been active moneylenders, they may have staked the residents of House K in some of their ventures. Moreover, House N residents occur as witnesses to some of the more important documents of the Ninlil-zimu family. The first to move into the space dominated by House K, then, were not kinsmen, but people providing particular services or who were brought in under the patronage of the dominant family.

When Hammurabi conquered southern Mesopotamia, one of his policies seems to have been to undermine the more autonomous elements of late Isin-Larsa society. This practice, well documented in Larsa[11] and elsewhere,[12] can also be seen both in the Ninlil-zimu texts and in the archaeology of TA. TB, already closely associated with state institutions, remained largely unaffected. Two events recorded in the texts testify to the weakening of TA's dominant lineage at that time: first, the challenge by one branch of the family, backed by Hammurabi, against the current leadership; and second, the division, reallotment, and sale of a large block of unbuilt urban property which had been owned in common by all members of the lineage since they first settled in Nippur nearly one and a half centuries earlier. Both of these events not only reflect the inability of the lineage to maintain a community of interest, but show further their inability to come to an agreement. In the first instance, the council of Nippur was called on to decide the case, while in the second, a final settlement was only arrived at after a year of wrangling.

Although it seems unlikely that any of the land under dispute in these instances was located in TA, the ability of the Ninlil-zimu family living in House K to dictate to the residents of the neighborhood was in eclipse. When Houses H and I were built, reducing the open area to a mere T-intersection, their owners seem to have been brought in not by the Ninlil-zimu family but by the one-time clients of that family, those living in Houses F and N. This is not to indicate that the residents of House K had abandoned all interest in the area; when House G was put up for sale, it found a ready purchaser in Ekur-andul, a member of one of the minor branches of the Ninlil-zimu family. However, the text which records this transaction does not indicate that the Ninlil-zimu leadership was at all instrumental in helping their kinsman acquire this property.

Further evidence for the lessening control of the lineage over TA is seen in the construction of the last house to be built in the area, House E. This was occupied by a woman, almost certainly a *nadītum*. The *nadītum* institution seems to have been controlled by a limited

[11] Fritz R. Kraus, *Briefe aus dem Archive des Šamaš-hazir* (Leiden: E. J. Brill, 1968).

[12] Norman Yoffee, *The Economic Role of the Crown in the Old Babylonian Period* (Malibu: Undena Publications, 1977).

number of Nippur lineages, and the Ninlil-zimu family was not one of them. Thus the construction of a house in TA by a *nadītum* must signify the intrusion of a member of a different kin group, although she would still have been the daughter of a property owner and not of a temple administrator or craftsman.

By the tenth year of Samsuiluna, TA was still physically dominated by House K, in spite of the filling in of the open area; and over half of the residents still had ties of kinship or clientage with members of the dominant family.

But this pattern was to change in the following year when what was probably a disruption of the water supply added to the already existing strains in Nippur society. In TA, those who had first settled as clients of the Ninlil-zimu family were the first to leave, implying that their patronage had been withdrawn as a response to the worsening economic climate. The scribal school was shut, never to open again, and the outsiders living in House N left, perhaps going to Iaḫalpilum, where they apparently owned some property. Moreover, Ekur-andul, the minor member of the dominant family, abandoned House G, while much of House I fell into the hands of an entrepreneur who hoped to profit from the disaster. In short, all or almost all of those who had once been tied to the residents of House K had left, leaving only the interlopers, such as the *nadītum* who owned House E, living in the area. Furthermore, the texts belonging to the remaining members of the Ninlil-zimu family indicate that even they abandoned all contact with other kinsmen. In the closing years of the Old Babylonian occupation of Nippur, Ninlil-zimu's descendants concentrated their resources in temple offices—property allied to urban institutions—and forged closer ties with those remnants of other families that had retained sufficient holdings to ride out the storm.

After a few years, economic conditions improved and TA was reoccupied, but by that time the Ninlil-zimu family had moved away, and House K was no longer a residential building. As TA was rebuilt we find no evidence for ties of kinship or clientage holding the neighborhood together. Nevertheless, the residents of TA were still drawn from the ranks of small property owners, indicating that even in the absence of a dominant family, the character of the neighborhood remained unchanged.

Even TB residents, with their ties to one or more large risk-sharing urban institutions, were not unaffected by the economic upheaval experienced by the city during the reign of Samsuiluna, but for only some TB residents was this economic crisis an unmitigated evil. Although those responsible for scribal education left the city, and famine and disease may have carried away some of their infants, some found new economic opportunities in the plight of the small property owners who had abandoned their holdings when fleeing the city. While much privately held agricultural land had apparently become worthless, presumably due to a lack of irrigation water, temple offices retained some, if not all, of their previous value. The social, political, and economic unrest allowed some TB residents, previously excluded from the property-owning group, to acquire temple offices for themselves.

Thus the economic crisis radically altered the nature of both neighborhoods. TA, dominated by a large lineage, found itself abandoned by the minor kinsmen and clients, who were then replaced by outsiders and entrepreneurs. Similarly, the dominant institution in TB found that some of its one-time dependents took advantage of the situation to establish their own economic independence. Regrettably, Nippur was completely abandoned within two decades of these events, so we have no means of telling how these neighborhoods might, or might not, have been refocussed.

The two domestic sequences from Nippur allow several generalizations which may prove valid for Mesopotamian neighborhoods in general. First, neighborhoods seem to have been occupied by quite small, distinct groups, formed around a defining kernel—a family or institution. These kernels must have served the same risk-sharing functions as the corporate kin groups that have been observed in rural Iraq today. Indeed, in the case of the residents of TA, it appears that like the immigrants to the later, Islamic, cities, they attempted to maintain village ways in an urban setting. The second point—which is one also made by students of Islamic culture—is that these neighborhoods had a dynamic of their own. In TB, one was dealing with an old, established population. The TB residents were probably closely enough tied to urban institutions that they would remain when others fled back to the countryside at times of urban weakness, as shown by their tenacity in the face of the economic crisis of 1739 B.C. The residents of TA, on the other hand, retained both a memory of rural life and ties to the land, enabling many of them to revert to the tribal hinterland in times of trouble. Those that remained, replaced kinship with institutional ties and substituted urban property holdings for private agriculture.

Adams[13] has suggested that biological models of the antithetical strategies of stability and resilience may be applied to ancient Mesopotamian society and history. The strategy of stability—or better, maximization—is that pursued by centralized states attempting to draw resources and manpower towards the focus of power:

> Over the short run . . . , the 'success' of the system is evident in massive, specialized networks of commodity production and distribution, in population and urban growth, in the proliferation of monumental public buildings, and in the hypertrophy of administrative personnel and bureaucratic procedures.[14]

Unfortunately, as argued by Yoffee,[15] an inherent tendency towards fragmentation coupled with the lack of acceptable means for legitimizing centralized power led such systems to collapse after a few generations. It is at the point of collapse that the resilient strategy becomes desirable, as embodied in "tribally organized, semi-nomadic elements . . . with . . . an emphasis on mobility, military prowess, and the maintenance of a spectrum of subsistence options that balanced herding with limited cultivation."[16] Although Adams notes "that the connection between nomads and sedentaries was a two-way street, with individuals and groups moving back and forth along this continuum as a response to environmental and social pressures that never could produce an equilibrium,"[17] he is less concerned with the mechanism of the transition of society from centralization to decentralization, from maximization to resilience. Information on the structure of Mesopotamian cities and on the organization of urban neighborhoods can provide some clues as to how these shifts of emphasis were effected. Two interrelated questions must be asked. First, under what circumstances was it possible for basic urban institutions to emerge relatively unscathed after a considerable period of decentralization, and second, how did the tribal groups retain enough of their structure in the face of urban dominance to emerge as the dominant mode once the maximizing strategy had run its course? Clearly a system whereby both elements were ensured survival during the dominance of the other must be envisaged. The Nippur data suggest that cities at times of maximization were composed of a number of small cells which fell into *at least* two categories. On the one hand were the old, established neighborhoods tied to stable state institutions and occupied by diehard urbanites, while on the other were the new areas, united by a mixture of kinship and clientage and occupied by those who maintained ties with their rural origins.[18] After several generations, the members of the latter type might forget their

[13] Robert McC. Adams, "Strategies of Maximization, Stability and Resilience in Mesopotamian Society, Settlement and Agriculture," *Proceedings of the American Philosophical Society* 122 (1978):329-35.

[14] Ibid., p. 331.

[15] Yoffee, *Economic Role*, pp. 145-50.

[16] Adams, "Maximization and Resilience," p. 334.

[17] Ibid., p. 334.

[18] The separation between different segments of Mesopotamian society is stressed by Johannes Renger, "Interaction of Temple, Palace, and 'Private Enterprise' in the Old Babylonian Economy," in *State and Temple Economy in the Ancient Near East I*, ed. Edward Lipinski, Orientalia Lovaniensia Analecta, vol. 5 (Leuven: Department Orientalistiek, 1979), pp. 249-56.

rural roots and replace kinship with institutional ties,[19] but if the political climate made maximization a less desirable strategy, they could return to the countryside. In the first chapters of this book the need for flexibility in the ancient Mesopotamian social system was stressed, especially the flexibility of risk-sharing in agricultural production. The neighborhood system outlined above not only preserves such flexibility, but at the same time, under favorable conditions, permits the dominance of the maximizing mode, normally the antithesis of risk-sharing, without destroying the basis of the resilient mode when the system collapsed. It is clearly too simplistic to assume that Mesopotamian neighborhoods were of only two types, with TA and TB as archetypes. However, it seems worthwhile to think of cities as composed of a number of social groups, or cells, normally organized into physical neighborhoods and varying in flexibility and urban commitment. As political and economic conditions varied these cells could be added or sloughed off as needed, providing both continuity of urban traditions in times of weakness and cohesion of the city-state in times of strength. Furthermore, such a scheme would explain one of the incongruities of the textual record from Mesopotamia. While archives abound describing the administration and functioning of specific urban institutions—temples, palaces, and the like—we have virtually no records of the administration of cities as units. Other than occasional references to city councils and mayors, whose major functions are often judicial, the record of civil administration is minimal. This pattern of documentation could be explained if the overarching administrative structure was indeed weak, merely tying together the basic institutions which were embedded in the various residential quarters. In many respects such a pattern would suggest that the internal structure of the cities was as loosely organized as the broader political structure of the state in times of political centralization. Just as the city-states were the basic building blocks of the Mesopotamian nation-state, so were the neighborhoods the basic building blocks of the cities. Finally, if such a concept is correct, it might help to explain the difficulty often encountered both in generalizing from particular textual archives and in relating the results of archaeological surveys to the picture of urban life revealed in excavations and texts. A single archive usually provides a detailed picture of the activities of a single institution or urban cell over a relatively short period of time. What is not revealed is its history or how it compares with the other cells in the same city. Also similarities in the texts generated by the more flexible social groups may mask the more significant differences which result from differing stages in their evolution. For example, although the private documents of the early Ninlil-zimu family differ not at all in form from those of the property owners still living at Nippur in the later years of Samsuiluna, the basic organization of the two groups was quite different. A combined archaeological and Assyriological approach is needed to articulate the long-term trends revealed by survey data with the detailed snapshots provided by Assyriological research. To generalize from the TA example, the transformation of a flexible, kin-oriented group into one more stable and institutionally based might take two centuries or so. Since the record of Mesopotamian history indicates that a period of economic and political stability lasting that long was extremely rare, cycles of urban migration and emigration must have been a fairly constant feature of ancient Mesopotamian life. On the other hand, except for the earliest stages in Mesopotamian history, archaeological reconnaissance tends to analyze sites grouped in spans of close to a half-millennium, each one of which must have encompassed more than one cycle of urban migration and emigration. Only when such data are combined with textual sources can the mechanisms of change in Mesopotamian society be understood. When survey, archaeological, and archival studies are taken in isolation, the dynamic remains hidden.

[19] Although not interpreted in this way, this seems to be the pattern seen by Michael J. Desroches in Dilbat (*Aspects of the Structure of Dilbat during the Old Babylonian Period* [Ann Arbor: University Microfilms, 1978]), where the population replaces their concern with real estate with office holding.

APPENDIX I

Concordance of Level Designations

Locus	Published Level	Field Level		Present Level
		TA		
144		VIII-1		XA-1
	X-3	VIII-2		XA-2
150	VIII	VIII-1		XA fill
	(IX)			
	(X-1)			
	X-2	VIII-2		XA-2
	X-3)	(IX-1)	213	XB-1
	(X-4)	(IX-2)	213	XB-2
	(X-4 fdn.)		213	XB fdn.
	(XI-1)	(X-1)	213	XB fdn.
	(XI-2)	(X-2)	213	XB fdn.
151	VIII	VIII-1		XA fill
	(IX)			
	(X-1)			
	X-2	VIII-2		XA-2
	(X-3)	(VIII-3)		XA-3
	X-4	IX-1 floor	212	XB-1
	(XI-1)	(IX-1)	212	XB-2
		X-1	212	XB fdn.
	XI-2	X-2	212	XI
152	VIII	VIII-1		XA-1
		(VIII-2)		XA-2
	(IX)			
		VIII-3		XA-3
153	(X-1)	(VIII-1)		XA fill
	X-2	VIII-2		XA-2
	(X-3)	(VIII-3)		XA-3
	X-3 fdn.	IX-1		XB-1
		below IX-1		XB-2
	XI-1	X-1		XI-1

Locus	Published Level	Field Level		Present Level
154	VIII	VIII-1 fill		XA-1 fill
	X-1	fill below VIII-1		XA-2
	X-2			
		VIII-3		XA-3
	X-3			
	X-4	IX-1 floor	153	XB-1
	(XI-1)			
		(IX-2)	153	XB fdn.
	(XI-2)			
155	X-1	VIII-1		XA-1
	(X-2)			
	X-3	VIII-2		XA-2
	X-4	IX		XI-1
		X-1		XI fdn.
	X-4 fdn.			
		X-2		XI fdn.
156	X-1	VIII-1		XA-1
	(X-2)			
	X-3	VIII-2		XA-2
		(VIII-3)		XA-3
	X-4	IX-1		XB-1
		(IX-2)		XB-2
	(XI-1)	(X-1)		XI-1
	(XI-2)	(X-2)		XI-2
157	(X-1)	(VIII-1)		XA-1
	(X-2)	(VIII-2)		XA-2
	X-3	VIII-3		XA-3
	X-4	IX-1		XI-1
	(X-4 fdn.)	(X)		XI fdn.
158	X-1	VIII-1		XA-1
	X-2	VIII-2		XA-2
	(X-3)	(IX-1)		XB-1
	X-4	IX-2		XB-1
		(IX-3)		
	XI-1			XI-1
		X-1		
	(XI-2)			
	(XII-1)	(XI-1)		
	(XII-2)	(XI-2)		
	(XIII-3)	(XI-3)	234	XIIB-1
159	(X-1)			
		(VIII-1)		XA-1
	(X-2)			
		(VIII-2)		XA-2
	(X-3)			

Locus	Published Level	Field Level	Present Level
160	X-1	VIII-1	XA-1
	(X-2)	(VIII-2)	XA-2
	(X-3)	(VIII-3)	
			XB-1
	(X-4)	(IX-1)	
			XB-2
	X-4 fdn.	IX-2	
	XI-1	X-1 floor	XI-1
	(XI-2)	(X-2)	XI-2
161	X-1	VIII-1	XA-1
	(X-2)		
		(VIII-2)	XB-1
	(X-3)		
162	IX	VIII high	XA fill
	(X-1)	(VIII-1)	XA-1
		VIII-2	XA-2
	X-2		
		VIII-3	XA-3
163	(X-1)	(VIII-1)	XA-1
	(X-2)	(VIII-2)	XA-2
	(X-3)	(IX-1)	XB-1
	X-4	IX-2	XB-2
	XI-1		
		X-1	XI-1
	XI-2		
		(X-2)	XI-2
164	(X-1)	(VIII-1)	XA-1
	X-2	VIII-2	XA-2
		(IX-1)	XB-1
		(X)	XI fill
165	(X-1?)	(VIII-2)	XA-1
166			XA fill
	X-1	VIII-1	
			XA-1
	X-2		
		VIII-2	XA-2
	X-3		
167	(X-1)		
		(VIII-1)	XA-1
	(X-2)		
		VIII-2	XA-2
	X-3		
		VIII-3	XA-3
	X-4	IX-1	200 XB-1

Locus	Published Level	Field Level	Present Level
168	X-2	VIII-1	XA-2
	(X-3)	VIII-2	XA-3
	X-4	IX-1	XB-1
			XB-2
			XI-1
169	X-1	VIII-1	XA fill
	(X-2)	(VIII-2)	XA-1
	(X-3)	(VIII-3)	XA-2
170	(X-1)		
		(VIII-1)	XA fill
	(X-2)		
	X-3	VIII-2	XA-2
	(X-4)	(IX-1)	XB-1
	(XI-1)	(IX-2)	XB-2
	(XI-2)	(X-1)	XI-1
171	VIII		
		VIII-1 fill	XA fill
	IX		
	(X-1)	(VIII-1)	XA-1
	(X-2)	(VIII-2)	XA-2
	(X-3)	(VIII-3)	XA fdn.
172	(X-1)		
		(VIII-1)	XA-2
	(X-2)		
	X-3	VIII-2	XA-3
173		(VIII-1)	XA-1
	X-1		
	X-2	VIII-2	XA-2
	X-3		
	(X-4)	(VIII-3)	201 XA-3
174		(VIII-1)	XA-1
	X-1		
		VIII-2	XA-2
	X-2		
	(X-3)	(VIII-3)	XA-3
	X-4	IX-1	XI-1
	X-4 fdn.	X-1 floor	XI-2
175	VIII	VIII high	XA fill
		(VIII-1)	XA-1
176	VIII	VIII-1 high	
			XA-1
	(X-1)	(VIII-1)	
	X-2	VIII-2	XA-2

Locus	Published Level	Field Level	Present Level
	X-3	VIII-3	XA-3
	X-3 fdn.	IX-1	XB fdn.
177	X-1	VIII-1	XA-1
	(X-2)	(VIII-2)	XA-2
178	X-1	VIII-1	XA-1
	X-2		
	X-3	VIII-2	
	X-4	VIII-3	XA-2
179	X-1	VIII-1	XA-1
	(X-2)	(VIII-2)	XA-2
	(X-3)	(VIII-3)	XA-3
	X-4	IX-1	XB fdn.
180	VIII	VIII-1 fill	XA fill
	(X-1)		
	(X-2)	(VIII-1)	XA-1
	(X-3)		
		VIII-2	XA-2
	X-4		
		VIII-3	XA-3
		IX fill	XB fdn.
	X-4		
		X-1	XI fdn.
181	X-1	VIII-1	XA-1
	X-2	VIII-2	XA-2
	(X-3)		
	X-4	VIII-3	XA-3
		IX-1	XI fill
	X-4 fdn.		
		X-1	
			XI-1
	XI-1	X-1 floor	
		(X-2)	XI-2
	XI-2	X-3	XI-3
182	X-1	below VIII-1	XA-1
		(VIII-2)	XA-2
	(X-2)		
		(VIII-3)	XA-3
	X-3	IX-1	205 XI fill
183	(X-1)	(VIII-1)	XA-1
	X-2	VIII-2	XA-2
184	X-1	VIII-1	184/189 XA-1
	X-2	VIII-2	XA-2
		(VIII-3)	XA-3

Locus	Published Level	Field Level		Present Level
	(X-3)			
		(IX-1)		XI fill
	(X-4)	(IX-2)		XI-1
	XI-1	X-1		XI-1
	XI-2	X-2		XI-2
185	X-1	VIII-1		XA-1
	X-2	VIII-2		XA-2
	(X-3)	(VIII-3)		XA-3
	X-4	IX-1		XI-1
		below IX-1		
	X-4 fdn.			XI fdn.
		X fill		
186	(X-1)			
		(VIII-1)		XA-1
	(X-2)			
		(VIII-2)		XA-2
	(X-3)			
	X-4	VIII-3		XA-3
	X-4 fdn.	IX-1		XB fdn.
		(X-1)		
				XI fdn.
		(X-2)		
187	(X-1)	(VIII-1)		XA-1
	X-2	VIII-2		XA-2
	(X-3)			
	X-4	VIII-3		XA-3
	X-4 fdn.	X-1		XI fdn.
188	(X-1)	(VIII-1)		XA-1
	X-2	VIII-2		XA-2
	(X-3)			
	X-4	VIII-3		XA-3
	X-4 fdn.	X-1		XI-1
	(XI-1)			
	XI-2	X-2		XI-2
189	X-1	VIII-1	184/189	XA-1
	(X-2)	(VIII-2)		XA-2
	(X-3)			XI fill ???
	(X-4)	(X-1)		XI-1
	XI-1	X-2		XI-2
				XI-3
190	(X-1)	(VIII-1)		
				XA-1
	X-2	VIII-2		
	(X-3)			

Locus	Published Level	Field Level	Present Level
		high VIII-3	
		VIII-3	XA-2
		(IX)	XA-3
	XI-1	X-1 floor	XI fill
	(XI-2)	(X-2)	188 XI-1
191	X-1	VIII-1	XA-1
	(X-2)	(VIII-2)	XA-2
	(X-3)	(IX)	XI fill
	X-4	X-1	XI-1
	(XI-1)		
	XI-2		
		X-2	XI-2
	XI-3		
		X-3	XI-3
192	(X-1)	(VIII-1)	XA-1
	(X-2)	(VIII-2)	XA-2
	(X-3)	(IX-1)	XI fill
	(X-4)	(IX-2)	XI-1
	(XI-1)	(X-1)	XI-2
	(XI-2)	(X-2)	XI-3
193	(X-1)	(VIII-1)	XA fill
	X-2		
		VIII-2	XA-2
	X-3		
		VIII-3	XA-3
		(X-1)	XI-1
194	X-3	IX-1	XB-1
	(X-4)	(IX-2)	XB-2
	XI-1	X-1	XI-1
		(XI-1)	XIIA-1
		(XI-2)	XIIA-2
		XII-1	XIIB-1
		XII-2	XIIB-2
195	X-4 fdn.	X-1	XI
	XII-1	XI-1	XIIB-1
196		(IX-1)	XB-1
	X-4 fdn.	IX-2	XB-2
	XI-1	X-1	XI-1
	(XI-2)	(X-2)	XI-2
	(XII-1)	(XI-1)	XIIA-1
	(XII-2)	(XI-2)	XIIA-2
	XII-3	XI-3	XIIA-3
	XIII-1	XII-1	XIIA fdn.

Locus	Published Level	Field Level	Present Level
197	(X-3)	(IX-1)	XB-1
	X-4	IX-2	XB-2
	XI-1	X-1 floor	XI-1
	XI-1 fdn.	X-2	XI-2
	XII-1	XI-1 floor	XIIA-1
		(XI-2)	XIIA-2
		(XI-3)	XIIA-3
198	X-4	IX-1	XB-1
	X-4 fdn.	IX-2	XB-2
		(X-1)	XI-1
		(X-2)	XI-2
		(X-3)	XI-3
		(XI-1)	XIIA-1
		(XI-2)	XIIA-2
		(XI-3)	XIIA-3
199		(IX-1)	XB-1
		(IX-2)	XB-2
		(X-1)	XI-1
	XI-2	X-2 and above	XI-2
	(XII-1)	(XI-1)	XIIA-1
	(XII-2)	(XI-2)	XIIA-2
	XII-3	XI-3	XIIA-3
200		IX-1 fill	
	X-4		XB fdn.
		IX-2	
	X-4 fdn.	ash from IX-2 fill	XI fill
	XI-1	X-1	XI-1
	XI-1 fdn.	X-2 floor	XI-2
		(XI-1)	XIIA-1
201	X-4	IX-1	XI-1
	(X-4 fdn.)	(X-1)	XI fdn.
202	X-4	IX-1	XI fill
	XI-1	X-1	XI-1
		(X-2)	XI-2
203	X-3	IX-1	XI fill
	X-4	IX-2	XI-1
	XI-1	X-1	XI-2
204		(VIII-2)	XA-2
	X-3	IX-1	XA-3
205	X-3	IX-1	XI fill
	X-4	X-1 fill	XI-1 fill
	XI-1	X-2	XI-2
	XI-2	X-3	XI-3
	XII-1	XI-1	XIIB-1

Locus	Published Level	Field Level	Present Level
206		(VIII-1)	
	X-3	VIII-2	179 XA-2
		VIII-3	179 XA-3
	X-4		
		IX	179 XI-1
207	X-4 fdn.	X	XI fdn.
	XII-1	XI-1	XIIB-1
	XII-2	XI-2	XIIB-2
	XIII-1	XII-1	XIII-1
	XIII-2	XII-2	XIII-2
208	X-4	IX-1	XB-1
209	X-4	IX-1	XB-1
		(IX-2)	XB-2
	sub X-4	IX-3	
			XI-1
	XI-1	X-1 floor	
	XI-2	X-2	XI-2
	(XII-1)	(XI-1)	XIIB-1
	(XII-2)	(XI-2)	XIIB-2
	XIII-1	XII fill	XIII-1
	(XIII-2)	(XII)	XIII-2
210	X-4	IX-1	XI fill
		(X-1)	XI-1
211	(X-4)	(IX-1)	XB-1
	X-4 fdn.	IX-2	XB-2
	XI-1	X-1	XI-1
	XI-2	X-2	XI-2
	XI-3	X-3	XI fdn.
	XII-1	XI-1 fill	XIIA-1
	(XII-2)	(XI-2)	XIIA-2
	(XII-3)	(XI-3)	XIIA-3
212		151 IX-1	XB-1
		(151 IX-2)	XB-2
		151 X-1	XI-1
		151 X-2	XI fdn.
213		(152 IX-1)	XB-1
		(152 IX-2)	XB-2
		(152 X-1)	XI-1
		(152 X-2)	XI fdn.
214	XI-1	X-1	XI-1
	XI-2	X-2	XI-2
215	XII-2	XI fill	XI

Locus	Published Level	Field Level	Present Level
216	XII-2	XI-1 floor	XIIB-1
217	XIII-1	XII-1	XIII-1
218	XII-2	XI-1	XIIB-1
		XI-2	XIIB-2
	XIII-1	XII-1	XIII-1
	XIII-2	XII-2	XIII-2
219	XII-1	XI-1	XIIB-1
	(XII-2)	(XI-2)	XIIB-2
	(XIII-1)	(XII-1)	XIII-1
	XIII-2	XII-2	XIII-2
220	(XII-1)	(XI-1)	XIIB-1
	XII-2	XI-2	XIIB-2
			XIII-1[a]
			XIII-2[a]
221		(XI)	XIIB-1
	(XIII-1)	(XII-1)	XIII-1[a]
	XIII-2	XII-2	XIII-2[a]
222	(XII-1)	(XI-1)	XIIB-1
	XII-2	XI-2	XIIB-2
	(XIII-1)	(XII-1)	XIII-1[a]
	XIII-2	XII-2	XIII-2[a]
223	XII-1	XI-1	XIIB-1
	XII-2	XI-2	222 XIIB-2
224		(XI-1)	XIIB-1
		(XI-2)	XIIB-2
225		(XI-1)	XIIB-1
		(XI-2)	XIIB-2
		(XI-3)	XIIB-3
	XIII-1	XII-1	XIII-1
		(XII-2)	XIII-2
226			XIIB-1
		(XI)	
			XIIB-2
	XIII-1	XII-1	XIII-1
	XIII-2	XII-2	XIII-2
227		(XI-1)	XIIB-1
		(XI-2)	XIIB-2
		(XII-1)	XIII-1
		(XII-2)	XIII-2

[a] Loci 220, 221, and 222 are to be treated together.

Locus	Published Level	Field Level	Present Level
228		(XI)	XIIB-1
	XIII-2	XII-1	XIII-1
229	XII-2	XI fill	XIIB fill
		(XI-1)	XIIB-1
230	XII-2 fill		XIIB fill
		XI fill	
	XII-2		XIIB-1
	(XII-3)	(XI-2)	XIIB-2
		(XII-1)	XIII-1
	(XIII-1)		
		(XII-2)	XIII-2
	XIII-2	XII-2	XIII-3
	(XIV)	(XIII)	XIV
	XV	XIV	XV
231	XII-2	XI-1	XIIB-1
		(XI-2)	XIIB-2
			XIII-2[b]
232		(XI-1)	XIIB-1
		(XI-2)	XIIB-2
		(XII-1)	XIII-1[c]
		(XII-2)	XIII-2[c]
233	XII-2	XI-1	XIIB-1
	(XIII-1)	(XI-2)	XIIB-2
	XIII-2	XII-1	XIII-1[c]
		(XII-2)	XIII-2[c]
234	XII-1	XI-1	XIIB-1
		(158 XII-1)	XIII-1
		(158 XII-2)	XIII-2
235		(XI-1)	XIIA-1
		(XI-2)	XIIA-2
	XII-3	XI-3	XIIA-3
236		(XI)	XIIB-1
		(XII)	XIII
237			XIII-1
			XIII-2
			XV
238			XIII-1
			XIII-2

[b] Together with locus 229.
[c] Loci 232 and 233 are to be treated together.

Locus	Published Level	Field Level	Present Level
239			XIII-2
240			XIII
241			XIII-2
243			XIII-2
244			XIII-2
		TB	
1	I-1	I-1	I-1
	I-2	(I-2)	I-2
	II-1	(II-1)	II-1
	II-2	II-2	II fdn.
2	D	D	D
	E	E	E
	I-1	I-1	I-1
	I-2	I-2	I-2
	29 II-1	II-1	29 II-1
	70 III	III	70 III
3	I-1	I-1	I-1
	17 I-2	(I-2)	17 I-2
	17 II-1	II-1	17 II-1
	17 II-2	II-2	17 II-2
4	D	D	D
	E	E	E
	5 I-1	I-1	5 I-1
5	D?	1	D?
	E	E	E
	I-1	I-1	I-1
6	E	E	E
	I-1	I-1	I-1
7	E	E	E
	I-1	I-1	I-1
8	I-1	I-1	I-1
	I-2	I-2	30 I-2
9	I-1	I-1	I-1
	I-2	I-2	30 I-2

Locus	Published Level	Field Level	Present Level
10	I-1	I-1	I-1
	I-2	I-2	I-2
	II-1	II-1	II-1
	II-2	II-2	II-2
	III-1	III-1	
			II fdn.
	III-2	III-2	
11	I-1	I-1	I-1
12	I-1	I-1	I-1
	I-2	I-2	I-2
	II-1	II-1	II-1
	II-2	II-2	II-2
	III-1	III-1	
			II fdn.
	III-2	III-2	
13	I-1	I-1	I-1
	I-2	I-2	I-2
	106 II-1	II-1	106 II-1
14	I-1	I-1	I-1
	I-2	I-2	I-2
	II-1	II-1	II-1
	II-2	II-2	II-2
15	E	E	E
	I-1	I-1	5 I-1
	87 I-2	I-2	87 I-2
	120 II-1	II-1	120 II-1
	187 III-1	III-1	187 III-1
	187 III-2	III-2	187 III-2
16	D	D	D
	E	E	E
	20 I-1	I-1	20 I-1
17	I-1	I-1	I-1
	I-2	I-2	I-2
	II-1	II-1	II-1
	II-2	II-2	II-2
		III	II fdn.
18	I-2	I-2	I-2
	II-1	II-1	II-1
	II-2	II-2	II-2
	153 III	III	153 III

Locus	Published Level	Field Level	Present Level
19		C/D	
	I-1	I-1	I-1
	I-2	I-2	I-2
	II-1	II-1	II-1
	II-2	II-2	II-2
	153 III	III	153 III
20	D	D	D
	E-1	E	E-1
	E-2	F	E-2
	I-1	I-1	I-1
		I-2	I-2
21	I-1	I-1	I-1
	I-2	I-2	12 I-2
	II-1	II-1	12 II-1
	II-2	II-2	II-2
22	I-1	I-1	I-1
	I-2	I-2	I-2
	II-1	II-1	II-1
	II-2	II-2	II-2
23	intrusive	intrusive	intrusive
24	D	D	D
	E-1	E	E-1
	E-2	F	E-2
	I-1	I-1	I-1
	I-2	I-2	I-2
25	D	D	D
	E	E	E
	I-1	I-1	I-1
	I-2	I-2	I fdn.
26	D	D	D
27	D	D	D
28	D?	D	2 D
	II-1	II-1	2 II-1
	II-2	II-2	II-2
29	II-1	II-1	II-1
	II-2	II-2	II-2
30	I-2	I-2	I-2
	II-1	II-1	II-1
	II-2	II-2	II-2

Locus	Published Level	Field Level	Present Level
31	I-1	I-1	I-1
	I-2	I-2	I-2
	II-1	II-1	II-1
	II-2	II-2	II-2
32	I-2	I-2	I-2
	II-1	II-1	II-1
	II-2	II-2	II-2
39	D	D	D
	E	E	E
40	D	D	D
	E	E	E
41	D	D	D
	E-1	E	E-1
	E-2	F	E-2
42	D	D	D
	E	E	E
	I-1	I-1	I-1
	I-2	I-2	I-2
	II-1	II-1	II-1
	II-2	II-2	II-2
43	D	D	D
	E	E	E
	I-1	I-1	I-1
	I-2	I-2	I-2
44	D	D	26 D
	E	E	E
	I-1	I-1	I-1
	I-2	I-2	I-2
45		D	
	I-1		I-1
		I-1	
	I-2	I-2	I-2
	II-1	II-1	II-1
	II-2	II-2	II-2
46	E-1	E	E-1
	E-2	I-1	E-2
47	D	D	D
	E	E	E
	I-1	5 I-1	5 I-1

Locus	Published Level	Field Level	Present Level
48	D	D	D
	E	E	E
		F	
	I-1		I-1
	I-2	I-2	I-2
49	D	D	42 D
	E	E	42 E
50	I-1	I-1	I-1
	I-2	I-2	I-2
	II-1	II-1	II-1
	II-2	II-2	II-2
	III fdn.	III fdn.	II fdn.
51	E-2	F	
			I-1
	I-1	I-1	
	I-2	I-2	I-2
	II-1	II-1	II-1
	II-2	II-2	II-2
	III-1	III-1	
			II fdn.
	III-2	III-2	
52	I-1	I-1	I-1
	I-2	I-2	I-2
	II-1	II-1	II-1
	II-2	II-2	II-2
	III-1	III-1	
			II fdn.
	III-2	III-2	
53	D	D	D
	E	E	E
	I-1	I-1	I-1
	I-2	I-2	I-2
54	D	D	D
	E	E	E
55	D	D	D
	E	E	E
	83 I-1	I-1	83 I-1
56	D	D	D
	E-1	E	E-1
	E-2	F	E-2
	I-1	I-1	I-1
	I-2	I-2	I-2

Locus	Published Level	Field Level	Present Level
57	I-1	I-1	I-1
	I-2	I-2	I-2
	II-1	II-1	II-1
	II-2	II-2	II-2
58	E	E	E
	I-1	I-1	I-1
59	I-1	I-1	I-1
	I-2	I-2	I-2
	II-1	II-1	II-1
	II-2	II-2	II-2
	III	III	II fdn.
60	I-1	I-1	I-1
	I-2	I-2	I-2
	II-1	II-1	II-1
		II-2	
	II-2		II-2
		II-2a	
	III	III	II fdn.
61	I-1	I-1	I-1
	I-2	I-2	I-2
	II-1	II-1	II-1
		II-2	
	II-2		II-2
		II-2a	
	III	III	II fdn.
63	D	D	D
	E	E	E
	I-1	I-1	I-1
	I-2	I-2	I-2
64	D	D	42 D
	E	E	42 E
	I-1	I-1	42 I-1
	I-2	I-2	42 I-2
65	E-1	E	E-1
	E-2	F	E-2
	I-1	I-1	I-1
	I-2	I-2	I-2
66	D	D	D
	E-1	E	E-1
	E-2	F	E-2
	I-1	I-1	I-1
	I-2	I-2	I-2

Locus		Published Level	Field Level		Present Level
67		D	D		D
		E	E		E
		I-1	I-1		I-1
		I-2	I-2		I-2
68		D	D		D
		E	E		E
		I-1	I-1		I-1
69		I-1	I-1		I-1
		I-2	I-2		I-2
		II-1	II-1		II-1
		II-2	II-2		II-2
		III	III		II fdn.
70	29	II-1	II-1	29	II-1
	29	II-2	II-2	29	II-1
		III-1			
			III-1		III-1
		III-2			
		IV-1	IV high		III-2
71		D	D		D
		E	E	72	E
72		D	D		D
		E	E		E
		I-1	I-1		I-1
		I-2	I-2	92	I-2
73		D	D		D
		E	E		E
	83	I-1	I-1	83	I-1
74		D	D		D
		E	E		E
		I-1	I-1		I-1
		I-2	I-2		I-2
75		D	D		D
		E-1	E		E-1
		E-2	F		E-2
		I-1	I-1		I-1
		I-2	I-2		I-2
76		D	D		D
		E-1	E		E-1
		E-2	F		E-2
		I-1	I-1		I-1
		I-2	I-2		I-2

Locus	Published Level	Field Level	Present Level
77	D	D	D
	E-1	E	E-1
	E-2	F	E-2
	I-1	I-1	I-1
	I-2	I-2	I-2
79	I-2	I-2	I-2
80	I-2	I-2	I-2
81	I-1	I-1	I-1
	I-2	I-2	I-2
82	I-2	I-2	I-2
	II-1	II-1	II-1
	II-2	II-2	II-2
83	I-1	I-1	I-1
	I-2	I-2	I-2
84		I-1	68 I-1
	I-2	I-2	I-2
85	47 I-1	I-1	5 I-1
	I-2	I-2	I-2
86	I-1	I-1	I-1
	I-2	I-2	I-2
87	I-2	I-2	I-2
88	I-2	I-2	I-2
89	I-1	I-1	20 I-1
	I-2	I-2	I-2
90	I-1	I-1	I-1
	I-2	I-2	I-2
91	I-1	I-1	I-1
	I-2	I-2	I-2
92	I-1	I-1	I-1
	I-2	I-2	I-2
93	I-1	I-1	I-1
	I-2	I-2	I-2
94	I-2	I-2	I-2

Locus	Published Level	Field Level	Present Level
95			D
			E
			I-1
	I-2	I-2	I-2
96			D
			E
			I-1
	I-2	I-2	I-2
97	I-2	I-2	I-2
98		I-1	5 I-1
	I-2	I-2	I-2
99	I-1	I-1	I-1
	I-2	I-2	I-2
100	I-1	I-1	I-1
	I-2	I-2	I-2
101	II-2	II-2	II-2
	III-1		
		III-1	III-1
	III-2		
102	I-2	I-2	I-2
103	I-2	I-2	I-2
104	II-1	II-1	II-1
	II-2	II-2	II-2
105	II-1	II-1	II-1
	II-2	II-2	II-2
106	II-1	II-1	II-1
	II-2	II-2	II-2
107	II-1	II-1	II-1
	II-2	II-2	II-2
108	II-1	II-1	II-1
	II-2	II-2	II-2
109	II-1	II-1	II-1
	II-2	II-2	II-2
110	II-1	II-1	II-1
	II-2	II-2	II-2

Locus	Published Level	Field Level	Present Level
111	II-1	II-1	II-1
	II-2	II-2	II-2
112	II-1	II-1	II-1
	II-2	II-2	II-2
113	II-1	II-1	II-1
	II-2	II-2	II-2
	III	III	II fdn.
114	II-1	II-1	II-1
	II-2	II-2	502 II-2
		III	167 III
115	II-1	II-1	II-1
	II-2	II-2	II-2
116	II-1	II-1	II-1
	II-2	II-2	II-2
117	II-1	II-1	II-1
	II-2	II-2	502 II-2
	III	III	172/168 III
118	II-1	II-1	II-1
	II-2	II-2	502 II-2
	III	III	167 III
119	II-1	II-1	120 II-1
	II-2	II-2	120 II-2
120	II-1	II-1	II-1
	II-2	II-2	II-2
		III-1	187 III-1
121	II-1	II-1	II-1
	II-2	II-2	II-2
	III-1	III-1	
			II fdn.
	III-2	III-2	
122	II-1	II-1	II-1
	II-2	II-2	II-2
123	II-1	II-1	II-1
	II-2	II-2	II-2
124	II-1	II-1	II-1
	II-2	II-2	502 II-2

Locus	Published Level	Field Level	Present Level
125	II-1	II-1	II-1
	II-2	II-2	502 II-2
126	II-1	II-1	II-1
	II-2	II-2	502 II-2
127	II-1	II-1	II-1
	II-2	II-2	II-2
	?	III-1	169 III-1
128	II-1	II-1	II-1
	II-2	II-2	II-2
	III-1	III-1	III-1
	III-2	III-2	III-2
129	II-1	II-1	I fdn.
	II-2	II-2	II fdn.
130	II-1	II-1	II-1
	II-2	II-2	II-2
131	II-1	II-1	I fdn.
	II-2	II-2	II fdn.
132	II-1	II-1	II-1
	II-2	II-2	II-2
133	II-1	II-1	I fdn.
	II-2	II-2	II fdn.
134	II-1	II-1	I fdn.
	II-2	II-2	II fdn.
135	II-1	II-1	II-1
136	II-1	II-1	II-1
	II-2	II-2	II-2
	III	III	II fdn.
137	II-1	II-1	II-1
	II-2	II-2	II-2
	III	III	II fdn.
138	II-1	II-1	I fdn.
	II-2	II-2	II fdn.
139	II-1	II-1	II-1
	II-2	II-2	II-2
	III	III	II fdn.

Locus	Published Level	Field Level		Present Level
140	II-1	II-1		II-1
	II-2	II-2	502	II-2
	III fdn.	III high		III
141	II-1	II-1		II-1
	II-2	II-2		II-2
	III fdn.	III high		III
142	II-1	II-1		II-1
	II-2	II-2		II-2
	III	III		II fdn.
143	II-1	II-1		II-1
	II-2	II-2		II-2
	III fdn.	III		III
144	II-1	II-1		II-1
	II-2	II-2		II-2
	III fdn.	III	141	III
145	II-1	II-1		I fdn.
	II-2	II-2		II fdn.
146	II-1	II-1		I fdn.
	II-2	II-2		II fdn.
147	D	D		D
	E	E		E
148	II-1	II-1		I fdn.
	II-2	II-2		II fdn.
149	II-1	II-1		I fdn.
	II-2	II-2		II fdn.
150	I-1	I-1	86	I-1
	II-1	II-1		II-1
	II-2	II-2	120	II-2
151	D	D		D
	E	E		E
152	I-1	I-1		I-1
	I-2	I-2		I-2
	II-1	II-1		II-1
	II-2	II-2		II-2
153	II-1	II-1	30?	II-1
	II-2	II-2	30?	II-2

Locus	Published Level	Field Level	Present Level
	III-1	III	III-1
	III-2	III-1	III-2
154	III	III	III fdn.
155	III	III	II fdn.
156		III high	
	III-1		III-1
		III-1	
	206 IV-1	IV-1	III-2
157	II-1	II-1	II-1
	II-2	II-2	II-2
158	II-1	II-1	159 II-1
	II-2	II-2	II-2
160	III	II-2	
			II fdn.
	III-1	III-1	
161	III	III	III fdn.
162	III-1	III high	
			III-1
	III-2	III-1	
163	III-1	III high	III-1
164	III-2	III high	III-2
	III	III	III disturbed
165	III	III	164 III disturbed
166	III-1	III-1	III-1
	III-2	III-2	III-2
167		III-1	
	III-1		III-1
		III-2	
168	III-1	III-1	
			III-1
	III-2	III-2	
169		II-2	
	III-1		
		III-1	III-1
	III-2	III-2	

Locus	Published Level	Field Level	Present Level
170	III	III	II fdn.
171	III-1	III high	III-1
	III-2		
172	III-1	III-1	III-1
	III-2	III-2	
	IV-1	IV high	229 III fdn.
173	III-1	III-1	III-1
	III-2	III-2	III-2
174	III-1	III high	III-1
	III-2		
175	III-1	III	III-1
	III-2		
176	II-2	II-2	II-2
		III-1	II fdn.
	III	III-2	III fdn.
177	III-1	III-1	III-1
	III-2	III-2	
178	III-1	III-1	III-1
	III-2	III-2	III-2
179	III-1	III-1	III
	III-2	III-2	
180	III-1	III-1	III
	III-2	III-2	
181	III-1	III-1	II fdn.
	III-2	III-2	
182	III-1	III high	III-1
	III-2	III	225 III fdn.
183	III-1	III-1	III-1
	III-2	III-2	III-2

Locus		Published Level	Field Level		Present Level
184		III-1	III high		III-1
		III-2	III	225	III fdn.
185		III-1	III-1		
					III-1
		III-2	III-2		
186		III-1	III-1		III-1
		III-2	III-2		III-2
187		III-1	III-1		III-1
		III-2	III-2		III-2
188		III	III		II fdn.
189		III-1			
			III		III-1
		III-2			
190		III-1			
			III		III
		III-2			
191		?	III high	167	III-1
			IV high		III-2
		IV-1			
			IV-1		IV-1
196		IV-1	IV intrusive	178	III-2
200			II fdn.	180	II fdn.
201			IV high		III-2
		IV-1			
			IV-1		IV-1
203		III-2	III-2	101	III-1
			IV high		III-2
		IV-1			
			IV-1		IV-1
206			IV high/fill		III-2
		IV-1			
			IV-1		IV-1
207	153	III-2	III	153	III-1
			IV high		III-2
		IV-2			
			IV-1		IV-1
213	153	III	III	153	III

Locus	Published Level	Field Level	Present Level
216	III-2	III	III-1
	IV-1	IV high	
			III-2
		IV fill	
	IV-2	IV-1	
			IV-1
		IV-2	
217		IV high	III-2
	IV-1		
		IV-1	IV-1
220	IV-1	IV high	III-2
223		IV high/fill	III-2
	IV-1		
		IV-1	IV-1
224		IV high	III fdn.
	IV-1		
		IV-1	IV-1
225	III	III	
			III fdn.
	IV-1	IV high	
229	IV-1	IV high	III fdn.
230	IV-1	IV high	III fdn.

NOTE: Level designations in parentheses had no objects recorded from them. In these circumstances correlations between levels as assigned in the field and in OIP 78 were more difficult. Underlined locus numbers indicate a change in locus designation.

APPENDIX II

OBJECT CATALOG

Abbreviations

AmSi	=	Amar-Sîn	IlIl	=	Iluma-ilu	Si	=	Samsuiluna
BuSi	=	Būr-Sîn	IšDa	=	Išme-Dagan	SiEr	=	Sîn-erībam
DaIl	=	Damiq-ilišu	IšEr	=	Išbi-erra	SiId	=	Sîn-Iddinam
EnBa	=	Enlil-bāni	ItPi	=	Iter-pīša	Šu	=	Šulgi
Ha	=	Hammurabi	LiEn	=	Lipit-Enlil	ŠuIl	=	Šu-ilišu
IbSi	=	Ibbi-Sîn	RiSi	=	Rīm-Sîn	ŠuSi	=	Šu-Sîn
IdDa	=	Iddin-Dagan	RiSi II	=	Rīm-Sîn II	UrNi	=	Ur-Ninurta

TA

Findspot and Description	Type	OIP 78 Reference
144 unknown function		
XA-1 floor		
3D 191 chariot fragment	F-9	
XA-2		
3D 240 clay bottle top with seal impression	T-12	
3P 197 jar	P-U	pl. 94:10
3P 201 dish	P-7(?)	
3N-T 106 literary text		
3N-T 109 business document		
150 subsidiary room, disturbed in XA-2		
XA-1		
3D 187 copper/bronze ring	T-2	
3N-T 66 school text		
XA-2		
3P 178 beaker	P-39	
151 entrance chamber		
XA-2		
3D 234 chariot fragment	F-9	
152 court and main room, disturbed		
XA-1		
3D 211 head of an animal figurine	F-5	
153 court, disturbed in VIII-1		
XA-2		
3N 174 plaque showing figure	F-20	pl. 135:3
3N-T 103 court case (Si 6) = Text 60		

Findspot and Description	Type	OIP 78 Reference
XB-1		
3N 271 cylinder seal	T-12	pl. 112:14
3N 279 bull-man plaque	F-14	pl 136:9
3D 449 clay cone		
3D 450 crude figurine	F-4	pl. 131:8
3P 394 potstand	P-34	
XI fill		
3D 439 head of a female figurine	F-1	
3D 440 bronze nail fragment		
XI-1		
3N 277 feet of a seated figurine	F-3	pl. 134:1
3D 462 nude female plaque fragment	F-11	pl. 127:8
154 main room		
XA-1		
3D 186 bone instrument		
XA-2		
3N 153 bronze point	T-3	pl. 154:10, p. 101
155 entrance chamber		
XA-1		
3N 107 painted goddess plaque	F-12	pl. 134:6
3N 125 copper/bronze drill	T-7	pl. 153:14, p. 104
XA-2 fill		
3D 238 chariot fragment	F-9	
3D 239 figurine	F-4	
156 street		
XA-1		
3D 194 figurine fragment	F-4	
3D 213 shell bead	T-1	
XA-2		
3D 233 animal figurine fragment	F-8	
3P 174 small beaker	P-39A	
XB-1		
3N 290 goddess plaque	F-12	pl. 134:7
3D 434 male figurine fragment	F-2	pl. 130:9
3D 435 bronze fragment		
3D 436 bird figurine fragment	F-5	
3P 369 jar with pointed base	P-40C	pl. 96:9
XI fill		
3D 467 nude female plaque	F-11	
3N-T 215 literary text		
157 XA-1 and VIII-2 main room, XA-3 entrance chamber		
XA-1 (intrusive?)		
3N 149 ovoid hematite weight	T-10	p. 110
XA-3		
3N 258 erotic scene on plaque	F-19	pl. 137:6
3N-T 209 school text		
158 XA-1 main room, XA-2 to XI-2 entrance chamber		
XA-1		
3P 109 dish	P-7(?)	
3P 110 dish	P-7(?)	
3P 111 dish	P-7(?)	
3P 112 dish	P-7(?)	

Findspot and Description	Type	OIP 78 Reference
XA-2		
3P 185 small dish	P-21	
3P 186 small dish	P-21	
3P 187 small dish	P-21	
XB-2		
3P 382 "flowerpot"	P-34	pl. 93:14
3P 383 potstand	P-41	pl. 97:3
XI-1		
3N 299 hematite barrel weight	T-10	p. 109
160 entrance chamber		
XA-1		
3P 117 dish	P-21	
3P 135 beaker	P-39	
XB-2		
3P 381 warped vessel	P-U	
XI-1		
3D 460 animal figurine	F-5	pl. 141:4
161 court		
XA-1		
painted sherd	P-24	
painted sherd	P-24	
162 court		
XA-1		
3N 122 bronze pin	T-2	
XA-2		
3N 152 ram figurine fragment	F-5	
XA-3		
3P 219 small pot	P-35	
3P 220 small dish	P-21	
3N-T 186 school text		
3N-T 187 literary text		
163 subsidiary room, disturbed in XA and XI		
XB-2		
3D 441 flint	T-4	p. 103
3P 372 miniature pot	P-M	pl. 94:9
3P 376 tubular vase	P-27	
3P 378 beaker	P-39A	pl. 95:10
3P 411 jar with pointed base	P-40C	pl. 96:8
3N-T 234 school text		
3N-T 235 literary text		
XI-1		
3N 278 rattle	T-13	
3P 413 cup	P-39	
XI-2		
3P 426 jar	P-U	
164 main room in XA-1, street below, disturbed in XA-1		
XA-1 (intrusive?)		
3P 182 small Kassite jar*		
3P 183 Kassite jar*		

* This vessel belongs in OIP 78 pottery type 46B.

Findspot and Description	Type	OIP 78 Reference
165 unknown function, disturbed		
XA-1		
3N-T 68 Kassite business document		
166 open area, disturbed		
XA-1		
3D 195 female figurine fragment	F-1	
bronze fragment		
painted sherd	P-24	
XA-2		
3P 176 beaker	P-39	
3P 177 large burial jar	P-25	pl. 89:11
3P 180 painted pot	P-24	
3P 181 painted pot	P-24	
3P 188 large bowl	P-32	
3P 189 dish	P-7(?)	
3P 190 beaker	P-39	
3N-T 104 school text		
167 street		
XA-2		
3P 192 beaker	P-39	
heavy pot	P-U	
XA-3		
3D 246 base of seated figure	F-3	pl. 134:3
3P 191 beaker	P-39	
3P 200 dish	P-7(?)	
168 street, disturbed in XA-1		
XA-1		
3D 198 plaque fragment	F-20	p. 92
3D 199 figurine fragment	F-4	pl. 131:7
3N-T 71 school text		
XB-1		
3D 408 head of male figurine	F-2	pl. 130:8
169 unknown function, disturbed		
XA fill		
3N 176 bronze blade	T-5	pl. 155:1
3N-T 73 school text		
170 main room		
XA-3		
3D 261 figurine head	F-6	
171 unclear function		
XA fill		
3D 197 seal impression	T-12	
172 unclear function		
XA-2		
3N-T 72 inheritance document = Text 6		
XA-3		
3N-T 105 school text		
173 main room		
XA-2		
3N 124 stone stamp seal	T-12	
unfinished shell object	T-1	
3P 148 beaker	P-39A	

Findspot and Description	Type	OIP 78 Reference
3P 150 deep bowl	P-31	
3P 152 tall jar with pointed base	P-40	
3P 161 large shallow bowl	P-30	pl. 93:9
3P 166 tall vase	P-U	pl. 96:12
3P 179 large jar	P-U	
3P 221 dish	P-7(?)	
3P 233 beaker	P-39	
3P 234 beaker	P-39	
3N 205 painted pot	P-24	
large bowl	P-U	
3N-T 74 account (RiSi 42)		
3N-T 75 receipt		
174 courtyard, perhaps disturbed in XA		
XA drain		
3D 443 seal impression	T-12	pl. 120:11
lead fragment		
XA-1		
3N-T 76 literary text		
XA-2		
3N 128 bronze chisel	T-6	pl. 153:7
3P 146 dish	P-7(?)	
3N-T 77 account (Šu 48)		
XI-1		
3N 283a hematite duck weight	T-10	p. 109
3N 283b hematite plano-convex disk weight	T-10	p. 109
3N 284 limestone ovoid weight	T-10	p. 109
3N 286 diorite duck weight	T-10	p. 109
3D 438 spindle whorl	T-11	
oyster shell		
3P 370 large jar	P-U	
3P 371 miniature pot	P-2	pl. 80:3
3P 375 ribbed potstand	P-42	pl. 97:4
3P 379 beaker	P-39(?)	
3P 388 large shallow bowl	P-30	pl. 93:4
3P 389 large shallow bowl	P-30(?)	
3P 390 small jar	P-U	
3P 391 white pot	P-U	
3P 392 painted pot	P-24	
3P 393 painted pot	P-24	
3N-T 221 field rental (RiSi II) = Text 29		p. 76
3N-T 222 silver loan (Si 1) = Text 28		p. 76
3N-T 223 grain loan (Ha 43) = Text 27		p. 76
3N-T 224 business document		
3N-T 225 court case = Text 40		
3N-T 226 account		
3N-T 246 field rental (Si 10) = Text 32		p. 76
3N-T 247 account		
3N-T 248 wool loan = Text 33		
XI-2		
3N 330 hematite duck weight	T-10	p. 109
3P 395 ribbed potstand	P-42	pl. 97:5
3P 408 painted pot	P-24	pl. 88:19

Findspot and Description	Type	OIP 78 Reference
3P 409 painted pot	P-24	
3N-T 863 house exchange (RiSi 59) = Text 20		pl. 120:8, 10; p. 76
3N-T 864 grain loan (Si 5) = Text 23		p. 76
3N-T 865 grain payment (Si 7) = Text 25		p. 76
3N-T 866 house sale (ItPi) = Text 37		p. 76
3N-T 867 inheritance document (Si 10) = Text 31		p. 76
3N-T 868 silver loan = Text 39		
3N-T 869 house sale (RiSi 37) = Text 18		pl. 120:9, p. 76
3N-T 870 field rental (Si 7) = Text 38		p. 76
3N-T 871 betrothal text (Si 11) = Text 34		p. 76
3N-T 872 house exchange (RiSi 59) = Text 21		p. 76
3N-T 873 court case = Text 24		
3N-T 874 court case (LiEn) = Text 36		
3N-T 875 adoption text (Si) = Text 30		
3N-T 876 court case (Ha 42) = Text 22		p. 76
3N-T 877 house sale = Text 19		
3N-T 878 grain loan = Text 41		
3N-T 879 account		
3N-T 880 business document		
3N-T 881 business document		
3N-T 882 court case (UrNi) = Text 35		
3N-T 883 letter		
3N-T 884 house sale (Si 7) = Text 26		p. 76
175 unclear function, disturbed		
XA fill		
4 globular frit beads	T-1	
1 cylindrical frit bead	T-1	
4 frit bead fragments	T-1	
176 entrance chamber		
XA-1		
3N 260 (3D 216) male figurine fragment	F-2	pl. 130:11
XA-2		
3D 225 seal impression	T-12	
XA-3		
3N-T 114 field rental (Si 11) = Text 59		p. 76
XI foundations		
duck weight	T-10	
177 open area		
XA-1		
3N 259 (3D 215) male plaque	F-13	pl. 135:4
178 main room		
XA-1		
3D 219 heavy polished stone object		
3N-T 91 house exchange (Si 17) = Text 45		pl. 76
3N-T 92 house sale (Si 12) = Text 43		p. 76
3N-T 93 house sale (Si 16) = Text 44		
3N-T 94 inheritance document (Si 8) = Text 42		pl. 76
XA-2		
3N 146a hematite barrel weight	T-10	p. 109
3N 146b hematite barrel weight	T-10	p. 109
3N 146c hematite barrel weight	T-10	p. 109

Findspot and Description	Type	OIP 78 Reference
3N 146d hematite barrel weight	T-10	p. 109
3N 146e hematite boar's head weight	T-10	p. 109
3P 149 large jar (drain)	P-U	pl. 93:6
3P 158 small pot	P-35	
3P 159 bottle	P-37	
3P 160 bottle	P-37	pl. 95:1
3N 136 painted pot	P-24	pl. 88:23
bottle with flared rim	P-37(?)	
3N-T 80 literary text		
179 storeroom(s), disturbed		
XA wall		
3N 234 limestone cylinder weight	T-10	p. 110
XA-1		
3N 139 bronze forked pin	T-2	pl. 154:10
3P 420 tall cylindrical pot	P-U	pl. 96:3
3N-T 844 house sale (Si 7) = Text 54		
3N-T 845 manumission (RiSi 51) = Text 53		
3N-T 846 account		
3N-T 847 exchange text = Text 55		
XA-2		
3N-T 213 literary text		
XA-3		
3D 472 male figurine fragment	F-2	
XA foundations		
3N 305 male plaque	F-13	pl. 135:9
3D 433 part of skirted figure	F-4	
3D 475 bronze needle	T-9	p. 106
3P 422 small cup	P-U	pl. 96:2
3N-T 218 receipt		
3N-T 815 account		
180 main room		
XA fill		
3D 224 lapis bead	T-1	p. 98
3D 226 loom weight	T-10	p. 112
XA-2		
3D 349 tablet clay with design		pl. 148:10, p. 112
XA-3		
3D 357 bronze pin	T-2	p. 101
3N-T 179 school text		
3N-T 182 literary text		
3N-T 183 literary text		
3N-T 184 business document (Si 8)		p. 76
3N-T 185 contract (Ha 31) = Text 58		
XI fill		
3N-T 812 literary text		
3N-T 813 literary text		
XI foundations		
3N 325 inset stone	T-1	pl. 151:24, p. 105
3N 326 bronze awl	T-6	pl. 156:15, p. 102
3D 496 clay figurine	F-4	pl. 131:5
3D 497 bronze sleeve		
3N-T 852 marriage contract (RiSi 30) = Text 1		

Findspot and Description	Type	OIP 78 Reference
181 main room, disturbed in XI		
XA wall		
3N-T 204 bulla		
XA-1		
3D 223 large bead	T-1	
XA-2		
3N 157 hematite plano-convex disk weight	T-10	p. 109
3D 263 whetstone fragment	T-8	p. 110
3D 264 bull figurine fragment	F-5	
weight	T-10	
carnelian fragment	T-1	
3P 198 beaker	P-39A	pl. 95:11
3P 204 tall beaker	P-38	pl. 95:7
3P 214 large pot	P-36	pl. 94:14
3P 217 large pot	P-36	pl. 94:13
XA-3		
3D 332 bronze fragment		
3P 287 small bowl	P-21	
3N-T 150 literary text		
3N-T 151 school text		
3N-T 152 literary text		
3N-T 153 school text		
3N-T 154 school text		
XI fill		
3P 432 ridged pot	P-24	
XI-1		
3P 430 red potlike bowl	P-U	pl. 94:3
3P 431 small pot	P-35	
3P 444 jar	P-U	pl. 94:17
3P 445 small pot	P-35	
3P 446 ridged pot	P-24	
3N-T 790–792 three literary texts		
XI-2		
3P 460 small jar with pointed base	P-40C	
XI-3		
3N 334 male plaque	F-13	
182 main room		
XA-2		
3N 198 long bronze pin	T-2	p. 101
183 unclear function, XA-1 disturbed		
XA-2		
3P 167 "flowerpot"	P-34	pl. 93:12
184 subsidiary room		
XA-1		
3N 143 small cylinder seal	T-12	pl. 113:4
3N 151 erotic scene on plaque	F-19	pl. 137:7
seal impression	T-12	
3P 168 pot	P-24	
3N-T 87 house exchange (IlIl 1) = Text 12		p. 76
3N-T 88 allocation of temple offices (RiSi 54) = Text 11		p. 76
3N-T 89 house rental (Si 27) = Text 14		p. 76

Findspot and Description	Type	OIP 78 Reference
3N-T 90 orchard sale (Si 7) = Text 13		p. 76
3N-T 96 adoption (Si 8) = Text 15		p. 76
3N-T 97 house sale (RiSi 38) = Text 17		p. 76
3N-T 98 house sale (BuSi) = Text 16		
XA-2		
3N-T 117–119 three literary/school texts		
XI-2		
3P 449 tall beaker	P-38	pl. 95:5, p. 116
3P 451 tall beaker	P-39B	p. 116
3P 452 tall beaker	P-39B	p. 116
3P 453 tall beaker	P-39B	p. 116
3P 462 tall beaker	P-39B	p. 116
3P 463 tall beaker	P-39B	p. 116
3P 464 tall beaker	P-39B	p. 116
3N-T 723–728 six literary texts		
3N-T 740–743 four lexical texts		
3N-T 744 loan (SiId) = Text 7		
3N-T 745 lexical text		
3N-T 746 lexical text		
3N-T 747 account		
3N-T 748 school text		
3N-T 886 lexical text		p. 116
3N-T 887 literary text		
XI-3		
3P 448 small pot	P-35	p. 116
3P 450 small pot	P-35	p. 116
3N-T 722 literary text		
3N-T 729–739 eleven literary/school texts		
3N-T 923–924 eighteen literary/school text fragments		
185 subsidiary room, disturbed		
XA-1		
3N-T 81 contract concerning field property? = Text 52		
3N-T 82 field rental = Text 51		
3N-T 83 field rental (Si 7) = Text 49		p. 76
3N-T 84 house rental (Si 8) = Text 50		p. 76
3N-T 85 house sale (Si 17) =Text 46		
3N-T 86 house sale (Si 18) = Text 47		p. 76
3N-T 95 grain payments (RiSi 30) = Text 48		p. 76
XA-2		
3N-T 78 witness list (Ha 38) = Text 56		p. 76
3N-T 79 business document		
XI foundation		
3D 457 inscribed stone fragment		
3D 458 glazed disk fragment		
186 subsidiary room, disturbed		
XA-3		
3N-T 168 school text		
3N-T 169 literary text		
XI foundations		
3N 321 rattle	T-13	
3D 476 two pin fragments	T-2	

Findspot and Description	Type	OIP 78 Reference
3P 423 small pot	P-35	
3P 424 small pot	P-35	pl. 94:5
3P 425 painted pot	P-24	
3N-T 814 letter		
187 court		
XA-2		
3N 175 hematite barrel weight	T-10	p. 110
3D 480 stone spindle whorl	T-11	p. 111
XA-3		
3N 192 plaque showing shepherd	F-16	pl. 138:2
3P 458 large jar	P-U	pl. 97:1
3N-T 128–131 four literary/school texts		
3N-T 156–158 three literary/school texts		
3N-T 159 silver loan (Ha 38) = Text 57		p. 76
XI foundations		
3N 307 baked clay cylinder seal	T-12	pl. 112:12
3D 503 plaque	F-20	
3D 504 male figurine fragment	F-2	
clay stopper		
plaque	F-20	
188 court, disturbed in XI fill		
XA-2		
3N 219 cylinder seal	T-12	pl. 113:2
XA-3		
3D 358 double spiral bronze ring	T-2	p. 100
3P 307 jar	P-U	pl. 95:3
3P 309 deep bowl	P-31	pl. 93:8
3N-T 160 school text		
3N-T 162–166 five literary/school texts		
3N-T 167 account (Si 27)		p. 76
3N-T 177 school text		
3N-T 178 school text		
XI fill		
3P 436 burial jar	P-25	pl. 89:5
3P 437 burial jar	p-25	pl. 89:7
3P 438 burial jar	P-25(?)	
3P 439 tray	P-20	pl. 88:1
XI-1		
3N 318 model chariot fragment	F-9	pl. 149:10
3P 433 tall beaker	P-39B	
3P 434 shallow bowl with carinated rim	P-8B	
3P 435 beaker	P-39A	
XI-2		
3D 523 model chariot wheel	F-10/T-11	
3D 524 model chariot wheel	F-10/T-11	
3D 525 model chariot wheel	F-10/T-11	
3D 526 spindle whorl	T-11	p. 111
3P 461 beaker	P-39B	pl. 148:3
3N-T 766 literary text		
3N-T 767 letter		
3N-T 768–775 eight literary/lexical/school texts		

Findspot and Description	Type	OIP 78 Reference
189 subsidiary room		
XA-1		
3D 247 macehead	T-3	cf. p. 105
3D 299 erotic scene on plaque	F-19	
3P 171 stone bowl	T-14	
3P 203 painted sherds	P-24	
XI-2		
3N-T 749–765 seventeen lexical/literary texts		
3N-T 925–926 thirteen lexical/literary texts		
190 entrance chamber		
XA-1		
3P 173 small pot	P-35	
painted pot	P-24	
XA-2		
bead	T-1	
3N-T 123–125 three literary texts		
3N-T 126 letter		
3N-T 127 account		
3N-T 155 business document (Si 13)		p. 76
3N-T 160 school text		
XI fill		
3D 473 female plaque	F-11	
191 subsidiary room		
XA-1		
3P 175 beaker	P-39	
XI-1		
3N 308 head of male figurine	F-2	pl. 130:5
3N-T 657–671 fifteen literary texts		
3N-T 687–692 six literary/lexical texts		
3N-T 916–917 eighty-four literary/school texts		
3N-T 920 thirty-four literary/school texts		
XI-2		
3N-T 672–682 eleven literary texts		
3N-T 683 letter		
3N-T 684 letter		
3N-T 685 business document		
3N-T 686 literary text		
3N-T 693–721 twenty-nine lexical/literary texts		
3N-T 885 lexical text		p. 116
3N-T 918–919 ninety-one literary/school texts		
3N-T 921–922 seventy-one literary/school texts		
XI-3		
3D 553 plaque fragment	F-20	p. 116
192 court		
193 unclear function, disturbed		
XA-2		
3N 193 lion plaque	F-15	
3D 283 stone disk		
3P 231 bottle	P-37(?)	
3P 280 miniature bowl	P-M	pl. 93:5
XA-3		
3N-T 205 letter		

Findspot and Description	Type	OIP 78 Reference
194 court/entrance chamber		
XB		
3P 476 potstand	P-41	
3P 478 potstand	P-41	pl. 97:2
XI-1		
3D 463 spindle whorl	T-11/F-10	
195 subsidiary room, disturbed		
XI		
3N 291 nude female plaque	F-11	pl. 127:10
3D 459 chariot fragment	F-9	
3D 464 nude female plaque	F-11	
3D 465 chariot fragment	F-9	
196 main room		
XB-2		
3N-T 230 literary text		
3N-T 231 school text		
XI-1		
3N-T 810 literary text		
3N-T 811 literary text		
XIIA-3		
3N 424 cylinder seal	T-12	pl. 112:4
3N 428 carved shell inlay		pl. 153:19, p. 105
3D 623 blue bead	T-1	
3D 624 whetstone fragment	T-8	p. 110
3P 548 tubular vase	P-27	
3P 550 tubular vase	P-27	
3P 551 dish	P-U	
3N-T 858 hire of workers = Text 5		
3N-T 859 distribution of kislaḫ = Text 4		
3N-T 860 business document		
XIIA foundation		
3N 429 nude female plaque	F-11	pl. 127:4
197 entrance chamber, disturbed in XB		
XB-2		
3N-T 232 school text		
3N-T 236 literary text		
3N-T 237 letter		
3N-T 238–245 eight literary/school texts		
XI-1		
3N 292 driver plaque	F-18	pl. 138:6
XI-2		
3N-T 804 Rim-Sin cone		
XIIIA-1		
head of animal figurine	F-5	
198 subsidiary room, disturbed in XB		
XB-1		
3P 385 small pot	P-35(?)	
XB-2		
3D 444 head of animal figurine	F-5	
199 subsidiary room		
XI-2		
3N 287 bull-man plaque, head only	F-14	pl. 136:10
3P 419 beaker	P-39A	

Findspot and Description	Type	OIP 78 Reference
XIIB-3		
3N-T 851 literary text		
200 subsidiary room, disturbed		
XB-1		
3N 269 plaque	F-20	pl. 135:2
3N-T 214 account		
XB-2		
3N-T 284–289 six literary/school texts		
XI fill		
3N 300 stone half-dome gaming piece		p. 104
XI-2		
3D 471 head of female figurine	F-4	pl. 126:9
201 main room		
XA-3		
3N 145 bone object—hollow tube with white chalk at narrow end		pl. 154:8, p. 112
crystal bead	T-1	
XB-1		
3N-T 208 receipt (Ha 38)		p. 76
3N-T 217 school text		
202 subsidiary room, disturbed		
XI fill		
3P 373 dish	P-U	pl. 93:2
3P 374 deep bowl	P-31	pl. 93:7
3P 398 large pot	P-36	pl. 94:11
3P 473 pot	P-U	
203 entrance chamber		
XI fill		
3P 380 red burnished ware jar	P-U	
3N-T 233 letter		pl. 120:12
3N-T 816 grain loan (RiSi 22) = Text 8		p. 76
3N-T 817–819 three lexical texts		
204 unclear function		
XA-3		
3N-T 220 literary text		
205 main room		
XI fill		
3N 293 cylinder seal	T-12	pl. 112:13
3D 437 figurine fragment	F-6	
3P 368 miniature pot	P-M	pl. 94:16
3P 377 beaker	P-39A	
3P 384 large jar	P-U	pl. 94:2
3P 386 bowl	P-U	
3P 387 small pot	P-26	pl. 90:13
3P 396 platter	P-U	pl. 93:1
3P 397 dish	P-7(?)	
3N-T 211 literary text		
3N-T 212 mathematical text		
3N-T 216 literary text		
3N-T 219 grain loan = Text 9		
3N-T 229 school text		
3N-T 290 school text		

Findspot and Description	Type	OIP 78 Reference
XI-1		
3P 403 beaker	P-39	
3P 404 plate	P-U	pl. 96:1
3P 405 beaker	P-39	
3P 406 tall jar with pointed base	P-40	pl. 96:7
3N-T 249–276 twenty-eight literary/school texts		
3N-T 283 model cone		
XI-2		
3N-T 291–427 one hundred thirty-seven literary/school texts		
3N-T 776–789 fourteen lexical/literary texts		
3N-T 900–901 sixty literary/school texts		
XI-3		
3N 303 male plaque	F-13	pl. 134:9, p. 116
3N 304 nude female plaque	F-11	pl. 127:9, p. 116
3N 329 bone chisel (stylus?)	T-6	pp. 104, 116
3N 340 lion plaque	F-15	pl. 142:10, p. 116
3N 343 model chariot wheel	F-10/T-11	p. 116
3N 345 male plaque	F-13	pl. 136:2, p. 116
3D 533 lower part of nude female plaque	F-11	p. 116
3D 534 small figurine fragment	F-4	pl. 131:6, p. 116
3P 459 bowl	P-U	p. 116
3P 465 painted pot	P-24	p. 116
3N-T 428–434 seven lexical/literary texts		
3N-T 435 letter		
3N-T 436–469 thirty-four lexical/literary texts		
3N-T 470 business document		
3N-T 471–494 twenty-four literary texts		
3N-T 495 business document		
3N-T 496–560 sixty-six literary/lexical/mathematical texts		
3N-T 561 adoption = Text 10		
3N-T 562–631 seventy literary/lexical/mathematical texts		
3N-T 632 business document		
3N-T 633–656 twenty-four prisms		
3N-T 902–915 five hundred twenty-one literary/school texts		
XIIA-1 fill		
3P 515 beaker	P-39A	
3P 516 jar with pointed base	P-40	
3P 517 jar	P-U	
3P 518 pot	P-U	pl. 90:18
XIIB fill		
3N 390 duck weight	T-10	p. 109
3D 603 bed or toy fragment	F-8(?)	
3N-T 842 silver loan (SiId 7) = Text 3		
206 see locus 179		
207 see locus 230		
208 unclear function		
XB-1		
3N 294 Early Dynastic cylinder seal	T-12	pl. 113:1

Findspot and Description	Type	OIP 78 Reference
209 court		
XB-2		
3P 400 jar with pointed base	P-40	
3P 402 jar with pointed base	P-40	
3P 407 small pot	P-35	
XI-1		
3D 466 carved stone		
XI-2		
3P 418 beaker	P-39	
XII-1		
3D 622 female figurine	F-1	
XII-2		
3N 433 cylinder seal	T-12	
3D 640 seal impression	T-12	
3N-T 853 literary text		
3N-T 854 literary text		
210 unclear function		
XI fill		
3N-T 228 Ur III account		
211 court		
XB-2		
3N 280 bull-man plaque	F-14	p. 92
XI-1		
3N 306 bronze needle	T-9	p. 106
3D 461 male figurine	F-2	
3D 470 plaque fragment showing presentation scene	F-17	opp. pl. 133:5
bone ring	T-1	
3P 412 tall beaker	P-U	pl. 96:11
XIIA-1		
3P 542 tubular vase	P-27	
XIIA-2		
3N 430 model boat	F-9	pl. 144:9
3D 639 model bed fragment	F-8	
3N-T 861 school text		
3N-T 862 account		
XIIA-3		
3D 637 seal impression	T-12	pl. 120:4
3D 638 seal impression	T-12	
212 subsidiary room, disturbed		
XB-1		
3N 263 model bed	F-8	pl. 144:5
3D 442 bone awl	T-6	
213 subsidiary room, disturbed		
XI foundation		
3P 455 beaker	P-39	
3P 456 jar with pointed base	P-40	
3P 457 beaker	P-39A	
214 subsidiary room, disturbed		
XI-1 cut		
3P 477 burial jar	P-25	pl. 89:8, p. 144
3P 479 very large bowl	P-33	pl. 93:11
3P 480 very large bowl	P-33(?)	

Findspot and Description	Type	OIP 78 Reference
3P 481 very large bowl	P-33(?)	
3P 482 red vase	P-U	pl. 94:18
3P 483 burial jar	P-25	pl. 89:9, p. 144
3P 484 burial jar	P-25	pl. 89:10, p. 144
XIIB-1		
3D 474 male figurine fragment	F-2	pl. 130:6
216 subsidiary room		
XIIB-1		
3N 389 long hematite barrel weight	T-10	p. 109
217 main room?		
XIII-1		
3D 603 model bed fragment	F-8	
3P 519 miniature pot	P-M	
3P 520 vase	P-28	pl. 91:17
3P 521 jar	P-U	pl. 91:13
3P 526 jar	P-U	pl. 91:12
218 open area, disturbed		
XIIB-1		
3N 391 plaque showing lutist	F-16	pl. 138:5
XIIB-2		
3N 399 cylinder seal	T-1	pl. 112:5
XIII-1		
3N 421 bronze bracelet	T-2	p. 99
3N 422 bone inlay		p. 105
3N 423 bull-man plaque	F-14	pl. 136:8
3D 621 loom weight	T-10	
XIII-1 cut (3B* 92)		
3P 585 vase	P-U	p. 144
3P 586 jar	P-U	pl. 90:16, p. 144
3P 587 jar	P-U	p. 144
XIII-2		
3N 412 plaque fragment	F-20	pl. 137:9
3N 431 nude female plaque fragment	F-11	
3D 628 bone blade	T-6	
3D 629 snake head on plaque	F-15	pl. 142:6
shell		
fish jaw		
3P 547 small pot	P-U	pl. 91:4
3N-T 857 letter		
219 court		
XIIB-1		
3N 396 seated figurine	F-3	pl. 139:3
3D 582 model chariot wheel	F-10/T-11	
3D 583 seal impression	T-12	
3D 626 plaque fragment	F-20	pl. 139:2
3D 627 stone fragment		
XIII-2		
3D 641 model boat fragment	F-9	
3D 642 nude female plaque	F-11	

* B = burial

Findspot and Description	Type	OIP 78 Reference
220 open area, disturbed		
XIIB-2		
3D 607 figurine fragment	F-6	
3P 534 tubular vase	P-27	
XIII cut		
3P 543 burial jar	P-25(?)	
3P 544 burial jar	P-25(?)	
3P 545 bottle	P-37(?)	
3P 546 round-based jar	P-19B(?)	
XIII cut (3B 70)		
jar	P-U	p. 144
XIII-1		
3N 434 plaque	F-20	pl. 133:8
3D 666 seal impression	T-12	pl. 119:15
3D 667 unbaked clay square		
3D 668 model chariot fragment	F-9	
3D 669 male plaque fragment	F-13	pl. 135:7
3D 670 female figurine fragment	F-1	
3N-T 850 account		
XIII-2		
3N 442 rattle	T-13	
3N 455 half of limestone macehead	T-3	pl. 154:25, p. 105
3D 616 figurine fragment	F-6	
3P 552 vase	P-U	pl. 91:5
3P 553 small flat pot	P-U	pl. 90:7
3P 556 spout	P-U	
3P 562 fragment of small stone bowl	T-14	
221 subsidiary room, disturbed		
222 open area, disturbed		
XIIB-2		
3N 415 cylinder seal	T-12	pl. 112:6
3N 419 model bed	F-8	pl. 144:6
XIIB foundation		
3N-T 849 lexical text		
223 unclear function		
225 court, disturbed		
XIII-1 cut (3B 73)		
3P 575 jar with pointed base	P-40C(?)	p. 144
3P 580 pot	P-U	p. 144
226 subsidiary room, disturbed		
XIII cut (3B 74)		
3N 463 erotic scene on plaque	F-19	opp. pl. 137:4
3N 464 male figurine fragment	F-2	pl. 130:3
3D 618 model chariot wheel	F-10/T-11	
jar	P-U	p. 144
XIII-1		
3D 619 model chariot wheel	F-10/T-11	
3D 620 figurine fragment	F-4	
XIII-2		
3N 468 granite barrel weight	T-10	p. 109
3N 469 plaque showing lutist	F-16	pl. 138:1
3D 659 bead	T-1	p. 98

Findspot and Description	Type	OIP 78 Reference
3D 679 whetstone	T-8	p. 110
3D 680 model chariot wheel	F-10/T-11	
3D 681 model chariot wheel	F-10/T-11	
3P 563 miniature pot	P-M	pl. 92:10
227 main room in XIIB, entrance chamber in XIII		
228 subsidiary room		
XIII-1		
3P 574 jar	P-U	pl. 90:17
229 court in XIII, main room(?) in XIIB		
XIIB fill		
3D 590 male figurine	F-2	
230 court in XIIB, main room in XIII, disturbed in XIIB		
XIIB fill		
3N-T 855 silver loan (EnBa) = Text 2		
XIIB-1		
3N 460 stone stamp seal	T-12	
3D 665 stone bead	T-1	
bone ring	T-1	
5 shell beads	T-1	
XIII-1 cut		
3N 488 beads, some shell, 2 carnelian, 3 or 4 frit	T-1	
3P 581 jar	P-U	
3P 582 jar with pointed base	P-40	
XIII-2		
3N 448 cylinder seal	T-12	pl. 111:15
XIII-3		
3N 466 cylinder seal	T-12	pl. 111:16
3N 467 bone animal amulet	T-1	pl. 147:7, p. 99
3D 676 model chariot wheel	F-10/T-11	p. 111
3D 677 female plaque fragment	F-11	
XV		
bead	T-1	
bead	T-1	
3N-T 889 account (IbSi)		pl. 120:9, p. 75
231 court in XIII, subsidiary room in XIIB		
XIIB-1		
3N 417 limestone statue fragment		pl. 145:3
XIIB-2		
3D 657 male figurine fragment	F-2	
232 subsidiary room		
233 subsidiary room, disturbed		
XIIB-1		
3D 650 bone awl	T-6	p. 102
3D 651 bone awl	T-6	p. 102
XIIB-1 cut		
3N 470 beads	T-1	
XIII-1 cut (3B 75)		
pot	P-U	p. 144
pot	P-U	p. 144
234 unclear function		
XIIB-1		
3D 615 stone loom weight	T-10	p. 112
3P 533 beaker	P-39A	pl. 95:16

Findspot and Description	Type	OIP 78 Reference
235 main room		
XIIA-3		
3N 461 plaque fragment showing charioteer	F-18	pl. 138:7
3D 678 animal figurine	F-5	
236 unclear function		
XIII-2		
3D 686 plaque fragment	F-20	pl. 134:4
237 subsidiary room		
238 subsidiary room		
239 unclear function, disturbed		
XIII cut (3B 72)		
3P 582 jar with pointed base	P-40	p. 144
240 unclear function		
241 unclear function, disturbed		
XIII cut (3B 71)		
3N 488 frit, carnelian, and white and black stone beads	T-1	p. 144
3P 581 jar	P-U	p. 144
242 subsidiary room		
243 subsidiary room, disturbed		
XIII cut (3B 92)		
3P 585 pot	P-U	p. 144
3P 586 pot	P-U	p. 144
3P 587 pot	P-U	p. 144
244 main room		
— dump		
3N-T 210 grain loan = Text 61		

APPENDIX II (continued)

TB

Findspot and Description	Type	OIP 78 Reference
1 unknown function		
I-1		
1N 168 stone chisel	T-6	p. 103
1N 170 hematite boar's head weight	T-10	pl. 147:17, p. 109
2P 24 small dish	P-21	
1N 171 small dish	P-21	
1N 172 dish	P-7	
1N 173 small dish	P-21	
1N 174 dish	P-7	
1N 175 small dish	P-21	
1N 176 dish	P-7	
2N-T 388 god list		
2N-T 389 god list		
2 open area, disturbed		
D		
2N-T 167 adoption contract (EnBa X) = Text 62		
D/E		
2N 98 shallow bowl with carinated rim	P-8B	
I-1		
2N 176 iron point	T-3	
2N 177 copper ornament	T-2	
2P 66 bowl	P-U	pl. 90:5
1N 215 beaker	P-39	
3 subsidiary room, disturbed		
I-1		
2D 1 female(?) figurine fragment	F-1(?)	
2D 5 copper/bronze ring	T-2	p. 100
4 unknown function, disturbed		
D/E		
2N-T 14 literary text		
2N-T 15 literary text		
2N-T 17 lexical text		
5 street		
I-1		
2N 325 copper/bronze ring	T-2	p. 100
2N 333 male figurine fragment	F-2	pl. 130:4
2N 656 (2D 187) flint blade	T-4	p. 103
2D 188 stone palette fragment		
2N-T 172 school text		
2N-T 414 school text		
2N-T 424 business document		
6 entrance chamber		
E		
2N 322 bronze fishhook		pl. 153:16, p. 104
I-1		
2N 332 female figurine fragment	F-1	pl. 124:1
2N-T 412 school text		

Findspot and Description	Type	OIP 78 Reference
2N-T 413 account of sheep		
7 unknown function, disturbed		
8 court, disturbed		
I-1		
2D 2 female figurine fragment	F-1	
2D 4 female plaque fragment	F-11	
2N-T 94 account of barley expenditure		
9 subsidiary room, disturbed		
10 court		
I-1		
2N-T 71 receipt (AmSi 5)		p. 75
I-2		
2N 857 (2D 65) seated figurine fragment	F-3	
II fill		
2N 338 pottery rattle	T-13	pl. 149:16
2D 386 rider figurine fragment	F-4	
2N 950 (2P 406) shallow bowl with carinated rim	P-8B	
II-1		
2N 69 plaque fragment showing head of dog	F-15	pl. 142:5
2N-T 41 school text		
2N-T 54 account of murder trial (UrNi)		p. 75
2N-T 55 literary text		
2N-T 56 lexical text		
2N-T 131 mathematical text		
2N-T 391 school text		
2N-T 497 school text		
2N-T 498 school text		
2N-T 499 mathematical text		
2N-T 500 mathematical text		
2N-T 501 school text		
2N-T 502 school text		
2N-T 503 school text		
II-2		
2N-T 496 school text		
2N-T 550 literary text		
II foundations		
2N 497 stone duck weight	T-10	pl. 147:16, p. 109
2N 626 bronze blade, bone handle	T-5	p. 103
2N 865 (2D 395) head of male figurine	F-2	
2D 410 female figurine fragment	F-1	
2P 428 dish	P-7(?)	
2P 451 large jar—mended	P-14A	
2P 462 shallow red bowl with carinated rim	P-8B	pl. 82:19
2N 423 strainer fragments	P-6	
2N 951 (2P 409a) shallow bowl with carinated rim	P-8B	pl. 82:23
2N 1032 (2P 409b) small bowl	P-22	pl. 88:9
2N-T 685 silver loan (Ha 31) = Text 65		
11 unknown function, disturbed		
I-1		
2N 320 copper ring	T-2	p. 100
2D 54 bowl	P-U	
2D 55 bowl	P-U	

Findspot and Description	Type	OIP 78 Reference
12 main room		
I-1		
2N-T 390 mathematical text		
2N-T 396 literary text		
I-2		
2N-T 468 lexical text		
2N-T 789 school text		
II-1		
2D 867 seal impression	T-12	pl. 119:9
2D 868 seal impression	T-12	pl. 119:10
2D 869 seal impression	T-12	
2P 10 tall beaker	P-38	
2P 18 miniature pot fragment	P-M	pl. 92:14
2N 73 small gray-ware pot	P-35(?)	
2N-T 18 school text		
2N-T 19 lexical text		
2N-T 23 school text		
2N-T 24 school text		
2N-T 25 school text		
2N-T 26 lexical text		
2N-T 27 mathematical text		
2N-T 28 school text		
2N-T 30 mathematical text		
2N-T 31 lexical text		
2N-T 32 lexical text		
2N-T 34 letter		
2N-T 35 mathematical text		
2N-T 36 lexical text		
2N-T 38 lexical text		
2N-T 42 school text		
II foundations		
2N 789 (2D 449) nude female plaque	F-11	pl. 127:1
2N-T 596 receipt (AmSi 1)		p. 75
13 subsidiary room		
14 unknown function, disturbed in I		
I wall		
2N-T 403 letter		
II-1		
2D 374 female figurine fragment	F-1	
2N 944 (2P 389) large jar	P-14A	pl. 84:8
2N-T 22 account of offerings		
inscribed brick		
II-2		
clay bottle stopper		
2P 344 shallow red bowl with carinated rim	P-8B	
2P 347 small bowl	P-22	
2N 949 (2P 392) shallow bowl with carinated rim		
2N-T 548 literary text		
15 entrance chamber, disturbed		
16 entrance chamber in D, unknown function in I, disturbed		
E		
2N-T 166 administrative document		

Findspot and Description	Type	OIP 78 Reference
17 storeroom in I-1, main room in I-2 and II, disturbed in I		
II-1		
2P 362 miniature jar	P-M	
2N-T 37 school text		
2N-T 40 list of temples		
2N-T 43 school text		
2N-T 44 field rental (ŠuIl 23) = Text 66		
2N-T 440 law code		
II-2		
2N 565 blank cylinder seal	T-12	
2N 593 (2D 464) stone head	T-1	
2D 572 seal impression	T-12	
II foundations		
2N 670 (2D 486) bone awl	T-6	p. 102
unfinished bead	T-1	
18 subsidiary room, disturbed		
II-1		
2N 66 bone awl	T-6	pl. 153:1, p. 102
II-2		
2P 388 small pot	P-35	
19 subsidiary room, disturbed in I		
II-2		
2N 546 black stone weight	T-10	p. 109
2N 839 (2D 382) female figurine fragment	F-1	
2D 381 female figurine fragment	F-1	
2D 473 shell ring	T-1	
2N 1033 (2P 601) small bowl	P-22	
20 entrance chamber		
D		
2N 68 iron bracelet	T-2	p. 99
2N 128 iron drill head	T-7	p. 104
2N 92 (2P 46) painted pot	P-24	
5 painted sherds	P-24	
red painted sherd	P-U	
2N-T 84 literary text		
2N-T 85 literary text		
2N-T 86 literary text		
2N-T 87 literary text		
E-1		
2N 301 cylinder seal	T-12	pl. 112:9
2N 861 (2D 76) male figurine fragment	F-2	
2N-T 169 account of flour		
2N-T 174 mathematical text		
E-2		
2N 175 bone needle	T-9	p. 106
I-1		
2N 329 bone needle	T-9	
2N 330 female plaque fragment	F-11	
pottery chariot wheel	F-10/T-11	
bent copper/bronze nail		
2N-T 136 literary text		
2N-T 191 Ur III food account		

Findspot and Description	Type	OIP 78 Reference
21 subsidiary room, disturbed in I		
II-1		
2N 859 (2D 283) model chariot	F-9	pl. 144:7
2D 284 flint core	T-4	
2N 998 (2P 356) tubular vase	P-27	
22 open area in I, court in II, disturbed		
I-1		
2P 33 shallow bowl with carinated rim	P-8B	
2P 34a small bowl	P-22	
2P 35 dish	P-7	
2P 36 small dish	P-21	
2P 37 small dish	P-21	
2P 38 dish	P-7	
2P 39 dish	P-7(?)	
2P 40 small dish	P-21	
2P 41 small dish	P-21	
2P 42 small dish	P-21	
2P 43 small dish	P-21	
2P 44 small dish	P-21	
2P 45 small dish	P-21	
2N 876 (2P 61) bowl	P-U	
2N 904 (2P 15) dish	P-7	
2N 905 (2P 16) dish	P-7	
2N 1035 (2P 134) large bowl	P-32	
2N 1049 (2P 34b) beaker	P-39A	pl. 95:8
2N 1094 (2P 115) painted pot	P-24	pl. 88:16
2N-T 250 school text		
I-2		
2N 234 ovoid stone weight	T-10	pl. 156:4, p. 109
II-1		
2N 395 model bed	F-8	pl. 144:2
II-2 cut (1B 247)		
2P 396 large jar	P-U	pl. 90:15, p. 135
2N 926 (2P 391) small pot	P-35	pl. 94:7, p. 135
II-2		
2N 597 large bead	T-1	
round-based jar, used as drain	P-19B	pl. 87:6
2N-T 734 inscribed brick (AmSi)		
2N-T 739 inscribed brick (AmSi)		
23 well—intrusive from higher levels		
24 main room in E and I-1, court in I-2, disturbed in D and E		
E-2		
2D 875 (2P 118) alabaster vase fragment	T-14	pl. 107:13
2P 119 dish	P-7	pl. 82:14
I-1		
2N-T 181 business document		
25 subsidiary room in E and I-1, entrance chamber in I-2		
E		
2N 706 (2D 412) nude female plaque	F-11	
three painted sherds	P-24	
2N-T 320 school text		
2N-T 321 school text		

Findspot and Description	Type	OIP 78 Reference
I-1		
2N 746 (2D 149) figurine head and arm	F-4	
26 court		
D		
2N 139 bronze pin	T-2	
2N 847 (2D 66) plaque fragment showing 4 human feet	F-20	
28 subsidiary room, disturbed		
29 court, disturbed		
II-1		
2P 509 round-based jar	P-19A	
2N-T 62 lexical text		
II-2		
2N 791 (2D 261) bull-man plaque fragment	F-14	pl. 136:5
1N 220 small dish	P-21	
1N 221 small dish	P-21	
30 court, disturbed		
I-2		
2N 180 lion plaque fragment	F-15	
2N 580 (2D 112) lapis bead	T-1	
2D 99 model chariot	F-9	
figurine fragment	F-6	
bronze point	T-3	
clay cone		
2N 999 (2P 111) tubular vase	P-27	pl. 91:10
2N-T 130 silver loan (RiSi 8) = Text 67		p. 75
II-1		
2N 126 bronze point	T-3	pl. 154:12, p. 101
2D 64 nude female plaque	F-11	
2D 258 sack-shaped figurine	F-20	
2D 259 flint blade	T-4	
2P 349 small bowl	P-22	
2N-T 39 lexical text		
2N-T 64 school text		
2N-T 65 school text		
II-2		
2D 390 female figurine fragment	F-1	pl. 133:2
2D 391 bead	T-1	
2D 392 gray stone macehead	T-3	
oval platter	P-U	pl. 92:16
II		
2N 389 plaque showing divine standard	F-17	pl. 138:9
2N 390 lion plaque	F-15	pl. 142:8
2N 417 stone weight	T-10	pl. 156:7, p. 109
2D 308 copper/bronze sheet and disk		
2P 363 incised stone bowl fragment	T-14	
II intrusive (1B 249)		
2P 496 beaker	P-39A	
31 main room		
II-1		
2N-T 543 school text		
2N-T 738 inscribed brick (Šu)		

Findspot and Description	Type	OIP 78 Reference
II-2		
2N 671 (2D 475) bone awl	T-6	
2D 474 lapis bead	T-1	
2D 877 (2P 412) stone cup	T-14	pl. 107:12
32 subsidiary room, disturbed		
39 unknown function, disturbed		
D		
2D 95 model chariot fragment	F-9	
40 unknown function, disturbed		
41 unknown function, disturbed		
D		
2N 94 (2P 47) painted vase	P-28	pl. 91:16
2N 900 (2P 63) dish	P-7	
two painted sherds	P-24	
bowl		
2N-T 129 lexical text		
2N-T 137 letter		
2N-T 138 school text		
2N-T 141 lexical text		
E-1		
2N 314 stone weight	T-10	pls. 147:18, 156:3; p. 109
2N 315 copper/bronze spatula	T-5	pl. 154:4, p. 107
2N 858 (2D 177) half a lid with human figure	F-3	pl. 126:4
2N-T 212 literary text		
E-2		
2N 164 figurine fragment	F-4	
42 street		
D		
2N 149 bone awl	T-6	p. 102
E		
2N 217 sickle blade	T-4	p. 103
2N 231 gold-leaf cover	T-2	
2D 192 seal impression	T-12	
2P 241 small jar*		
2N-T 202 lexical text		
2N-T 203 lexical text		
2N-T 204 lexical text		
2N-T 205 lexical text		
2N-T 206 lexical text		
2N-T 221 account of flour for the cult		
2N-T 231 school text		
2N-T 251 lexical text		
2N-T 252 lexical text		
2N-T 253 school text		
2N-T 254 school text		
2N-T 255 lexical text		
2N-T 259 illegible tablet		
2N-T 263 school text		

* This vessel falls into OIP 78 pottery type 45A.

Findspot and Description	Type	OIP 78 Reference
2N-T 308 metrological text		
2N-T 309 prism		
2N-T 313 hire of a boat (school text)		
2N-T 314 school text		
I-1		
2N 331 lion figurine fragment	F-5	pl. 141:7
2D 208 copper/bronze disk	T-2	
2N-T 372 metrological text		
2N-T 373 mathematical text		
2N-T 399 account of flour for the cult		
I-2		
2N 323 glazed bead	T-1	
II-2		
2N 889 (2D 354) male figurine fragment	F-2	
2D 362 copper/bronze fragment		
43 subsidiary room, disturbed		
II		
broken hematite weight	T-10	
44 main room/court in I-1, main room in I-2, disturbed		
I-1		
2N-T 96 school text		
45 entrance chamber		
I-1		
2P 58 tall jar with pointed base	P-40A	pl. 96:5
2N 899 (2P 62) dish	P-7	
II-1		
2N 110 god plaque fragment	F-14	pl. 136:7
2N-T 110 literary text		
2N-T 111 literary text		
2N-T 112 literary text		
2N-T 113 literary text		
2N-T 114 literary text		
2N-T 115 mathematical text		
2N-T 116 mathematical text		
2N-T 118 school text		
2N-T 119 literary text		
2N-T 120 account		
2N-T 121 literary text		
2N-T 122 school text		
II-2		
2N-T 490 school text		
2N-T 491 school text		
46 unknown function, disturbed		
47 unknown function, disturbed		
E		
2N 251 nude female plaque	F-11	pl. 127:7
2P 158 glazed pot	P-U	
48 entrance chamber, disturbed in D and E		
D		
2N-T 549 literary text		
2N-T 790 contract (now lost)		

Findspot and Description	Type	OIP 78 Reference
E-1		
2N 901 (2P 147) dish	P-7	
E-2		
painted sherds	P-24	
2N-T 235 school text		
2N-T 236 account of expenditures		
I-1		
2P 289 dish	P-7	pl. 82:15, p. 116
2N 1002 (2P 126) pot	P-35	p. 116
painted sherds	P-24	
2N-T 346 business document		p. 116
50 subsidiary room		
II-1		
2N 212 figurine with scratched design	F-4	
2P 128 miniature bowl	P-M	
2N 925 (2P 129) small pot	P-35	
dish	P-7(?)	
2N-T 159 administrative text about work gang		
II-2 wall		
2N 828 (2D 504) male figurine	F-2	pl. 130:1
II		
2P 480 tall jar	P-18	
II foundations		
2P 623 3 broken jars	P-U	
51 court		
I-1		
2N-T 472 school text		
2N-T 473 literary text		
I-2		
2N 997 (2P 355) cylindrical vase	P-27	pl. 91:9
2N-T 469 account		
2N-T 470 field rental(?) (DaII 8) = Text 63		
2N-T 471 field rental(?) = Text 64		
II-1		
three-sided stone object		
carnelian bead	T-1	
II-2		
2D 361 flint	T-4	p. 103
2P 460 round-based jar	P-19A	pl. 87:1
2N 1099 (2P 415) round-based jar	P-19A	
2N-T 541 account of libations		
II foundations		
2D 878 (2P 489) alabaster vase	T-14	pl. 107:11
2N 1065 (2P ?) jar	P-14B	pl. 84:12
52 main room		
II-1		
2N 197 piece of iron		
2N 198 limestone stamp seal	T-12	pl. 116:16
2N 199 green stone bead	T-1	
2D 311 two pieces of copper/bronze bracelet	T-2	p. 99
II foundation		
2N 768 (2D 453) god plaque	F-14	pl. 136:6
2N 810 (2D 450) animal figurine head	F-5	

Findspot and Description	Type	OIP 78 Reference
IV cut (1B 287)		
2P 632 large jar	P-14A	p. 139
2P 635 large jar	P-14B	pl. 84:10, p. 139
2N 30 (2P 636) tall jar	P-18	pl. 86:10, p. 138
2N 945 (2P 634) large jar	P-14A	p. 138
2N 948 (2P 633) large jar	P-14A	p. 138
53 entrance chamber in D and E, subsidiary room in I		
E		
2P 211 small dish	P-21	
2P 212 shallow bowl with carinated rim	P-8B	
2P 225 beaker	P-39A	
2N 1048 (2P 223) beaker	P-39A	pl. 95:13
2N 1087 (2P 224) beaker	P-39	
2N-T 331 school text		
2N-T 380 two literary texts		
I-1		
2P 215 small dish	P-21	p. 116
2N 902 (2P 213) dish	P-7	p. 116
2N 956 (2P 214) small dish	P-21	p. 116
2N 1051 (2P 226) beaker	P-39	
I-2		
2N-T 409 school text		
54 unknown function, disturbed		
E		
2N-T 230 Ur III text		
55 unknown function, disturbed		
E-1		
2N 860 (2D 181) model bed	F-8	
2P 275 small dish	P-21	
2N 1083 (2P 250) painted vase	P-28	pl. 91:15
2N 1096 (2P 247) pot	P-24	pl. 88:18
painted sherds	P-24	
2N-T 229 grain loan (Si 7) = Text 95		
2N-T 398 account of expenditures		
2N-T 404 grain loan (Ha) = Text 96		
2N-T 405 school text		
E-2		
2N 782 (2D 116) female figurine	F-1	
56 main room		
E		
2N 708 (2D 202) model chariot	F-9	
2N 922 (2P 234) Kassite goblet	P-46a	pl. 98:12
2N 1088 (2P 229) tall beaker	P-39B	pl. 95:17
2N-T 171 literary text		
I-1		
2N 335 ram figurine fragment	F-5	
2N 898 (2P 288) dish	P-7	
2N-T 439 grain loan (Ha) = Text 93		p. 75
57 main room, disturbed in I		
I-1		
2N-T 189 lexical text		
2N-T 196 literary text		

Findspot and Description	Type	OIP 78 Reference
I-2		
2N 785 (2D 179) female figurine fragment	F-1	pl. 124:2, p. 115
2N 1086 (2P 151) tall beaker	P-39B	p. 115
saucer		p. 115
58 subsidiary room, disturbed		
59 subsidiary room		
I-2		
2N 1097 (2P 162) painted pot	P-24	pl. 88:22
II-2		
2P 594 sherd	P-U	
60 subsidiary room		
II-2		
2N-T 542 receipt		
II foundations		
2N 954 (2P 457) small dish	P-21	pl. 88:7
2N-T 599 literary text		
61 subsidiary room, disturbed in I		
63 court, disturbed in D and E		
D		
small flat bowl	P-7(?)	
ceramic rattle, broken	T-13	
E		
2N-T 213 literary text		
I-1		
2P 133 painted pot	P-24	p. 116
2P 136 dish	P-7(?)	p. 116
2P 159 dish	P-7	p. 116
2P 209 small dish	P-21	p. 116
2P 210 broken beaker	P-39B	p. 116
2N 1067 (2P 137) pot	P-24	pl. 88:15, p. 116
2N 1095 (2P 135) dish	P-7	p. 116
saucer	P-7(?)	p. 116
2N-T 207 school text		p. 116
2N-T 209 school text		p. 116
2N-T 211 school text		p. 116
2N-T 216 lexical text		p. 116
2N-T 217 lexical text		p. 116
2N-T 218 account, list of fields		p. 116
2N-T 219 school text		p. 116
2N-T 220 school text		p. 116
2N-T 223 mathematical text		p. 116
2N-T 224 lexical text		p. 116
2N-T 225 school text		p. 116
2N-T 238 account of expenditures		p. 116
2N-T 242 literary text		p. 116
2N-T 243 school text		p. 116
2N-T 256 lexical text		p. 116
2N-T 257 lexical text		p. 116
2N-T 258 school text		p. 116
2N-T 278 literary text		p. 116
2N-T 279 literary text		p. 116
2N-T 381 school text		p. 116

Findspot and Description	Type	OIP 78 Reference
2N-T 382 school text		p. 116
2N-T 383 school text		p. 116
2N-T 384 school text		p. 116
I-2		
2N-T 450 school text		
65 subsidiary room, disturbed in D and E		
E-2		
2N 777 (2D 110) oxen figurine	F-5	
2N-T 366 lexical text		
2N-T 367 lexical text		
I-1		
2N 324 cylinder seal	T-12	pl. 112:3
I-2		
2N 337 stone tool		pl. 156:12, p. 112
2N 342 shell necklace found in 2P 274	T-1	pl. 147:3, p. 98
2N 704 (2D 180) female plaque fragment	F-11	
2P 274 small bottle	P-13	
2N-T 407 business document (list)		
66 court, disturbed in D, E, and I-1		
E-1		
2N 289 bead-shaped stamp seal	T-12	
2N 927 (2P 232) small pot	P-35	pl. 94:8
2D 876 (2P 255) stone bowl	T-14	
E-2		
2N 1001 (2P 204) small pot	P-35	
2N-T 332 literary text		
2N-T 333 literary text		
I-1		
2N 284 hematite weight	T-10	pl. 156:5
2N 707 (2D 201) model chariot	F-9	
2D 160 clay seal impression	T-12	
2D 161 hemispherical clay stamp seal	T-12	
2D 169 seal impression	T-12	pl. 120:2
2D 170 seal impression	T-12	
2D 209 copper/bronze pin	T-2	
2P 143 dish	P-7	
2P 144 dish	P-7	
2N 1068 (2P 145) pot	P-24	pl. 88:17
2N-T 267 lexical text		
2N-T 269 lexical text		
I-2		
2D 233 two seal impressions	T-12	
67 subsidiary room, disturbed in D, E, and I-1		
I-1		
2N 209 female musician figurine fragment	F-4	pl. 126:1, p. 116
2N-T 244 Kassite(?) administrative text		p. 116
I-2		
2P 243 cup	P-39C	pl. 95:19, p. 115
68 court, disturbed in D		
D fill		
2N 259 copper/bronze blade	T-4	
2N 260 small green stone chisel	T-6	

Findspot and Description	Type	OIP 78 Reference
2N 261 small green stone chisel	T-6	
2N 647 (2D 269) copper/bronze nail		
2N 775 (2D 454) pottery rattle	T-13	
2N-T 262 lexical text		
D floor		
2N 299 stone duck weight	T-10	pl. 147:15, p. 109
2N 312 bronze arrowhead	T-3	
2N 775 (2D 454) pottery rattle		
2D 224 bitumen basket		
2N-T 411 school text		
E		
2P 216 small cup		
2N-T 319 school text		
I-1		
2P 299 large pot	P-U	pl. 92:15
2N 11 (2P 319) small jar found in 2P 299	P-U	
dish found in 2P 299	P-7(?)	
dish found in 2P 299	P-7(?)	
2N-T 340 lexical text		
69 subsidiary room, disturbed		
I-1		
2N 666 (2D 184) stone fish-net sinker	T-10	pp. 112, 116
2N 667a (2D 185) stone loom weight	T-10	pp. 112, 116
2N 667b (2D 186) whetstone	T-8	pp. 110, 116
2N-T 392 economic document		p. 116
2N-T 393 letter		p. 116
2N-T 394 account of cattle in the temple of Ninurta (RiSi 22)		p. 116
2N-T 395 account, list of cattle		p. 116
70 court		
III-1		
2N 606 (2D 489) 5 shell rings	T-1	p. 115
2D 490 shell ring	T-1	p. 115
2P 709 shallow bowl with carinated rim	P-8B	
1N 245 saucer	P-U	
1N 246 jar	P-U	pl. 92:5
1N 247 saucer	P-U	
1N 280 shallow dish with carinated rim	P-8B	
III-2		
2N 465a carnelian bead with gold cap	T-1	pl. 150:6, p. 98
2N 465b copper pin wrapped in gold leaf	T-2	p. 101
2N 566 (2D 593) lapis pendant	T-1	
2N 640 (2D 671) copper/bronze blade	T-5	pl. 155:5, p. 103
2D 511 female figurine fragment	F-1	
2D 578 flint	T-4	p. 102
2P 741 round-based jar	P-19A	
2N 1008 (2P 708) strainer	P-6	
2N 1101 (2P 739) round-based jar	P-19B	pl. 87:3
2N-T 730 lexical text		
71 unknown function, disturbed		
E cut (1B 188)		
2P 775 large burial jar containing skeleton	P-25	pl. 89:6, p. 131

Findspot and Description	Type	OIP 78 Reference
72 unknown function, disturbed		
E		
2D 155 decorated stone fragment		
2N-T 232 lexical text		
I-1		
2D 215 hexagonal pottery prism		
2N-T 370 school text		
73 unknown function, disturbed		
E		
2N-T 228 bulla (amounts and names)		
74 subsidiary room		
D		
2N 869 (2D 153) figurine head	F-4	
2N 911 (2P 155) tall beaker	P-38	
I-1		
2P 207 dish	P-7(?)	
2P 208 dish	P-7	
2P 220 potstand	P-U	pl. 92:8
2P 221 beaker	P-39	
2N 913 (2P 222) tall beaker	P-38(?)	pl. 95:6
2N 1100 (2P 605) round-based jar	P-19A	
75 main room		
E-2		
2N 279 cylinder seal	T-12	pl. 112:7
2N 280 hematite boar's head weight	T-10	p. 109
2N 334 hematite weight	T-10	pls. 147:19, 156:6; p. 109
2N 801 (2D 205) male figurine	F-2	
2P 206 bottle	P-37	pl. 95:2
2P 487 large rounded pot	P-U	
2N-T 323 receipt (ŠuSi 5)		p. 75
2N-T 329 business document (Si 11)		p. 75
2N-T 374 temple office redemption (Si 24) = Text 84		p. 75
2N-T 375 temple office sale (Si X) = Text 85		p. 75
2N-T 376 literary text		
2N-T 377 temple office sale = Text 90		
2N-T 378 temple office sale = Text 91		
2N-T 379 lexical text		
2N-T 764 temple office sale = Text 88		p. 75
2N-T 765 lump of clay		p. 75
2N-T 766 temple office sale (Si 23) = Text 83		p. 75
2N-T 767 temple office redemption (Si 12) = Text 80		p. 75
2N-T 768 temple office sale(?) (Si 12) = Text 77		p. 75
2N-T 769 temple office sale (Si 11) = Text 75		p. 75
2N-T 770 temple office sale (Si 11) = Text 73		p. 75
2N-T 771 temple office sale (Si 10) = Text 72		
2N-T 772 temple office sale (Si 10) = Text 71		p. 75
2N-T 773 temple office sale (Si 14) = Text 81		p. 75
2N-T 774 temple office sale (Si 12) = Text 78		p. 75
2N-T 775 temple office exchange = Text 86		p. 75
2N-T 775C (2N-T 781???) temple office sale (Si 11) = Text 76		p. 75

Findspot and Description	Type	OIP 78 Reference
2N-T 776 temple office sale = Text 89		p. 75
2N-T 777 temple office sale = Text 87		p. 75
2N-T 778 temple office sale (Si 3) = Text 70		p. 75
2N-T 779 temple office sale (Si 3) = Text 69		p. 75
2N-T 780 temple office sale (Si 12) = Text 79		p. 75
2N-T 781 "illegible lump of clay," now lost		p. 75
2N-T 782 temple office sale (Si 11) = Text 74		p. 75
2N-T 783 temple office sale = Text 68		
2N-T 788 sale document(?) (Si 14) = Text 82		p. 75
I-1		
2N-T 385 literary text		
76 court, disturbed		
D		
2N 800 (2D 195) male figurine	F-2	pl. 130:7
animal horn		
2P 268 small dish	P-21	pl. 88:8
2N-T 341 field rental (Si 10) = Text 92		
E-1		
2N-T 338 lexical text		
2N-T 368 business document		
E-2		
2N 302 cylinder seal	T-12	pl. 112:8
2P 235 large jar	P-U	
2N-T 350 administrative document		
77 subsidiary room, disturbed in D and E		
I-1		
2N 292 cylinder seal	T-12	pl. 115:8, p. 116
2N 700 (2D 200) pottery chariot wheel	F-10	pl. 149:12, p. 116
2P 231 wide jar with pointed base	P-40B	pl. 96:6, p. 116
2P 269 small dish	P-21	p. 116
2N 903 (2P 272) dish	P-7	p. 116
2N 920 (2P 230) beaker	P-39A	pl. 95:9, p. 116
2N 955 (2P 271) small dish	P-21	p. 116
2N-T 351 account of expenditures		p. 116
2N-T 352 business document		p. 116
2N-T 361 adoption record		p. 116
2N-T 362 literary text		p. 116
2N-T 369 receipt (bulla)		p. 116
I-2		
2D 183 green stone polisher fragment	T-8	pp. 112, 115
2P 293 dish	P-7	p. 115
2P 294 dish	P-7	p. 115
2P 295 dish	P-7	p. 115
79 main room, disturbed		
I-2		
2N 596 (2D 194) long cylindrical bead	T-1	
2P 253 small pot with 4 feet	P-U	
2N-T 417 business document (Si)		
80 main room/subsidiary room		
81 unknown function, disturbed		
I-1		
2N-T 406 literary text		
2N-T 408 account of flour for the cult		

Findspot and Description	Type	OIP 78 Reference
2N-T 410 record of loans		
2N-T 415 literary text		
82 subsidiary room, disturbed		
83 street		
I-1		
2N 339 nude female plaque	F-11	pl. 127:6
2N 693 spindle whorl	T-11	p. 111
I-2		
2N 296 animal figurine	F-5	pl. 140:9
2D 176 female figurine	F-1	
2N 916 (2P 246) painted cup	P-39C	pl. 95:18
84 court, disturbed		
I-2		
2N-T 416 administrative text		
85 unknown function, disturbed		
86 unknown function, disturbed		
I-1		
2D 323 seal impression	T-12	
2D 324 curved flint blade	T-4	p. 103
87 open area		
I-2		
2N 353 nude female plaque	F-11	pl. 127:5
88 subsidiary room, disturbed		
I-2		
2D 282 female figurine fragment	F-1	
89 entrance chamber, disturbed		
I-2		
2N-T 435 grain account (Ur III?)		
2N-T 436 Ur III grain account		
2N-T 437 Ur III account of beer and bread		
90 unknown function, disturbed		
91 court		
I-1		
2N-T 419 account of payments (RiSi 22)		p. 75
2N-T 420 account of payments		
2N-T 421 silver loan = Text 97		
2N-T 422 account of grain payments		
2N-T 423 account of flour payments		
I-2		
2N 303 cylinder seal	T-12	pl. 112:2
92 unknown function, disturbed		
I-2		
2D 329 three seal impressions	T-12	pls. 119:16, 18; 120:3
93 court		
I-2		
2N 380 painted seated figurine fragment	F-3	pl. 146:1
2D 248 seal impression	T-12	pl. 120:1
2P 322 "table"	P-29	pl. 92:13
94 unknown function, foundations		
I foundations		
2D 245 heavy copper/bronze piece		
95 entrance chamber		

Findspot and Description	Type	OIP 78 Reference
96 unknown function		
97 unknown function, disturbed		
98 open area, disturbed		
99 subsidiary room		
100 main room, disturbed		
101 main room		
III-1		
2D 400 female figurine fragment	F-1	p. 115
2D 401 model chariot fragment	F-9	p. 115
2P 400 small bowl	P-22	p. 115
2P 530 small bowl	P-22	
102 subsidiary room, disturbed		
103 entrance chamber		
104 main room		
II-2		
2N 426 chalky cylinder seal		
2N-T 544 account		
105 court		
II-1		
2N 702 (2D 275) nude female plaque	F-11	
2N 764 (2D 274) plaque fragment showing boatman	F-16	pl. 138:4
2D 291 broken pottery rattle	T-13	
II-2		
2P 348 small bowl	P-22	
106 main room		
II-1		
2P 11 round-based jar	P-19A	
2N-T 20 mathematical text		
2N-T 21 bulla with seal impression	T-12	
2N-T 60 lexical text		
107 court		
II-2		
2P 405 tubular vase	P-27	
108 court, disturbed		
II-1		
2N 803 (2D 272) female figurine	F-1	
2D 321 three seal impressions	T-12	
2P 339 shallow bowl with carinated rim	P-8B	
II-2		
2N-T 494 bulla		
2N-T 495 Ur III account		
II-2 cut (1B 248)		
2P 408 pot	P-U	pl. 92:1, p. 135
109 main room, disturbed in II-1		
II-1		
2N 392 stone statue		pl. 146:2
2N 871 (2D 299) female figurine head	F-1	pl. 131:10
2D 298 bull-man plaque	F-14	
110 subsidiary room		
II-2		
2N 401 cylinder seal	T-12	pl. 111:12, p. 115
2D 349 pottery disk		p. 115

Findspot and Description	Type	OIP 78 Reference
II		
2N 396 plaque showing rider on donkey	F-16	pl. 137:10, p. 115
111 main room, disturbed		
II-2		
2N 678 (2D 529) copper/bronze nail		p. 105
2N 734 (2D 257) female figurine fragment	F-1	
112 entrance chamber		
II-1		
2P 352 small bowl	P-22	
II-2		
2D 267 bone awl	T-6	p. 102
113 entrance chamber		
114 entrance chamber		
115 subsidiary room		
II-2		
2D 344 seal impression	T-12	
2P 377 shallow bowl with carinated rim	P-8B	
116 subsidiary room		
II-2		
2N 436 horn		
2N 437 back half of lion plaque	F-15	pl. 142:9
2N 522 broken cylinder seal	T-12	pl. 111:13
2D 345 small animal figurine	F-5	
2P 375 shallow bowl with carinated rim	P-8B	
117 subsidiary/main room		
118 unknown function		
120 open area		
II-1		
2N 429 copper ring	T-2	p. 100
2N 739 (2D 273) seated figurine fragment	F-3	pls. 126:12, 149:1
2N 863 (2D 351) male figurine head	F-2	pl. 130:2
2D 285 model chariot fragment	F-9	
2D 326 seal impression	T-12	
2D 327 two seal impressions	T-12	
2D 328 three seal impressions	T-12	pl. 119:13, 14
2D 330 sixteen seal impressions	T-12	pl. 119:11, 12
2D 347 four seal impressions	T-12	
2D 352 female figurine fragment	F-1	
2D 375 seal impression	T-12	
2P 461 round-based jar	P-19A	
2N-T 447 lexical text		
2N-T 452 bulla		
2N-T 453 school text		
2N-T 459 school text		
2N-T 460 school text		
2N-T 461 literary text		
2N-T 462 school text		
2N-T 463 school text		
2N-T 464 school text		
2N-T 465 school text		
2N-T 466 lexical text		
2N-T 467 school text		

Findspot and Description	Type	OIP 78 Reference
II		
2N 787 (2D 277) female figurine fragment	F-1	
2N 864 (2D 276) figurine (man's head)	F-2	
2N 278 female figurine fragment	F-1	
121 unknown function		
II-1		
2D 412 seal impression	T-12	
II-2		
2D 346 two seal impressions	T-12	
2D 367 seal impression	T-12	
2P 378 small bovine-footed tripod	P-U	
2P 382 dish	P-U	pl. 88:4
2N-T 504 inscribed jar sealing		
2N-T 505–524 nineteen school/lexical/literary/ mathematical texts		
2N-T 534 literary text		
2N-T 535 economic document		
2N-T 536–538 three school texts		
II foundations		
2D 409 figurine	F-4	
2D 426 seal impression	T-12	
2D 501 bead	T-1	
122 entrance chamber		
II-1		
2N 701 (2D 297a) female figurine	F-1	pl. 127:3
2D 297b figurine	F-4	
123 main room		
II-1		
2N 428 animal figurine	F-5	
124 open area, disturbed		
II-1		
2N-T 451 letter		
2N-T 540 receipt for loaves (SiEr 1)		p. 75
125 unknown function, disturbed		
126 court		
II-1		
2N 774 (2D 455) pottery rattle	T-13	
2D 325 seal impression	T-12	
2P 380 shallow bowl with carinated rim	P-8B	
127 unknown function		
128 entrance chamber, disturbed		
II-2		
2N 438 seated figurine	F-3	pl. 126:5
III intrusive		
2N 482 cylinder seal	T-12	pl. 111:10
129 unknown function, foundations		
II foundations		
2D 358 eight seal impressions	T-12	
copper/bronze earring(?)	T-2	
130 court, disturbed		
131 unknown function, foundations		
I foundations		
2P 301 round-based jar	P-19A	

Findspot and Description	Type	OIP 78 Reference
2N 18 (2P 316) small jar	P-U	pl. 91:6
II foundations		
2P 414 odd-shaped heavy pottery object	P-U	pl. 92:17
132 subsidiary room		
133 unknown function, foundations		
II foundations		
2N 646 (2D 388) long copper/bronze pin	T-2	p. 101
2N 771 (2D 360) female figurine fragment	F-1	
134 unknown function, foundations		
II foundations		
2N 867 (2D 356) male figurine head	F-2	pl. 131:11
2P 300 round-based jar	P-19A	pl. 87:2
whetstone fragment	T-8	
135 unknown function		
136 main room, disturbed in II-1		
II-2		
2P 655 round-based jar	P-19A	p. 115
2N 917 (2P 390) vase	P-U	pl. 89:2, p. 115
II foundations		
2N 653 (2D 383) figurine—mask	F-7	pl. 132:8
137 court		
II-2		
2N 663 (2D 348) stone fish-net sinker	T-10	pp. 112, 115
broken green stone whorl	T-11	
138 unknown function, foundations		
II foundations		
2N 373 long copper/bronze needle	T-8	p. 106
139 main room, disturbed in II-1		
140 entrance chamber		
II-1		
2N-T 449 silver loan (BuSi) = Text 94		p. 75
141 court		
II-1		
2N 427 cylinder seal	T-12	pl. 111:14
2N 699 (2D 292) pottery chariot wheel	F-10/T-11	
2D 280 female figurine	F-1	
II-2		
2D 393 bone or shell ring	T-1	
2D 355 animal figurine fragment	F-5	
2N-T 539 business document, list of houses		
142 subsidiary room		
II-1		
2N 378 plaque showing presentation scene	F-17	pl. 133:5, p. 115
2N 379 copper/bronze sickle blade	T-5	pl. 154:1, pp. 107, 115
2N 402 small hematite weight	T-10	pp. 109, 115
2N 403 copper/bronze shaft pin	T-2	pp. 101, 115
2N 406 carnelian duck weight, found in 2P 335	T-10	pp. 109, 115
2D 309a small copper/bronze spatula	T-5	pp. 107, 115
2D 309b fragment of flint blade	T-4	pp. 103, 115
2P 335 small bowl	P-22	p. 115
2P 341 small dish	P-21	p. 115
2P 342a cylindrical vase	P-27	p. 115

Findspot and Description	Type	OIP 78 Reference
2P 342b cylindrical vase	P-27	p. 115
2N 992 (2P 342c) cylindrical vase	P-27	p. 115
2N 993 (2P 342d) cylindrical vase	P-27	p. 115
2N 994 (2P 342e) cylindrical vase	P-27	p. 115
2N 995 (2P 342f) cylindrical vase	P-27	pl. 91:7, p. 115
143 unknown function, disturbed		
II-1		
2N 414a copper/bronze pin	T-2	pl. 152:8, p. 101
2N 414b copper/bronze rod	T-2	
2D 316 fragment of flint	T-4	p. 103
2D 317 round clay disk, gaming piece		p. 104
2D 318 seal impression	T-12	
II-2 cut (1B 271)		
2P 737 round-based jar	P-19A	p. 137
144 unknown function, disturbed in II-1		
II-2		
2N 769 (2D 404) male figurine	F-2	pl. 131:9
2P 411 miniature jar	P-M	pl. 90:12
145 unknown function, foundations		
146 unknown function, foundations		
147 subsidiary room		
D		
2P 302 large pot	P-U	see pl. 90:1
2P 307 vase	P-28	
2P 337 miniature pot	P-M	pl. 94:4
2N 928 (2P 311) small pot	P-35	pl. 94:6
two bowls	P-U	
E		
2N 349 broken cylinder seal	T-12	pl. 112:10
148 unknown function, foundations		
II foundations		
2D 478 unfinished stone bead	T-1	
149 unknown function, foundations		
II foundations		
2N 770 (2D 357) female figurine	F-1	
150 unknown function, disturbed		
151 unknown function		
152 unknown function, disturbed		
I-1		
2N 788 (2D 376) nude female plaque	F-11	
2D 377 egg-shaped stone, sling stone(?)	T-3	
2P 393 bitumen cup		
II-1 cut		
2P 560 bottom bowl from infant burial	P-U	
2P 597 top bowl from infant burial	P-U	
2P 598 top bowl from infant burial	P-U	
2P 599 top bowl from infant burial	P-U	
2P 643 top bowl from infant burial	P-U	
2P 644 bottom bowl from infant burial	P-U	
2P 645 top bowl from infant burial	P-U	

Findspot and Description	Type	OIP 78 Reference
153 court, disturbed		
III cut (1B 249)		
2P 496 beaker	P-39A	pl. 95:15, p. 135
round-based jar	P-19A	p. 135
jar	P-U	
bowl	P-U	
III-1		
2N 433 glazed bead	T-1	
2N 558 forked copper point	T-3	pl. 154:13, p. 112
2N 567a silver wire fragment, interlocked	T-2	
2N 567b strings of beads	T-1	
2N 567c black stone pendant	T-1	pl. 150:48, p. 99
2N 595 (2D 458) incised bored stone bead	T-1	pl. 150:21, p. 98
2N 625 (2D 389) copper ring	T-2	p. 100
2N 651 (2D 302b) copper/bronze chisel	T-6	p. 103
2N 657 (2D 302a) flint	T-4	p. 103
2N 696 (2D 585) seated animal figurine	F-5	pl. 140:8
2N 793 (2D 253) bull-man plaque, head	F-14	pl. 136:4
2N 806 (2D 256) female figurine	F-1	pl. 123:6
2D 369 seal impression	T-12	
2D 480 large black bead	T-1	
2P 346 miniature cup	P-M	pl. 90:11
2P 369 miniature pot	P-M	
2P 384 dish with wood fragments	P-7	
2P 394 tall beaker	P-38	
2P 507 2 pieces of alabaster	T-14	
2N-T 555 receipt of cult flour (ŠuIl 1)		p. 75
2N-T 556 receipt of loaves (ŠuIl 9)		p. 75
2N-T 557 receipt of loaves (ŠuIl 6)		p. 75
2N-T 558 receipt of barley flour (ŠuIl 6)		p. 75
2N-T 559 receipt of prebends (IšEr 11)		
2N-T 560 receipt of temple income, sheep (IdDa)		p. 75
2N-T 561 receipt of temple income, sheep (IdDa)		p. 75
2N-T 562 receipt of temple income, sheep (IdDa)		p. 75
2N-T 563 receipt of temple income, sheep (IdDa)		p. 75
2N-T 564 receipt of temple income, sheep (IdDa)		p. 75
2N-T 565 receipt of temple income, sheep (IdDa)		p. 75
2N-T 566 receipt of temple income for 12 months, sheep (IdDa)		p. 75
2N-T 567 receipt of loaves (IdDa)		
2N-T 568 receipt of temple(?) income (IdDa)		
2N-T 569 receipt		
2N-T 570 account of expenditures, loaves		
2N-T 571 receipt of loaves		
2N-T 572 account of temple income, loaves		
2N-T 573 receipt of temple income, sheep		
2N-T 574 receipt		
2N-T 575 receipt of loaves		
2N-T 576 receipt of loaves		
2N-T 577 order for the providing of loaves for cult purposes		
2N-T 578 receipt of temple(?) income, loaves (IdDa)		

Findspot and Description	Type	OIP 78 Reference
2N-T 579 receipt		
2N-T 580 receipt of temple(?) income, loaves		
III-2		
2N 521 decorated clay bead	T-1	pl. 150:20, p. 98
2D 385 animal figurine		
2D 685 two seal impressions	T-12	pl. 119:7
2N-T 616 receipt of bitumen (ŠuSi 3)		
IV cut (1B 288)		
2N 1057 (2P 640) miniature jar	P-M	pl. 88:15, p. 139
IV cut (1B 290–291)		
2P 668 jar	P-14B	p. 139
2P 671 shallow bowl with carinated rim	P-8B	p. 139
2P 672 shallow bowl with carinated rim	P-8B	p. 139
2P 673 shallow bowl with carinated rim	P-8B	p. 139
2P 674 shallow bowl with carinated rim	P-8B	p. 139
2P 676 shallow bowl with carinated rim	P-8B	p. 139
2P 677 shallow bowl with carinated rim	P-8B	p. 139
2P 678 shallow bowl with carinated rim	P-8B	p. 139
2P 679 shallow bowl with carinated rim	P-8B	p. 139
2P 680 shallow bowl with carinated rim	P-8B	p. 139
2P 683 shallow bowl with carinated rim	P-8B	p. 139
2P 684 shallow bowl with carinated rim	P-8B	p. 139
2P 685 shallow bowl with carinated rim	P-8B	p. 139
2P 686 shallow bowl with carinated rim	P-8B	p. 139
2P 687 shallow bowl with carinated rim	P-8B	p. 139
2P 688 shallow bowl with carinated rim	P-8B	p. 139
2P 689 shallow bowl with carinated rim	P-8B	p. 139
2P 690 shallow bowl with carinated rim	P-8B	p. 139
2P 691 shallow bowl with carinated rim	P-8B	p. 139
2P 692 shallow bowl with carinated rim	P-8B	p. 139
2P 694 large vase	P-14B	p. 139
2P 695 saucer	P-U	p. 139
2P 696 round-based jar	P-19A	p. 139
2P 698 tall jar	P-18	pl. 86:11, p. 139
2P 699 vase	P-U	p. 139
2N 32 (2P 682) vase	P-15	pl. 85:4, p. 139
2N 34 (2P 669) calcite bowl	T-14	pl. 107:10, p. 139
2N 990 (2P 697) vase	P-15	p. 139
2N 1023 (2P 693) pot	P-U	p. 139
2N 1045 (2P 675) shallow bowl with carinated rim	P-8B	pl. 82:20, p. 139
2N 1064 (2P 681) large vase	P-14B	pl. 84:13, p. 139
2N 1075 (2P 670) large vase	P-14B	p. 139
IV cut (1B 292)		
2P 743 reddish jar	P-U	p. 139
saucer	P-8B/ P-21	p. 139
saucer	P-8B/ P-21	p. 139
saucer	P-8B/ P-21	p. 139

Findspot and Description	Type	OIP 78 Reference
IV cut (3B 13a–b)		
3D 19 bronze ring	T-2	p. 141
3P 14 pot	P-12	p. 141
3P 23 tall jar	P-18	p. 141
3P 24 round-based jar	P-19B	p. 141
broken jar	P-U	p. 141
154 unknown function, foundations		
III foundations		
2N 550 stone weight	T-10	p. 109
2P 383 shallow bowl with carinated rim	P-8B	
2P 403 pot	P-U	
155 unknown function, foundations		
II foundations		
2D 263 2 lapis beads	T-1	
2D 264 worked bone		
2D 265 stamp-seal impression	T-12	
obsidian fragment	T-5	
IV cut (1B 287)		
2D 782 figurine legs	F-4	
2P 632 large jar	P-14A	p. 139
2P 635 large jar	P-14B	pl. 84:10, p. 139
2N 30 (2P 636) tall jar	P-18	pl. 86:10, p. 138
2N 945 (2P 634) large jar	P-14A	p. 138
2N 948 (2P 633) large jar	P-14A	p. 138
156 main room		
III-1		
2P 427 large jar	P-U	pl. 92:3, p. 115
2N 996 (2P 345) cylindrical vase	P-27	pl. 91:8, p. 115
157 subsidiary room		
II-1		
2N 432 white fruit cylinder seal	T-12	
II-2		
2N 790 (2D 287) male plaque fragment	F-13	pl. 138:3
2D 288 clay knuckle(?)		
2P 370 miniature goblet	P-23	pl. 88:14
2N-T 489 stamped brick (AmSi)		
2N-T 525 school text		
2N-T 526 list of personal names		
2N-T 527 literary text		
2N-T 529 school text		
158 main room, disturbed		
II-1		
2D 258 figurine fragment	F-6	
2D 259 flint	T-4	p. 103
159 court, disturbed		
II-1		
2P 357 miniature vase	P-M	
160 unknown function, foundations		
II foundations		
2N 533 stone weight	T-10	p. 109
2N 607 (2D 468) shell ring, found in 2P 416		

Findspot and Description	Type	OIP 78 Reference
2N 658 (2D 459) flint blade	T-4	
2D 411 seal impression	T-12	
2D 460 bead	T-1	
2D 469 bead	T-1	
2D 477 bead	T-1	
2P 416 dish, containing 2N 607	P-7	
large jar	P-U	
161 unknown function		
162 subsidiary room		
III-1		
2D 379 model bed	F-8	p. 115
2D 446 model bed	F-8	p. 115
2P 395 small dish	P-21	p. 115
2P 399a small dish	P-21	p. 115
2P 399b shallow bowl with carinated rim	P-8B	p. 115
2P 399c shallow bowl with carinated rim	P-8B	p. 115
2P 399d shallow bowl with carinated rim	P-8B	p. 115
2N 946 (2P 477) large vase	P-14B	p. 115
163 entrance chamber		
III-1		
2P 401 small bowl, mended	P-22	p. 115
2N 1034 (2P 402) small bowl, mended	P-22	p. 115
164 unknown function, foundations		
165 unknown function, foundations		
166 street		
III		
2N 499 hematite weight	T-10	p. 109
2N 500 copper/bronze cap to vessel		
2D 548 beads	T-1	
167 open area		
III-1		
2N 467 sherd incised with a figure		pl. 148:1
2N 535 small stone weight	T-10	p. 109
2N 564 stone fragment, decorated		
2N 598 (2D 472) black bead	T-1	
2N 737 (2D 730) white stone macehead fragment	T-3	
2D 405 nude female plaque	F-11	
2D 413 female figurine	F-1	
2D 432 female figurine fragment	F-1	
2D 515 bone awl	T-6	p. 102
figurine fragment	F-6	
2P 410 miniature jar containing 2 copper/bronze fragments		
2P 438 miniature vessel	P-M	
2P 491 decorated pottery fragment		
2P 508 three stone bowl fragments	T-14	
2P 513 large vase	P-14B	pl. 84:11
2P 519 stone sherd	T-14	
2P 603 round-based jar	P-19B	pl. 87:5
2P 745 jardiniere	P-U	
2N 952a (2P 490a) small bowl	P-22	

Findspot and Description	Type	OIP 78 Reference
2N 952b (2P 490b) shallow bowl with carinated rim	P-8B	
2N 952c (2P 490c) small bowl	P-22	
2N-T 591 letter		
2N-T 592 receipt (ŠuSi 1)		p. 75
168 entrance chamber		
III-1		
2N 670 bone point	T-3	
169 court		
III-1		
2N 542 half of lapis cylinder seal	T-12	pl. 111:11
2N 843 (2D 380) female figurine fragment	F-1	
2P 398 tall jar	P-18	
2P 407 shallow bowl with carinated rim	P-8B	
2P 624 green ware vessel	P-U	
2N 988 (2P 404) lower part of chalice	P-23	
170 unknown function, foundations		
II foundations		
2D 510 model bed fragment, in 2P 512	F-8	
2P 512 beaker, contained 2D 510 and a human vertebra	P-39A	pl. 95:12
2P 604 round-based jar	P-19A	
171 subsidiary room		
III-1		
2P 444 tall beaker	P-38	
2N 957 (2P 445a) small dish	P-21	pl. 88:6, p. 115
2P 445b shallow bowl with carinated rim	P-8B	
172 main room		
III-1		
2N 819 (2D 396) lower part of figurine	F-6	
decorated clay object	F-20	
2P 413 large heavy mixing bowl	P-U	
jar	P-U	
173 unknown function, disturbed		
174 subsidiary room		
175 subsidiary room/entrance chamber		
III		
2N 888 (2D 488) female figurine head	F-1	pl. 133:1, p. 115
2N 1066 (2P 500) tall jar	P-18	p. 115
176 unknown function, disturbed		
II-2		
2P 435 bowl	P-U	
III foundations		
2D 438 clay chariot wheel	F-10/T-11	
2P 527 vessel	P-U	
177 open area, disturbed		
III-1		
2N 669 (2D 485) bone awl	T-6	p. 102
2N 814 (2D 420) goat figurine fragment	F-5	
2D 402 female plaque fragment	F-11	
2D 419 female figurine fragment	F-1	
2D 421 figurine fragment	F-4	
2D 422 figurine fragment	F-4	
2D 443 base of vase	P-U	pl. 89:3

Findspot and Description	Type	OIP 78 Reference
178 unknown function, disturbed		
III-1		
2N 799 (2D 403) small male figurine	F-2	pl. 129:8
2D 495 small bead	T-1	
2P 425 bowl	P-U	
2P 426 dish	P-7	
III-2		
2N-T 613 receipt of weaver's rations		
2N-T 627 receipt of royal prebend (flour), temple income (IdDa)		
2N-T 628 receipt of flour, temple income		
2N-T 629 account of expenditures, loaves		
2N-T 630 receipt of loaves		
IV cut (1B 276)		
2N 466a crude figurine	F-4	pl. 126:3, p. 138
2N 466b crude figurine	F-4	pl. 126:2, p. 138
ovoid clay cylinder		p. 138
ovoid clay cylinder		p. 138
179 unknown function, disturbed		
III		
2N 872 (2D 414) male figurine	F-2	pl. 129:9
2D 413 seal impression	T-12	
2N-T 586 receipt of grain (AmSi 7)		p. 75
2N-T 588 literary text		
180 unknown function, disturbed		
III		
2D 487 bone ring	T-1	
181 unknown function, disturbed		
II foundations		
2D 417 female figurine fragment	F-1	
2D 418 female figurine fragment	F-1	
2P 441 shallow bowl with carinated rim	P-8B	
2P 442 shallow bowl with carinated rim	P-8B	
2P 518a stone vase fragment	T-14	
2P 518b stone vase fragment	T-14	
2P 518c stone vase fragment	T-14	
2N 987 (2P 447) chalice fragment	P-23	
2N-T 582 literary text		
2N-T 583 literary text		
2N-T 584 literary text		
182 main room		
III-1		
2P 424 beaker	P-39A	pl. 95:14
183 unknown function		
III-1		
2D 407 figurine, broken head mended	F-4	
2D 408 black stone polisher	T-8	p. 112
2N 986 (2P 422) broken chalice	P-23	pl. 88:12
184 subsidiary room, disturbed		
III-1		
2D 406 female plaque fragment	F-11	pl. 127:2
2D 482 copper/bronze pin	T-2	p. 101

Findspot and Description	Type	OIP 78 Reference
2P 420 shallow bowl with carinated rim	P-8B	
2P 421 shallow bowl with carinated rim	P-8B	
185 unknown function		
III-1		
2N 509 bronze bracelet	T-2	pl. 151:16, p. 99
2N 985 (2P 423) mended chalice	P-23	pl. 88:13
186 unknown function, disturbed		
III-1		
bronze bracelet	T-2	
2P 429 dish	P-7	
2N 985 (2P 423) chalice	P-23	
dish	P-7(?)	
187 unknown function, disturbed		
III-1		
2N 488 cylinder seal	T-12	pl. 111:8
2N 502 erotic scene on plaque	F-19	pl. 137:4
2N 517 round stone		pl. 156:16, p. 112
2N 736 (2D 775) stone macehead	T-3	pl. 154:26, p. 105
2D 416 female figurine	F-1	
2D 434 model chariot fragment	F-9	
2P 439 dish	P-7	
2N-T 593 list of personal names		
2N-T 594 list of personal names		
2N-T 595 receipt of temple expenditures		
2N-T 784 school text		
2N-T 785 school text		
2N-T 786 school text		
III-2		
2N 780 (2D 714) model bed fragment	F-8	pl. 144:1
2D 713 copper/bronze blade	T-5	
2D 715 legs of figurine	F-1(?)	
2N-T 697 letter		
188 unknown function, disturbed		
II foundations		
2N 490 copper/bronze cylinder seal	T-12	pl. 111:9
189 unknown function		
III-1		
2N 845 (2D 415) animal figurine head	F-5	
190 unknown function, disturbed		
III		
2N 481 cylinder seal	T-12	pl. 111:7
2N 767 (2D 451) female plaque fragment	F-11	pl. 126:6
2D 430 model chariot fragment	F-9	
2D 435 painted cylindrical clay object		
2D 500 clay ball		
2N-T 585 mathematical text		
191 unknown function, disturbed		
III-1		
2N 535 animal plaque mold	F-15	
2N 688 (2D 835) bone pin	T-2	p. 101
2N 797 (2D 571) base of plaque		
2N 808 (2D 595) animal figurine head	F-5	

Findspot and Description	Type	OIP 78 Reference
2D 570 figurine head	F-4	
2D 796 animal figurine fragment	F-5	
2D 797 seal impression	T-12	
2P 547a small dish	P-21	
2P 547b small dish	P-21	
201 subsidiary room, disturbed		
III-2		
2N 495 plaque showing god	F-14	
2D 852 small blue frit beads	T-1	
2P 611 shallow bowl with carinated rim	P-8B	
2N 1042 (2P 629) shallow bowl with carinated rim	P-8B	
2N-T 668 account		
2N-T 687 school text		
2N-T 688 school text		
2N-T 689 loan of silver (IbSi)		
203 main room, disturbed		
III-2		
2N 583 five red carnelian beads	T-1	
2N 584 small gold ring	T-2	
2N 735 (2D 576) drill head	T-7	pl. 153:15, p. 104
drill head	T-7	
2P 533 shallow bowl with carinated rim	P-8B	
IV cut (1B 282)		
bronze cup fragment		p. 138
IV cut (1B 289)		
2N 592 (2D 778b) three pendants: 1 frog-shaped, 2 pot-shaped		pl. 147:5, 6, p. 139
2N 610 (2D 778a) stone and shell beads	T-1	p. 139
2N 619 (2D 779) small copper/bronze ring	T-2	p. 139
2N 822a three bronze bracelets	T-2	p. 139
2N 822b three shell rings	T-1	p. 139
five shell rings	T-1	p. 139
206 main room, disturbed?		
III-2		
2N 471 lapis pendant with incised human head	T-1	pl. 147:9, p. 98
2N 476 two gold earrings	T-2	pl. 151:4, p. 99
2N 501 bronze digging tool		pl. 154:23, p. 112
2N 527 small gold disk	T-2	p. 104
2N 530 white limestone cylinder seal	T-12	
2N 611 (2D 611) string of shell rings, 1 shell bead	T-1	
2N 612 (2D 624) string of 6 shell rings and 1 stone bead	T-1	
2N 616 (2D 625) copper/bronze rings with glazed beads	T-1/T-2	p. 100
2D 626 piece of agate	T-1	
2D 627 shell rings and a shell	T-1	
2D 688 seashell bead	T-1	
2P 485 jar	P-17	pl. 86:3
2P 486a shallow bowl with carinated rim	P-8B	
2P 486b shallow bowl with carinated rim	P-8B	
2P 567 large jar	P-14A	
2P 568 little deep bowl	P-U	
2P 572 miniature pot	P-M	

Findspot and Description	Type	OIP 78 Reference
2P 574 limestone piece of incense burner	T-14	
2P 600 shallow bowl with carinated rim	P-8B	
2P 601 shallow bowl with carinated rim	P-8B	
2P 602 shallow bowl with carinated rim	P-8B	
2P 627 shallow bowl with carinated rim	P-8B	
2P 628a shallow bowl with carinated rim	P-8B	
2P 628b shallow bowl with carinated rim	P-8B	
2N-T 647 receipt		
2N-T 648 receipt for barley (AmSi 1)		
2N-T 649 estimate of date yields		
2N-T 650 account of food		
2N-T 651 temple account (IšDa)		
2N-T 652 temple account (IšDa)		p. 75
2N-T 653 temple account		
2N-T 654 account of beer for cult purposes		
2N-T 655 account		
2N-T 656 account		
2N-T 657 account		
2N-T 658 receipt of horns (AmSi 1)		p. 74
207 court, disturbed		
III-2		
2N 513 (2D 634) broken clay chariot wheel	F-10	
2N 556 two hematite weights	T-10	
2N 638 (2D 614) long broken lapis bead	T-1	
2N 643 (2D 613) copper/bronze pin	T-2	pl. 152:6, p. 101
2N 779 (2D 635) prow of model boat	F-9	
2N 820 (2D 647) chariot model	F-9	
2D 646 spindle whorl	T-11	
2D 648 bead	T-1	
2P 580 half of miniature pot	P-M	pl. 90:9
2P 581 shallow bowl with carinated rim	P-8B	
2N 1003 (2P 570) small bottle	P-13	
2N-T 679 school text		
2N-T 680 account of expenditure of loaves		
216 court, disturbed		
III-1		
2D 766a seal impression	T-12	
2D 766b seal impression	T-12	
2D 767 figurine fragment	F-4	
2D 768a two shell rings	T-1	
2D 768b two beads	T-1	
2D 768c copper/bronze ring	T-2	
2D 769 top of male figurine	F-2	
2P 630 molded rim fragment on sherd	P-U	
III-2		
2N 459 cylinder seal	T-12	pl. 111:1
2N 462 copper/bronze sickle	T-5	pl. 154:2, p. 107
2N 543 cylinder seal	T-12	pl. 111:2
2N 824 (2D 741) female plaque	F-11	
2D 700 two beads	T-1	
2D 798 seal impression	T-12	

Findspot and Description	Type	OIP 78 Reference
2D 799 seal impression	T-12	
2D 800 seal impression	T-12	
2D 803 copper/bronze ring	T-2	
2D 804 bone awl	T-6	p. 102
2D 806 clay stopper		
2D 807 two shells	T-1	
2D 808 seal impression	T-12	
2D 814 seal impression	T-12	
2D 815 seal impression	T-12	
2D 816 lapis and shell beads	T-1	
seal impression	T-12	
animal figurine	F-5	
bead	T-1	
2P 667 small decorated pottery lid	P-U	
2P 720 shallow bowl with carinated rim	P-8B	
2P 740 large jar	P-19B	
2N 1060 (2P 617) miniature pot	P-M	
III-2 cut (1B 295–297)		
2P 726 small bowl	P-22	pl. 88:10, p. 139
2P 728 large vase	P-14B	p. 139
2P 730 large vase	P-14B	p. 139
2P 731 large reddish vase	P-14B	p. 139
2N 1069 (2P 727) large vase	P-14B	p. 139
2N 1077 (2P 729) round jar	P-U	pl. 90:1, p. 139
217 court		
III-2		
2N 710 (2D 709) stone weight	T-10	p. 109
2N 724 (2D 751) spindle whorl	T-11	p. 111
2N 795 (2D 696) goddess plaque	F-12	
2N 817 (2D 710) animal figurine	F-5	
2N 884 (2D 697) erotic scene on plaque	F-19	pl. 137:1
2D 711 bone point	T-3	
2D 752 pottery spindle whorl	T-11/F-10	
2D 753 copper/bronze fragment		
2D 754 bead	T-1	
2D 755 shell rings	T-1	
2N-T 681 order for release of person from service		
220 open area, disturbed		
III-2		
2N 452 lower half of plaque	F-17(?)	pl. 135:5
2N 621 (2D 791) copper/bronze ring fragments	T-2	p. 100
2N 723 spindle whorl	T-11	p. 111
2D 780a bead	T-1	
2D 780b bone ring	T-1	
2D 789 female figurine fragment	F-1	
2D 790 animal figurine fragment	F-5	
2P 637 dish	P-7	
2P 641 stone vase	T-14	
2N 29 (2P 657) greenish ware bowl	P-U	pl. 88:5
2N 36 (2P 658) reddish ware bowl	P-U	

Findspot and Description	Type	OIP 78 Reference
221 open area, disturbed		
IV cut (1B 299)		
2N 562 copper knife	T-5	pl. 155:6, p. 140
2P 746 shallow bowl with carinated rim	P-8B	p. 140
2P 747 shallow bowl with carinated rim	P-8B	p. 140
2P 748 pot	P-U	p. 140
2P 749 shallow bowl with carinated rim	P-8B	p. 140
2P 750 round-based jar	P-14B	p. 140
2P 751 shallow bowl with carinated rim	P-8B	
2P 752 round-based jar	P-14B	p. 140
2P 762 vase	P-U	p. 140
2P 764 vase	P-U	p. 140
IV cut (1B 302)		
shell beads	T-1	p. 140
bronze bracelet fragment	T-2	p. 140
jar	P-U	p. 140
223 unknown function, foundations		
III foundations		
2D 801 seal impression	T-12	
2D 802 cylinder seal fragment	T-12	
2P 642 dish	P-7	
2N 7 (2P 719) candlestick	P-U	pl. 92:11
2N-T 705 receipt		
224 unknown function, foundations		
III foundations		
2D 817 seal impression	T-12	
2D 818 seal impression	T-12	
2P 659 large jar	P-14A(?)	
2P 666 stone jar fragment	T-14	
2P 723 half of alabaster vase	T-14	
2N-T 702 letter		
225 unknown function, foundations		
III foundations, intrusive		
2N 453 hematite cylinder seal	T-12	pl. 111:4
2N 454 stone cylinder seal	T-12	pl. 111:5
2D 805 three beads	T-1	
2P 660 large jar	P-14A	
2P 662 shallow reddish bowl with carinated rim	P-8B	
2P 663 shallow greenish bowl with carinated rim	P-8B	
2N 1040 (2P 661) shallow bowl with carinated rim	P-8B	
229 unknown function, foundations		
III foundations		
2N 608 (2D 601) one large and 5 small beads	T-1	
2D 599a seal impression	T-12	
2D 599b seal impression	T-12	
2D 600 flint	T-4	
2D 837 figurine fragment	F-1	
2P 734 shallow bowl with carinated rim	P-8B	

Findspot and Description	Type	OIP 78 Reference
230 unknown function, foundations		
III foundations, cut (1B 301)		
2N 953 (2P 732) shallow bowl with carinated rim	P-8B	p. 140
2N 773 (2P 733) greenstone jar	T-14	pl. 107:8, p. 140
502 open area		
II-2		
2N 439 head and body of painted pottery statue, other half in TB 93	F-3	pl. 146:1
2N 544 whetstone	T-8	
2N 705 (2D 353) top of female plaque	F-11	
2D 338 blue bead	T-1	
2D 339 female figurine fragment	F-1	
2D 341 pierced painted pottery ring		
2D 342 clay indented pellet		
2D 343 bone awl	T-6	p. 102
2D 350 seal impression	T-12	
2D 364 lapis bead	T-1	
2D 366 seal impression	T-12	pl. 119:8
2D 371 worn figurine fragment, head(?)	F-4(?)	
bone awl		
copper/bronze fragment		
copper/bronze fragment		
2P 376 small bowl	P-22	
2N-T 544 lexical text		

APPENDIX III

TYPOLOGIES

POTTERY

Type	Field Type	Description	OIP 78 Reference
P-2		miniature pot	pl. 80:3
P-6	49	strainer	see pl. 82:10–11
P-7	29	dish	pl. 82:14–15
P-8B	33	shallow bowl with carinated rim	pl. 82:19–20, 23
P-12	44	pot	see pl. 83:8–10
P-13	41	small bottle	pl. 83:15
P-14A	36B	large jar	pl. 84:8
P-14B	36A	large jar	pl. 84:10–13
P-15	40	vase	pl. 85:4
P-17	42A	jar	pl. 86:3
P-18	46	tall jar	pl. 86:10–11
P-19A	47	round-based jar	pl. 87:1–2
P-19B	47B	round-based jar	pl. 87:3, 5–6
P-20		tray	pl. 88:1
P-21	31	small dish	pl. 88:6–8
P-22	32	small bowl	pl. 88:9–10
P-23	50	chalice	pl. 88:12–14
P-24	35	pot, usually painted	pl. 88:15–20, 22–23
P-25		large burial jar	pl. 89:5, 7–11
P-26		small pot	pl. 90:13
P-27	48	tubular vase	pl. 91:7–10
P-28	42B	vase, usually painted	pl. 91:15–17
P-29		"table"	pl. 92:13
P-30		large, shallow bowl	pl. 93:4, 9
P-31		deep bowl	pl. 93:7–8
P-32		large bowl	pl. 93:10
P-33		very large bowl	pl. 93:11
P-34		"flowerpot"	pl. 93:12–14
P-35	43	small pot, sometimes painted	pl. 94:5–8
P-36		large pot	pl. 94:11, 13–14
P-37		bottle	pl. 95:1–2
P-38	39	tall beaker, sometimes painted	pl. 95:5–8
P-39A	38A	beaker	pl. 95:8–16
P-39B	38B	tall beaker	pl. 95:17
P-39C	38B	cup, sometimes painted	pl. 95:18–19
P-40A	37	tall jar with pointed base	pl. 96:5
P-40B	37	wide jar with pointed base	pl. 96:6
P-40C	37	jar with pointed base	pl. 96:7–8
P-41		potstand	pl. 97:2–3

P-42		ribbed potstand	pl. 97:4–5
P-46A	26	Kassite goblet	pl. 98:12
P-U		untyped vessel	
P-M	min	miniature vessel	pls. 88:15; 90:6, 10–12; 92:7, 10, 14; 93:5; 94:4, 9, 16

TOOLS

Type	Description	OIP 78 Reference
T-1	jewelry (lapidary work): beads, pendants, etc.	pls. 147:3, 5–7, 9; 150:1–6, 20–21, 48; 151:24
T-2	jewelry (metalwork): rings, bracelets, pins, etc.	pls. 151:4, 16; 152:6, 8; 154:11
T-3	weapons: arrowheads, maceheads, etc.	pl. 154:10, 12–14, 25–26
T-4	flint blades, cores	
T-5	metal blades	pls. 155:1, 5–6; 156:1–2
T-6	awls, chisels	pls. 153:7; 156:15
T-7	drills, drill heads	pl. 153:14–15
T-8	whetstones, polishers	pl. 156:8
T-9	needles	see pl. 153:29–30
T-10	weights	pls. 147:15–19; 156:3–7
T-11	spindle whorls	pl. 156:11
T-12	seals, seal impressions	pls. 111:1–4, 7–16; 112:1–10, 12–14; 113:1–2, 4; 115:8; 116:16; 119:7–16, 18; 120:1–4, 8–12
T-13	rattles, whistles	pl. 149:16; see pl. 149:17
T-14	stone bowls	pl. 107:8–13

FIGURINES AND PLAQUES

Type	Description	OIP 78 Reference
F-1	nude female figurine	pls. 123:6–7; 124:1–3; 131:10; 133:1–2
F-2	male figurine	pls. 129:8–9; 130:1–9, 11; 131:9, 11
F-3	seated human figurine	pls. 126:4–5, 12; 134:1, 3; 146:1; 149:1
F-4	miscellaneous human figurine	pls. 126:1–3, 9; 131:5–8; 134:4; 139:3
F-5	animal figurine	pls. 140:8–9; 141:4, 6–7
F-6	miscellaneous figurine	
F-7	mask	pl. 132:8
F-8	model bed, model chair	pl. 144:1–2, 5–6
F-9	model chariot, model boat	pls. 144:7, 9; 149:10
F-10	chariot wheel	pl. 149:12
F-11	nude female plaque	pls. 126:6; 127:1–2, 4–10
F-12	goddess plaque	pl. 134:6–7
F-13	male plaque	pls. 134:9; 135:4, 7, 9; 136:2; 138:3
F-14	bull-man or god plaque/figurine	pl. 136:4–10
F-15	animal plaque	pl. 142:5–6, 8–10
F-16	secular scene on a plaque	pls. 137:10; 138:1–2, 4–5
F-17	religious scene on a plaque	pls. 133:5; 134:5; 138:9
F-18	warrior scene on a plaque	pl. 138:6–7
F-19	erotic scene on a plaque	pl. 137:1, 4, 6–7
F-20	miscellaneous plaque	pls. 133:8; 135:2–3; 137:9; 139:2

APPENDIX IV

Text Catalog

Abbreviations

BuSi	= Būr-Sîn	RiSi	= Rīm-Sîn
DaIl	= Damiq-ilišu	RiSi II	= Rīm-Sîn II
EnBa	= Enlil-bāni	Si	= Samsuiluna
Ha	= Hammurabi	SiId	= Sîn-iddinam
IlIl	= Iluma-ilu	ŠuIl	= Šu-ilišu
ItPi	= Iter-pīša	UrNi	= Ur-Ninurta
LiEn	= Lipit-Enlil		

N.B. Dates are listed as follows: year/month/day.

Text 1 (3N-T 852, IM 58763). Marriage contract. Damiq-ilišu marries SAL-kalla and adopts her three children. 13 witnesses. Bur-gul seals of both husband and wife impressed on all faces of the case and on the side, top, and end of the tablet. RiSi 30/7/- (1793 B.C.). Findspot: TA 180 XI fdn.

Text 2 (3N-T 855, IM 58765). Silver loan. The god Sîn lends 7 shekels of silver to Šeš-kalla, to be returned in the third month. 3 witnesses. Unsealed. EnBa b/3/- (1860–1837 B.C.). Findspot: TA 230 XIIB fill.

Text 3 (3N-T 842, IM 58753). Silver loan. Gud-kuta lends 1 shekel of silver belonging to the Ninurta Gate without interest to Šeš-aldug. 4 witnesses. Bur-gul seal of the borrower impressed on both edges and on one end. SiId 7/2/- (1843 B.C.). Findspot: TA 205 XIIB fill.

Text 4 (3N-T 859, IM 58769). Division of property. Abba-kalla, Im-ši-ŠI KA-Damu, and Lu-Dingirra divide a kislaḫ plot. Unwitnessed. Unsealed. Undated (ca. 1880 B.C.). Findspot: TA 196 XIIA-3.

Text 5 (3N-T 858, IM 58768). Hire of workers. Enlil-maš-zu pays 5 workers. Unwitnessed. Unsealed. Undated (ca. 1840 B.C.). Findspot: TA 196 XIIA-3.

Text 6 (3N-T 72, UM 55-21-23). Inheritance document fragment(?) Imgur-[ ] and [ ]-da-gi$_4$-ia inherit fields and other property. Neighbors and witnesses not preserved. *Bur-gul* seal of heirs impressed on the edge. Date not preserved. Findspot: TA 172 XA-2.

Text 7 (3N-T 744, IM 58672). Loan. Sîn-nāši and Nūr-[ ] give a field to Šeš-aldug as a security for a loan. 3 witnesses. Burgul seal of Sin-naši impressed on the edge. SiId X/3/- (1849–1843 B.C.). Findspot: TA 184 XI-2.

Text 8 (3N-T 816, IM 58733). Grain loan. Dingir-mansum lends 1 and ⅕ gur 20 silá of grain without interest to Bēlum-muštal. 2 witnesses. Bur-gul seal of the lender impressed on the edge and ends. RiSi 22/10/1 (1801 B.C.). Findspot: TA 203 fill.

Text 9 (3N-T 219, IM 58383). Grain loan. Narām-[ ] lends 1 gur 1 pi 3 bán of grain with interest of 4 pi 2 bán to Tarībatum. 2 witnesses preserved. Unsealed. Date not preserved. Findspot: TA 205 XI fill.

Text 10 (3N-T 561, IM 58553). Adoption. An adoption including a gift of property. Names of the participants not preserved. 1 neighbor. No witnesses preserved. Seal not preserved. Date not preserved. Findspot: TA 205 XI-3.

Text 11 (3N-T 88, UM 55-21-240). Allocation of temple offices. Two offices are divided between Ur-Lulal, Agûa, and Ubar-Bau. 8 witnesses. Bur-gul seal of the recipients impressed on the top and edge. RiSi 54/9/- (1769 B.C.). Findspot: TA 184 XA-1.

Text 12 (3N-T 87, UM 55-21-239). House exchange. Ninurta-rīm-ilī gives a 1 sar 16 gín house plot to Ištar-kīma-ilija in exchange for a 1 sar plot and 1 shekel of silver. 2 neighbors. 5 witnesses. Bur-gul seals of both participants impressed on the edge, both ends, and on the reverse above and below the date. IlIl 1/7/16 (1721 B.C.). Findspot: TA 184 XA-1.

Text 13 (3N-T 90, UM 55-21-242). Orchard sale. Nippur-gamil and Aḫu-waqar sell a 9 sar 3⅔ gìn 15 še plot in the nanga orchard. No neighbors. 4 witnesses. Bur-gul seal of the sellers impressed on the edge, on the preserved end, and on the reverse between the witness list and the date. Si 7/11/- (1743 B.C.). Findspot: Ta 184 XA-1.

Text 14 (3N-T 89, UM 55-21-241). House rental. Ninnutum rents a house to Ina-Ekur-magir for an annual rent of ¼ shekel of silver. 3 witnesses. Stone seal impressed lightly on the edge and ends. Si 27/10/13 (1723 B.C.). Findspot: TA 184 XA-1.

Text 15 (3N-T 96, UM 55-21-246). Adoption. Ipqu-Damu(?) adopts Enlil-abī and makes him coheir with Šamaš-šemi. 10 witnesses. Bur-gul seal of the two sons impressed on the edge and end. Si 16/4/20 (1734 B.C.). Findspot: TA 184 XA-1.

Text 16 (3N-T 98, UM 55-21-248). House sale. Udugmu and Nin-keš sell a 1⅔ sar house plot and a 1 sar kislaḫ plot to Lu-Ninurta and Lugal-keš for 8 shekels of silver. 1 neighbor. 4 witnesses. Bur-gul seal of Udugmu impressed on the end. BuSi c/9/- (1895–1874 B.C.). Findspot: TA 184 XA-1.

Text 17 (3N-T 97, A30143). House sale. Ur-dukuga sells a ⅚ sar house plot with door and lock to Amurru-bāni for 8 shekels of silver. 6 witnesses. Bur-gul seal of the seller impressed on the edge and ends of the tablet, and on the edge, ends, and the reverse between the witness list and the date on the case. RiSi 48/4/- (1775 B.C.). Findspot: TA 184 XA-1.

Text 18 (3N-T 869, IM 58779). House sale. Iltāni and Eani sell a ruined house plot (ki-šub-ba) to Sapḫum-lipḫur for 1⅙ shekels of silver. 2 neighbors. 7 witnesses. Two stone seals impressed on all surfaces of the tablet, especially on the two ends and on the reverse between the witness list and the date. RiSi 37/8/- (1786 B.C.). Findspot: TA 174 XI-2.

Text 19 (3N-T 877, IM 58787). House sale. Sapḫum-lipḫur sells a 2 sar ruined house plot (ki-šub-ba) to Amurru-šemi for 2½ shekels of silver. 4 neighbors. 9 witnesses. Stone seal impressed on the end and edges; superscription of witness. Date not preserved. Findspot: TA 174 XI-2.

Text 20 (3N-T 863, IM 58773). House exchange. Sapḫum-lipḫur gives a 1 sar ruined house plot (ki-šub-ba) to Amurru-šemi in exchange for a similar plot. 2 neighbors. 9 witnesses. Stone seals of Sîn-šaruḫ and one other impressed on the edges and ends of both tablet and case. Superscription of the witnesses Iṣidarê and Damiq-ilišu. RiSi 59/10/- (1764 B.C.). Findspot: TA 174 XI-2.

Text 21 (3N-T 872, IM 58782). House exchange; counterpart of Text 20. Amurru-šemi gives a 1 sar ruined house plot (ki-šub-ba) to Sapḫum-lipḫur in exchange for a similar plot. 2 neighbors. 8 witnesses. Stone seal of Sîn-šaruh impressed on the edge and ends. RiSi 59/10/- (1764 B.C.). Findspot: TA 174 XI-2.

Text 22 (3N-T 876, IM 58786). Court case. Amurru-šemi and Watar-pîša contest the sale of a ruined house plot (ki-šub-ba). 4 neighbors. 9 witnesses. Stone seals of Watar-pîša and at least 6 witnesses impressed on all edges. Ha 43/7/17 (1750 B.C.). Findspot: TA 174 XI-2.

Text 23 (3N-T 864, IM 58774). Grain loan. Bēltani lends 2 gur 2 bán of grain with interest to Amurru-šemi. 4 witnesses. Stone seal impressed on all edges; superscription of borrower. Si 5/9/- (1745 B.C.). Findspot: TA 174 XI-2.

Text 24 (3N-T 873, IM 58783). Court case. Amurru-šemi disinherits Ilī-u-Šamaš. 10 witnesses. Bur-gul seal of Ilī-u-Šamaš impressed on all preserved edges. Date not preserved. Findspot: TA 174 XI-2.

Text 25 (3N-T 865, IM 58775). Payment of grain. Amurru-šemi collects a total of 11 gur 1 bán of grain from 9 people to enable him to pay for a house that he had bought from Apil-Amurru. 6 witnesses. Stone seals of 4 of the witnesses impressed on all uninscribed surfaces. Si 7/3/- (1743 B.C.). Findspot: TA 174 XI-2.

Text 26 (3N-T 884, IM 58794). House sale. Apil-Amurru sells a ruined house plot (ki-šub-ba) to Amurru-šemi for X shekels of silver. 1 neighbor. 4 witnesses. Stone seals of 3 of the witnesses impressed all over the tablet. Si 7/6/20 (1743 B.C.). Findspot: TA 174 XI-2.

Text 27 (3N-T 223, IM 58386). Grain loan. Mār-erṣetim lends 1 gur of grain with interest and 4 bán without interest to Sîn-magir. 2 witnesses. Unsealed. Ha 43/2/26 (1750 B.C.). Findspot: TA 174 XI-1.

Text 28 (3N-T 222, IM 58385). Silver loan. The god Šamaš lends 1 shekel of silver without interest to Mār-erṣetim. 2 witnesses. Unsealed. Si 1/3/25 (1749 B.C.). Findspot: TA 174 XI-1.

Text 29 (3N-T 221, IM 58384). Field rental. Mār-erṣetim rents a total of 4 gán of field property from Enlil-issu. 2 neighbors. 3 witnesses. Stone seal of Aplum impressed on both ends, on one side, and on the reverse between the witness list and the date. Superscription of a witness. RiSi II/8/25 (1741 B.C.). Findspot: TA 174 XI-1.

Text 30 (3N-T 875, IM 58785). Adoption. Enlil-nīšu and Aḫātum adopt Ninurta-abī. 8 witnesses. Bur-gul seal of the adoptee impressed on the only end preserved. Si ?/-/- (1749–1721 B.C.). Findspot: TA 174 XI-2.

Text 31 (3N-T 867, IM 58777). Inheritance document. Nūr-Ištar and Enlil-nīšu inherit house (in Iaḫalpilum), kislaḫ, and field property from Nabi-Enlil. 3 neighbors. 10 witnesses. Bur-gul seal of the heirs impressed on both ends and on the edge. Si 10/10/12 (1740 B.C.). Findspot: TA 174 XI-2.

Text 32 (3N-T 246, IM 58401). Field rental. Sābîja rents a 1 gán field plot in the apin-nu-zu field for 3 years to Nannatum for one-fourth of the crop. 3 witnesses. 2 stone seals impressed on the ends of the tablet and on all surfaces of the case. Si 10/8/8 (1740 B.C.). Findspot: TA 174 XI-1.

Text 33 (3N-T 248, IM 58403). Wool loan. Nannatum lends 1 *mina* of wool to Adija. 2 witnesses. Unsealed. Date not preserved/10/-. Findspot: TA 174 XI-1.

Text 34 (3N-T 871, IM 58781). Betrothal. Ištar-lamassī and Sîn-abušu are betrothed. The witnesses receive a gift of oil. 13 witnesses. Unsealed. Si 11/6/23 (1739 B.C.). Findspot: TA 174 XI-2.

Text 35 (3N-T 882, IM 58792). Court case. Reassignment of inheritance between Ubar-Enlil and Puzur-Ninšubur. 1 neighbor. 7 witnesses. Bur-gul seals of both participants impressed on ends, on edge, and on the reverse between the witness list and the date. UrNi X/6/- (1923–1896 B.C.). Findspot: TA 174 XI-2.

Text 36 (3N-T 874, IM 58784). Court case. Settling the final payment for a 1 sar house plot that had been sold (?) by Lamaša, Ur-Ningizzida, and Lu-Ninsun to Ama-kalla. 1 neighbor. 3 witnesses. Bur-gul seal of Ur-Ningizzida impressed on edge, on ends, and on the reverse between the witness list and the date. LiEn a/-/- (1873–1869 B.C.). Findspot: TA 174 XI-2.

Text 37 (3N-T 866, IM 58776). House sale. Nuska-mālik, Aḫu-waqar, Bulālum, Warad-ilišu, Elali, and Warad-Amurru sell a 16 gín house and kislaḫ plot to Ibnija for 6 shekels of silver. 1 neighbor. 5 witnesses. Bur-gul seals of the sellers impressed on the edge and ends. ItPi X/12/- (1833–1831 B.C.). Findspot: TA 174 XI-2.

Text 38 (3N-T 870, IM 58780). Field rental. Ubar-x rents a 12 gán field plot to Ilija for one-third of the crop. 4 witnesses. Stone seal impressed on ends and edge. Si 7/4/- (1743 B.C.). Findspot: TA 174 XI-2.

Text 39 (3N-T 868, IM 58778). Silver loan. The god Šamaš lends 1 shekel of silver from the é-dub without interest to Ea-tajjār. 3 witnesses. Unsealed. Undated. Findspot: TA 174 XI-2.

Text 40 (3N-T 225, IM 58388). Court case. Concerns the support of a boy by Ipquša(?). 7 witnesses. Unsealed. Undated. Findspot: TA 174 XI-1.

Text 41 (3N-T 878, IM 58788). Grain loan. 4 gur of grain are lent. 3 witnesses. No seal impressions preserved. Date not preserved. Findspot: TA 174 XI-2.

Text 42 (3N-T 94, A30142). Inheritance document. Enlil-mansum, Ṭāb-balāṭu, Ur-dukuga, and Enlil-galzu inherit house property from Illu-nāši. 1 neighbor. 9 witnesses. Bur-gul seal of the heirs on all four edges. Si 8/4/20 (1742 B.C.). Findspot: TA 178 XA-1.

Text 43 (3N-T 92, A30140). House sale. Ṭāb-balāṭu sells a ⅚ sar house plot to Ipqu-Enlil for 6 shekels of silver. 1 neighbor. 4 witnesses. Bur-gul seal of the seller impressed on the top and edges, and between the witness list and the date. Si 12/5/18 (1738 B.C.). Findspot: TA 178 XA-1.

Text 44 (3N-T 93, A30141). House sale. Ipqu-Enlil sells a ⅓ sar house plot to Enlil-nīšu and Etel-pî-Ištar for X shekels of silver. 1 neighbor. 6 witnesses. Bur-gul seal of the seller impressed on the edges and ends of the tablet and case where preserved. Si 16/-/2 (1734 B.C.). Findspot: TA 178 XA-1.

Text 45 (3N-T 91, UM 55-21-423). House exchange. Enlil-galzu gives a 10 gín house plot to Ipqu-Enlil in exchange for a 10 gín house plot and ½ shekel of silver. 3 neighbors. 6 witnesses. Bur-gul seal of both participants impressed on one edge and both ends of the tablet, and on all surfaces of the case. Si 17/3/- (1733 B.C.). Findspot: TA 178 XA-1.

Text 46 (3N-T 85, A30138). House sale. Ipqu-Enlil sells a 10 gín house plot to Enlil-nīsŭ and Etel-pî-Ištar for 1⅙ shekels of silver. 1 neighbor. 6 witnesses. Bur-gul seal of the seller impressed on all sides of the tablet and case. Si 17/3/- (1733 B.C.). Findspot: TA 185 XA-1.

Text 47 (3N-T 86, A30139). House sale. Enlil-nīšu buys Etel-pî-Ištar's share of a ⅚ sar house plot that they had owned in partnership for 2⅔ shekels of silver. 1 neighbor. 6 witnesses. Bur-gul seal of the seller impressed on one side, on both ends, and on the reverse between the witness list and the date, and on the edge of the case where preserved. Si 18/5/25 (1732 B.C.). Findspot: TA 185 XA-1.

Text 48 (3N-T 95, UM 55-21-245). Record of silver payments. BI.KU?-[ ] gives silver to Balilum, Šakkan-kurra, and Urdatum. 4 witnesses. Unsealed. RiSi 30/10/14 (1793 B.C.). Findspot: TA 185 XA-1.

Text 49 (3N-T 83, A30136). Field rental. Apil-Adad rents a 3 gán field plot to Ilī-erībam for a share of the crop. 3 witnesses. Stone seal of the lessor impressed on all preserved edges and on the reverse between the witness list and the date. Si 7/3/9 (1743 B.C.). Findspot: TA 185 XA-1.

Text 50 (3N-T 84, A30137). House rental. Rīm-Adad rents a house for 1 year to Ilī-erībam for a rent of 1¼ shekels of silver. 3 witnesses. Stone seal impressed on the top, on both sides, and on the reverse between the witness list and the date. Si 8/5/6 (1742 B.C.). Findspot: TA 185 XA-1.

Text 51 (3N-T 82, UM 55-21-238). Field rental. Ippatum rents a 1½ gán field plot to Etel-pî-Ištar for one-third of the crop. 3 witnesses. Stone seal impressed on all preserved surfaces of the case. Date not preserved/8/-. Findspot: TA 185 XA-1.

Text 52 (3N-T 81, UM 55-21-237). Concerns fields and grain. Warad-Sîn and Ilī-erībam participate. Badly damaged. Findspot: TA 185 XA-1.

Text 53 (3N-T 845, IM 58756). Manumission. Ur-dukuga frees a slave. 11 witnesses. Bur-gul seal of Ur-dukuga impressed on ends, on edge, and on the reverse between the witnesses list and the date. RiSi 51/8/- (1772 B.C.). Findspot: TA 179 XA-1.

Text 54 (3N-T 844, IM 58754). House sale. Apil-Adad and Dannam-išu sell a 1 sar ruined house plot (ki-šub-ba) to Nabi-Enlil and Ekuritum for 3 shekels of silver. 2 neighbors. 10 witnesses. Stone seal of a witness impressed on the edge. Si 7/2/- (1743 B.C.). Findspot: TA 179 XA-1.

Text 55 (3N-T 847, IM 58757). Property exchange. Nabi-Enlil and the heirs of Abum-waqar exchange property. Witnesses, seal, and date all or largely destroyed. Findspot: TA 179 XA-1.

Text 56 (3N-T 78, UM 55-21-235). Witness list fragment. Remains of 5 witnesses. No seal impression preserved. Ha 38/12/- (1755 B.C.). Findspot: TA 185 XA-2.

Text 57 (3N-T 159, IM 58346). Silver loan. Lipit-Ištar lends 1 shekel of silver without interest to Etel-Pî-Enlil. 3 witnesses. Stone seal impressed on ends and edges. Ha 38/10/13(?) (1755 B.C.). Findspot: TA 187 XA-3.

Text 58 (3N-T 185, IM 58357). Witness list fragment. 6 witnesses preserved. Bur-gul seal of Šamaš-nūrī and Geme-Nuska impressed on the edge and between the witness list and the date. Ha 31/12/10(?) (1762 B.C.). Findspot: TA 180 XA-3.

Text 59 (3N-T 114, UM 55-21-255). Field rental. Imgur-Sîn rents a 2 gán field plot to [ ]-Dagan for a share of the crop. 1 neighbor. 3 witnesses. Stone seal impressed on the end and edge and on the reverse between the witness list and the date. Superscriptions of the lessor and of one of the witnesses. Si 11/3/3 (1739 B.C.). Findspot: TA 176 XA-3.

Text 60 (3N-T 103, UM 55-21-433). Cultivation contract. Sîn-imguranni and Apil-Adad agree to the cultivation and maintenance of two fields. 4 witnesses. Unsealed. Si 6/5/- (1744 B.C.). Findspot: TA 153 XA-2.

Text 61 (3N-T 210, IM 58379). Grain loan. Ninurta-[ ] lends 2 gur 2 bán of grain with interest to ^{d}EN-[ ]. 4 witnesses. Unsealed. Ha 42/11/- (1751 B.C.). Findspot: TA dump.

Text 62 (2N-T 167, IM 65519). Adoption. Lamassatum adopts (or is adopted by) Lu-Nuska. 4 witnesses. Traces of a seal impression on the edge and end. EnBa g/-/- (1860–1837 B.C.). Findspot: TB 2 D.

Text 63 (2N-T 470, IM 58018). Field rental (or sale). A 15 gán field plot is rented. 1 neighbor. 2 witnesses preserved. Unsealed. DaIl 8/8/- (1808 B.C.). Findspot: TB 51 I-2.

Text 64 (2N-T 471, IM 58019). Concerns a field plot. Mār-erṣetim and Šagubum own a total of 6 gán of field property. 2 neighbors. No witnesses preserved. Bur-gul seal impressed on the edge and between lines 1′ and 3′. Date not preserved. Findspot: TB 51 I-2.

Text 65 (2N-T 685, UM 55-21-129). Silver loan. Ešumeša-gamil lends ½ shekel 2 še of silver without interest to Balṭuka. 3 witnesses. Unsealed. Ha 31/11/- (1762 B.C.). Findspot: TB 10 II fdn.

Text 66 (2N-T 44, IM 57829). Field rental. Utu-ḫegal rents to Šunaja a 9 gán field plot for an annual rent of 40 gur of grain for each 18 gán rented and an extra payment of 10 gur of grain. 1 neighbor. 3 witnesses. Stone seal impressed on the edge and end. ŠuIl 23/3/- (1872 B.C.). Findspot: TB 17 II-1.

Text 67 (2N-T 130, IM 57849). Silver loan. The god Enlil lends 1 shekel of silver with interest of 1/6 shekel 6 še of silver, added to a previous loan, to Anne-babdu. 2 witnesses. Unsealed. RiSi 8/5/- (1815 B.C.). Findspot: TB 30 I-2.

Text 68 (2N-T 783, UM 55-21-169). Temple office sale. Damiq-ilišu sells at least two offices, the inheritance of Ḫabannatum(?).[1] 10 witnesses. Seal of Ḫabannatum impressed on the edges where preserved. Date not preserved. Findspot: TB 75 E-2.

Text 69 (2N-T 779 + (2N-T 799, UM 55-21-166). Temple office sale. Ipqatum sells one office in the É-kur-ra for 7½ days to Atta and Imgur-Ninurta for 5⅔ shekels of silver. 7 witnesses. Bur-gul seal of the seller impressed on the edge, on the ends, and on the reverse between the witness list and the date Si 3/6/- (1747 B.C.). Findspot: TB 75 E-2.

Text 70 (2N-T 778, UM 55-21-165). Temple office sale. Ubar-Šamaš sells 4 offices in the Šamaš temple for 10 days each to Atta and Imgutum for ½ mina ½ shekel of silver. 8 witnesses. Bur-gul seal of the seller impressed on the edges and ends of the case and tablet and on

[1] The remains now preserved are consistent with Ḫabannatum as the seller, but Albrecht Goetze ("The Archive of Ātta from Nippur," *Journal of Cuneiform Studies* 18 [1964]) gives the seller as Damiq-ilišu. It is quite possible that the tablet has deteriorated since Goetze looked at it.

the reverse of the case between the witness list and the date Si 3/11/- (1747 B.C.). Findspot: TB 75 E-2.

Text 71 (2N-T 772, UM 55-21-162). Temple office sale. Nuska-nišu sells 2 or more offices in the Nuska temple with their perbend field for 5 days each to Atta for 10½ shekels of silver. 5 witnesses. Bur-gul seal of the seller impressed on the edges of the tablet and case and on the ends and the reverse between the witness list and the date on the tablet. Si 10/8/11 (1740 B.C.). Findspot: TB 75 E-2.

Text 72 (2N-T 771, UM 55-21-161). Temple office sale. Igmil-Sîn sells 6 offices in the Šamaš temple for 5 days each to Šamaš-muballiṭ for 9½ shekels of silver. 5 witnesses. Bur-gul seal of the seller impressed on the ends and edges of the case and tablet. Si 10/8/11 (1740 B.C.). Findspot: TB 75 E-2.

Text 73 (2N-T 770, UM 55-21-160). Temple office sale. Sîn-imguranni and Tarībatum sell 5 offices in the Lugal-aba temple for 20 days each to Adad-tajar for 11½ shekels of silver. 7 witnesses. Bur-gul seal of the sellers impressed on the edges, ends, and reverse between the witness list and the date of both tablet and case. Si 11/3/15 (1739 B.C.). Findspot: TB 75 E-2.

Text 74 (2N-T 782, UM 55-21-168). Temple office sale. Ilīma-lulim and Abī-ikkua sell 5 offices in the Šamaš temple for 5 days each to Atta for 8½ shekels of silver. 7 witnesses. Bur-gul seal of the sellers impressed on the edges and ends of both tablet and case where preserved. Si 11/4/11 (1739 B.C.). Findspot: TB 75 E-2.

Text 75 (2N-T 769, UM 55-21-159). Temple office sale. Ilī-iddinam sells 6 offices in the Šamaš temple for 5 days each to Atta for 6 shekels of silver. 6 witnesses. Bur-gul seal of the seller impressed on the edges and ends of the tablet and case where preserved. Si 11/10/1 (1739 B.C.). Findspot: TB 75 E-2.

Text 76 (2N-T 775C, A30091C). Temple office sale. Abija and ? sell one for more offices in the Ninlil/Ninurta temple for 2 or more days to Atta for 4⅓ shekels of silver. 4 witnesses. Illegible bur-gul seal impressed on the edges, ends, and reverse between the witness list and the date where preserved. Si 11/11/9 (1739 B.C.). Findspot: TB 75 E-2.

Text 77 (2N-T 768, A30088). Sale. Atta purchases something. 8 witnesses. No seal preserved. Si 12/-/- (1738 B.C.). Findspot: TB 75 E-2.

Text 78 (2N-T 774, A30089). Temple office sale. Lipit-Ištar sells 3 offices in the Inanna-anaka temple for 15 days each to Atta for ⅓ mina 5 shekels of silver. 6 witnesses. Bur-gul seal of the seller impressed on the edges and ends of the tablet and case. Si 12/5/15 (1738 B.C.). Findspot: TB 75 E-2.

Text 79 (2N-T 780, UM 55-21-167). Temple office sale. Aluttaḫi and Damiq-ilišu sell 3 or 4 offices in the Lugal(aba) and Ab-kù-maḫ temples for 22½ days each to Atta for 5⅓ shekels of silver. 5 witnesses. Bur-gul seal of the seller impressed on the edges, ends, and reverse between the witness list and the date on the tablet and case. Si 12/6/21 (1738 B.C.). Findspot: TB 75 E-2.

Text 80 (2N-T 767, A30087). Temple office redemption. Enlil-NI-[ ] sells temple offices in the Šamaš temple to Atta for 5 shekels of silver. 5 witnesses. Bur-gul seal of the seller(?) impressed on the edge of the case where preserved. Si 12/8/6 (1738 B.C.). Findspot: TB 75 E-2.

Text 81 (2N-T 773, UM 55-21-163). Temple office sale. Tarībatum sells 6 offices in the Šamaš temple for 10 days each to Atta for 7½ shekels of silver. 5 witnesses. Bur-gul seal of the seller impressed on the edges, ends, and reverse between the witness list and the date on both tablet and case. Si 14/11/24 (1736 B.C.). Findspot: TB 75 E-2.

Text 82 (2N-T 788, UM 55-21-171). Sale? Concerns 2 offices and an 8½ gán orchard plot, the inheritance of Imgur-Ninurta. 1 neighbor. 5 witnesses. Bur-gul seal of Damu-erībam and Ninurta-muballiṭ impressed on the edge and end. Si 14/12/6 (1736 B.C.). Findspot: TB 75 E-2.

Text 83 (2N-T 766, A30086). Temple office sale. Annum-pî-Ištar and KA-Ninurta sell 4 offices in the Lugal-aba and Ab-kù-maḫ temples belonging to Ḫunābatum and Annum-pî-Ištar for

22½ days to Sîn-magir for 5 shekels of silver. 7 witnesses. Bur-gul seal of KA-Ninurta impressed on the edge of the case. Si 23/-/14 (1727 B.C.). Findspot: TB 75 E-2.

Text 84 (2N-T 374, IM 57972). Temple office redemption. Sîn-magir sells 4 offices in the Lugal-aba and Ab-kù-maḫ temples for 22½ days each to Atta for 5⅓ shekels 15 še of silver. 8 witnesses. Bur-gul seal of the seller impressed on the reverse between the witness list and the date. Ends and edges not preserved. Si 24/3/26 (1726 B.C.). Findspot: TB 75 E-2.

Text 85 (2N-T 375, IM 58956). Temple office sale. Sîn-[ ] sells offices in the Šamaš temple for 30 days each to Atta. 5 witnesses. Bur-gul seal of the seller impressed on the edge. Si X/12/13 (1749–1721 B.C.). Findspot: TB 75 E-2.

Text 86 (2N-T 775, A30091). Temple office exchange. Damu-iddinam (and [ ]-i-bi-[ ]?) exchange temple offices with Enlil-nīšu (and Alijatum?). 3 witnesses preserved. Bur-gul seal of the participants impressed on the edge and ends of the tablet and case. Date not preserved. Findspot: TB 75 E-2.

Text 87 (2N-T 777, UM 55-21-164). Temple office sale. Lipit-Ištar sells offices for 15 days each to ? for ⅓ mina 5 shekels of silver. 6 witnesses. Bur-gul seal of the seller(?) impressed on the reverse between the witness list and the date. Edges and ends not preserved. Date not preserved. Findspot: TB 75 E-2.

Text 88 (2N-T 764, A30085). Temple office sale. Damu-iddinam sells offices in the Šamaš temple with their prebend field for 36(?) days each to Atta for X minas 8 shekels of silver. 7 witnesses. Bur-gul seal of the seller impressed on the edge where preserved. Date not preserved. Findspot: TB 75 E-2.

Text 89 (2N-T 776, A30092). Temple office sale. Apil-Šamaš sells 5 offices in the Šamaš temple for 10 days each to Atta for 10⅓ shekels of silver. 6 witnesses. Bur-gul seal of the seller impressed on the ends of the tablet and on the edges of the tablet and case. Date not preserved/6/-. Findspot: TB 75 E-2.

Text 90 (2N-T 377, IM 57974). Temple office sale. Nabi-Šamaš and Annum-pî-Šamaš sell 4 or more offices in the Šamaš temple for 5 days each to Atta for 6⅔ shekels of silver. Fragments of 3 witnesses preserved. Bur-gul seal of the sellers impressed on the edge and ends. Date not preserved. Findspot: TB 75 E-2.

Text 91 (2N-T 378, IM 57975). Temple office sale. Iddin-Ištar sells 2 or more offices in the Šamaš temple for 5 days each to Atta for 4½ shekels of silver. Traces of 2 witnesses preserved. Seal not preserved. Date not preserved. Findspot: TB 75 E-2.

Text 92 (2N-T 341, IM 57952). Field rental. Lamassatum rents a 3 gán plot to Nūr-Šamaš for a share of the crop. Nūr-Šamaš will also pay 1 gur of grain. 1 neighbor. 3 witnesses. Unsealed. Si 10/-/7 (1740 B.C.). Findspot: TB 76 D.

Text 93 (2N-T 439, IM 58010). Grain loan. Enlil-[ ] lends 50 silá of grain with interest to Lipit-[ ]. Traces of 2 witnesses. Stone seal impressed on edges and ends. Ha X/9/- (1762–1750 B.C.). Findspot: TB 56 I-1.

Text 94 (2N-T 449, IM 58013). Silver loan. Kuritum and Ku-Enlil lend ½ shekel of silver without interest to Šeš-dugga. If the loan is not repaid by the third month, interest will be charged. 2 witnesses. Traces of a stone(?) seal impressed on the edge. BuSi a/10/- (1895–1874 B.C.). Findspot: TB 140 II-1.

Text 95 (2N-T 229, IM 57884). Grain loan. Sîn-erībam lends grain with interest to ? 1 witness preserved. Unsealed. Si 7/10/- (1743 B.C.). Findspot: TB 55 E.

Text 96 (2N-T 404, IM 57987). Grain loan. Names of participants broken. 2 witnesses. Unsealed. Ha X/12/- (1762–1750 B.C.). Findspot: TB 55 E.

Text 97 (2N-T 421, IM 57996). Silver loan. Lugal-murube lends 10 or more shekels of silver at 25% interest, to be added to a previous loan, to Ummi-waqrat and Sîn-rēmēnī, to be repaid in the third month. Several seals impressed on the edge and ends. Witness list not preserved. Date not preserved. Findspot: TB 91 I-1.

APPENDIX V

Index of Personal Names

ABBREVIATIONS

so.	=	son of	hu.	=	husband of
da.	=	daughter of	wi.	=	wife of
fa.	=	father of	n.d.	=	no date
mo.	=	mother of	NI.	=	no genealogical or professional information
br.	=	brother of			
si.	=	sister of			

NOTE: The terms for professions (scribe, mason, etc.) have been translated in this appendix. However, where an individual is identified by the office that he owns, the office name is left untranslated since such translations add only confusion to an already complex situation. Kinship terms may be combined; e.g., fa.fa. means father's father.

A

a-[ ]
fa. é-a-tu-ri-im. 1734. Text 15: rev. 11.
fa. ^{d}nin-urta-ga-<mil>. 1743. Text 13: rev. 3′.

a-[ ]-a
bur-gul (seal-cutter), so. ^{d}nin-urta-ga-mil.
1747. Witness. Text 70: tablet rev. 13; case rev. 8′.

a-ab-ba
fa. ^{d}nanna-zi. 1760. BE 6/2 10: 37.

a-ab-ba-a-(a)
so. a-ḫi-ša-gi$_4$-iš.
1747. Witness. Text 69: tablet rev. 6.
fa. u-bar-^{d}šamaš. n.d. Text 40: obv. 3.
dub-sar (scribe).
1780. Witness. PBS 8/1 38: 22.
1769. Witness. Text 11: rev. 12.

a-ab-ba-dingir
so. [ ]-lú-ti.
1789. Witness. *ARN* 31: rev. 13′.

a-ab-ba$^{?}$-DÙG.um$^{?}$
NI. n.d. Neighbor. *ARN* 20: v 12 (joins OIMA 1 52).

a-ab-ba-kal-la

so. a-gu-ú-a.

n.d. Witness. *ARN* 22: rev. 6.

so. ^{d}nin-líl-zi-mu, br. KA-^{d}da-mu, im-ši-ŠI, and lú-dingir-ra.

n.d. With his brothers he inherits from his father. *ARN* 20 = OIMA 1 52: I 17′, IV 8′, V 2, VI 22, VII 1.

n.d. With his brothers he divides a plot of unimproved land (kislaḫ). Text 4: obv. 2.

fa. ^{d}en-líl-maš-zu, ^{d}da-mu-a-zu, and lú-^{d}nin-urta.

1867. His sons inherit from him. PBS 8/2 169 + *ARN* 23: = seal.

1860–1837. TIM 4 27: 21.

a-ap-pa-a-a

gudu$_4$ ^{d}inanna, so. i-bi-^{d}sìn.

1739. Witness. Text 74: tablet rev. 7; case rev. 9′.

1738. Witness. Text 78: tablet rev. 5′; case rev. 7.

a-ap-pa-tum (a-ap-pa-a-tum, a-ab-ba-tum)

bur-gul (seal-cutter).

1739. Witness. Text 75: tablet rev. 10; BE 6/2 35: 21; BE 6/2 37: 19; Cornell 8: 23; Cornell 19: rev. 6′; Cornell 20: 20′; OIMA 1 18: 28 (case of *ARN* 96); OIMA 1 19: 22; N1119: 4′.

1749–1721. Witness. Text 85: rev. 9′.

a-at-ta-a

^{lú}ŠIM, so. na-ra-am-^{d}sìn, br. ^{d}en-líl-na-da, ip-qú-^{d}en-líl, ip-qú-er-ṣe-tim, and im-gur-^{d}nin-urta (im-gu-tum).

1747. With his brother im-gur-^{d}nin-urta he buys a temple office from ip-qá-tum. Text 69: tablet obv. 6; case 5′.

1747. With his brother im-gu-tum he buys a temple office from u-bar-^{d}šamaš. Text 70: tablet obv. 8; case obv. 8.

1740. He buys a temple office from ^{d}nuska-ni-šu. Text 71: case obv. 9.

1739. He buys a temple office from ì-lí-ma-lu-lim and a-bi-ik-ku-ú-a. Text 74: case obv. 10.

1739. He buys a temple office from ì-lí-i-din-nam. Text 75: tablet obv. 6; case 6.

1739. He buys a temple office from a-bi-ia and lú-[ ]. Text 76: obv. 5.

1738. Purchaser. Text 77; obv. 1′.

1738. He buys a temple office from li-pí-it-ištar. Text 78: tablet obv. 7; case obv. 7.

1738. He buys a temple office from a-lu-ut-ta-ḫi and da-mi-iq-ì-lí-šu. Text 79: tablet obv. 9; case obv. 8′.

1738. He buys a temple office from ^{d}en-líl-NI-[ ]. Text 80: case 6′.

1737. Witness. BE 6/2 40: 19.

1736. He buys a temple office from ta-ri-ba-tum. Text 81: tablet obv. 7; case obv. 8.

1726. He buys a temple office from ^{d}sìn-ma-gir. Text 84: obv. 7.

1749–1721. He buys a temple office from ^{d}sìn-[ ]. Text 85: obv. 5′.

n.d. He buys a temple office from ^{d}da-mu-i-din-nam. Text 88: obv. 8.

n.d. He buys a temple office from a-píl-^{d}šamaš. Text 89: tablet obv. 7; case 6′.

n.d. He buys a temple office from na-bi-^{d}šamaš and an-nu-um-pi$_4$-^{d}šamaš. Text 90: obv. 8′.

n.d. He buys a temple office from i-din-ištar. Text 91: obv. 6′.

so. ^{d}nanna-[ ].

1739. Witness. Text 73: tablet rev. 5.

fa. ^{d}sìn-īriš(APIN). 1760. BE 6/2 10: 45.

a-ba-[ ]
fa. a-píl-ì-lí-šu. 1734. Text 15: rev. 10.

a-ba-^{d}en-líl-gin$_7$
NI. 1737. He receives ^{d}sìn-a-bu-šu's titles from ^{d}nanna-tum at ^{d}sìn-a-bu-šu's death. BE 6/2 42: 9, 14.

a-ba-^{d}nanna-gin$_7$
fa. ^{d}da-mu-i-din-nam. n.d. Text 86: seal; Text 88: obv. 6.

ab-bu-tu-tum
NI. 1784. With ši-pa-ta he may be a neighbor of a-ḫu-wa-qar. PBS 8/1 28: tablet 4.

a-bi-ia
so. [ ]-^{d}nin-urta, br. lú-[ ].
1739. With his brother he sells a temple office to a-at-ta-a. Text 76: obv. 3, 10.

a-bi-ik-ku-ú-a
wi. ib-ni-é-a, mo. ì-lí-ma-lu-lim.
1739. She and her son sell a temple office to a-at-ta-a. Text 74: tablet obv. 7; case obv. 9, seal.

a-bi-ì-lí
fa. ^{d}en-líl-ma-an-s[um]. 1789. *ARN* 31: rev. 10′.

a-bu-ia-tum
fa. a-píl-^{d}amurru. 1743. Text 25: seal.

a-bu-ra-an(?)
fa. a-wi-ìl-tum. 1895–1874. Text 94: rev. 8.

a-bu-ú-a-tum
so. ilum-ga-mil.
1793. Witness. Text 1: tablet rev. 18.

a-bu-um-wa-qar (a-bu-wa-qar)
so. lú-^{d}iškur.
1793. Witness. Text 1: tablet rev. 10.
1787. Witness. *ARN* 31: rev. 11′.
fa. ma-ri-er-ṣe-tim, ku-bu-tum, ì-lí-tu-ra-am, ta-ri-bu-um, and nu-úr-ištar.
1741. Text 29: obv. 8; *ARN* 125: obv. 9.
1739. BE 6/2 30: 5.
1738. Text 43: rev. 2.
n.d. Text 55: obv. 9′.

abzu-ḫé-gál
fa. é-a-ta-a-a-ar. 1740. Text 31: rev. 12.

^{d}adad-ra-bi
so. da-ma-gu-gu.
1816–1794. Witness. PBS 8/1 18: 21.
fa. ì-lí-ù-^{d}šamaš. 1743. *ARN* 82: obv. 8.
fa. ma-ri-er-ṣe-tim and mu-tum-ilum, "br." u$_4$-du$_7$-du$_7$.
1760. He had been given a field plot by his u$_4$-du$_7$-du$_7$ in exchange for a temple office, now contested by his sons. BE 6/2 10: 3, 9, 32.
NI. 1786. Witness. Text 18: obv. 14.

^{d}adad$^{?}$-šar$^{?}$-ì-lí
fa. ì-lí-ù-^{d}šamaš. n.d. Text 19: rev. 9.

^{d}adad-šar-ru-um

uku-uš (gendarme), so. i-šum-a-bi.

1760. He asks the king, Hammurabi, to write to the Nippur council on behalf of ma-ri-er-ṣe-tim and mu-tum-ilum. BE 6/2 10: 11.

^{d}adad-ta-a-a-ar

so. ḫu-mu-ru-um.

1739. He buys a temple office from ^{d}sìn-im-gur-an-ni and ta-ri-ba-tum. Text 73: tablet obv. 9′; case obv. 9.

1737. Witness. OECT 8 7: 24.

ad-da-[ ]

NI. 1860–1837. Witness. Text 62: rev. 2′.

ad-da-dùg-ga (a-ad-da-dùg-ga)

nu-èš. fa. ^{d}nuska-ni-šu and lú-^{d}ama-a-ra-zu, hu. ištar-la-ma-sí.

1746. BE 6/2 22: 7.

1742. BE 6/2 28: 31.

1740. Text 71: case rev. 2′.

1739. Text 74: case rev. 10′.

1738. Text 77: rev. 8′.

1737. BE 6/2 40: 25, 26.

1732. Text 47: tablet rev. 7; case rev. 3′.

1726. Text 84: rev. 6′.

fa. u-bar-ru-um. 1843. Text 3: rev. 10.

a-di-ia

NI. n.d. He borrows wool from ^{d}nanna-tum. Text 33: obv. 2.

a-gu-ú-a

so. lugal$^{?}$-ma-an-[sum].

1769. He divides two temple offices with ur-^{d}lú-làl and u-bar-^{d}ba-ú. Text 11: obv. 12, seal.

fa. a-ab-ba-kal-la. n.d. *ARN* 22: rev. 6.

fa. be-el-šu-nu.

1762. Text 58: 3′.

1755. *ARN* 70: rev. 9.

1751. OIMA 1 12: 20.

fa. [ ]-ì-lí-šu. 1738. Text 77: rev. 7′.

a-ḫa-tum

wi. ^{d}en-líl-ni-šu.

1749–1721. With her husband she adopts ^{d}nin-urta-a-bi. Text 30: obv. 4′, 10′.

a-ḫa-u-ta

NI. 1743. Witness. Text 13: rev. 2′.

a-ḫi-[ ]

fa. nu-úr-^{d}šamaš. n.d. Text 19: rev. 12.

a-ḫi$^{?}$-^{d}da-mu

fa. i-bi-^{d}en-líl. 1739. Text 34: obv. 12.

a-ḫi-ia

fa. ḫa-bil-ki-nu-um. 1739. Text 73: tablet rev. 8.

a-ḫi-lu-mu-ur

NI. 1743. Witness. Text 54: rev. 10.

a-ḫi-ša-gi$_4$-iš (a-ḫi-ša-<gi$_4$>-iš)
so. ^{d}nanna-zi-mu, br. i-din-ia-tum.
1758. BE 6/2 11: 26.
fa. a-ab-ba-a. 1747. Text 69: tablet rev. 6.
fa. ni-in-nu-tum and nu-úr-^{d}šamaš. n.d. OIMA 1 48: 10, seal.
bur-gul (seal-cutter)
1783. Witness. BE 6/2 7: 25.
1775. Witness. Text 17: tablet rev. 13; case rev. 4.
NI. 1762–1750. Witness. Text 96: rev. 1.

a-ḫu-ni
fa. ì-lí-damiq. 1721. Text 12: rev. 3.

a-ḫu-šu-nu
so. ur-^{d}en-nu-gi$_4$, br. zi-ia-tum and na-bi-^{d}šamaš.
1783. He sells a temple office to his brothers. BE 6/2 7: 5, 7, 14, seal.
1755. Witness. BE 6/2 14: 22.
fa. kù-^{d}nin-šubur. 1923–1896. Text 35: rev. 8.
fa. ^{d}sìn-im-gur-an-ni, ta-ri-ba-tum, and ^{d}en-nu-gi$_4$-ga-mil.
1739. Text 73: tablet obv. 6′, 8′, 15′, rev. 9; case obv. 6, 8, rev. 1′ seal.
fa. ^{d}šamaš-li-wi-ir. 1740. Text 72: tablet rev. 6; case rev. 6.

a-ḫu-um
ra-bi-a-nu-um (mayor). so. ^{d}sìn-i-ri-ba-am.
1750. Witness. Text 22: rev. 9, seal.

a-ḫu-wa-qar (a-ḫu-um-wa-qar)
so. la-ma-ša, br. ^{d}nuska-ma-lik, bu-la-lum, warad-ì-lí-šu, e-la-lí, and warad-^{d}amurru.
1833–1831. With his brothers he sells a house plot to ib-ni-ia. Text 37: obv. 5, 8, seal.
so. ma-an-nu-um-ba-la-^{d}šamaš.
1785. He sells a house plot to ^{d}nanna-ma-an-sum. PBS 8/1 28: tablet 5, 6, 14; case 7, 8.
so. ^{d}sin-ì-din-nam, br. ni-ip-pu-ur-ga-mil.
1743. With his brother he sells an orchard plot. Text 13; obv. 7, seal.
so. ŠU.BA.AN.DINGIR so.so. a-wi-il-ì-lí.
1750. Witness. Text 22: rev. 14.

a-lí-a-bu-ša
da. SAL-kal-la, da.da. dingir-kù-ta, si. nu-úr-kab-ta and ì-lí-tu-ra-am.
1793. With her brothers she is adopted by her stepfather, da-mi-iq-ì-lí-šu. Text 1: tablet obv. 6, 13, rev. 2.

a-lí-ia-tum
wi. ì-lí-i-din-nam, mo. ^{d}en-líl-ni-šu.
n.d. With her son she exchanges temple offices with [ ]-i-bi-[ ] and ^{d}da-mu-i-din-nam(?). Text 86: seal.

a-lí-ilum
gudu$_4$-^{d}nin-líl-lá.
1749–1721. Witness. Text 85: rev. 7′.
NI. n.d. Witness. Text 87: rev. 5′.

a-lí-wa-aq-rum
fa. ni-in-nu-tum. n.d. Text 40: obv. 2.

a-lu-um
so. ur-kù-zu.
1843. Witness. Text 3: rev. 7.

a-lu-um-[ ]-zu
NI. 1755. Witness. Text 56: 3.

a-lu-ut-ta-ḫi
da. a-píl-ì-lí-šu, wi. da-mi-iq-ì-lí-šu.
1738. With her husband she sells a temple office to a-at-ta-a. Text 79: tablet obv. 4, 7, 14; case obv. 3′, 6′, 14′, seal.

ama-kal-la
wi. šeš-kal-la.
1873–1869. She settles a claim on her house with a payment of silver. Text 36: obv. 3.

amar-^{d}da-mu
fa. ta-ri-bu-um. 1742. Text 42: rev. 12.

^{d}amurru-[ ]
NI. 1743. Neighbor of a-píl-^{d}amurru. Text 26: obv. 3.

^{d}amurru-ba-ni
so. ^{d}sìn-ri-me-ni.
1775. He buys a house plot from ur-du$_{6}$-kù-ga. Text 17: tablet obv. 8; case obv. 6.

^{d}amurru-še-mi
so. ú-ba-a-a-tum.
1745. He borrows grain from be-el-ta-ni. Text 23: obv. 4, edge.
n.d. He buys a house plot from sà-ap-ḫu-um-li-ip-ḫu-ur. Text 19: obv. 3, 9.
NI. 1764. He exchanges house plots with sà-ap-ḫu-um-li-ip-ḫu-ur. Text 20: tablet obv. 8; case obv. 11; Text 21: obv. 4, 7.
NI. 1750. Neighbor of wa-tar-pi-ša and enters into a dispute with him over a house plot. Text 22: obv. 4, 6, rev. 3.
NI. 1743. He receives grain from several people to pay for a house bought from a-píl-^{d}amurru. Text 25: rev. 7.
NI. 1743. He buys a house plot from a-píl-^{d}amurru. Text 26: obv. 3, 8.
NI. n.d. In the past he had adopted ì-lí-ù-^{d}šamaš, he now disinherits him. Text 24: obv. 3, 14′, rev. 2.

a-na-tum
NI. 1751. Witness. Text 61: rev. 5.

an-na-[ ]
fa. [ ]-li-tum. 1740. Text 71: case rev. 1′.

an-né-ba-ab-du$_{7}$
so. ^{d}en-líl-ḫé-gal.
1772. Witness. Text 53: obv. 17.
so. ^{d}en-líl-maš-zu.
1816–1794. Witness. PBS 8/1 18: 19.
n.d. Witness. *ARN* 22: rev. 3.
fa. ^{d}en-líl-dingir.
1783. BE 6/2 6: 21.
1755. *ARN* 70: seal.
1754. BE 6/2 16: 11.
n.d. *ARN* 176: obv. 12.

fa. ú-qá-ilam.
1793. Text 1: tablet rev. 16.
n.d. PBS 8/1 92: 22.
fa. warad-uruk^{ki}. 1860–1837. YOS 14 321: rev. II 4′.
NI. 1860–1837. His and lú-dingir-ra's field is inherited by ^{d}da-mu-a-zu. YOS 14 321: obv. II 6.
NI. 1815. He borrows silver from the god Enlil. Text 67: obv. 5.

a-nu-um-pi$_4$-ištar
da. e-te-el-pi$_4$-^{d}nuska, si. ḫu-na-ba-tum.
1727. With her sister and KA-^{d}nin-urta she sells a temple office to ^{d}sìn-ma-gir. Text 83: tablet obv, 6, 8.

an-nu-um-pi$_4$-^{d}šamaš
so. ì-lí-ma, br. na-bi-^{d}šamaš.
n.d. With his brother he sells a temple office to a-at-ta-a. Text 90: obv. 4′, 6′, seal.

a-píl-[ ]
NI. 1785. Witness. PBS 8/1 28: 17.

a-píl-^{d}adad
so. na-pa-al-aš-šu.
1744. With sin-im-gur-an-ni he comes to an agreement over a rented field. Text 60: obv. 5, 10, rev. 2, 4.
fa. ^{d}en-líl-is-sú and na-bi-^{d}en-líl. 1741. Text 29: obv. 6, 7, rev. 3.
sanga lugal-du$_6$-kù-ga, so. ri-im-^{d}adad.
1743. He rents a field plot to [ ]-tu/i-ri. Text 49: obv. 4, 5, seal.
bur-gul (seal-cutter)(?).
n.d. Witness. Text 68: case 13′.
NI. 1743. With da-an-na-am-i-šu he sells a house plot to na-bi-^{d}en-líl and e-ku-ri-tum. Text 54: obv. 6, 8.

a-píl-^{d}amurru
nimgir (herald), so. a-bu-ia-tum.
1743. Witness. Text 25: rev. 14, seal.
NI. 1744. With his brother's wife mārat-er-ṣe-tim he borrows grain from mār-er-ṣe-tim. *ARN* 81: obv. 4.
NI. 1743. ^{d}amurru-še-mi buys his house and a-si-rum already lives in it. Text 25: obv. 13, rev. 9.
NI. 1743. He sells a house plot to ^{d}amurru-še-mi. Text 26: obv. 5, 6.

a-píl-ilim
so. da-mi-iq-ì-lí-šu.
1758. Witness. BE 6/2 11: 25.

a-píl-ì-lì-šu
so. a-ba-[ ].
1734. Witness. Text 15: rev. 10.
fa. a-lu-ut-ta-ḫi. 1738. Text 79: tablet obv. 5, 7, 8; case 4′, seal.
dub-sar (scribe), so ^{d}nuska-ni-šu.
1742. Witness. Cornell 18: 21.
1738. Witness. OECT 8 9: 23; OIMA 1 22: 17.
1737. Witness. BE 6/2 41: 22.
^{lú}ŠIM ^{d}en-líl-lá, so. ur-[ ].
1738. Witness. Text 78: tablet rev. 2′; case rev. 3.

1733. Witness. Text 45: tablet rev. 6; Text 46: tablet rev. 7; case rev. 7; BE 6/2 47: 12.
1727. Witness. BE 6/2 58: 17.
ugula-é-(d)mah̬.
1742. Witness. Text 42: rev. 8.
1739. Witness. Text 75: tablet rev. 5; BE 6/2 30: 1.
1737. Witness. BE 6/2 42: 16; PBS 8/2 133: 28.
1734. Witness. Text 44: tablet rev. 5′; case rev. 5′.
1732. Witness. Text 47: tablet rev. 3.
1721. Witness. BE 6/2 64: 20.
n.d. Witness. Text 24: rev. 4; Text 89: rev. 6.
NI. 1801. Witness. Text 8: rev. 3.

a-píl-ša
so. warad-ìr-ra.
1785. Witness. PBS 8/1 28: 21.
fa. bé-la-nu-um.
1750. Text 22: rev. 15.
1743. Text 25: seal.

a-píl-ᵈšamaš
so. ì-lí-ia-tum.
1749–1721. Witness. Text 30: rev. 9.
so. nu-úr-ᵈšamaš
1750. Witness. Text 22: rev. 12, seal.
so. ur-da-tum.
n.d. He sells a temple office to a-at-ta-a. Text 89: tablet obv. 4, 6, rev. 1; case: 3′, 5′, seal.
fa. ì-lí-i-qí-ša-am. 1747. Text 70: tablet rev. 12; case rev. 7′.

ap-lum
NI. 1743. Witness. Text 54: rev. 7.
NI. n.d. Witness. Text 9: rev. 1.

arad-ᵈen-líl-lá
fa. KA-ᵈnin-urta. 1843. Text 3: rev. 4.
fa. sa-al-lu-h̬u-um. 1739. Text 74: tablet rev. 11; case rev. 12′.
nu-èš
1739. Witness. Text 34: obv. 6.
NI. 1895–1874. Neighbor of u_4-dùg-mu. Text 16: obv. 2.

arad-ᵈimin-bi
fa. ì-lí-iš-me-a-ni. 1740. Text 71: tablet rev. 7; case rev. 5′.

arad-ᵈinanna
dub-sar (scribe).
1733. Witness. Text 45: tablet rev. 9; Text 46: tablet rev. 10; case rev. 10.

arad-ᵈnanna
so. é-a?-[ ].
1867. Witness. *ARN* 23: IV 2′ (joins PBS 8/2 169).
šu-[ ].
1785. Witness. PBS 8/1 28: 18.
NI. 1785. Witness. PBS 8/1 28: 19.

ar-na-bu-um
fa. ^{d}nanna-me-ša$_{4}$. 1775. Text 17: tablet rev. 6; case obv. 16.

a-sa-la-x
NI. 1745. Witness. Text 38: rev. 4.

a-si-rum
NI. 1743. Lives in a-píl-^{d}amurru's house. Gives grain to ^{d}amurru-še-mi so that he can buy a-píl-^{d}amurru's house. Text 25: obv. 12.

at-ta-tum
fa. ^{d}sìn-i-din-nam. 1762. Text 65: rev. 3.

a-wi-a-nu-um
fa. ilum-réʾûm. 1923–1896. Text 35: rev. 6.

a-wi-ia
fa. ha-ṣí-rum. 1769. Text 11: rev. 8.

a-wi-ia-tum
fa. a-píl-^{d}amurru. 1743. Text 25: seal.
fa. KA-^{d}nin-urta. 1727. Text 83: seal.
^{lú}ŠIM ^{d}en-líl-lá.
1737. Witness. BE 6/2 42: 17; BE 6/2 43: 32.
1728. Witness. BE 6/2 57: 25.

a-wi-il-[ ]
fa. im-gu-ia-tum. n.d. OIMA 1 48: 7.

a-wi-il-ì-lí
fa. ŠU.BA.AN.DINGIR, fa.fa. a-ḫu-wa-qar. 1750. Text 22: seal.

a-wi-il-ištar
dub-sar (scribe).
1743. Witness. Text 13: rev. 5′.

a-wi-i[l-s]in
fa. ba-li-lum. 1793. Text 48: obv. 2.

a-wi-ìl-tum
so. a-bu-ra-an.
1895–1874. Witness. Text 94: rev. 7.

a-wi-li-ia (a-wi-il-ia, awīli^{lí}-ia)
so. i-[ ]-lum.
1772. Witness. Text 53: rev. 12.
bur-gul (seal-cutter), so. ur-^{d}ba-ú.
1773. Witness. PBS 8/2 116: 32.
1760. Witness. BE 6/2 10: 48; PBS 13 67: rev. 7.
1755. Witness. *ARN* 70: rev. 11.
1752. Witness. *ARN* 72: tablet rev. 5′; [case rev. 9].
1746. Witness. *ARN* 78: rev. 8; BE 6/2 23: 34; BE 6/2 24: 36.
1745. Witness. OIMA 1 13 + Ni 9244 + N 968: 29; PBS 8/2 129: 37.
1744. Witness. Cornell 4: rev. 17′.
1743. Witness. Text 13: rev. 4′.
1742. Witness. Text 42: rev. 15; Cornell 18: 20.
1741. Witness. OECT 8 19: 25.

1740. Witness. Text 31: rev. 15. Text 71: tablet rev. 8; case rev. 6′. Text 72: tablet rev. 9; case rev. 10. Cornell 21: 21. OECT 8 11: 26. OECT 8 16: 21.
1739. Witness. Text 74: tablet rev. 12; case rev. 14′. *ARN* 92: rev. 6. *ARN* 95: rev. 6. *ARN* 97: rev. 8. BE 6/2 32: 30. BE 6/2 33: 21. BE 6/2 34: 20. Cornell 12: 27.
1738. Witness. Text 43: rev. 7. Text 78: tablet rev. 7′; case rev. 9. Text 79: tablet rev. 10; case rev. 10′. BE 6/2 38: 22. OECT 8 1: 21. OECT 8 5: 23. OIMA 1 21: 20. OIMA 1 22: 18. PBS 8/2 135: tablet 22; case 5. TIM 4 25: 20. TIM 4 54: 19. Toledo: 17.
1737. Witness. BE 6/2 40: 30; BE 6/2 41: 21; BE 6/2 43: 35.
1736. Witness. BE 6/2 44: 27.
1734. Witness. Text 15: rev. 17; Text 44: tablet rev. 11′, case rev. 12′.
1733. Witness. Text 45: tablet rev. 8; Text 46: tablet rev. 9; case rev. 9.
1732. Witness. BE 6/2 48: 43.
1727. Witness. Text 83: tablet rev. 10.
1726. Witness. PBS 13 66: rev. 3′.
1725. Witness. OIMA 1 28: 39.
1724. Witness. *ARN* 103: VI 26.
1723. Witness. PBS 8/2 146: 45.
1722. Witness. PBS 8/1 91: 22; PBS 8/2 138: 22.
1721. Witness. Text 12: rev. 7; BE 6/2 68: 26.
1749–1721. Witness. *ARN* 110: rev. 7′; Cornell 6: IV 12.
n.d. Witness. Text 87: rev. 10′; Text 88: rev. 6′; Text 89: tablet rev. 10; OIMA 1 67: 4′.

fa. é-a-ba-ni. 1769. Text 11: rev. 7.

u g u l a é - s i k i l.

n.d. Witness. Text 40: rev. 12.

B

ba-al-ṭù-ka

agrig.

1762. Borrows silver from é-šu-me-ša$_4$-ga-mil. Text 65: obv. 4.

ba-ḫur-tu-um

NI. 1867. Neighbor of ^{d}da-mu-a-zu. PBS 8/2 169: III 11 (joins *ARN* 23).

ba-li-lum

so. a-wi-i[l-s]in.

1793. Receives silver from BI-KU$^{?}$-[ ]. Text 48: obv. 2.

BAR/MAŠ-ku-ta(?)

fa. i-pí-iq-é-a. 1793. Text 1: tablet rev. 15.

ba-zi-ia

fa.br. ì-lí-i-din-nam. 1743. Text 25: obv. 7.

be-el-šu-nu

so. a-gu-ú-a.

1762. Witness. Text 58: 3′.
1755. Witness. *ARN* 70: rev. 9.
1751. Witness. OIMA 1 12 + N1176 + N1094: 20.

be-el-ta-ni

l u k u r - ^{d}n i n - u r t a (*nadītum*), da. ^{d}en-líl-na-da.

1745. She lends grain to ^{d}amurru-še-mi. Text 23: obv. 2.

l u k u r - ^{d}n i n - u r t a (*nadītum*), da. pa-ni-ra-bi.

1743. She gives grain to ^{d}amurru-še-mi for him to buy a house. Text 25: obv. 1.

be-la-nu-um (bé-la-nu-um)
so. a-píl-ša.
1750. Witness. Text 22: rev. 15, seal.
1743. Witness. Text 25: rev. 13, seal.
so. ra$^{?}$-an-ḫu-um.
n.d. Witness. Text 19: rev. 13.
fa. ú-ba-a-a-tum. 1739. OIMA 1 19: 4, 5, 13, seal.
dub-sar (scribe).
1764. Witness. Text 20: tablet rev. 9; case rev. 13.
NI. 1743. Witness. Text 26: rev. 7.

ba-lí-da-a-a-an
so. ḫu-nu-bu-um.
n.d. Witness. *ARN* 22: rev. 4.

be-lí-ga-si-it
NI. n.d. Neighbor. OIMA 1 52: II 7′ (joins *ARN* 20).

be-lum
fa. mu-na-wi-rum. 1721. Text 12: rev. 5.

be-lum-mu-uš-ta-al
NI. 1800. He borrows grain from dingir-ma-an-sum. Text 8: obv. 3.

be-lu-ú
NI. 1755. Witness. Text 57: rev. 2.

bi-ga-ma$^{?}$-tum
NI. n.d. Property that he had inherited is now inherited by one of the sons of ^{d}nin-líl-zi-mu. OIMA 1 52: II 5′ (joins *ARN* 20).

BI.[ ].DINGIR
fa. ta-na-nu-um. Text 22: seal.

bi-ia-tum
da. še-ga-^{d}NIN-[ ].
n.d. Text 41: rev. 5.

BI-KU$^{?}$-[ ]
NI. 1793. Gives grain to ba-li-lum, ^{d}šákkan-kur-ra and ur-da-tum. Text 48: rev. 1.

bi-tu-ú-a-a
fa. ib-ni-ia. 1833–1831. Text 37: rev. 1.

bu-la-lum
so. la-ma-ša, br. ^{d}nuska-ma-lik, a-ḫu-wa-qar, warad-ì-lí-šu, e-la-lí and warad-^{d}amurru.
1833–1831. With his brothers he sells a house plot to ib-ni-ia. Text 37: obv. 6, 9.
fa. ur-^{d}[ ]. 1808. Text 63: rev. 4′.

bur-^{d}ma-ma
fa. i-da-tum.
1723. Text 14: rev. 2.
1749–1721. PBS 8/2 155: 11.

bu-sa-nu-um
fa. warad-^{d}sìn. 1789. *ARN* 31: rev. 8′.

D

da-an-gá-ta
fa. šeš-dùg-ga. 1895–1874. Text 94: obv. 6.

da-an-na-am-i-šu
NI. 1743. With a-píl-^{d}adad he sells a house plot to na-bi-^{d}en-líl and e-ku-ri-tum. Text 54: obv. 7, 9.

da-da-kal-la
fa. i-bi-^{d}en-líl.
1755. *ARN* 70: rev. 8.
1739. Text 34: obv. 10.

da-du-um
NI. 1737. Father of the neighbors of ^{d}sìn-iš-me-a-ni. BE 6/2 43: 9.

da-ga-a-a-tum
NI. 1739. Witness. Text 59: rev. 1.

da-ga$^{?}$-a$^{?}$-ni
NI. n.d. Witness. Text 41: rev. 3.

^{d}da-gán-ma-an-sum
BA$^{?}$-ZA$^{?}$.
n.d. Neighbor. Text 10: 7.

da-gi$_4$-x
br(?). im-gur-^{d}s[ì]n.
n.d. Inherits(?). Text 6: seal.

da-ma-gu-gu
fa. ^{d}adad-ra-bi, fa.fa. ma-ri-er-ṣe-tim and mu-tum-ilum.
1816–1794. PBS 8/1 18: 21.
1755. BE 6/2 14: 5.
1739. BE 6/2 30: 15.

da-mi-iq-ì-lí-šu (dam-qí-ì-lí-šu)
so. ^{d}nin-urta-ma-an-sum.
1738. Witness. Text 77: rev. 4′.
so. ip-qú-ša.
1793. He marries SAL-kal-la and adopts her children nu-úr-kab-ta, ì-lí-tu-ra-am, and a-lí-a-bu-ša. Text 1: tablet obv. 2, 7, 10, 17, seal.
so. ^{d}sìn-e-ri-ba-am.
n.d. He sells a temple office. Text 68: no longer preserved.
fa. é-a-i-din-nam. 1755. BE 6/2 14: 21, edge.
fa. ^{d}en-líl-gal-zu.
1739. BE 6/2 30: 8.
1738. BE 6/2 38: 3.
fa. ^{d}nanna-zi-mu. 1762. PBS 8/1 82: 17.
fa. šu-mu-um-li-ib-ši. 1739. OIMA 1 19: 21; N1119: 3.
hu. a-lu-ut-ta-ḫi
1738. With his wife he sells a temple office to a-at-ta-a. Text 79: tablet obv. 6, 15; case obv. 5′, 7′, seal.
hu. na-ru-ub-tum, fa. a-píl-ilim.
1758. With his wife he exchanges house plots with na-bi-^{d}šamaš. BE 6/2 11: 4, 12, 18, 25, seal.

dub-sar (scribe).
n.d. Witness. *ARN* 176: rev. 8′.
NI. 1764. Witness. Text 20: tablet rev. 4; case rev. 8, edge; Text 21; rev. 5.
NI. n.d. One of the coheirs of i-din-^{d}da-mu. *ARN* 142: seal.
NI. n.d. Witness. Text 68: tablet rev. 9′; case 11′.

dam-qum (see da-mi-iq-ì-lí-šu)
fa. ^{d}sìn-i-din-nam. 1743. Text 25: obv. 9.

^{d}da-mu-[ ]
fa. e-te-ia-tum. 1726. Text 84: rev. 7′.

^{d}da-mu-a-zu
so. a-ab-ba-kal-la, br. ^{d}en-líl-maš-zu and lú-^{d}nin-urta.
1867. With his brothers he inherits from his father. PBS 8/2 169: I 2, III 15, IV 10, seal + *ARN* 23: III 11′, 13′.
1860–1837. He and ^{d}en-líl-maš-zu divide an inheritance. YOS 14 321: obv. II 17, rev. I 1′.
1860–1837. Witness. TIM 4 27: 21.
fa. ^{d}nin-líl-zi-mu and lú-šag$_5$-ga(?).
1816–1794. PBS 8/1 18: 7, seal.
n.d. *ARN* 22: obv. 4, rev. 7, seal; OIMA 1 48: 6.

^{d}da-mu-DU-[ ]
NI. 1734. Witness. Text 15: rev. 14.

^{d}da-mu-e-ri-ba-am
so. ri-[ ].
1747. Witness. Text 70: [tablet rev. 11]; case rev. 6′.
NI. 1736. With ^{d}nin-urta-mu-ba-lí-iṭ he does something with im-gur-^{d}nin-urta's property. Text 82: seal.
NI. 1736. Witness. Text 81: tablet rev. 7; case rev. 9.

^{d}da-mu-ga-[ ]
NI. 1734. Witness. Text 15: rev. 13.

^{d}da-mu-gal-zu (^{d}da-mu-ia)
so. ḫu-pa-tum.
1744. Witness. Text 60: rev. 7.
1742. Witness. Text 42: rev. 9.
1737. Witness. PBS 8/2 133: 31.
fa. ^{d}šamaš-mu-ba-lí-iṭ. 1740. Text 72: tablet obv. 7; case obv. 8.

^{d}da-mu-i-din-nam
so. a-ba-^{d}nanna-gin$_7$.
n.d. With [ ]-i-bi-[ ] he exchanges temple offices with ^{d}en-líl-ni-šu and a-lí-ia-tum(?). Text 86: tablet obv. 2′, seal.
n.d. He sells a temple office to a-at-ta-a. Text 88: obv. 5, 7, seal.
dub-sar (scribe).
1762. Witness. *ARN* 65: rev. 19.
1760. Witness. BE 6/2 10: 47.
1755. Witness. BE 6/2 14: 32.
^{lú}ŠIM ^{d}en-líl-lá (^{lú}kaš-tin-na). so. ^{d}en-líl-dingir, br. i-na-é-kur-ra-bi.
1739. Witness. Text 34: rev. 4.
1739. He buys a temple office from ú-ba-a-a-tum. OIMA 1 19: 6.

1738. He buys a field plot from his brother. OIMA 1 22: 7.
1738. He buys a field plot from u_4-ta-u_{18}-lu-me-ša_4. OIMA 1 23: obv. 8.
1737. Witness. BE 6/2 43: 33.
n.d. He redeems a field plot from ni-in-nu-tum and nu-úr-dšamaš. OIMA 1 48: 12.
NI. 1762. Witness. Text 58: 6′.

dda-mu-ma-an-sum
gudu4 dnin-líl-lá.
1745. Witness. OIMA 1 13: 20 (duplicate PBS 8/2 154, q.v. Ni 9244, case).

dda-mu-ú-a
so. den-líl-ma-an-sum.
1738. Witness. Text 77: rev. 5′.
fa. den-líl-NI-[ ]. 1738. Text 80: case 4′.

DINGIR-[ ]
NI. 1743. Witness. Text 49: rev. 1.

dingir-da-nu-me-a
fa. im-gur-dsìn. n.d. PBS 8/1 92: 19.

dingir-kù-ta
so. nam-maḫ-abzu.
n.d. Witness. PBS 8/1 92: 21.
fa. SAL-kal-la, mo.fa. nu-úr-kab-ta, ì-lí-tu-ra-am, and a-lí-a-bu-ša.
1793. Text 1: tablet obv. 1, seal.

dingir-lú-ti
descendant of im-ši-ŠI.
1745. His heirs and the heirs of dnin-líl-zi-mu, den-líl-za-me-en, and dnin-urta-ma-an-sum divide a plot of unimproved property (kislaḫ). OIMA 1 13: 14. PBS 8/2 154: seal (q.v. Ni 9244, case).

dingir-ma-an-sum
so. dnanna-an-dùl.
n.d. Witness. Text 24: rev. 6.
so. dsìn-na-ṣi-ir, br. ilum-īriš(APIN).
1767. With his brother he inherits from his father. *ARN* 46: obv. 13, 16, seal.
fa. li-pí-it-ištar.
1738. Text 78: tablet obv. 5, 12; case obv. 5, 12, seal.
n.d. Text 87: obv. 4′, seal.
fa. na-bi-den-líl.
1740. Text 31: rev. 10.
1738. Text 43: rev. 4.
fa. dnanna-ma-an-sum.
1739. BE 6/2 30: 6.
1734. Text 44: tablet rev. 7′; case rev. 7′.
gudu4 dnin-líl-lá.
1745. OIMA 1 13: 21; PBS 8/2 129: 34 (q.v. Ni 9244, case).
lúŠIM dnin-líl-lá, so. i-lu-ni.
1739. Witness. Text 34: obv. 7; Text 75: tablet rev. 9.
1737. Witness. BE 6/2 40: 22.

ugula dag-gi4-a.
n.d. Role unclear. Text 40: obv. 1.

NI. 1801. He lends grain to be-lum-mu-uš-ta-al. Text 8: obv. 2.
NI. 1745. Witness. Text 38: rev. 1.
NI. 1749–1721. Witness. Text 30: rev. 11.

dingir-mu-silim
fa. ^{d}nin-urta-ga-mil. 1739. Text 73: tablet rev. 4.

dingir-ra-[ ]
so. ur-[ ].
1755. Witness. Text 56: 4.

du-ga-a-a
fa. ip-qú-^{d}da-mu. 1767. *ARN* 46: obv. 11.

dug$_4$-ga-dùg-ga
dub-sar (scribe).
1873–1869. Witness. Text 36: rev. 7.

DÙL-$^{!}$a-GU
fa. i-din-^{d}en-líl. 1739. Text 34: obv. 11.

du-qá-qum
fa. ur-du$_6$-kù-ga. 1772. Text 53: seal.

E

é-a$^{?}$-[ ]
fa. arad-^{d}nanna. 1867. *ARN* 23: IV 2 (joins PBS 8/2 169).

é-a-ba-ni
so. awīli^{lí}-ia.
1769. Witness. Text 11: rev. 7.

é-a-i-din-nam
so. dam-qí-ì-lí-šu.
1755. Witness. BE 6/2 14: 21, edge.
so. ṣi-lí-^{d}šamaš.
1721. Witness. Text 12: rev. 4.

é-a-li-ri-im
so. a-[ ]
1734. Witness. Text 15: rev. 11.

é-a-na-ṣir
NI. 1750. Neighbor of wa-tar-pi-ša. Text 22: obv. 2.

é-a-ni
NI. 1786. With il-ta-ni, he sells a house plot to sà-ap-ḫu-um-li-ip-ḫu-ur. Text 18: obv. 6.

é-a-ta-a-a-ar
so. abzu-ḫé-gál.
1740. Witness. Text 31: rev. 12.
NI. n.d. He borrows silver from the god Šamaš. Text 39: obv. 4.

é-a-tu-ra-am
so. ip-qú-ša.
1742. He divides his father's estate with his adoptive brother é-a-ta-a-a-ar. BE 6/2 28: 8, 14, 15, 16, 23.
NI. n.d. Role unclear. Text 40: rev. 7.

e$^{?}$-ku-ia
fa. za-ri-qum. n.d. Text 19: rev. 14.

é-kur-an-dùl
so. i-din-^{d}da-mu.
1751. He exchanges house plots with i-din-^{d}nin-urta. OIMA 1 12: 4, 10, 15, seal.

e-ku-ri-tum
NI. 1743. With na-bi-^{d}en-líl he buys a house plot from a-píl-^{d}adad and da-an-na-am-i-šu. Text 54: obv. 11.

e-ku-ú-a
so. dam-qum, br. mu-na-wi-rum.
1739. He rents an orchard plot from a-wi-il-ištar and ilum-da-mi-iq. PBS 8/2 128: 8.
nu-èš, so. ^{d}nanna-zi-mu.
1720. He buys a house plot from ḫ̮i-du-tum and na-ra-am-tum. PBS 8/1 89: 6.

e-la-a
fa. ta-ri-ba-tum.
1736. Text 81: tablet obv. 5; case obv. 6, seal.
n.d. Text 89: tablet rev. 8.

e-la-lí(-im) (e-la-DINGIR, e-la-li)
so. ^{d}EN-[ ].
1762. Witness. Text 58: 4′.
so. la-ma-ša, br. ^{d}nuska-ma-lik, a-ḫ̮u-wa-qar, bu-la-lum, warad-ì-lí-šu, and warad-^{d}amurru.
1833–1831. With his brothers he sells a house plot to ib-ni-ia. Text 37: obv, 7, 10, seal.
fa. iz-kur-^{d}šamaš (iz-ku-rum).
1743. Text 25: rev. 2.
n.d. BE 6/2 66: 19.
gala.
1742. Witness. Text 50: rev. 3.

el-le-tum
so. ilum-na-ši.
1739. Witness. BE 6/2 30: 4.
fa. zalag-^{d}nanna-ni-ì-dùg. 1755. BE 6/2 14: 26.
gudu$_{4}$ ^{d}nin-líl-lá, so. lú-^{d}nin-urta.
1739. Witness. Text 74: tablet rev. 8.
1738. Witness. Text 77: rev. 6′.
1726. Witness. Text 84: rev. 1′.
1749–1721. Witness. Text 85: rev. 5′.

^{d}EN-[ ]
fa. e-la-lí. 1762. Text 58: 4′.
fa. nun-di. 1785. PBS 8/1 28: 2.
NI. 1751. He borrows grain from ^{d}nin-urta-[ ]. Text 61: obv. 4.

e-ne-ia
so. nam-maḫ̮-^{d}ba-ú.
1793. Witness. Text 1: tablet rev. 11.

^{d}en-líl-[ ]
so. ì-lí-i-[ ].
1738. Text 80: seal.

so. ur-du$_6$-kù-ga.
n.d. Witness. *ARN* 176: rev. 4′.
NI. 1762–1750. He lends grain to li-pí-it-[ ]. Text 93: obv. 3.

^{d}en-líl-a-bi
so. ^{d}nin-urta-a-bi.
1734. He is adopted by ip-qú-^{d}da-mu and divides property with ^{d}šamaš-še-mi. Text 15: obv. 1, 10, rev. 1, seal.
fa. li-pí-it-^{d}en-líl.
1739. Witness. Text 74: tablet rev. 9; case rev. 13′.

^{d}en-líl-á-maḫ
fa. šeš-kal-la. 1860–1837. Text 2: obv. 6.
fa. šeš-ma-kal. n.d. PBS 8/1 92: 16.

^{d}en-líl-be-el-ì-lí
NI. 1752. Neighbor of ^{d}sìn-ma-gir. Witness. BE 6/2 18: 2, 17.

^{d}en-líl-dingir
so. an-né-ba-ab-du$_7$.
1783. Witness. BE 6/2 6: 21.
1755. He exchanges field plots with i-din-^{d}nin-urta. *ARN* 70: obv. 7.
1754. Witness. BE 6/2 16: 11.
n.d. He redeems a field plot from ^{d}nanna-á-daḫ. *ARN* 176: obv. 12.
fa. ^{d}da-mu-i-din-nam and i-na-é-kur-ra-bi.
1739. OIMA 1 19: 7.
1738. OIMA 1 22: 5, seal; OIMA 1 23: obv. 9.
n.d. OIMA 1 48: 12.
^{d}en-líl-en-nam
so. ì-lí-i-din.
n.d. Witness. PBS 8/1 92: 24.

^{d}en-líl-gal-zu
so. da-mi-iq-ì-lí-šu (dam-qí-ì-lí-šu)
1739. Witness. BE 6/2 30: 8.
1738. Neighbor of lugal-ḫé-gál and ^{d}nin-urta-e-mu-qá-a. BE 6/2 38: 2.
so. ilum-na-ši, br. ^{d}en-líl-ma-an-sum, ṭāb-ba-la-ṭù, and ur-du$_6$-kù-ga.
1742. With his brothers he inherits from his father. Text 42: rev. 2, seal.
1740. Witness. Text 71: tablet rev. 5; case rev. 3′.
1733. He exchanges house plots with ip-qú-^{d}en-líl. Text 45: tablet obv. 2, 3, 13; case obv. 3, seal.
1733. Neighbor of ip-qú-^{d}en-líl. Text 46: tablet obv. 3; case obv. 2.
1732. Neighbor of ^{d}en-líl-ni-šu and e-tel-pi$_4$-ištar. Text 47: tablet obv. 2; case obv. 2.
nu-èš.
1742. Neighbor of ^{d}en-líl-ma-an-sum. Text 42: obv. 1.
NI. n.d. Neighbor. *ARN* 20: III 11′ (joins OIMA 1 52).

^{d}en-líl-gi-mi-il-la-a-ni
NI. 1762. Witness. Text 65: rev. 1.

^{d}en-líl-gú-gal
fa. ^{d}nanna-me-ša$_4$.
1810. PBS 8/1 12: 32.
1800. OIMA 1 7: 9.
n.d. PBS 8/1 92: 17.

^{d}en-líl-ḫé-gál (^{d}en-líl-ḫe-gal)
so. ^{d}EN-[ ].
n.d. Witness. PBS 8/2 168: 28.
fa. an-né-ba-ab-du$_{7}$. 1772. Text 53: obv. 17.
fa. ^{d}sìn-iš-me-[a-ni] and ^{d}sìn-e-ri-ba-a[m].
1789. His sons inherit from him. *ARN* 31: rev. 3′, seal.

^{d}en-líl-i-tu-ra-am
nu-èš.
1727. Witness. Text 83: tablet rev. 6; case 5′.

^{d}en-líl-is-sú
so. a-píl-^{d}adad, br. na-bi-^{d}en-líl.
1741. He rents an inherited field to mār-erṣetim. Text 29: obv. 5, 7.

^{d}en-líl-ki-sag-[ ]
fa. ip-qú-ša. 1793. Text 1: tablet rev. 8.

^{d}en-líl-lá-bí-dug$_{4}$
dub-sar (scribe).
1751. Witness. OIMA 1 12: 23.

^{d}en-líl-la-ma-sí
NI. 1739. Witness. Text 34: rev. 6.

^{d}en-líl-ma-an-sum
so. a-bi-ì-lí.
1789. Witness. *ARN* 31: rev. 10′.
so. ilum-na-ši, br. ṭāb-ba-la-ṭù, ur-du$_{6}$-kù-ga, and ^{d}en-líl-gal-zu.
1742. With his brothers he inherits from his father. Text 42: obv. 7, 8, seal.
so. lú-^{d}inanna.
n.d. Witness. *ARN* 22: rev. 8.
so. ^{d}nin-urta-ma-an-sum.
n.d. Witness. Text 68: case 9′.
fa. ^{d}sìn-iš-me-a-ni, br.(?) i-na-é-kur-ra-bi, fa.fa. igi-šag$_{5}$.
1737. BE 6/2 43: 17, lower edge, seal.
fa. ^{d}da-mu-ú-a. 1738. Text 77: rev. 5′.
gudu$_{4}$ ^{d}nin-líl-lá, so. lú-^{d}nin-urta.
1739. Witness. Text 74: case rev. 7′; Text 75: tablet rev. 6.
1738. Witness. OIMA 1 22: 15.
1737. Witness. BE 6/2 41: 17.
1732. Witness. Text 47: tablet rev. 4.
1724. Witness. BE 6/2 59: 14; OIMA 1 29: 19′.
^{lú}ŠIM.
1760. Witness. BE 6/2 10: 44.
NI. 1736. Witness. Text 82: rev. 3′.
NI. n.d. Witness. Text 87: rev. 8′; OIMA 1 58: 7.

^{d}en-líl-maš-zu
so. a-ab-ba-kal-la, br. ^{d}da-mu-a-zu and lú-^{d}nin-urta.
1867. With his brothers he inherits from his father. *ARN* 23: II 12 + PBS 8/2 169: IV 2, 15, seal.
1860–1837. He and ^{d}da-mu-a-zu divide an inheritance. YOS 14 321: obv. I 12, II 3.
so. lú-^{d}inan[na].

1867. Witness. *ARN* 23: IV 6′ (joins PBS 8/2 169).
fa. an-né-ba-ab-du$_7$.
1816–1794. PBS 8/1 18: 19.
n.d. *ARN* 22: rev. 3.
NI. 1816–1794. Neighbor of ^{d}nin-líl-zi-mu. PBS 8/1 18: 2.
NI. n.d. Hires workers. Text 5: rev. 2.

^{d}en-líl-me-ša$_4$
fa. puzur$_4$-^{d}amurru. 1895–1874. Text 16: rev. 3.

^{d}en-líl-mu-ba-lí-iṭ
so. i-din-^{d}[ ].
1740. Witness. Text 72: tablet rev. 7; case rev. 7.
dub-sar (scribe).
1738. Witness. Text 77: rev. 10′(?).
1738. Witness. Text 78: tablet rev. 8′; case 10. Text 79: tablet rev. 11; case rev. 11′. OIMA 1 23: rev. 3′.
1736. Witness. Text 81: tablet rev. 10; case rev. 11.
1727. Witness. BE 6/2 58: 23.
1726. Witness. PBS 13 66: rev. 3′.
1725. Witness. OIMA 1 28: 40 (case is ARN 102).
1723. Witness. Text 14: rev. 3; PBS 8/2 127: 13.
1722. Witness. PBS 13 19: rev. 2.
Witness. BE 6/2 64: 25.
1749–1721. Witness. Text 85: rev. 8′.
n.d. Witness. Text 87: rev. 9′; Text 88: rev. 7′.

^{d}en-líl-mu-da-mi-iq
so. ri-im-ištar.
1733. Witness. BE 6/2 47: 17.
1727. Witness. Text 83: tablet rev. 8; case 8′. BE 6/2 58. 18.
1726. Witness. Text 84: rev. 4′.
1749–1721. Witness. OIMA 1 29: 22′.
NI. 1732. Witness. Text 47: tablet rev. 6.

^{d}en-líl-na-da
so. na-ra-am-^{d}sìn, br. a-at-ta-a, ip-qú-^{d}da-mu, ip-qú-er-ṣe-tim, and im-gur-^{d}nin-urta (im-gu-tum).
1746. Witness. BE 6/2 22: 11, seal.
1739. Witness. Text 75: tablet rev. 8.
fa. be-el-ta-ni. 1745. Text 23: obv. 3.
lú-gurušda.
1746. Witness. BE 6/2 24: 31.
1744. Witness. *ARN* 81: rev. 1.

^{d}en-líl-na-ṣi-ir
fa. ^{d}sìn-ma-gir.
1727. Text 83: tablet obv. 11.
1726. Text 84: obv. 5, 6, 11, seal.

^{d}en-líl-na-ši
so. ilum-e-te-lum.
1793. Witness. Text 1: tablet rev. 7.

^{d}en-líl-NI-[ ]

so. ^{d}da-mu-ú-a.

1738. He sells a temple office for redemption to a-at-ta-a. Text 80: case 3′, 5′, 10′.

^{d}en-líl-ni-šu

so. ì-lí-i-din-nam and a-lí-ia-tum.

n.d. With his mother(?) he exchanges temple offices with [ ]-i-bi-[ ] and ^{d}da-mu-i-din-nam. Text 86: seal.

so. im-gur-^{d}nin-urta, br. e-tel-pi$_{4}$-ištar.

1734. With his brother he buys a house plot from ip-qú-^{d}en-líl. Text 44: tablet obv. 6, case obv. 5′.

1733. With his brother he is a neighbor of ip-qú-^{d}en-líl. Text 45: tablet obv. 6.

1733. With his brother he buys a house plot from ip-qú-^{d}en-líl. Text 46: tablet obv. 8; case obv. 6.

1732. He buys his brother's share of a house plot from him. Text 47: tablet obv. 4, 7.

so. na-bi-^{d}en-líl, br. nu-úr-ištar.

1740. With his brother he inherits from his father. Text 31: rev. 2, seal.

so. ^{d}sìn-ga-mil

1738. Witness. OIMA 1 22: 16.

hu. a-ḫa-tum.

1749–1721. With his wife he adopts ^{d}nin-urta-a-bi. Text 30. obv. 3′, 9′.

NI. n.d. Witness. Text 51: tablet rev. 6.

^{d}en-líl-za-me-en

so. lú-ga-tum.

1734. Witness. Text 15: rev. 8.

NI. 1744. His heirs inherit. OIMA 1 13: 8, 10, seal; PBS 8/2 154: seal; Ni 9244: seal.

^{d}en-nu-gi$_{4}$-ga-mil

so. a-ḫu-šu-nu, br. ^{d}sìn-im-gur-ra-an-ni and ta-ri-ba-tum.

1739. Witness. Text 73: tablet rev. 9.

e-ri-iš-tum

NI. 1726. She is the mother(?) of the original owner of a temple office which is now redeemed by a-at-ta-a. Text 84: obv. 4.

é-šar-ga-mil

so. wa-ra-sú-nu, br. nu-rum-li-ṣi, ku-um-bu-lum, and ^{d}sìn-iš-me-a-ni.

1755. Witness. BE 6/2 14: 30.

e-šu-me-ša$_{4}$-ga-mil

NI. 1762. He lends silver to ba-al-ṭù-ka. Text 65: obv. 3.

e-te-ia

fa. ^{d}sìn-a-ḫi-i-din-nam. 1747. Text 69: tablet rev. 5.

e-te-ia-tum

so. ^{d}da-mu-[ ].

1726. Witness. Text 84: rev. 7′.

e-te-el-ḪÉ$^{?}$-TI$^{?}$

dub-sar (scribe).

1762. Witness. Text 65: rev. 4.

e-te-el-pi$_{4}$-^{d}en-líl

NI. 1755. He borrows silver from li-pí-it-ištar. Text 57: obv. 4.

e-tel-pi$_4$-ištar (e-te-el-pi$_4$-ištar, e-te-er$^!$-pi$_4$-ištar)

so. im-gur-^{d}nin-urta, br. ^{d}en-líl-ni-šu.

1734. With his brother he buys a house plot from ip-qú-^{d}en-líl. Text 44: tablet obv. 6; case obv. 6′.

1733. With his brother he is a neighbor of ip-qú-^{d}en-líl. Text 45: tablet obv. 7.

1733. With his brother he buys a house plot from ip-qú-^{d}en-líl. Text 46: tablet obv. 8; case obv. 7.

1732. He sells his share of a house to his brother. Text 47: tablet obv. 4, 6, 8, 10; case obv. 4′, 8′, 10′.

NI. n.d. He rents a field from ip-pa-tum. Text 51: tablet obv. 5.

e-tel-pi$_4$-^{d}nin-urta

so. ^{d}nanna-ma-an-sum.

1741. Witness. *ARN* 125: rev. 1.

e-tel-pi$_4$-^{d}nuska

fa. ḫu-na-ba-tum and an-nu-um-pi$_4$-ištar. 1727. Text 83: tablet obv. 5.

G

ga-mi-lum

NI. n.d. Text 24: rev. 11.

geme$_2$-^{d}nuska

da. ^{d}sìn-ma-gir.

1762. Role unclear. Text 58: seal.

gi-mil-ì-lí

NI. 1764. Neighbor of ^{d}amurru-še-mi. Text 21: obv. 2.

gìr-ni-ì-sá (gìr-ni-ì-šag$_5$)

so. lú-sig$_5$.

1746. Witness. BE 6/2 21: 9.

so. ^{d}nanna-ma-an-sum.

1775. Witness. Text 17: tablet rev. 12.

fa. ^{d}sìn-i-din-nam. 1772. Text 53: rev. 6.

fa. ^{d}sìn-li-di-iš. 1833–1831. Text 37: rev. 12.

fa. šu-mi-a-ḫi-ia. 1750. Text 27: rev. 3.

gub-ba-ni-dùg

NI. 1867. Neighbor of ^{d}da-mu-a-zu. PBS 8/2 169: II 6, III 12 (joins *ARN* 23).

gud-ku-ta

da. ^{d}nanna-ma-an-sum.

1843. She lends silver to šeš-al-dùg. Text 3: obv. 4.

H

ḫa-an-da-at-ru-um

NI. 1789. Neighbor of ^{d}sìn-iš-me-[a-ni]. *ARN* 31: obv. 7.

ḫa-ba-na-tum (ḫa-ba-an-na-tum)

lukur-^{d}nin-urta (*nadītum*).

n.d. Her inheritance is sold by da-mi-iq-ì-lí-šu(?). Text 68: tablet obv. 4′(?), 11′, seal.

ḫa-bil-ki-nu-um

so. a-ḫi-ia.

1739. Witness. Text 73: tablet rev. 8.

ḫa-DU-NI?-IM?
NI. 1872. Neighbor of šu-na-a-a. Text 66: obv. 2.

ḪAR-^{d}EN-[ ]
NI. n.d. Father of a neighbor of ma-ri-er-ṣe-tim and ša-ga-bu-um. Text 64: 6

ḫa-ṣí-rum
so. a-wi-ia.
1769. Witness. Text 11: rev. 8.

ḫé-a-[ ]
NI. n.d. Witness. OIMA 1 56: 10′.

ḫi-ba-ab-tum
nu-èš, fa. ḫi!-du-tum. 1745. Text 23: rev. 2.

ḫi!-du-tum
lukur ^{d}nin-urta (*nadītum*), da. ḫi-ba-ab-tum.
1745. Witness. Text 23: rev. 1.

ḪI.TAR-^{d}iškur(?)
so. u-bar-[ ].
1736. Neighbor of im-gur-^{d}nin-urta. Text 82: obv. 6.
bur-gul (seal-cutter).
1758. Witness. BE 6/2 11: 27.
1739. Witness. *ARN* 86: rev. 8′; OECT 8 6: 20.
1738. Witness. Cornell 7: 21; OECT 8 2: 23; OECT 8 9: 22; OECT 8 10: 25; OIMA 1 23: rev. 4′.
1737. Witness. OECT 8 7: 26; PBS 8/2 153: 24.

ḫu-[ ]
fa. ^{d}nin-urta-ni-šu. 1744. Text 60: rev. 8.

ḫu-ba-bu-um
NI. 1867. Land that he had once bought is now inherited by ^{d}da-mu-a-zu and lú-^{d}nin-urta. PBS 8/2 169 II 8 + *ARN* 23: III 4′.

ḫu-mu-rum (ḫu-mu-ru-um)
fa. ^{d}adad-ta-a-a-ar.
1739. Text 73: tablet obv. 10.
1737. OECT 8 7: 24.

ḫu-na-ba-tum
da. e-te-el-pi$_4$-^{d}nuska, si. a-nu-um-pi$_4$-ištar.
1727. With her sister and KA-^{d}nin-urta she sells a temple office to ^{d}sìn-ma-gir. Text 83: tablet obv. 4, 7.

ḫu-nu-bu-um
fa. be-lí-da-a-a-an. n.d. *ARN* 22: rev. 4.

ḫu-pa-tum
fa. ^{d}da-mu-gal-zu (=^{d}da-mu-ia)
1744. Text 60: rev. 7.
1742. Text 42: rev. 9.
1737. PBS 8/2 133: 31.
fa. ^{d}sìn-īris (APIN). 1760. BE 6/2 10: 42.

I

i-[ ]-lum
fa. a-wi-li-ia. 1772. Text 53: rev. 12.
ib-ba-tum
NI. 1743. Witness. Text 54: rev. 6.

i-bi-^{d}[ ]
NI. n.d. Witness. Text 68: case 1′.

i-bi-^{d}en-líl (=ib-ni-^{d}en-líl?)
so. a-ḫi$^{?}$-^{d}da-mu.
1739. Witness. Text 34: obv. 12.
so. da-da-kal-la.
1755. Witness. *ARN* 70: rev. 8.
1739. Witness. Text 34: obv. 10.
so. ^{d}sìn-[ ].
n.d. Witness. *ARN* 176: rev. 6′.
fa. ì-lí-i-din-nam.
1739. Text 75: tablet obv. 4, 5, 11, seal.
1738. OECT 8 2: 22.
^{lú}ŠIM ^{d}en-líl-lá.
1739. Witness. OIMA 1 19: 19.
1737. Witness. BE 6/2 43: 34.

i-bi-ia
fa. ma-áš-qum. n.d. PBS 8/1 92: 4, 5, 13, seal.
fa. šeš-al-dùg. 1843. Text 3: obv. 7, seal.
fa. zi-na-tum. 1793. Text 48: rev. 5.

i-bi-^{d}nin-šubur
fa. ma-ri-er-ṣe-tim.
1742. Text 42: rev. 11.
n.d. PBS 8/2 176: 17.
bur-gul (seal-cutter).
1744. Witness. Text 60: rev. 10.

i-bi-^{d}nin-urta
fa. ma-ri-er-ṣe-tim. 1769. Text 11: rev. 6.

i-bi-^{d}sìn
fa. a-ap-pa-a-a.
1739. Text 74: tablet rev. 7; case rev. 9′.
1738. Text 78: tablet rev. 5′; case rev. 7.

ib-ni-é-a
so. zi-ia-tum, hu. a-bi-ik-ku-ú-a, fa. ì-lí-ma-lu-lim.
1739. Text 74: tablet obv. 6; case obv. 4, 7, seal.

ib-ni-^{d}en-líl
dub-sar (scribe).
1737. Witness. BE 6/2 43: 36.
1736. Witness. BE 6/2 44: 28.
1722. Witness. BE 6/2 61: 10.
1721. Witness. Text 12: rev. 6; BE 6/2 68: 27.

ib-ni-ia
so. bi-tu-ú-a-a.
1833–1831. He buys a house plot from ^{d}nuska-ma-lik, a-ḫu-wa-qar, e-la-lí, warad-^{d}amurru, bu-la-lum, and warad-ì-lí-šu. Text 37: obv. 3, rev. 1.
so. KA-^{d}nin-urta.
1843. Witness. Text 3: rev. 5.

i-da-tum
so. bur-^{d}-ma-ma.
1723. Witness. Text 14: rev. 1.
1749–1721. Neighbor of ìl-šu-ba-ni. PBS 8/2 155: 11.

i-di-ia-tum
so. lú-^{d}nin-urta.
1738. Witness. Text 43: rev. 5.

i-din-[ ]
fa. i-din-^{d}i-šum. 1923–1896. Text 35: rev. 5.

i-din-^{d}[ ]
fa. ^{d}en-líl-mu-ba-lí-iṭ. 1740. Text 72: tablet rev. 7; case rev. 8.
fa. ma-an-nu-um-ki-ma-é-a. 1740. Text 31: rev. 14.

i-din-^{d}adad
so. lú-[ ].
1923–1896. Witness. Text 35: rev. 3.

i-din-^{d}da-mu
so. ^{d}nin-urta-zi-mu.
n.d. With da-mi-iq-ì-lí-šu and others(?) he inherits from his father. *ARN* 142: 4′$^{?}$, 7′$^{?}$, seal.
fa. é-kur-an-dùl. 1751. OIMA 1 12: 4, seal.

i-din-^{d}en-líl
so. DÙL-la-GU.
1739. Witness. Text 34: obv. 11.
fa. ṣi-lí-ištar. 1923–1896. Text 35: rev. 7.
nu-èš, so. na-<bi>-^{d}en-líl.
1755. Witness. *ARN* 70: rev. 7.
nu-èš, so. ^{d}sìn-e-ri-ba-am.
1760. Witness. BE 6/2 10: 40.
1743. Witness. PBS 8/2 147: tablet 9; case 8.
1738. Witness. BE 6/2 39: tablet 20.
1731. Witness. BE 6/2 49: 43.
nu-èš.
n.d. Witness. Text 33: rev. 1.

i-din-ia-tum
so. ^{d}nanna-zi-mu, br. a-ḫi-ša-<gi$_{4}$>iš.
1758. Witness. BE 6/2 11: 24.

i-din-ištar
so. ì-lí-[ ].
n.d. He sells a temple office to a-at-ta-a. Text 91: obv. 4′, 5′, 10′.

i-din-^{d}i-šum

so. i-din-[ ].

1923–1896. Witness. Text 35: rev. 5.

bur-gul (seal-cutter).

1783. Witness. BE 6/2 6: 24.

1769. Witness. Text 11: rev. 11.

1768. Witness. *ARN* 44: rev. 24.

1767. Witness. *ARN* 45: rev. 17.

1762. Witness. Text 58: 7′.

i-din-^{d}nin-šubur

so. ^{d}sìn-ma-gir.

1772. Witness. Text 53: rev. 1.

i-din-^{d}nin-urta

so. ì-lí-ia-a-tum.

1740. Neighbor of nu-úr-ištar and ^{d}en-líl-ni-šu. Text 31: obv. 4, 17.

fa. na-bi-^{d}en-líl. 1727. Text 83: tablet rev. 9.

nu-èš, so. ^{d}sìn-ma-gir.

1755. He exchanges field plots with ^{d}en-líl-dingir. *ARN* 70: obv. 5, 6, 14, rev. 4, seal.

1751. He exchanges house plots with é-kur-an-dùl. OIMA 1 12: 3, 8, 9, 14, seal.

i-din-^{d}nuska$^{?}$

fa. ì-lí-di-e-ki. 1743. Text 25: seal.

i-din-^{d}sìn

so. ki-ág-ga, br. lugal-á-zi-da.

1873–1869. Witness. Text 36: rev. 5.

so. ^{d}sìn-i-din-nam.

1751. Witness. OIMA 1 12: 21.

1744. Witness. OIMA 1 14: 15.

i-di-šum

bur-gul (seal-cutter).

1749. Witness. TIM 4 24: 18.

1747. Witness. Text 69: tablet rev. 8.

1744. Witness. PBS 8/2 132: 18.

1739. Witness. Text 73: tablet rev. 11; case rev. 2′.

1738. Witness. BE 6/2 39: tablet 24.

1737. Witness. OECT 8 8: 21; PBS 8/2 133: 33.

1736. Witness. Text 81: tablet rev. 9; case 10; Text 82: rev. 7′.

1724. Witness. BE 6/2 59: tablet 18; TIM 4 19:12.

igi-^{d}nanna-šè-al-gub

NI. 1762. Witness. PBS 8/1 81: 10; PBS 8/1 82: 25.

igi-šag$_{5}$

so. i-na-é-kur-ra-bi, fa.br.so.(?) ^{d}sìn-iš-me-a-ni.

1737. He divided his grandfather's(?) estate with his cousin. BE 6/2 43: 6, 7, 14, seal.

ig-mil-^{d}sìn

so. ip-qú-er-ṣe-tim.

1740. He sells a temple office to ^{d}šamaš-mu-ba-lí-iṭ. Text 72: tablet obv. 4, 5, 12; case obv. 4, 6, seal.

NI. n.d. Witness. Text 68: tablet rev. 8′; case 8′.

ì-lí-[ ]
so. šu-[ ].
1800. Witness. Text 8: rev. 1.
fa. i-din-ištar. n.d. Text 91: obv. 5′.
fa. [ ]-ba-a-a-ba. n.d. Text 55: obv. 3.
NI. 1755. Witness. Text 56: 6.
NI. 1743. Witness. Text 49: rev. 2.

ì-lí-a-wi-li
so. [lu]gal-ní-te-ni.
1741. Witness. *ARN* 125: rev. 3.

ì-lí-di-e-ki
ra-bi-a-nu (mayor), so. i-din-^{d}nuska$^{?}$.
1743. Witness. Text 25: rev. 11, seal.

ì-lí-di-im-ti
fa. i-ṣi-da-ri-e and ^{d}sìn-ša-ru-uḫ.
1764. Text 21: seal.
n.d. Text 19: seal.

ì-lí-é-a-[ ]
NI. 1743. Witness. Text 38: rev. 3.

ì-lí-ekallī^{li}
fa. ^{d}sìn-im-gur-an-ni. 1739. Text 34: obv. 9.

ì-lí-e-ri-ba-am (ì-lí-i-ri-ba-am)
so. $^{\langle d\rangle}$nin-urta-[ ].
1749–1721. Witness. Text 30: rev. 10.
fa. ip-qú-é-a and ^{d}sìn-i-din-nam. 1740. Text 31: rev. 7.
bur-gul (seal-cutter).
1739. Witness. BE 6/2 36: 22.
1738. Witness. Text 80: rev. 4′.
1736. Witness. BE 6/2 45: 24.
NI. 1793. Witness. Text 48: rev. 7.
NI. 1743. He rents a field from a-píl-^{d}adad. Text 49: obv. 7.
NI. 1742. He rents a house from ri-im-^{d}adad. Text 50: obv. 4.
NI. n.d. Text 52: 13′.

ì-lí-i-[ ]
fa. ^{d}en-líl-[ ]. 1738. Text 80: seal.

ì-lí-ia
dam-gàr (merchant).
1743. He rents a field from u-bar-^{d}x-x. Text 38: obv. 5.

ì-lí-ia-tum (ì-lí-ia-a-tum)
fa. a-píl-^{d}šamaš. 1749–1721. Text 30: rev. 9.
fa. i-din-^{d}nin-urta. 1740. Text 31: obv. 4, 17.
fa. ur-du$_{6}$-kù-ga.
1747. Text 69: tablet rev. 4.
1746. PBS 8/1 86: tablet 13; case 16.
1742. Text 42: rev. 10.
1739. *ARN* 96: obv. 3, 12; OIMA 1 18: 3, 12 (case).

dub-sar (scribe).
1745. Witness. Text 23: rev. 7.
NI. n.d. Text 55: rev. 6.

ì-lí-i-din
fa. ^{d}en-líl-en-nam. n.d. PBS 8/1 92: 24.

ì-lí-i-din-nam
so. i-bi-^{d}en-líl.
1739. He sells a temple office to a-at-ta-a. Text 75: tablet obv. 4, 5, 11; case 4, 5, 10, seal.
1738. Witness. OECT 8 2: 22.
so. pa-ap-pa-[a].
1751. Witness. OIMA 1 12: 22.
so. ^{d}sìn-ga-mil.
1772. Witness. Text 53: rev. 7.
br.so. ba-zi-ia.
1743. He gives grain to ^{d}amurru-še-mi so that he can buy a house. Text 25: obv. 6.
fa. ^{d}en-líl-ni-šu, hu. a-lí-ia-tum. n.d. Text 86: seal.
fa. ^{d}nanna-ma. 1745. PBS 8/2 129: 29.
fa. nu-ri-ia-tum. n.d. Text 19: rev. 11.
fa. nu-úr-^{d}adad (=nu-úr-ia-tum). 1743. Text 26: seal.
uku-uš (gendarme).
1769. Witness. Text 11: rev. 10.
NI. 1786. Witness. Text 18: rev. 4.
NI. 1764. Neighbor of sà-ap-ḫu-um-li-ip-ḫu-ur. Text 20: tablet obv. 3; case obv. 3.
NI. 1743. Witness. Text 95: rev. 1′.

ì-lí-i-lu-ta(?)
dub-sar (scribe).
1743. Witness. Text 54: rev. 13.

ì-lí-i-ma
so. sin-gal-zu.
1750. Witness. Text 22: rev. 11.

ì-lí-ip-pa-al-sà(-am)
so. lú-^{d}nin-urta.
1762. Witness. PBS 8/1 82: 20.
so. ur-du$_{6}$-kù-ga.
1744. Witness. Text 60: rev. 9.
dub-sar (scribe).
1742. Witness. Text 42: rev. 16.

ì-lí-i-qí-ša-am
simug (smith), so. a-píl-^{d}šamaš.
1747. Witness. Text 70: tablet rev. 12; case rev. 7′.

ì-lí-iš-me-a-ni (ì-lí-iš-me-a-an-ni)
šidim (mason), so. arad-^{d}imin-bi.
1740. Witness. Text 71: tablet rev. 6; case rev. 4′.
NI. 1739. Witness. Text 59: rev. 2; BE 6/2 30: 10.
NI. n.d. Witness. Text 40: rev. 18.

ì-lí-ma

fa. an-nu-um-pi$_4$-^{d}šamaš and na-bi-^{d}šamaš. n.d. Text 90: obv. 5′, 7′, seal.

ì-lí-ma-a-bi

so. sa-mi-ia.

1741. His temple office is given by mār-er-ṣe-tim to šeš-al-dùg. *ARN* 125: obv. 5, seal.

ì-lí-ma-a-ḫi

fa. ta-ri-bu-um. 1769. Text 11: rev. 9.

ì-lí-ma-ilum

NI. 1743. Neighbor of a-píl-^{d}adad. Text 49: obv. 3.

ì-lí-ma-lu-lim

so. ib-ni-é-a and a-bi-ik-ku-ú-a, so.so. zi-ia-tum.

1739. He sells a temple office to a-at-ta-a. Text 74: case obv. 6, 8, seal.

ì-lí-tu-ra-am

so. a-bu-um-wa-qar, br. ku-bu-tum, ma-ri-er-ṣe-tim, ta-ri-bu-um, and nu-úr-ištar.

n.d. With his brothers he exchanges something with na-bi-^{d}en-líl. Text 55: obv. 6′.

so. SAL-kal-la, da.so. dingir-kù-ta, br. nu-úr-kab-ta and a-lí-a-bu-ša.

1793. With his siblings he is adopted by his stepfather da-mi-iq-ì-lí-šu. Text 1: tablet obv. 5, 12, rev. 1.

bur-gul (seal-cutter).

1748. PBS 8/2 142: 31.

1740. Text 32: rev. 4′.

gudu$_4$.

n.d. Neighbor(?). Text 10: 8.

NI. 1751. Witness. Text 61: rev. 3.

NI. 1749. Witness. Text 28: rev. 2.

ì-lí-ù-^{d}šamaš (ì-lí-ù-$^{\langle d \rangle}$šamaš)

so. ^{d}adad$^{?}$-šar$^{?}$-ì-lí.

n.d. Witness. Text 19: rev. 8.

so. ma-ar-ti-er-ṣe-tim.

n.d. He had been adopted by ^{d}amurru-še-mi and is now disinherited. Text 24: obv. 1, 17′, seal.

so. ^{d}nin-urta-ga-mil.

1740. Witness. Text 31: rev. 11.

dub-sar (scribe).

1751. Witness. Text 61: rev. 6; TIM 4 28: 12.

1750. Witness. *ARN* 75: rev. 4.

1746. Witness. BE 6/2 24: 37.

1739. Witness. Text 59: rev. 3; BE 6/2 32: 31.

1737. Witness. PBS 8/2 153: 25.

n.d. Witness. PBS 8/2 155: 41(?).

NI. 1743. Witness. Text 26: rev. 8.

il-la-la

so. lugal-murub$_4$-e.

1810. Witness. PBS 8/1 12: 33.

ìl-šu-ba-ni

so. ip-qú-^{d}sìn.

1743. Witness. Text 54: rev. 8, seal.

ìl-šu-i-[ ]
NI. 1761. Witness. PBS 8/1 83: 16.

ìl-šu-ib-ni-šu (ìl-šu-ib-bi-šu, ìl-šu-i-bi-šu)
so. maḫ-mu-da.
n.d. Witness. Text 24: rev. 5.
fa. ^{d}nuska-ni-šu. 1722. PBS 8/2 138: 9.
fa. ^{d}sìn-ma-gir. 1750. Text 27: rev. 5.
gudu$_{4}$ ^{d}nin-líl-lá.
1726. Witness. Text 84: rev. 2′.
NI. 1727. Witness. Text 83: case 6′.

il-ta-ni
NI. 1786. With é-a-ni she sells a house plot to sà-ap-ḫu-um-li-ip-ḫu-ur. Text 18: obv. 4, 5.

ilum-da-mi-iq (ì-lí-damiq)
so. a-ḫu-ni.
1721. Witness. Text 12: rev. 3.
fa. ma-an-na-šu. 1743. Text 25: seal.
NI. 1743. With nu-úr-^{d}šamaš he gives grain to ^{d}amurru-še-mi so that he can buy a house plot. Text 25: obv. 4.

ilum-du-gu-ul (ilum^{lum}-du-gu-ul)
GÌR-NÍTA
1764. Witness. Text 20: tablet rev. 3; case rev. 7. Text 21: rev. 3.

ilum-e-te-lum
fa. ^{d}en-líl-na-ši. 1793. Text 1: tablet rev. 7.

ilum-ga-mil
fa. a-bu-ú-a-tum. 1793. Text 1: tablet rev. 18.

ilum-na-ši
fa. el-le-tum. 1739. BE 6/2 30: 4.
fa. ^{d}en-líl-gal-zu, ^{d}en-líl-ma-an-sum, ṭāb-ba-la-ṭù, and ur-du$_{6}$-kù-ga.
1742. Text 42: rev. 3, seal.
1740. Text 71: tablet rev. 5; case rev. 3′.
1738. Text 43: obv. 3, seal.
1733. Text 45: tablet obv. 2, 3; case obv. 3′, seal. Text 46: tablet obv. 4; case obv. 2.
NI. 1751. Neighbor of i-din-^{d}nin-urta. OIMA 1 12: 7.

ilum-rēʾûm
so. a-wi-a-nu-um.
1923–1896. Witness. Text 35: rev. 6.

i-lu-ni
fa. dingir-ma-an-sum.
1739. Text 34: obv. 7; Text 75: tablet rev. 9.
1737. BE 6/2 40: 22.

i-lu-su-na-da
NI. 1786. Witness. Text 18: rev. 2.

im-[ ]
fa. ^{d}sìn-[ ]. 1749–1721. Text 85: seal.

im-x-a-tum(?)
fa. ^{d}nin-urta-a-bi. 1749–1721. Text 30: seal.

im-gu-ia-tum
so. a-wi-il-[ ].
n.d. He had bought a field plot in the past from ^{d}nin-líl-zi-mu which is now redeemed by ^{d}da-mu-i-din-nam. OIMA 1 48: 7.

im-gur-ì-lí-šu
ugula-é
n.d. Witness. Text 89: tablet rev. 6.

im-gur-^{d}nin-urta (=im-gu-tum)
so. na-ra-am-^{d}sìn, br. a-at-ta-a.
1747. With his brother he buys a temple office from ip-qá-tum. Text 69: tablet obv. 6; case 6′.
fa. ^{d}en-líl-ni-šu and e-tel-pi$_{4}$-ištar.
1734. Text 44: tablet obv. 7; case obv. 7′.
1733. Text 46: tablet obv. 9; case obv. 8.
1732. Text 47: seal.
nu-èš, so. lú-^{d}nin-urta.
1783. Witness. BE 6/2 6: 19.
n.d. Witness. Text 68: tablet rev. 4′; case 2′.
NI. 1736. Inherits. Text 82: obv. 7.

im-gur-^{d}sìn (im-gur-sin)
so. dingir-da-nu-me-a.
n.d. Witness. PBS 8/1 92: 19.
so. ^{d}sìn-ma-gir.
1739. He rents a field to [ ]-^{d}da-gan. Text 59: obv. 4, 5, edge.
fa. ri-im-ištar. n.d. OIMA 1 48: 4.
br. da-gi$_{4}$-x(?).
n.d. He inherits(?) Text 6: seal.

im-gu-ru-um (im-gu-rum)
so. ur-du$_{6}$-kù-ga.
1789. Witness. *ARN* 31: rev. 12′.
fa. e-tel-pi$_{4}$-ištar. 1732. Text 47: seal.
fa. ma-an-nu-ma-ḫir-šu. 1760. BE 6/2 10: 43.
NI. 1785. Witness. PBS 8/1 28: 20.

im-gu-tum (=im-gur-^{d}nin-urta)
so. ur-du$_{6}$-kù-ga.
n.d. Witness. Text 68: case 4′.
so. na-ra-am-^{d}sìn, br. a-at-ta-a.
1747. With his brother he buys a temple office from u-bar-^{d}šamaš. Text 70: tablet obv. 8; case obv. 8.

im-gu-ú-a
fa. ip-qú-ì-lí-šu. 1739. Text 34: obv. 8.
fa. na-bi-^{d}šamaš.
1758. Neighbor of da-mi-iq-ì-lí-šu. BE 6/2 11: 2, 11.
1752. *ARN* 72: case rev. 4.
1746. BE 6/2 23: 25.
1724. *ARN* 103: VI 20.
fa. ri-im-ištar.
1755. *ARN* 70: obv. 4.
1739. *ARN* 96: obv. 4; OIMA 1 18: 4 (case).

im-ši-ŠI

so. ^{d}nin-líl-zi-mu, br. KA-^{d}da-mu.

1745. He and his brother agree over shares of a plot of unimproved property (kislaḫ). PBS 8/2 129: tablet 11, 19; case 7, seal.

ancestor of ^{d}nin-líl-zi-mu, dingir-lú-ti, ^{d}en-líl-za-me-en, ^{d}nin-urta-ma-an-sum, im-ši-ŠI, and KA-^{d}da-mu.

1745. OIMA 1 13: 15 (duplicate PBS 8/2 154, q.v. Ni 9244, case).

gudu$_4$. so. ^{d}nin-líl-zi-mu, br. a-ab-ba-kal-la, KA-^{d}da-mu, and lú-dingir-ra.

1867. Neighbor of ^{d}en-lil-maš-zu, ^{d}da-mu-a-zu, and lú-^{d}nin-urta. *ARN* 23: I 1; II 13, 15 (joins PBS 8/2 169).

1860–1837. His property is inherited by ^{d}en-líl-maš-zu. Witness. YOS 14 321: obv. I 3, rev. I 9′.

n.d. With his brothers he inherits from his father. *ARN* 20 + OIMA 1 52: I 18′, IV 7’, VI 12, 15, VII 5, 8.

n.d. With his brothers he divides a plot of unimproved property (kislaḫ). Text 4: obv. 4.

i-na-é-kur-ma-gir

NI. 1723. He rents a house from ni-in-nu-tum. Text 14: obv. 3.

i-na-é-kur-ra-bi

so. ^{d}en-líl-dingir, br. ^{d}da-mu-i-din-nam.

1738. He sells a field plot to his brother. OIMA 1 22: 4, 6, 11, seal.

fa. igi-šag$_5$, br.(?) ^{d}en-líl-ma-an-sum.

1737. BE 6/2 43: 6.

nu-èš

1740. Witness. Text 32: rev. 3′.

^{d}inanna-[ ]

fa. [ ]-um. n.d. Text 10: 1.

^{d}inanna-ma-an-sum

so. ma-nu-um-ma-ḫir-šu, br. ma-nu-um-ma-ḫir-šu.

n.d. Witness. Text 40: rev. 15.

inim-kù-ga-ni

so. ^{d}nanna-gú-gal, br. lú-ur-sag-gal, and pa$_4$-šeš-ma-an-sum.

1800. With lú-ur-sag-gal he sells a field plot to pa$_4$-šeš-ma-an-sum. *ARN* 27: obv. 4, 6, rev. 1, seal.

n.d. He had sold a field plot in the past to lú-ur-sag-gal and pa$_4$-šeš-ma-an-sum. *ARN* 176: obv. 4.

i-pí-iq-é-a

so. BAR/MAŠ-kù-ta(?)

1793. Witness. Text 1: tablet rev. 15.

ip-pa-tum

NI. n.d. He rents a field to e-te-el-pi$_4$-ištar. Text 51: tablet obv. 3, 4; case obv. 2.

ip-qá-tum

so. kù-^{d}nin-gal, br. ni-id-nu-ša.

1744. Witness. BE 6/2 26: IV 20.

1749–1721. Witness. Text 30: rev. 6.

so. li-bur-ra-am.

1760. Witness. BE 6/2 10: 38.

so. u_4-du_7-du_7, br. [d]iškur-gìr-ra.
1760. As a result of a court case he and his brother give a house plot to ma-ri-er-ṣe-tim and mu-tum-ilu. BE 6/2 10: 29.
1755. Witness. BE 6/2 14: 27.
1739. With ma-ri-er-ṣe-tim and mu-tum-ilum he asks for a new trial. BE 6/2 30: 17.
so. ur-du_6-kù-ga.
1747. He sells a temple office to a-at-ta-a and im-gur-[d]nin-urta. Text 69: tablet obv. 3, 5, 12; case 4′, seal.
1739. He rents a field plot from [d]da-mu-i-din-nam. BE 6/2 29: 4, 6.
fa. [ ]-ištar. 1742. Text 50: rev. 2.
fa. ma-an-nu-um-ma-ḫir[!]-šu. *ARN* 125: rev. 4.
[lú]x.
1793. Witness. Text 48: rev. 6.

ip-qú-[ ]
fa. u_4-ta-u_{18}-lu-ḫé-ti. 1740. Text 71: tablet rev. 11.

ip-qú-[d]da-mu
so. na-ra-am-[d]sìn, br. a-at-ta-a.
1737. Witness. PBS 8/2 133: 30.
1736. Witness. Text 81: tablet rev. 6; case rev. 7.
1726. Witness. Text 84: rev. 3′.
1749–1721. Witness. Text 85: rev. 6′.
n.d. Witness. Text 88: rev. 4′.
fa. im-gur-[d]šamaš.
1800. *ARN* 27: rev. 6.
1786. *ARN* 35: rev. 4.
fa. [d]nanna-á-daḫ. n.d. *ARN* 112: rev. 3; *ARN* 176: seal.
fa. [d]šamaš-še-mi, hu. ta-bi-ia.
1734. Adopts(?) [d]en-líl-a-bi and divides his property between his real and adoptive sons. Text 15: rev. 5, seal.

ip-qú-é-a
so. ì-lí-i-ri-ba-am, br. [d]sìn-i-din-nam.
1740. Witness. Text 31: rev. 7.

ip-qú-[d]en-líl
nu-èš, so. lú-[d]nin-urta.
1738. He buys a house plot from ṭāb-ba-la-ṭù-um. Text 43: obv. 5.
1737. Witness. BE 6/2 43: 30.
1734. He sells a house plot to [d]en-líl-ni-šu and e-te-el-pi_4-ištar. Text 44: tablet obv. 3, 5, 12; case obv. 4′, 5′, seal.
1733. He exchanges house plots with [d]en-líl-gal-zu. Text 45: tablet obv. 8, 13, seal.
1733. He sells a house plot to [d]en-líl-ni-šu and e-tel-pi_4-ištar. Text 46: tablet obv. 5, 7, rev. 1; case obv. 3, 5, rev. 1, seal.
1732. He had sold a house plot in the past to [d]en-líl-ni-šu and e-tel-pi_4-ištar. Text 47: tablet obv. 3; case obv. 3′.
NI. n.d. Witness. Text 89: tablet rev. 11.

ip-qú-er-ṣe-tim
so. na-ra-am-[d]sìn.
1747. Witness. Text 69: tablet rev. 3; Text 70: tablet rev. 10; case rev. 5′.

1745. Witness. OIMA 1 13: 24 (duplicate PBS 8/2 154, q.v. Ni 9244, case); PBS 8/2 129: tablet 28.
fa. ig-mil-^{d}sìn. 1740. Text 72: tablet obv. 4, 5, 13; case obv. 5, 6, seal.

ip-qú-ì-lí-šu
so. im-gu-ú-a.
1739. Witness. Text 34: obv. 8.

ip-qú-^{d}inanna (ip-qú-ištar)
so. ta-ri-bu-um.
1762. Witness. PBS 8/2 125: tablet 15; case 17.
1758. Witness. BE 6/2 12: 26.

ip-qú-^{d}nin-šubur
šabra.
1750. Witness. Text 22: rev. 16.

ip-qú-^{d}sìn
fa. ìl-šu-ba-ni. 1743. Text 54: seal.

ip-qú-ša
so. ^{d}en-líl-ki-sag$^{?}$-[ ].
1793. Witness. Text 1: tablet rev. 8.
fa. da-mi-iq-ì-lí-šu. 1793. Text 1: tablet obv. 2, seal.
fa. ^{d}sìn-re-me-ni. 1833–1831. Text 37: rev. 11.
gudu$_4$ ^{d}nin-líl-lá.
1810. Witness. PBS 8/1 12: 29.
1762. Witness. PBS 8/1 81: 2.
NI. 1734. Witness. Text 15: rev. 18.
NI. n.d. He supports boy(?). Text 40: obv. 8, rev. 3.

ip-qú-ú-a-tum (ip-qú-a-tum)
so. ^{d}nanna-zi-mu
1793. Witness. Text 1: tablet rev. 6.
1789. Witness. *ARN* 31: rev. 9′.

ìr-ra-na-da
NI. 1872. Witness. Text 66: rev. 2.

i-ṣi-da-ri-e (i-ṣi-id$^{!}$-ri-e)
šabra, so. ì-lí-di-im-ti, br. ^{d}sìn-ša-ru-uḫ.
1764. Witness. Text 20: tablet rev. 1; case rev. 5, edge; Text 21: rev. 1.

^{d}iškur-gìr-ra (^{d}iškur-im$^{!}$-gir-ra)
fa. i-din-^{d}adad. 1737. BE 6/2 40: 20.
gudu$_4$ ^{d}nin-líl-lá, so. u$_4$-du$_7$-du$_7$, br. ip-qá-tum.
1760. He gives a house plot to ma-ri-er-ṣe-tim and mu-tum-ilum as a result of a court case. BE 6/2 10: 28.
1745. Witness. OIMA 1 13: 19 (duplicate of PBS 8/2 154, q.v. Ni 9244, case); PBS 8/2 129: 27.

ištar-ki-ma-ì-lí-ia
so. u-bar-^{d}ba-ú, br. ^{d}nin-urta-ri-im-ì-lí.
1721. He exchanges house plots with his brother. Text 12: obv. 8, 13, seal.

ištar-la-ma-sí
da. ^{d}nanna-tum(?).
1739. She is betrothed to ^{d}sìn-a-bu-šu. Text 34: obv. 2.
NI. 1739. With her mother she is a witness. Text 34: rev. 2.

i-šum-a-bi
fa. ^{d}adad-šar-ru-um. 1760. BE 6/2 10: 12.

iz-kur-^{d}šamaš (iz-ku-rum)
so. e-la-ilum (a-la-lí-im)
1743. He gives grain to ^{d}amurru-še-mi so that he can buy a house. Text 25: rev. 1.
n.d. Witness. BE 6/2 66: 19.

K

KA-[ ]-TU
fa. kù-^{d}nin-urta. 1816–1794. PBS 8/1 18: 23.

KA-^{d}da-mu
so. ^{d}nin-líl-zi-mu, br. a-ab-ba-kal-la, im-ši-ŠI, and lú-dingir-ra.
1867. Neighbor of ^{d}en-líl-maš-zu, ^{d}da-mu-a-zu, and lú-^{d}nin-urta. PBS 8/2 169: III 17, IV 16 + *ARN* 23: I 2, 13, 14.
1860–1837. Neighbor of ^{d}en-líl-maš-zu. YOS 14 321: obv. I 9.
n.d. With his brothers he inherits from his father. *ARN* 20 + OIMA 1 52: I 19′, VI 10, 16, 21, VII 3, 9.
n.d. He divides a plot of unimproved property (k i s l a ḫ) with his brothers. Text 4: rev. 3.
so. ^{d}nin-líl-zi-mu, br. im-ši-ŠI.
1745. He and his brother agree over shares of a plot of unimproved property (k i s l a ḫ). PBS 8/2 129: 2, 18, 20, seal.

KA-^{d}en-líl-lá
fa. lú-dingir-ra.
1867. *ARN* 23: IV 5′ (joins PBS 8/2 169).
1860–1837. Hussey: 6, 9, seal; YOS 14 321: rev. I 16′.

KA-^{d}nanna
NI. 1860–1837. Text 62: rev. 3′.

KA-^{d}nin-urta
so. arad-^{d}en-líl-lá.
1843. Witness. Text 3: rev. 3.
so. a-wi-ia-tum.
1727. With ḫu-na-ba-tum and an-nu-um-pi$_{4}$-ištar he sells a temple office to ^{d}sìn-ma-gir. Text 83: tablet obv. 9, seal.
fa. ib-ni-ia. 1843. Text 3: rev. 6.
n u - è š.
1810. Witness. PBS 8/1 12: 31.
u g u l a(?).
n.d. Witness. Text 68: case 5′.

K[A]-^{d}nus[ka]
NI. n.d. Neighbor of ma-áš-qum. PBS 8/1 92: 2.

ki-ág-ga
fa. lugal-á-zi-da and i-din-^{d}sìn. 1873–1869. Text 36: rev. 3.

ku-[ ]
NI. 1736. Witness. Text 82: rev. 5′.

ku-bu-tum (ku-ub-bu-tum)
so. a-bu-um-wa-qar, br. ta-ri-bu-um, ì-lí-tu-ra-am, ma-ri-er-ṣe-tim, and nu-úr-ištar.
n.d. With his brothers he exchanges something with na-bi-^{d}en-líl. Text 55: obv. 6′.
fa. ni-in-nu-tum. 1740. Text 72: tablet rev. 8; case rev. 9.

kù-^{d}en-líl(-lá)
NI. 1895–1874. With ku-ri-tum he lends silver to šeš-dùg-ga. Text 94: obv. 4.
NI. n.d. Neighbor. *ARN* 20: II 15′ (joins OIMA 1 52).

KU-gu-za-na
fa. ú-ṣí-na-wi-ir. 1895–1874. Text 94: rev. 6.
NI. 1867. Witness. *ARN* 23: IV 7′ (joins PBS 8/2 169).
NI. 1860–1837. Witness. Text 2: rev. 6.

kù-^{d}nin-gal
fa. ip-qá-tum and ni-id-nu-ša.
1744. BE 6/2 26: IV 20.
1749–1721. Text 30: rev. 6.

kù-^{d}nin-ìmma
dub-sar (scribe).
1746. Witness. BE 6/2 22: 15.
1744. Witness. OIMA 1 14: 17.
1742. Witness. BE 6/2 28: 34.
1740. Witness. Text 32: rev. 5′.
1739. Witness. BE 6/2 30: 13.
1749–1721. Witness. Cornell 6: IV 11.
n.d. Witness. Text 39: rev. 3.

kù-^{d}nin-šubur
so. a-ḫu-šu-nu. 1923–1896. Witness. Text 35: rev. 8.

kù-^{d}nin-urta
nu-èš. so. KA-[ ]-TU.
1816–1794. PBS 8/1 18: 23.

ku-ri-tum
NI. 1895–1874. With kù-^{d}en-líl she lends silver to šeš-dùg-ga. Text 94: obv. 3.

ku-um-bu-lum
so. wa-ra-sú-nu, br. ^{d}sìn-iš-me-a-ni, nu-rum-li-ṣi, and é-šar-ga-mil.
1755. Witness. BE 6/2 14: 28.

L

la-x-x
fa. nu-ra-tum. 1793. Text 48: rev. 8.

^{d}lama-lama-ellat-su
so. ^{d}sìn-[ ].
n.d. Witness. *ARN* 176: rev. 7′.

la-ma-sà-tum
da. níg-ga-^{d}[ ].
1860–1837. She adopts or is adopted by lú-^{d}nuska. Text 62: obv. 1.

da. ^{d}nin-urta-mu-ša-lim.
1745. Witness. Text 23: rev. 3.
lukur ^{d}nin-urta (*nadītum*).
1740. She rents a field to nu-úr-^{d}šamaš. Text 92: obv. 4, 5.

la-ma-ša
so. ama-kal-la and šeš-kal-la.
1873–1869. With ur-^{d}nin-giz-zi-da and lú-^{d}nin-sún he receives a payment of silver as settlement of a claim on a house. Text 36: obv. 5, 13.
fa. ^{d}nuska-ma-lik, a-ḫu-wa-qar, bu-la-lum, warad-ì-lí-šu, e-la-lí, and warad-^{d}amurru. 1833–1831. Text 37: obv. 11, rev. 5, seals.

li-bur-ra-am
fa. ip-qá-tum. 1760. BE 6/2 10: 38.

li-pí-[it-]
NI. 1762–1750. He borrows grain from ^{d}en-líl-[ ]. Text 93: obv. 4.

li-pí-it-^{d}en-líl
so. ^{d}en-líl-a-bi.
1739. Witness. Text 74: tablet rev. 9; case rev. 13′.
NI. 1723. Witness. Text 14: obv. 8.

li-pí-it-ištar
so. dingir-ma-an-sum.
1738. He sells a temple office to a-at-ta-a. Text 78: tablet obv. [4], 6, 12; case obv. 4, 6, 12, seal.
n.d. He sells a temple office to ? Text 87: obv. 5′, 10′, 12′.
so. šu-nu-ma-ilum (šu-ma-ilum).
1739. Witness. BE 6/2 30: 9.
1737. Witness. PBS 8/2 133: 32.
1733. Witness. Text 45: tablet rev. 7; Text 46: tablet rev. 8; case rev. 8.
fa. ^{d}nuska-ni-šu. 1740. Text 71: tablet obv. 7; case obv. 6, 8, seal.
dub-sar (scribe).
1762–1750. Witness. Text 96: rev. 2.
1750. Witness. Text 22: rev. 17.
1739. Witness. BE 6/2 35: 20.
NI. 1755. He lends silver to e-te-el-pi$_{4}$-^{d}en-líl. Text 57: obv. 3.
NI. 1743. Witness. Text 54: rev. 11; Text 25: rev. 15.

lú-[ ]
so. [ ]-^{d}nin-urta, br. a-bi-ia.
1739. With his brother he sells a temple office to a-at-ta-a. Text 76: obv. 4.
fa. i-din-^{d}adad. 1923–1896. Text 35: rev. 3.
fa. ^{d}sìn-na-ši. 1849–1843. Text 7: seal.

lú-^{d}da-mu
fa. ur-^{d}šul-pa-é-a. 1860–1837. YOS 14 321: rev. I 11′.

lú-dingir-ra
so. KA-^{d}en-líl-lá.
1867. Witness. *ARN* 23: IV 5′ (joins PBS 8/2 169).
1860–1837. With the heirs of ur-^{d}šu-maḫ he sells a field plot to ìl-šu-mu-ba-lí-iṭ. Hussey: 5, 8, 17, seal.
1860–1837. Witness. YOS 14 321: rev. I 15′.

so. ^{d}nin-líl-zi-mu, br. a-ab-ba-kal-la, im-ši-ŠI, and KA-^{d}da-mu.
1860–1837. Witness. YOS 14 321: rev. I 13′.
n.d. With his brothers he inherits from his father. *ARN* 20 + OIMA 1 52: I 20′, V 3, VI 6, VII 27.
n.d. He divides a plot of unimproved property (kislaḫ) with his brothers. Text 4: rev. 5.
fa. lugal-murub$_4$-e. n.d. Text 97: 5.

lú-^{d}en-líl-lá
fa. u-bar-^{d}en-líl and puzur$_4$-^{d}nin-šubur.
1723–1896. His sons divide a left-over share of his estate. Text 35: seals.
agrig (^{d}en-líl-lá), so. é-lú-ti.
1741. Witness. OECT 8 19: 21.
1740. Witness. OECT 8 11: 23; OECT 8 16: 17.
1739. Witness. Cornell 12: 22; Cornell 20: 16′; OECT 8 21: 26.
1738. Witness. BE 6/2 38: 20; OECT 8 1: 18; OECT 8 2: 19; OECT 8 9: 19; OECT 8 10: 23.
1737. Witness. BE 6/2 41: 19; OECT 8 7: 19; OECT 8 8: 19.
1727. Witness. Cornell 23: 48.
1749–1721. Witness. BE 6/2 64: 21.
n.d. Witness. Text 89: tablet rev. 7; Cornell 16: 19.

lú-ga-a-a
NI. n.d. Text 24: rev. 8, 10.

^{d}lugal-[ ]
fa. ur-^{d}nin-giz-zi-da. 1873–1869. Text 36: seal.

lugal-a-[ ]
fa. lugal-kéš. 1898–1874. Text 16: rev. 4.

lugal-APIN
fa. warad-^{d}amurru. 1793. Text 1: tablet rev. 13.

lugal-á-zi-da
so. a-wi-ia-tum.
1758. Witness. BE 6/2 12: 33.
so. ki-ág-ga, br. i-din-^{d}sìn.
1873–1869. Witness. Text 36: rev. 3.

lugal-ezen
so. lugal-a-[ ].
1895–1874. Witness. Text 16: rev. 4.
so. lú-^{d}nin-ME, br. lú-^{d}nin-urta.
1895–1874. With his brother he buys a house plot from u$_4$-dùg-mu and nin-kéš. Text 16: obv. 8.
fa. lú-^{d}nin-nibru^{ki}. 1762. PBS 8/1 82: 19.

lugal$^{?}$-ma-an-[sum]
fa. a-gu-ú-a. 1768. Text 11: seal.

lugal-me-lám
fa. warad-^{d}amurru. n.d. PBS 8/1 92: 23.
nar, so. níg-DU.DU.
1867. Witness. *ARN* 23: IV 4′ (joins PBS 8/1 169).

lugal-murub$_4$-e
fa. il-la-la. 1810. PBS 8/1 12: 33.
bar-šu-gál, so. lú-dingir-ra.
n.d. He lends silver to um-mi-wa-aq-ra-at and ^{d}sìn-re-me-ni. Text 97: 4.

[lu]gal-ní-te-ni
fa. ì-lí-a-wi-li. 1741. *ARN* 125: rev. 4.

lugal-zi-mu
NI. 1762. He brings suit about a house. PBS 8/1 82: 1.

lú-ga-tum
fa. ^{d}en-líl-za-me-en. 1734. Text 15: rev. 9.
fa. na-bi-^{d}en-líl. 1745. PBS 8/2 129: tablet 35.

lú-^{d}inanna
fa. ^{d}en-líl-ma-an-sum. n.d. *ARN* 22: 8.
fa. ^{d}en-líl-maš-zu. 1867. *ARN* 23: IV 6′ (joins PBS 8/2 169).

lú-^{d}iškur
fa. a-bu-um-wa-qar (a-bu-wa-qar).
1793. Text 1: tablet rev. 10.
1789. *ARN* 31: rev. 11′.
fa. ^{d}sìn-na-ši.
n.d. *ARN* 22: rev. 9; PBS 8/1 92: 20.

lú-^{d}nanna
^{lú}ŠIM, so. nam-ma-ni-ì-šag$_5$.
1760. Witness. BE 6/2 10: 46.
n.d. Witness. Text 68: tablet rev. 2′; case 6′.

lu-^{d}nin-ME
fa. lú-^{d}nin-urta and lugal-ezen. 1895–1974. Text 16: obv. 9.

lú-^{d}nin-nibru^{ki}
so. lugal-ezen.
1762. Witness. PBS 8/1 82: 18.

lú-^{d}nin-sún
NI. 1873–1869. With ur-^{d}nin-giz-zi-da and la-ma-ša he receives a payment of silver as settlement of a claim on a house. Text 36: obv. 8, 15.

lú-^{d}nin-urta
so. a-ab-ba-kal-la, br. ^{d}en-líl-maš-zu and ^{d}da-mu-a-zu.
1867. With his brothers he inherits from his father. PBS 8/2 169: I 2, IV 13 (joins *ARN* 23).
1860–1867. ^{d}en-líl-maš-zu receives part of his inheritance. YOS 14 321: obv. I 11.
so. lú-^{d}nin-ME, br. lugal-ezen.
1895–1874. With his brother he buys a house plot from u$_4$-dùg-mu and nin-kéš. Text 16: obv. 7.
fa. el-le-tum.
1739. Text 74: tablet rev. 8.
1738. Text 77: rev. 6′.
fa. ^{d}en-líl-ma-an-sum.
1739. Text 74: case rev. 8′; Text 75: tablet rev. 7.
1737. BE 6/2 41: 18.

fa. i-di-ia-tum. 1738. Text 43: rev. 6.
fa. ì-lí-ip-pa-al-sà-am. 1762. PBS 8/1 82: 21.
fa. im-gur-^{d}nin-urta.
1783. BE 6/2 6: 20.
n.d. Text 68: case 3′.
fa. ip-qú-^{d}en-líl.
1734. Text 44: seal.
1733. Text 45: tablet obv. 8, case obv. 2, seal; Text 46: tablet obv. 6, case obv. 4, seal.
1732. Text 47: tablet obv. 3, case obv. 3.
fa. ^{d}nanna-ma-an-sum, ^{d}sìn-li-di-iš, ^{d}nin-urta-ri-im-ì-lí, and u_4-du_7-du_7.
1810. U_4-du_7-du_7 and ^{d}nin-urta-ri-im-ì-lí inherit from him. PBS 8/1 12: seal.
1816–1794. PBS 8/1 18: 9, 20.
1775. *ARN* 36: rev. 2.
1792–1763. *ARN* 48: rev. 7′(?).
n.d. *ARN* 22: obv. 3, 6, rev. 5.
fa. nu-ra-tum. 1738. Text 78: tablet rev. 4′; case rev. 5; Text 79: tablet rev. 8; case rev. 8′.
fa. ^{d}sìn-ma-gir.
1752. *ARN* 72: tablet rev. 3′; case rev. 7.
1747. PBS 8/2 179: 9.
1742. Text 42: rev. 13.

lú-^{d}nuska
NI. 1860–1837. He is adopted by (or adopts) la-ma-sà-tum. Text 62: obv. 3.

lú$^{?}$-sin$^{?}$
ÍL.ÍL$^{?}$. n.d. Neighbor. Text 10: 11.

lú-$šag_5$-ga (lu-sig_5)
so. ^{d}da-mu-a-zu(?).
n.d. Witness. *ARN* 22: rev. 7.
NI. 1816–1794. Neighbor of ^{d}nin-líl-zi-mu. PBS 8/1 18: 5.

lú-urí^{ki}-ma
fa. [ ]-ma-an-sum. OIMA 1 23: obv. 4.
NI. n.d. Neighbor of ^{d}nanna-á-daḫ. *ARN* 176: obv. 3.

lú-ur-sag-gal(-la)
so. ^{d}nanna-gú-gal, br. inim-kù-ga-ni and pa_4-šeš-ma-an-sum.
1800. With inim-kù-ga-ni he sells a field plot to pa_4-šeš-ma-an-sum. *ARN* 27: obv. 5, 7, seal.
n.d. He had sold a field plot in the past to pa_4-šeš-ma-an-sum and inim-kù-ga-ni. *ARN* 176: obv. 5.

M

ma-an-na-šu
so. ilum-da-mi-iq.
1743. Witness. Text 25: rev. 12, seal.
NI. 1743. Witness. Text 26: rev. 5, seal.

ma-an-nu-um-ba-la-^{d}šamaš
fa. a-ḫu-wa-qar. 1785. PBS 8/1 28: tablet obv. 5; case obv. 6.

ma-an-nu-um-ba-lum-^{d}šamaš
so. ^{d}nin-urta-ga-[ ].
1743. He gives grain to ^{d}amurru-še-mi so that he can buy a house. Text 25: obv. 10.

ma-an-nu-um-ki-ma-é-a
so. i-din-^{d}[ ].
1740. Witness. Text 31: rev. 14.
NI. n.d. Witness. Text 39: rev. 2.

ma-an-nu-um-ma-ḫir-šu (ma-nu-um-ma-ḫir-šu, ma-an-nu-ma-ḫir-šu)
so. im-gu-ru-um.
1760. BE 6/2 10: 43.
so. ip-qá-tum.
1741. Witness. *ARN* 125: rev. 5.
so. ma-an-nu-um-ma-ḫir-šu, br. ^{d}inanna-ma-an-sum.
n.d. Witness. Text 40: rev. 14.
fa. ši-i-di-iš-pu-um.
1745. Text 23: rev. 6.
dub-sar (scribe).
1739. Witness. BE 6/2 36: 23; PBS 8/2 128: 15.
1738. Witness. Text 80: tablet rev. 5′.
^{lú}ZI?-BU?, fa. ma-nu-um-ma-ḫir-šu and ^{d}inanna-ma-an-sum.
n.d. Witness. Text 40: rev. 13.

ma-an-nu-um-me-šu-li-ṣur
so. ^{d}nin-urta-qar-ra-ad.
1755. Witness. BE 6/2 14: 23.
uku-uš (gendarme).
n.d. Witness. PBS 8/2 178: 39.

^{d}ma-ar-ti-$^{d!}$a-nu(-um-mi)
mo(?). ^{d}sìn-a-ḫi-i-din-nam. 1743. Text 25: rev. 4.

ma-ar-ti-er-ṣe-tim
fa. ì-lí-ù-^{d}šamaš. n.d. Text 24: obv. 2, seal.

maḫ?-mu?-da
fa. ìl-šu-ib-ni-šu. n.d. Text 24: rev. 5.

ma-na-tum
fa. ḫi-du-tum, hu. na-ra-am-tum. 1720. PBS 8/1 89: 3, 11, seal.

ma-ni-ia (ma-an-ni-ia)
so. ú-ba-a-a.
1758. Witness. BE 6/2 12: 32.

mārat-er-ṣe-tim
NI. 1744. With her husband's brother, a-píl-^{d}amurru, she borrows grain from mār-er-ṣe-tim. *ARN* 81: obv. 5.

mār-er-ṣe-tim (ma-ri-er-ṣe-tim, mār-erṣetim)
so. a-bu-um-wa-qar, br. ku-bu-tum, ì-lí-tu-ra-am, ta-ri-bu-um, and nu-úr-ištar.
1741. He gives ì-lí-ma-a-bi's temple office to šeš-al-dùg. *ARN* 125: obv. 8.
1741. He rents a field plot from ^{d}en-líl-is-sú. Text 29: obv. 8.
1739. Witness. BE 6/2 30: 5.
n.d. With his brother he exchanges something with na-bi-^{d}en-líl. Text 55: obv. 7′.
so. ^{d}adad-ra-bi, so.so. da-ma-gu-gu, br. mu-tim-ilum.
1760. With his brother he brings suit against u$_4$-du$_7$-du$_7$ and wins. BE 6/2 10: 1, 31.
1755. He disputes a boundary wall with ^{d}sìn-iš-me-a-ni. BE 6/2 14: 4, 6, 17.
1739. With his brother and ip-qá-tum he asks for a new trial. BE 6/2 30: 15.

so. i-bi-^{d}nin-šubur
1742. Witness. Text 42: rev. 11.
n.d. Witness. PBS 8/2 176: 17.
so. i-bi-^{d}nin-urta.
1768. Witness. Text 11: rev. 6.
so.? warad-ì-lí-šu, br. ša-gu-bu-u[m].
n.d. With his brother he rents or sells a field. Text 64: 8.
NI. 1764. Witness. Text 20: tablet rev. 7, case rev. 11; Text 21: rev. 4.
NI. 1751. He borrows grain from tab-bi-ia. TIM 4 28: 5.
NI. 1750. He lends grain to ^{d}sìn-ma-gir. Text 27: obv. 3.
NI. 1749. He borrows silver from the god Šamaš. Text 28: obv. 2.
NI. 1744. He lends grain to mārat-er-ṣe-tim and a-píl-^{d}amurru. *ARN* 81: obv. 3.
NI. 1739. He borrows silver from the god Šamaš. PBS 8/2 150: 3.

ma-ṣa-am-ì-lí
fa. ur-^{d}sìn. 1895–1874. Text 16: rev. 1.

ma-ṣí-^{d}en-líl
NI. 1743. Neighbor of a-píl-^{d}adad and da-an-na-am-i-šu. Text 54: obv. 2, 4.

MAŠ-^{d}šamaš
^{lú}ŠIM(?).
n.d. Witness. Text 19: rev. 15.

ma-áš-qum
so. i-bi-ia.
n.d. He sells a house plot to [ ]-kab-ta. PBS 8/1 92: 4, 5, 12, seal.

mi-gir-^{d}en-líl
NI. 1743. Witness. Text 54: rev. 12.

mu-mu-ì-pà
fa. u_4-ta-u_{18}-lu-me-$ša_4$. 1738. OIMA 1 23: obv. 6, seal.
nu-èš.
1737. Witness. BE 6/2 43: 29.
1736. Witness. BE 6/2 44: 18.

mu-na-wi-rum
so. be-lum.
1721. Witness. Text 12: rev. 5.
NI. n.d. Witness. Text 40: rev. 17.

mu-tum-ilum
so. ^{d}adad-ra-bi, br. mār-erṣetim, so.so. da-ma-gu-gu.
1760. With his brother he contests the actions of u_4-du_7-du_7 and wins. BE 6/2 10: 2, 3.
1739. With his brother and ip-qá-tum he asks for a new trial. BE 6/2 30: 16.

N

na-bi-[ ]
fa. [lú-^{d}en-líl]-lá and [^{d}nin]-urta-ni-šu. 1738. Text 80: tablet rev. 2′, 3′.

na-bi-^{d}en-líl(-lá)
so. dingir-ma-an-sum.
1740. Witness. Text 31: rev. 10.
1738. Witness. Text 43: rev. 3.

so. i-din-^{d}nin-urta.
1727. Witness. Text 83: tablet rev. 9.
so. ^{d}sìn-na-ši.
n.d. He exchanges something with ku-bu-tum, ì-lí-tu-ra-am, ma-ri-er-ṣe-tim, ta-ri-bu-um, and nu-úr-ištar. Text 55: obv. 4′, 5′.
fa. i-din-^{d}en-líl. 1755. *ARN* 70: rev. 7.
fa. nu-úr-ištar and ^{d}en-líl-ni-šu.
1740. His sons inherit from him. Text 31: rev. 3.
gudu$_4$, so. a-píl-^{d}adad, br. ^{d}en-líl-is-sú.
1741. Neighbor of ^{d}en-líl-is-sú and witnesses. Text 29: rev. 3, edge.
nimgir (herald), so. lú-ga-tum.
1745. Witness. OIMA 1 13: 26 (duplicate PBS 8/2 154, q.v. Ni 9244, case); PBS 8/2 129: 35.
NI. 1743. With e-ku-ri-tum he buys a house plot from a-píl-^{d}adad and da-an-na-am-i-šu. Text 54: obv. 10.
NI. n.d. Witness. Text 68: case 12′.

na-bi-^{d}sìn
NI. n.d. Neighbor. OIMA 1 52: II 23′ (joins *ARN* 20).

na-bi-^{d}šamaš
so. ì-lí-ma, br. an-nu-um-pi$_4$-^{d}šamaš.
n.d. With his brother he sells a temple office to a-at-ta-a. Text 90: obv. 5′, 6′, seal.
so. im-gu-ú-a (im-gu-a).
1758. He exchanges house plots with da-mi-iq-ì-lí-šu and na-ru-ub-tum. BE 6/2 11: 6, 11, 17.
1752. Witness. *ARN* 72: case rev. 3.
1746. Witness. BE 6/2 23: 25.
1724. Witness. *ARN* 103: VI 19.
bur-gul (seal-cutter).
1785. Witness. *ARN* 34: rev. 6′.
1775. Witness. *ARN* 36: rev. 10.
1772. Witness. Text 53: rev. 10.
1793–1763. Witness. TIM 4 4: 45.
NI. 1742. Witness. Text 50: rev. 4.

nam-maḫ-abzu
fa. dingir-kù-ta. n.d. PBS 8/1 92: 21.
NI. 1873–1869. Neighbor of ama-kal-la. Text 36: obv. 2.
NI. 1867. Neighbor. *ARN* 23: II 5 (joins PBS 8/2 169).
NI. n.d. Neighbor. OIMA 1 52: V 8 (joins *ARN* 20).

nam-maḫ-^{d}ba-ú
fa. e-ne-ia. 1793. Text 1: tablet rev. 11.

nam-ma-ni-ì-sag$_5$
fa. lú-^{d}nanna.
1760. BE 6/2 10: 46.
n.d. Text 68: tablet rev. 3′; case 7′.

^{d}nanna-[ ]
fa. a-at-ta-a. 1739. Text 73: tablet rev. 5.
NI. n.d. Neighbor. *ARN* 142: 10′.

^{d}nanna-[ ]-lá-[ ]
NI. 1736. Witness. Text 82: rev. 6′.

^{d}nanna-[ ]-zi
NI. 1755. Witness. Text 56: 1.

^{d}nanna-a-a (=^{d}nanna-ma-an-sum, ^{d}nin-urta-ma-an-sum???)
fa. ^{d}nin-urta-ra-ʾì-im-ze-ri-im. Cornell 21: 7.
fa. sin-i-din-nam. 1816–1794. PBS 8/1 18: 22.

^{d}nanna-á-daḫ
so. ip-qú-^{d}da-mu.
n.d. He had bought a field plot from pa$_4$-šeš-ma-an-sum which he now sells for redemption to ^{d}en-líl-dingir. *ARN* 176: obv. 9, 10, 11, seal.
n.d. Witness. *ARN* 112: rev. 3.

^{d}nanna-an-dùl
fa. dingir-ma-an-sum. n.d. Text 24: rev. 6.

^{d}nanna-gú-gal
fa. inim-kù-ga-ni, lú-ur-sag-gal and pa$_4$-šeš-ma-an-sum.
1800. *ARN* 27: obv. 4, 6, 9, seal.
1798. TIM 4 17: 24.
n.d. *ARN* 176: obv. 6.
gala-maḫ.
1867. Witness. *ARN* 23: IV 3′ (joins PBS 8/2 169).

^{d}nanna-ibila-ma-an-sum
nu-èš.
1737. Witness. BE 6/2 43: 27.

^{d}nanna-kù-zu
NI. 1867. Neighbor of ^{d}en-líl-maš-zu. PBS 8/2 169: I 13 (joins *ARN* 23).
NI. n.d. He owns a hill that is inherited. *ARN* 20: IV 3′, 5′ (joins OIMA 1 52).

^{d}nanna-lú-ti
so. ṣi-lí-ištar.
1833–1831. Witness. Text 37: rev. 9.
fa. ^{d}sìn-a-bu-šu. 1737. BE 6/2 42: 2.
dub-sar (scribe).
1739. Witness. Text 73: tablet rev. 10; case rev. 3′.

^{d}nanna-ma
so. ì-lí-i-din-nam.
1745. Witness. PBS 8/2 129: tablet 29.

^{d}nanna-ma-an-sum
so. dingir-ma-an-sum.
1739. Witness. BE 6/2 30: 6.
1734. Witness. Text 44: tablet rev. 6′; case rev. 6′.
so. lú-^{d}nin-urta, br. ^{d}sìn-li-di-iš and u$_4$-du$_7$-du$_7$.
1816–1794. He buys an orchard plot from ^{d}nin-líl-zi-mu. PBS 8/1 18: 9.
1793–1763. Witness. *ARN* 48: rev. 8′.
n.d. He buys a field plot from ^{d}nin-líl-zi-mu. *ARN* 22: obv. 6.
so. nu-úr-[ ].

1793. Witness. Text 1: tablet rev. 9.
so. ur-gá-giš-šú-a.
1762. Witness. PBS 8/1 82: 22.
fa. e-tel-pi$_4$-^{d}nin-urta. 1741. *ARN* 125: rev. 2.
fa. gìr-ni-ì-sà. 1785. Text 17: tablet rev. 12.
fa. gud-ku-ta. 1843. Text 3: obv. 5.
fa. ^{d}nin-urta-ra-ʾì-im-ze-ri-im (q.v. ^{d}nanna-a-a and ^{d}nin-urta-ma-an-sum).
1739. Text 73: tablet rev. 7.
1737. OECT 8 7: 4, 6, seal.
n.d. Cornell 16: 5, seal.
dub-sar (scribe).
1868–1861. Witness. PBS 8/1 19: rev. 14.
1860. Witness. PBS 8/1 8: rev. 14.
1773. Witness. PBS 8/2 116: tablet 31; case 32.
1755. Witness. *ARN* 70: rev. 10.
gudu$_4$ ^{d}nin-líl-lá.
1745. Witness. OIMA 1 13: 22 (duplicate PBS 8/2 154, q.v. Ni 9244, case).
1736. Witness. BE 6/2 44: 22.
nu-èš.
n.d. Witness. Text 33: rev. 2.
NI. 1860–1837. Witness. Text 62: rev. 4′.
NI. 1785. He buys a house plot from a-ḫu-wa-qar. PBS 8/1 28: tablet 7; case 9.
NI. 1755. Witness. Text 57: rev. 3.

^{d}nanna-me-ša$_4$
so. ar-na-bu-um.
1785. Witness. Text 17: tablet rev. 5; case obv. 15.
so. ^{d}en-líl-gú-gal.
1810. Witness. PBS 8/1 12: 32.
1800. Witness. OIMA 1 7: 9.
n.d. Witness. PBS 8/1 92: 17.
dub-sar (scribe).
1923–1896. Witness. Text 35: rev. 9.
1860–1837. Witness. OIMA 1 3: 21.
n.d. Witness. *ARN* 18: rev. 8.
NI. n.d. Text 52: 10′.

^{d}nanna-šu-nam-al$^?$
NI. 1860–1837. Witness. Text 2: rev. 4.

^{d}nanna-tum (^{d}nanna-a-tum)
so. ZA.MU.
n.d. He lends wool to a-di-ia. Text 33: obv. 3.
fa. ištar-la-ma-sí. 1739. Text 34: obv. 5.
fa. ni-din-ištar (ni-di-in-ištar, ni-id-ni-ištar).
1745. PBS 8/2 129: tablet 32.
1742. Text 42: rev. 14; BE 6/2 28: 29.
1740. Text 31: rev. 9.
nu-èš.
1740. He rents a field plot from sa-bi-ia and his son. Text 32: obv. 5.
1737. He held ^{d}sin-a-bu-šu's offices until his death. BE 6/2 42: 5.

^{d}nanna-zi
  nu-èš. so. a-ab-ba.
    1760. Witness. BE 6/2 10: 37.

^{d}nanna-zi-mu
  so. da-mi-iq-ì-lí-šu.
    1762. Witness. PBS 8/1 82: 16.
  fa. i-din-ia-tum and a-ḫi-ša-<gi$_4$>-iš. 1758. BE 6/2 11: 24, 26.
  fa. ip-qú-ú-a-tum (ip-qú-a-tum)
    1793. Text 1: tablet rev. 6.
    1789. *ARN* 31: rev. 9′.
  fa. ^{d}sìn-i-din-nam. 1760. BE 6/2 10: 39.

na-pa-al-aš-šu
  fa. a-píl-^{d}adad. 1744. Text 60: obv. 6.

na-ra-am-^{d}[ ]
  NI. n.d. He lends grain to ta-ri-ba-tum. Text 9: obv. 3.

na-ra-am-^{d}sìn
  fa. a-at-ta-a, ip-qú-^{d}da-mu, im-gur-^{d}nin-urta (im-gu-tum), ip-qú-er-ṣe-tim, and ^{d}en-líl-na-da.
    1747. Text 69: tablet obv. 7, rev. 3; case 7′. Text 70: tablet obv. 9, rev. 10; case obv. 9, rev. 5′.
    1746. BE 6/2 22: 11.
    1745. OIMA 1 13: 24(?) (duplicate PBS 8/2 154, q.v. Ni 9244, case); PBS 8/2 129: tablet 28.
    1740. Text 71: tablet obv. 8; case obv. 10.
    1739. Text 74: tablet obv. 8; case obv. 10. Text 75: tablet obv. 6, rev. 8; case 6.
    1738. Text 77: rev. 3′. Text 78: tablet obv. 7; case obv. 7. Text 79: tablet obv. 9, case obv. 8′.
    1737. BE 6/2 40: 19; PBS 8/2 133: 30.
    1736. Text 81: tablet obv. 7, rev. 6; case obv. 9, rev. 7.
    1726. Text 84: obv. 7, rev. 3′.
    1749–1721. Text 85: rev. 6′.
    n.d. Text 88: obv. 8, rev. 4′. Text 89: tablet obv. 8; case 7′. Text 90: obv. 8′, Text 91: obv. 6′.
  NI. 1738. Text 77: rev. 3′.

na-ru-ub-tum
  wi. da-mi-iq-ì-lí-šu.
    1758. With her husband she exchanges house plots with na-bi-^{d}šamaš. BE 6/2 11: 5, 13, 19, seal.

^{d}nergal-īriš(APIN)
  NI. 1737. Father of neighbors of ^{d}sìn-iš-me-a-ni. BE 6/2 43: 11.

^{d}nergal-ib-ri
  NI. n.d. Neighbor. OIMA 1 52: II 9′ + *ARN* 20: III 9′.

^{d}nergal-ma-an-sum
  bur-gul (seal-cutter).
    1758. Witness. BE 6/2 12: 36.
    1744. Witness. BE 6/2 26: IV 24.
    1726. Witness. Text 84: rev. 8′.

ni-din-ištar (ni-di-in-ištar, ni-id-ni-ištar)
so. ^{d}nanna-tum (^{d}nanna-a-tum)
1745. Witness. PBS 8/2 129: tablet 32.
1742. Witness. Text 42: rev. 14; BE 6/2 28: 29.
1740. Witness. Text 31: rev. 9.

níg-DU.DU
fa. lugal-me-lám. 1867. *ARN* 23: IV 4′ (joins PBS 8/2 169).

níg-ga-^{d}[ ]
fa. la-ma-sà-tum. 1860–1837. Text 62: obv. 2.

níg-ga-^{d}nanna
NI. 1810. Neighbor of ^{d}nin-urta-ri-im-ì-lí. PBS 8/1 12: 13.

ni-in-nu-tum
so. a-ḫi-ša-gi$_{4}$-iš, br. nu-úr-^{d}šamaš.
n.d. With his brother he redeems a field plot to ^{d}da-mu-i-din-nam. OIMA 1 48: 9, 11, seal.
so. a-lí-wa-aq-rum.
n.d. Role unclear. Text 40: obv. 2.
so. ku-ub-bu-tum.
1740. Witness. Text 72: tablet rev. 8; case rev. 9.
NI. 1723. He rents a house to i-na-é-kur-ma-gir. Text 14: obv. 1, 2.

ni-ip-pu-ur-ga-mil
so. ^{d}sìn-i-din-nam, br. a-ḫu-um-wa-qar.
1743. With his brother he sells an orchard plot. Text 13: obv. 6, 9, seal.

nin-[ ]
NI. n.d. Witness. Text 19: rev. 7.

nin-kéš
wi. u$_{4}$-dùg-mu.
1895–1874. With her husband she sells a house plot to lú-^{d}nin-urta and lugal-kéš. Text 16: obv. 6.

^{d}nin-líl-zi-mu
so. ^{d}da-mu-a-zu, br. lú-šig$_{5}$(?).
1816–1794. He sells an orchard plot to ^{d}nanna-ma-an-sum. PBS 8/1 18: 7, 8, 13, seal.
n.d. He had sold a field plot in the past to zi-ia-tum. OIMA 1 48: 5.
n.d. He sells a field plot to ^{d}nanna-ma-an-sum. *ARN* 22: 4, 5, 11, seal.
descendant of im-ši-ŠI.
1745. With dingir-lú-ti, ^{d}en-líl-za-me-en, and ^{d}nin-urta-ma-an-sum he divides a plot of unimproved urban land (kislaḫ). OIMA 1 13: 5, 7, 13, seal (duplicate PBS 8/2 154, q.v. Ni 9244, case).
fa. a-ab-ba-kal-la, im-ši-ŠI, KA-^{d}da-mu, and lú-dingir-ra.
1860–1837. YOS 14 321: rev. I 10′, 14′.
n.d. His sons inherit from him. *ARN* 20: seal (joins OIMA 1 52).
fa. im-ši-ŠI and KA-^{d}da-mu. 1745. PBS 8/2 129: 11, 18.

^{d}nin-tu-ma-an-sum
so. ^{d}sìn-a-bi.
1747. Witness. Text 69: tablet rev. 7.
NI. n.d. Witness. Text 40: rev. 16.

^{d}nin-urta-[ ]
fa. ì-lí-e-ri-ba-am. 1749–1721. Text 30: rev. 10.
NI. 1751. He lends grain to ^{d}EN-[ ]. Text 61: obv. 3.

^{d}nin-urta-a-bi
so. im-x-a-tum.
1749–1721. He is adopted by ^{d}en-líl-ni-šu and a-ḫa-tum. Text 30: obv. 5′, 8′, seal.
fa. ^{d}en-líl-a-bi. 1734. Text 15: seal.
uku-uš (gendarme).
1755. Witness. BE 6/2 14: 31.

^{d}nin-urta-dingir
so. ^{d}sìn-ga-mil, br. ì-lí-i-din-nam.
1772. Witness. Text 53: rev. 8.

^{d}nin-urta-en-nam
dub-sar (scribe).
1895–1874. Witness. Text 16: rev. 5.

^{d}nin-urta-ga-mil
so. a-[ ].
1743. Witness. Text 13: rev. 3′.
so. dingir-mu-silim.
1739. Witness. Text 73: tablet rev. 3.
so. ma-an-nu-um-ba-lum-^{d}šamaš. 1743. Text 25: obv. 11.
so. ta-ri-bu-um, br. ^{d}sìn-e-ri-ba-am.
1775. Witness. Text 17: tablet rev. 11; case rev. 3.
n.d. He adopts (or is adopted by) a-ḫa-tum, zi-ia-a, and ilum-ḫa-bi-il. *ARN* 156: obv. 5, seal.
so. ur-du$_6$-kù-ga.
1739. Witness. BE 6/2 30: 11.
1727. Witness. Text 83: tablet rev. 7; case 7′.
1726. Witness. Text 84: rev. 5′.
fa. a-[ ]-a. 1747. Text 70: tablet rev. 13; case rev. 8′.
fa. ì-lí-ù-<^{d}>šamaš. 1740: Text 31: rev. 11.
bur-gul (seal-cutter).
1751. Witness. OIMA 1 12: 24.
NI. 1721. Neighbor of ^{d}nin-urta-ri-im-ì-lí. Text 12: obv. 2.
NI. n.d. Witness. Text 87: rev. 7′.

^{d}nin-urta-ma-an-sum
so. ta-ri-bu-um.
1741. Witness. OECT 8 19: 22.
1740. He sells a temple office to ^{d}nin-urta-ra-ʾì-im-ze-ri-im. Cornell 21: 4, 6, 12, seal.
1740. Witness. OECT 8 11: 24.
1738. Witness. Text 79: tablet rev. 9; case rev. 9′.
1737. He sells a temple office to ma-an-nu-um-me-šu-li-ṣur. OECT 8 8: 7, 9, 14, seal.
descendant of im-ši-ŠI.
1745. With ^{d}nin-líl-zi-mu, ^{d}en-lil-za-me-en, and dingir-lú-ti he divides a plot of unimproved property (kislaḫ). OIMA 1 13: 11 (duplicate PBS 8/2 154, q.v. NI 9244, case).
fa. da-mi-iq-ì-lí-šu. 1738. Text 77: rev. 4′.
fa. ^{d}en-líl-ma-an-sum. n.d. Text 68: case 10′.

fa. ^{d}nin-urta-ra-ʾì-im-ze-ri-im (q.v. ^{d}nanna-a-a and ^{d}nanna-ma-an-sum).
1737. BE 6/2 40: 28.
1721. BE 6/2 64: 3, 11; BE 6/2 68: 10.
n.d. BE 6/2 66: 9.

^{d}nin-urta-mu-ba-lí-iṭ
NI. 1736. With ^{d}da-mu-e-ri-ba-am he does something with im-gur-^{d}nin-urta's property. Text 82: seal.
dub-sar (scribe).
1740. Witness. Text 92: rev. 8.

^{d}nin-urta-mu-ša-lim
fa. la-ma-sà-tum. 1745. Text 23: rev. 4.
fa. ur-da-tum. 1734. Text 44: tablet rev. 8′; case rev. 10′.
dub-sar (scribe).
1793(?). Witness. *ARN* 55: rev. 11.
1747. Witness. Text 69: tablet rev. 9.
1746. Witness. *ARN* 78: rev. 7; PBS 8/1 86: tablet 18; case 22.
1734. Witness. Text 44: tablet rev. 10′; case rev. 11′.
gala-maḫ.
1744. Witness. BE 6/2 26: IV 18.
1737. Witness. BE 6/2 42: 15.
gudu$_4$ ^{d}nin-líl-lá.
1760. Witness. BE 6/2 10: 41.
nu-èš, so. ^{d}nanna-tum.
1736. Witness. BE 6/2 43: 31.
1733. Witness. Text 45: tablet rev. 5. Text 46: tablet rev. 6; case rev. 6.
1731. He had bought a field plot from a-píl-ì-lí-šu which is now challenged by šu-mu-um-li-ib-ši. BE 6/2 49: 9, 14, 36, 38, 40.
n.d. Witness. OIMA 1 67: 5′.
ugula é-sikil.
1745. Witness. OIMA 1 13: 23 (duplicate PBS 8/2 154, q.v. Ni 9244, case); PBS 8/2 129: 30.

^{d}nin-urta-ni-šu
so. ḫu-[ ].
1744. Witness. Text 60: rev. 8.
so. na-bi-[ ], br. lú-^{d}-en-líl-lá.
1738. Witness. Text 80: tablet rev. 3′.

^{d}nin-urta-qar-ra-ad
fa. ma-an-nu-um-me-šu-li-ṣur. 1755. BE 6/2 14: 24.
muḫaldim (baker).
1760. Neighbor of ma-ri-er-ṣe-tim and mu-tum-ilum. BE 6/2 10: 26.

^{d}nin-urta-ra-ʾì-im-ze-ri(-im) (^{d}nin-urta-ra-i-im-ze-ri-im)
so. ^{d}nanna-ma-an-sum (^{d}nanna-a-a) (=^{d}nin-urta-ma-an-sum?)
1740. He buys a temple office from ^{d}nin-urta-ma-an-sum. Cornell 21: 6.
1739. Witness. Text 73: tablet rev. 6.
1737. He sells a temple office to ma-an-nu-um-me-šu-li-ṣur. OECT 8 7: 3, 5, 13, seal.
n.d. He sells a temple office to ma-an-nu-um-me-šu-li-ṣur. Cornell 16: 4, 6, 13, seal.
so. ^{d}nin-urta-ma-an-sum (=^{d}nanna-ma-an-sum?)
1737. Witness. BE 6/2 40: 28.

1721. He buys a plot of unimproved property (kislaḫ) for redemption from ^{d}nin-urta-mu-ba-lí-iṭ, i-din-ištar, and na-ru-ub-tum. BE 6/2 64: 2, 10.
1721. He buys a field plot from ^{d}utu-an-dùl and i-da-tum. BE 6/2 68: 9.
n.d. He redeems a temple office from the gods Enki and Damgalnunna. BE 6/2 66: 8.
n.d. He sells temple office and field property for redemption. OIMA 1 45: obv. 5′.

^{d}nin-urta-ri-im-ì-lí
so. lú-^{d}nin-urta, br. u_4-du_7-du_7.
1810. With his brother he inherits from his father. PBS 8/1 12: 21.
so. u-bar-^{d}ba-ú, br. ištar-ki-ma-ì-lí-ia.
1721. He exchanges house plots with his brother. Text 12: obv. 3, 14, seal.
NI. 1760. Neighbor of ma-ri-er-ṣe-tim and mu-tum-ilum. BE 6/2 10: 25.

^{d}nin-urta-zi-mu
$gudu_4$ ^{d}nin-líl-lá.
1810. Witness. PBS 8/1 12: 28.
NI. n.d. Perhaps he is the father of i-din-^{d}da-mu. *ARN* 142: seal.

nun-di
ugula, so. ^{d}EN-[ ].
1785. Neighbor of a-ḫu-wa-qar, and witnesses. PBS 8/1 28: tablet 2, 16.

nu-ra-tum
so. la-x-x.
1793. Witness. Text 48: rev. 8.
so. ú-ba-a-a.
1740. Neighbor of nu-úr-ištar. Text 31: obv. 2.
$gudu_4$ ^{d}nin-líl-lá, so. lú-^{d}nin-urta.
1738. Witness. Text 78: tablet rev. 4′; case rev. 5; Text 79: tablet rev. 7; case rev. 7′.
1737. Witness. BE 6/2 42: 18.
n.d. Witness. Text 87: rev. 6′.

nu-ri-ia-tum (nu-úr-ia-tum) (=nu-úr-^{d}adad?)
so. ì-lí-i-din-nam.
1743. Witness. Text 26: rev. 6, seal.
n.d. Witness. Text 19: rev. 10.
NI. 1764. Witness. Text 20: tablet rev. 8; case rev. 12; Text 21: rev. 6.

nu-rum-lí-ṣi
so. wa-ra-sú-nu, br. ^{d}sìn-iš-me-a-ni, ku-um-bu-lum, and é-šar-ga-mil.
1755. Witness. BE 6/2 14: 29.

^{d}nuska-DU
NI. 1867. Neighbor of ^{d}da-mu-a-zu. *ARN* 23: III 9′ (joins PBS 8/2 169).

^{d}nuska-ma-an-sum
dub-sar (scribe).
1789. Witness. *ARN* 31: rev. 14′.

^{d}nuska-ma-lik
so. la-ma-ša, br. a-ḫu-wa-qar, bu-la-lum, warad-ì-lí-šu, e-la-lí, and warad-^{d}amurru.
1833–1831. With his brothers he sells a house plot to ib-ni-ia. Text 37: obv. 5, 8, seal.

^{d}nuska-ni-šu
so. ad-da-dùg-ga.
1742. Witness. BE 6/2 28: 31.
1740. Witness. Text 71: tablet rev. 4; case rev. 2′.

1739. Witness. Text 74: case rev. 10′.
1738. Witness. Text 77: rev. 8′.
1737. Witness. BE 6/2 40: 25.
1732. Witness. Text 47: tablet rev. 7; case rev. 3′.
1726. Witness. Text 84: rev. 6′.

so. li-pí-it-ištar.

1740. He sells a temple office to a-at-ta-a. Text 71: tablet obv. 5, 14; case obv. 5, 7, 16, seal.

dub-sar (scribe).

1744. Witness. Cornell 4: rev. 18′.
1741. Witness. OECT 8 19: 26.
1740. Witness. OECT 8 11: 27; OECT 8 16: 22.
1732. Witness. Text 47: tablet rev. 8.

^{d}nuska-tum

dam-gar (merchant).

1744. Witness. *ARN* 81: rev. 2.

nu-úr-[ ]

fa. ^{d}nanna-ma-an-sum. 1793. Text 1: tablet rev. 9.

NI. 1849–1843. With ^{d}sìn-na-ši he borrows something with a field as security from šeš-al-dùg. Text 7: obv. 1′, rev. 5′.

NI. 1749–1721. Witness. Text 30: rev. 12.

nu-úr-i-KI

fa. [ ]-DINGIR. n.d. Text 24: rev. 7.

nu-úr-ištar

so. a-bu-um-wa-qar, br. ku-bu-tum, ì-lí-tu-ra-am, ma-ri-er-ṣe-tim, and ta-ri-bu-um.

1738. Witness. Text 43: rev. 2.
n.d. With his brothers he exchanges property with na-bi-^{d}en-líl. Text 55: obv. 8′.

so. na-bi-^{d}en-líl, br. ^{d}en-líl-ni-šu.

1740. With his brother he inherits from his father. Text 31: obv. 14, 19, rev. 1, seal.

NI. 1749. Witness. Text 28: rev. 1.

nu-úr-kab-ta

so. SAL-kal-la, da.so. dingir-kù-ta, br. ì-lí-tu-ra-am and a-lí-a-bu-ša.

1793. With his siblings he is adopted by da-mi-iq-ì-lí-šu. Text 1: tablet obv. 5, 12, rev. 1.

nu-úr-^{d}nin-šubur

dub-sar (scribe).

1739. Witness. PBS 8/2 150: 12.
1738. Witness. TIM 4 22: 20.

nu-úr-^{d}sìn

fa. u-bar-^{d}šamaš. n.d. PBS 8/1 92: 18.

nu-úr-^{d}šamaš

so. a-ḫi-[ ].

n.d. Witness. Text 19: rev. 12.

so. a-ḫi-ša-gi$_{4}$-iš, br. ni-in-nu-tum.

n.d. With his brother he sells a field plot for redemption to ^{d}da-mu-i-din-nam. OIMA 1 48: 9, 11, seal.

br. si-ru-um.
1764. Witness. Text 20: tablet rev. 5; case rev. 9; Text 21: rev. 7.
fa. a-píl-^{d}šamaš. 1750. Text 22: rev. 12, seal.
uku-uš gú-en-na (gendarme).
1772. Witness. Text 53: rev. 9.
NI. 1743. With ilum-da-mi-iq he gives grain to ^{d}amurru-še-mi so that he can buy a house. Text 25: obv. 5.
NI. 1740. He rents a field plot from la-ma-sà-t[um]. Text 92: obv. 6, rev. 2.
NI. n.d. Neighbor of sà-ap-ḫu-um-li-ip-ḫu-ur. Text 19: obv. 2.

P

pa-ap-pa-a
fa. ì-lí-i-din-nam. 1751. OIMA 1 12: 22.

pa-ni-ra-bi
fa. be-el-ta-ni. 1743. Text 25: obv. 3.

pa$_4$-šeš-ma-an-sum
so. ^{d}nanna-gú-gal, br. inim-kù-ga-ni and lú-ur-sag-gal.
1800. He buys a field plot from his brothers. *ARN* 27: obv. 8.
n.d. He sold the field that he and lú-ur-sag-gal had bought from his brother inim-kù-ga-ni to ^{d}nanna-á-daḫ. *ARN* 176: obv. 6, 7, 8.

pa-zi-ga-ni-im
NI. 1872. Witness. Text 66: rev. 1.

pirig-^{d}iškur
NI. 1872. Role unclear. Text 66: obv. 7.

puzur$_4$-^{d}amurru
so. ^{d}en-líl-me-ša$_4$.
1895–1874. Witness. Text 16: rev. 2.

puzur$_4$-^{d}nin-šubur
so. lú-^{d}en-líl-[lá], br. u-bar-^{d}en-líl.
1923–1896. With his brother he divides an extra share of his father's estate. Text 35: obv. 8, 10. seal.

Q

qa-[ ]
NI. n.d. Neighbor of ma-ri-er-ṣe-tim and ša-gu-bu-um. Text 64: 4′.

qú-ub-li-tum
NI. 1867. Neighbor of lú-^{d}nin-urta. PBS 8/2 169: IV 11 (joins *ARN* 23).

R

ra$^{?}$-an-ḫu-um
fa. be-la-nu-um. n.d. Text 19: rev. 13.

re-ša-nu-um
fa. ^{d}sìn-i-din-nam. 1772. Text 53: rev. 3.

ri-[ ]
fa. ^{d}da-mu-e-ri-ba-am. 1747. Text 70: case rev. 6′.

ri-bi-tum
NI. 1786. Neighbor of il-ta-ni. Text 18: obv. 3.

ri-im-^{d}adad
fa. a-píl-^{d}adad. 1743. Text 49: seal.
NI. 1867. Neighbor of ^{d}da-mu-a-zu. PBS 8/2 169: II 5 (joins *ARN* 23).
NI. 1816–1794. Neighbor of ^{d}nin-líl-zi-mu. PBS 8/1 18: 3.
NI. 1742. He rents a house to ì-lí-e-ri-ba-am. Text 50: obv. 1, 2.

ri-im-ištar
so. im-gur-^{d}sìn.
n.d. Neighbor of ni-in-nu-tum and nu-úr-^{d}šamaš. OIMA 1 48: 3.
so. im-gu-ú-a.
1755. Neighbor of i-din-^{d}nin-urta. *ARN* 70: obv. 4.
1739. Neighbor of ^{d}da-mu-e-ri-ba-am and ^{d}nuska-ni-šu. *ARN* 96: obv. 4; OIMA 1 18: 4 (case).
fa. ^{d}en-líl-mu-da-mi-iq.
1733. BE 6/2 47: 16.
1727. Text 83: tablet rev. 8; BE 6/2 58: 18.
1726. Text 84: rev. 4′.
1724. OIMA 1 29: 22′.
NI. 1762. Witness. Text 58: 2′.

ri-ni-iq-tum
NI. 1786. Witness. Text 18: obv. 15.

S

sa-al-lu-ḫu-um
šidim (mason), so. arad-^{d}en-líl-lá.
1739. Witness. Text 74: tablet rev. 11; case rev. 11′.

sa-al-lu-ú
NI. 1737. Father of the neighbor of igi-šag$_{5}$. BE 6/2 43: 5.

sà-ap-ḫu-um-li-ip-ḫu-ur
so. ^{d}sìn-re-me-ni.
n.d. He sells a house plot to ^{d}amurru-še-mi. Text 19: obv. 7, 9.
NI. 1786. He buys a house plot from il-ta-ni and é-a-ni. Text 18: obv. 7.
NI. 1764. He exchanges house plots with ^{d}amurru-še-mi. Text 20: tablet obv. 5; case obv. 5, 10. Text 21: obv. 8.
NI. 1762. Witness. PBS 8/2 125: tablet 22; case 16.

sa-bi-ia
NI. 1740. With his son he rents a field plot to ^{d}nanna-tum. Text 32: obv. 3, 4.

SAL-kal-la
da. dingir-kù-ta, mo. nu-úr-kab-ta, ì-lí-tu-ra-am, and a-lí-a-bu-ša.
1793. She marries da-mi-iq-ì-lí-šu who adopts her children. Text 1: tablet obv. 1, 7, 11, 16; case 3, seal.

^{d}sìn-[ ]
so. im-[ ].
1749–1721. He sells a temple office to a-at-ta-a. Text 85: obv. 4′, seal.
fa. i-bi-^{d}en-líl. n.d. *ARN* 176: rev. 6′.
fa. ^{d}lama-lama-elat-su. n.d. *ARN* 176: rev. 7′.

fa. wa-tar-pi-ša. 1750. Text 22: seal.
NI. n.d. He is hired by ^{d}en-líl-maš-zu. Text 5: obv. 8.

^{d}sìn-a-bi
fa. ^{d}nin-tu-ma-an-sum. 1747. Text 69: tablet rev. 7.

^{d}sìn-a-bu-šu
so. ^{d}nanna-lú-ti.
1737. His offices go to ^{d}nanna-tum before his death and to a-ba-^{d}en-líl-gin$_7$ after. BE 6/2 42: 1, 8, 11.
NI. 1739. He is betrothed to ištar-la-ma-sí. Text 34: obv. 3.
NI. 1739. Witness. Text 34: rev. 3.

^{d}sìn-a-ḫi-i-din-nam
so. ^{d}ma-ar-ti-$^{d!}$a-nu(-um-mi).
1743. He gives grain to ^{d}amurru-še-mi so that he can buy a house. Text 25: rev. 3.
so. e-te-ia.
1747. Witness. Text 69: tablet rev. 5.

^{d}sìn-be-el-ap-lim
dub-sar (scribe).
1741. Witness. Text 29: rev. 4.

^{d}sìn-be-el-ì-lí
NI. 1860–1837. Witness. Text 2: rev. 5.

sin-da-a-a-an-ni-im
NI. 1743. Witness. Text 54: rev. 5.

^{d}sìn-en-nam
<so.> ^{d}utu-^{d}en-líl-lá.
1793. Witness. Text 1: tablet rev. 17.
fa. u-bar-^{d}šamaš. 1747. Text 70: tablet obv. 6, 7; case obv. 6, 7, 5, seal.
fa. ^{d}utu-^{d}en-líl-lá. 1740. Text 31: rev. 13.

^{d}sìn-e-ri-ba-am (^{d}sìn-i-ri-ba-am, sin-e-ri-ba-am)
so. ^{d}en-líl-ḫé[gál], br. ^{d}sìn-iš-me-[a-ni].
1789. With his brother he inherits. *ARN* 31: seal.
so. ta-ri-bu-um, br. ^{d}nin-urta-ga-mil.
1775. Witness. Text 17: tablet rev. 9; case rev. 1.
fa. a-ḫu-um. 1750. Text 22: seal.
fa. da-mi-iq-ì-lí-šu. n.d. Text 68???
fa. i-din-^{d}en-líl.
1760. BE 6/2 10: 40.
1743. PBS 8/2 147: tablet 10; case 9.
1738. BE 6/2 39: tablet 20.
1731. BE 6/2 49: 43.
fa. ^{d}sìn-re-me-ni. 1741. *ARN* 125: rev. 8.
gudu$_4$ ^{d}nin-líl-lá.
1810. Witness. PBS 8/1 12: 30.
nu-èš, so. [ ]-ma-an-sum.
1738. Witness. Text 79: tablet rev. 6; case rev. 5′.
1736. Witness. BE 6/2 43: 28; BE 6/2 44: 19.
1733. Witness. Text 45: tablet rev. 4. Text 46: tablet rev. 5; case rev. 5.
ugula ^{sal}NAR.BALAG

1743. Lends grain. Text 95: obv. 2.

^{d}sìn-e-ri-im-šu
fa. ^{d}sìn-li-di-iš. 1772. Text 53: rev. 5.

sin-gal-zu
fa. ì-lí-i-ma. 1750. Text 22: rev. 11.

^{d}sìn-ga-mil (^{d}sìn-ga-mi-il, sin-ga-mil)
fa. ^{d}en-líl-ni-šu. 1738. OIMA 1 22: 16.
fa. ì-lí-i-din-nam and ^{d}nin-urta-dingir. 1772. Text 53: rev. 7.
fa. ta-ri-bu-um. 1740. Text 92: rev. 7.
NI. 1750. Neighbor of wa-tar-pi-ša. Text 22: obv. 3.

^{d}sìn-gi$_{4}$-im-la-an-ni
lú-èš.
1745. Witness. OIMA 1 13: 25 (duplicate PBS 8/2 154, q.v. Ni 9244, case); PBS 8/2 129: tablet 33.

^{d}sìn-ḫa-zi-ir
NI. 1741. Neighbor of ^{d}en-líl-is-sú. Text 29: obv. 4.

^{d}sìn-i-di-iš
NI. n.d. Witness. Text 41: rev. 4.

^{d}sìn-i-din-nam (sin-i-din-nam)
so.at-ta-tum.
1762. Witness. Text 65: rev. 2.
so. dam-qum.
1743. He gave grain to ^{d}amurru-še-mi so that he could buy a house. Text 25: obv. 8.
so. gìr-ni-ì-ša.
1772. Witness. Text 53: rev. 6.
so. ì-lí-i-ri-ba-am, br. ip-qú-é-a.
1740. Witness. Text 31: rev. 8.
so. ^{d}nanna-a-a.
1816–1794. Witness. PBS 8/1 18: 22.
so. ^{d}nanna-zi-mu
1760. Witness. BE 6/2 10: 39.
so. re-ša-nu-um.
1772. Witness. Text 53: rev. 2.
fa. i-din-^{d}sìn.
1751. OIMA 1 12: 21.
1744. OIMA 1 14: 15.
fa. ni-ip-pu-ur-ga-mil and a-ḫu-um-wa-qar. 1743. Text 13: obv. 8, seal.
fa. ^{d}sìn-ma-gir(?). 1749–1721. Text 30: rev. 8.
NI. 1743. Witness. Text 49: rev. 3.
NI. 1739. Neighbor of im-gur-^{d}sìn. Text 59: obv. 3.

^{d}sìn-i-din-na-aš-šu
NI. 1923–1896. Witness. Text 35: rev. 4.

^{d}sìn-im-gur-ra-an-ni (^{d}sìn-im-gur-an-ni, sin-im-gur-an-ni)
so. a-ḫu-šu-nu, br. ta-ri-ba-tum.
1739. With his brother he sells a temple office to ^{d}adad-ta-a-a-ar. Text 73: tablet obv. 5′, 7′, 14′; case 5, 7, seal.

so. ì-lí-ekallī^{li}.
1739. Witness. Text 34: obv. 9.
dub-sar (scribe).
1758. Witness. BE 6/2 11: 28.
1737. Witness. BE 6/2 42: 19.
NI. 1744. With a-píl-^{d}adad he comes to an agreement over a rented field. Text 60: obv. 2.
NI. 1739. Witness. Text 34: rev. 1.
NI. 1734. Witness. Text 15: rev. 12.
NI. n.d. Witness. Text 89: tablet rev. 9.

^{d}sìn-i-qí-ša-am
uku-uš (gendarme).
1762. Witness. PBS 8/1 82: 24.

^{d}sìn-iriš(APIN)
so. a-at-ta-a.
1760. Witness. BE 6/2 10: 45.
so. ḫu-pa-tum.
1760. Witness. BE 6/2 10: 42.
fa. tab-bi-ia. 1751. TIM 4 28: 4.

^{d}sìn-iš-me-a-ni
so. ^{d}en-líl-ḫé-[gál], br. ^{d}sìn-e-ri-ba-a[m].
1789. With his brother he inherits from his father. *ARN* 31: seal.
so. ^{d}en-líl-ma-an-sum, fa.br.so.(?) igi-šag$_{5}$.
1737. With his cousin he inherits from his grandfather(?). BE 6/2 43: 17, 21, seal.
nagar (carpenter), so. wa-ra-as-sú-nu, br. ku-um-bu-lum, nu-rum-li-ṣi, and é-šar-ga-mil.
1755. He disputes a boundary wall with ma-ri-er-ṣe-tim. BE 6/2 14: 2, 8, 11, 16.
NI. 1769. Witness. Text 11: rev. 5.

sin-i-tu-ra-am
NI. n.d. Neighbor. Text 10: 14.

^{d}sìn-li-di-iš
so. gìr-ni-ì-sá.
1833–1831. Witness. Text 37: rev. 12.
so. lú-^{d}nin-urta, br. ^{d}nanna-ma-an-sum and u$_{4}$-du$_{7}$-du$_{7}$.
n.d. Neighbor of ^{d}nin-líl-zi-mu. *ARN* 22: obv. 3.
so. ur-du$_{6}$-kù-ga.
1775. Witness. Text 17: tablet rev. 7; case obv. 17.
uku-uš (gendarme), so. ^{d}sìn-e-ri-im-šu.
1772. Witness. Text 53: rev. 4.

^{d}sìn-ma-gir (sin-ma-gir)
so. ^{d}en-líl-na-ṣi-ir.
1727. He buys a temple office from ḫu-na-ba-tum, an-nu-um-pi$_{4}$-ištar, and KA-^{d}nin-urta. Text 83: tablet obv. 10.
1726. He sells a temple office to a-at-ta-a. Text 84: obv. 5, 6, 11, seal.
so. ìl-šu-i-bi-šu.
1750. Witness. Text 27: rev. 4.
so. lú-^{d}nin-urta.
1752. Witness. *ARN* 72: tablet rev. 3′; case rev. 7.
1747. Witness. PBS 8/2 179: 8.

1742. Witness. Text 42: rev. 13.
so. si[n]-i-d[in-na]m?.
1749–1721. Witness. Text 30: rev. 8.
fa. geme$_2$-^{d}nuska, hu ^{d}šamaš-nu-ri.
1762. Text 58: seal.
fa. i-din-^{d}nin-šubur. 1772. Text 53: rev. 1.
fa. i-din-^{d}nin-urta.
1755. *ARN* 70: obv. 5, 6, seal.
1751. OIMA 1 12: seal.
fa. im-gur-^{d}sìn. 1739. Text 59: obv. 4.
gudu$_4$ ^{d}nin-líl-lá, so. ^{d}da-mu-ma-an-sum.
1737. Witness. PBS 8/2 133: 29.
1733. Witness. BE 6/2 47: 11.
1732. Witness. Text 47: tablet rev. 5; case rev. 2′.
NI. 1751. Witness. Text 61: rev. 4.
NI. 1750. He borrows grain from mār-erṣetim. Text 27: obv. 4.

^{d}sìn-na-ši
so. lú-^{d}iškur.
n.d. Witness. *ARN* 22: rev. 9; PBS 8/1 92: 20.
so. lú-[ ].
1849–1843. With nu-úr-[ ] he borrowed something and gave a field as security. Text 7: obv. 10′, rev. 4′, seal.
fa. na-bi-^{d}en-líl. n.d. Text 55: obv. 4′, 5′.

^{d}sìn-nu-úr-ma-tim
son of a šabra.
1833–1831. Witness. Text 37: rev. 10.

^{d}sìn-ra-bi
NI. 1815. Witness. Text 67: rev. 1.

^{d}sin-re-me-ni
so. ip-qú-ša.
1833–1831. Witness. Text 37: rev. 11.
so. ^{d}sìn-e-ri-ba-am.
1741. Witness. *ARN* 125: rev. 7.
so. um-mi-wa-aq-ra-at.
n.d. With his mother he borrows silver from lugal-murub$_4$-e. Text 97: 7.
fa. ^{d}amurru-ba-ni. 1775. Text 17: tablet obv. 9; case obv. 7.
fa. sà-ap-ḫu-um-li-ip-ḫu-ur. n.d. Text 19: obv. 8.
NI. n.d. Text 24: rev. 9.

^{d}sìn-ša-ru-uḫ
so. ì-lí-di-im-ti, br. i-ṣi-da-ri-e.
1764. Witness. Text 20: tablet rev. 2; case rev. 6; Text 21: rev. 2.
n.d. Text 19: seal.

^{d}sìn-šìr?-ma-tim
nimgir (herald).
1750. Witness. Text 22: rev. 13.

si-ru-um
br. nu-úr-^{d}šamaš
1764. Witness. Text 20: tablet rev. 6; case rev. 10; Text 21: rev. 8.

Ṣ

ṣi-lí-ištar
so. i-din-^{d}en-líl.
1923–1896. Witness. Text 35: rev. 7.
fa. ^{d}nanna-lú-ti. 1833–1831. Text 37: rev. 9.

ṣi-lí-^{d}šamaš
fa. é-a-i-din-nam. 1721. Text 12: rev. 4.

Š

ša-gi$_{4}$-iš-ki-nu-um
fa. ur-du$_{6}$-kù-ga. 1775. Text 17: tablet obv. 5, 7; case 4, 5, seal.

ša-gu-bu-u[m]
so?. warad-ì-lí-šu, br. ma-ri-er-ṣe-tim.
n.d. With his brother he rents or sells a field. Text 64: 9.

^{d}šákkan-kur-ra
so. ta-ri-bu-um, br. ur-da-tum.
1793. He receives grain from BI.KU?-[ ]. Text 48: obv. 4.

ša-ma-a-a-tum
NI. 1734. Witness. Text 15: rev. 15.

^{d}šamaš-li-we-er
g u d u$_{4}$, so. a-ḫu-šu-nu.
1740. Witness. Text 72: tablet rev. 5; case rev. 5.

^{d}šamaš-ma-gir
so. ^{d}utu-gal-zu.
1762. Witness. PBS 8/1 81: 8.
1745. Witness. OIMA 1 13: 27 (duplicate PBS 8/2 154, q.v. Ni 9244, case); PBS 8/2 129: tablet 31.
1744. Witness. BE 6/2 26: IV 22.
NI. n.d. Witness. Text 51: tablet rev. 7.

^{d}šamaš-mu-[ ]
NI. 1736. Witness. Text 81: tablet rev. 7; case rev. 8.

^{d}šamaš-mu-ba-lí-iṭ
so. ^{d}da-mu-gal-zu.
1740. He buys a temple office from ig-mil-^{d}sìn. Text 72: tablet obv. 6; case obv. 7.

^{d}šamaš-na-ṣ[ir]
NI. 1743. Witness. Text 38: rev. 2.

^{d}šamaš-nu-ri
wi. ^{d}sìn-ma-gir.
1762. Role unclear. Text 58: seal.

^{d}šamaš-ra-bi
so. ur-^{d}šul-pa-è-a.
1738. Witness. Text 78: tablet rev. 6′; case rev. 8.

^{d}šamaš-ri-bu-um
NI. 1786. Witness. Text 18: rev. 5.

^{d}šamaš-še-mi
so. ip-qú-^{d}da-mu and ta-bi-ia.
1734. He divides his father's estate with his adoptive brother ^{d}en-líl-a-bi. Text 15: obv. 7, rev. 1, seal.

šar-ri-ia
NI. 1786. Witness. Text 18: rev. 1.

šarrum-nūr$^{?}$-ma-tim
dub-sar (scribe).
1755. Witness. Text 57: rev. 4.

še-ga-^{d}NIN-[ ]
fa. bi-ia-tum. n.d. Text 41: rev. 6.

^{d}še-rum-ì-lí
NI. n.d. Witness. Text 51: rev. 5.

šeš-al-dùg
so. i-bi-ia.
1843. He borrows silver from gud-ku-ta. Text 3: obv. 6, seal.
NI. 1867. Neighbor of ^{d}da-mu-a-zu. PBS 8/2 169: III 10 (joins *ARN* 23).
NI. 1849–1843. He lends grain and gets a field plot as security from ^{d}sìn-na-ši and nu-úr-[ ]. Text 7: rev. 2′.
NI. 1741. He receives ì-lí-ma-a-bi's temple office from mār-er-ṣe-tim. *ARN* 125: obv. 3.

šeš-dùg-ga
so. da-an-gá-ta.
1895–1874. He borrows silver from ku-ri-tum and kù-^{d}en-lil. Text 94: obv. 5.

šeš-kal-la
so. ^{d}en-líl-á-maḫ.
1860–1837. He borrows silver from the god Sîn. Text 2: obv. 5.
hu. ama-kal-la. 1873–1869. Text 36: obv. 4.

šeš-ma-kal
so. ^{d}en-líl-á-maḫ.
n.d. Witness. PBS 8/1 92: 16.

ši-i-di-iš-pu-um
da. ma-an-nu-um-ma-ḫir-šu.
1745. Witness. Text 23: rev. 5.
ši-pa-ta
NI. 1785. With ab-bu-tu-tum he may be a neighbor of a-ḫu-wa-qar. PBS 8/1 28: tablet 3.

šu-[ ]
fa. ì-lí-[ ]. 1800. Text 8: rev. 2.

ŠU.BA.AN.DINGIR
so. a-wi-il-ì-lí, fa. a-ḫu-wa-qar.
1750. Text 22: rev. 14, seal.

^{d}šul-pa-è-a-na-ṣir
NI. 1739. Witness. BE 6/2 30: 7.

šu-mi-a-bi-im
NI. 1743. Witness. Text 54: rev. 9.

šu-mi-a-ḫi-ia
so. gìr-ni-ì-sà.
1750. Witness. Text 27: rev. 2.

šu-mu-um-li-ib-ši
gudu₄ ᵈnin-urta.
1741. Witness. Text 29: rev. 1.

šu-na-a-a
NI. 1872. He rents a field plot to ᵈutu-ḫe-gál. Text 66: obv. 4.

šu-nu-ma-ilum (šu-ma-ilum)
fa. li-pí-it-ištar.
1739. BE 6/2 30: 9.
1737. PBS 8/2 133: 32.
1733. Text 45: tablet rev. 7. Text 46: tablet rev. 8; case rev. 8.

T

ta-bi-ia (tab-bi-ia)
wi. ip-qú-ᵈda-mu, mo. ᵈšamaš-še-mi, adoptive mother of ᵈen-líl-a-bi. 1734. Text 15: rev. 2.
lukur ᵈnin-urta (*nadītum*), da. ᵈsìn-īriš(APIN).
1751. She lends grain to mār-erṣetim. TIM 4 28: 3.
1751. She lends grain to ì-lí-e-ri-ba-am. TIM 4 29: 3.

ta-na-nu-um
so. BI-[ ]-DINGIR.
1750. Witness. Text 22: rev. 10, seal.

ta-ra-am-ᵈsìn
NI. 1872. Witness. Text 66: rev. 3.

ta-ri-ba-tum
so. a-ḫu-šu-nu, br. ᵈsìn-im-gur-ra-an-ni.
1739. With his brother he sells a temple office to ᵈadad-ta-a-a-ar. Text 73: tablet obv. 6′, 8′, 15′; case obv. 6, seal.
so. e-la-a.
1736. He sells a temple office to a-at-ta-a. Text 81: tablet obv. 5, 6, 12; case obv. 5, 7, seal.
n.d. Witness. Text 89: rev. 8.
ra-bi-a-nu-um (mayor).
1743. Witness. Text 54: rev. 4.
NI. 1740. Neighbor of la-ma-sà-tum. Text 92: obv. 3.
NI. n.d. He borrows grain from na-ra-am-ᵈ[ ]. Text 9: obv. 4.

ta-ri-bu-um (ta-ri-bu)
so. a-bu-um-wa-qar, br. ku-bu-tum, ì-lí-tu-ra-am, ma-ri-er-ṣe-tim, and nu-úr-ištar.
n.d. With his brothers he exchanges something with na-bi-ᵈen-líl. Text 55: obv. 7′.
so. amar-ᵈda-mu.
1742. Witness. Text 42: rev. 12.
so. ì-lí-ma-a-ḫi.
1769. Witness. Text 11: rev. 9.
so. sin-ga-mil.
1740. Witness. Text 92: rev. 6.
fa. ᵈšákkan-kur-ra and ur-da-tum.

1793. Text 48: obv. 5.
fa. ^{d}nin-urta-ga-mil and ^{d}sìn-e-ri-ba-am.
1775. Text 17: tablet rev. 10; case rev. 2.
n.d. *ARN* 156: obv. 6, seal.
fa. ^{d}nin-urta-ma-an-sum.
1741. OECT 8 19: 22.
1740. Cornell 21: 13, seal; OECT 8 11: 24.
1738. Text 79: tablet rev. 9; case rev. 9′.
1737. OECT 8 8: 8.
gudu$_4$ ^{d}nin-líl-lá.
1739. Witness. BE 6/2 30: 3.
simug (smith).
1734. Witness. Text 44: tablet rev. 9′; case rev. 8′.
1749–1721. Witness. *ARN* 110: rev. 6′.
ugula dag-gi-a.
1754. Witness. BE 6/2 16: 16.
1746. Witness. BE 6/2 24: 32.
1739. Witness. BE 6/2 30: 2.

Ṭ

ṭāb-ba-la-ṭù(-um)
so. ilum-na-ši, br. ^{d}en-líl-ma-an-sum, ur-du$_6$-kù-ga, and ^{d}en-líl-gal-zu.
1742. With his brothers he inherits from his father. Text 42: obv. 11, 12, seal.
1738. He sells a house plot to ip-qú-^{d}en-líl. Text 43: obv. 3, 4, 10, seal.

U

ú-[ ]
fa. u-bar-^{d}šamaš. 1734. Text 15: rev. 16.

ú-ba-a-a
fa. nu-ra-tum. 1740. Text 31: obv. 2.
NI. n.d. Text 55: rev. 2′.

úba-a-a-tum
so. be-la-nu-um
1739. He sells a temple office to ^{d}da-mu-i-din-nam. OIMA 1 19: 3, 5, 13, seal.
fa. ^{d}amurru-še-mi.
1745. Text 23: obv. 5.
n.d. Text 19: obv. 4.
NI. 1786. Neighbor of il-ta-ni. Text 18: obv. 2.
NI. 1786. Witness. Text 18: rev. 3.
NI. 1764. Neighbor of sà-ap-ḫu-um-li-ip-ḫu-ur and ^{d}amurru-še-mi. Text 20: tablet obv. 2; case obv. 2. Text 21: obv. 3.

u-bar-[ ]
fa. ḪI.TAR$^{?}$-^{d}iškur. 1736. Text 82: obv. 6.

u-bar-^{d}x-x
NI. 1743. He rents a field plot to ì-lí-ia. Text 38: obv. 3, 4.

u-bar-^{d}ba-ú
fa. ^{d}nin-urta-ri-im-ì-lí and ištar-ki-ma-ì-lí-ia. 1721. Text 12: obv. 4, 9, seal.
NI. 1769. He divides two temple offices with ur-^{d}lú-làl and a-gu-ú-a. Text 11: rev. 4, seal.

u-bar-^{d}en-líl
so. lú-^{d}en-líl-lá, br. puzur$_4$-^{d}nin-šubur.
1923–1896. With his brother he divides a left-over inheritance share. Text 35: obv. 2, 9, seal.
NI. 1849–1843. Witness. Text 7: rev. 7′.

u-bar-ru-um (u-bar-rum)
so. a-ad-da-dùg-ga.
1843. Witness. Text 3: rev. 9.
uku-uš (gendarme).
1739. Witness. BE 6/2 30: 12.

u-bar-^{d}sìn
so. za-ba-bi-im
1793. Witness. Text 1: tablet rev. 14.

u-bar-^{d}šamaš
so. a-ab-ba-a.
n.d. Role unclear. Text 40: obv. 3.
so. nu-úr-^{d}sìn.
n.d. Witness. PBS 8/1 92: 18.
so. ^{d}sìn-en-nam.
1747. He sells a temple office to a-at-ta-a and im-gu-tum. Text 70: tablet obv. 5, 7, rev. 1; case obv. 5, 7, 14, seal.
so. ú-[ ].
1734. Witness. Text 15: rev. 16.

u$_4$-du$_7$-du$_7$
so. lú-^{d}nin-urta, br. ^{d}sìn-li-di-iš, ^{d}nanna-ma-an-sum, and ^{d}nin-urta-ri-im-ì-lí.
1810. With ^{d}nin-urta-ri-im-ì-lí he inherits from his father. PBS 8/1 12: 7, seal.
1816–1794. Witness. PBS 8/1 18: 20.
1775. Witness. *ARN* 36: rev. 2.
n.d. Witness. *ARN* 22: rev. 5.
gudu$_4$ ^{d}nin-líl-lá, fa. ^{d}iškur-gìr-ra and ip-qá-tum, "br." ^{d}adad-ra-bi.
1760. He had given a field plot to ^{d}adad-ra-bi in exchange for a temple office which is now disputed by mu-tum-ilum and ma-ri-er-ṣe-tim. BE 6/2 10: 8, 30, seal.
1755. BE 6/2 14: 27.
1739. BE 6/2 30: 17.

u$_4$-dùg-mu
hu. nin-kéš.
1895–1874. With his wife he sells a house plot to lú-^{d}nin-urta and lugal-ezen. Text 16: obv. 3, 4, 5, seal.

um-mi-ia-tum
NI. 1739. Witness. Text 34: rev. 5.

um-mi-wa-aq-ra-at
so. ^{d}sìn-re-me-ni.
n.d. With her son she borrows silver from lugal-murub$_4$-e. Text 97: 6.

ú-qá-ilam
so. an-né-ba-ab-du$_7$.
1793. Witness. Text 1: tablet rev. 16.
n.d. Witness. PBS 8/1 92: 22.

ur-[ ]
fa. a-píl-ì-lí-šu. 1738. Text 78: case rev. 4.
fa. dingir-ra-[ ]. 1755. Text 56: 5.
NI. 1860–1837. YOS 14 321: rev. II 2′.

ur-^{d}[ ]
so. bu-la-lum
1808. Witness. Text 63: rev. 3′.
NI. n.d. Neighbor. *ARN* 20: V 20 (joins OIMA 1 52).

ur-^{d}ba-ú
fa. a-wi-li-ia.
1760. BE 6/2 10: 48; PBS 13 67: rev. 8.
1755. *ARN* 70: rev. 11.
1745. OIMA 1 13: 29 (duplicate PBS 8/2 154; q.v. Ni 9244, case); PBS 8/2 129: tablet 37.
1742. Text 42: rev. 15.
1740. Text 31: rev. 15. Text 71: tablet rev. 9; case rev. 7′. Text 72: case rev. 11.
1739. Text 74: case rev. 14′.
1737. BE 6/2 40: 30.
1727. Text 83: tablet rev. 10.

ur-da-tum
so. ^{d}nin-urta-mu-ša-lim.
1734. Witness. Text 44: tablet rev. 8′; case rev. 9′.
so. ta-ri-bu-um, br. ^{d}šákkan-kur-ra.
1793. He receives grain from BI-KU$^{?}$-[ ]. Text 48: obv. 7.
fa. a-píl-^{d}šamaš. n.d. Text 89: tablet obv. 5; case 4′, seal.

ur-du$_{6}$-kù-ga
so. du-qá-qum.
1772. He frees a slave girl. Text 53: obv. 2, 10, 15, seal.
so. ìlí-ia-tum.
1747. Witness. Text 69: rev. 4.
1746. Witness. PBS 8/1 86: tablet 13; case 16.
1742. Witness. Text 42: rev. 10.
1739. He buys a field plot from ^{d}da-mu-e-ri-ba-am and ^{d}nuska-ni-šu. *ARN* 96: obv. 3, 12; OIMA 1 18: 3, 12.
so. ilum-na-ši, br. ^{d}en-líl-ma-an-sum, ṭāb-ba-la-ṭù, and ^{d}en-líl-gal-zu.
1742. With his brothers he inherits from his father. Text 42: obv. 15, 16, seal.
1738. Neighbor of ṭāb-ba-la-ṭù. Text 43: obv. 2.
so. ša-gi$_{4}$-iš-ki-nu-um.
1775. He sells a house plot to ^{d}amurru-ba-ni. Text 17: tablet obv. 4, 6, rev. 1; case obv. 4, 5, 11, seal.
so. ur-sukkal.
1833–1831. Witness. Text 37: rev. 8.
so. x-^{d}EN-[ ].
1749–1721. Witness. Text 30: rev. 7.
fa. ^{d}en-líl-[ ]. n.d. *ARN* 176: rev. 5′.
fa. ì-lí-ip-pa-al-sà. 1744. Text 60: rev. 9.
fa. im-gu-ru-um. 1789. *ARN* 31: rev. 12′.
fa. im-gu-tum. n.d. Text 68: case 4′.

fa. ip-qá-tum.
1747. Text 69: tablet obv. 4; case 3′, seal.
1739. BE 6/2 29: 5, 6.
fa. ^{d}nin-urta-ga-mil.
1739. BE 6/2 30: 11.
1727. Text 83: tablet rev. 7.
1726. Text 84: rev. 5′.
fa. ^{d}sìn-li-di-iš. 1775. Text 17: tablet rev. 8; case obv. 18.
nimgir (herald).
1740. Witness. Text 92: rev. 5.
NI. 1860–1837. Witness. Text 62: rev. 5′.
NI. 1815. Witness. Text 67: rev. 2.

ur-^{d}en-nu-gi$_{4}$
so. zi-ia-tum.
1793. Witness. Text 1: tablet rev. 12.
fa. a-ḫu-šu-nu, zi-ia-tum, and na-bi-^{d}šamaš.
1783. BE 6/2 7: 6, 9, seal.
1755. BE 6/2 14: 22; BE 6/2 15: 5.

ur-gá-giš-šú-a
fa. ^{d}nanna-ma-an-sum. 1762. PBS 8/1 82: 23.
dub-sar (scribe).
1808. Witness. TIM 4 23: 19.
1800. Witness. *ARN* 26: rev. 14.
1798. Witness. TIM 4 17: 26.
1775. Witness. Text 17: tablet rev. 13; case rev. 5.
1783. Witness. BE 6/2 6: 25.
n.d. Witness. *ARN* 52: rev. 17′; PBS 8/1 92: 25.
NI. 1775. Witness. Text 17: tablet rev. 13; case rev. 5.

ur-kù-zu
fa. a-lu-um. 1843. Text 3: rev. 8.
sanga ^{d}nanna.
1772. Witness. Text 53: rev. 11.

ur-^{d}lú-làl
NI. 1769. He divides two offices with a-gu-ú-a and u-bar-^{d}ba-ú. Text 11: obv. 6.

ur-^{d}nin-giz-zi-da
so. ^{d}lugal-[ ].
1873–1869. With lú-^{d}nin-sún and la-ma-ša he receives a payment of silver as settlement of a claim on a house. Text 36: obv. 7, 14, seal.

ur-^{d}sìn
so. ma-ṣa-am-ì-lí.
1895–1874. Witness. Text 16: rev. 1.

ur-sukkal
fa. ur-du$_{6}$-kù-ga. 1833–1831. Text 37: rev. 8.

ur-^{d}šul-pa-è-a
fa. ^{d}šamaš-ra-bi. 1738. Text 78: tablet rev. 6′; case rev. 8.
gudu$_{4}$, so. lú-^{d}da-mu.
1860–1837. Witness. YOS 14 321: rev. I 11′.

u-ṣí-na-wi-ir
so. KU-gu-za-na.
1895–1874. Witness. Text 94: rev. 5.

u_4-ta-u_{18}-lu-ḫé-ti
dub-sar (scribe), so. ip-qú-[ ].
1761. Witness. BE 6/2 13: 14.
1745. Witness. OIMA 1 13: 28 (duplicate PBS 8/2 154, q.v. Ni 9244, case); PBS 8/2 129: tablet 36.
1744. Witness. *ARN* 81: rev. 3; BE 6/2 26: IV 25.
1740. Witness. Text 31: rev. 16. Text 71: tablet rev. 10; case rev. 8′. Text 72: tablet rev. 10; case rev. 12.
1739. Witness. Text 74: tablet rev. 10; case rev. 15′. Text 75: tablet rev. 11; OIMA 1 19: 23.
1731. Witness. BE 6/2 49: 50.
1727. Witness. Text 83: tablet rev. 11.
1726. Witness. OIMA 1 27: rev. 2′.
1724. Witness. BE 6/2 59: tablet 19.
1749–1721. Witness. OIMA 1 29: 27′.
n.d. Witness. *ARN* 114: rev. 6′; N 1119: 5′.
NI. 1721. Neighbor of ištar-ki-ma-ì-lí-ia. Text 12: obv. 7.

u_4-ta-u_{18}-lu-me-$ša_4$
so. mu-mu-ì-pà.
1738. He sells a field plot to ^{d}da-mu-i-din-nam. OIMA 1 23: obv. 5, 7, seal.

^{d}UTU-[ ]
NI. 1849–1843. Witness. Text 7: rev. 8′.

^{d}utu-^{d}en-líl-lá
so. ^{d}sìn-en-nam.
1740. Witness. Text 31: rev. 13.
fa. ^{d}sìn-en-nam. 1793. Text 1: tablet rev. 17.

^{d}utu-gal-zu
fa. ^{d}šamaš-ma-gir.
1762. PBS 8/1 81: 8.
1745. OIMA 1 13: 27 (duplicate PBS 8/2 154, q.v. Ni 9244, case); PBS 8/2 129: tablet 31.
1744. BE 6/2 26: IV 22.

^{d}utu-ḫé-gál (^{d}utu-ḫe-gál)
NI. 1872. He rents a field plot from šu-na-a-a. Text 66: obv. 5.
NI. 1758. Neighbor of na-bi-^{d}šamaš. BE 6/2 11: 10.

W

warad-^{d}amurru
so. la-ma-ša, br. ^{d}nuska-ma-lik, a-ḫu-wa-qar, bu-la-lum, warad-ì-lí-šu, and e-la-lí.
1833–1831. With his brothers he sells a house plot to ib-ni-ia. Text 37: obv, 7, 10, seal.
so. lugal-īris(APIN).
1793. Witness. Text 1: tablet rev. 13.
so. lugal-me-lám.
n.d. Witness. PBS 8/1 92: 23.

warad-ì-lí-šu
so. la-ma-ša, br. ^{d}nuska-ma-lik, a-ḫu-wa-qar, bu-la-lum, e-la-lí, and warad-^{d}amurru.
1833–1831. With his brothers he sells a house plot to ib-ni-ia. Text 37: obv. 6, 9, seal.
fa(?). ma-ri-er-ṣe-tim and ša-gu-bu-u[m].
n.d. Text 64: seal.

warad-ìr-ra
fa. a-píl-ša. 1785. PBS 8/1 28: tablet 21.

warad-^{d}sìn
so. bu-sa-nu-um.
1789. Witness. *ARN* 31: rev. 8′.
NI. n.d. Text 52: 12′.

warda-uruk^{ki}
so. an-né-ba-ab-du$_{7}$.
1860–1837. Witness. YOS 14 321: rev. II 3′.

wa-ra-śu-nu (wa-ra-as-sú-nu)
fa. ^{d}sìn-iš-me-a-ni, ku-um-bu-lum, nu-rum-li-ṣi, and é-šar-ga-mil.
1755. BE 6/2 14: 3, 28.
nagar (carpenter).
1760. Neighbor of ma-ri-er-ṣe-tim and mu-tum-ilum. BE 6/2 10: 27.

wa-tar-pi$_{4}$-ša
so. ^{d}sìn-[ ].
1750. He has a dispute with ^{d}amurru-še-mi over a house plot. Text 22: obv. 5, 7, 11, rev. 4, seal.

we-e-di
fa. i-pí-iq-^{d}en-líl.
1860–1837. TIM 4 13: 2.
1751. TIM 4 28: 11.

Z

za-ba-bi-im
fa. u-bar-^{d}sìn. 1793. Text 1: tablet rev. 14.

zalag-^{d}nanna-ì-né-dùg
so. el-le-tum.
1755. Witness. BE 6/2 14: 25.

ZA.MU
fa. ^{d}nanna-tum. n.d. Text 33: obv. 3.

za-ri-qum
so. e-ku-ia.
n.d. Witness. Text 19: rev. 14.

zi-ia-tum
fa. ib-ni-é-a, fa.fa. ì-lí-ma-lu-lim.
1739. Text 74: case obv. 5.
fa. ur-^{d}en-nu-gi$_{4}$. 1793. Text 1: tablet rev. 12.
NI. n.d. Text 10: 2.

zi-na-tum
so. i-bi-ia.
1793. Witness. Text 48: rev. 5.

[ ]

[ ]-an-da-kal-[ ]
NI. 1736. Witness. Text 82: rev. 4′.

[ ]-ba-a-a-ba
so. ì-lí-[ ].
n.d. Neighbor of na-bi-^{d}en-lil(?). Text 55: obv. 3′.

[ ]-^{d}da-gan
NI. 1739. He rents a field plot from im-gur-^{d}sìn. Text 59: obv. 6.

[ ]-DINGIR
so. nu-úr-i-KI.
n.d. Witness. Text 24: rev. 7.

x-^{d}EN-[ ]
fa. [ur]-du$_6$-kù-ga. 1749–1721. Text 30: rev. 7.

[ ]-en-ia-tum
NI. n.d. Witness. Text 91: rev. 2′.

[ ]-^{d}en-líl-lá
so. na-bi-[ ], br. ^{d}nin-urta-ni-šu.
1738. Witness. Text 80: tablet rev. 2′.
ugula é-sikil.
1810. Witness. PBS 8/1 12: 26.

[ ]-ḫa-am-[ ]
NI. n.d. Witness. Text 86: tablet rev. 2.

[ ]-i-bi-[ ]
NI. n.d. He and ^{d}da-mu-i-din-nam exchange temple offices with ^{d}en-líl-ni-šu and a-lí-ai-tum(?). Text 86: tablet obv. 1.

[ ]-i-din-nam
NI. n.d. Text 24: rev. 12.

[ ]-ì-lí-šu
so. a-gu-ú-a.
1738. Witness. Text 77: rev. 7′.
NI. n.d. Witness. Text 19: rev. 6.

[ ]-ištar
so. ip-qá-tum.
1742. Witness. Text 50: rev. 1.

dub-sar (scribe).
1739. Witness. Text 76: rev. 5.

[ ]-kab-ta
so. [ ]-tum.
n.d. He buys a house(?) plot from ma-áš-qum. PBS 8/1 92: 6.

[ ]-la-du
NI. 1762. Witness. Text 58: 5′.

[ ]-li-tum
so. an-na-[ ].
1740. Witness. Text 71: tablet rev. 3; case rev. 1′.

[ ]-lú-ti(?)
fa. a-ab-ba-dingir. 1789. *ARN* 31: rev. 13′.

[ ]-ma-an-sum
fa. ^{d}sìn-e-ri-ba-am. 1738. Text 79: case rev. 6′.
so. l[ú-ú]ri^{ki}-ma$^{?}$.
1738. Neighbor of u_4-ta-u_{18}-lu-me-$ša_4$. OIMA 1 23: obv. 3.

[ ]-^{d}nanna
gudu$_4$ ^{d}nin-líl-lá.
1810. Witness. PBS 8/1 12: 27.

[ ]-^{d}nin-urta
fa.(?). a-bi-ia and lú-[ ]. 1739. Text 76: obv. 11.

[ ]-^{d}sìn
NI. 1860–1837. Text 62: seal.
NI. n.d. Text 86: seal.

[ ]-ta
NI. n.d. Neighbor of ma-áš-qum. PBS 8/1 92: 3.

[ ]-tu/i-ri
NI. 1743. He rents a field plot from a-píl-^{d}adad. Text 49: obv. 7.

[ ]-tum
fa. [ ]-kab-ta. n.d. PBS 8/1 92: 7.
NI. 1747. Text 70: tablet rev. 7, 8; case rev. 3, 4.

[ ]-um
so. ^{d}inanna-[ ].
n.d. Adopter or adoptee. Text 10: 1.
dub-sar (scribe).
1747. Witness. Text 70: case rev. 9′.

[ ]-UTU
NI. 1740. Witness. Text 71: tablet rev. 2.

APPENDIX VI

Suggested Corrections to Albrecht Goetze, "The Archive of Ātta from Nippur"[1]

Page 102

2N-T 778a does not now exist, but it appears that what Goetze calls 2N-T 778a is now marked 2N-T 776a and is actually the case to 2N-T 769.

2N-T 769:

Rev. 1, read ù ibila-a-ni a-na-me-a-bi.
Rev. 3, for gù-nu-gá-gá read inim nu-⸢gá⸣-gá-⸢a⸣.
Rev. 7, read dumu Lú-^{d}Nin-[urta].
Rev. 8, read igi [^{d}En]-líl-na-da dumu Na-ra-am-^{d}Sin.
Rev. 11, read igi u$_{4}$-ta-u$_{18}$-lu-ḫé-⸢ti⸣ dub-sar.
Rev. 15, read dùg-ga an ^{d}En-líl-bi-ta.

Page 105

2N-T 771:

Rev. 1, probably reads [bal-gub-ba]-bi-[šè].
Rev. 2, read ^{d}Utu-ka mu-⸢a⸣ [u$_{4}$-5-kam].

Page 106

Rev. 12, read mu Sa-am-su-i-lu-na lugal-⸢e⸣.
Rev. 15, read [ù] E-mu-ut-ba-lum^{ki}.

2N-T 773:

Rev. 4, read bal-⸢gub-ba⸣-bi-šè inim nu-gá-gá-[a].

Page 107

The list of offices for 2N-T 770 reads: nam gudu$_{4}$ nam ugula-é nam ì-d[u$_{8}$ na]m-kisal-luḫ ù nam-bur-šu-ma.

The list of offices for 2N-T 780 reads: nam gudu$_{4}$ nam ugula-é nam ⸢ì-du$_{8}$ nam kisal-luḫ⸣ ù ab-kù-maḫ-a é ^{d}lugal-ab-a.

3N-T 374 reads: nam gudu$_{4}$ nam ugula-é nam [ì-du$_{8}$$^{?}$] ù nam bur-šu-ma é ^{d}lugal-ab-[a] ù ^{d}ab-kù-maḫ-a.

Below he lists a second set of offices for 2N-T 780.

2N-T 762 is not part of this archive. Perhaps Goetze meant 2N-T 782, but at this time the obverse is too badly worn for one to tell whether the nam ì-du$_{8}$ was left out.

2N-T 772 reads: nam gudu$_{4}$ nam ^{lú}šim na[m].

pa-líl is better read ugula-é.

[1] *Journal of Cuneiform Studies* 18 (1964).

Page 108

2N-T 764 also has offices in the temple of the sun god.

Both the case and the tablet of 2N-T 770 give the temple as é ^{d}lugal-ab-a.

The temple ^{d}ab-zu-maḫ may be better read ^{d}ab-kù-mah.

Footnote 24: 2N-T 766 does not have the redemption clause cited here.

Page 109

The purchaser in 2N-T 770 is ^{d}adad-[ta]-⌜a-a-ar⌝.

1d. The phrase used in all cases is in-ši-in-sa$_{10}$, including 2N-T 377 and 770 tablet. 2N-T 778a, as noted above, is the case to 2N-T 769 and does not differ substantially from that text.

There is no text 2N-T 314 belonging to this archive, but since 2N-T 374 is a redemption text, I assume that this was the text intended; the phrase used is in-du$_{8}$, and I am sure that this same phrase was also used in 2N-T 767, but it is no longer preserved.

The poorly preserved remains of 2N-T 764 suggest that the temple involved was é-^{d}Utu; the number of days was probably 1 month, or a fraction of a month, and 6 days.

The price on 2N-T 378 is 4½ shekels; the number of days is probably 5.

Although admittedly fragmentary, the price on 2N-T 782 appears to be 8½ shekels.

The price on 2N-T 374 is 5⅓ shekels, 15 grains.

The office of 2N-T 779 was held for 7½ days.

Footnote 27: 2N-T 770 had the correct form of the verb, in-ne-en-lá. The phrase added to describe the objects of the deal is bal-gub-ba-ni.

2N-T 767 and 768 have dates of Samsuiluna 12.

List of Proper Names

A-ap-pa-a-a: Also occurs on 2N-T 782, tablet rev. 7 and on 2N-T 774, tablet rev. 5; case rev. 7.

A-bi-ik-ku: She also occurs on 2N-T 782 line 7, and her full name is A-bi-ik-ku-ú-a.

^{d}Adad-xxx: This name can be read ^{d}Adad-ta-a-a-ar.

A-ḫu-šu-nu: He is recorded as the father of ^{d}Sin-im-gur-ra-ni and Ta-ri-ba-tum on 2N-T 770 case lines 6, 8, and rev. 1′, tablet lines 6′, 8′, and 15′.

A-lí-^{d}En-lil: On 2N-T 777 at present all that can be read is A-lí-DINGIR. However, if a theocratic name followed, it cannot have been either Sin or Enlil. With both of these names the determinative DINGIR is combined with the EN of the name when written. In this instance the DINGIR stands alone. I suspect that, as in 3N-T 375, this name should be read A-lí-ilum; the traces that follow the name could be the beginning of a GUDU$_{4}$.

A-lu-ut-ta-tum: This name should be read A-lu-ut-ta-ḫi; in addition to being the daughter of A-píl-ì-lí-šu, she is also the wife of Da-mi-iq-ì-lí-šu.

Ama-x-la-x: This name can be read Ip-⌜qú?-ša?⌝.

AN-ma-an-sum: He is also recorded as the father of Li-pí-it-Ištar in 2N-T 774 line 12.

Anum-mu-de: He is the father of ^{d}Nin-urta-ga-mil in 2N-T 770.

An-nu-um-pī-^{d}x: Should be read An-nu-um-pī-^{d}Šamaš in 2N-T 377 and An-nu-um-pī-Ištar in 2N-T 766. An-nu-um-pī-Ištar is the sister of Ḫu-na-ba-tum and the daughter of E-te-el-pī-^{d}Nuska; she also occurs on line 8. An-nu-um-pī-^{d}Šamaš is the son of ì-lí-ma.

A-píl-É-a: Should be read a-ap-pa-a-a in 2N-T 774.

A-píl-ì-lí-šu: He does not appear on 2N-T 780, nor is his father's name recorded. In 2N-T 774 his father's name is Ur-[ ]. In 2N-T 780 he is the father of A-lu-ut-ta-ḫi.

A-wi-li-ia: He also occurs on 2N-T 776 rev. 11.

A-[ ]: Should be read Ur-[ ].

Da-mi-iq-ì-lí-šu: He is the son of ^{d}Nin-urta-ma-an-sum in 2N-T 768 and the husband of A-lu-ut-ta-ḫi in 2N-T 780.

^{d}Da-mu-e-ri-ba-am: He and his brother, probably ^{d}Nin-urta-mu-ba-lí-iṭ, seal the text. Since we do not know if this is a sale text, we cannot tell what role they played.

^{d}Da-mu-gal-zu: His name is recorded on 2N-T 771 tablet line 7 and case line 8.

^{d}Da-mu-ú-a: The son of ^{d}En-líl-ma-an-sum in 2N-T 768 is recorded in line 5 of the reverse and *may* be better read as a-gú-ú-a, but the fragmentary remains could be read either way, and the Nippur prosopography is no help.

E-la-a: He is recorded as the father of Ta-ri-ba-tum on line 5 of 2N-T 773 tablet and on line 6 of the case, as well as on the seal. He is also attested on 2N-T 776 rev. 8.

El-le-tum: His father's name is Lú-^{d}Nin-urta, and 2N-T 782 indicates that the gudu$_4$ ^{d}Nin-líl-lá and the son of Lú-^{d}Nin-urta are the same person.

^{d}En-líl-gal-zu: He is the son of Ilu-na-ši.

^{d}En-líl-i-tu-ra-am: He is also recorded a a nu-èš.

^{d}En-líl-ma-an-sum: The gudu$_4$ ^{d}Nin-líl-lá is the son of Lú-^{d}Nin-urta. The reference in 2N-T 777 was reverse line 8′, but since this is a very common name at Nippur, and since neither profession nor patronymic is preserved in this text, I am not sure that we are justified in making this identification here. In 2N-T 780, the name is better read [nu-ra]-tum, another gudu$_4$ son of Lú-^{d}Nin-urta. In 2N-T 783, he is the son of ^{d}Nin-urta-ma-an-sum.

^{d}En-líl-mu-ba-lí-iṭ: In 2N-T 788 the name should be read ^{d}Nin-urta-mu-ba-lí-iṭ, the brother of ^{d}Da-mu-e-ri-ba-am. The ^{d}En-lil-mu-ba-lí-iṭ in 2N-T 777 may not be a dub-sar. This name precedes that of the bur-gul, while the scribe's name usually follows that of the seal-cutter.

E-te-ia-tum: He is not a dub-sar but the son of ^{d}Da-mu-[ ].

E-te-el-pī-^{d}Nin-urta: In 2N-T 766 this name is better read as E-te-el-pī-^{d}Nuska. 2N-T 776 rev. 8 reads ⌜Ta-ri⌝-ba-tum dumu E-l[a-a], and the seal reads A-píl-^{d}[Šamaš] dumu Ur-da-tum. No other text in the archive has a name similar to E-te-el-pī-^{d}Nin-urta.

Ḫa-ba-(an)-na-tum: She is the lukur ^{d}Nin-urta.

Ḫu-na-ba-tum: She is the daughter of E-te-el-pī-^{d}Nuska and the sister of An-nu-um-pī-Ištar.

Ḫu-mu$^{?}$-ru-um: He is the father of ^{d}Adad-ta-a-a-ar.

I-bi-^{d}En-líl: Occurs on lines 4, 5, and 11 of 2N-T 769.

I-bi-^{d}Sîn: He is the father of A-ap-pa-a; he also occurs on 2N-T 774 rev. 5, case rev. 7.

Ib-ni-É-a: He is also the son of Zi-ia-tum and the husband of A-bi-ik-ku-ú-a; he occurs on 2N-T 782 tablet lines 6 and case lines 4 and 7.

I-din-Ištar: Occurs on lines 4′, 5′, and 10′.

Ì-lí-ba-aš-ti: Perhaps better read Ì-lí-ma-an-sum.

Ì-lí-i-din-nam: Occurs on 2N-T 769 lines 4, 5, and 11.

Ì-lí-iš-me-a-ni: Also described as a šidim.

Ì-lí-ia-tum: Occurs on 2N-T 779, tablet rev. 4.

Ì-lí-ma-lu-lim: He is the son of Ib-ni-É-a and A-bi-ik-kú-a.

Ilum-ma-^{d}Adad: Neither he nor his son appears in 2N-T 780.

Im-gur-^{d}Nin-urta: He is the son of Lú-^{d}Nin-urta.

Im-gu-ra-tum: Is better read Im-gur-^{d}Nin-urta.

Inim-^{d}Nin-urta: Probably an ugula.

Ip-qú-^{d}Da-mu: Also occurs on 2N-T 374 rev. 3′.

Li-pí-it-Ištar: He is the son of AN-ma-an-sum; he also occurs on 2N-T 777 lines 5′, 10′, and 12′.

Lú-^{d}Nin-líl-lá: Should be read Lú-^{d}Nin-urta. The name is not preserved in 2N-T 777 or 2N-T 375. In 2N-T 780 he is the father of Nu-ra-tum.

Na-bi-^{d}Šamaš: He is the son of Ì-lí-ma-an and brother of An-nu-um-pī-^{d}Šamaš.

Na-bi-[ ]: He is the father of Lú-^{d}En-líl-lá.

Na-ra-am-^{d}Sin: The alternate form of Im-gu-tum is Im-gur-^{d}Nin-urta. As father of Ip-qú-^{d}Da-mu he also occurs on 2N-T 374 rev 3 and 2N-T 778 case rev. 5. The Ur-xxx in 2N-T 374 should be read Ip-qu-^{d}Da-mu.

Na-ra-am-tum: Should be read Nu-ra-tum.

Na-[ ]: Perhaps should be read [^{d}]Nin-t[u]. It seems probable that ^{d}Nuska-ni-šu (which should be read DINGIR-šu-ì-lí-šu) was another witness, not the father.

^{d}Nin-líl-ma-an-sum: Should be read ^{d}Nin-urta-ma-an-sum. There is no particular reason to suppose that Da-mi-iq-ì-lí-šu and Na-bi-^{d}En-líl in 2N-T 783 were the brothers of ^{d}En-líl-ma-an-sum and therefore the sons of ^{d}Nin-urta-ma-an-sum. It is just as likely that they were identified simply by their professions.

^{d}Nin-líl-a-[ ]: Line 12 of 2N-T 775a should probably be read [nam gudu$_{4}$] ^{d}Nin-líl a-na-me[a-bi]. I read the seller's name in this text as A-bi-ia. However, the entire text is very badly worn and difficult to understand.

^{d}Nin-líl-xx-[ ]: This is better read ^{d}Nin-urta-ga-mil.

^{d}Nin-urta-ga-mil: He also occurs as the son of Anum-mu-de (or Dingir-mu-sillim?) in 2N-T 770 rev. 3.

Nu-ra-tum: He is also a son of Lú-^{d}Nin-urta and also occurs on 2N-T 780 rev. 8 and 2N-T 777 rev. 6.

^{d}Nuska-ni-šu: Is better read as DINGIR-šu-ib-ni-šu in 2N-T 374. 2N-T 772 rev. 4 has no possible mention of ^{d}Nuska-ni-šu.

Pir-ḫi-^{d}x: 2N-T 766 rev. 9 reads Na-bi-^{d}En-líl dumu I-din-^{d}Nin-urta.

Sí-ia-tum: He is the father of Ib-ni-É-a.

^{d}Sîn-ma-gir: He is also the purchaser in 2N-T 766 line 10.

^{d}Sîn-x-[ ]: Should be read ^{d}Sîn-im-gur-ra-ni.

^{d}Šamaš-i-qí-ša-am: The name in 2N-T 778 should be read Ì-lí-i-qí-ša-am.

^{d}Šamaš-ra-bi: He is the son of Ur-^{d}Šul-pa-é-a.

Ta-ri-ba-tum: He is recorded on 2N-T 773 lines 5, 6, and 12. Ta-ri-ba-tum son of E-la-a also occurs on 2N-T 776 rev. 8.

U-bar-^{d}Šamaš: Also occurs on rev. line 1.

Ur-^{d}Nin-líl: Should be read Ur-^{d}Nin-urta.

Ur- [ ]: Should be read Ur-^{d}Šul-pa-é-a.

Ur-x[x]xx: Should be read Ip-qú-^{d}Da-mu.

Ut-ta-gàl-lu-ḫé-ti: I cannot see his patronymic. He also occurs on 2N-T 769 rev. 11 and 2N-T 766 rev. 11.

Warad-^{d}En-líl: In 2N-T 766 this should be read Na-bi-^{d}En-líl, and his patronymic should be read I-din-^{d}Ninurta.

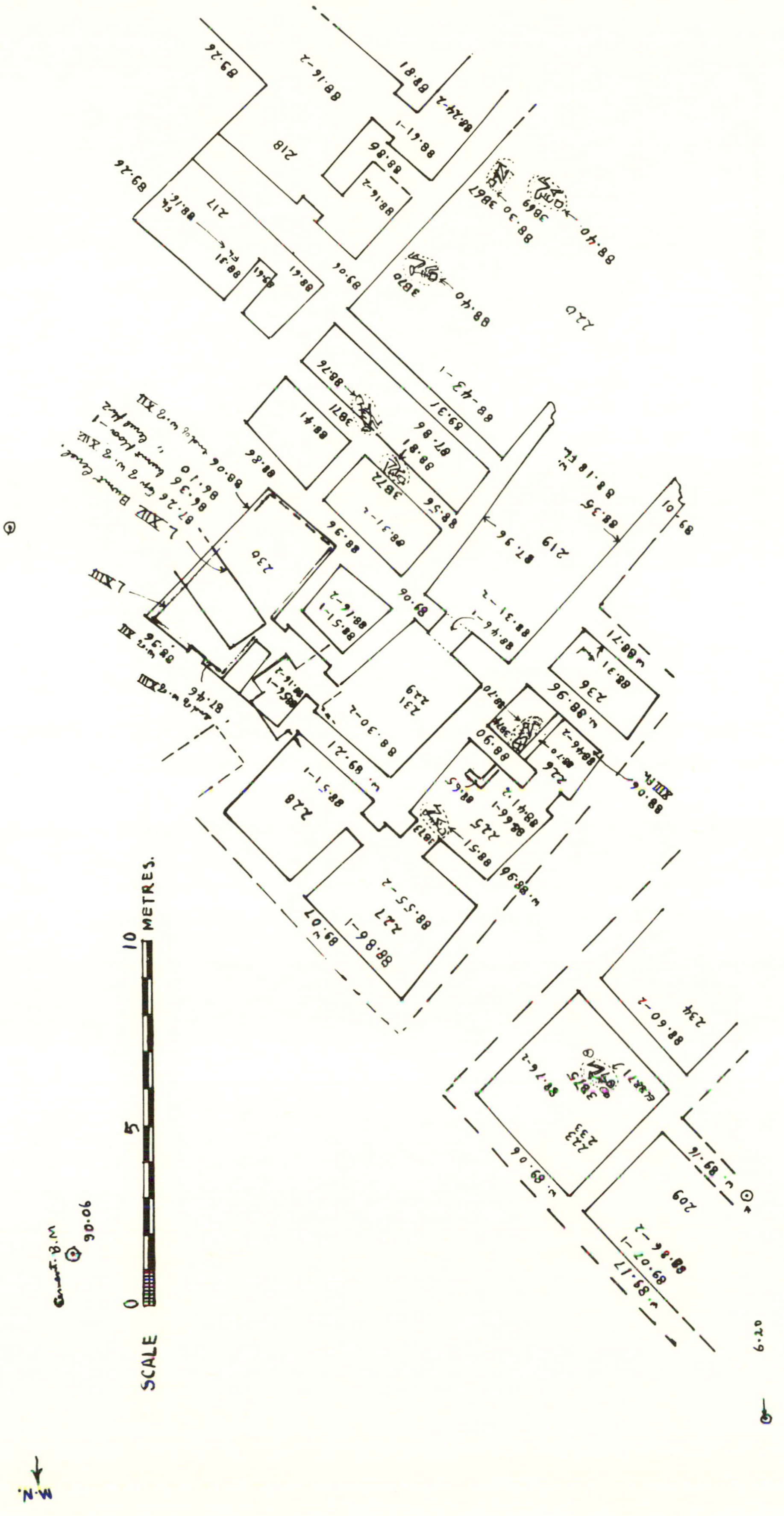

Field Plan: Area TA, Level XII

PLATE 2

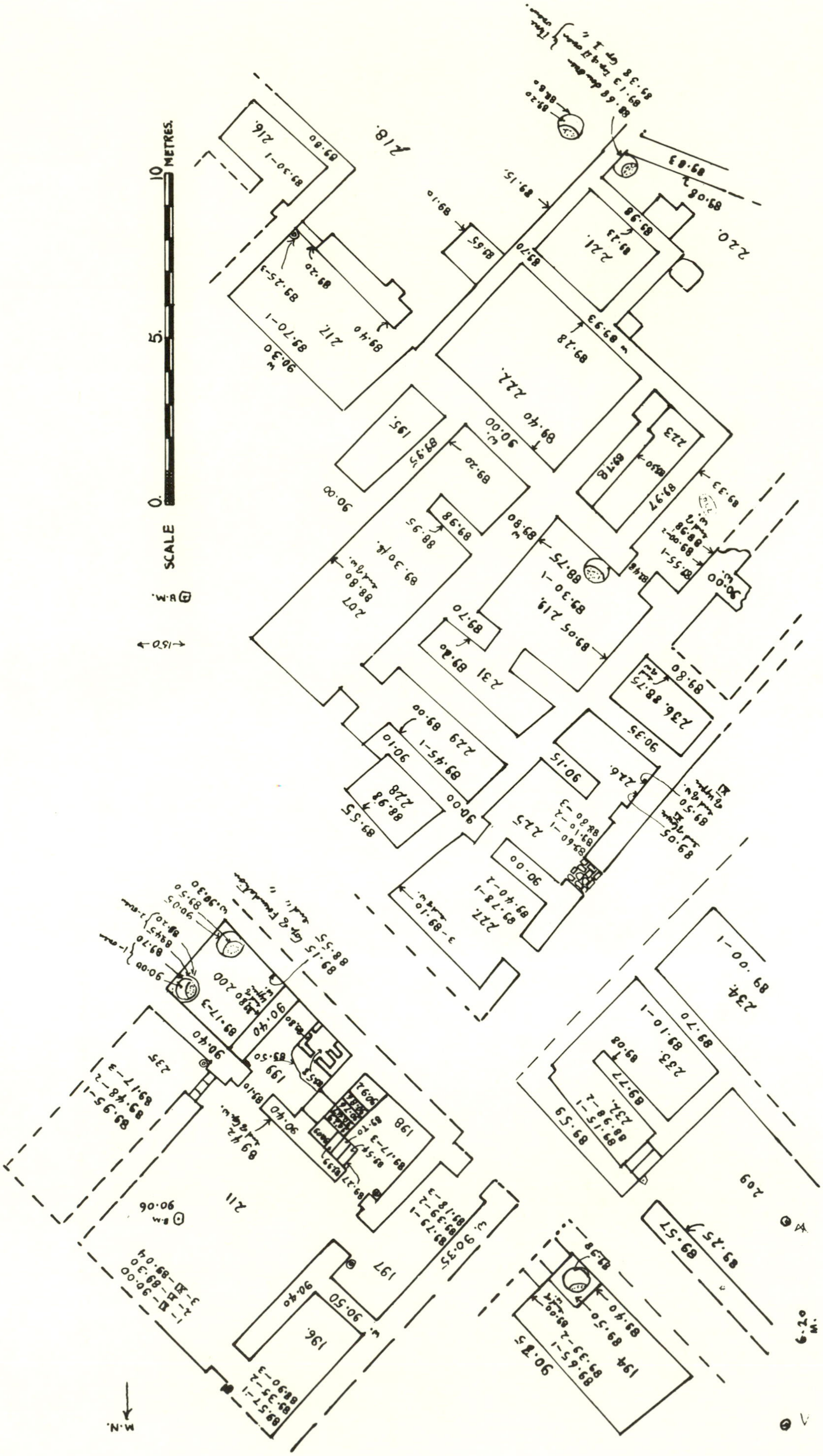

Field Plan: Area TA, Level XI

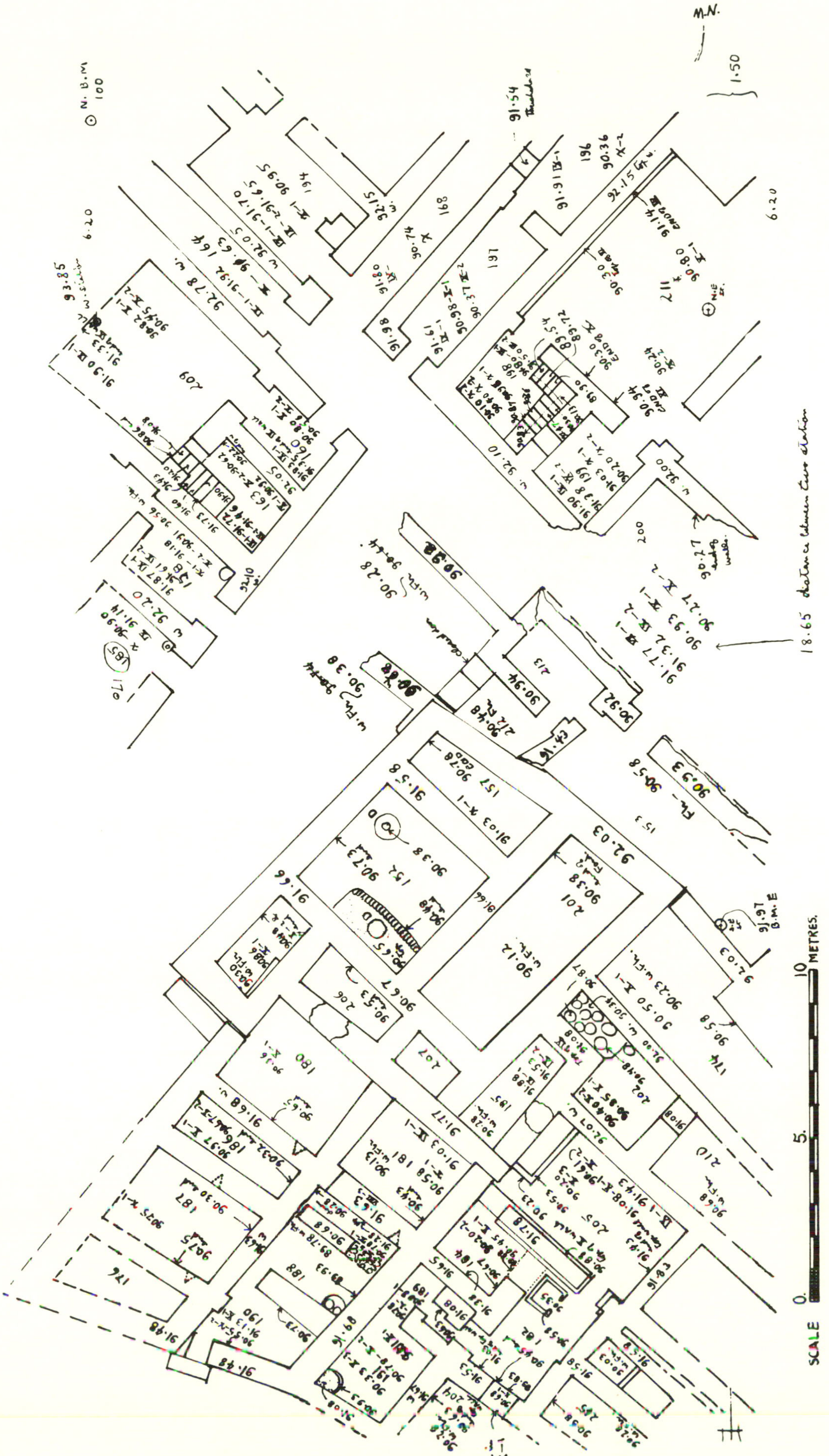

Field Plan: Area TA, Levels X and IX

PLATE 4

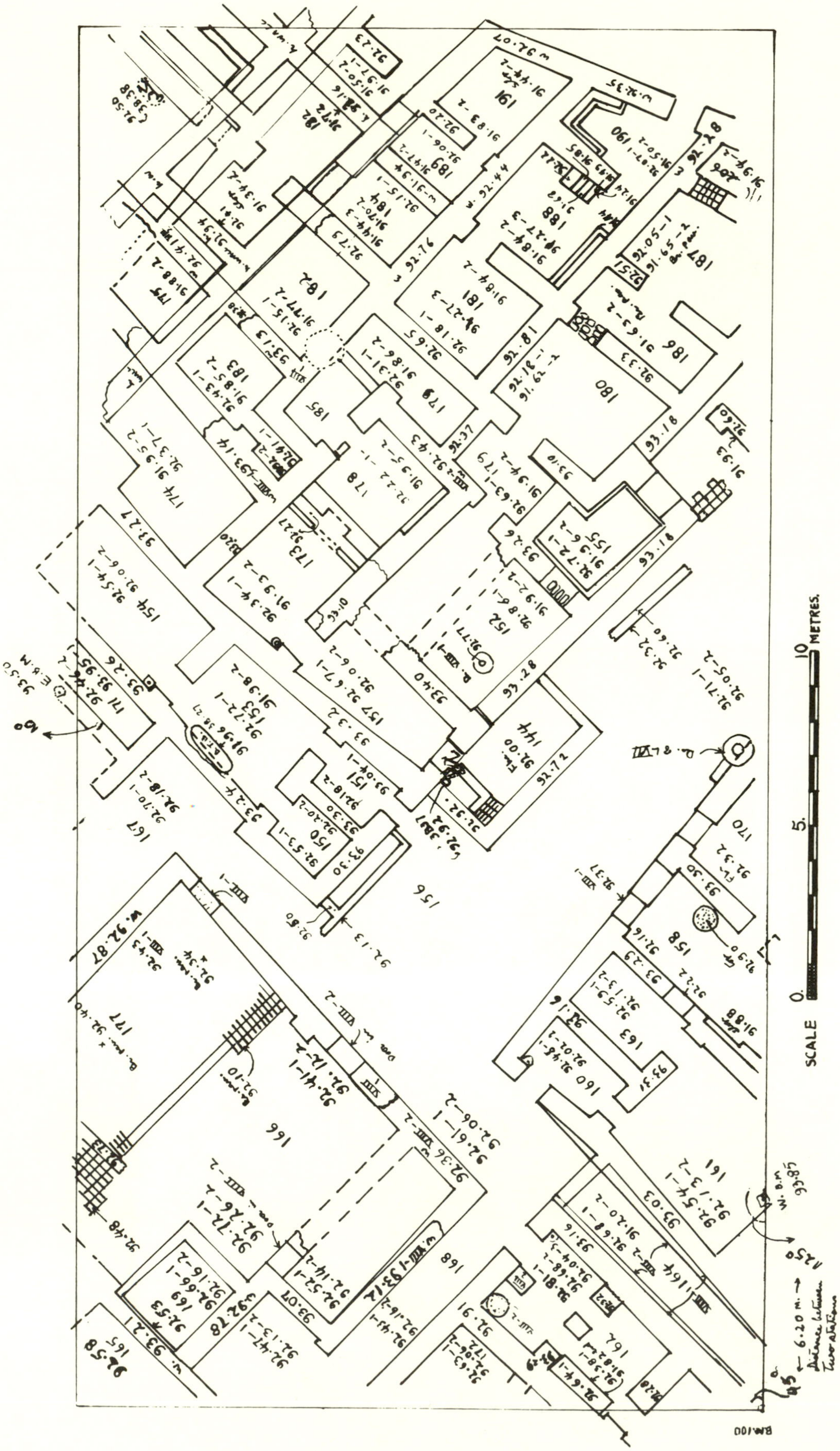

Field Plan: Area TA, Level VIII

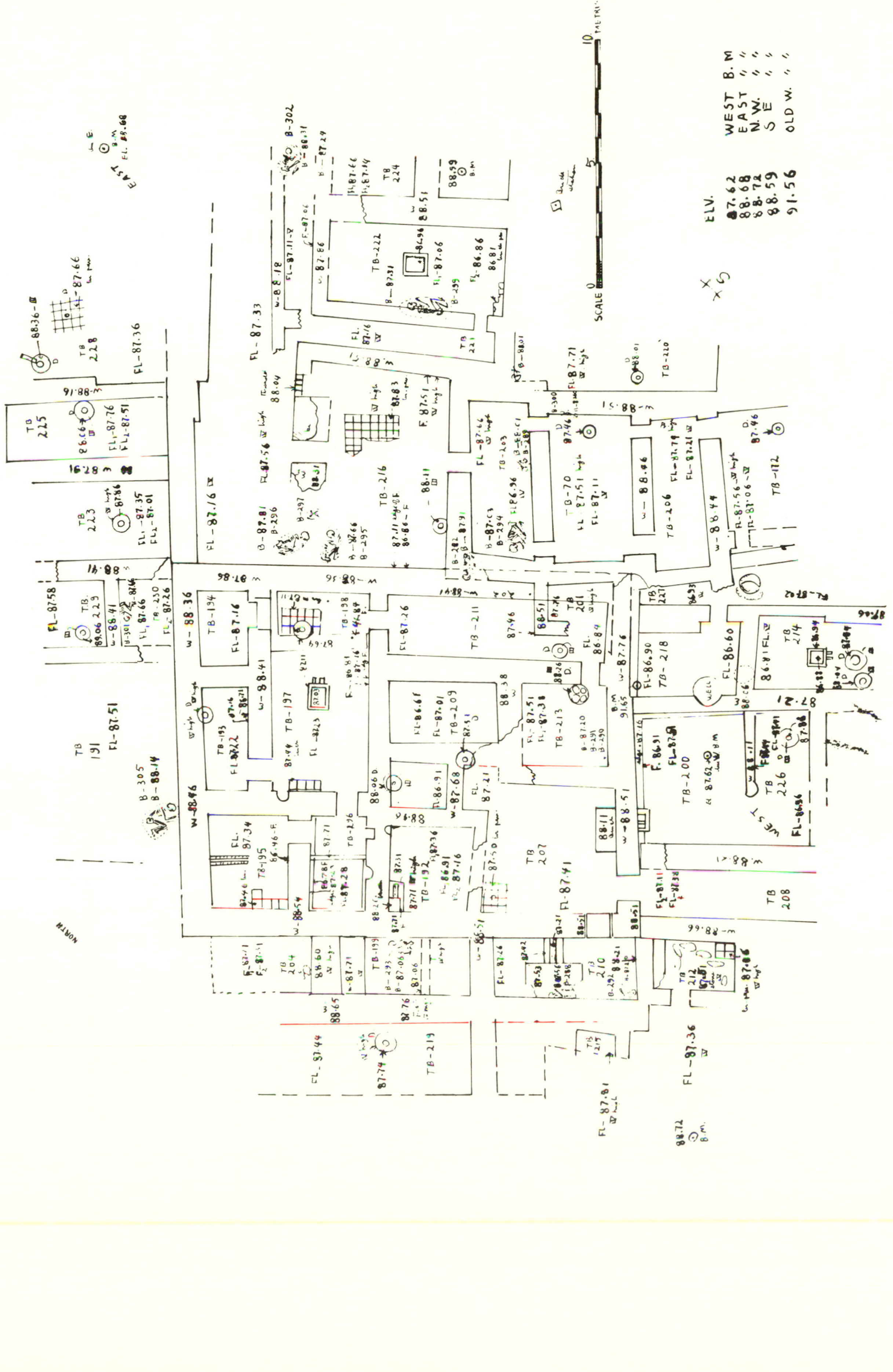

Field Plan: Area TB, Level IV

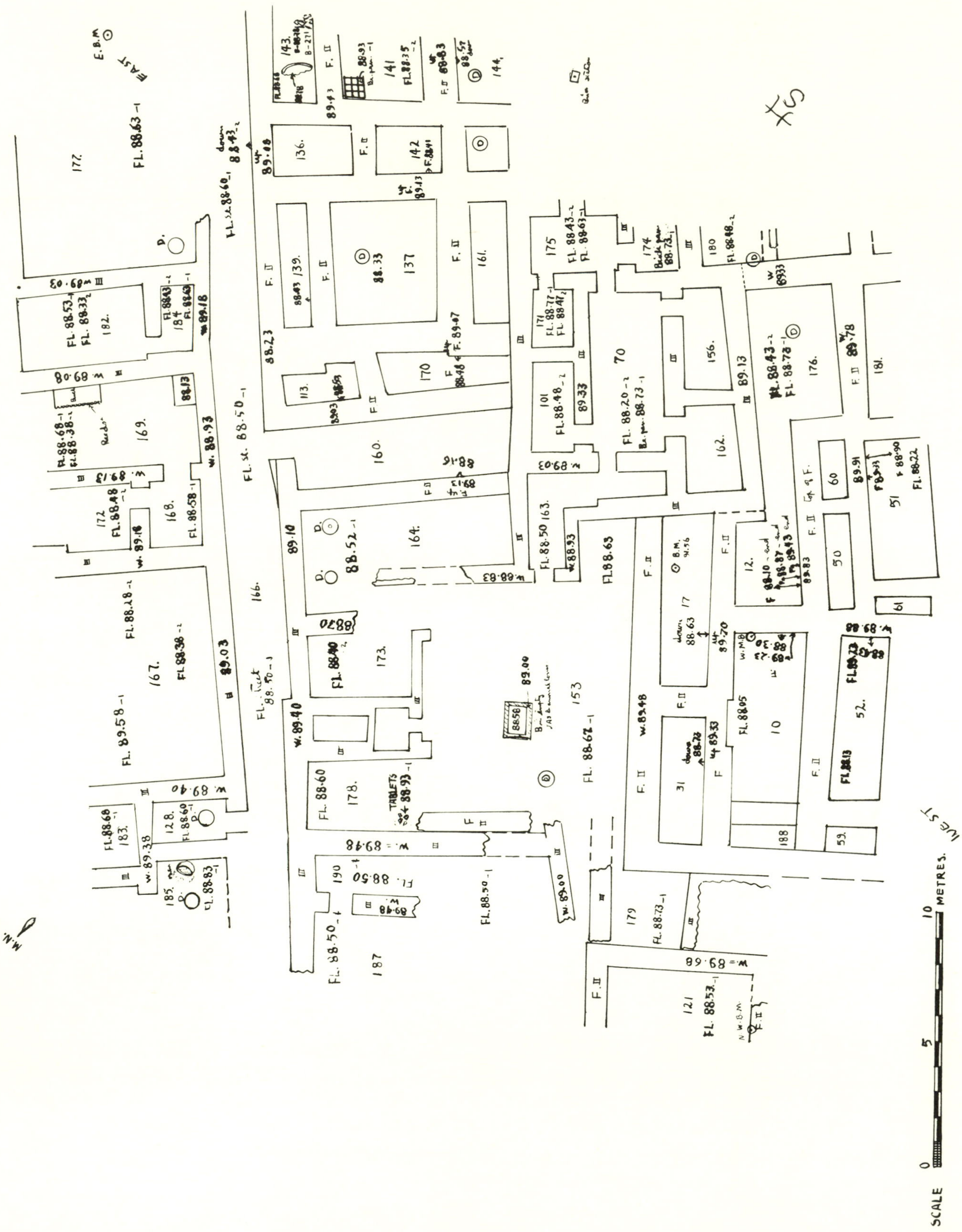

Field Plan: Area TB, Level III

Field Plan: Area TB, Level II, Floors 1 and 2

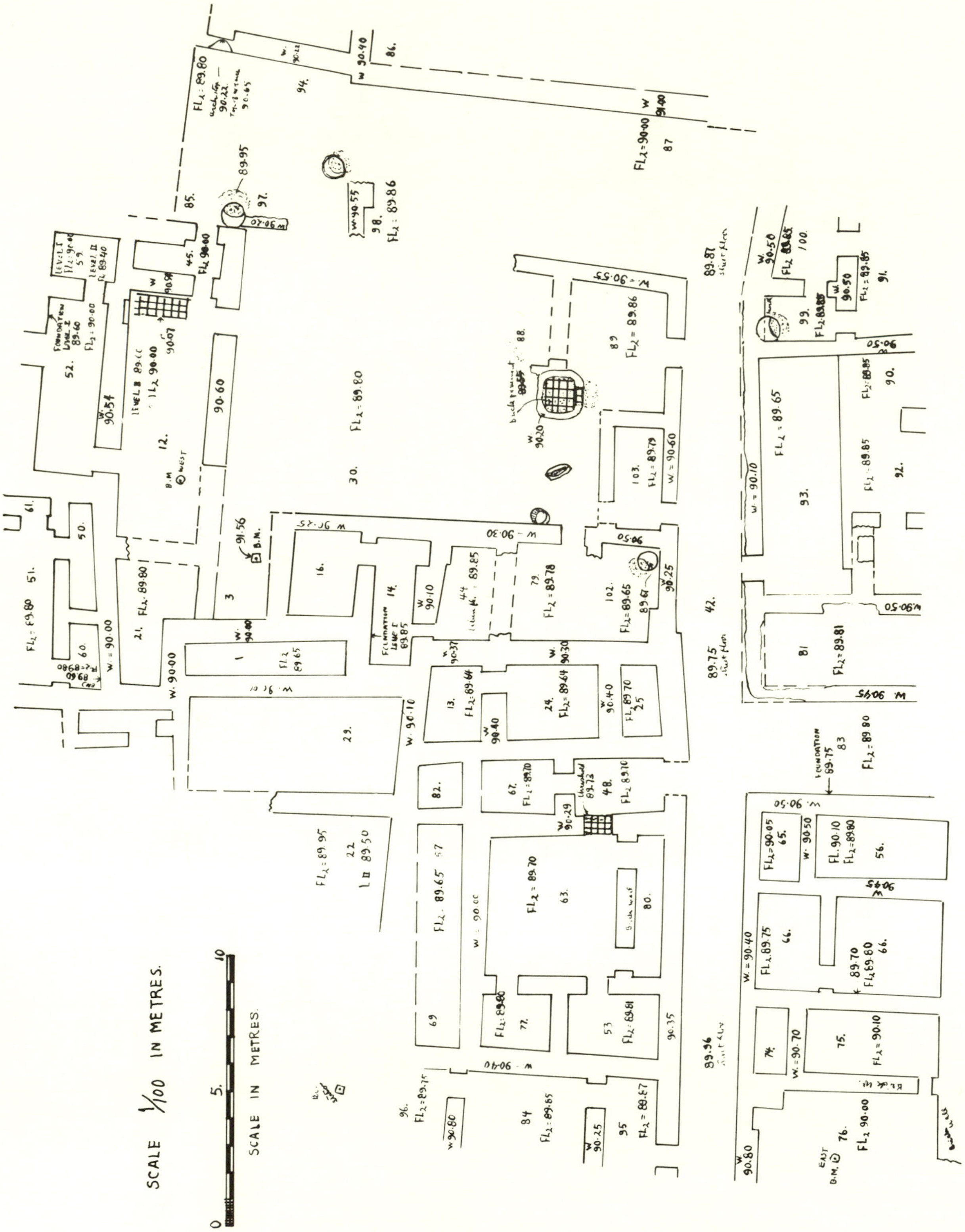

Field Plan: Area TB, Level I, Floor 2

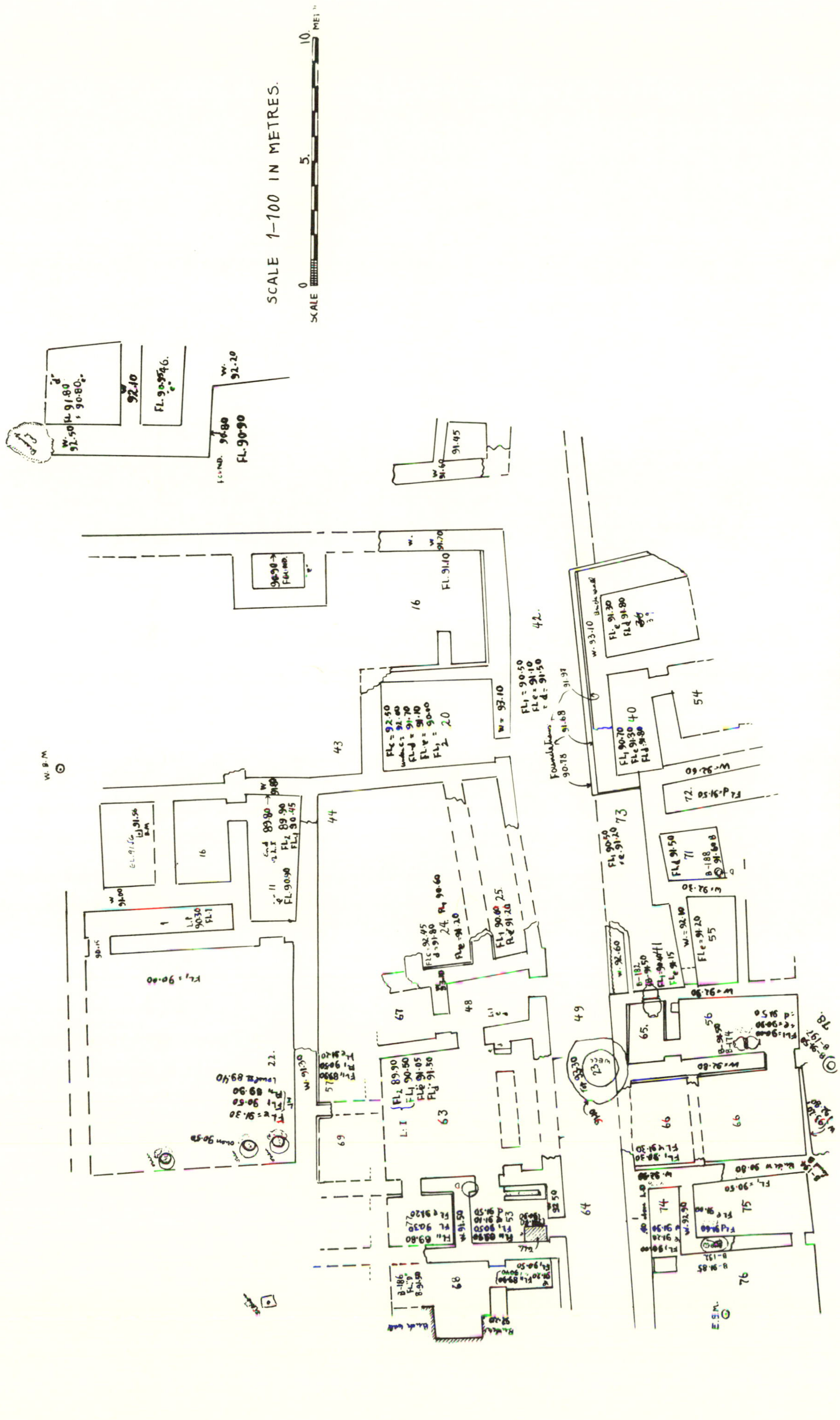

Field Plan: Area TB, Levels D and E

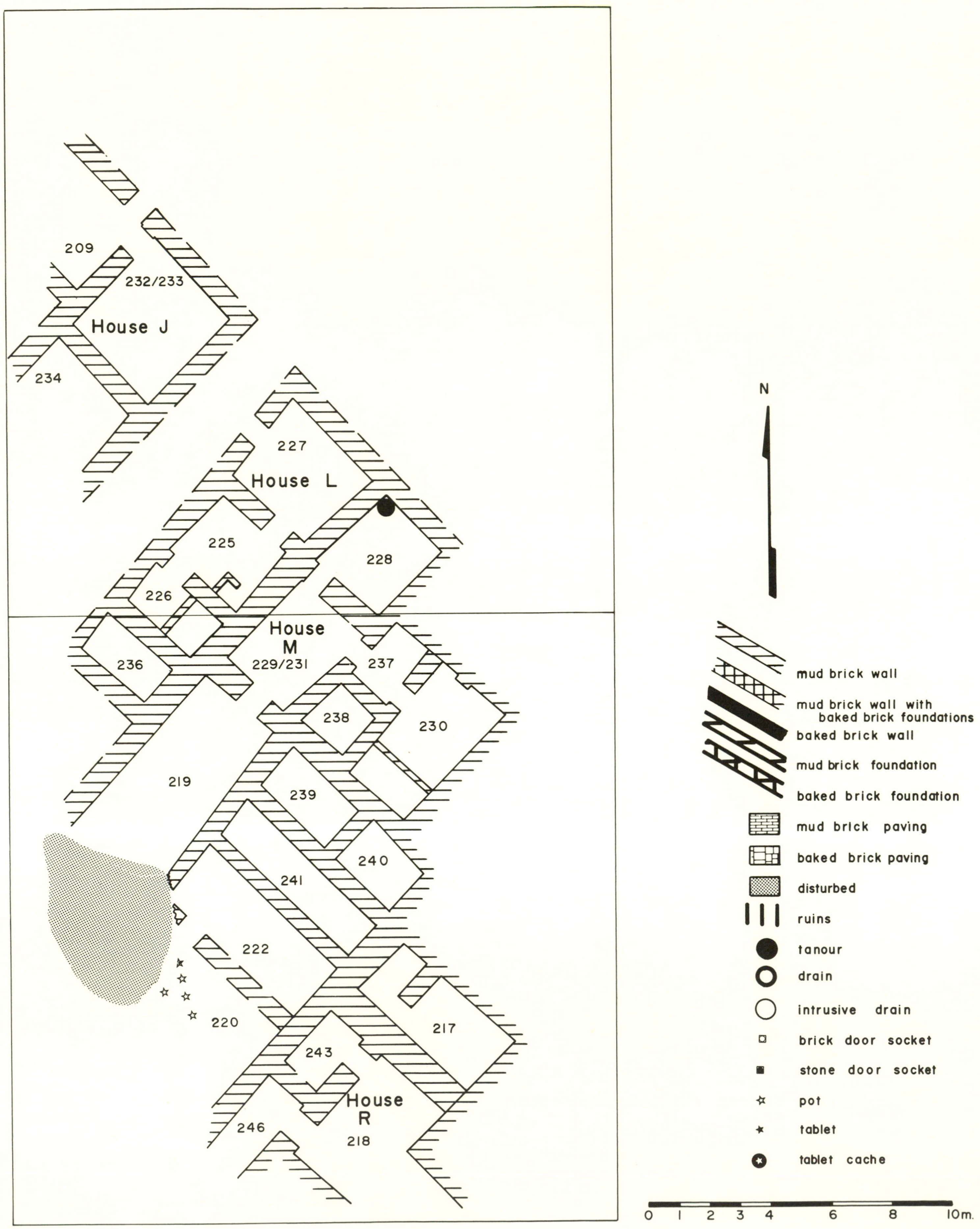
209
232/233
House J
234
227
House L
225
228
226
House
M
229/231
236
237
238
230
219
239
240
241
222
220
217
243
House
R
246
218
N
mud brick wall
mud brick wall with
baked brick foundations
baked brick wall
mud brick foundation
baked brick foundation
mud brick paving
baked brick paving
disturbed
ruins
tanour
drain
intrusive drain
brick door socket
stone door socket
pot
tablet
tablet cache
0 1 2 3 4 6 8 10m.

Area TA, Level XIII, Floor 2

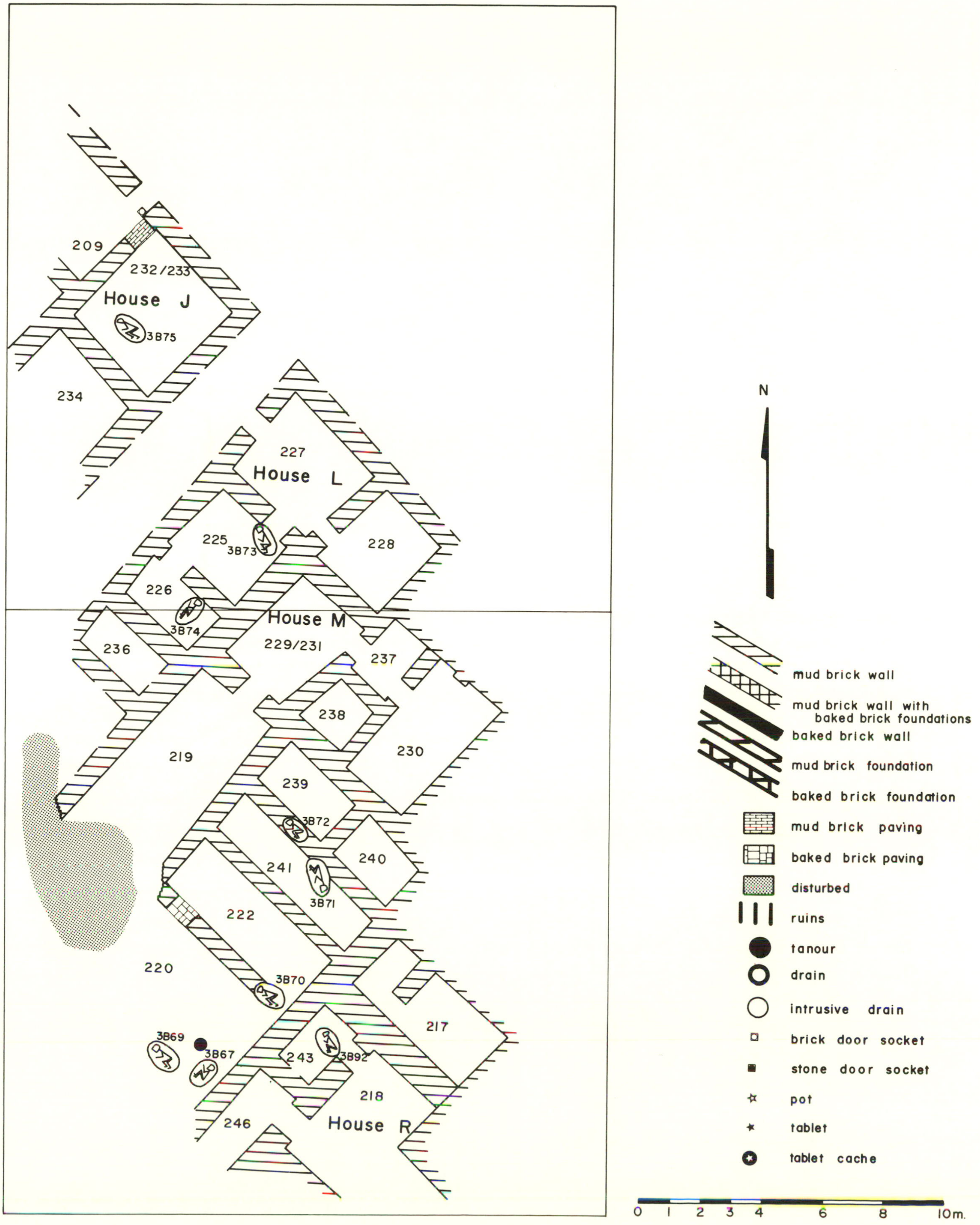

Area TA, Level XIII, Floor 1

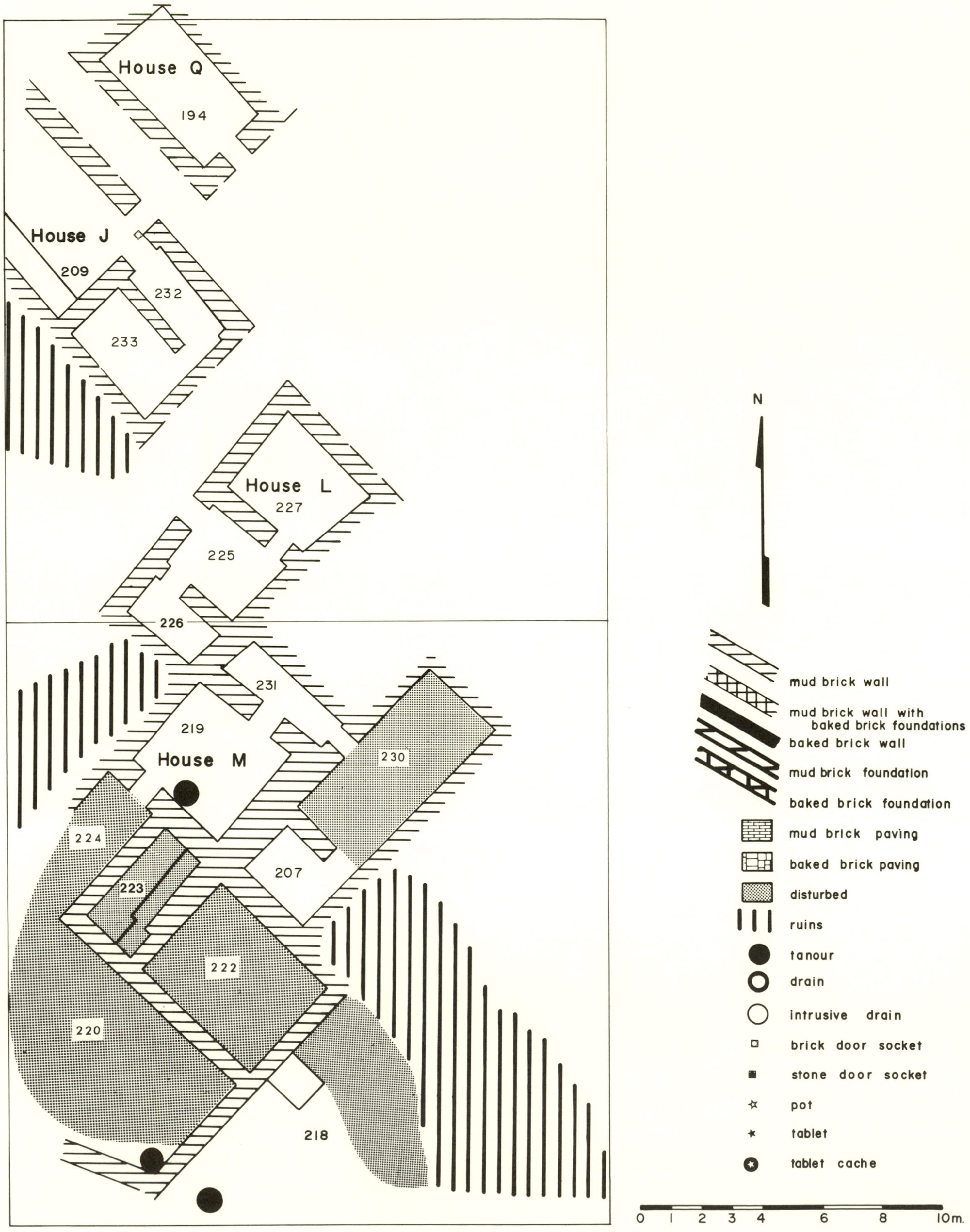

Area TA, Level XIIB, Floor 2

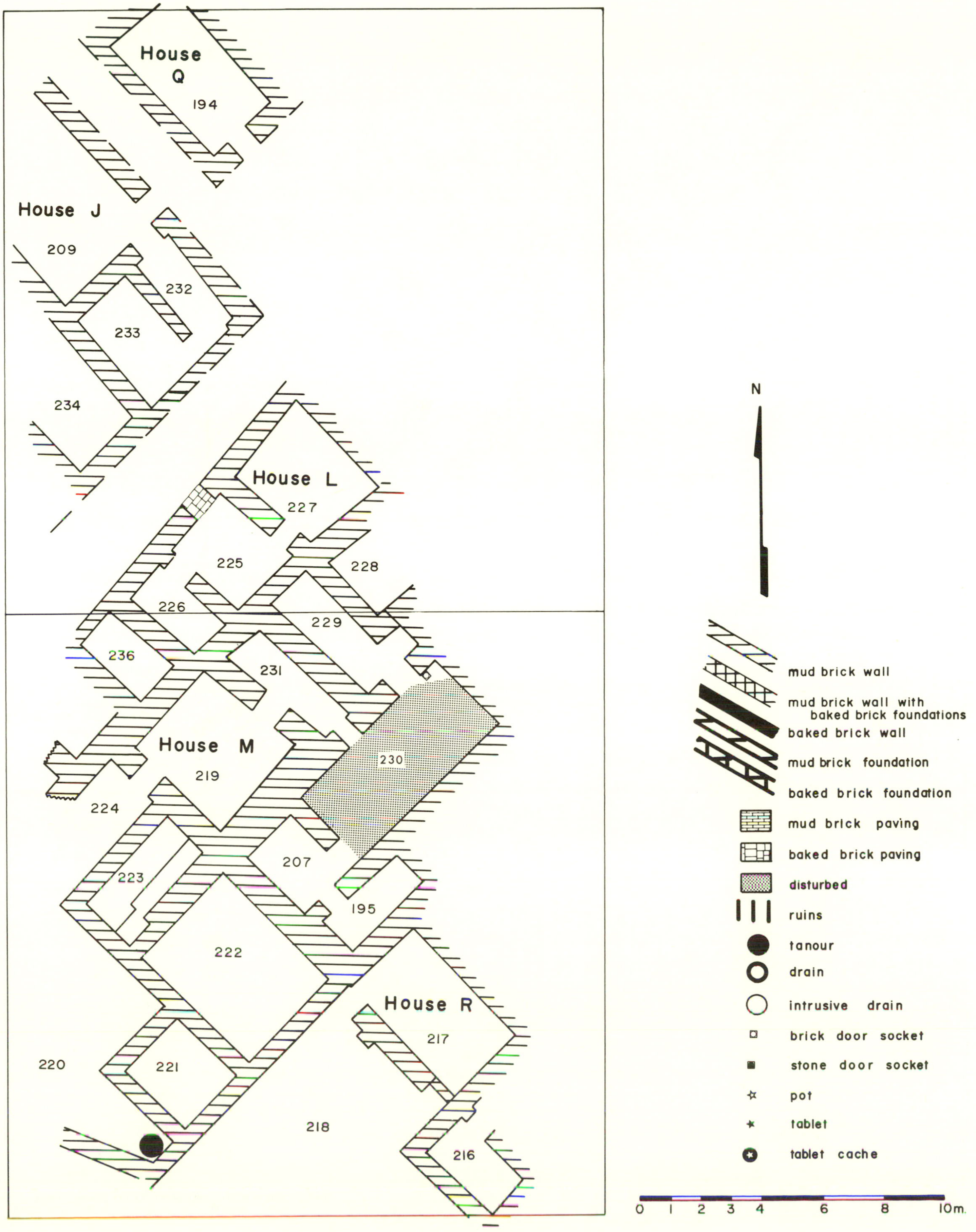

Area TA, Level XIIB, Floor 1

PLATE 14

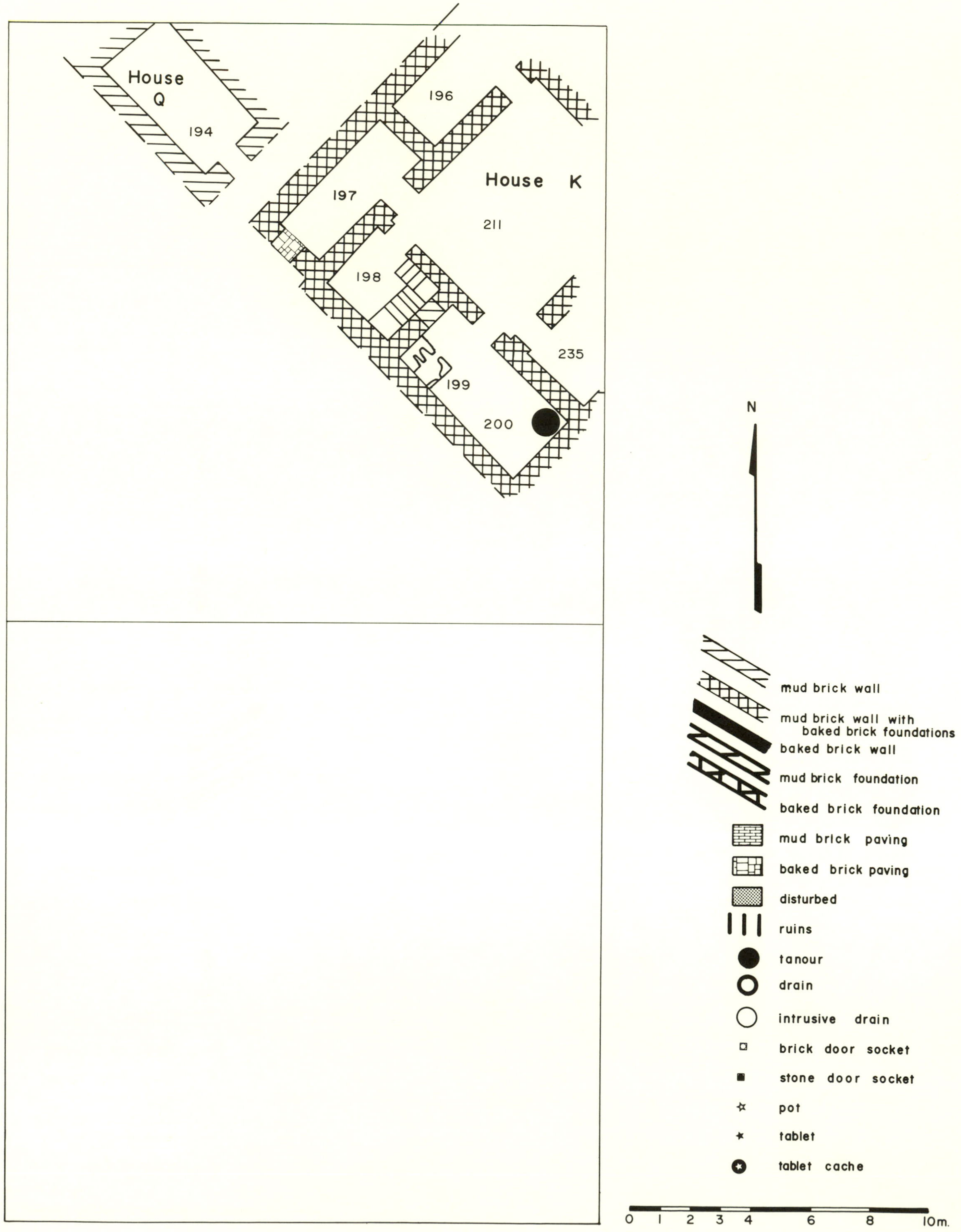

Area TA, Level XIIA, Floor 3

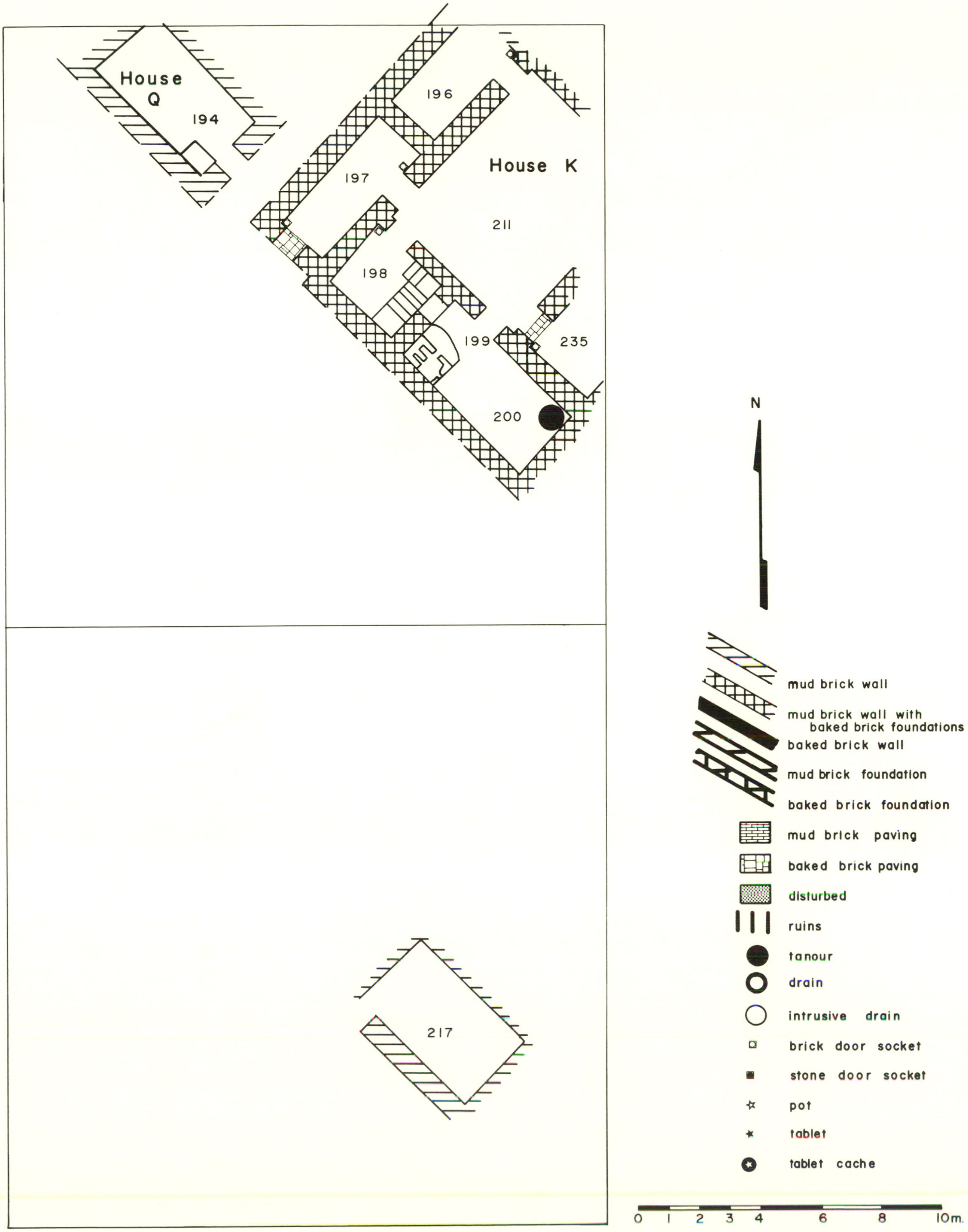

Area TA, Level XIIA, Floor 2

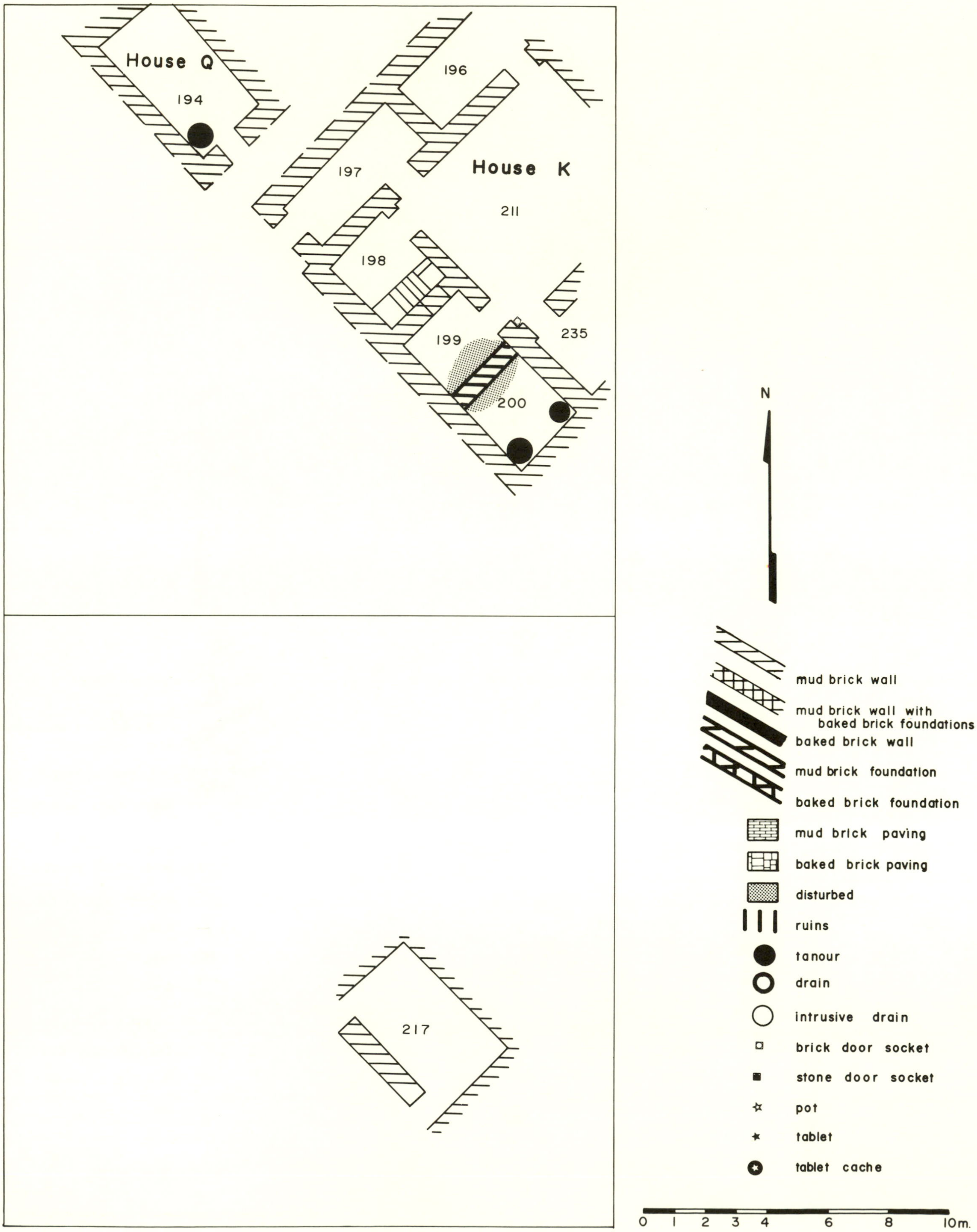

Area TA, Level XIIA, Floor 1

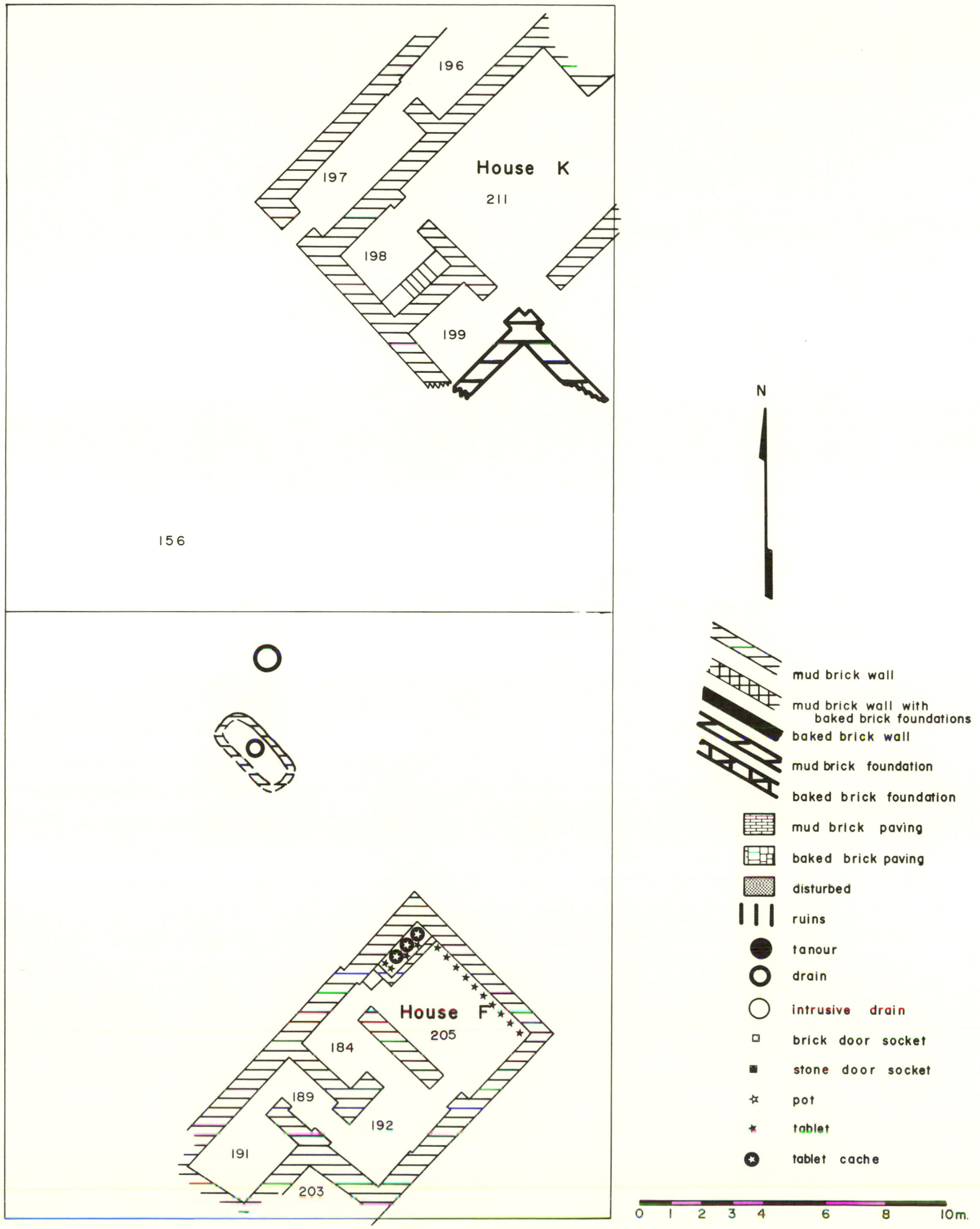

Area TA, Level XI, Floor 3

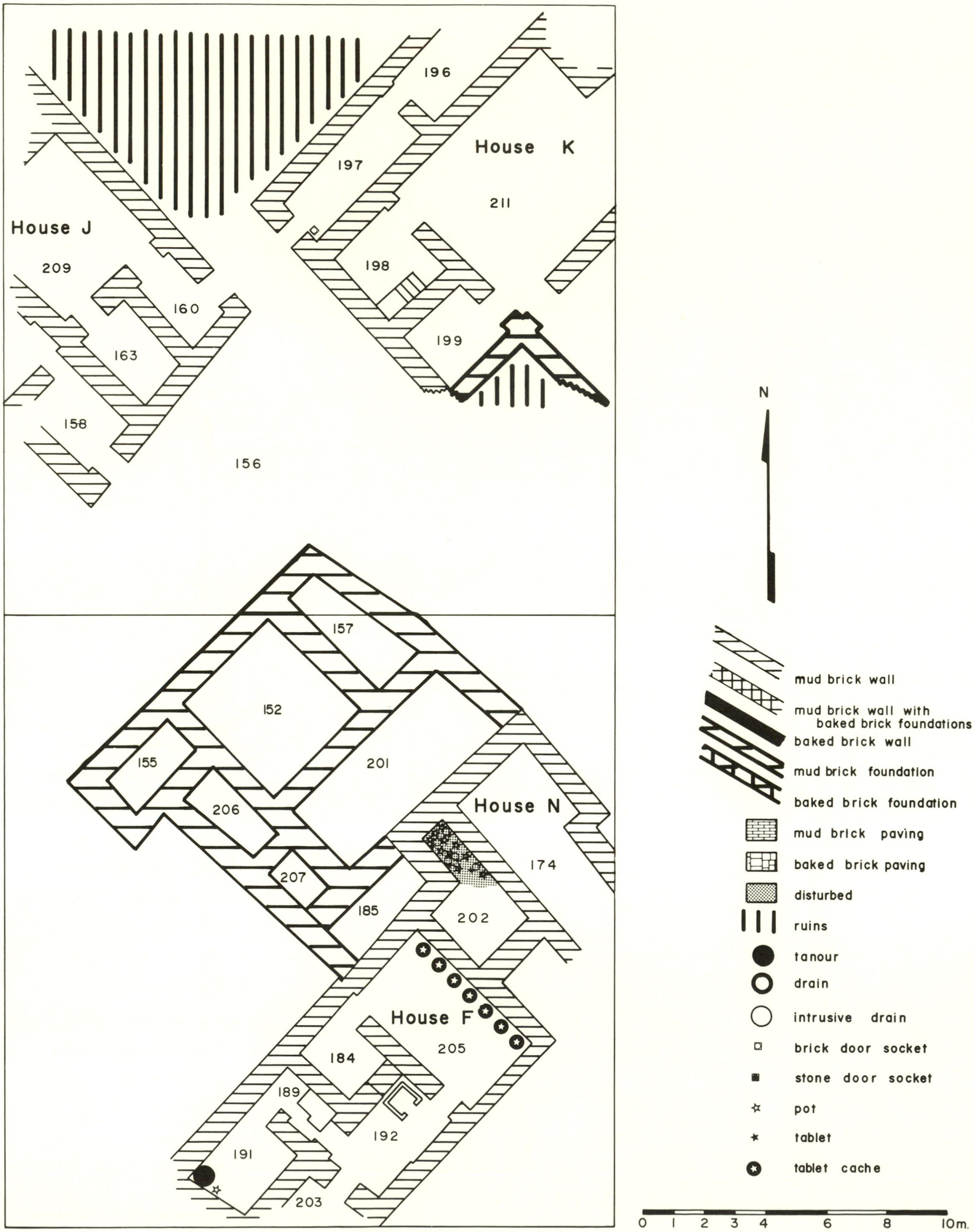

Area TA, Level XI, Floor 2

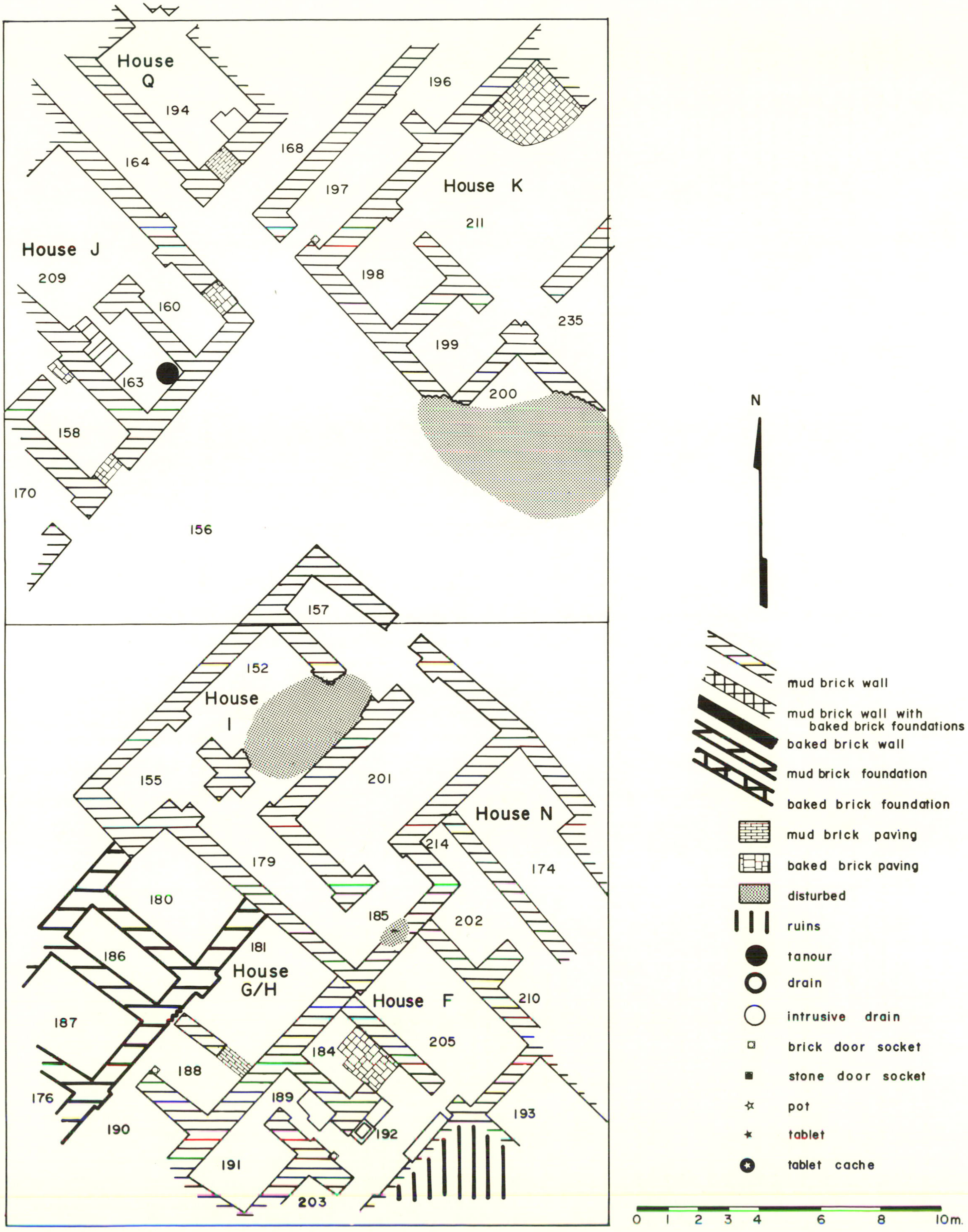

Area TA, Level XI, Floor 1

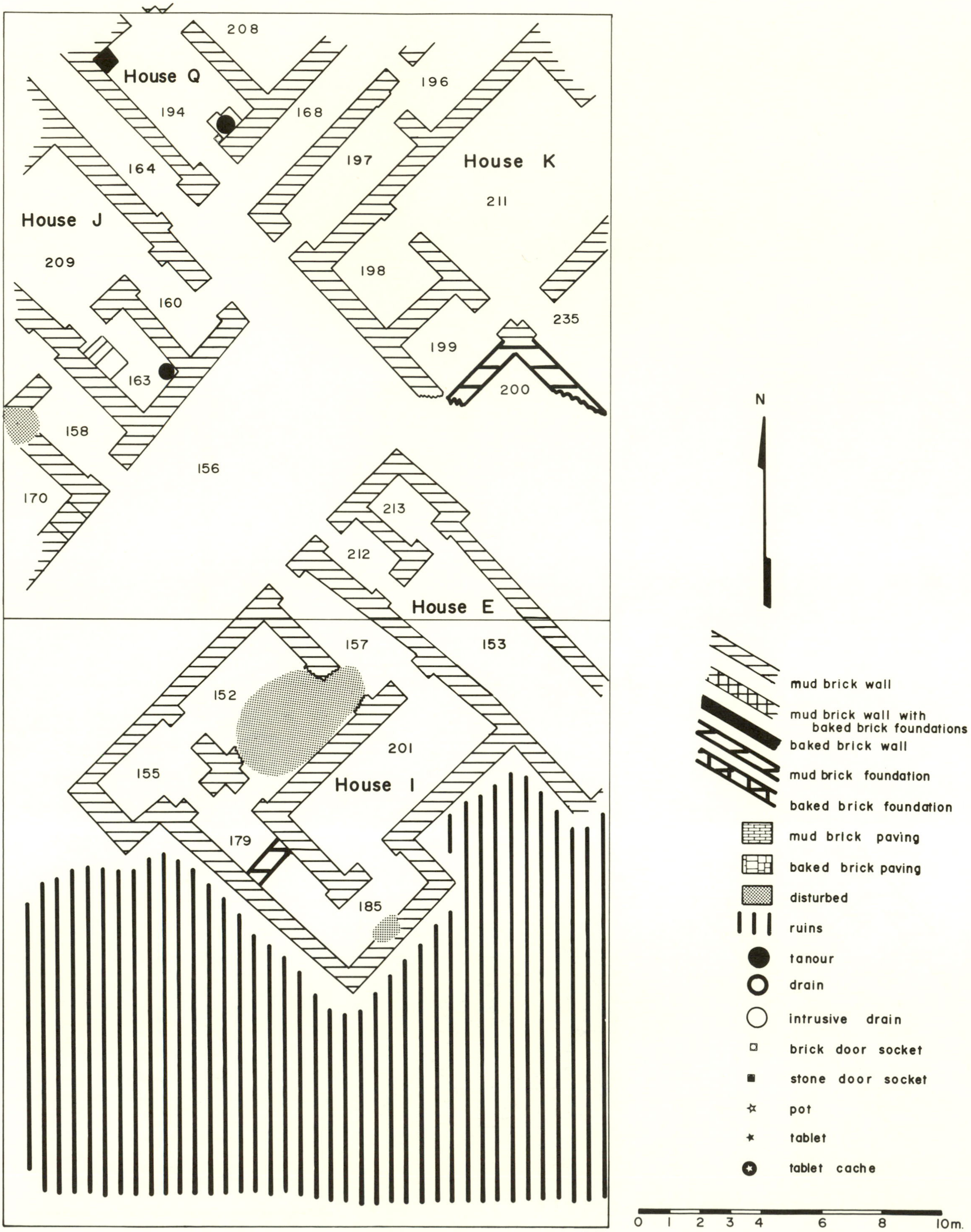

Area TA, Level XB, Floor 2

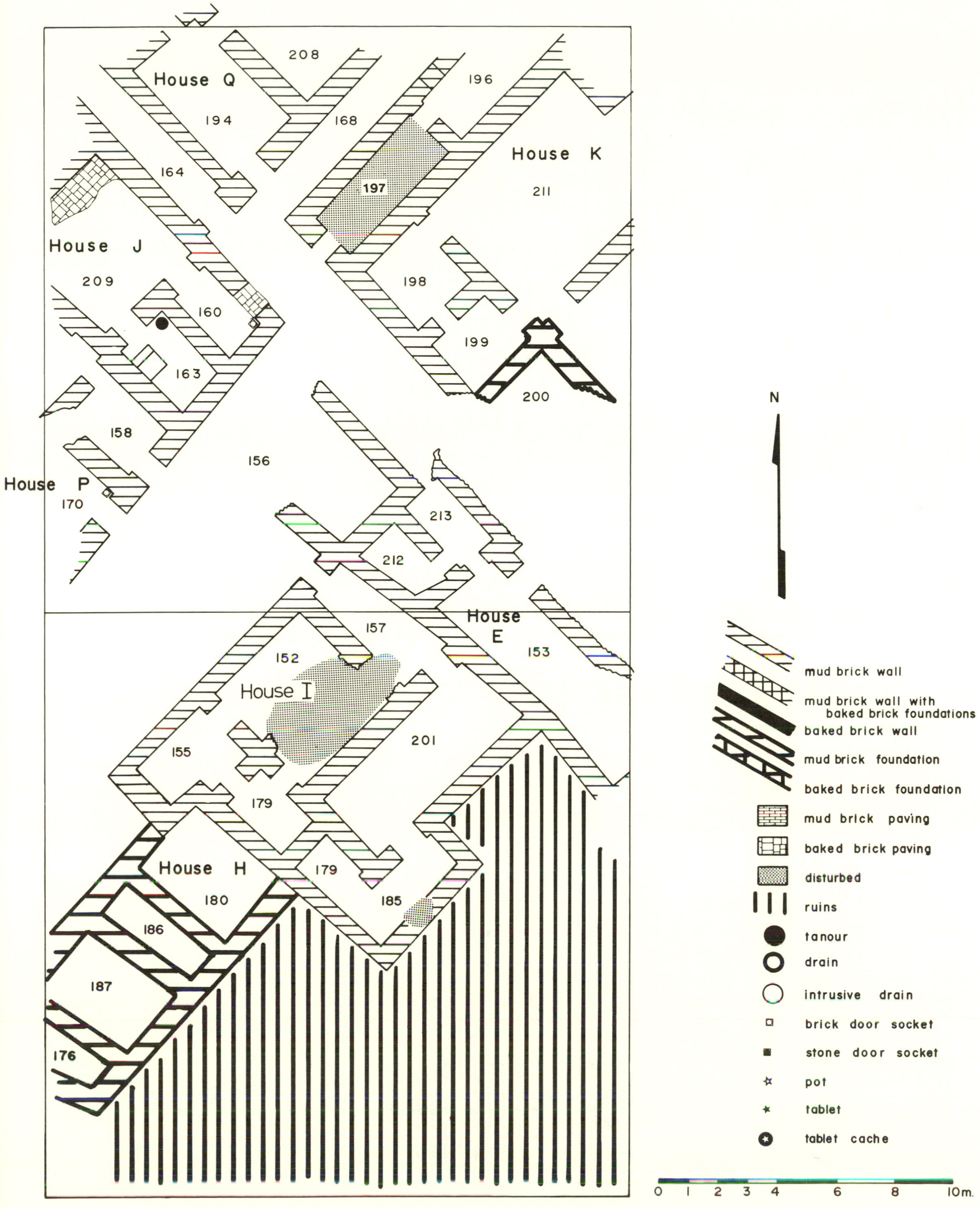

Area TA, Level XB, Floor 1

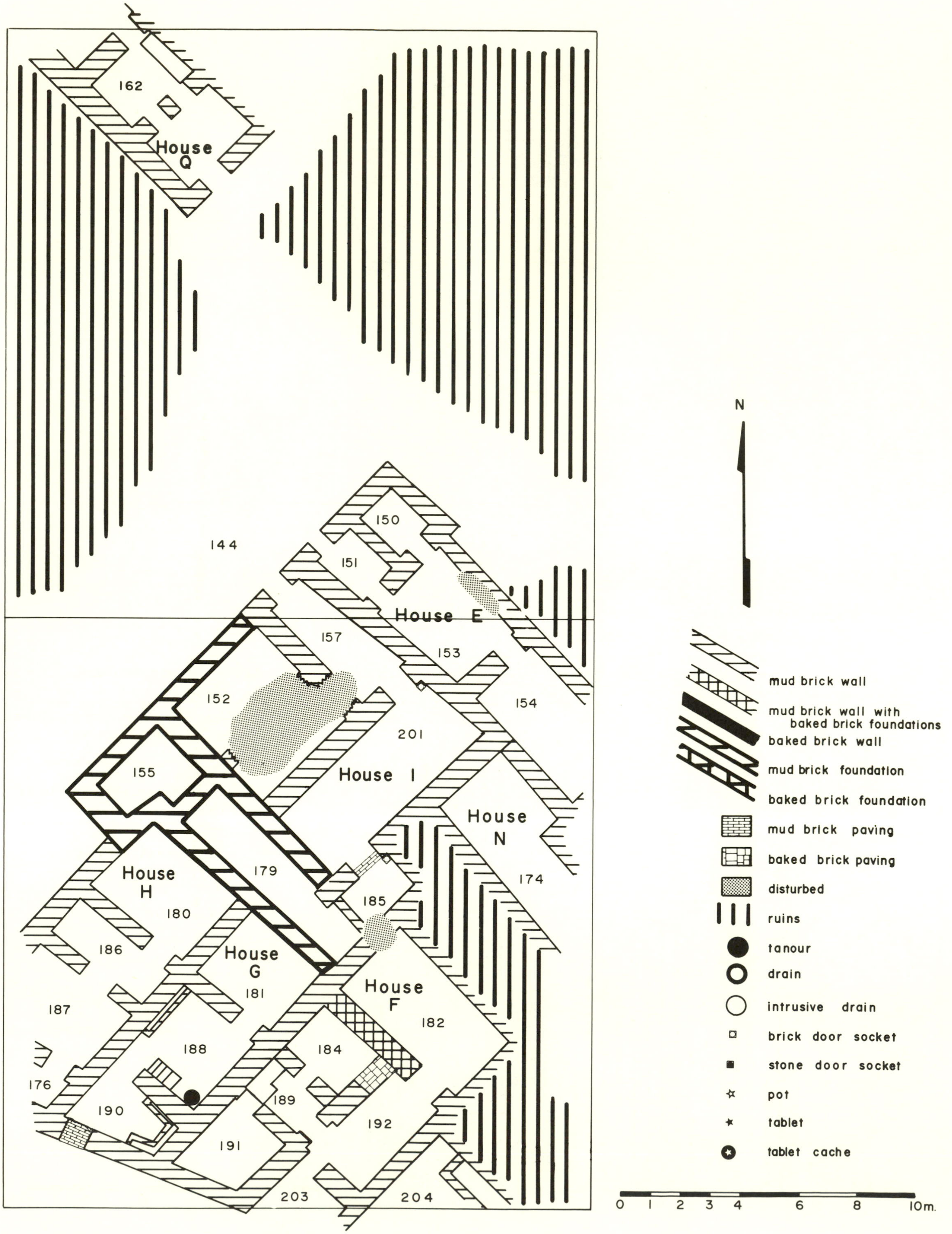

Area TA, Level XA, Floor 3

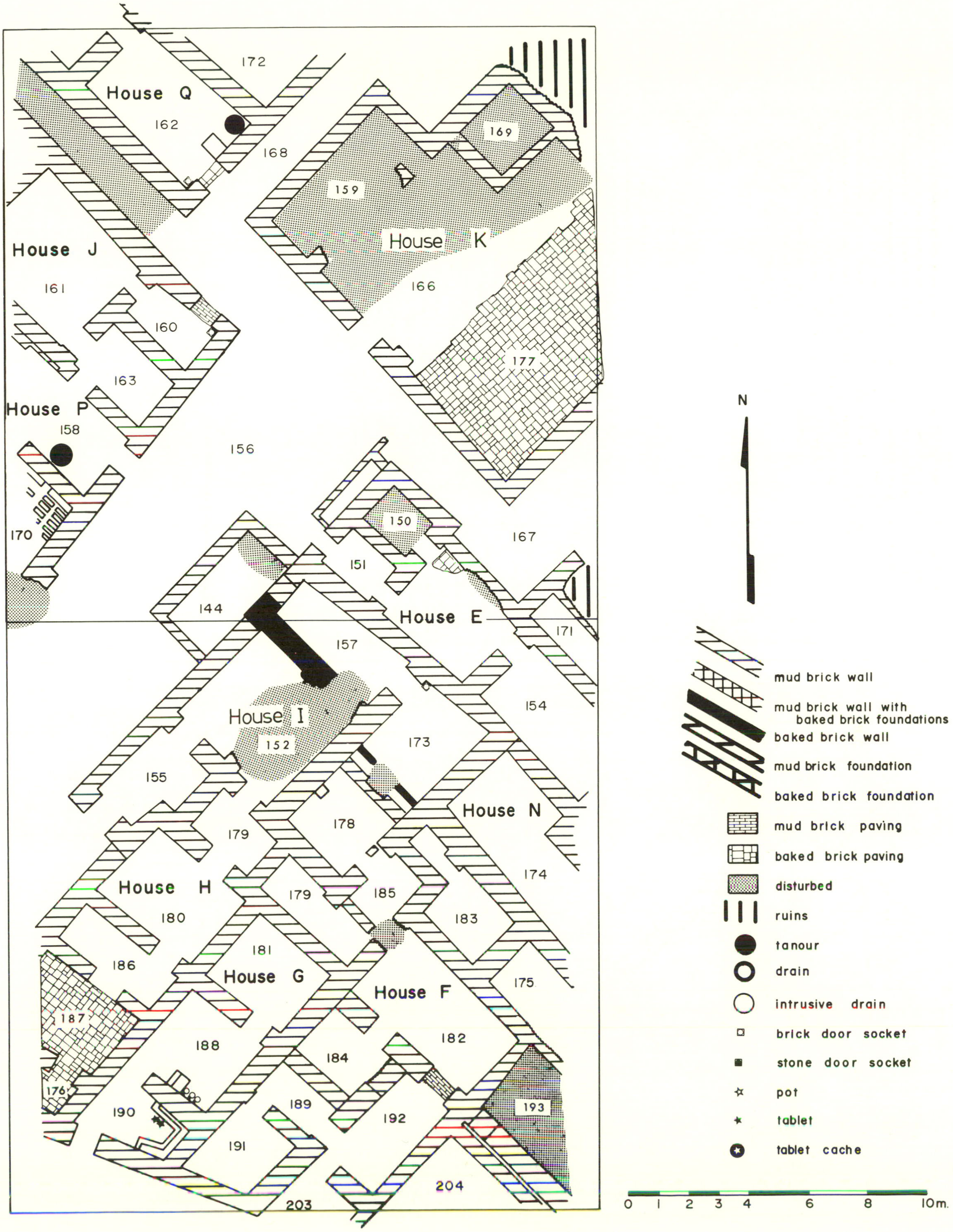

172
House Q
162
168
169
159
House J
House K
161
166
160
177
163
House P
158
156
N
170
150
167
151
144
House E
171
157
154
House I
152
173
155
House N
178
179
174
House H
179
185
180
183
181
186
House G
175
House F
187
188
182
184
176
189
193
190
192
191
204
203
mud brick wall
mud brick wall with baked brick foundations
baked brick wall
mud brick foundation
baked brick foundation
mud brick paving
baked brick paving
disturbed
ruins
tanour
drain
intrusive drain
brick door socket
stone door socket
pot
tablet
tablet cache
0 1 2 3 4 6 8 10m.

Area TA, Level XA, Floor 2

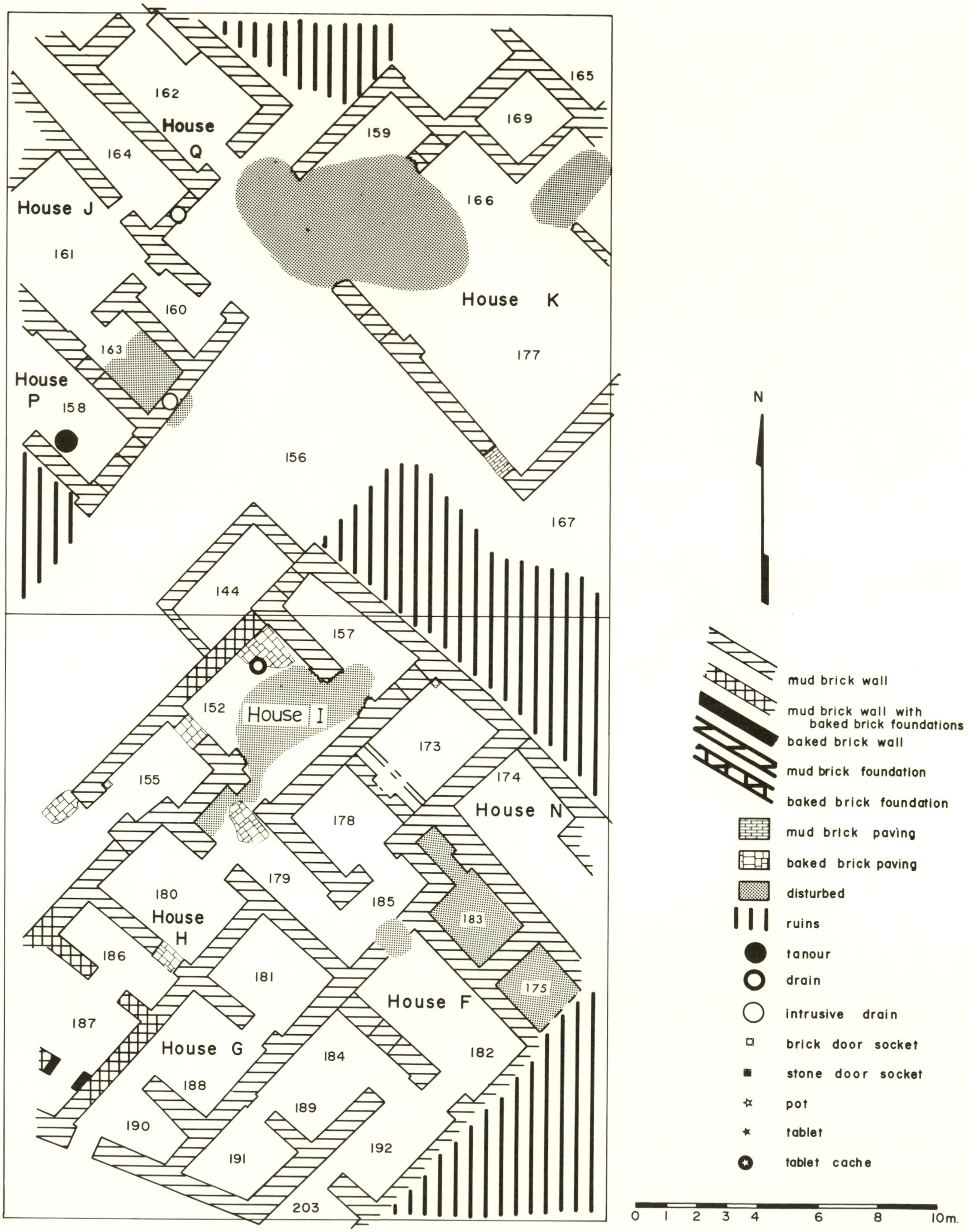

Area TA, Level XA, Floor 1

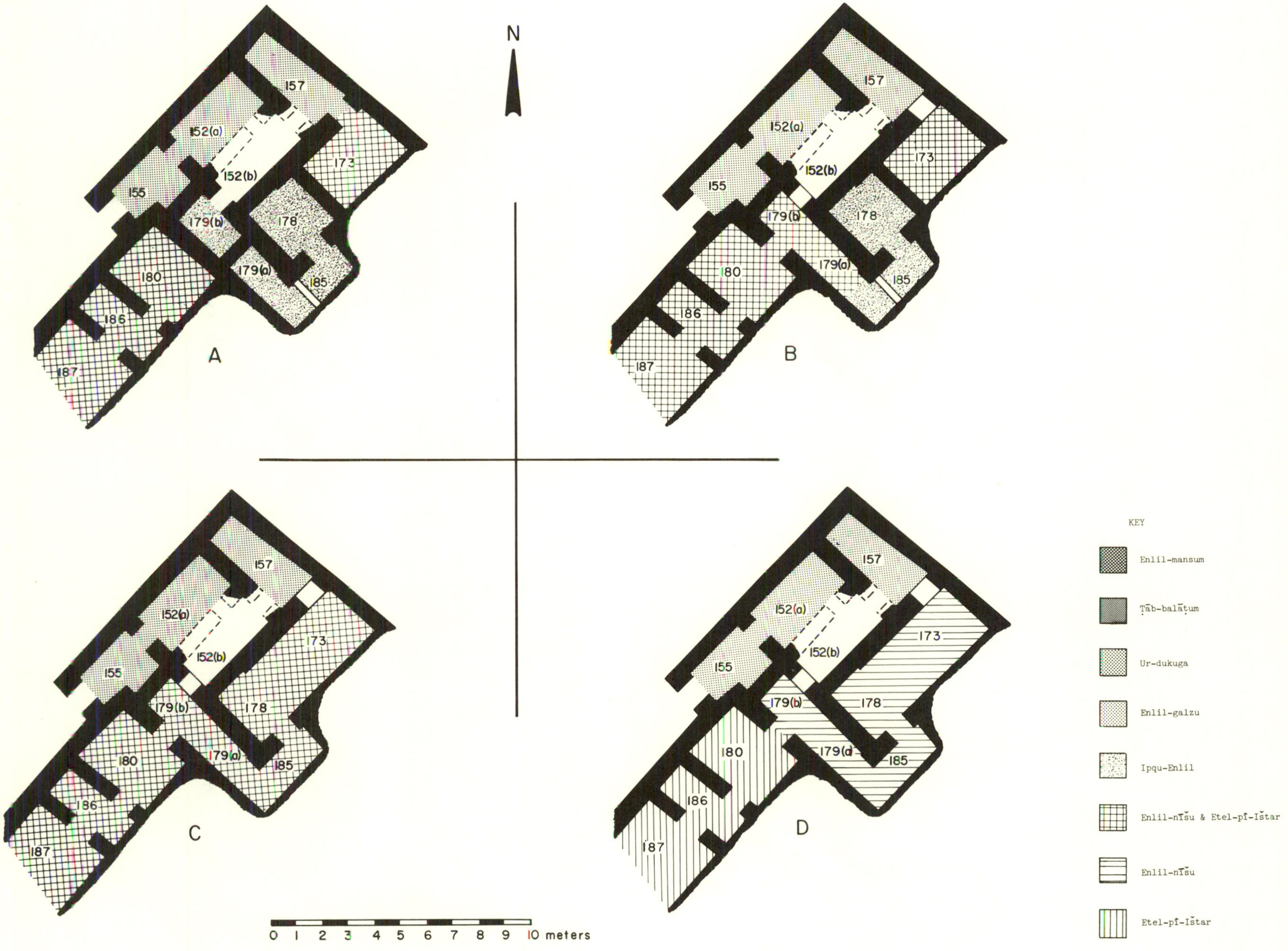

House I Transactions

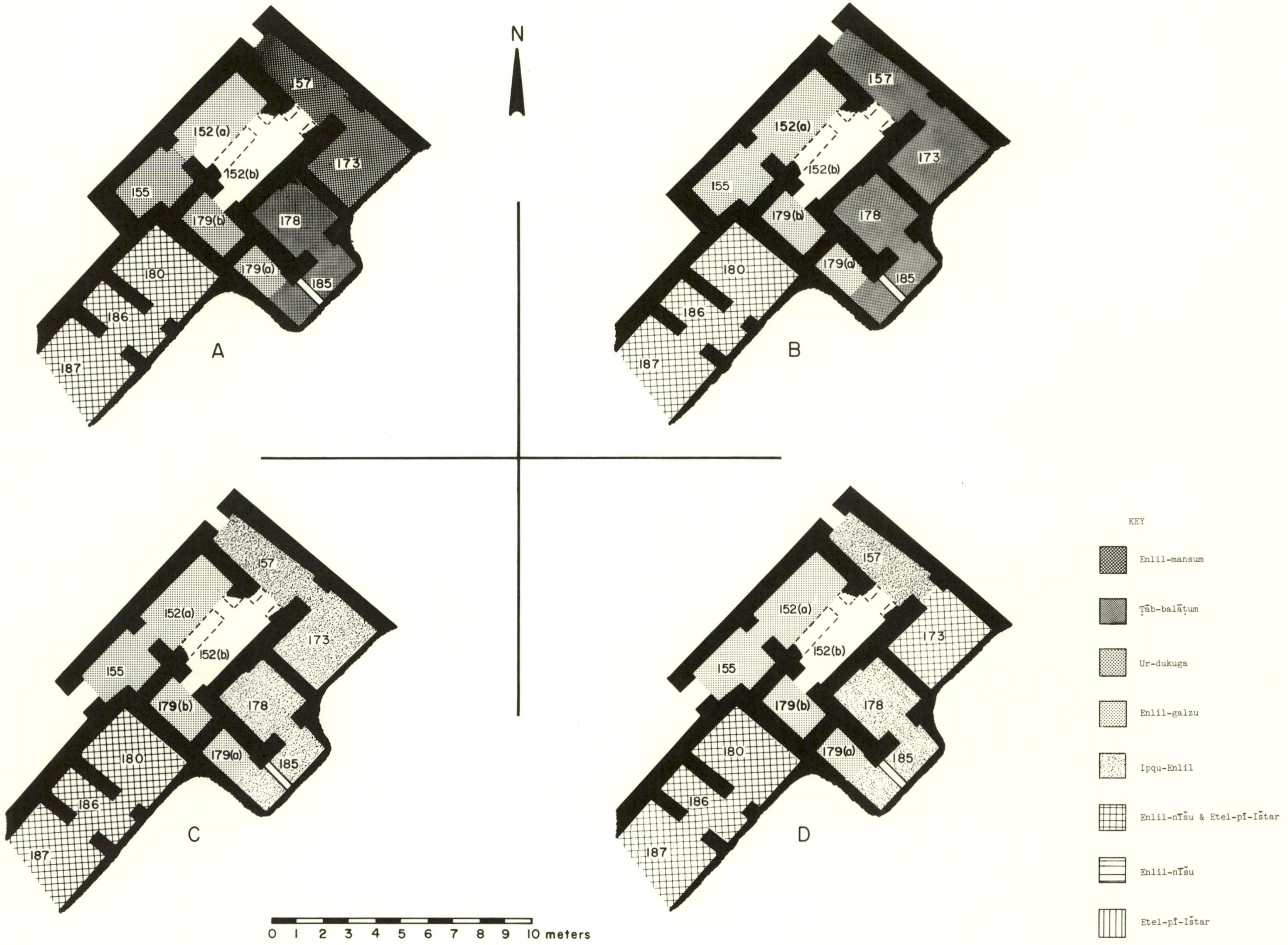

House I Transactions

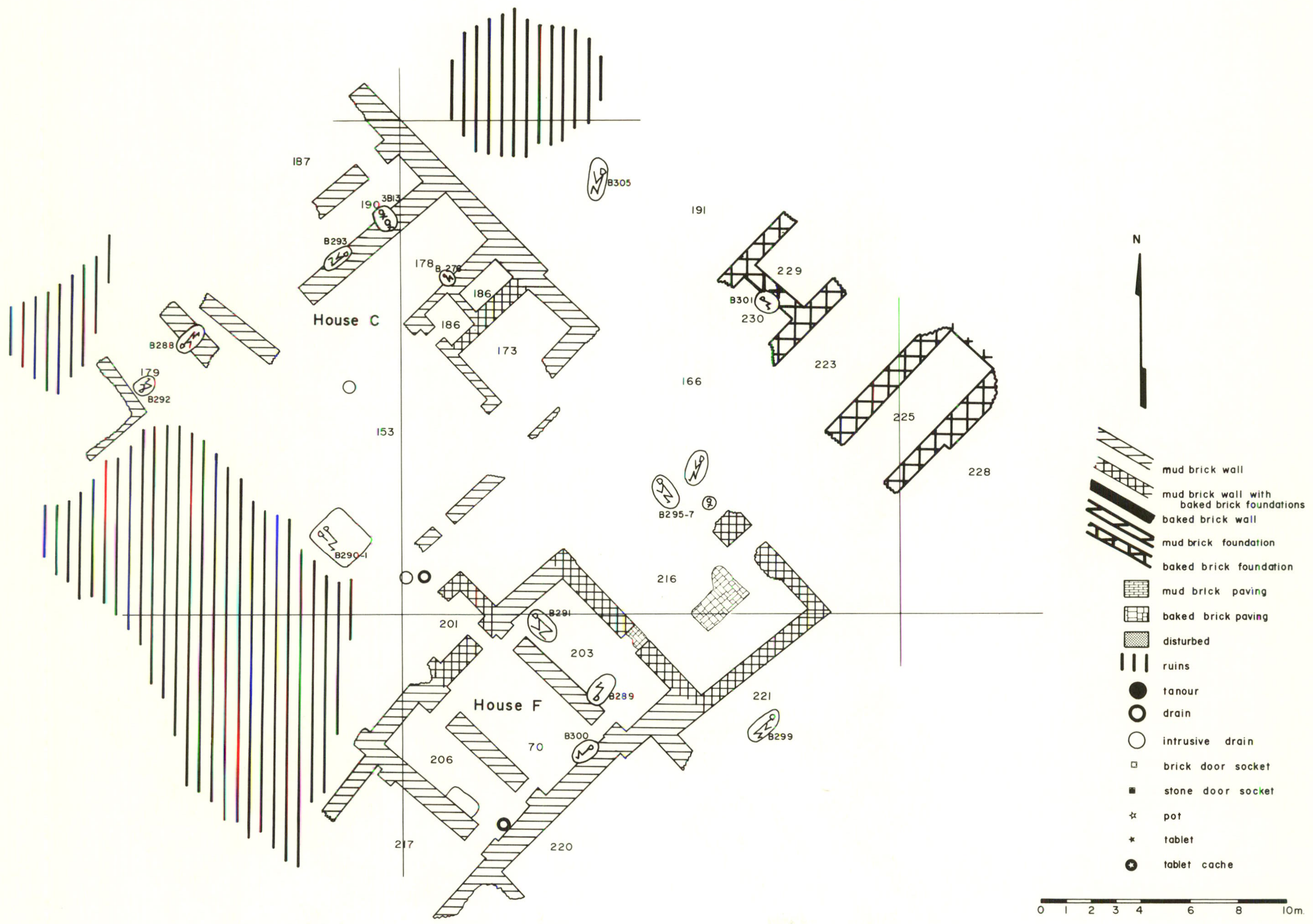

Area TB, Level III, Floor 2

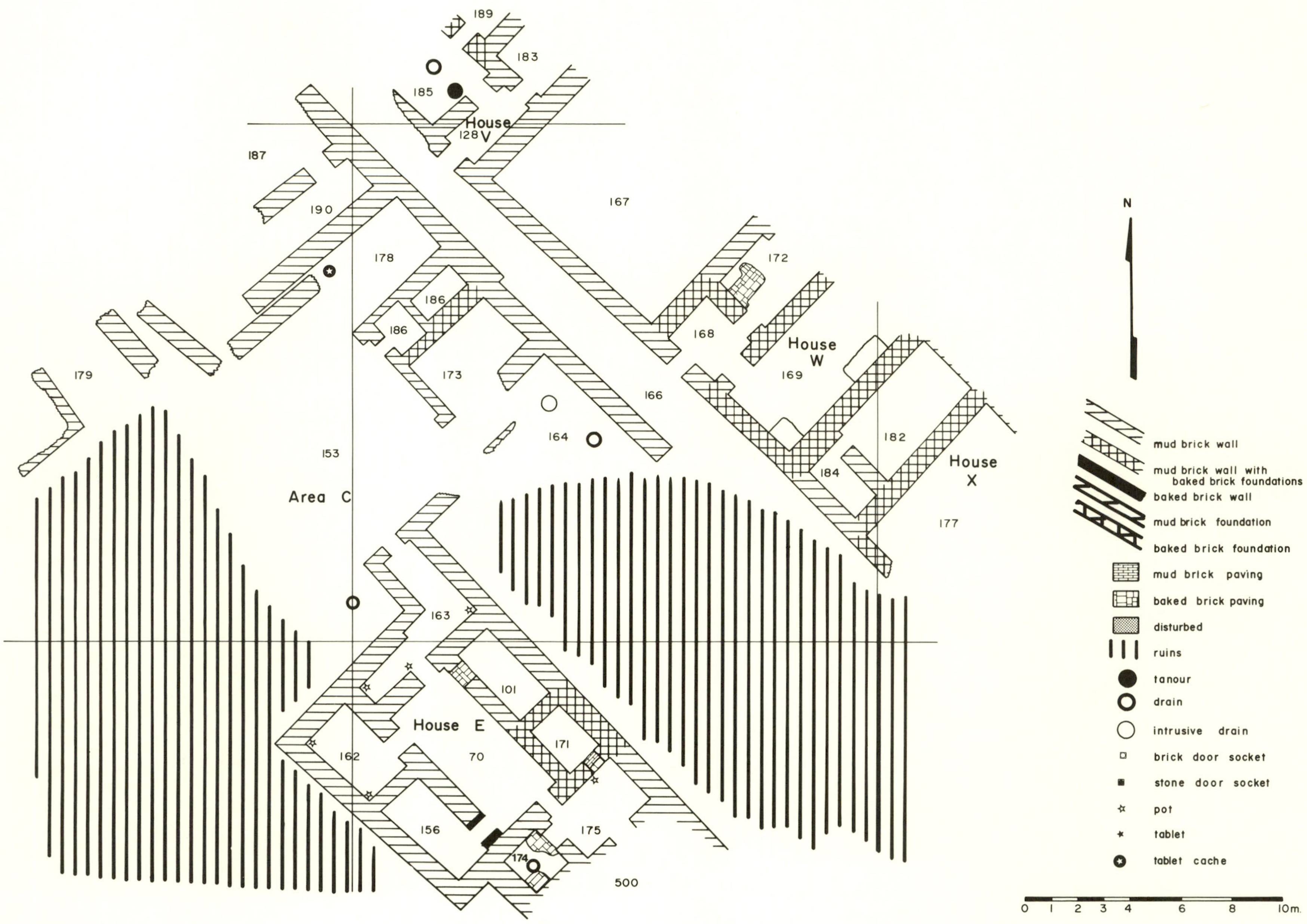

Area TB, Level III, Floor 1

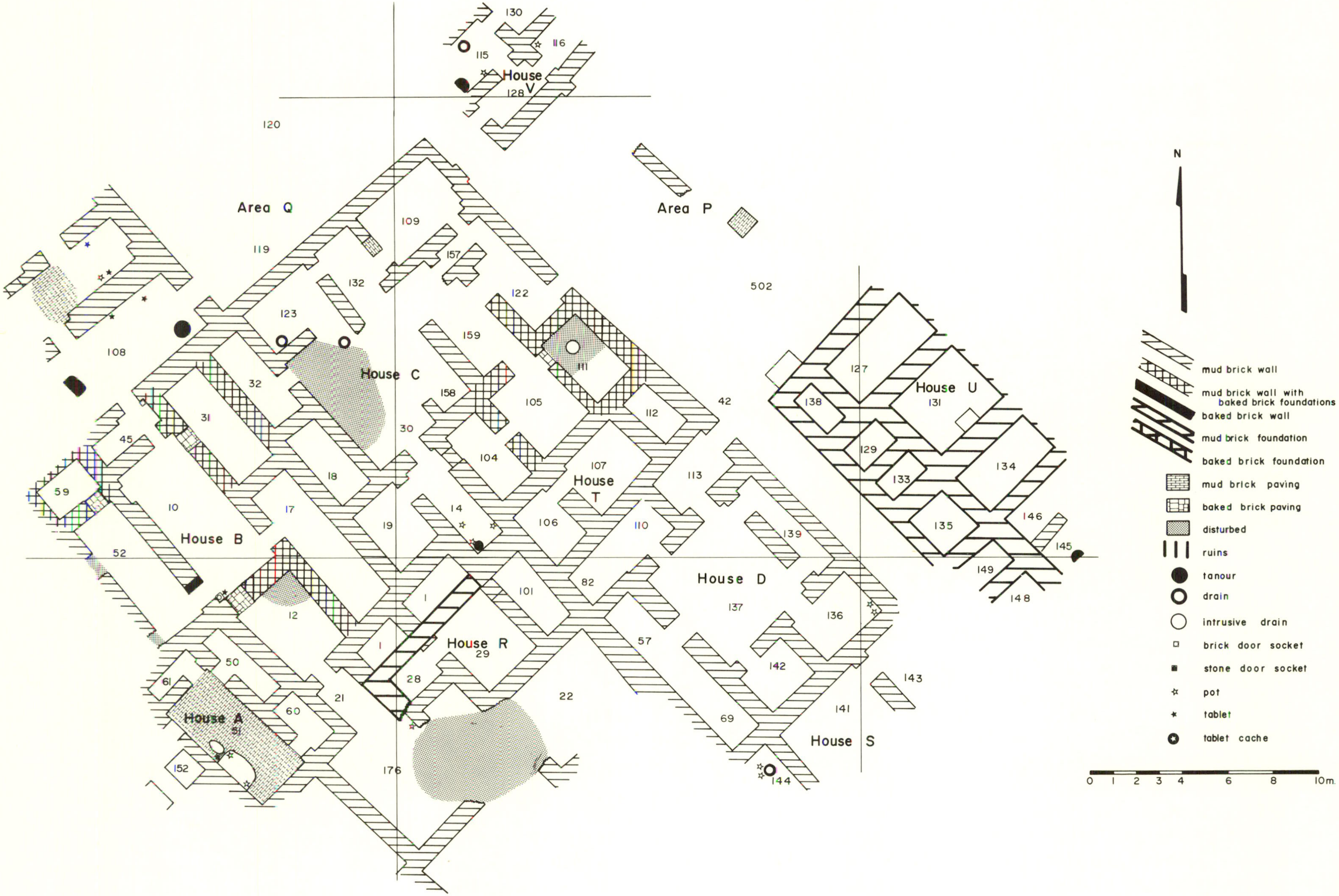

Area TB, Level II, Floor 2

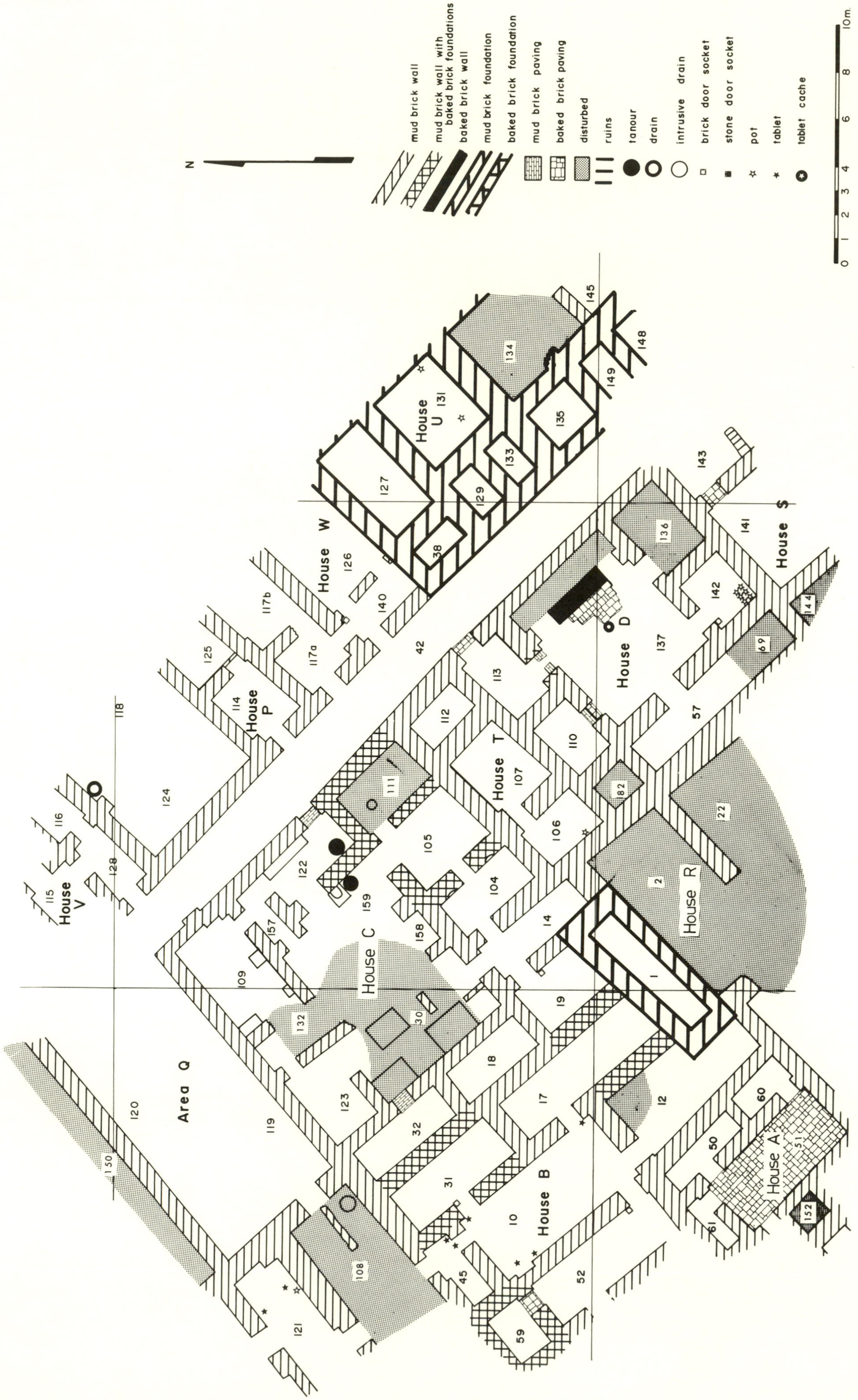

Area TB, Level II, Floor 1

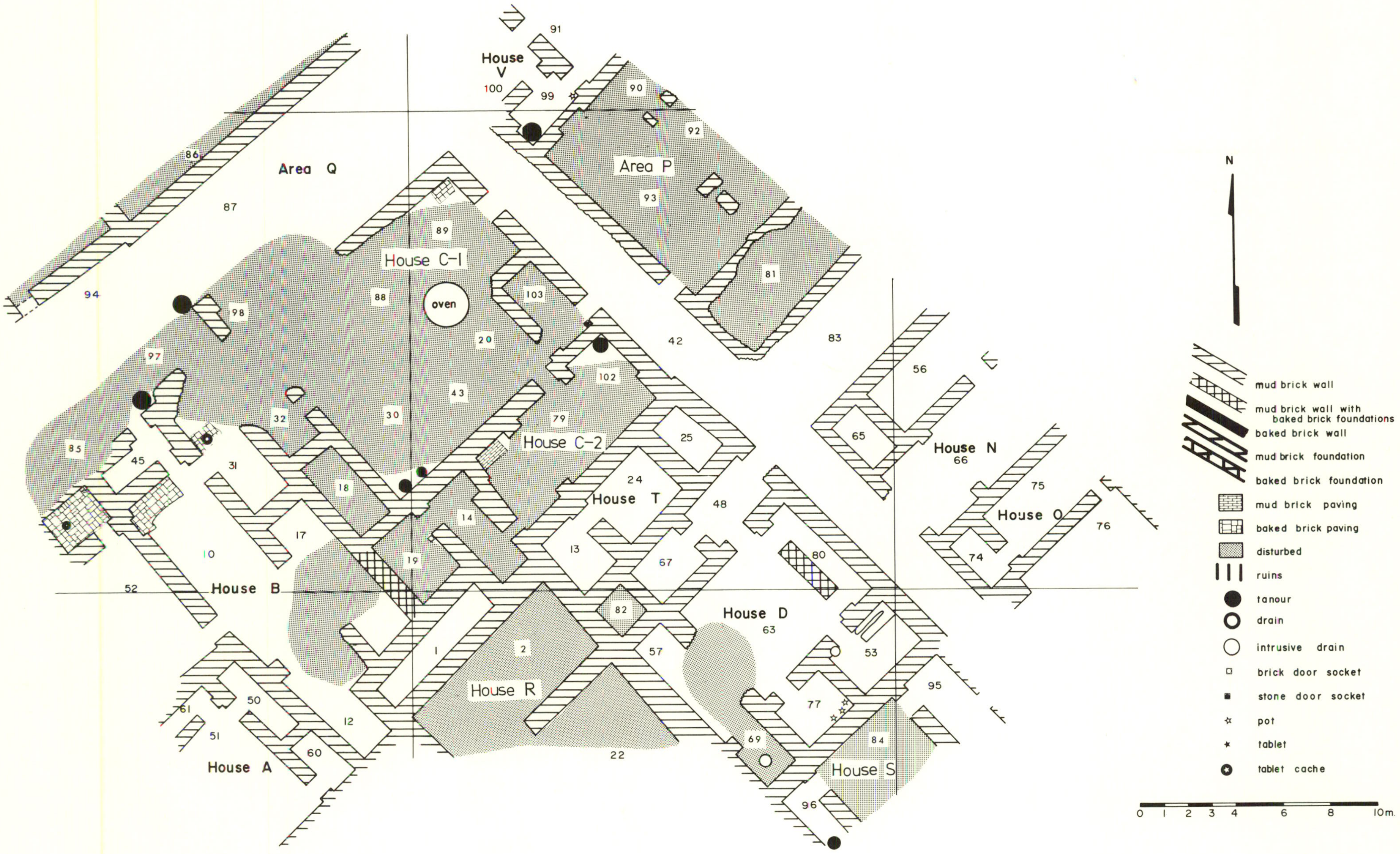
House V
91
100
99
90
92
Area P
93
81
Area Q
86
87
94
House C-I
89
88
oven
103
20
98
97
42
83
102
43
30
32
79
House C-2
25
85
45
31
18
14
24
House T
48
10
17
19
13
67
80
52
House B
82
House D
63
1
2
57
53
House R
61
50
77
95
51
12
69
84
60
22
House A
House S
96
56
65
House N
66
75
House O
74
76
N
mud brick wall
mud brick wall with baked brick foundations
baked brick wall
mud brick foundation
baked brick foundation
mud brick paving
baked brick paving
disturbed
ruins
tanour
drain
intrusive drain
brick door socket
stone door socket
pot
tablet
tablet cache
0 1 2 3 4 6 8 10m.

Area TB, Level I, Floor 2

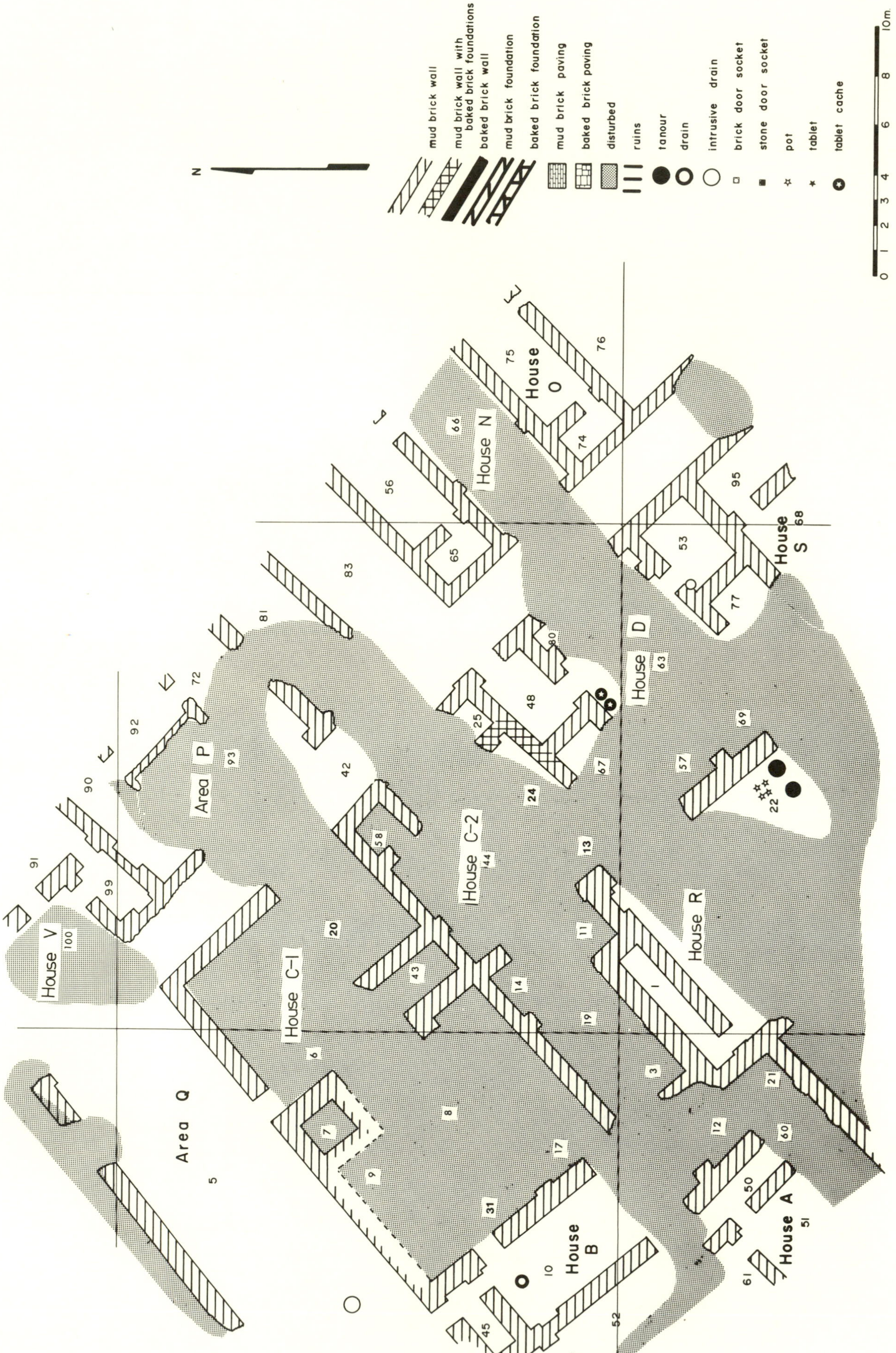

Area TB, Level I, Floor 1

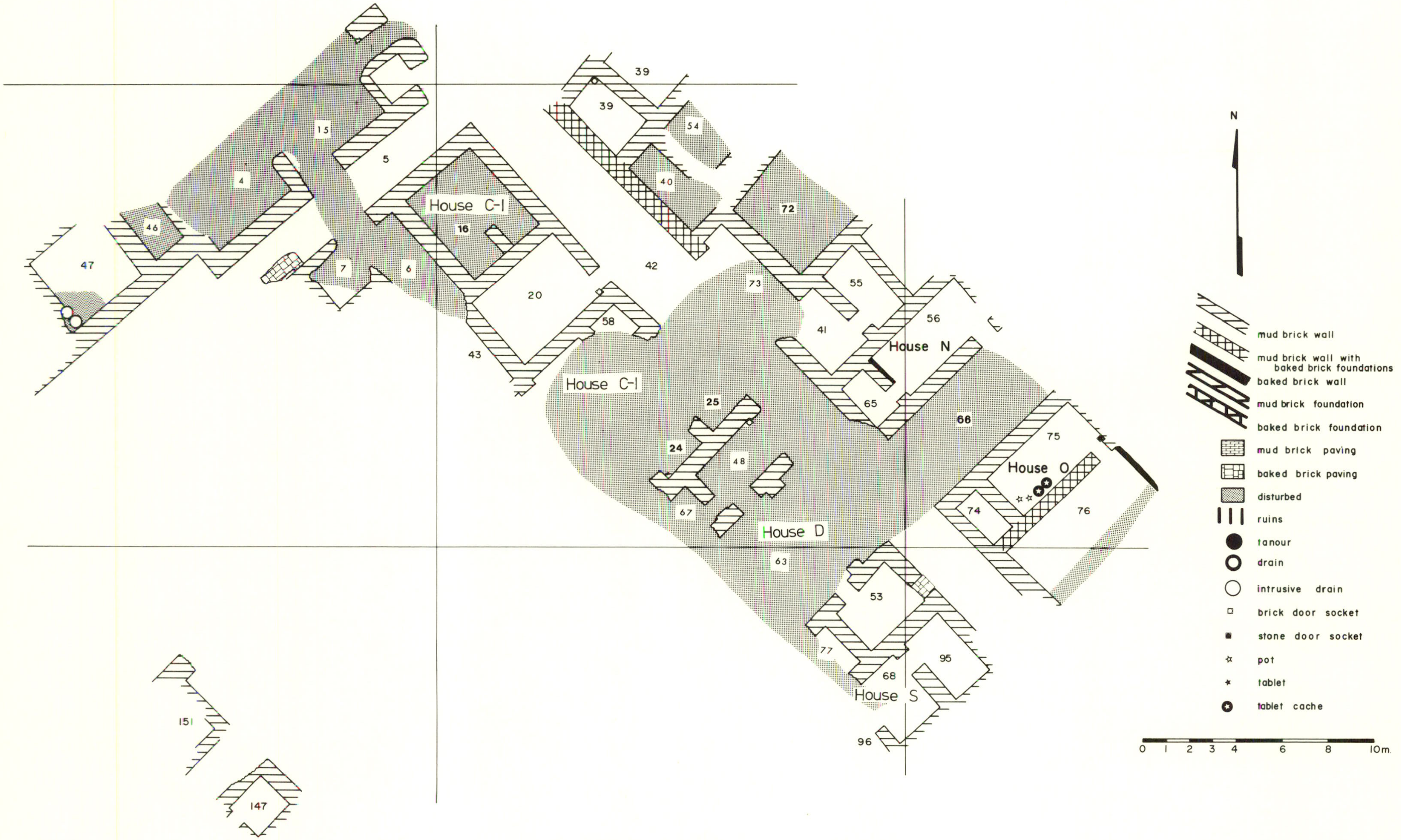

Area TB, Level E, Floors 1 and 2

PLATE 34

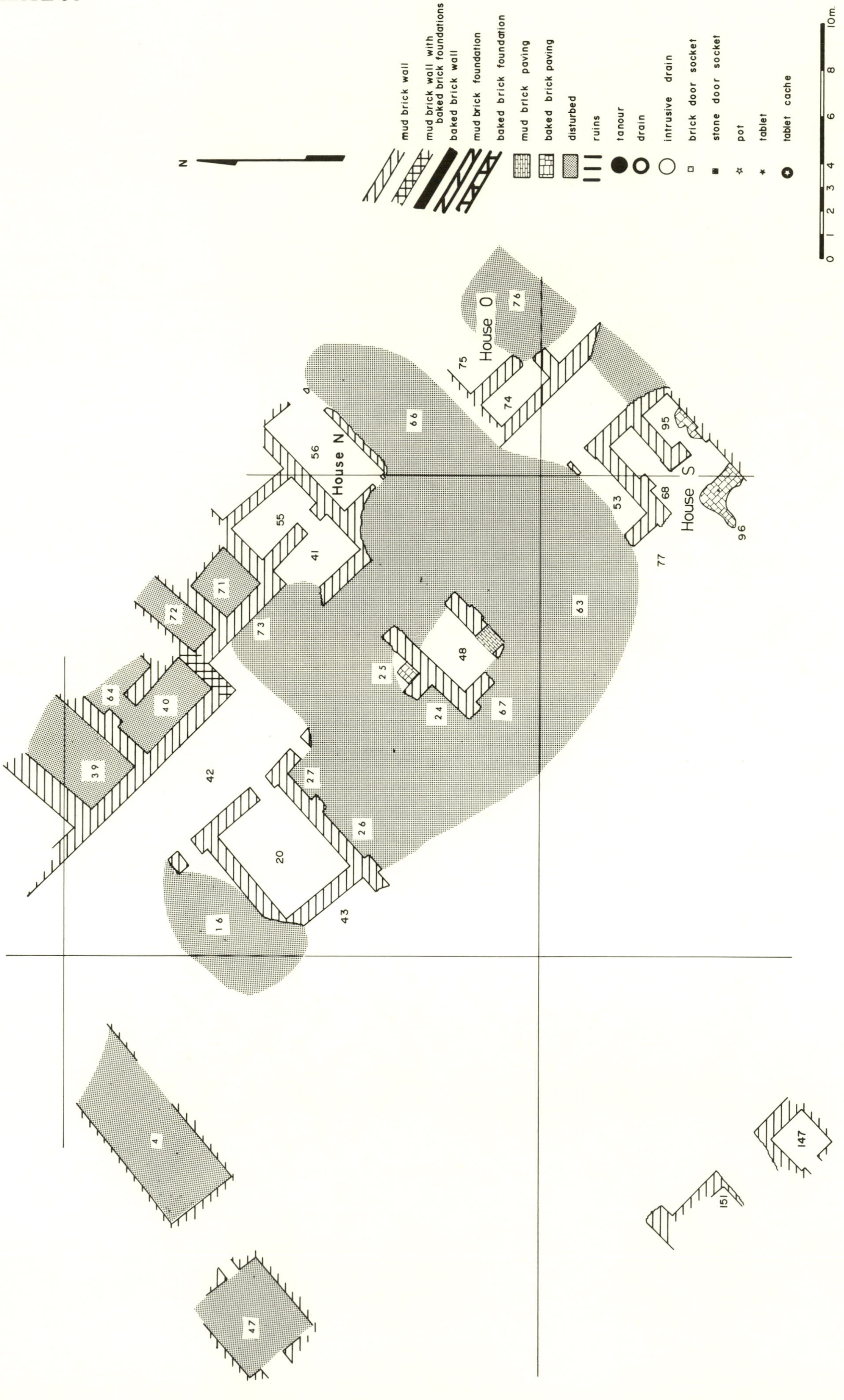

Area TB, Level D

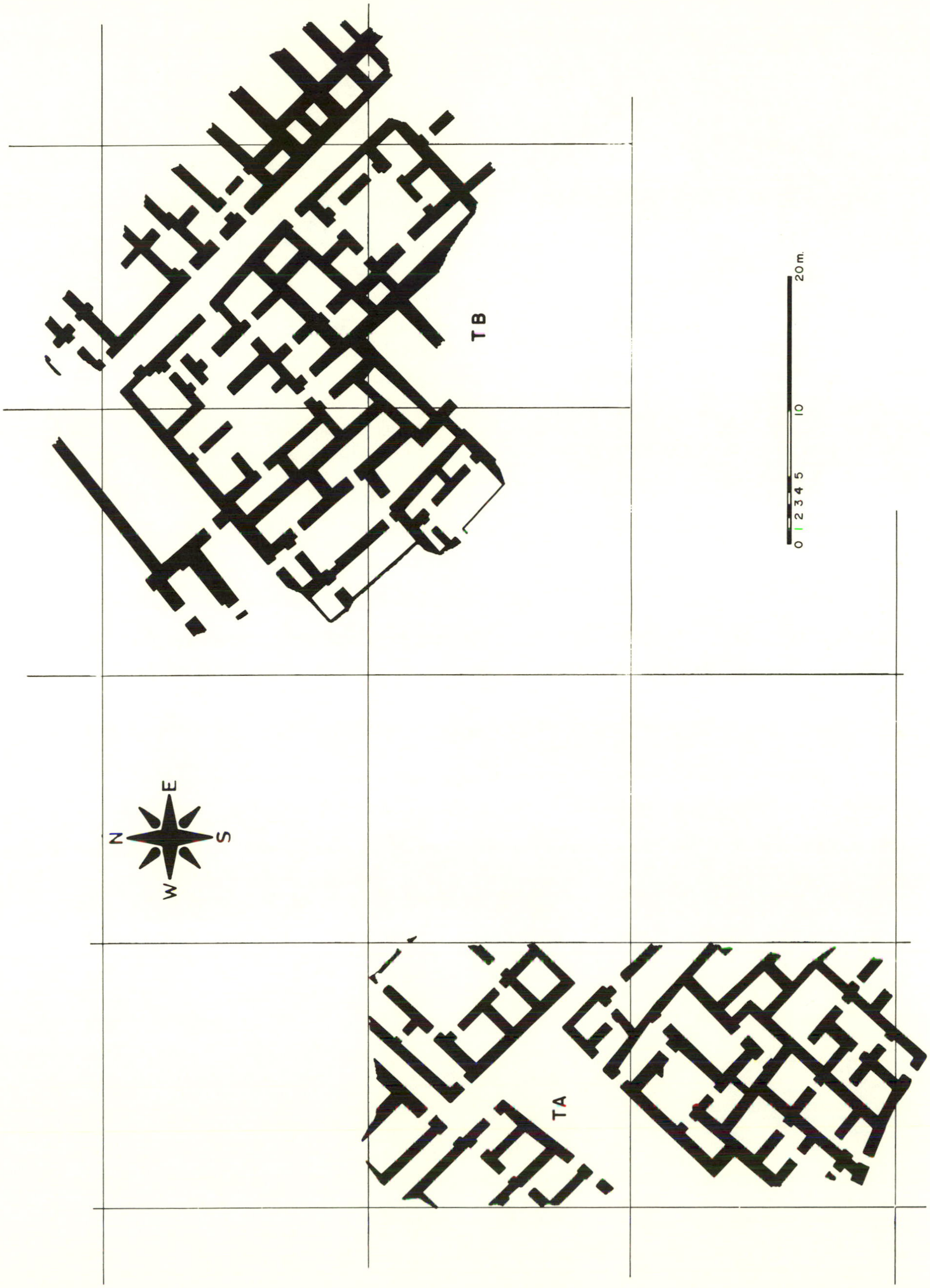

Areas TA and TB

TEXT 1

TABLET

obv.

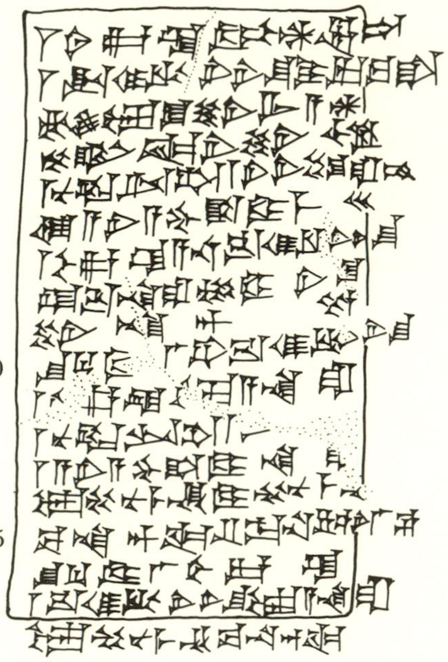

rev.

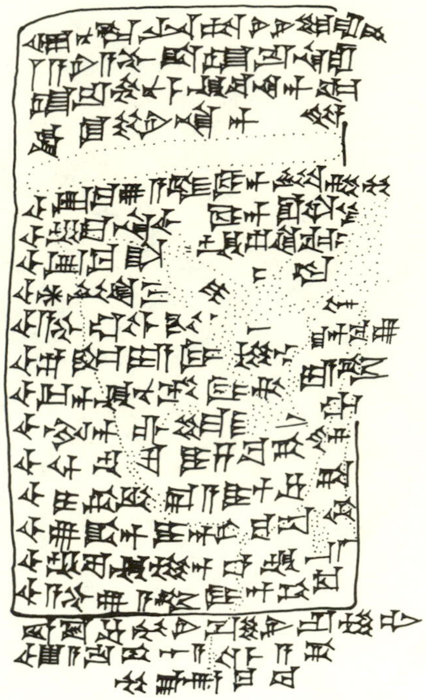

SEALS

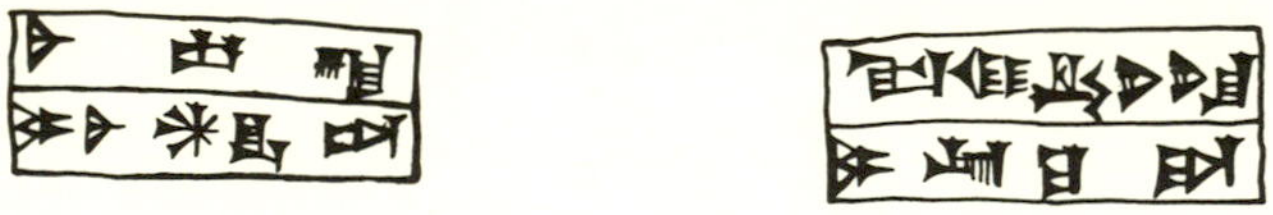

CASE

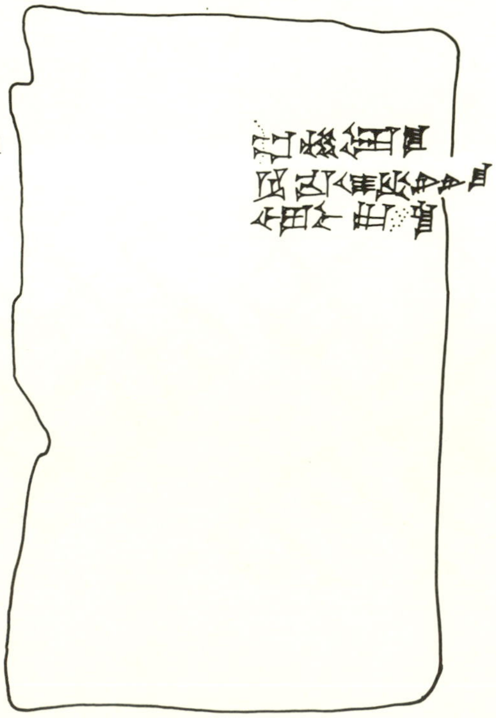

TEXT 2

obv.

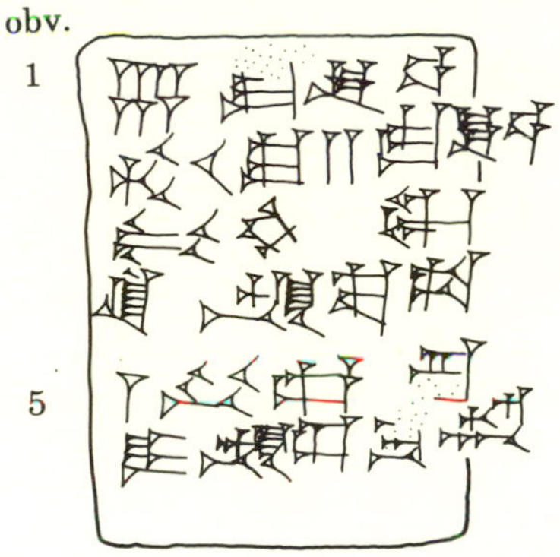

rev.

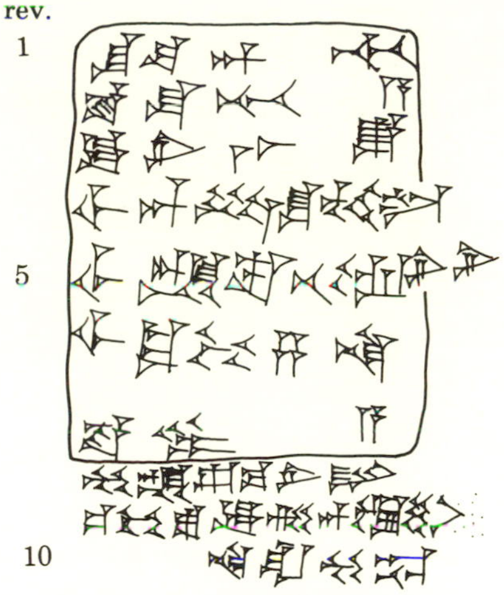

TEXT 3

obv.

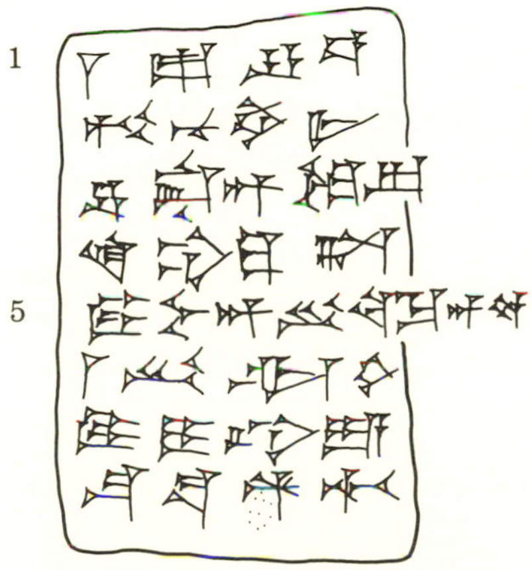

rev.

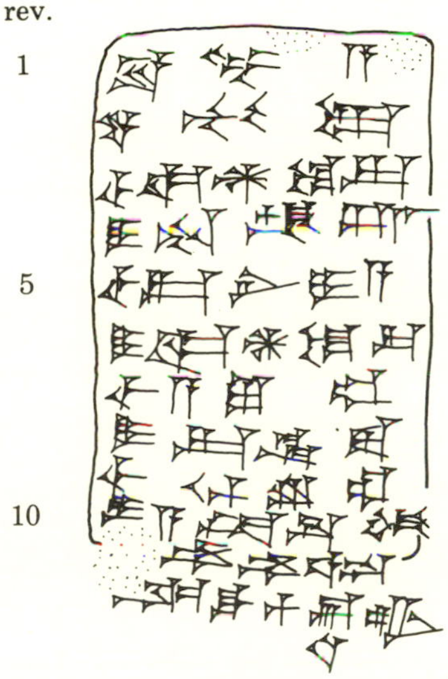

SEAL

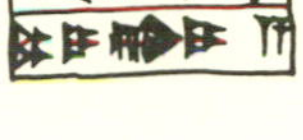

TEXT 4

obv.

1

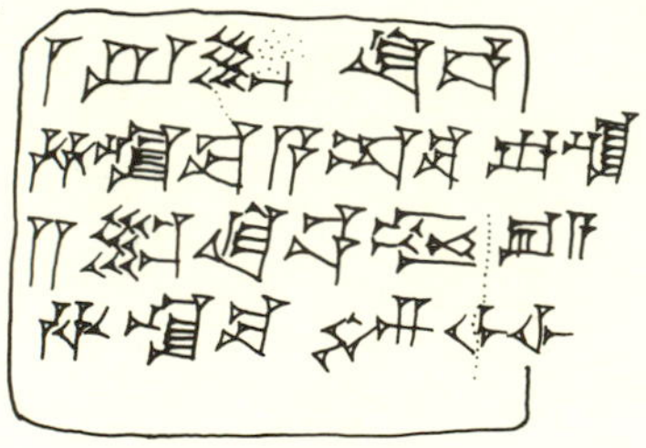

rev.

1

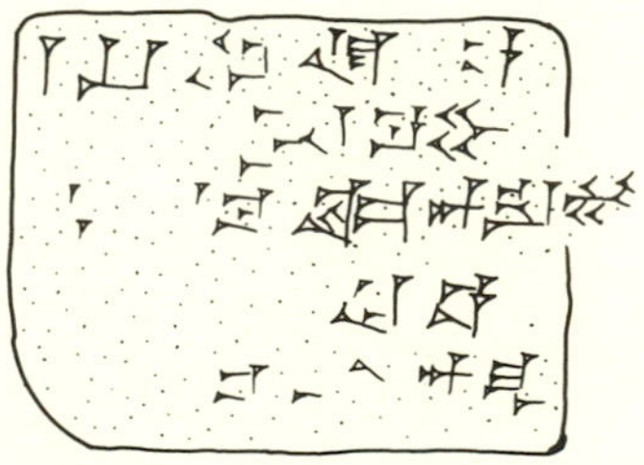

TEXT 5

obv.

1

5

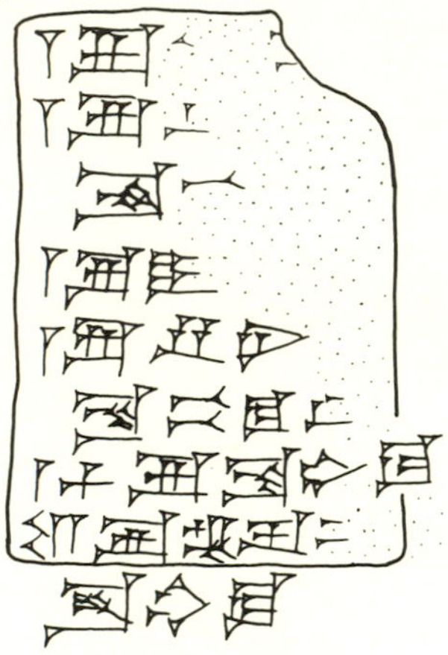

rev.

1

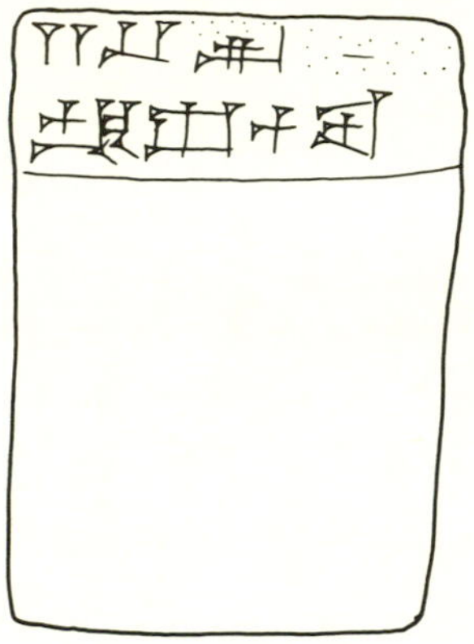

TEXT 6

1′

5′

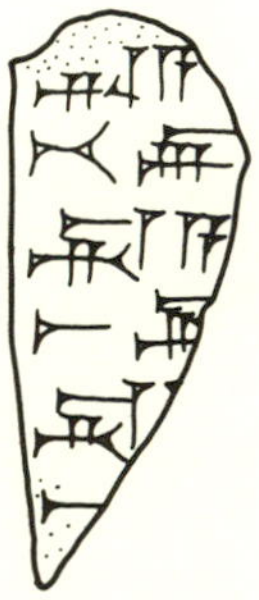

SEAL

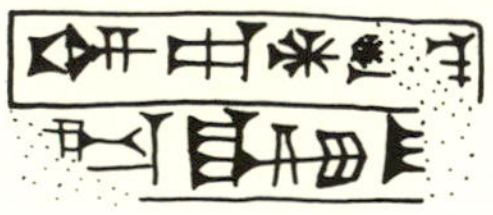

TEXT 7

obv.

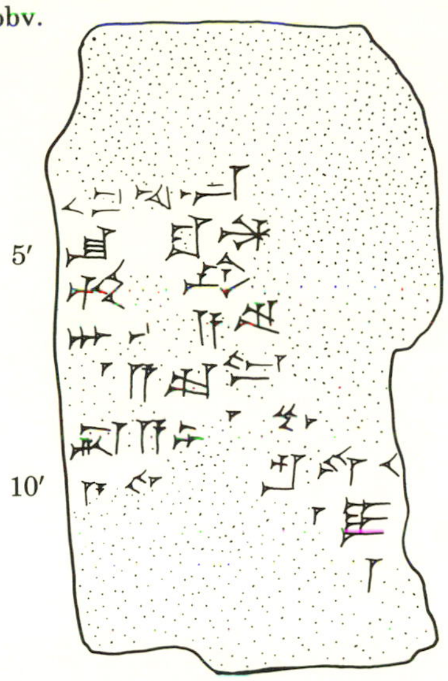

rev.

SEAL

TEXT 8

obv.

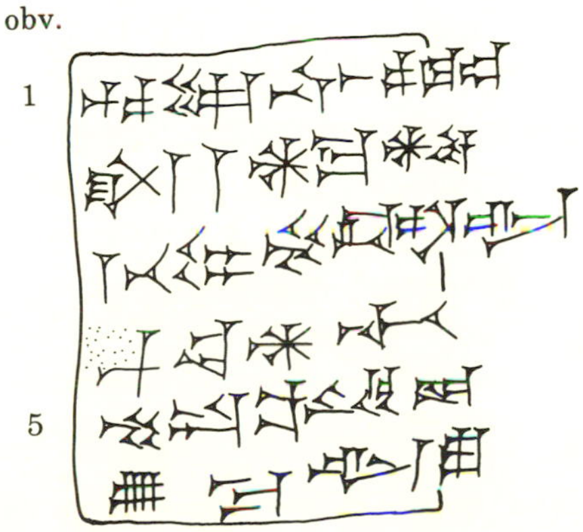

rev.

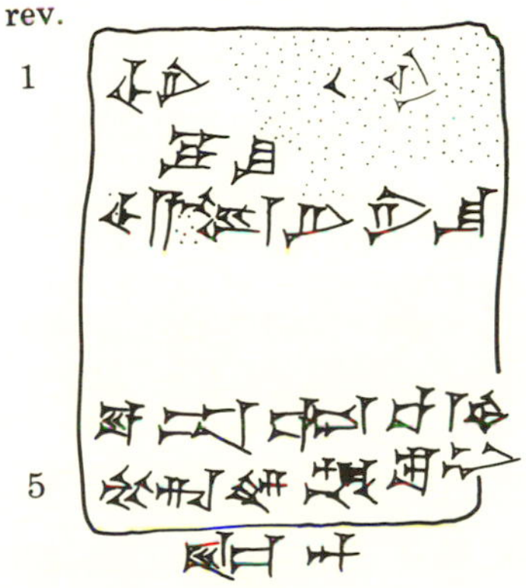

SEAL

TEXT 9

obv.

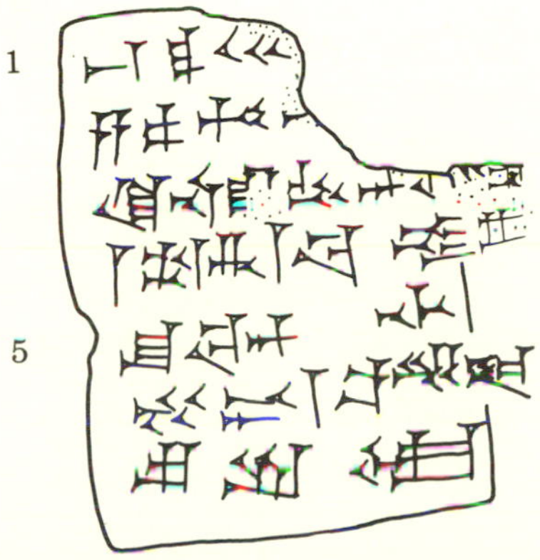

rev.

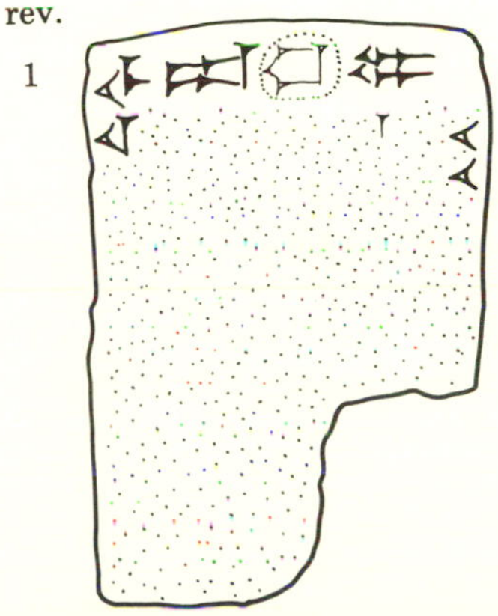

TEXT 10

obv.

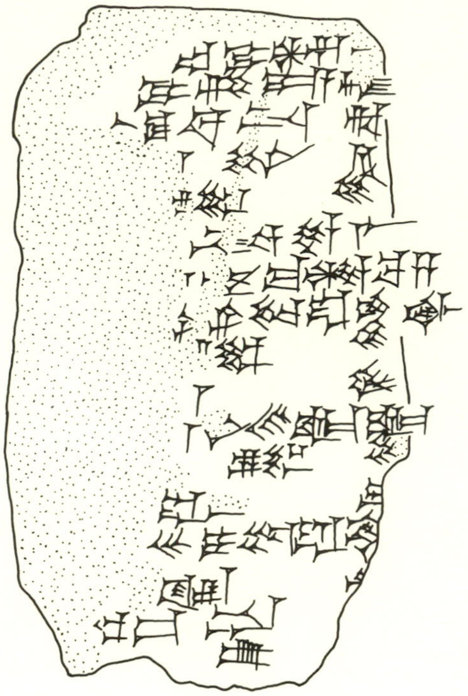

TEXT 11

obv.

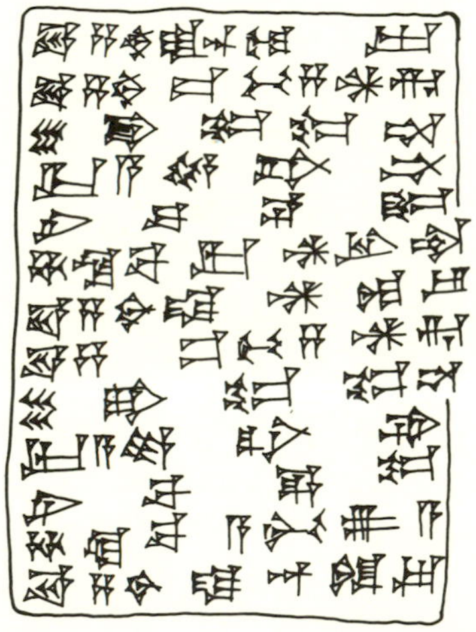

rev.

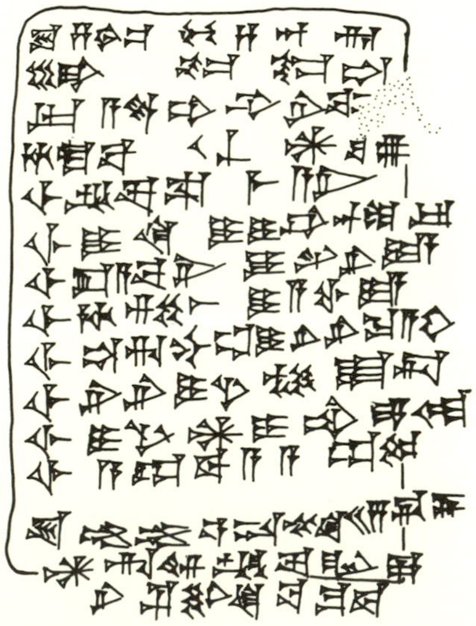

SEAL

TEXT 12

obv.

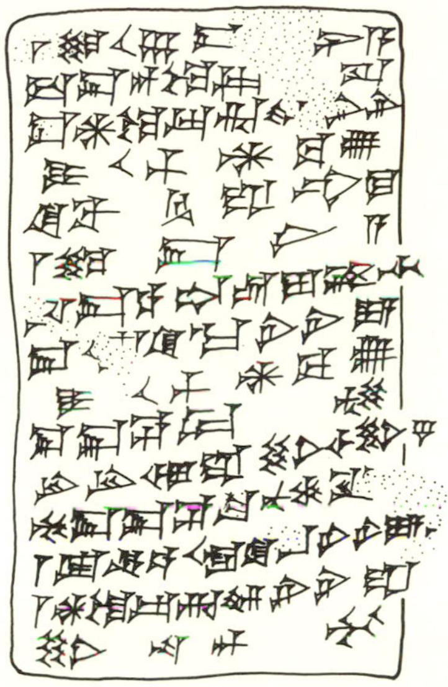

rev.

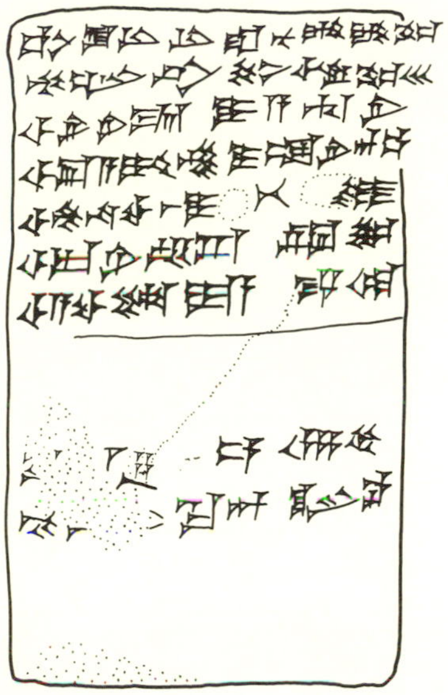

SEALS

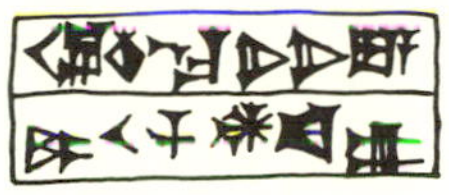

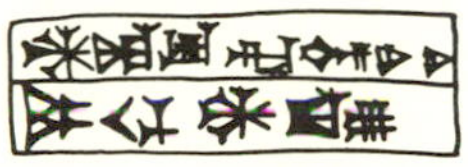

TEXT 13

obv.

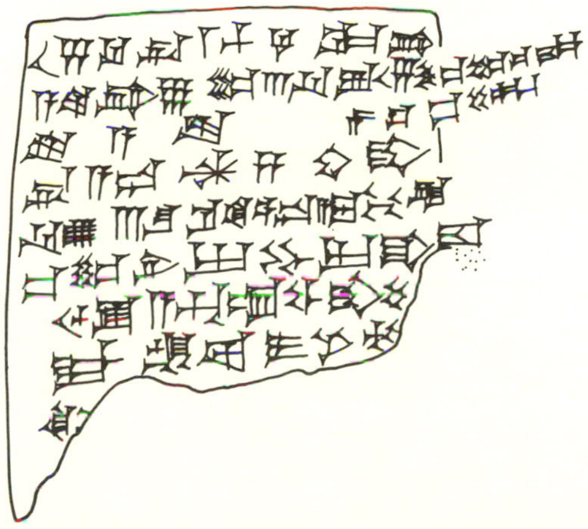

rev.

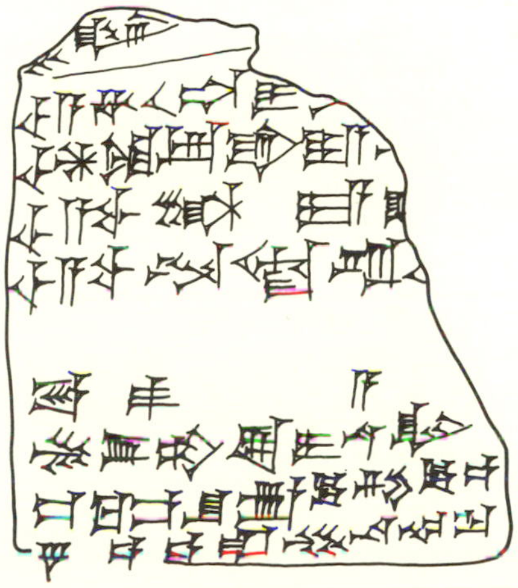

SEAL

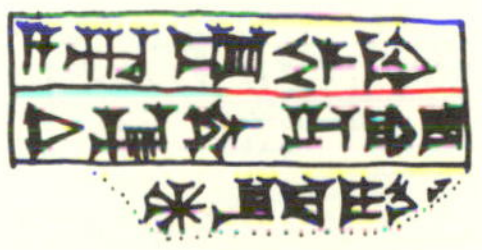

TEXT 14

obv.

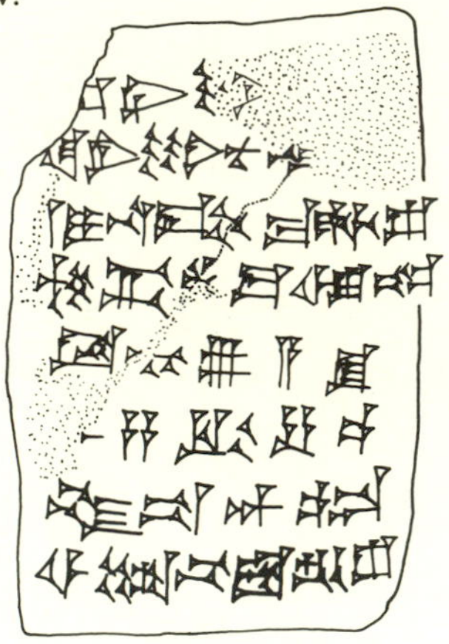

rev.

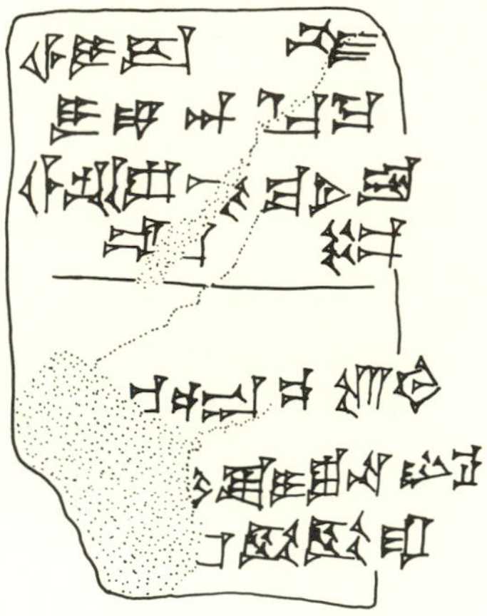

SEAL

TEXT 15

obv.

rev.

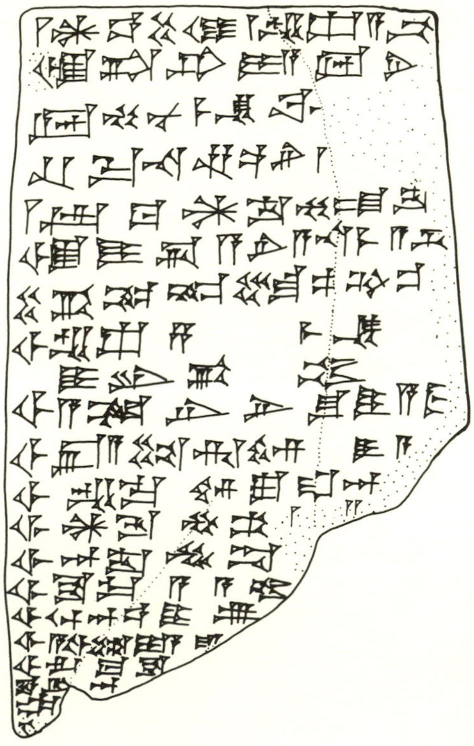

SEAL

TEXT 16

obv.

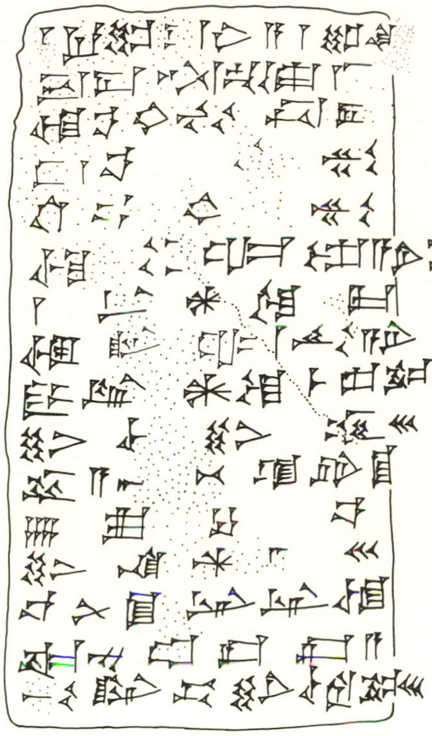

rev.

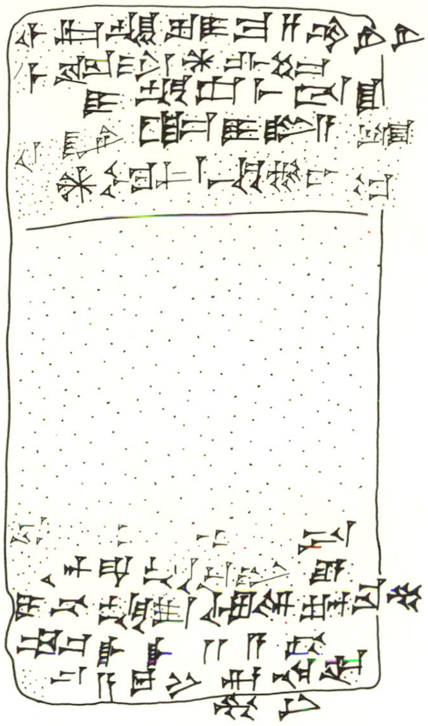

SEAL

TEXT 17

TABLET

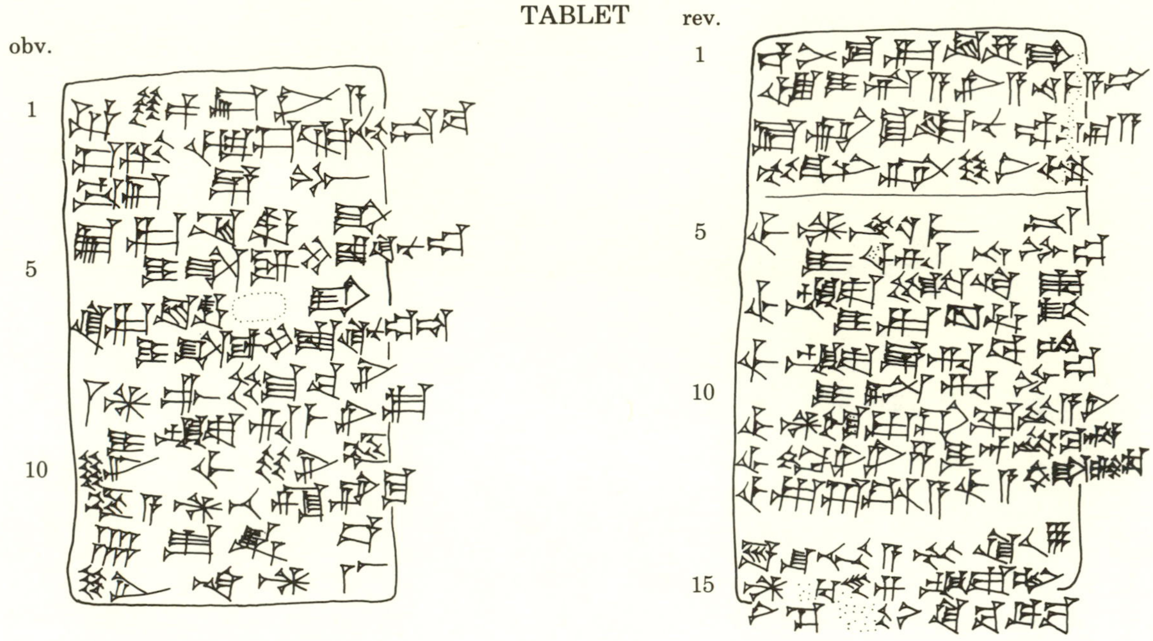

SEAL

CASE

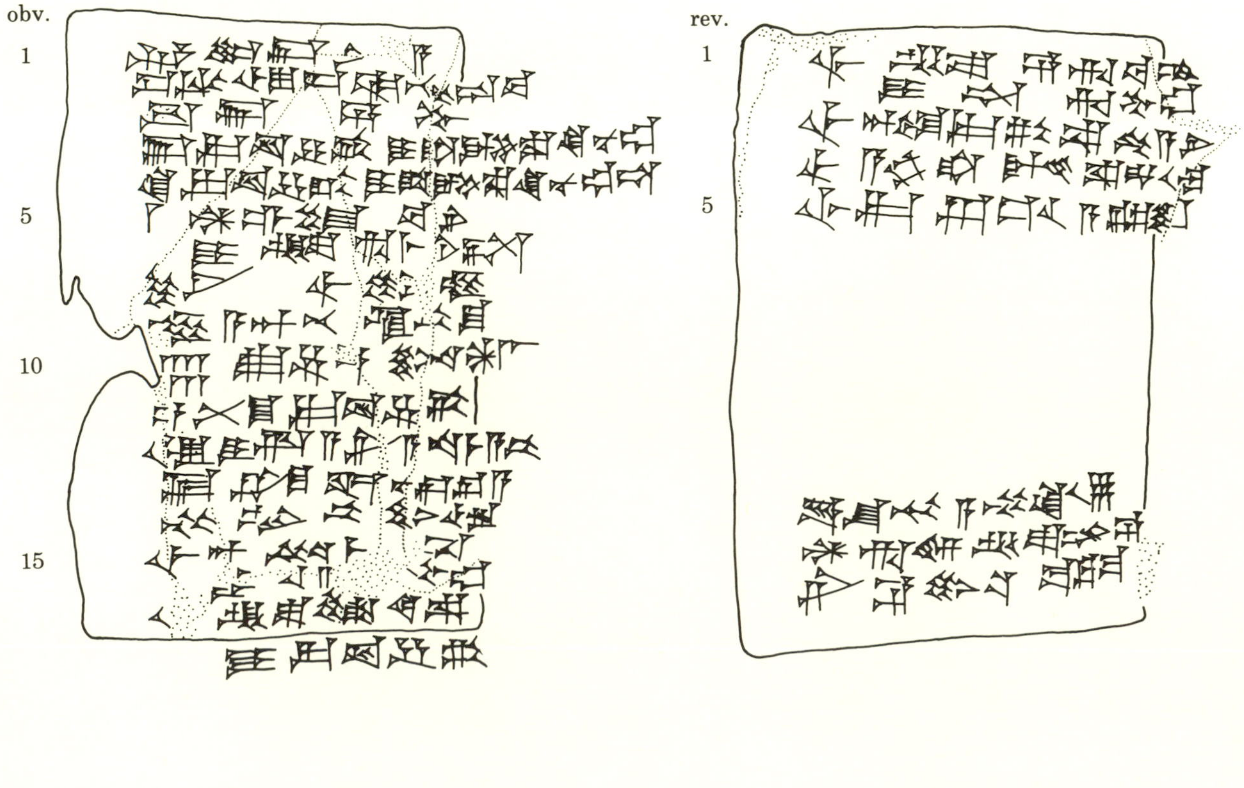

TEXT 18

obv.

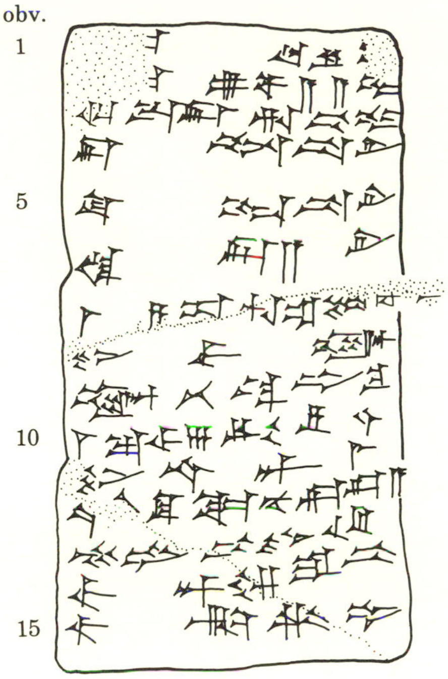

rev.

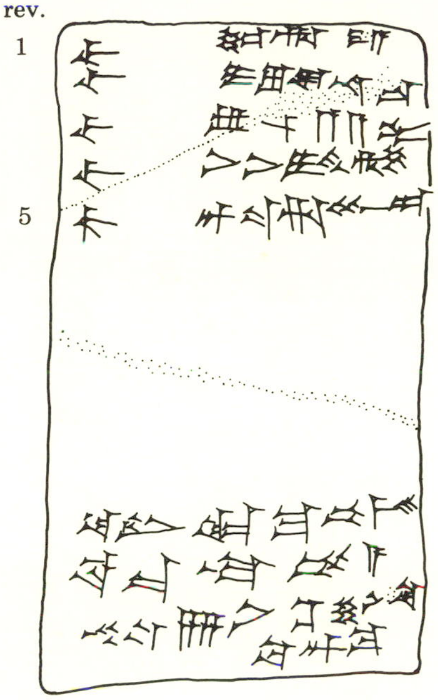

SEALS

TEXT 19

obv.

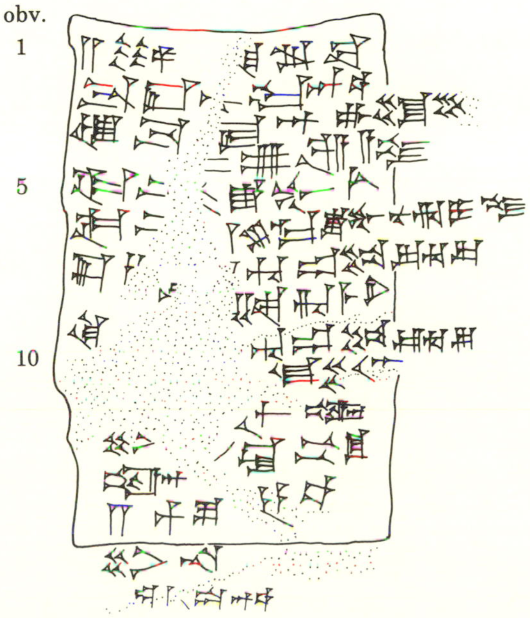

rev.

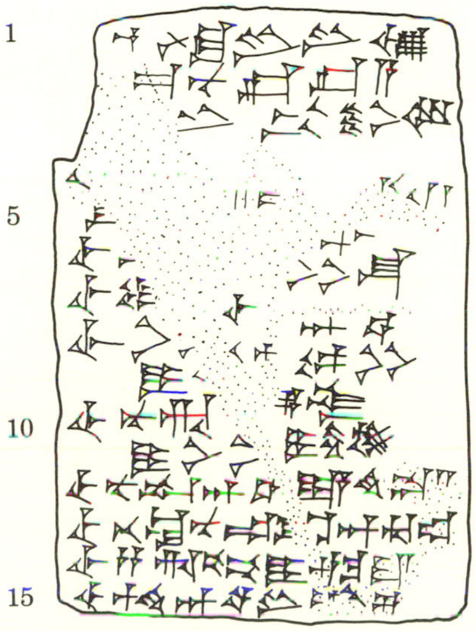

SEAL

TEXT 20

TABLET

obv.

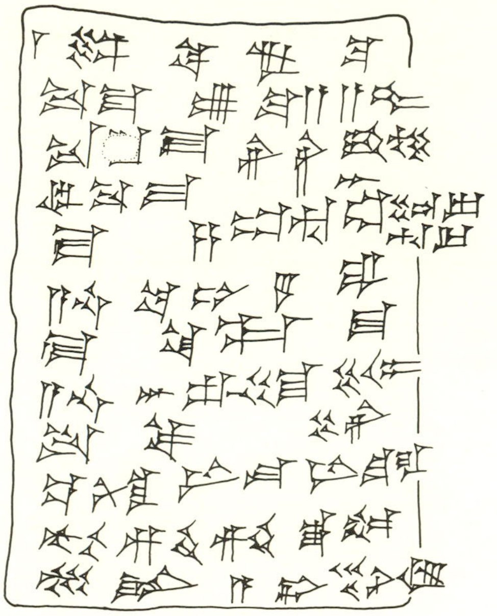

rev.

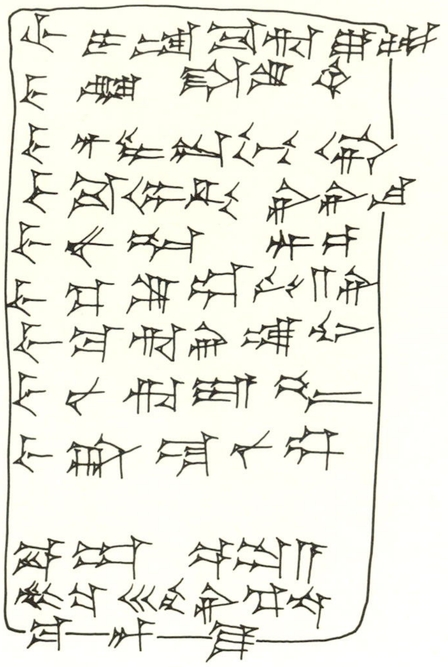

CASE

obv.

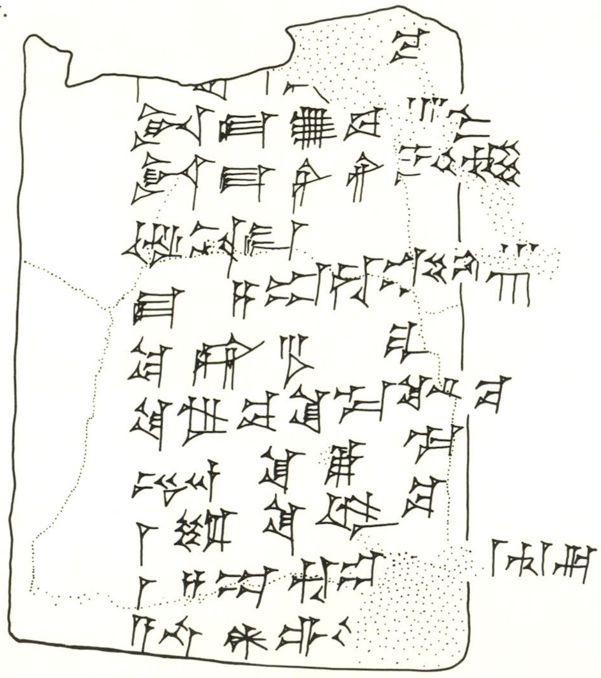

rev.

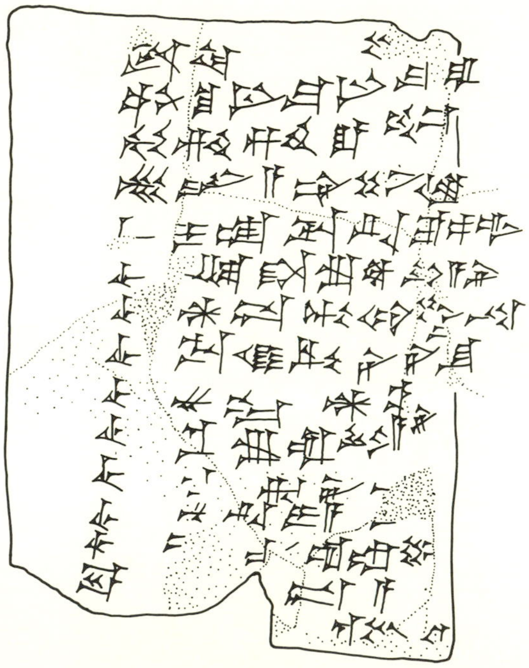

SEALS

TEXT 21

obv.

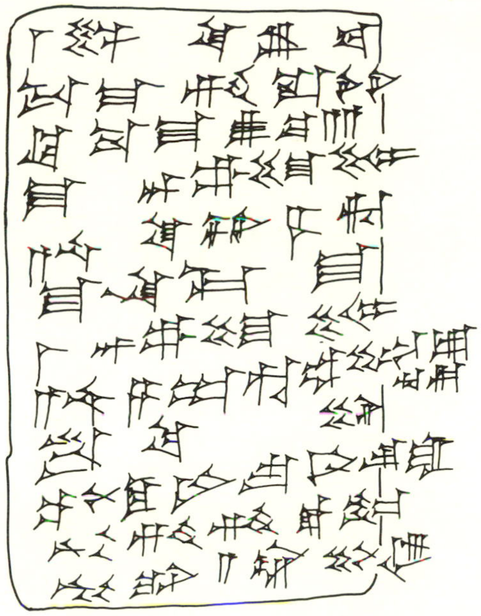

rev.

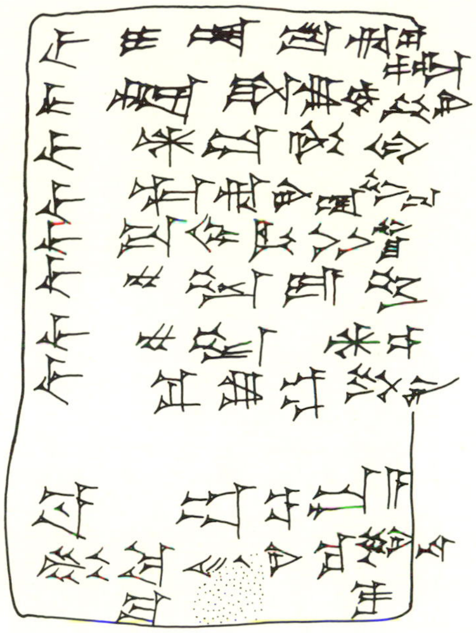

SEALS

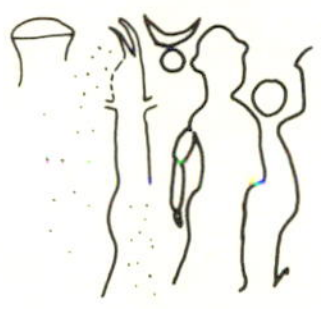

TEXT 22

obv.

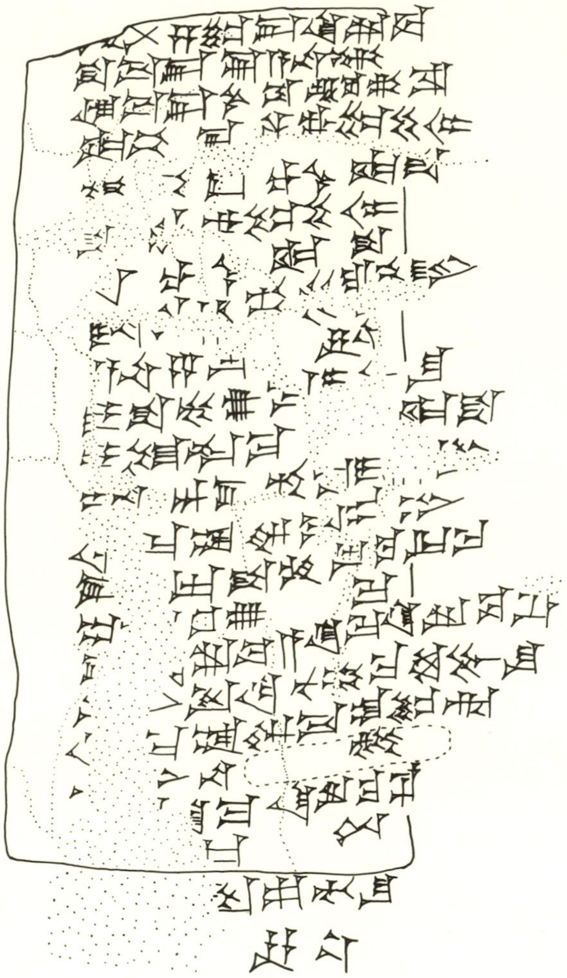

rev.

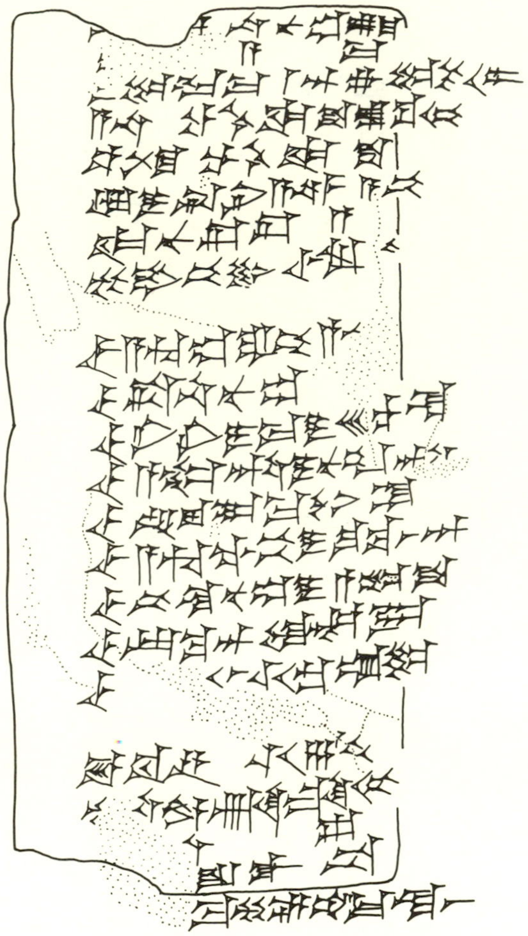

SEALS

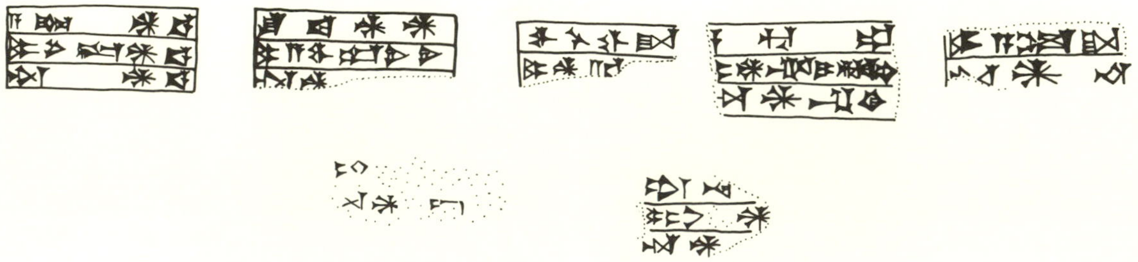

TEXT 23

obv.

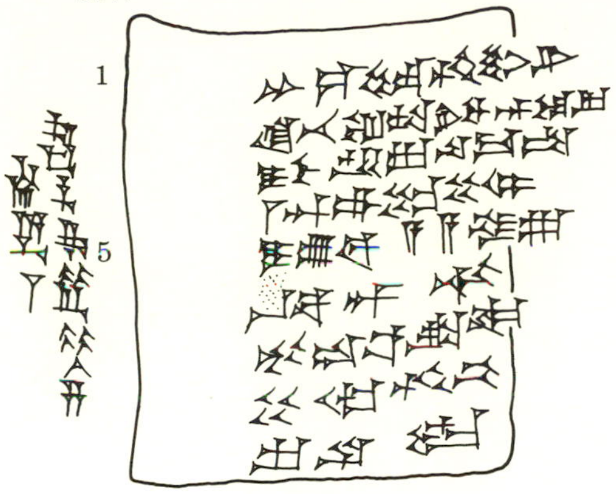

rev.

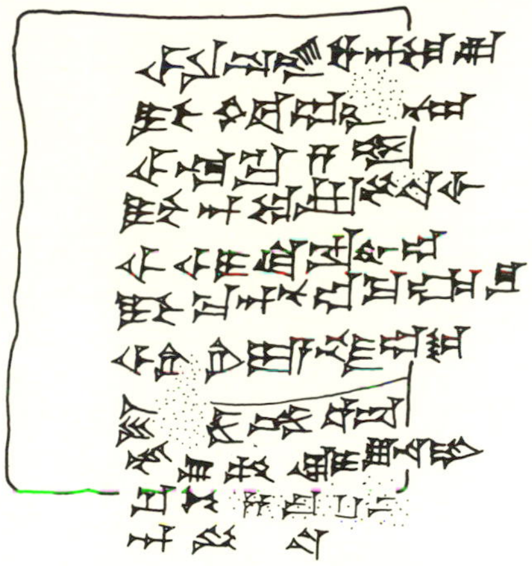

SEAL

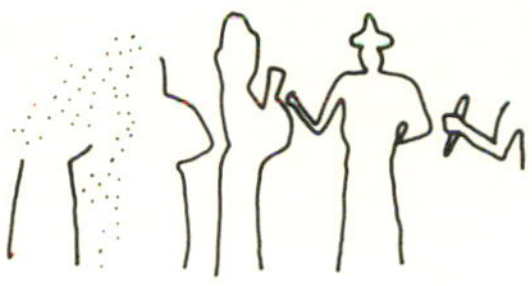

TEXT 24

TABLET

obv.

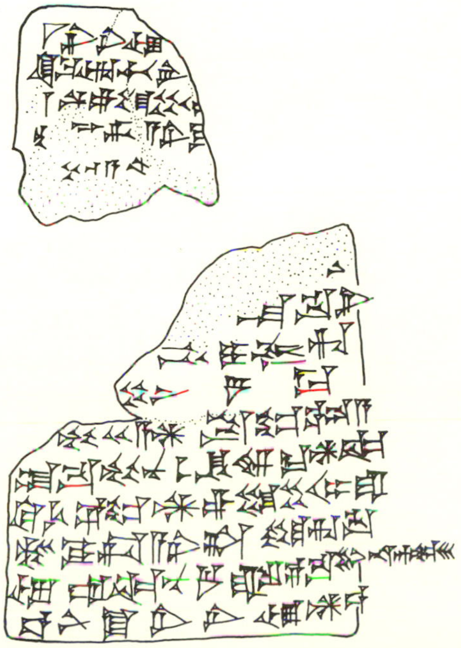

rev.

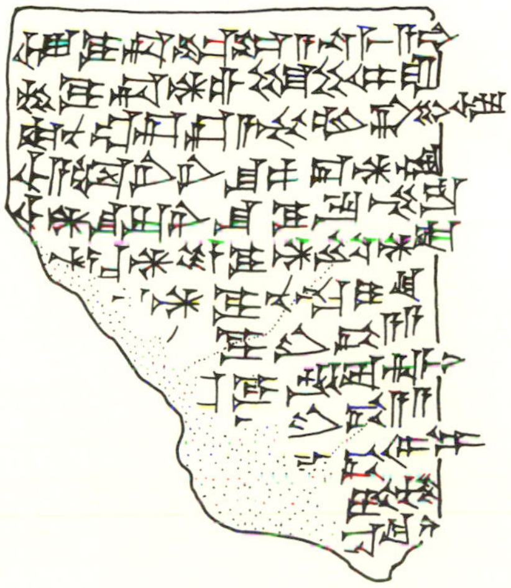

SEAL

CASE

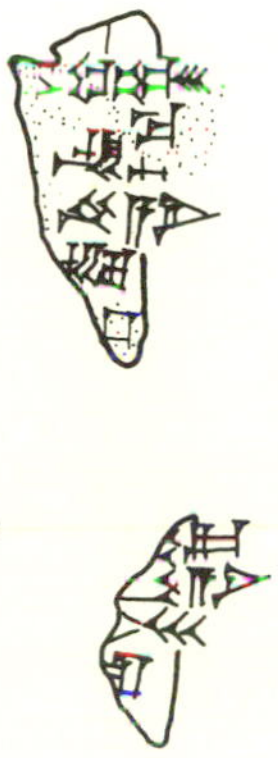

TEXT 25

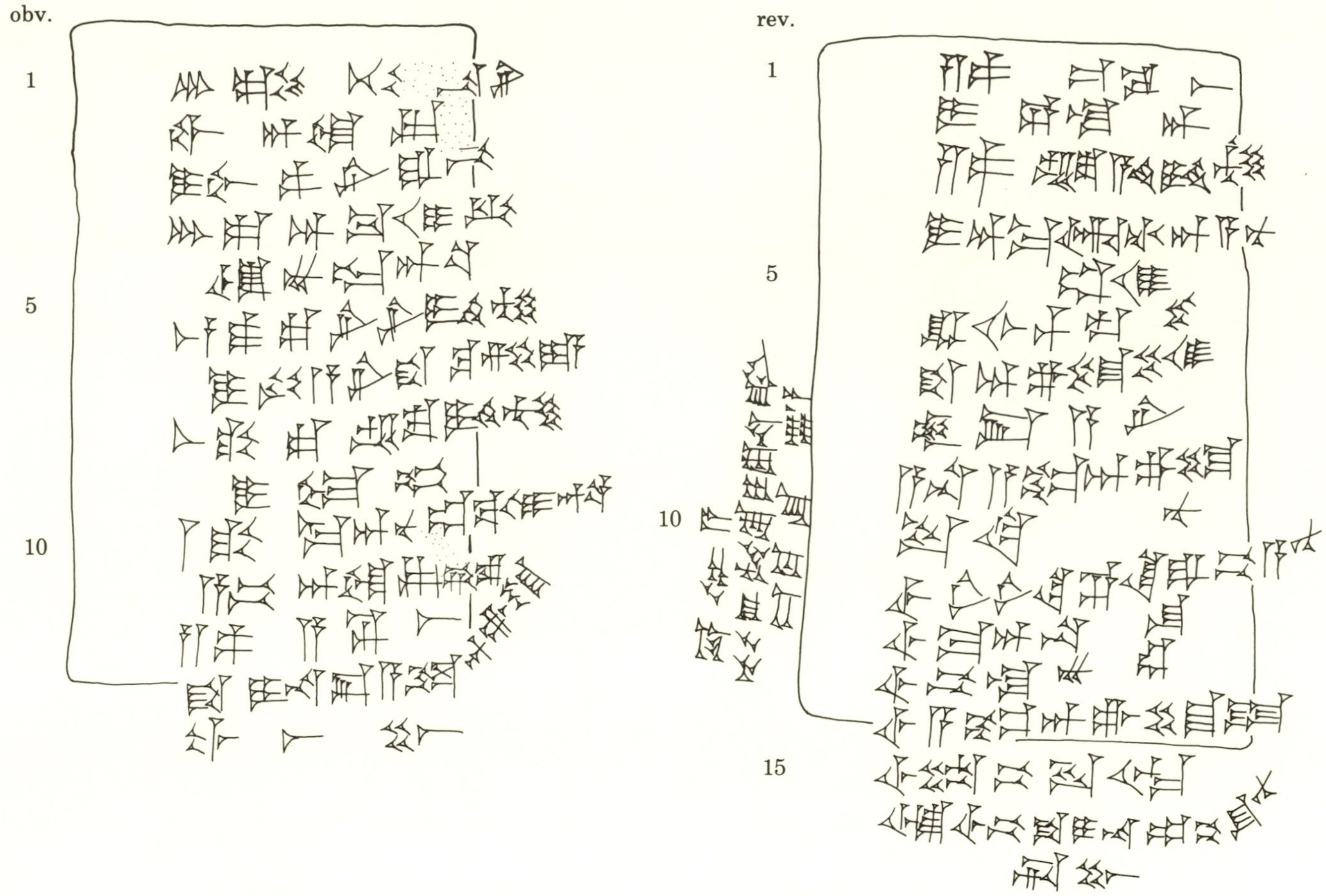

SEALS

TEXT 26

obv.

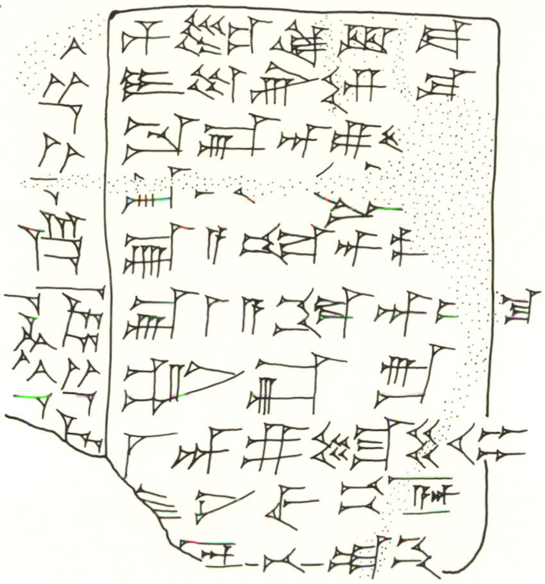

rev.

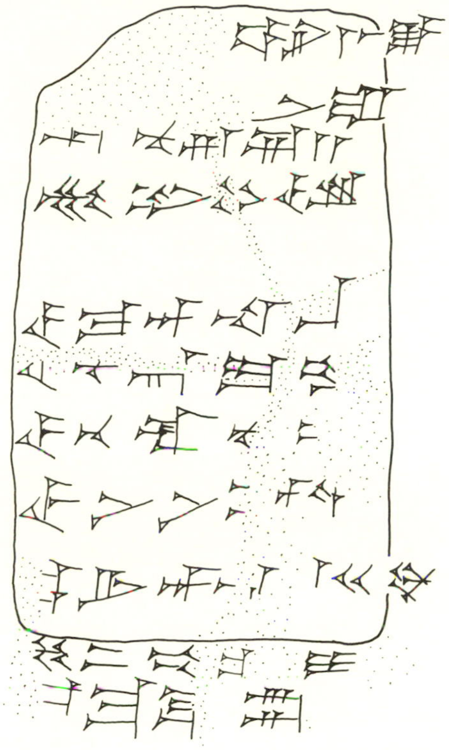

SEALS

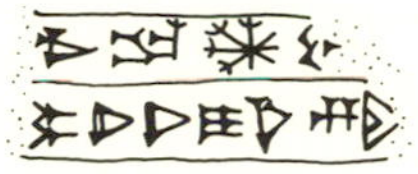

TEXT 27

obv.

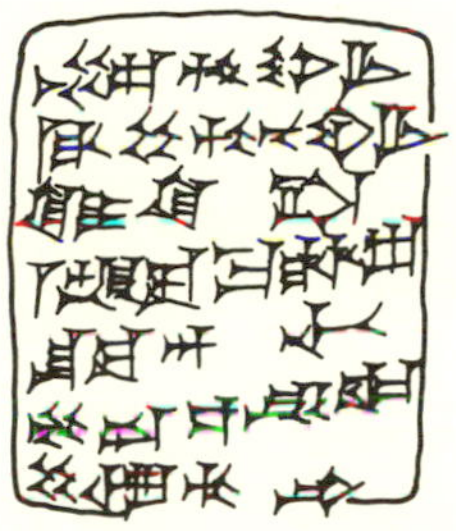

rev.

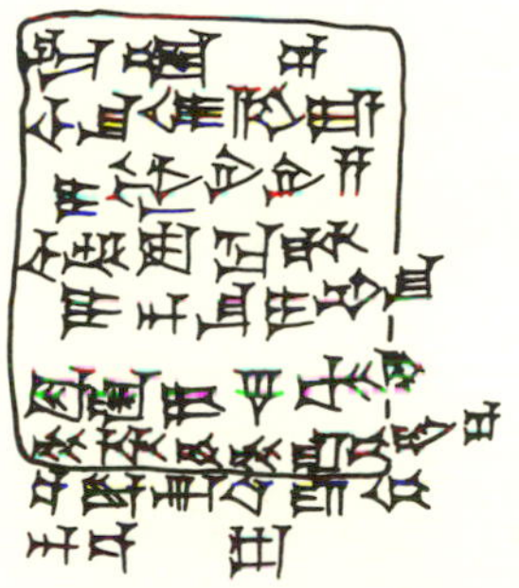

TEXT 28

obv.

rev.

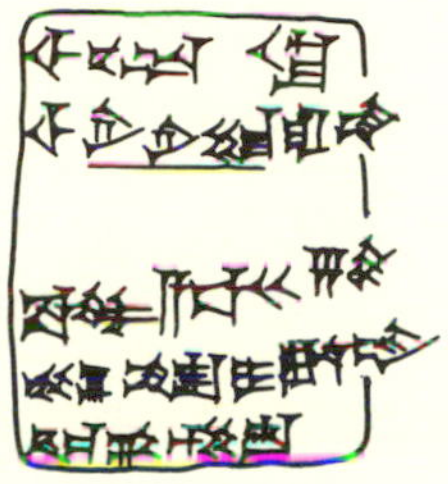

TEXT 29

obv.

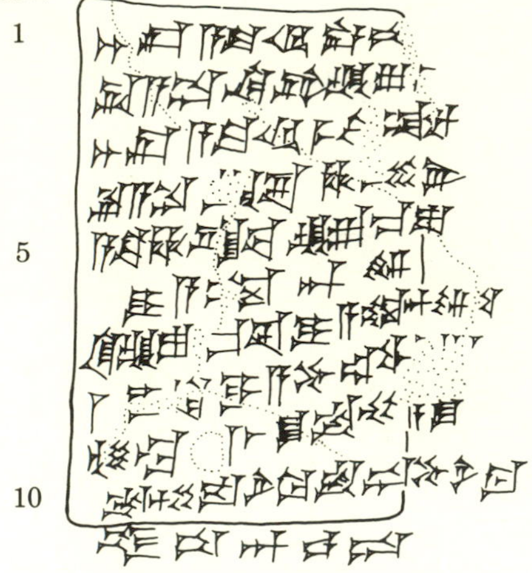

rev.

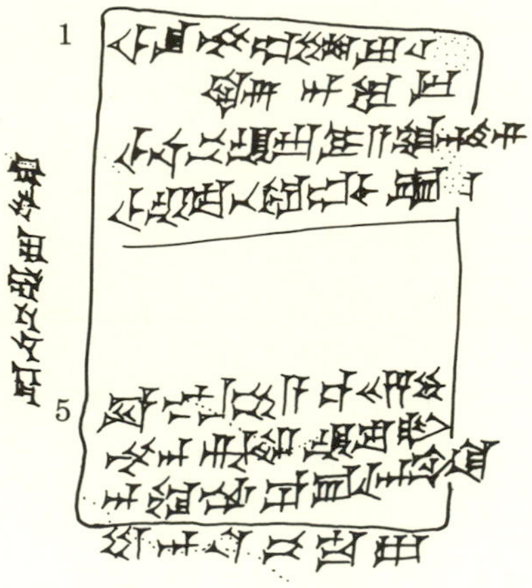

SEAL

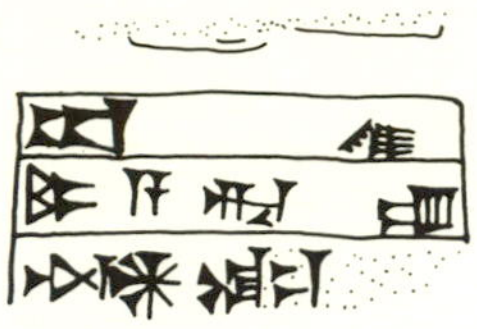

TEXT 30

obv.

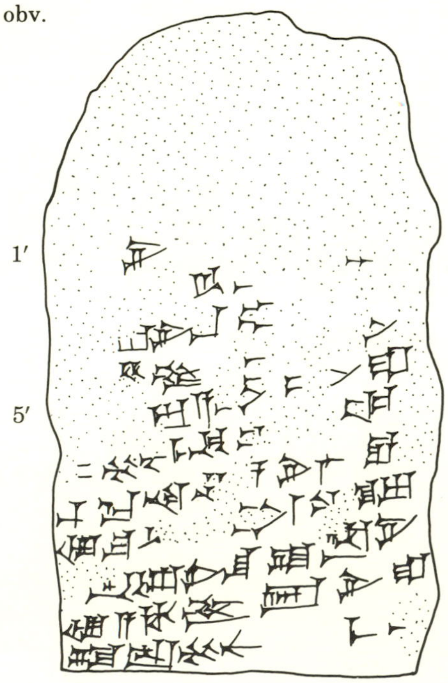

rev.

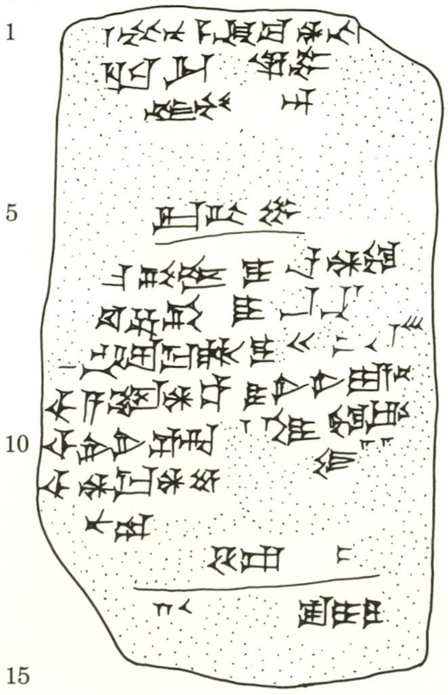

SEAL

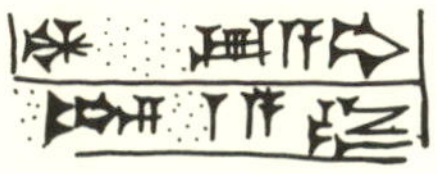

TEXT 31

obv.

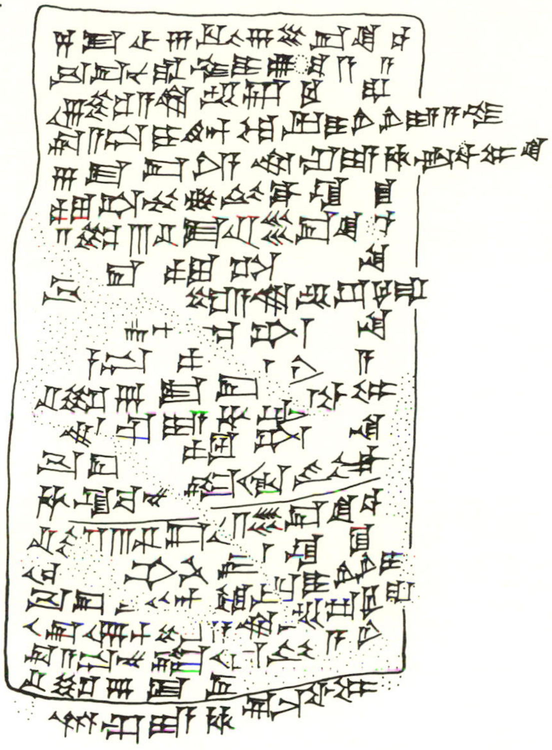

rev.

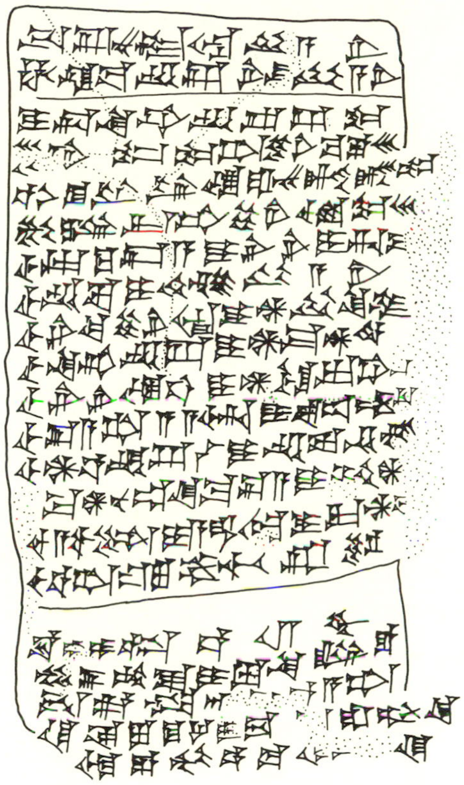

SEAL

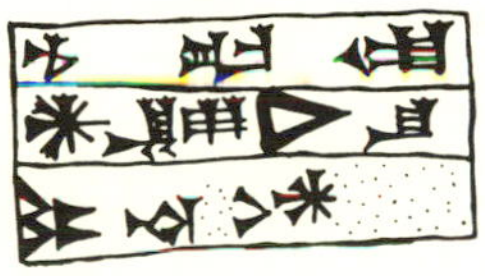

TEXT 32

TABLET

obv.

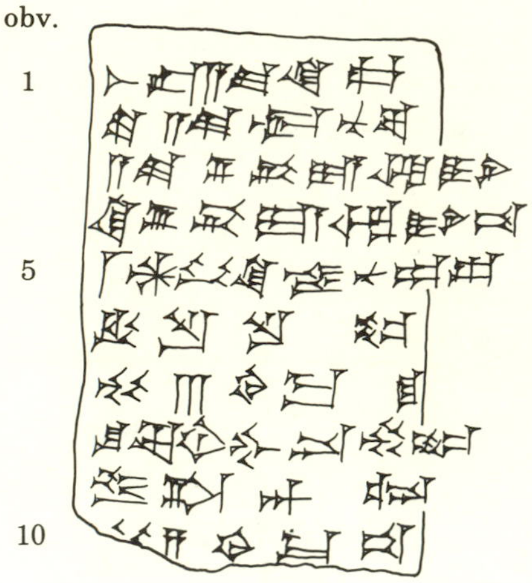

rev.

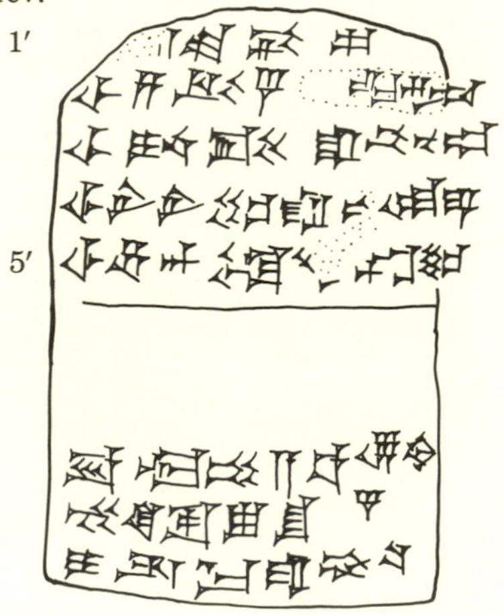

CASE

obv.

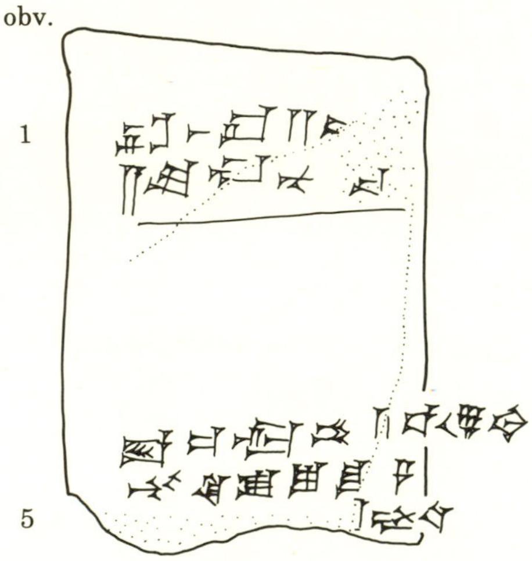

SEALS

TEXT 33

obv.

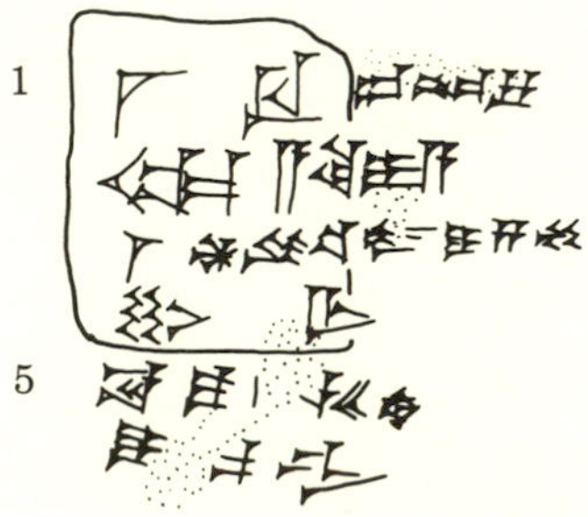

rev.

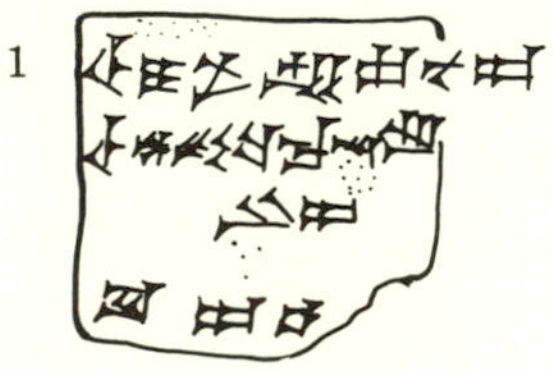

TEXT 34

obv.

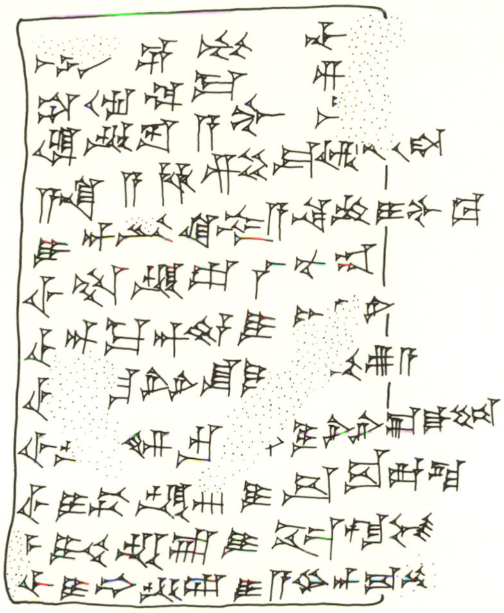

rev.

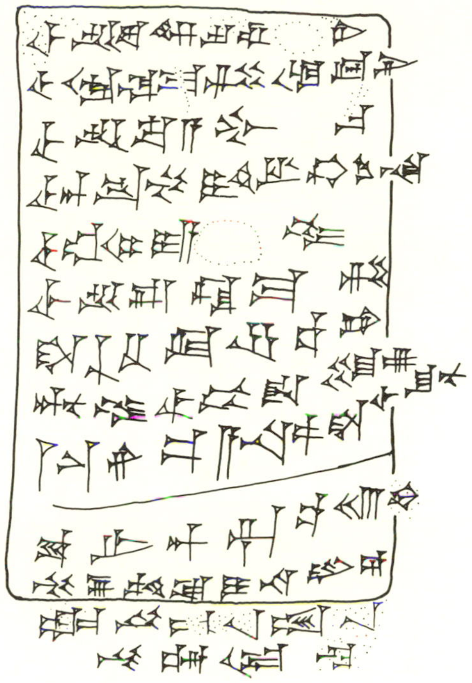

TEXT 35

obv.

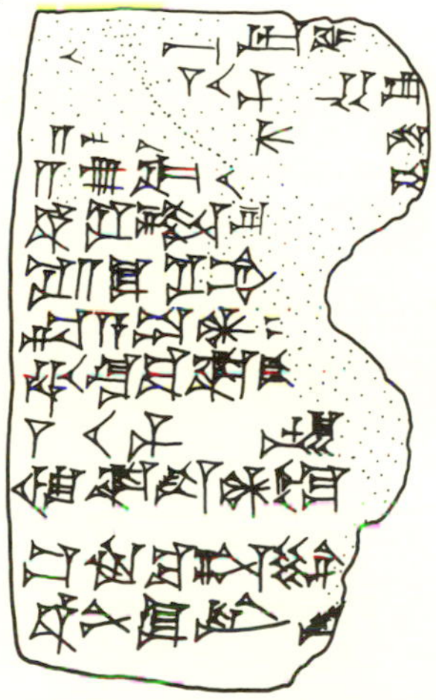

rev.

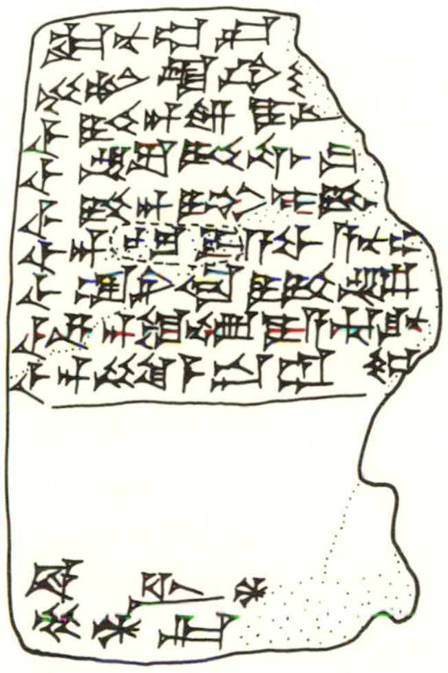

SEALS

TEXT 36

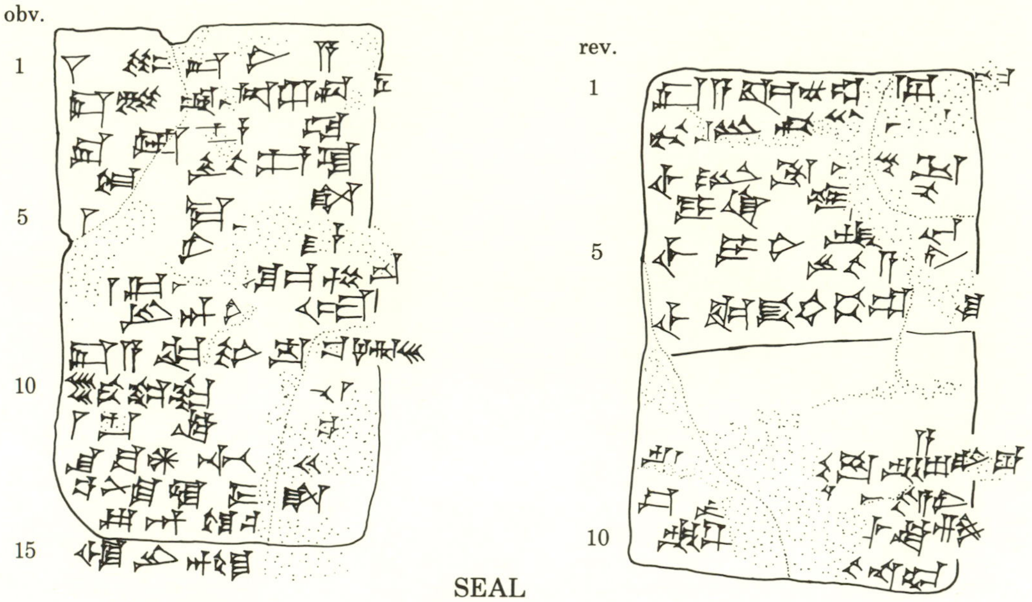

SEAL

TEXT 37

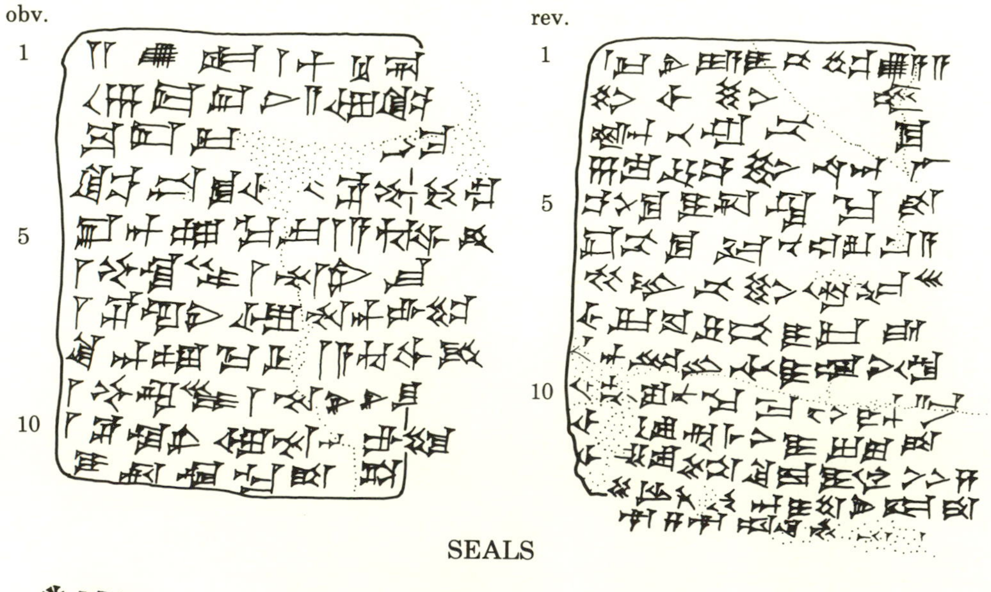

SEALS

TEXT 38

obv.

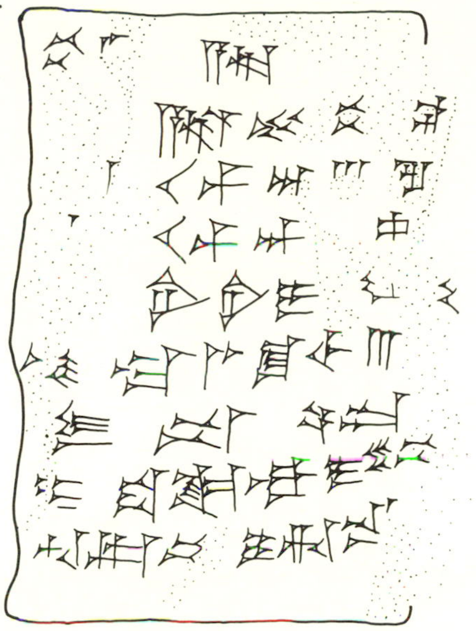

rev.

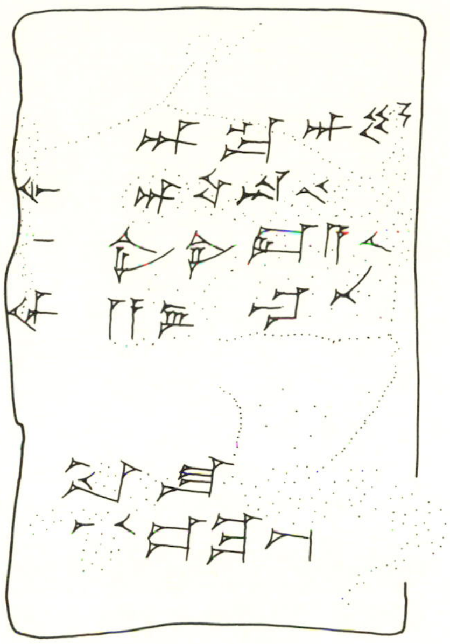

SEAL

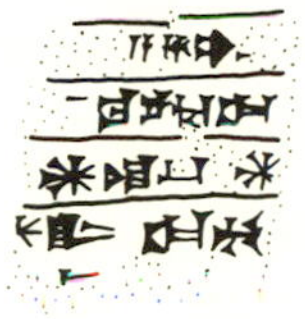

TEXT 39

obv.

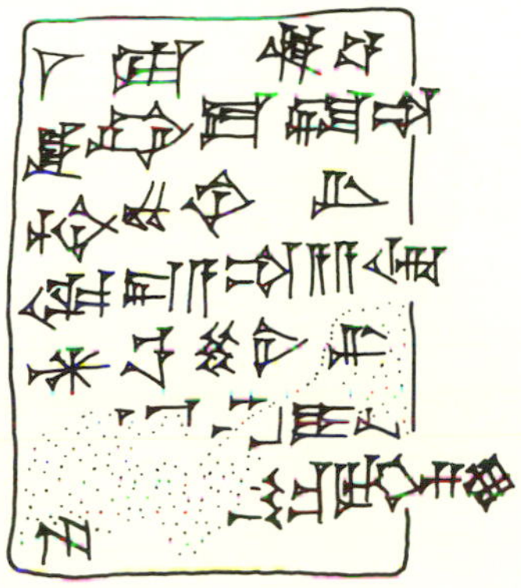

rev.

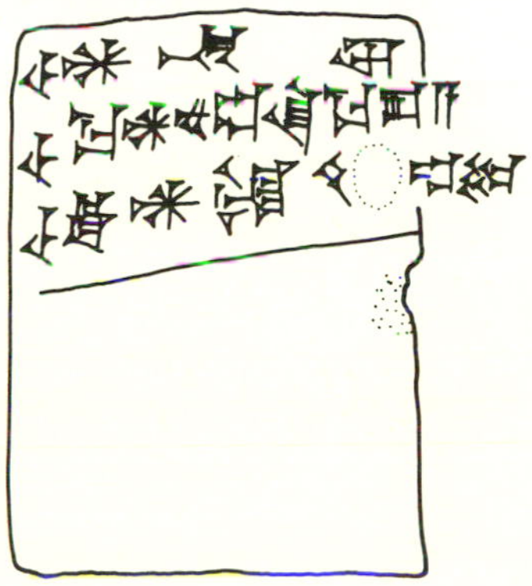

TEXT 40

obv.

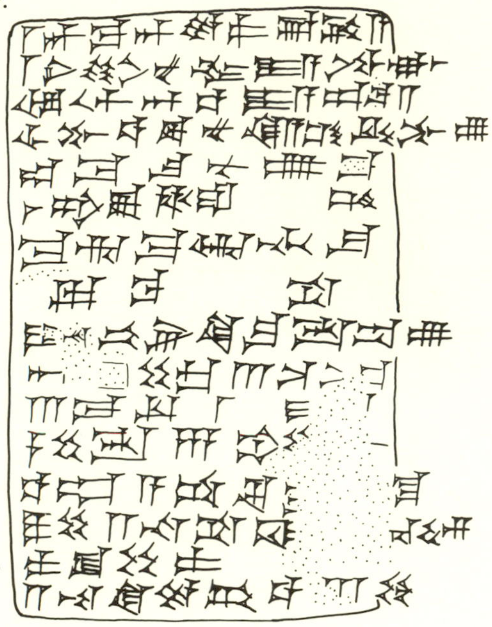

rev.

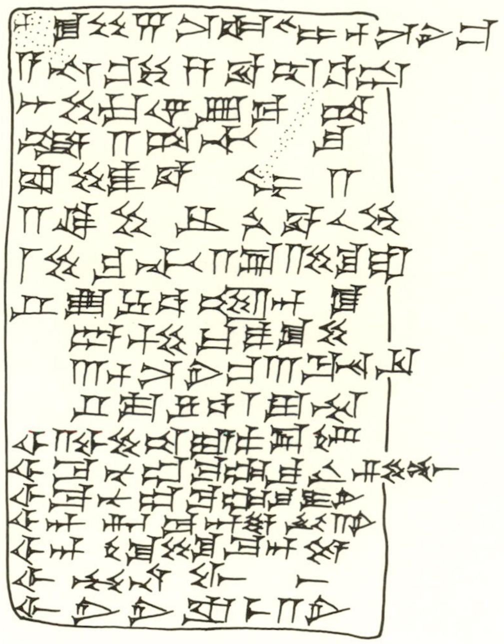

TEXT 41

obv.

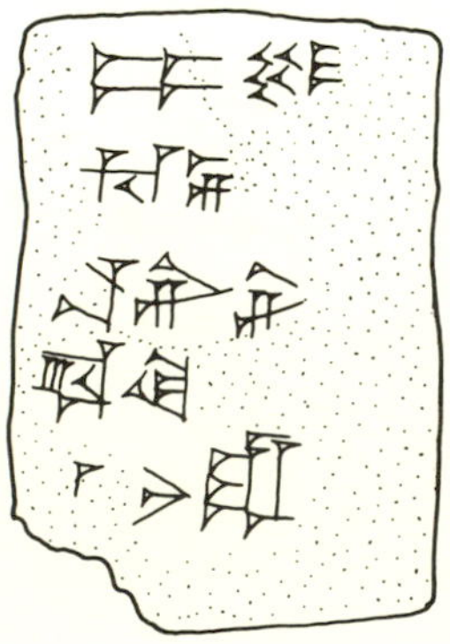

rev.

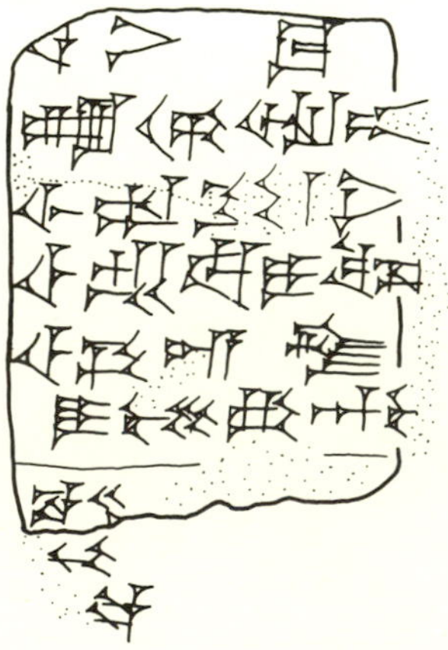

TEXT 42

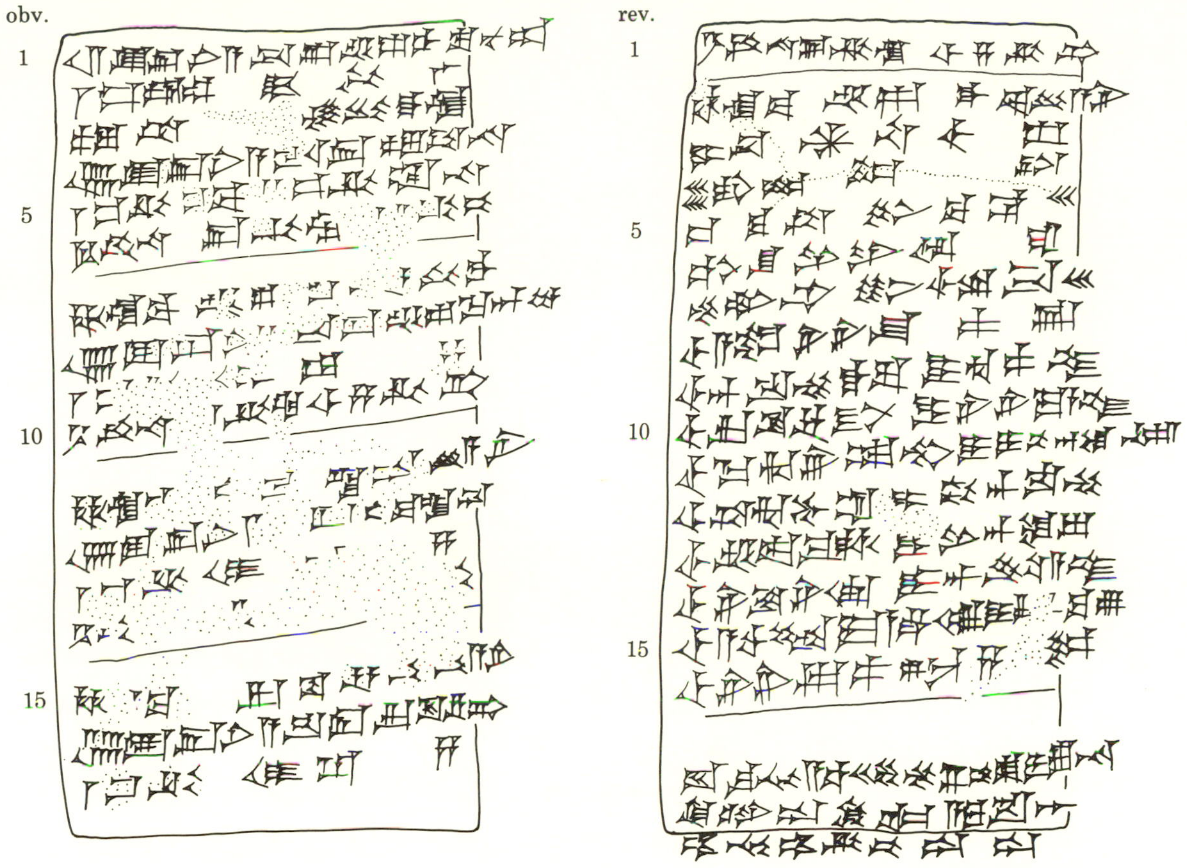

SEAL

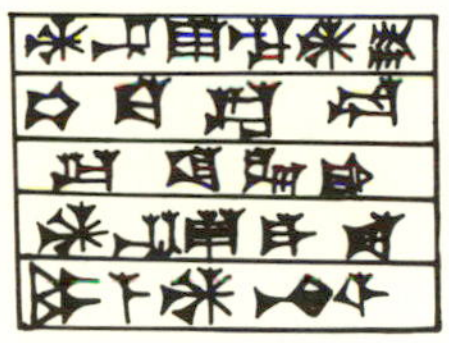

TEXT 43

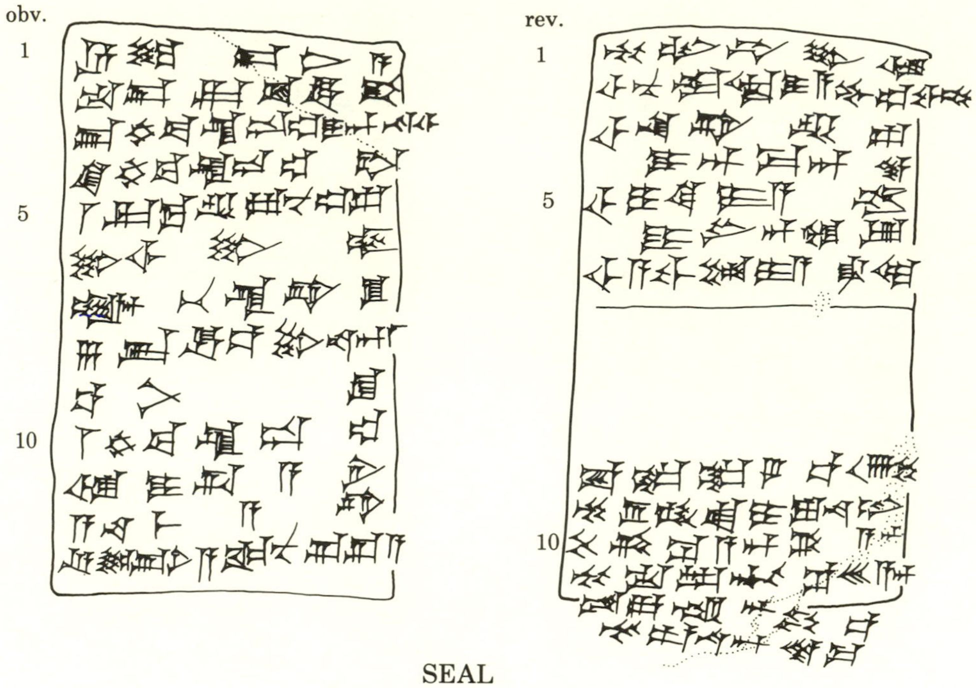

SEAL

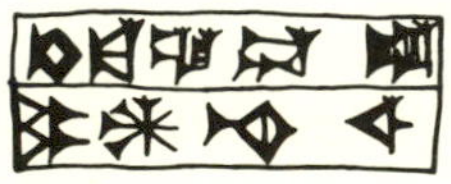

TEXT 44

TABLET

obv.

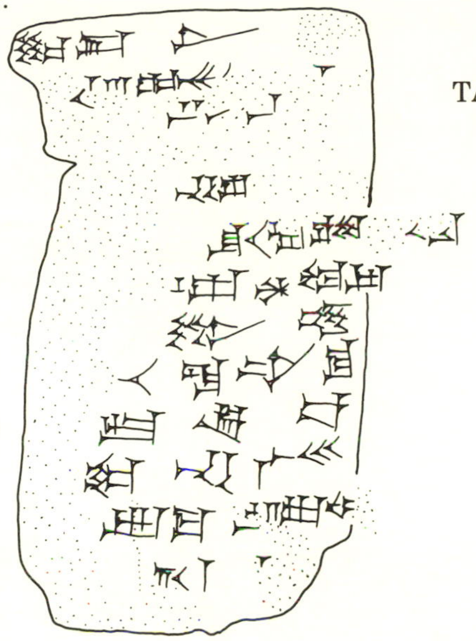

rev.

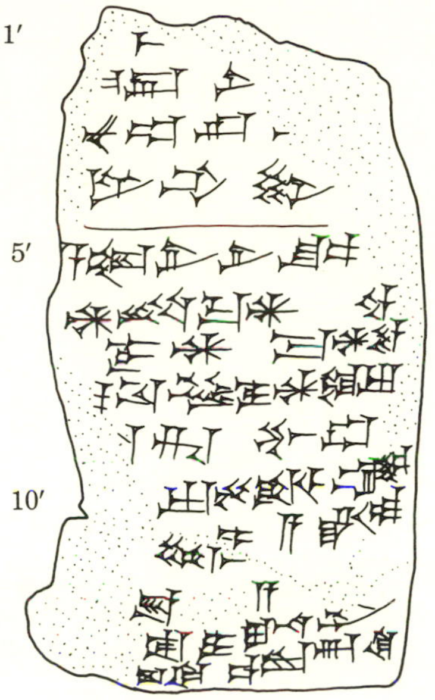

CASE

obv.

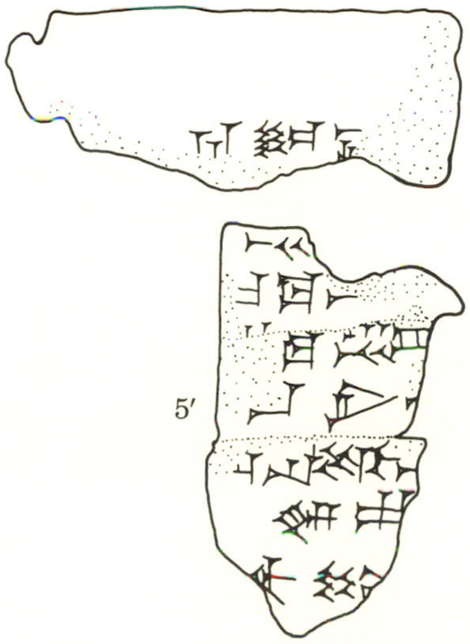

rev.

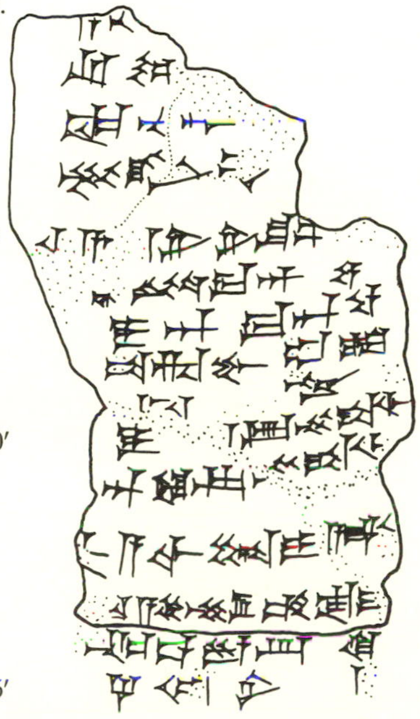

SEAL

TEXT 45

TABLET

obv.

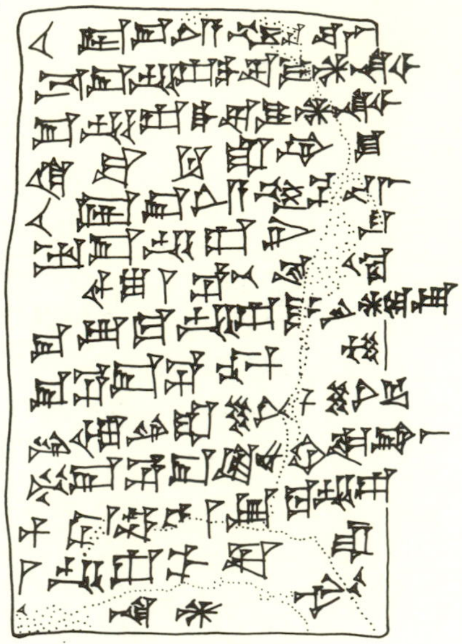

rev.

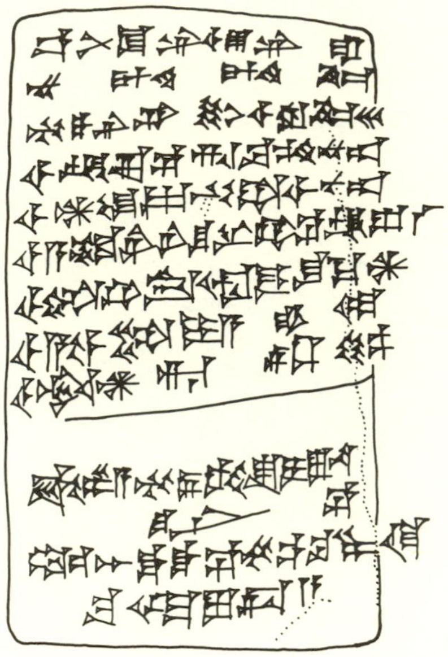

CASE

obv.

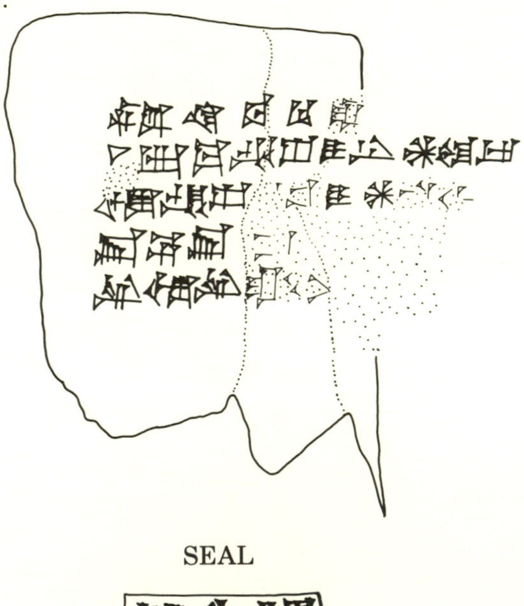

SEAL

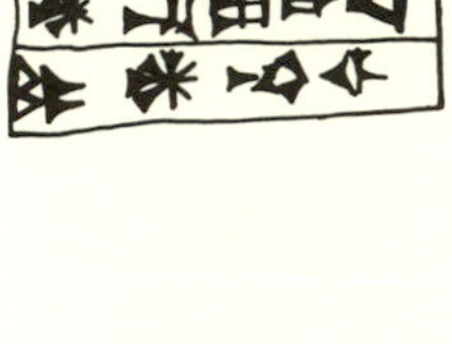

rev.

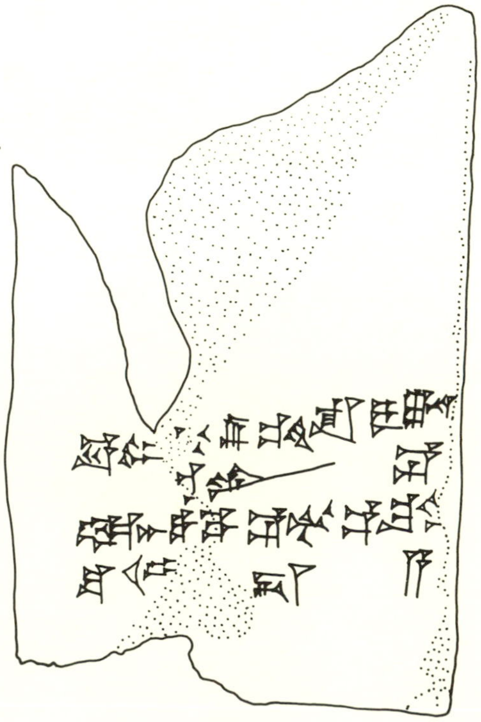

TEXT 46

TABLET

obv.

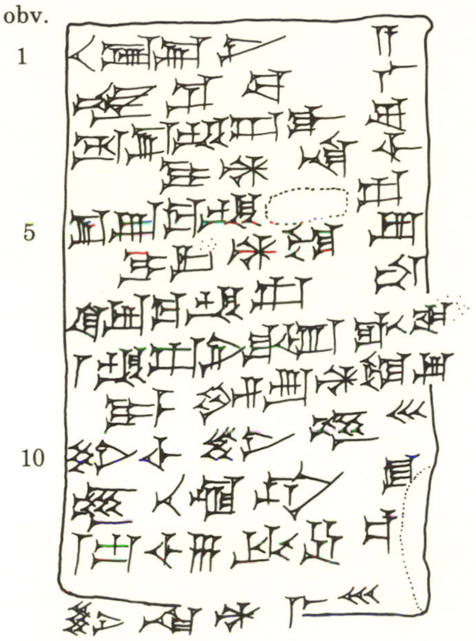

rev.

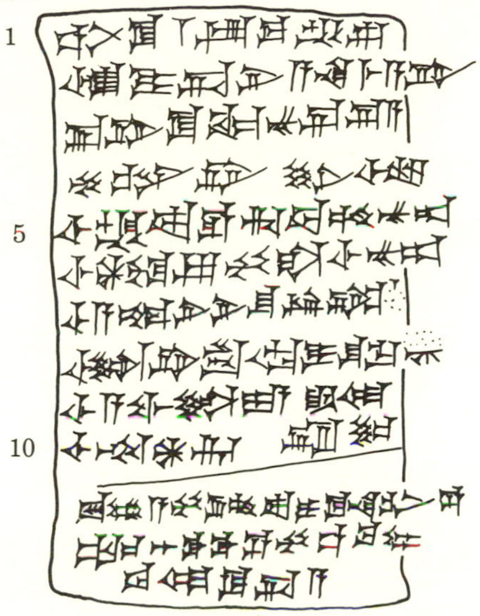

SEAL

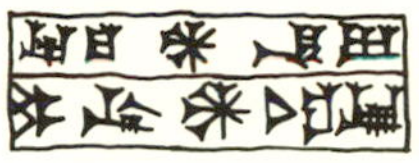

CASE

obv.

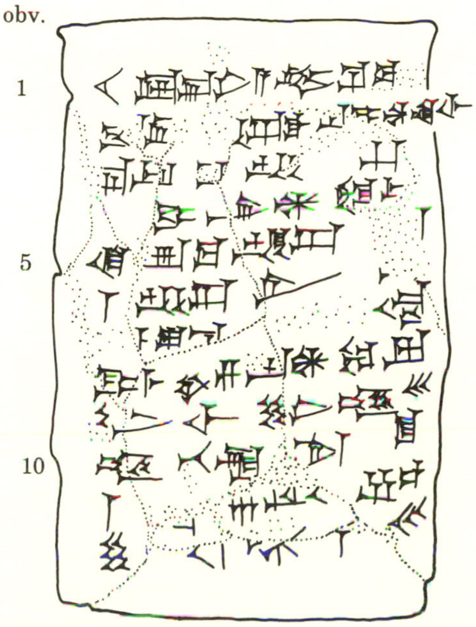

rev.

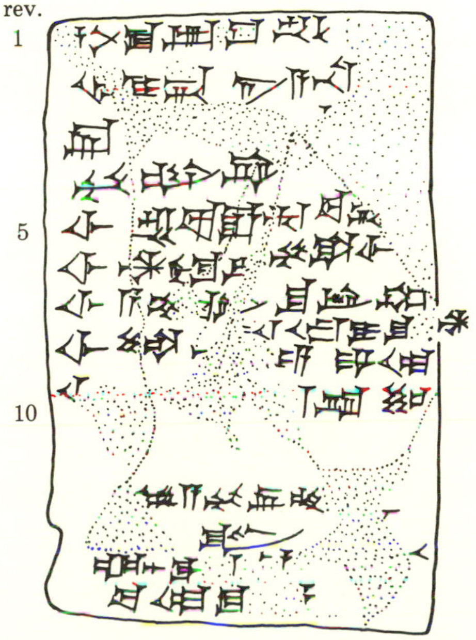

TEXT 47

TABLET

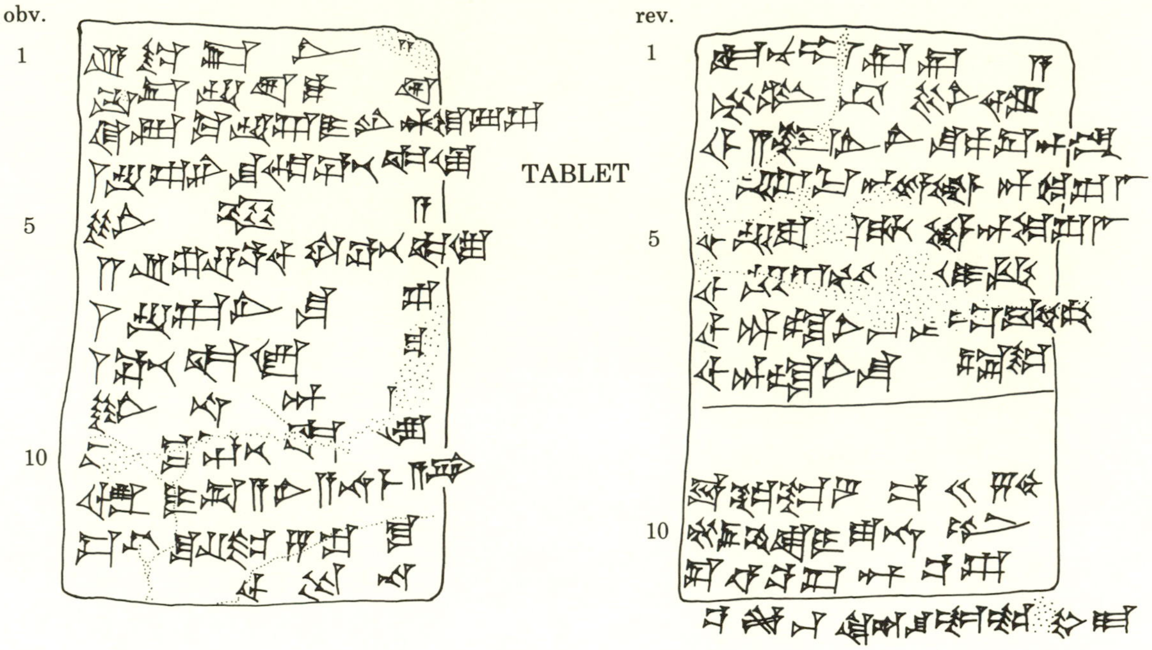

SEAL

CASE

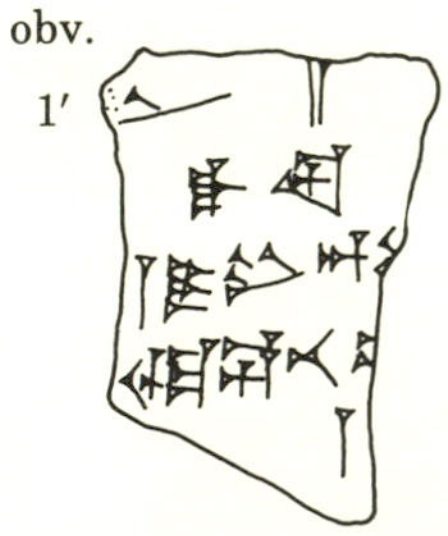

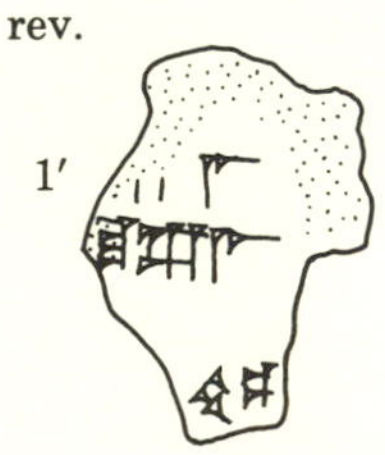

TEXT 48

obv.

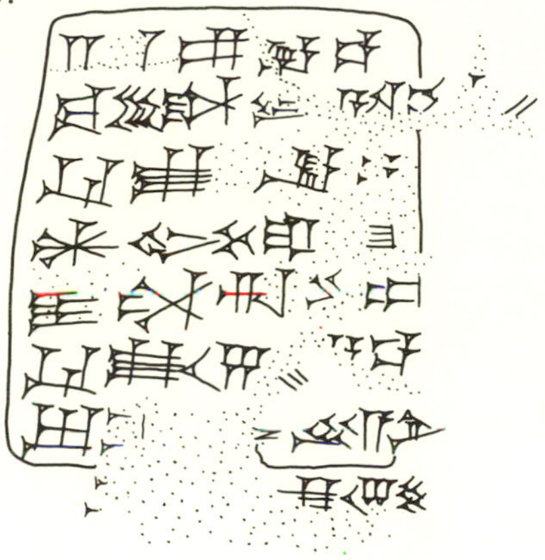

rev.

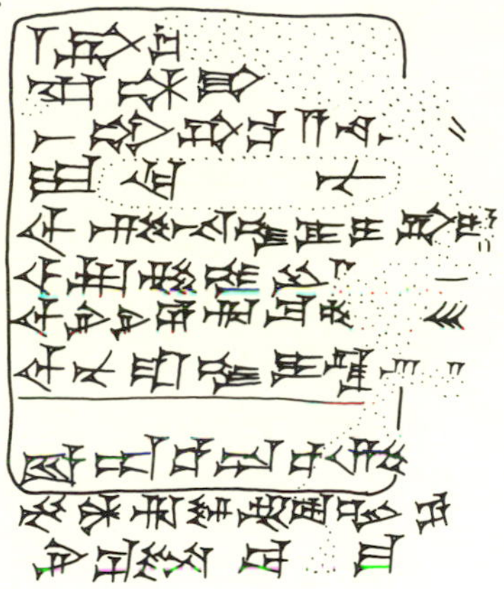

TEXT 49

obv.

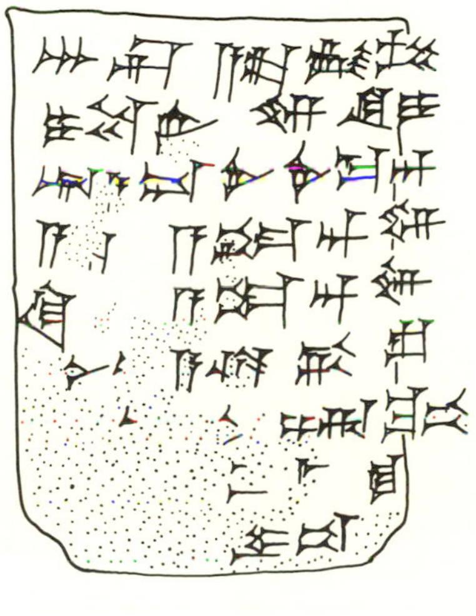

rev.

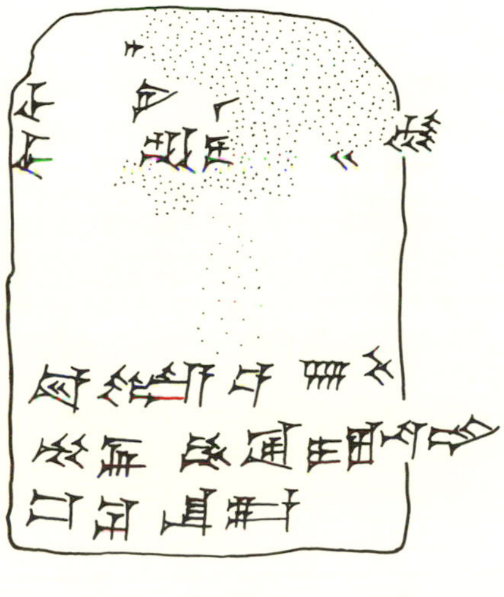

SEAL

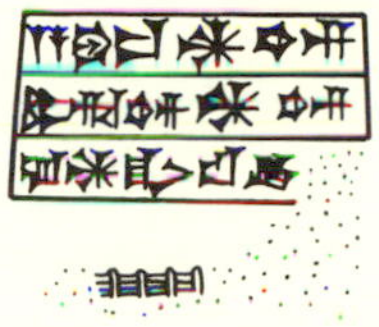

TEXT 50

obv.

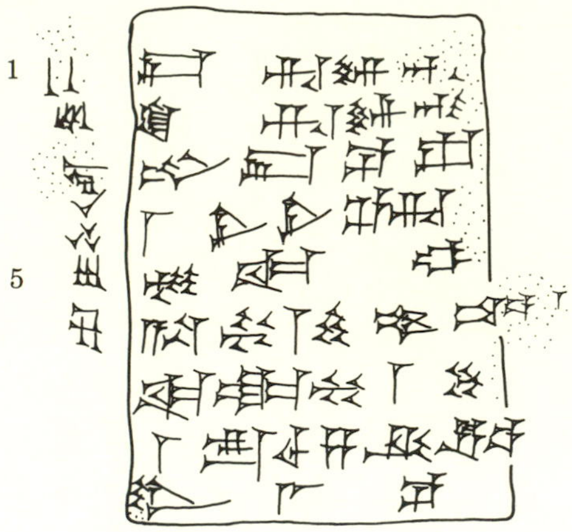

rev.

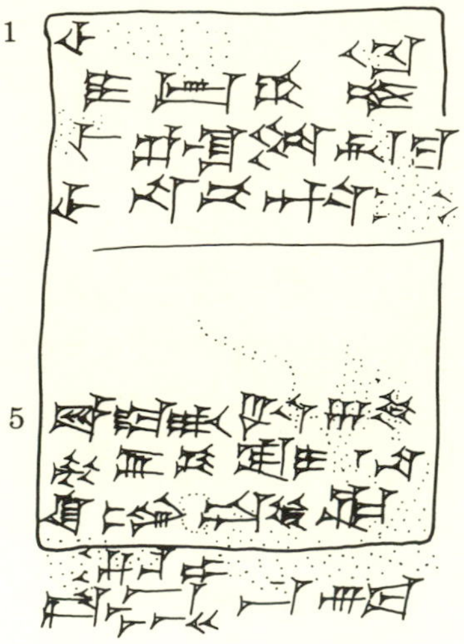

SEAL

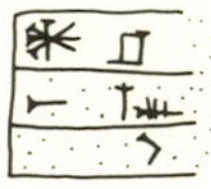

TEXT 51

TABLET

obv.

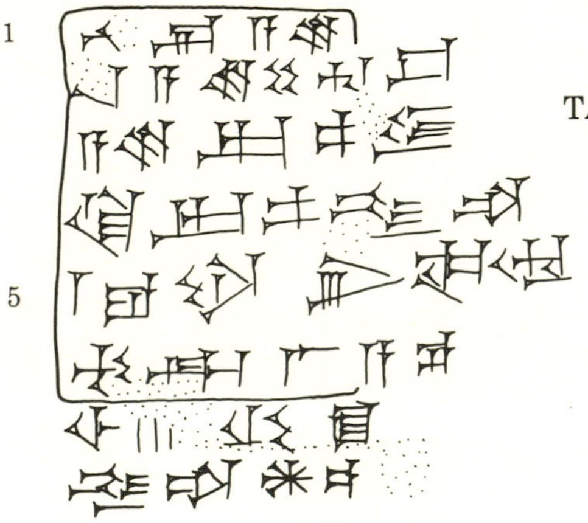

rev.

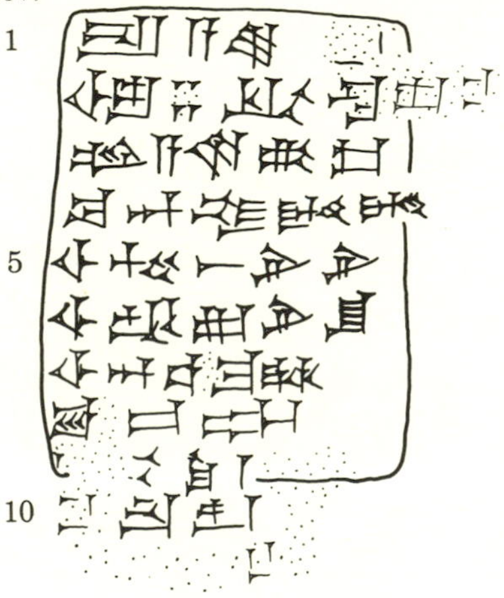

CASE

obv.

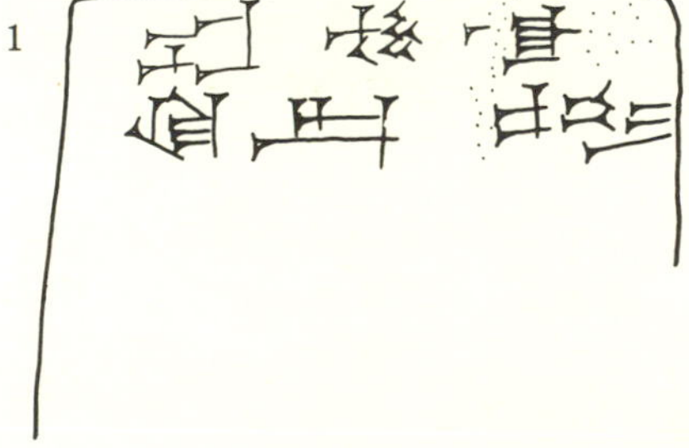

SEAL

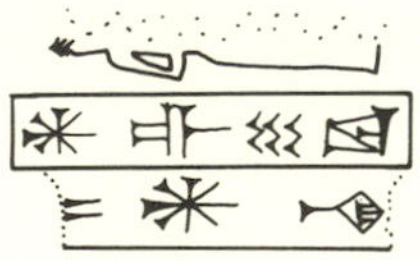

TEXT 52

obv.

1

5

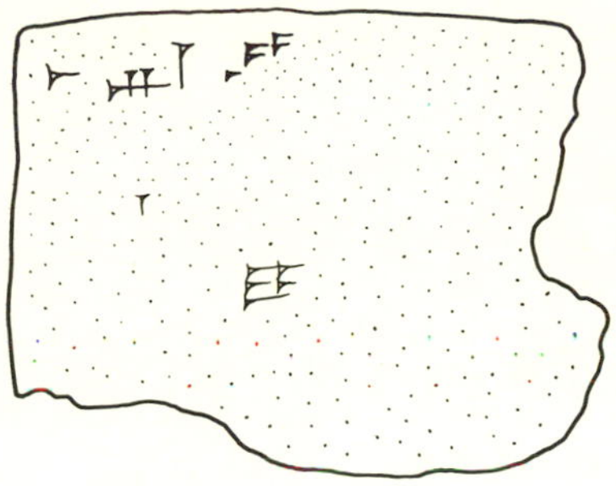

10′

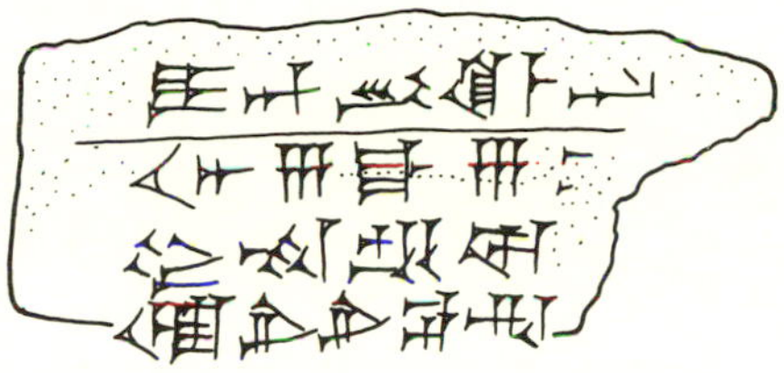

TEXT 53

obv.

1

5

10

15

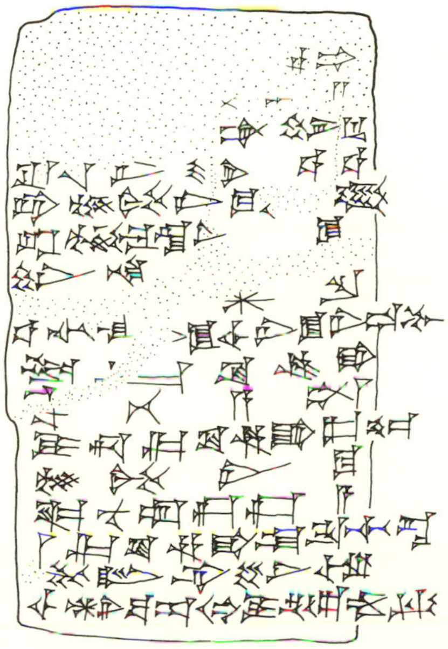

rev.

1

5

10

15

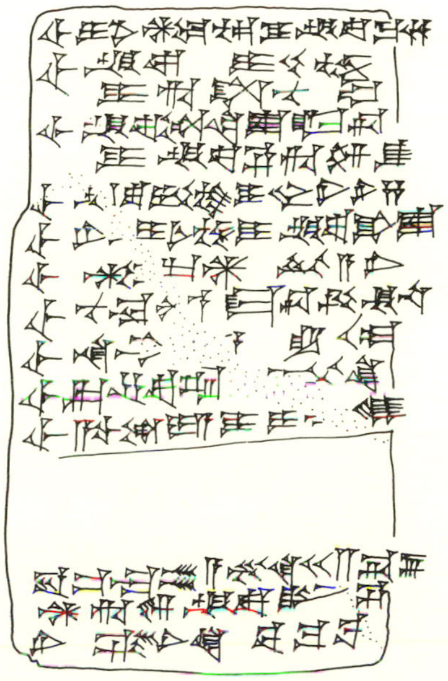

SEAL

TEXT 54

obv.

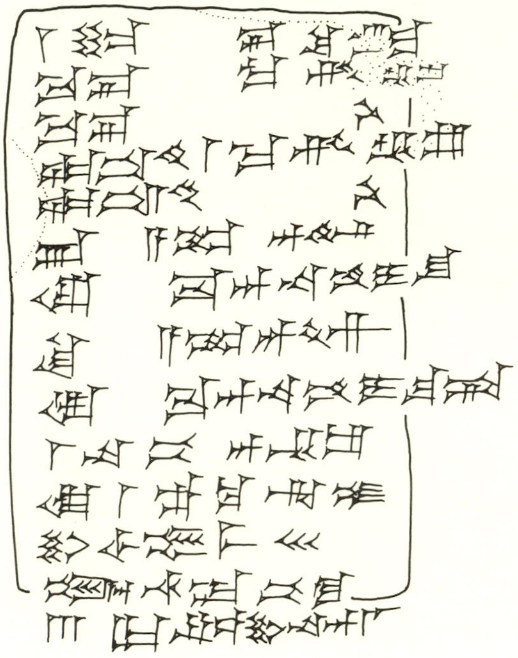

rev.

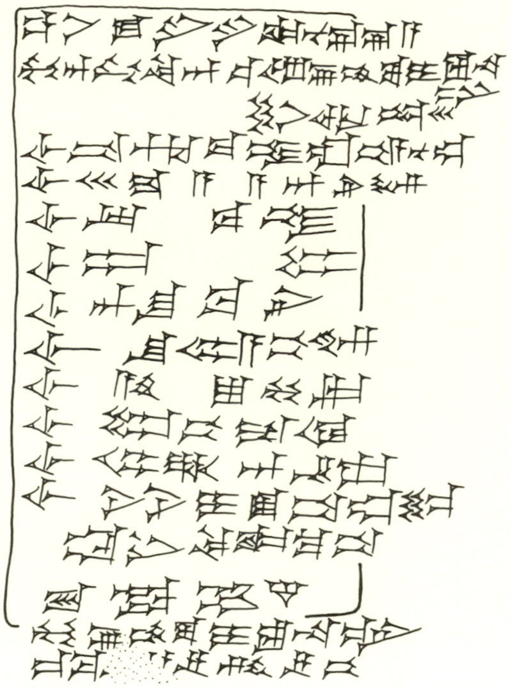

SEAL

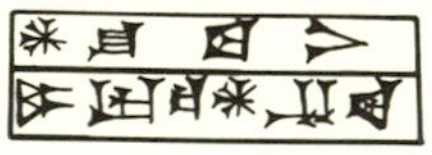

TEXT 55

obv.

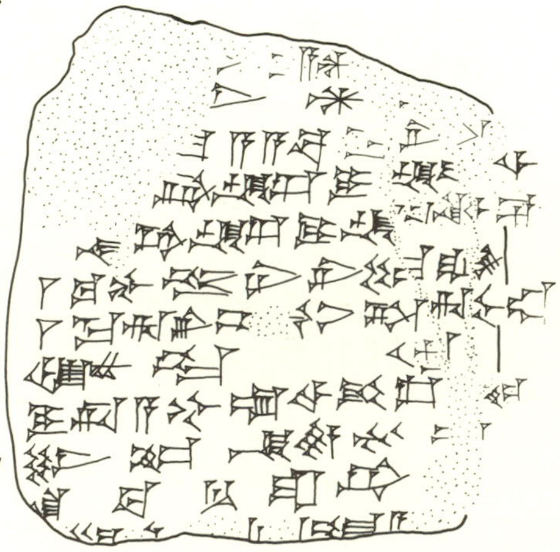

rev.

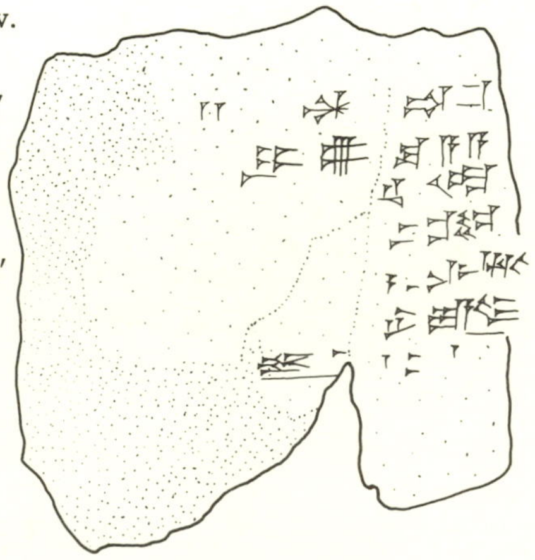

TEXT 56

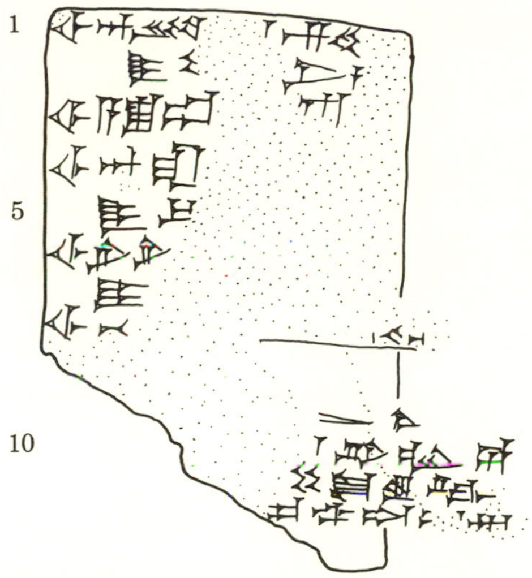

TEXT 58

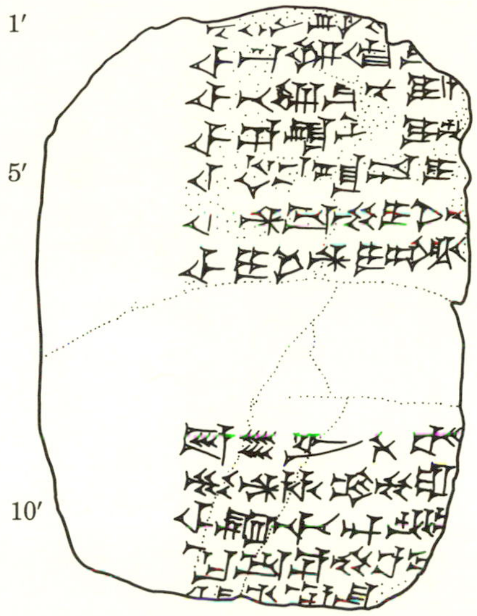

SEAL

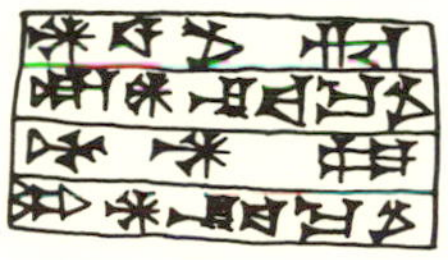

TEXT 57

obv.

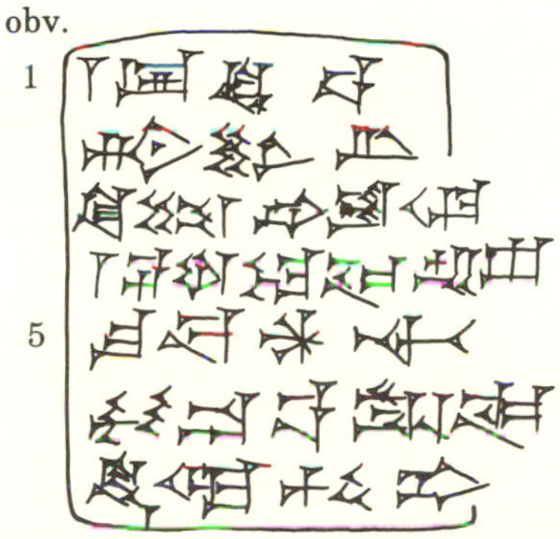

rev.

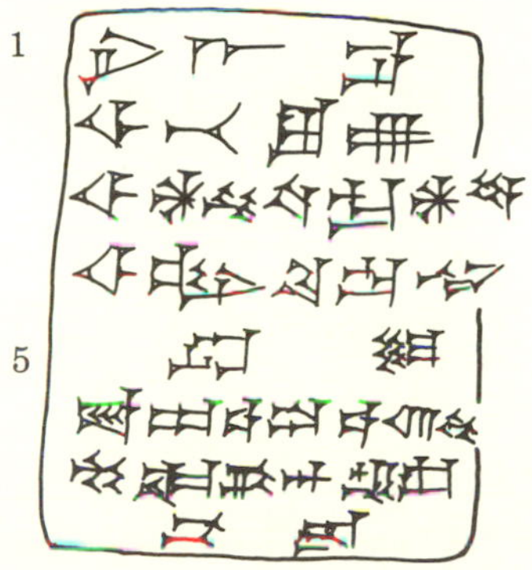

SEAL

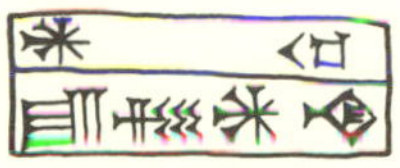

TEXT 59

obv.

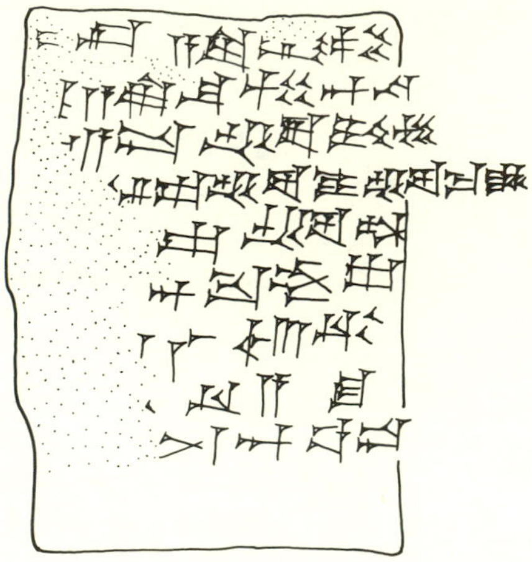

rev.

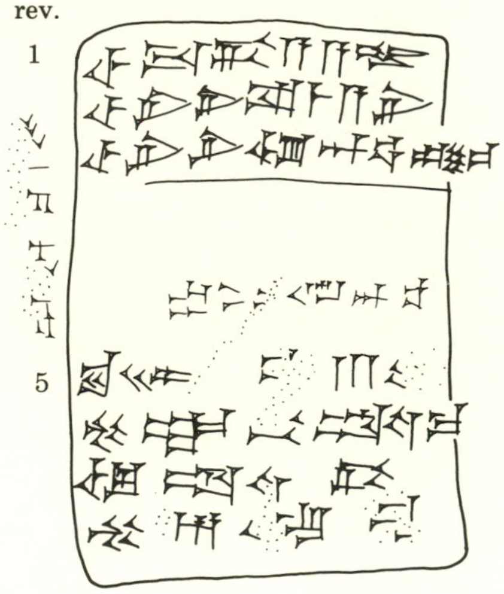

SEAL

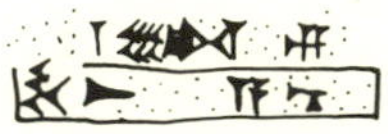

TEXT 60

obv.

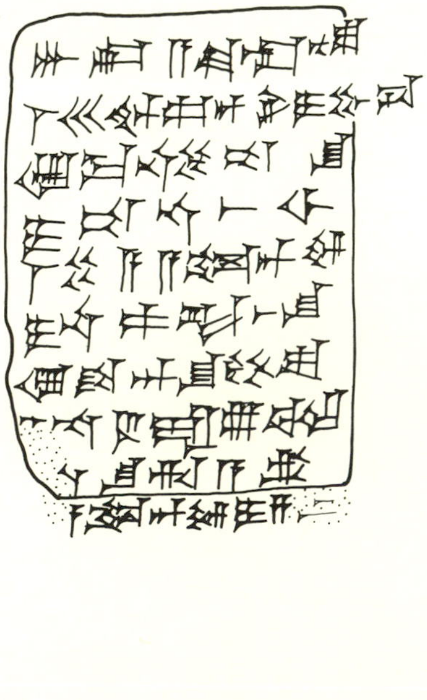

rev.

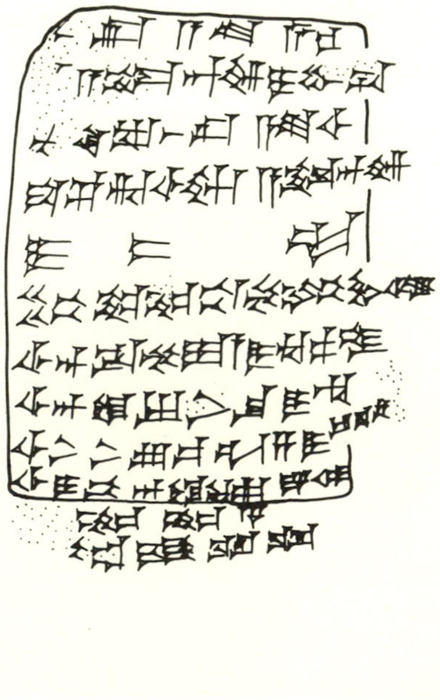

TEXT 61

obv.

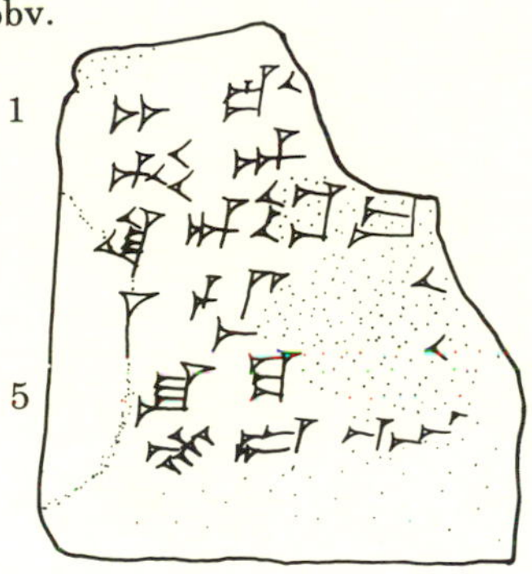

rev.

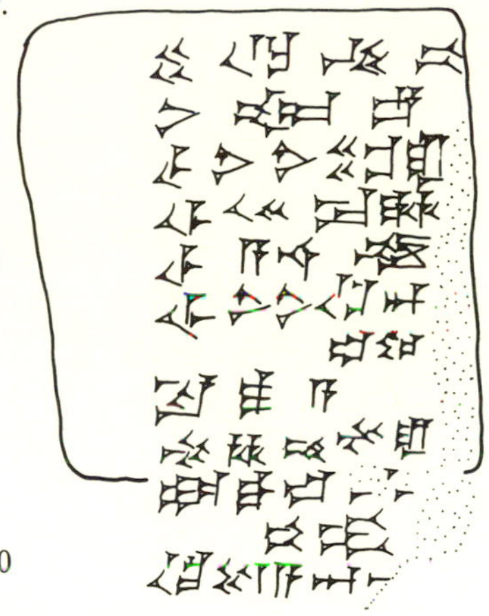

TEXT 62

obv.

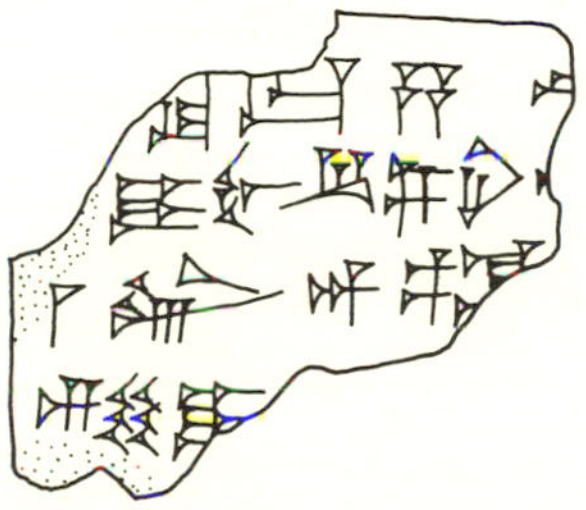

rev.

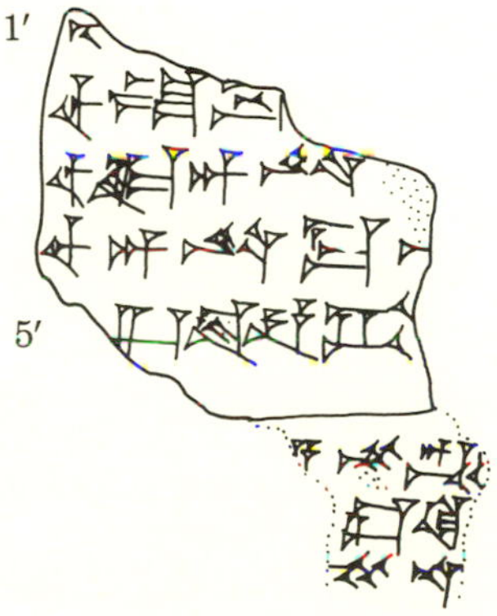

SEAL

TEXT 63

obv.

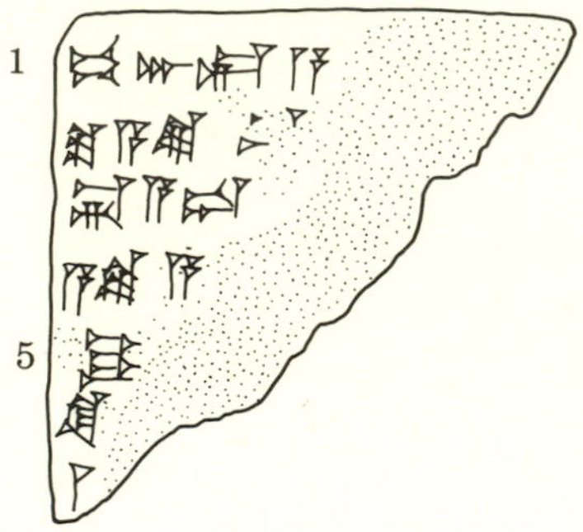

rev.

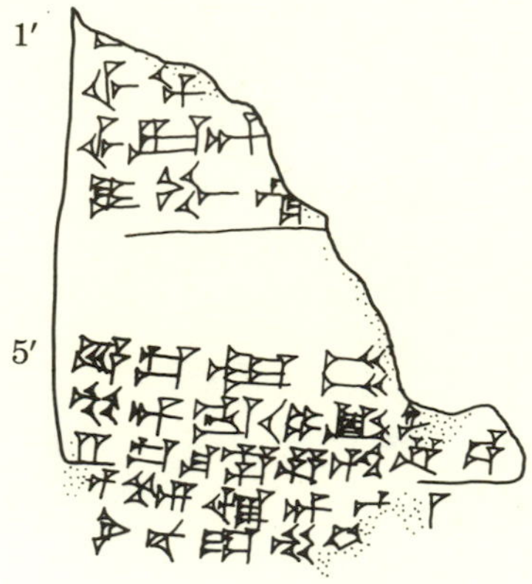

TEXT 64

obv.

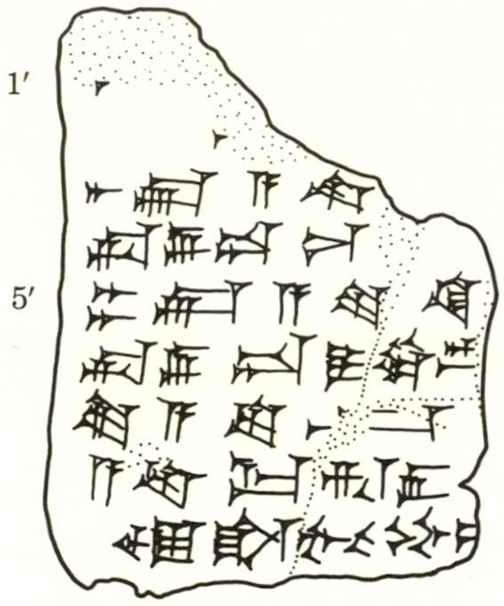

SEAL

TEXT 65

obv.

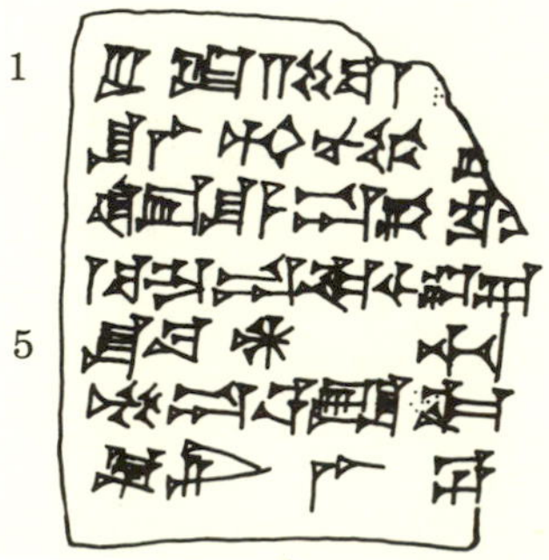

rev.

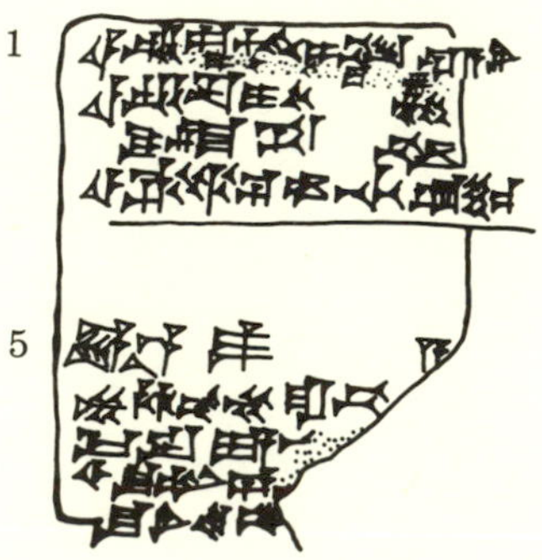

TEXT 66

obv.

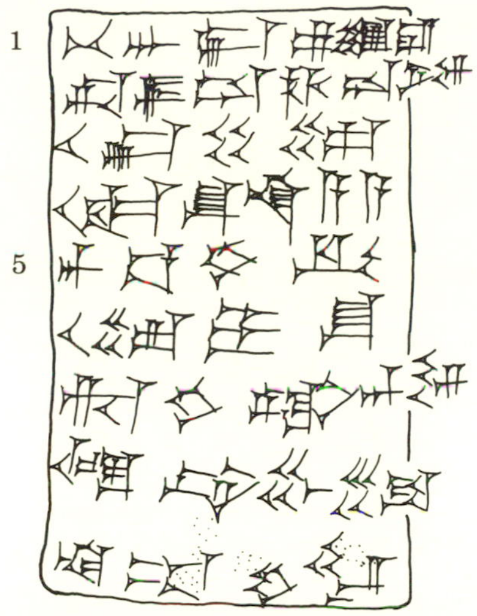

rev.

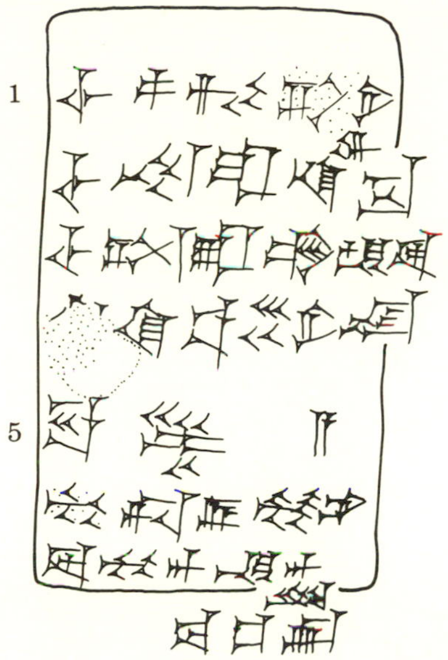

SEAL

TEXT 67

obv.

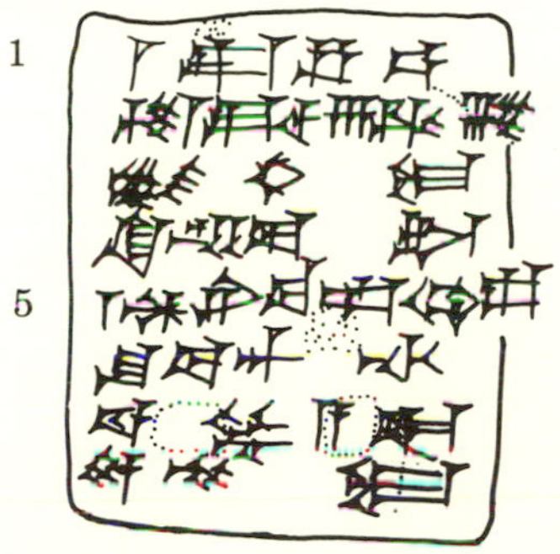

rev.

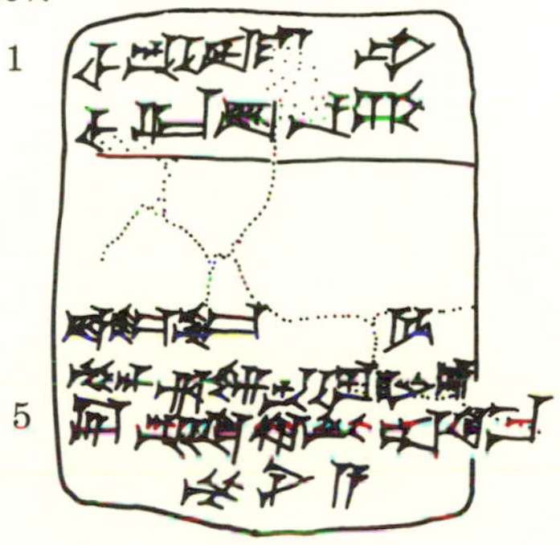

TEXT 68

TABLET

obv.

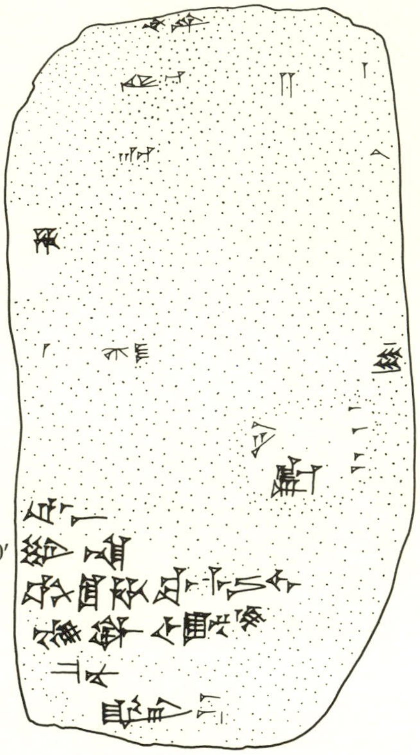

rev.

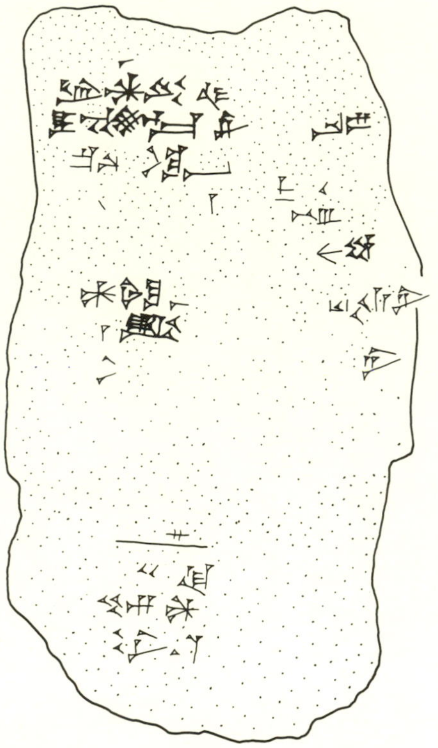

SEAL

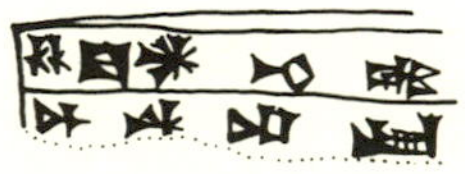

CASE

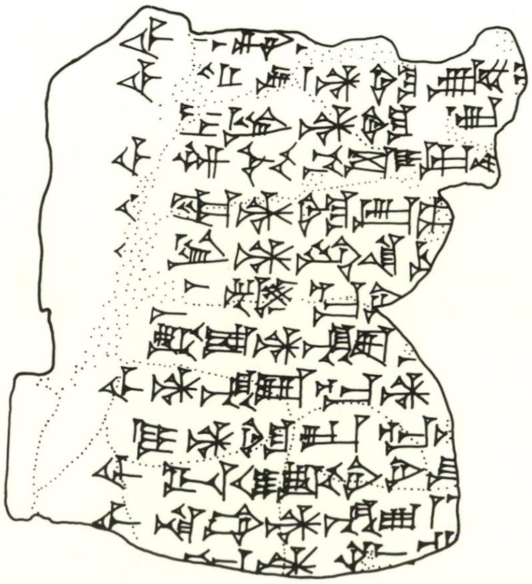

TEXT 69

TABLET

obv.

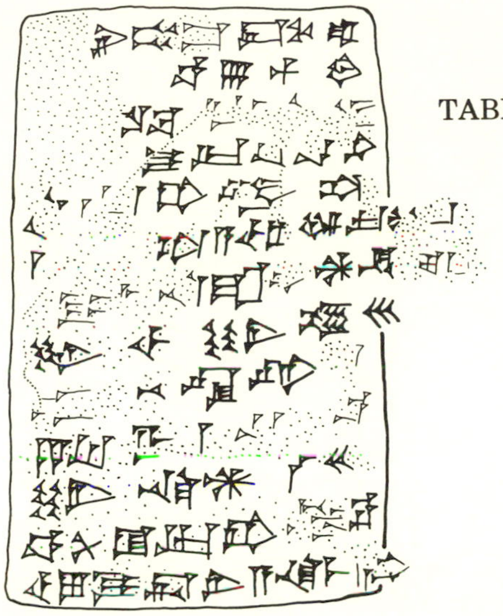

rev.

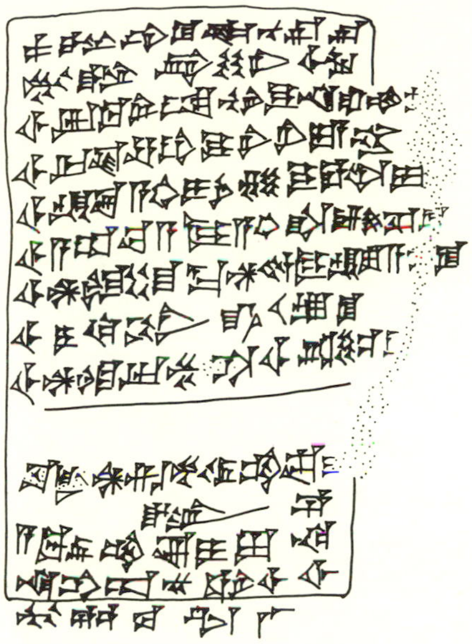

SEAL

CASE

TEXT 70

TABLET

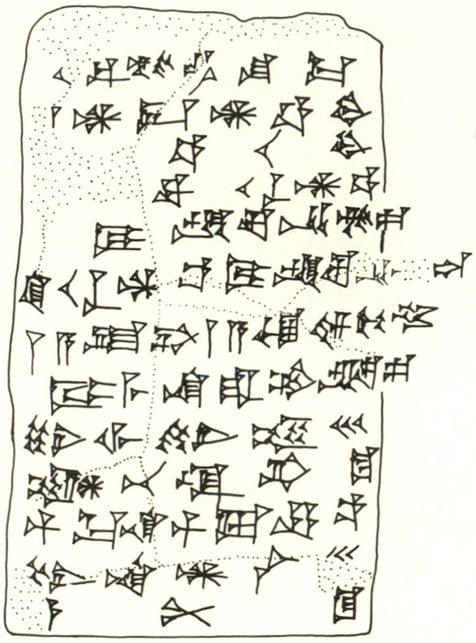

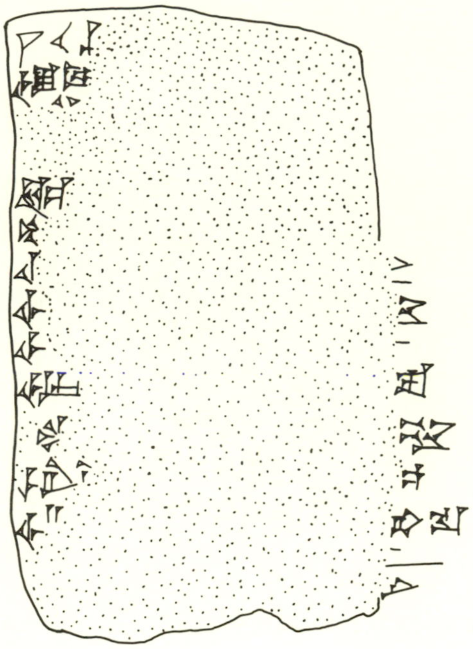

CASE

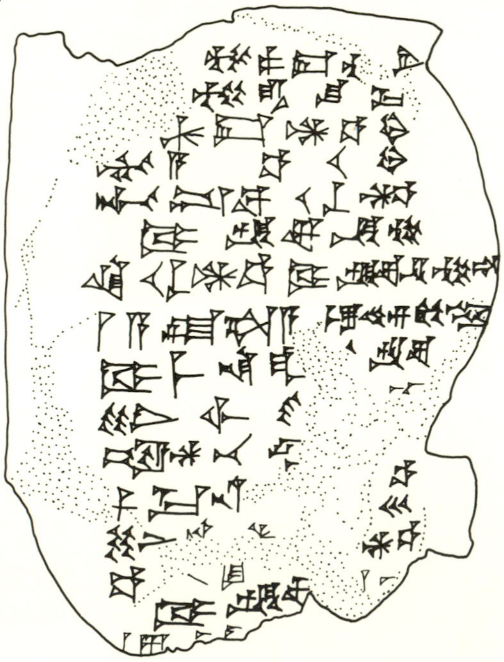

SEAL

TEXT 71

TABLET

obv.

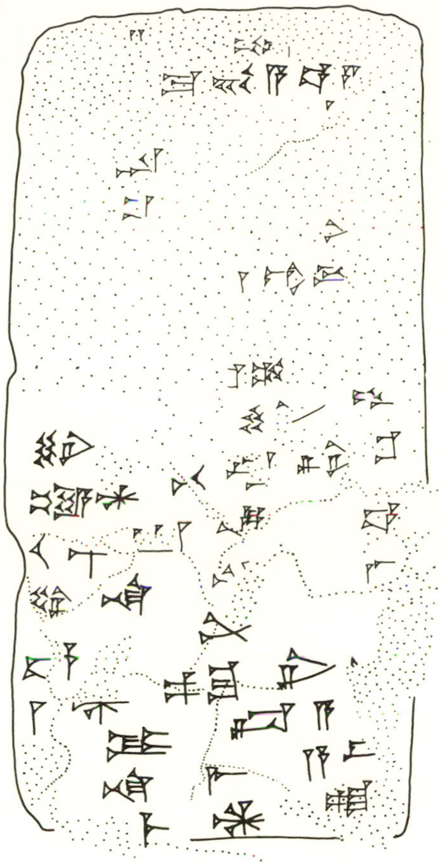

rev.

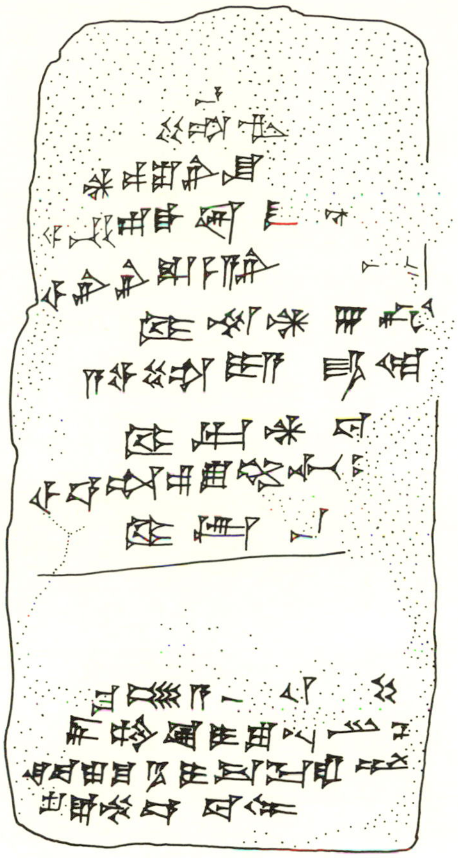

TEXT 71 (continued)

CASE

obv.

rev.

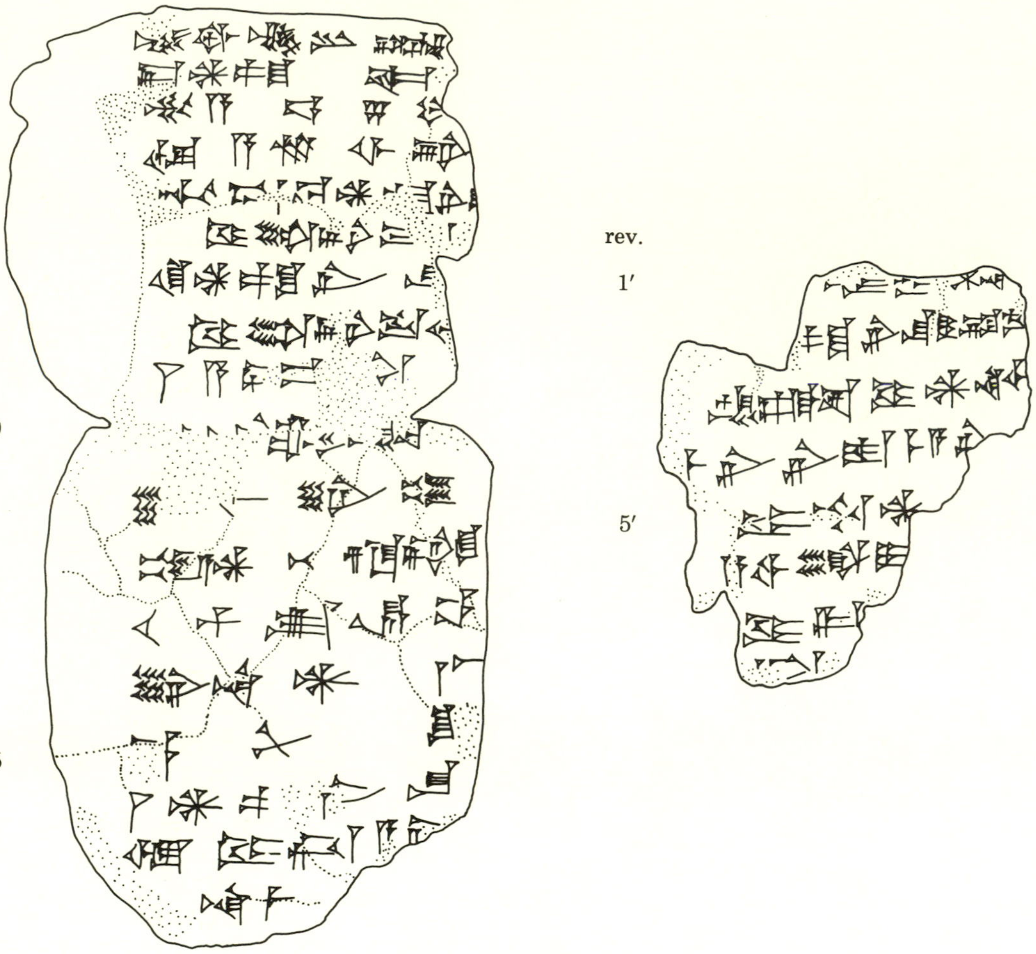

SEAL

TEXT 72

TABLET

obv.

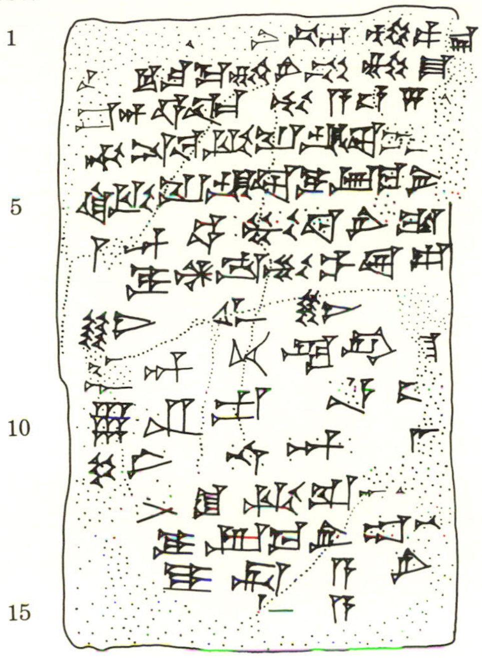

rev.

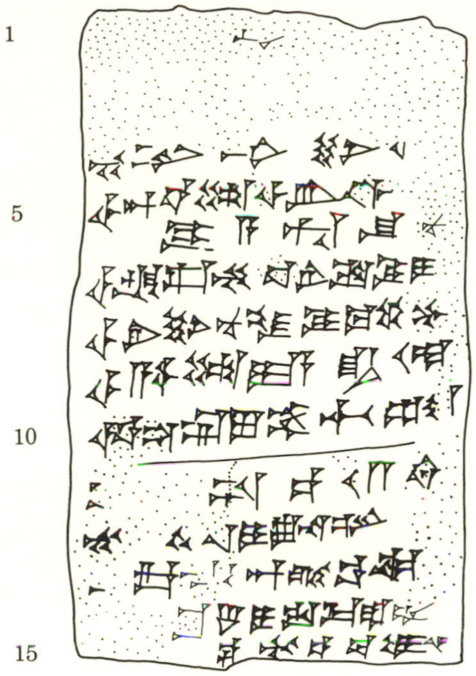

CASE

obv.

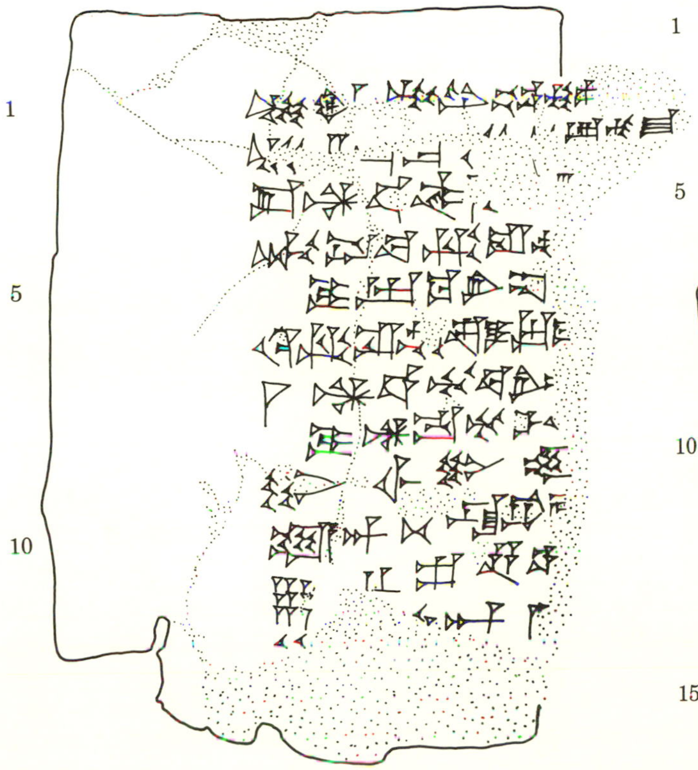

rev.

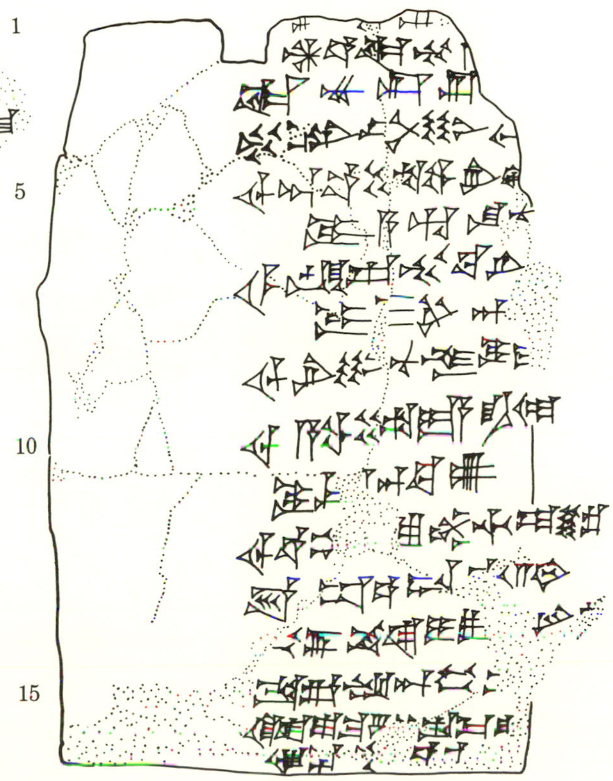

SEAL

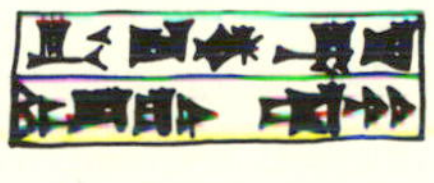

TEXT 73

obv.

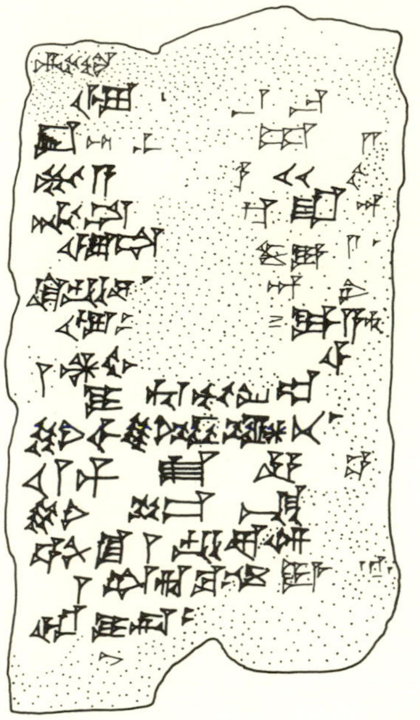

rev.

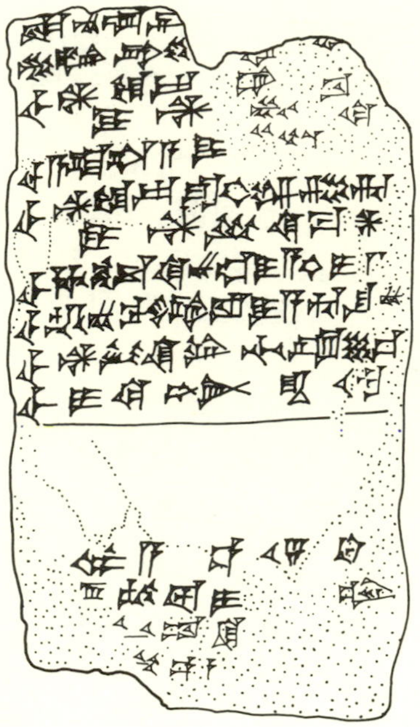

SEAL

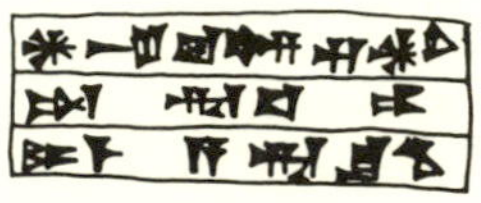

CASE

obv.

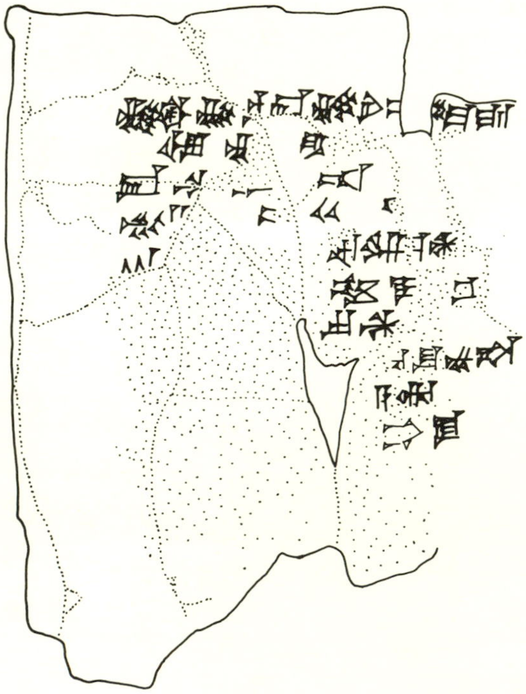

rev.

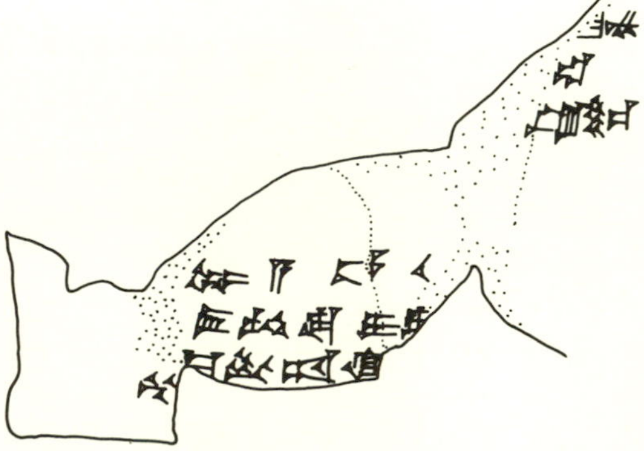

TEXT 74

TABLET

obv.

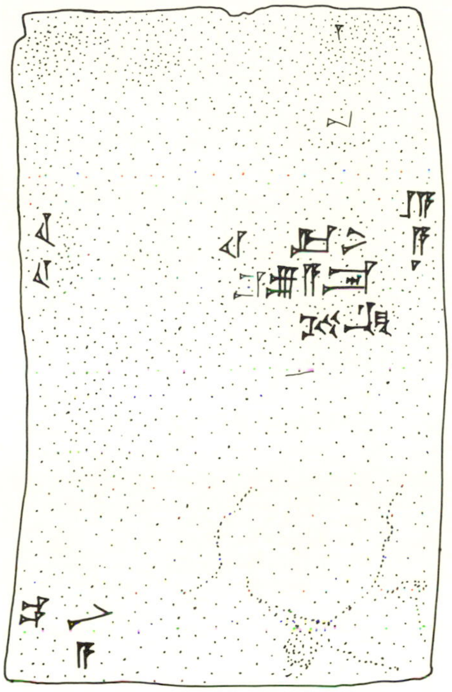

rev.

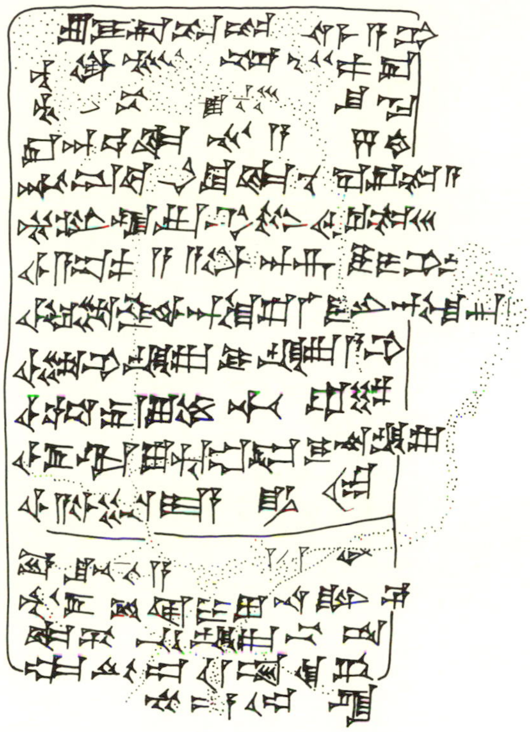

CASE

obv.

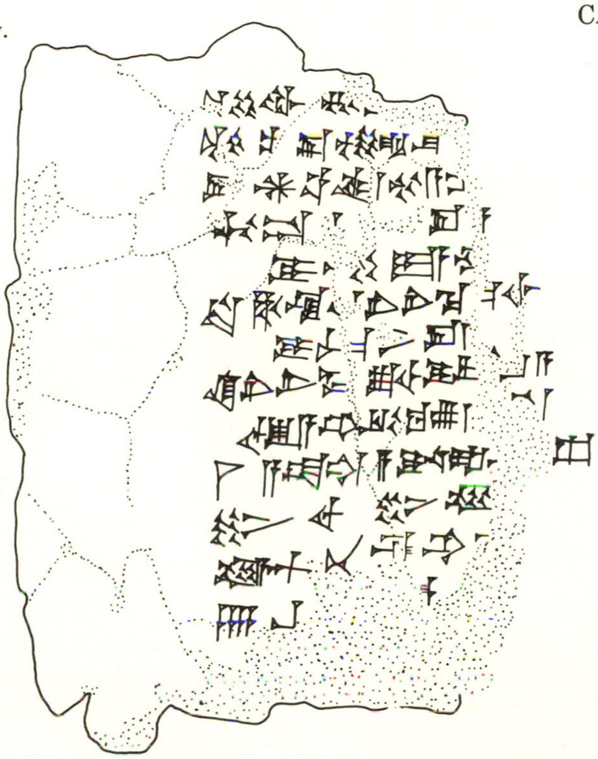

rev.

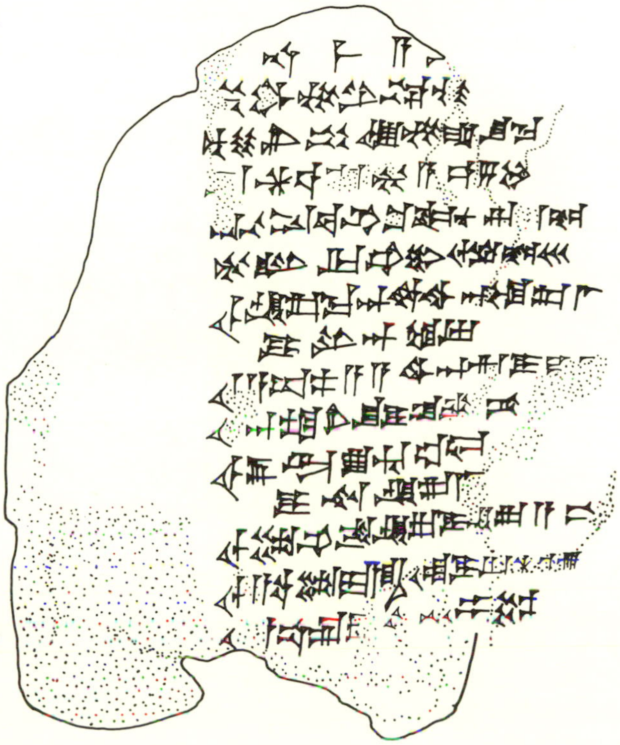

SEAL

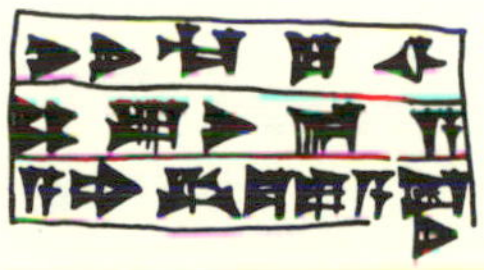

PLATE 82

TEXT 75

TABLET

obv.

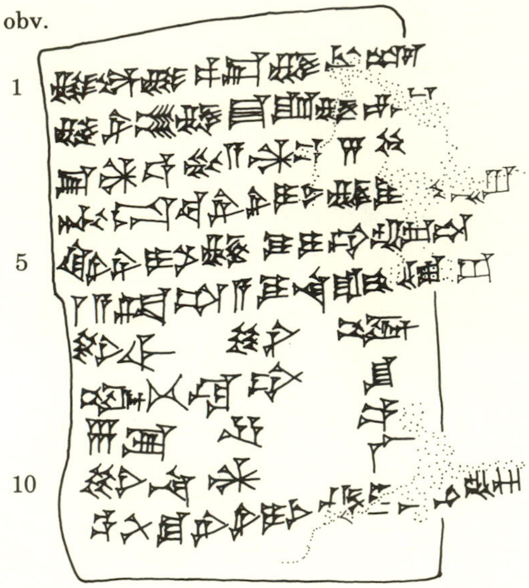

rev.

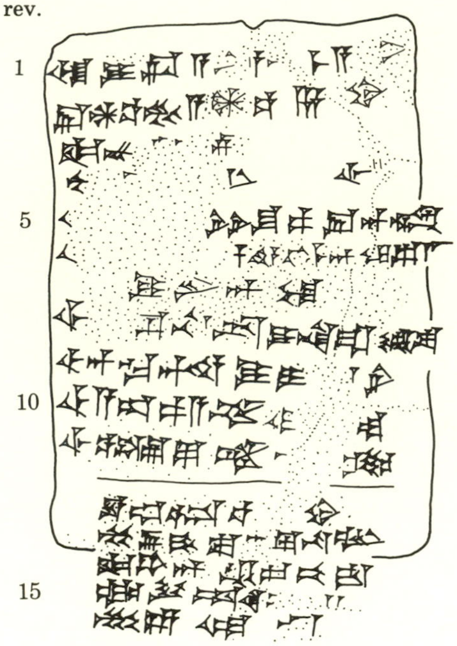

CASE

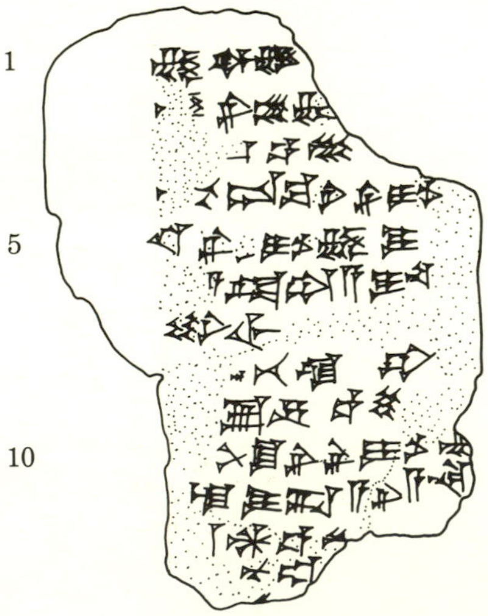

SEAL

TEXT 76

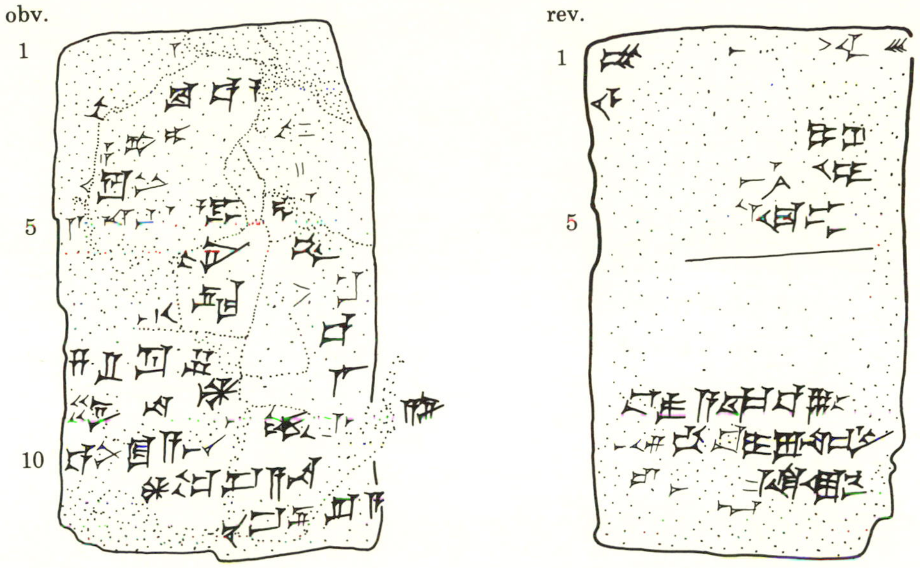

TEXT 77

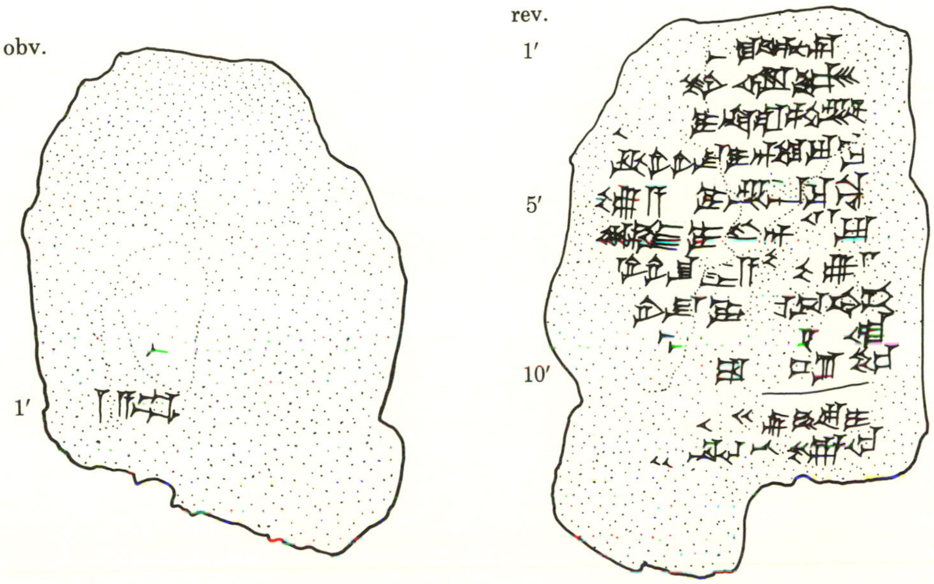

TEXT 78

TABLET

obv.

1

5

10

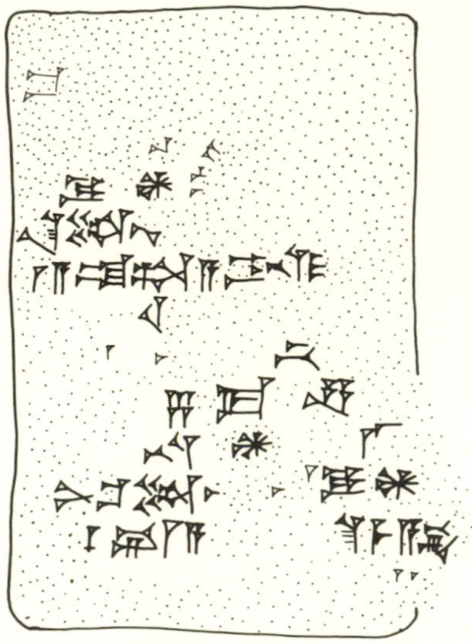

rev.

1′

5′

10′

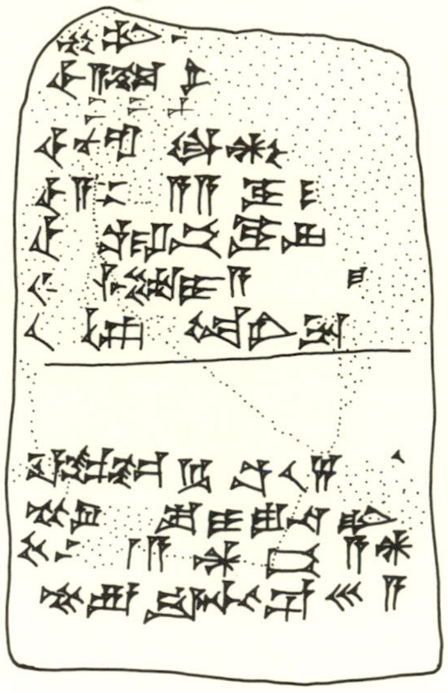

CASE

obv.

1

5

10

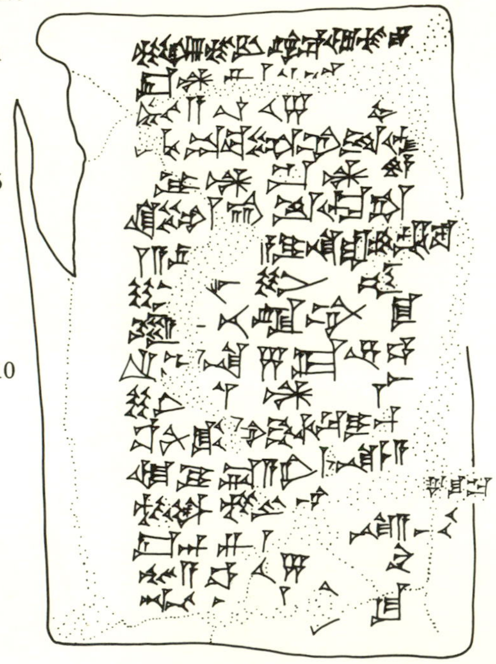

rev.

1

5

10

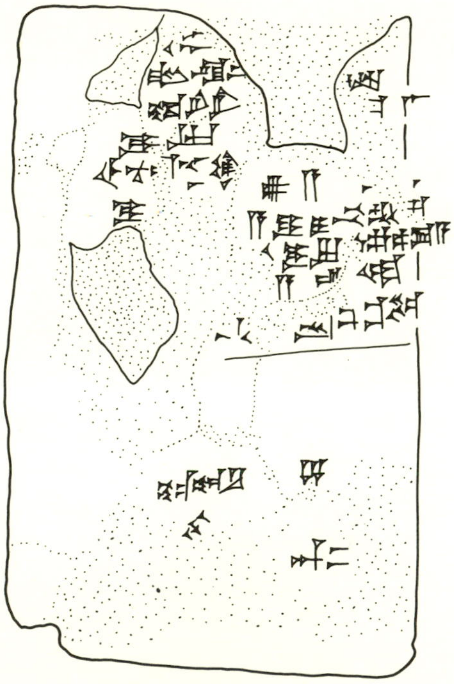

SEAL

TEXT 79

TABLET

obv.

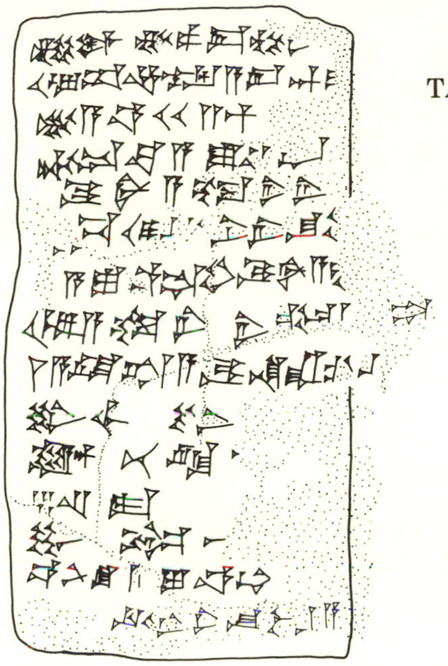

rev.

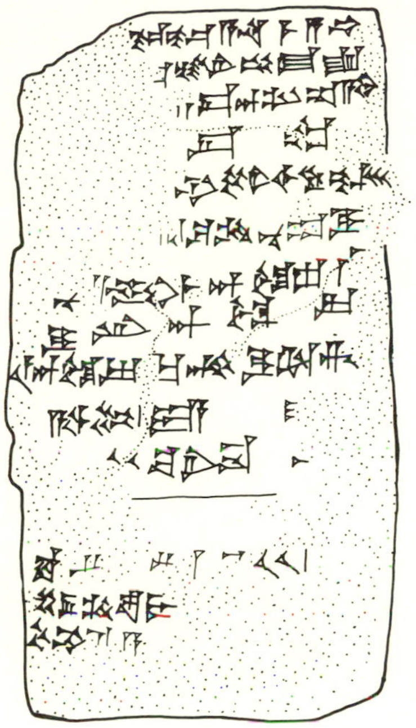

CASE

obv.

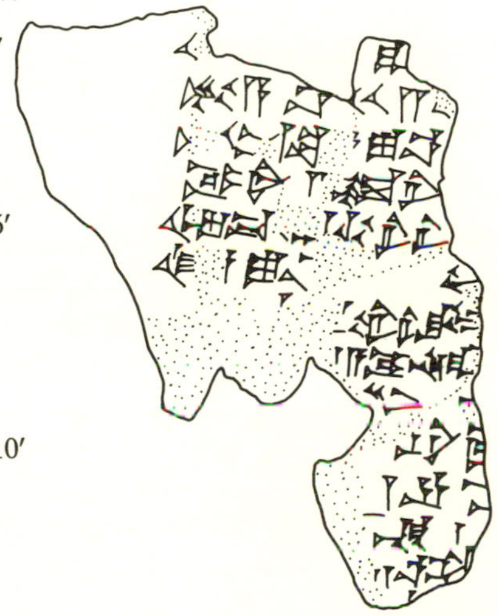

rev.

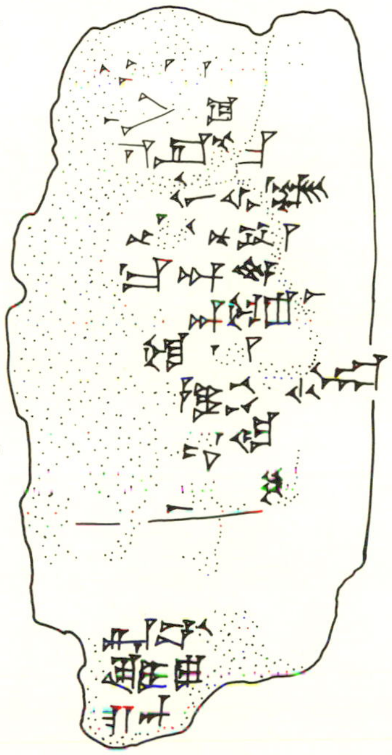

SEAL

TEXT 80

CASE

obv.
1′
5′
10′

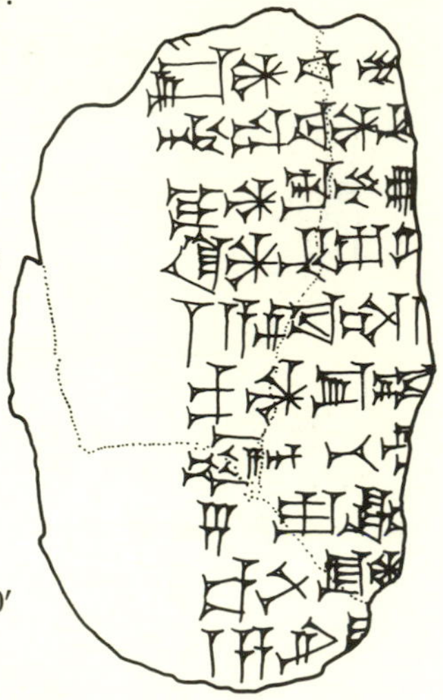

TABLET

rev.
1′
5′

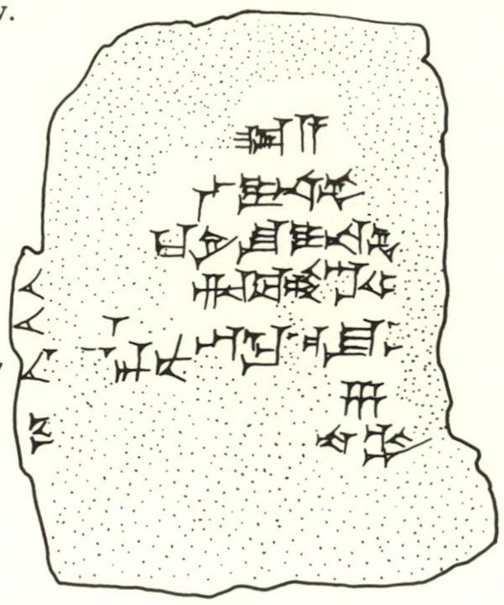

SEAL

TEXT 82

obv.
1
5

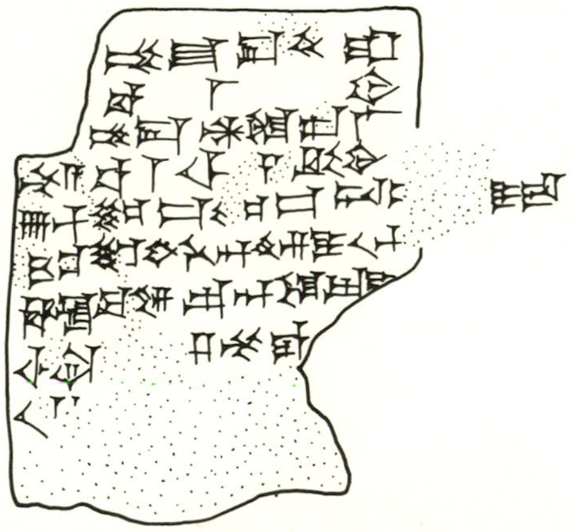

rev.
1′
5′
10′

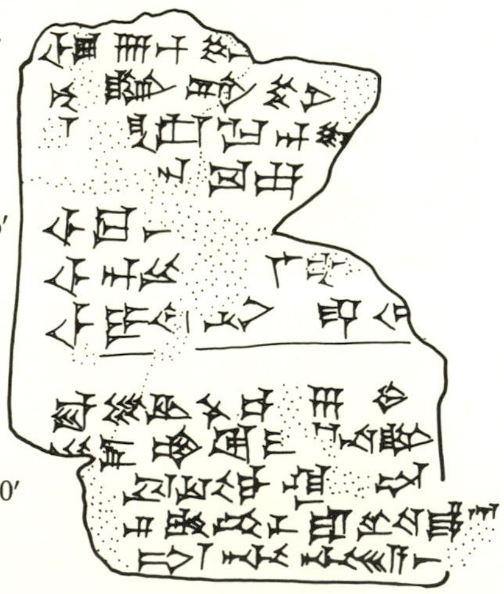

SEAL

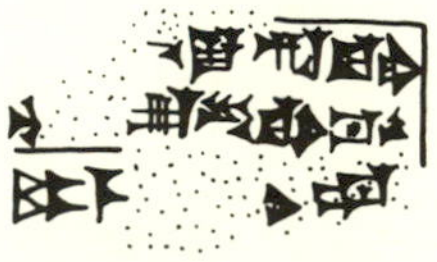

TEXT 81

TABLET

obv.

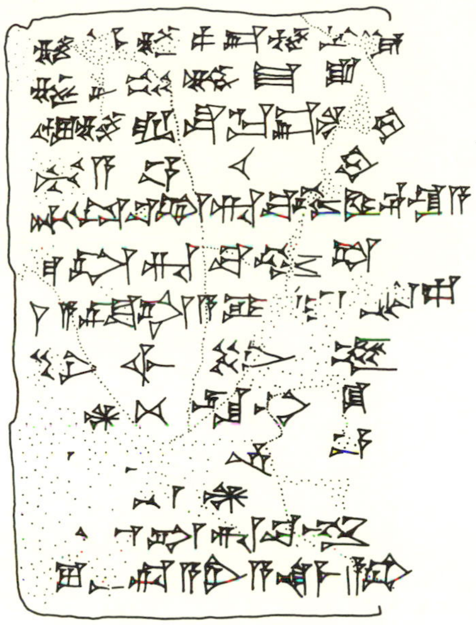

rev.

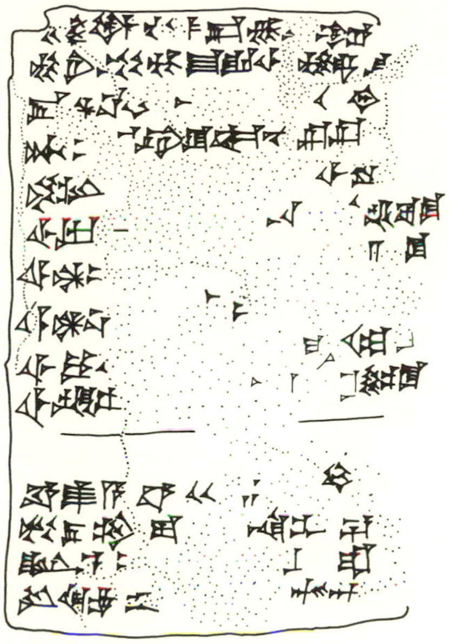

CASE

obv.

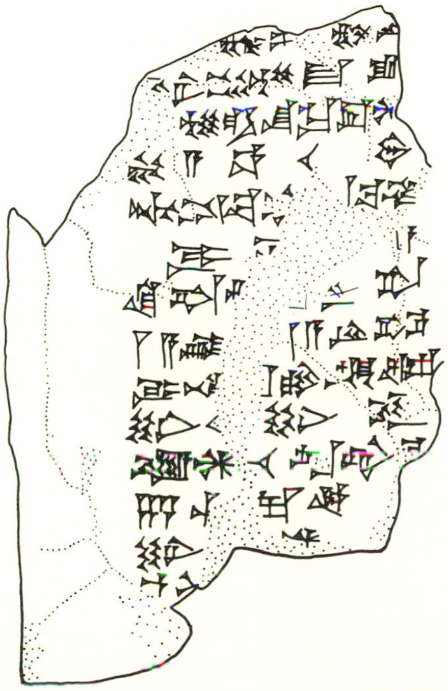

rev.

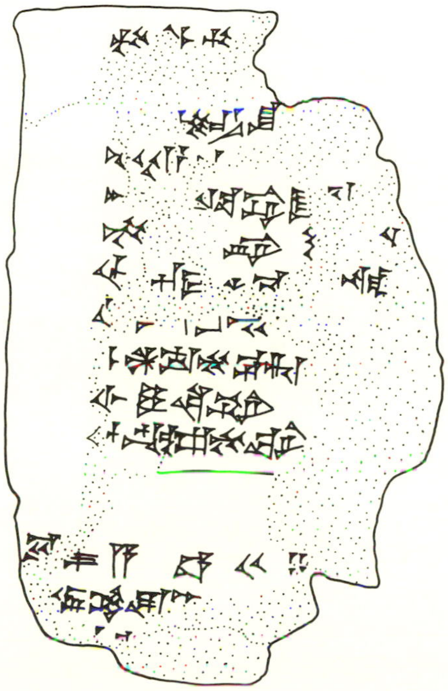

SEAL

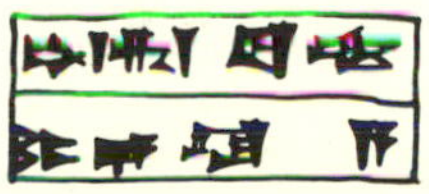

TEXT 83

TABLET

obv.

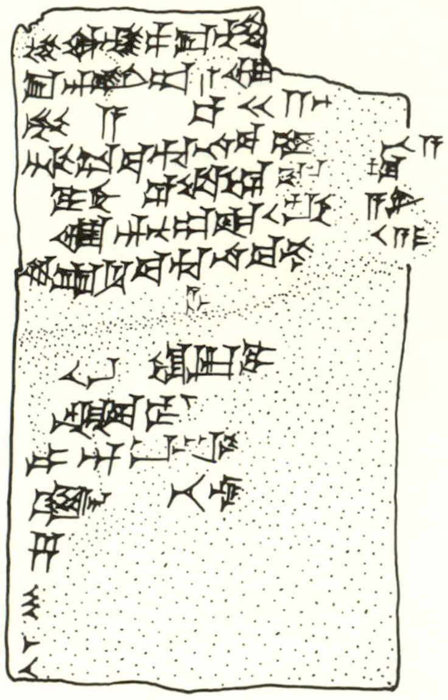

rev.

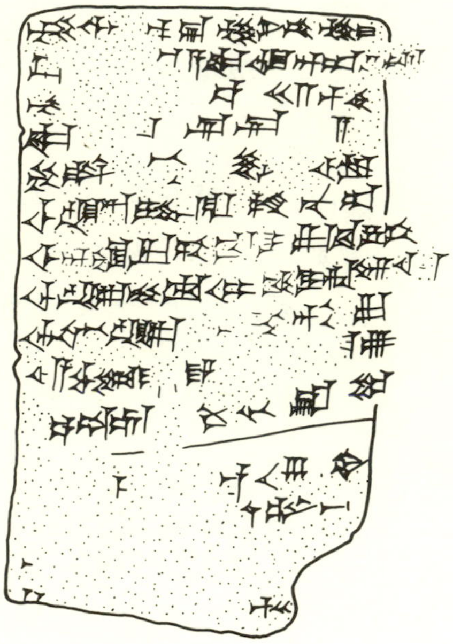

CASE

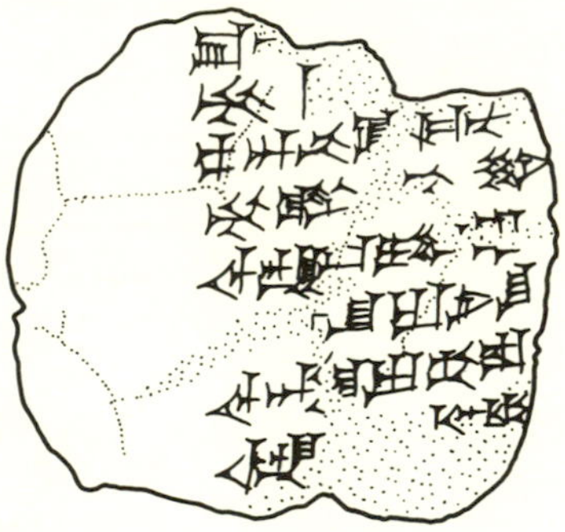

SEAL

TEXT 84

obv.

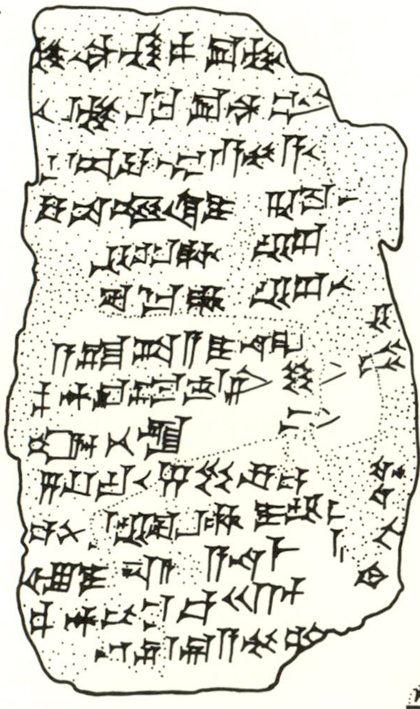

rev.

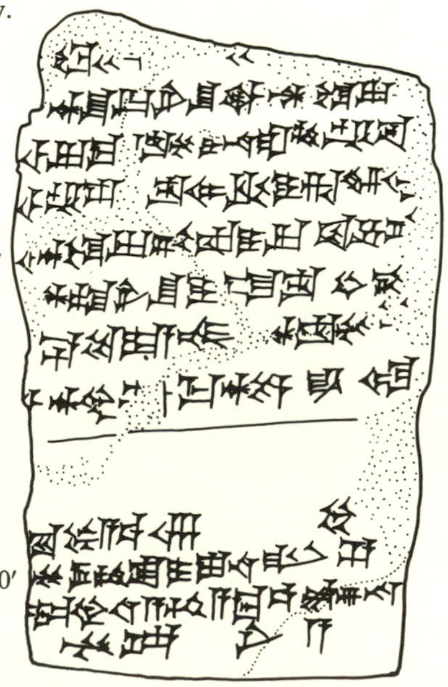

SEAL

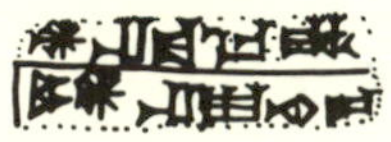

TEXT 85

obv.

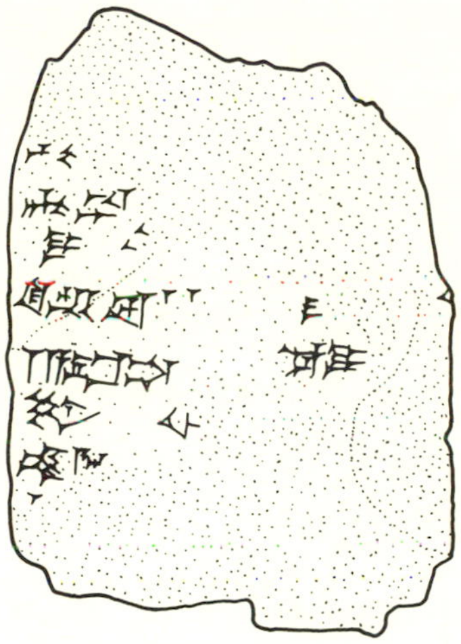

rev.

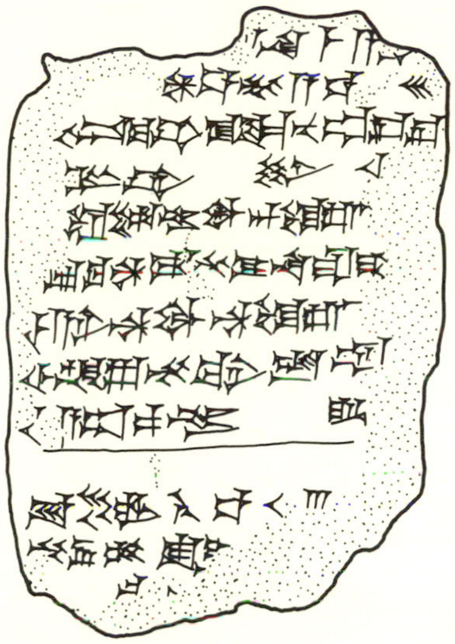

SEAL

TEXT 86

obv.

TABLET

rev.

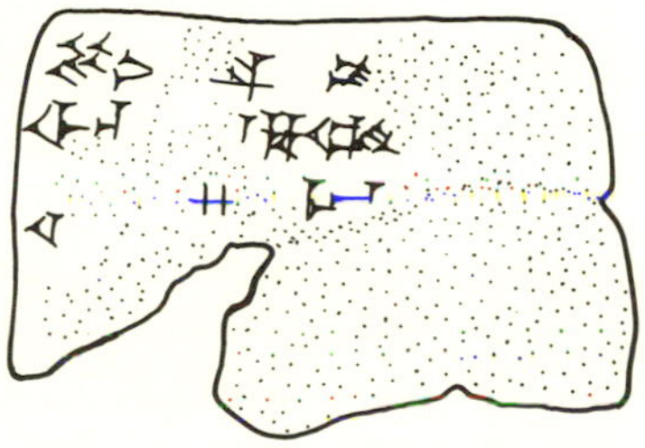

CASE

SEALS

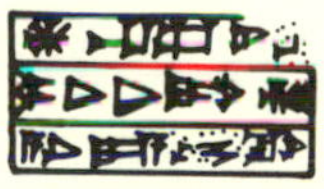

TEXT 87

obv.

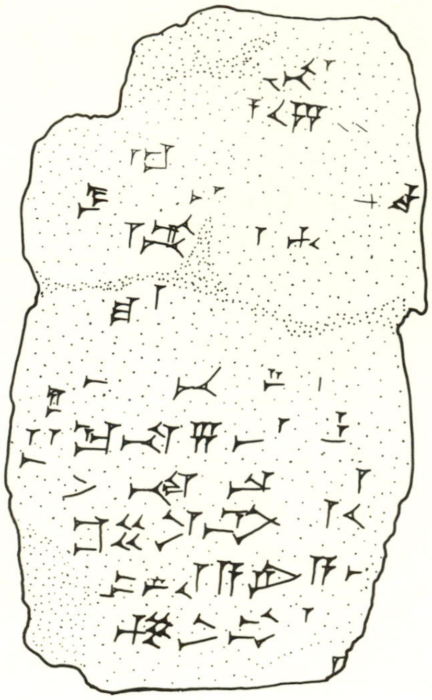

rev.

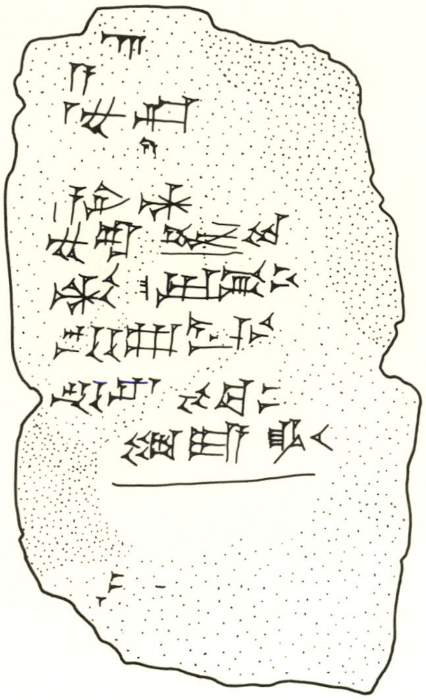

SEAL

TEXT 88

obv.

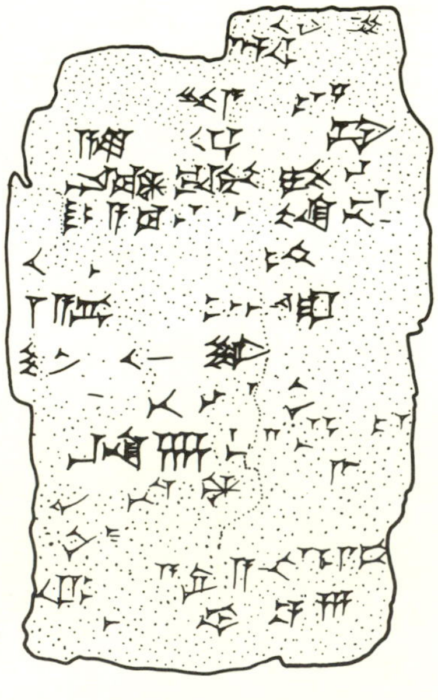

rev.

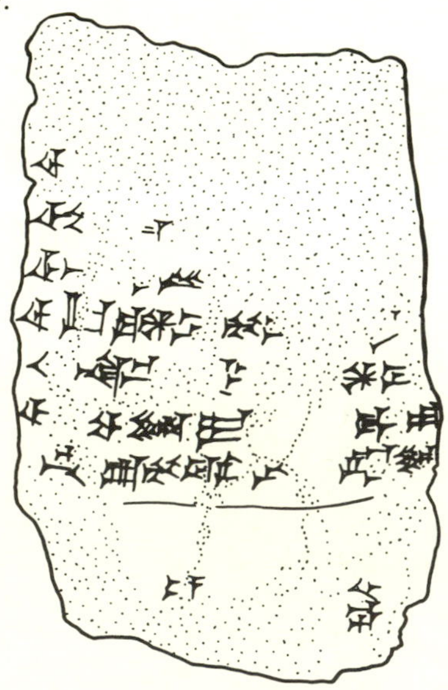

SEAL

TEXT 89

TABLET

obv.

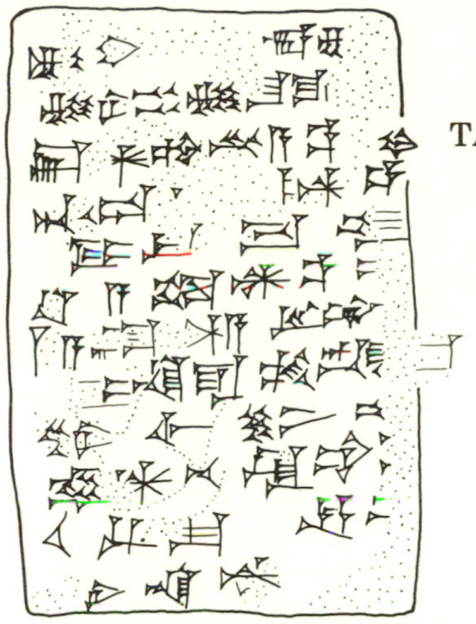

rev.

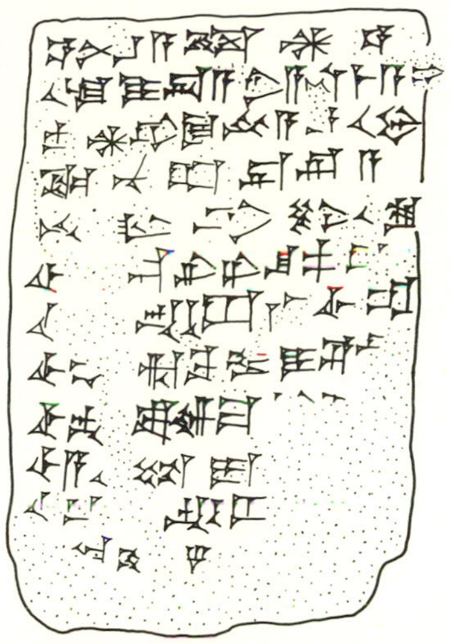

CASE

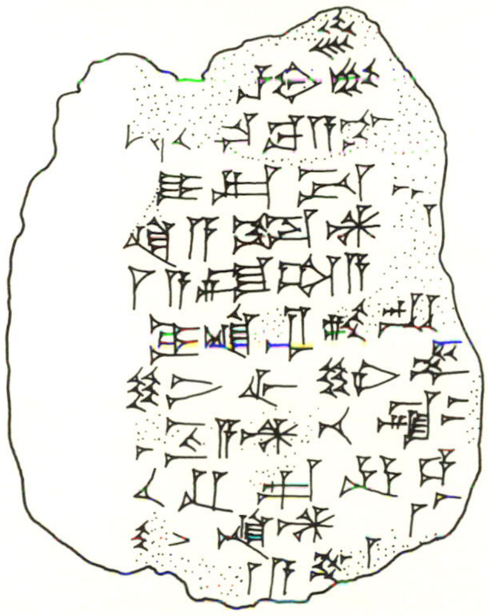

SEAL

TEXT 90

obv.

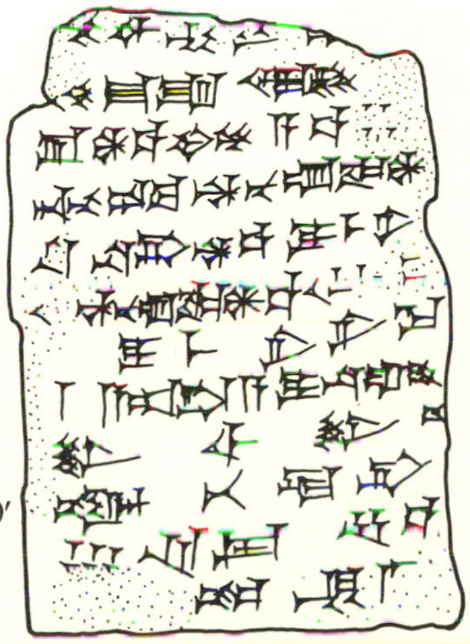

rev.

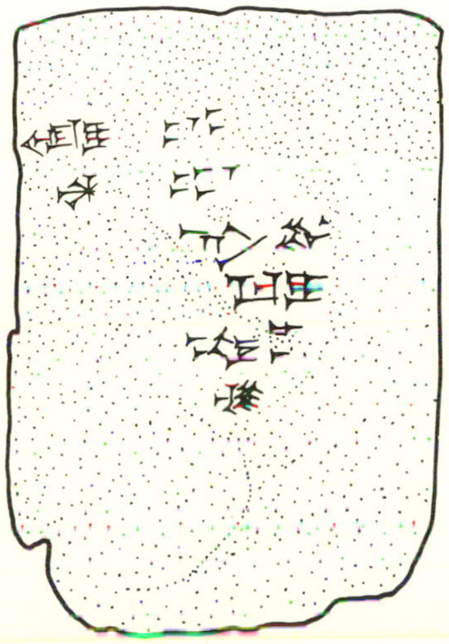

SEAL

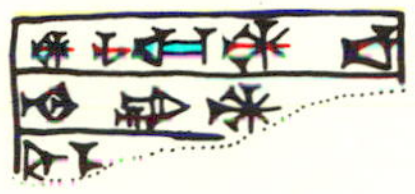

TEXT 91

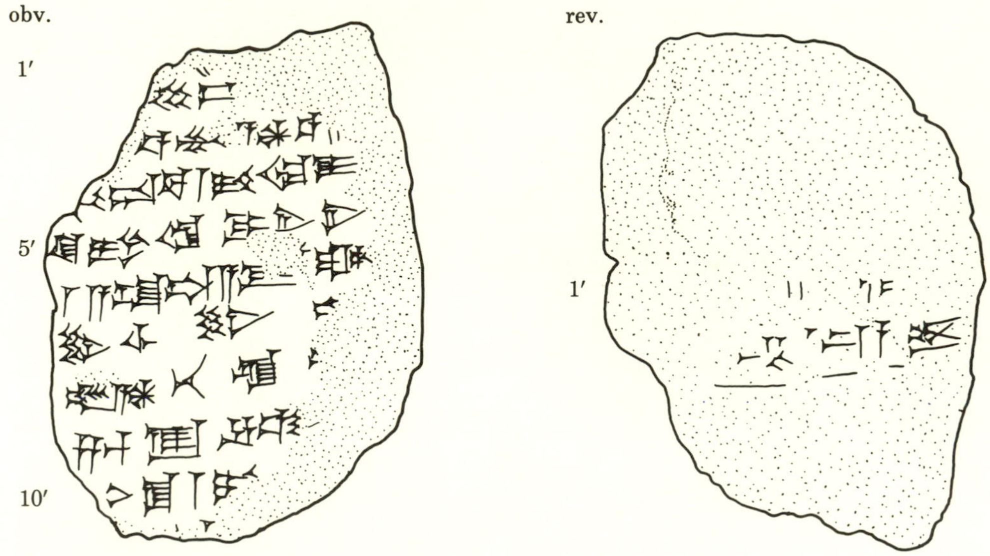

TEXT 92

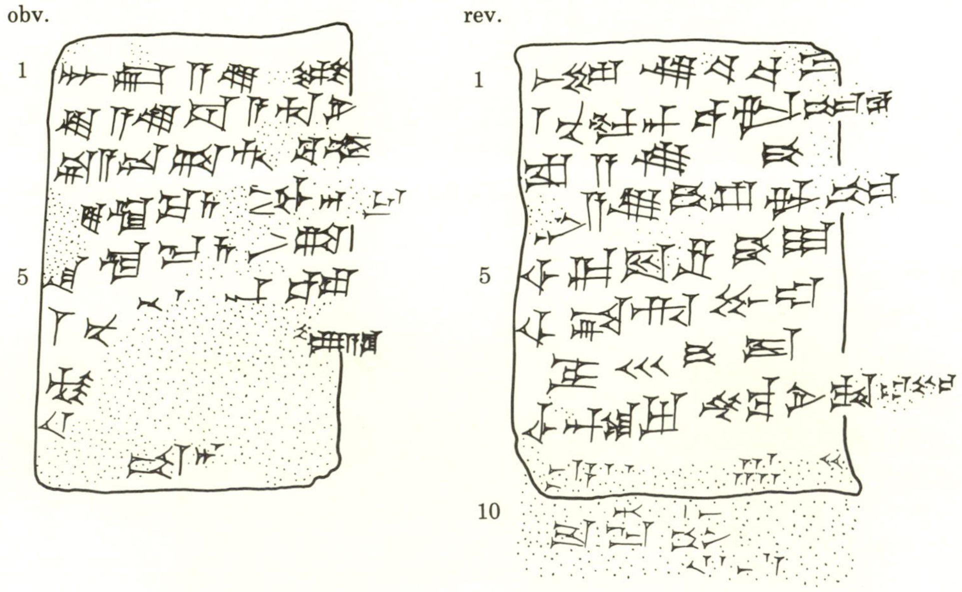

TEXT 93

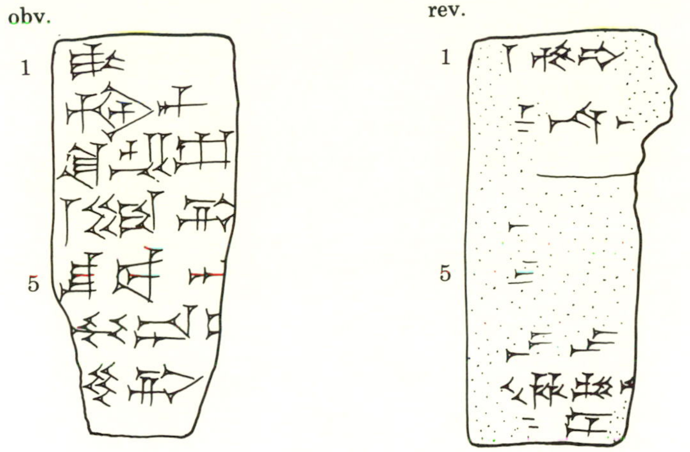

SEAL

TEXT 94

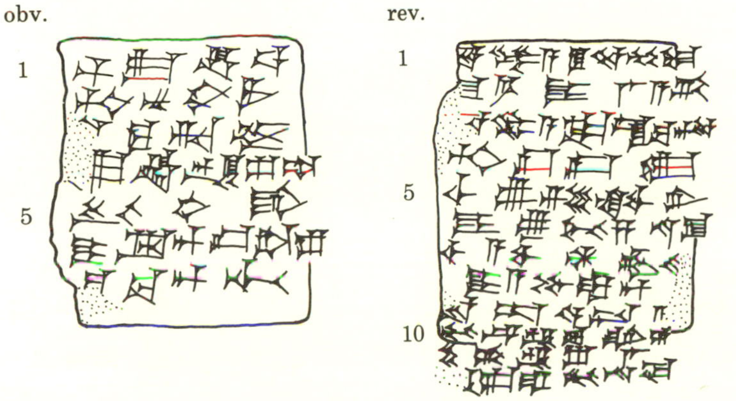

SEAL

TEXT 95

obv.

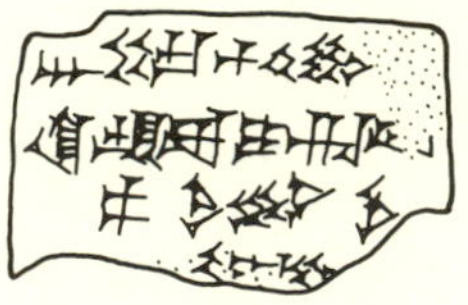

rev.

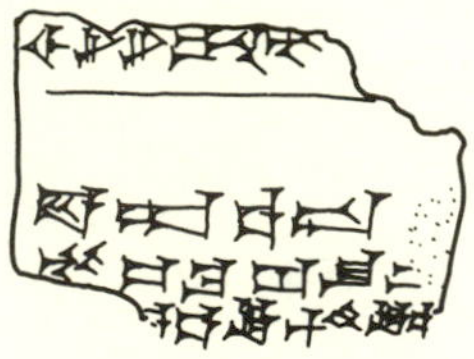

TEXT 96

obv.

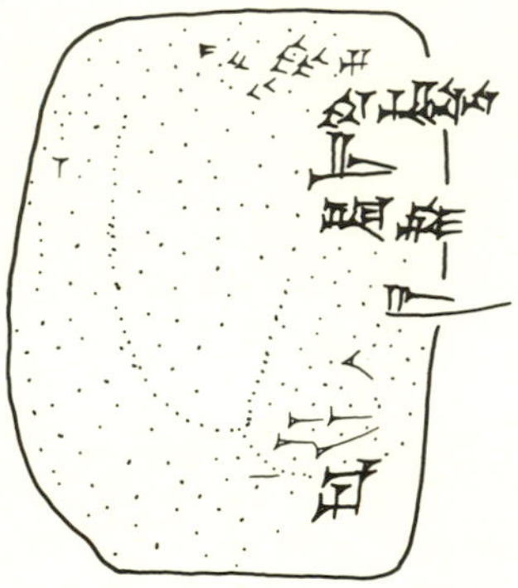

rev.

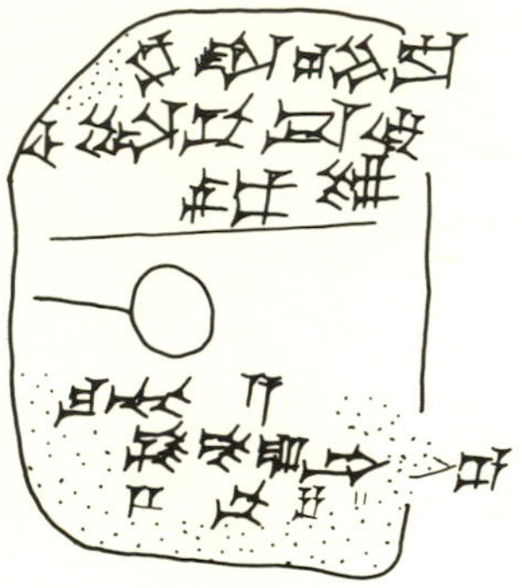

TEXT 97

rev.

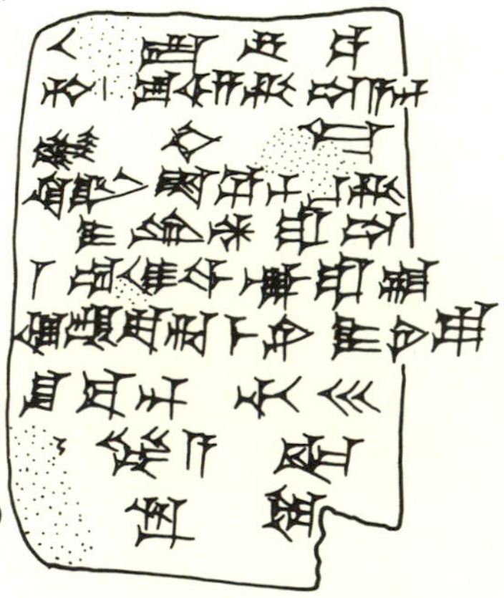

SEALS